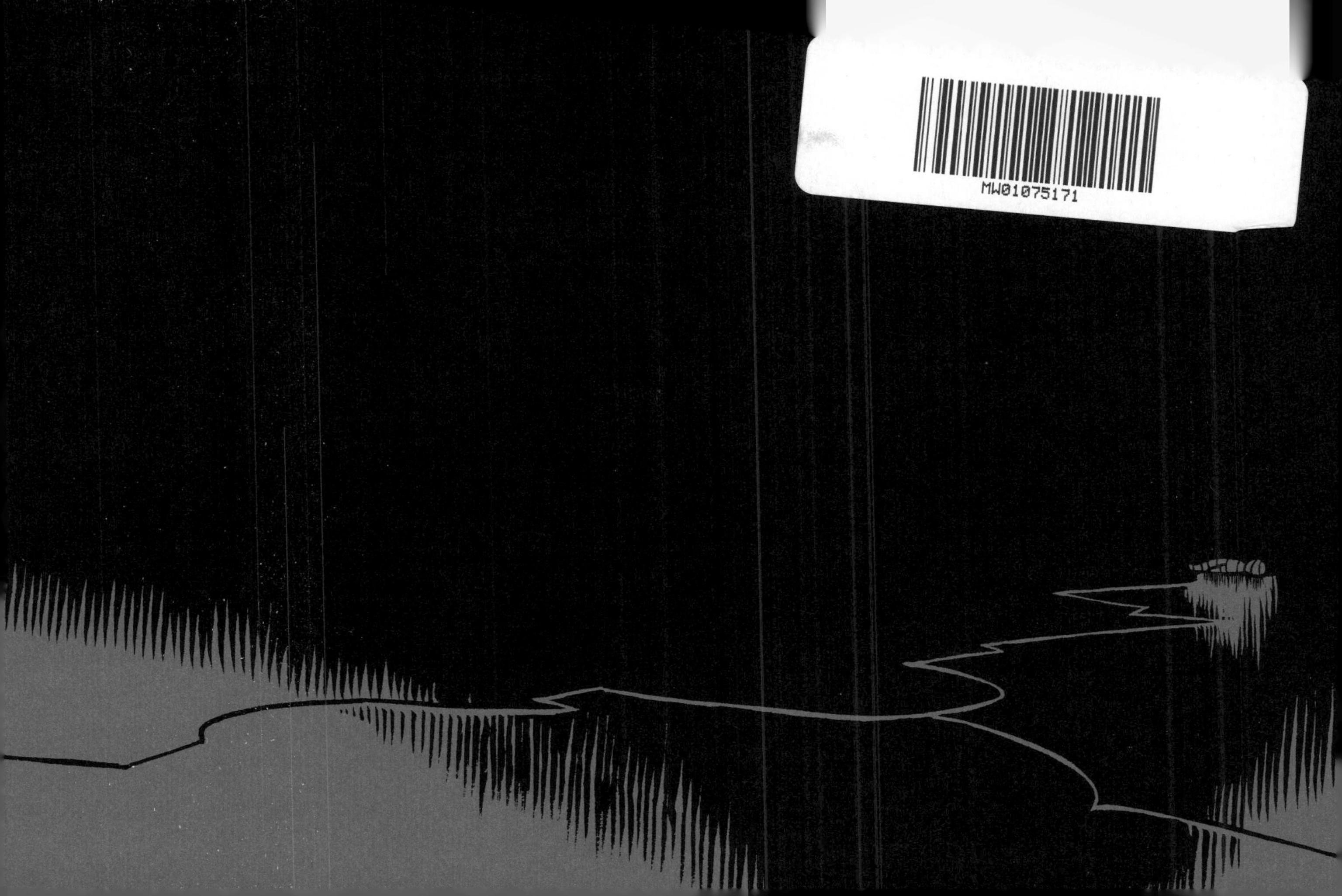

Heck

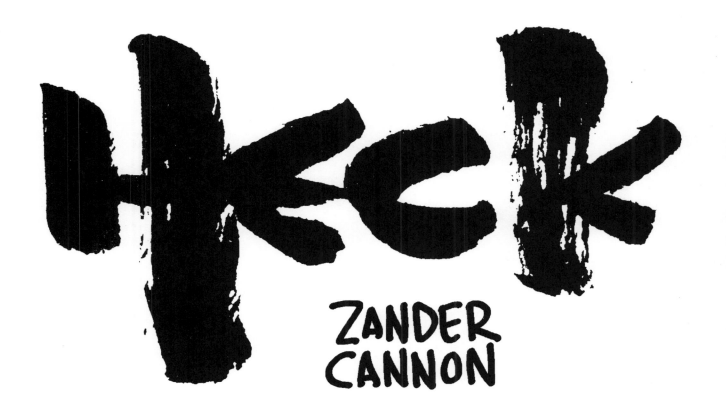

ZANDER CANNON

Published by
Top Shelf Productions
PO Box 1282
Marietta, GA 30061-1282
USA

Publishers: Chris Staros and Brett Warnock.

Visit our online catalog at www.topshelfcomix.com.

First Printing, July 2013. Printed in China.

for JIN,
WHO CAME HOME
AT JUST THE RIGHT
TIME

and for JULIE,
OF COURSE,
FOREVER

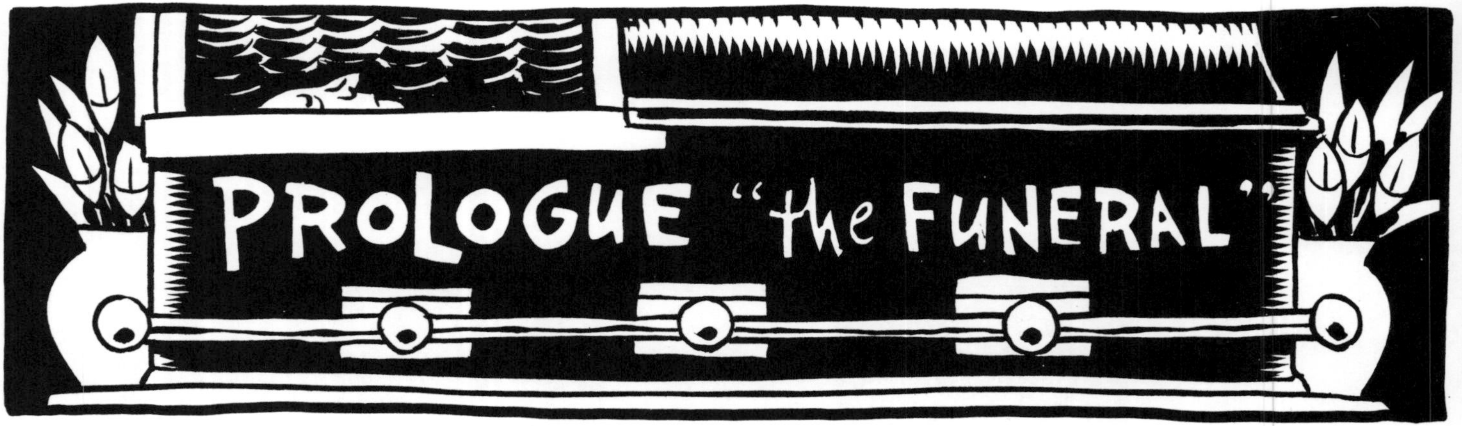
PROLOGUE "the FUNERAL"

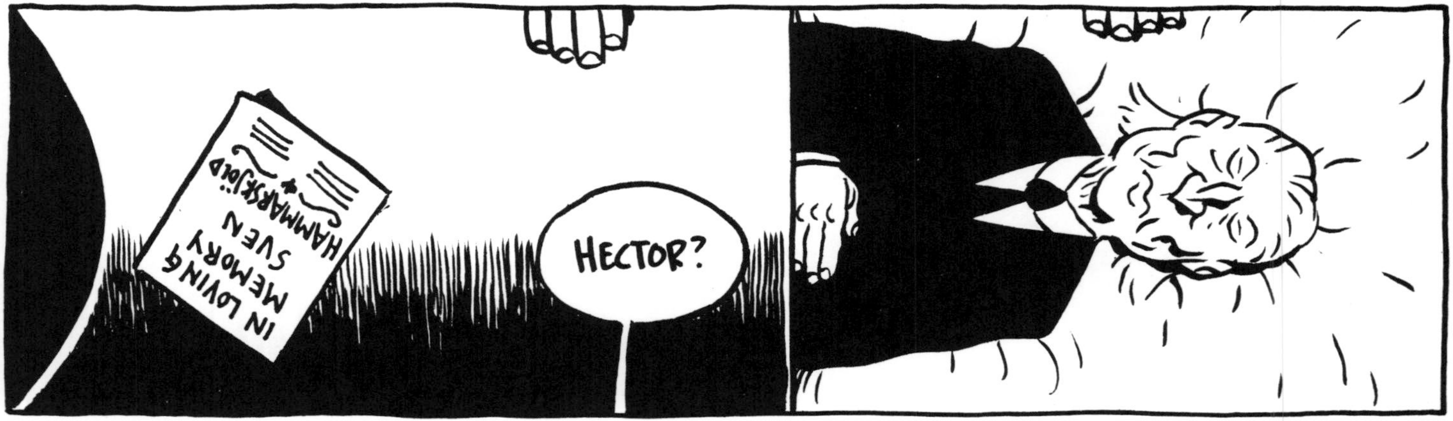
IN LOVING
MEMORY
SVEN
HAMMARSKJÖLD
HECTOR?

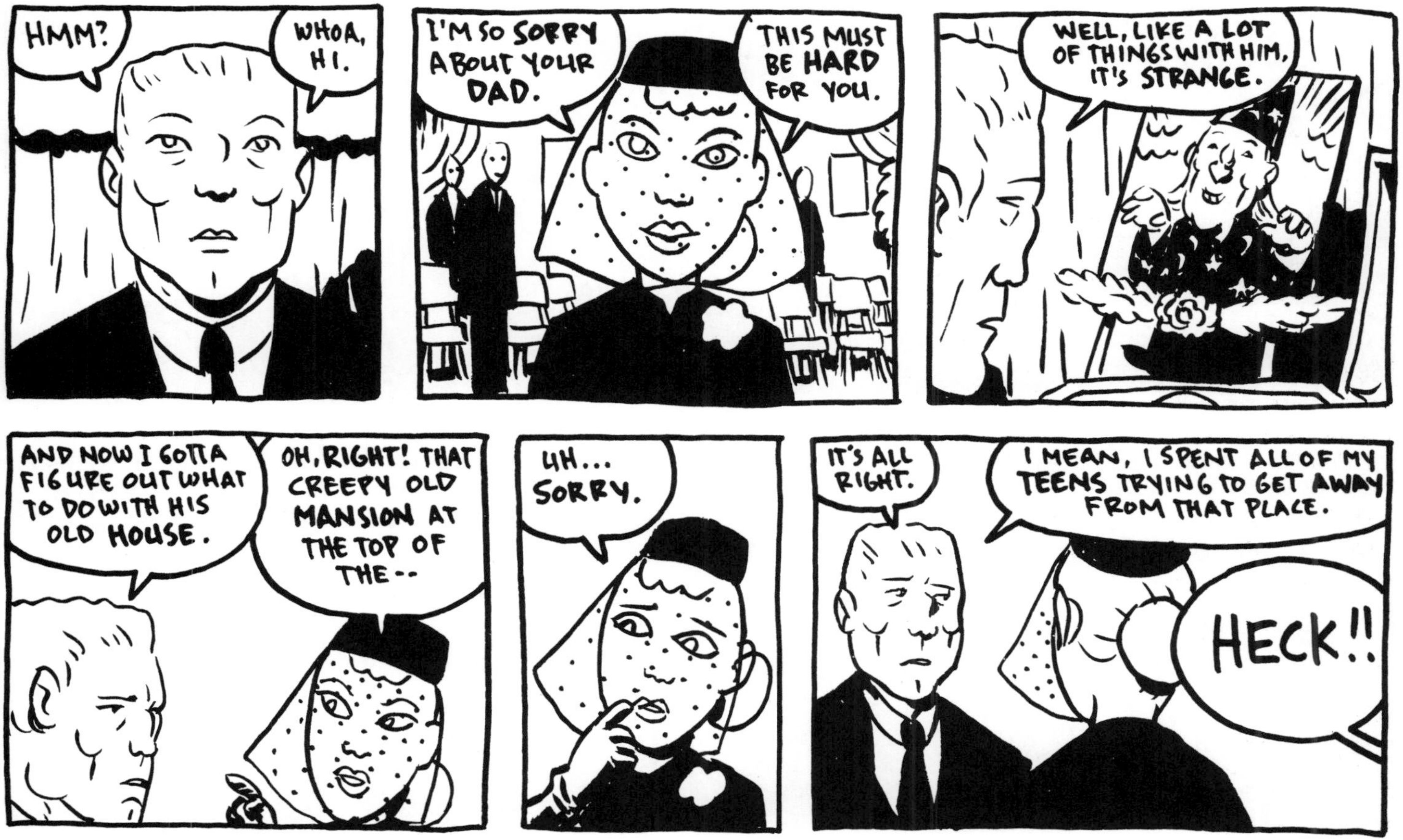
HMM?
WHOA, HI.
I'M SO SORRY ABOUT YOUR DAD.
THIS MUST BE HARD FOR YOU.
WELL, LIKE A LOT OF THINGS WITH HIM, IT'S STRANGE.
AND NOW I GOTTA FIGURE OUT WHAT TO DO WITH HIS OLD HOUSE.
OH, RIGHT! THAT CREEPY OLD MANSION AT THE TOP OF THE--
UH... SORRY.
IT'S ALL RIGHT.
I MEAN, I SPENT ALL OF MY TEENS TRYING TO GET AWAY FROM THAT PLACE.
HECK!!

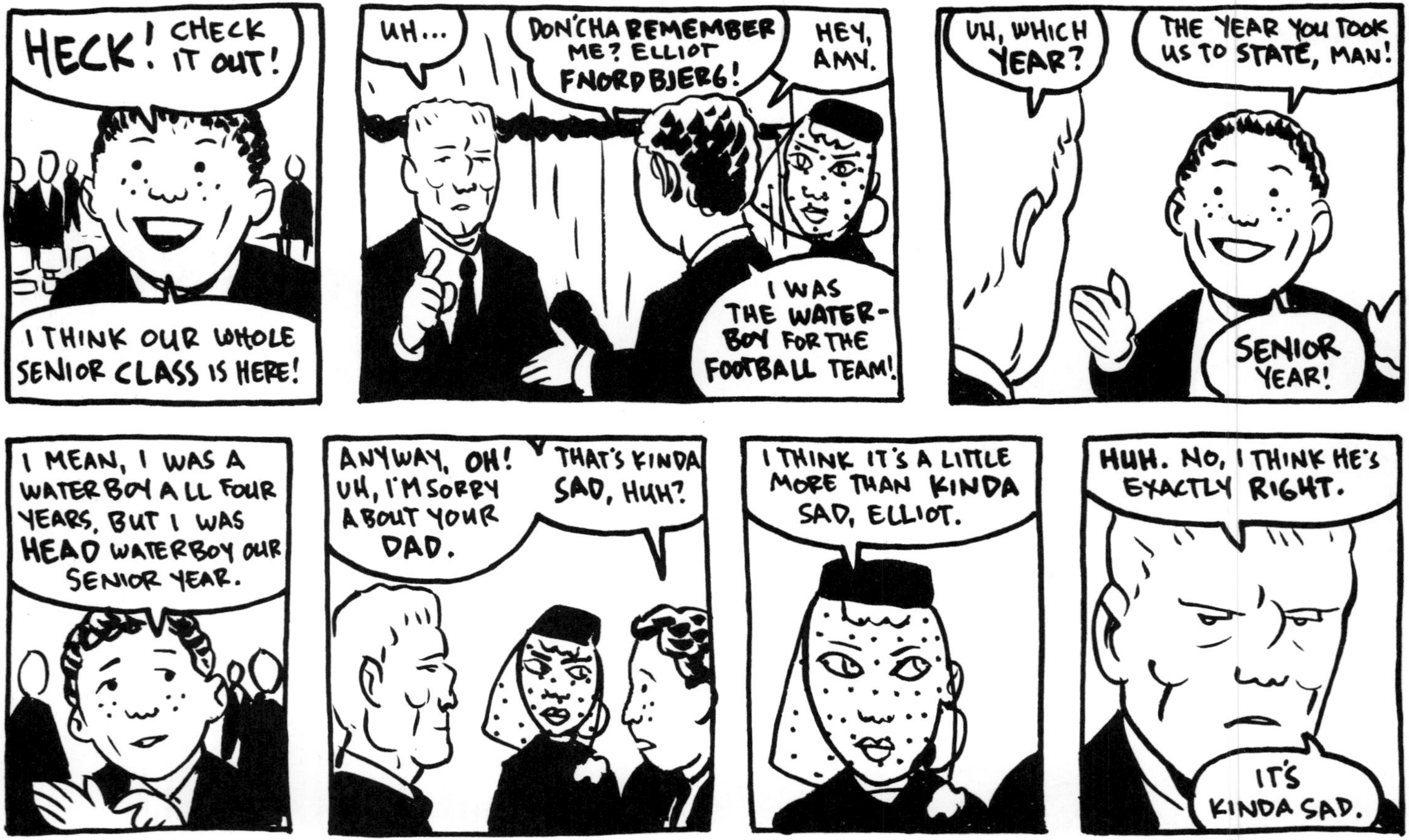
HECK! CHECK IT OUT!
I THINK OUR WHOLE SENIOR CLASS IS HERE!
UH...
DON'CHA REMEMBER ME? ELLIOT FNORDBJERG!
HEY, AMY.
I WAS THE WATER-BOY FOR THE FOOTBALL TEAM!
UH, WHICH YEAR?
THE YEAR YOU TOOK US TO STATE, MAN!
SENIOR YEAR!
I MEAN, I WAS A WATERBOY ALL FOUR YEARS, BUT I WAS HEAD WATERBOY OUR SENIOR YEAR.
ANYWAY, OH! UH, I'M SORRY ABOUT YOUR DAD.
THAT'S KINDA SAD, HUH?
I THINK IT'S A LITTLE MORE THAN KINDA SAD, ELLIOT.
HUH. NO, I THINK HE'S EXACTLY RIGHT.
IT'S KINDA SAD.

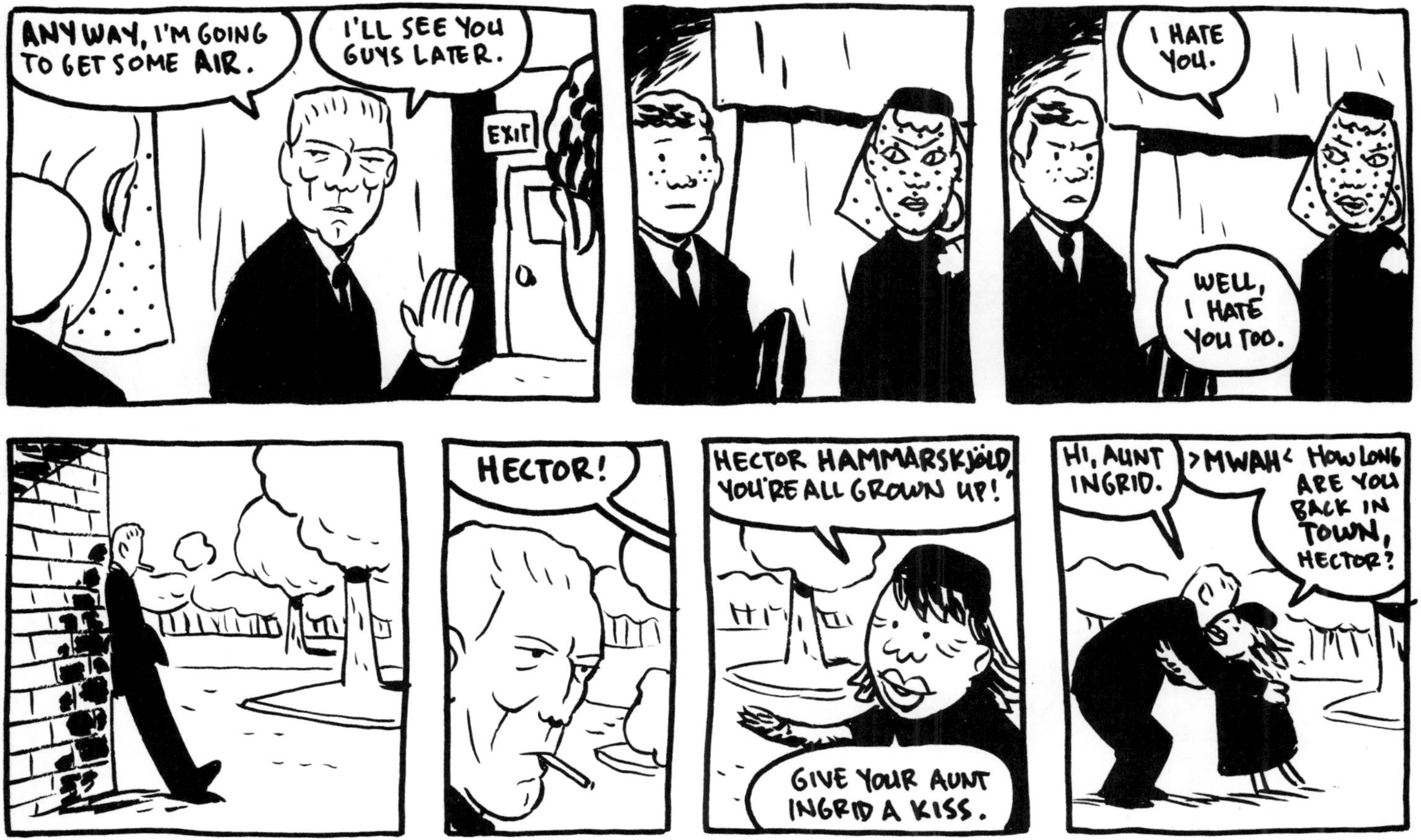
ANYWAY, I'M GOING TO GET SOME AIR.
I'LL SEE YOU GUYS LATER.
EXIT
I HATE YOU.
WELL, I HATE YOU TOO.
HECTOR!
HECTOR HAMMARSKJÖLD, YOU'RE ALL GROWN UP!
GIVE YOUR AUNT INGRID A KISS.
HI, AUNT INGRID.
>MWAH< HOW LONG ARE YOU BACK IN TOWN, HECTOR?

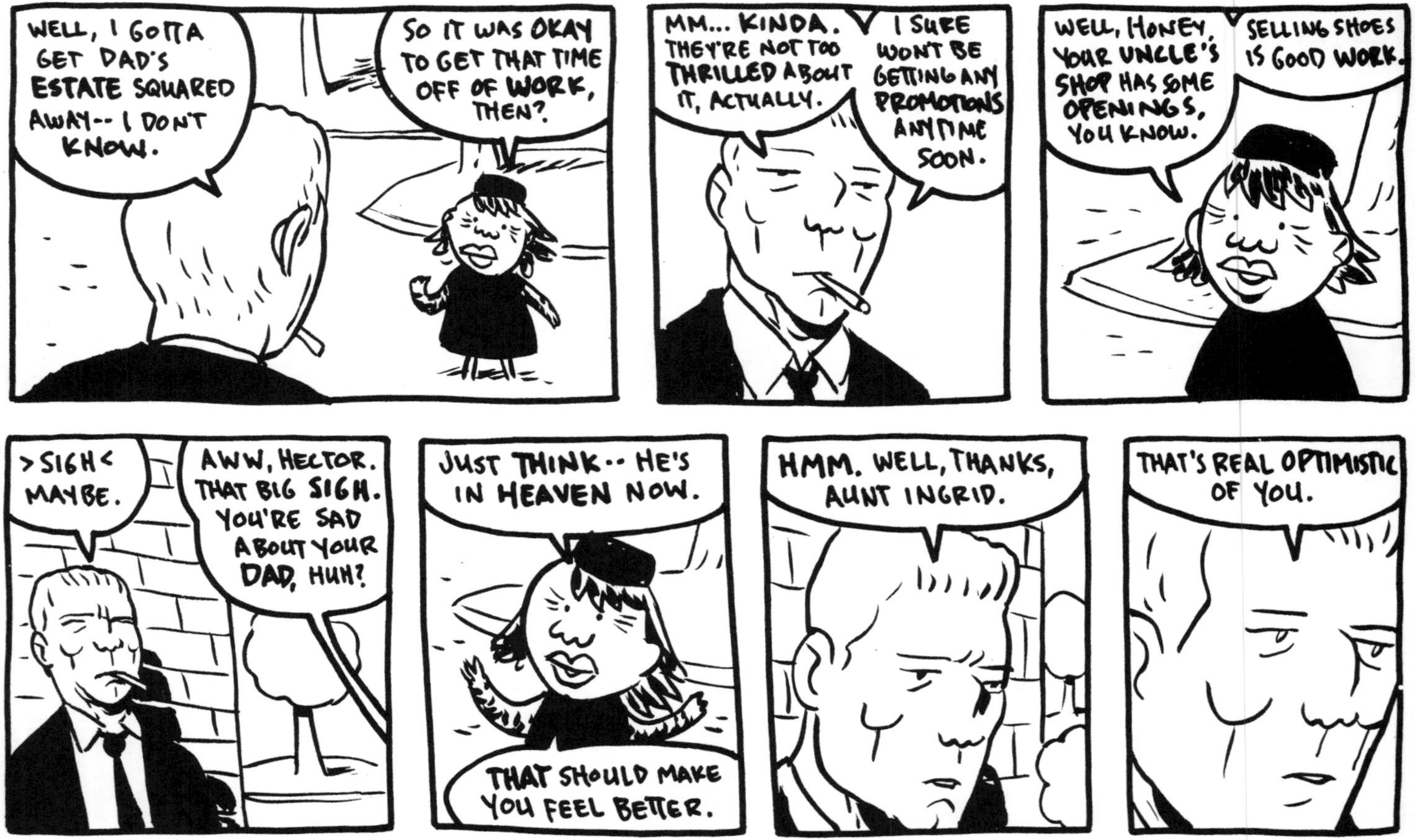
WELL, I GOTTA GET DAD'S ESTATE SQUARED AWAY-- I DON'T KNOW.
SO IT WAS OKAY TO GET THAT TIME OFF OF WORK, THEN?
MM... KINDA. THEY'RE NOT TOO THRILLED ABOUT IT, ACTUALLY.
I SURE WON'T BE GETTING ANY PROMOTIONS ANYTIME SOON.
WELL, HONEY, YOUR UNCLE'S SHOP HAS SOME OPENINGS, YOU KNOW.
SELLING SHOES IS GOOD WORK.
>SIGH< MAYBE.
AWW, HECTOR. THAT BIG SIGH. YOU'RE SAD ABOUT YOUR DAD, HUH?
JUST THINK-- HE'S IN HEAVEN NOW.
THAT SHOULD MAKE YOU FEEL BETTER.
HMM. WELL, THANKS, AUNT INGRID.
THAT'S REAL OPTIMISTIC OF YOU.

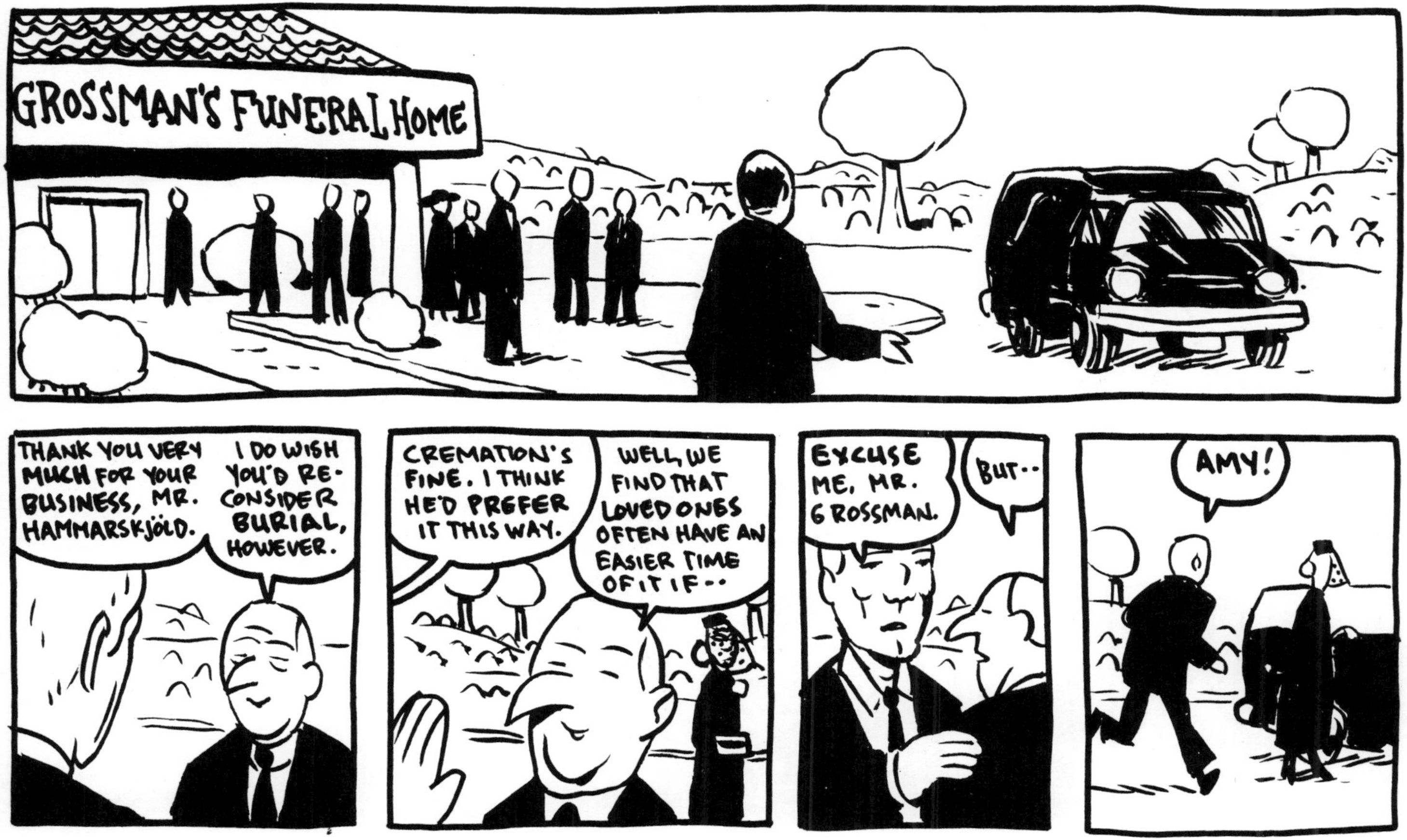
GROSSMAN'S FUNERAL HOME
THANK YOU VERY MUCH FOR YOUR BUSINESS, MR. HAMMARSKJÖLD.
I DO WISH YOU'D RE-CONSIDER BURIAL, HOWEVER.
CREMATION'S FINE. I THINK HE'D PREFER IT THIS WAY.
WELL, WE FIND THAT LOVED ONES OFTEN HAVE AN EASIER TIME OF IT IF--
EXCUSE ME, MR. GROSSMAN.
BUT--
AMY!

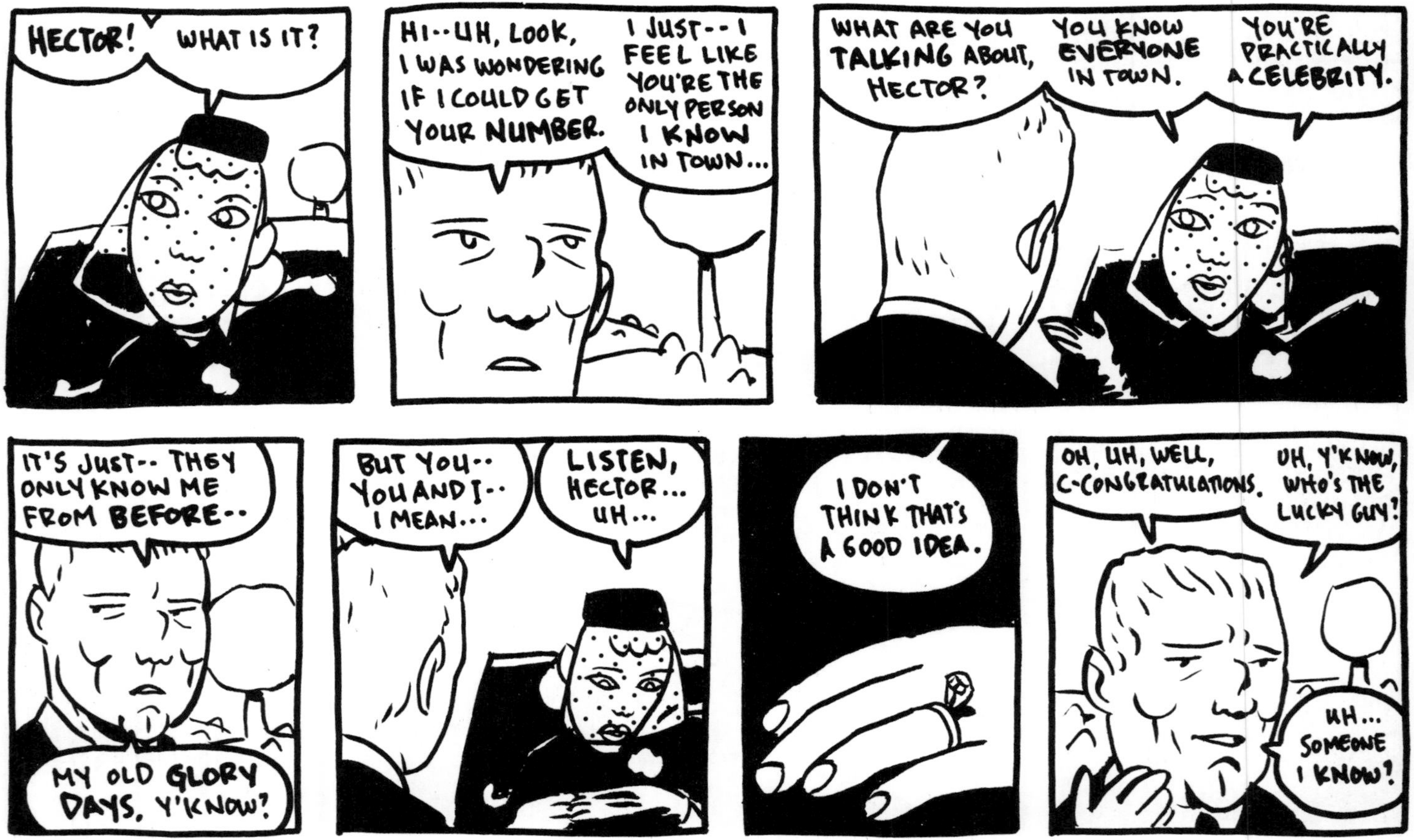
HECTOR!
WHAT IS IT?
HI--UH, LOOK, I WAS WONDERING IF I COULD GET YOUR NUMBER.
I JUST--I FEEL LIKE YOU'RE THE ONLY PERSON I KNOW IN TOWN...
WHAT ARE YOU TALKING ABOUT, HECTOR?
YOU KNOW EVERYONE IN TOWN.
YOU'RE PRACTICALLY A CELEBRITY.
IT'S JUST-- THEY ONLY KNOW ME FROM BEFORE--
MY OLD GLORY DAYS, Y'KNOW?
BUT YOU-- YOU AND I-- I MEAN...
LISTEN, HECTOR... UH...
I DON'T THINK THAT'S A GOOD IDEA.
OH, UH, WELL, C-CONGRATULATIONS.
UH, Y'KNOW, WHO'S THE LUCKY GUY?
UH... SOMEONE I KNOW?

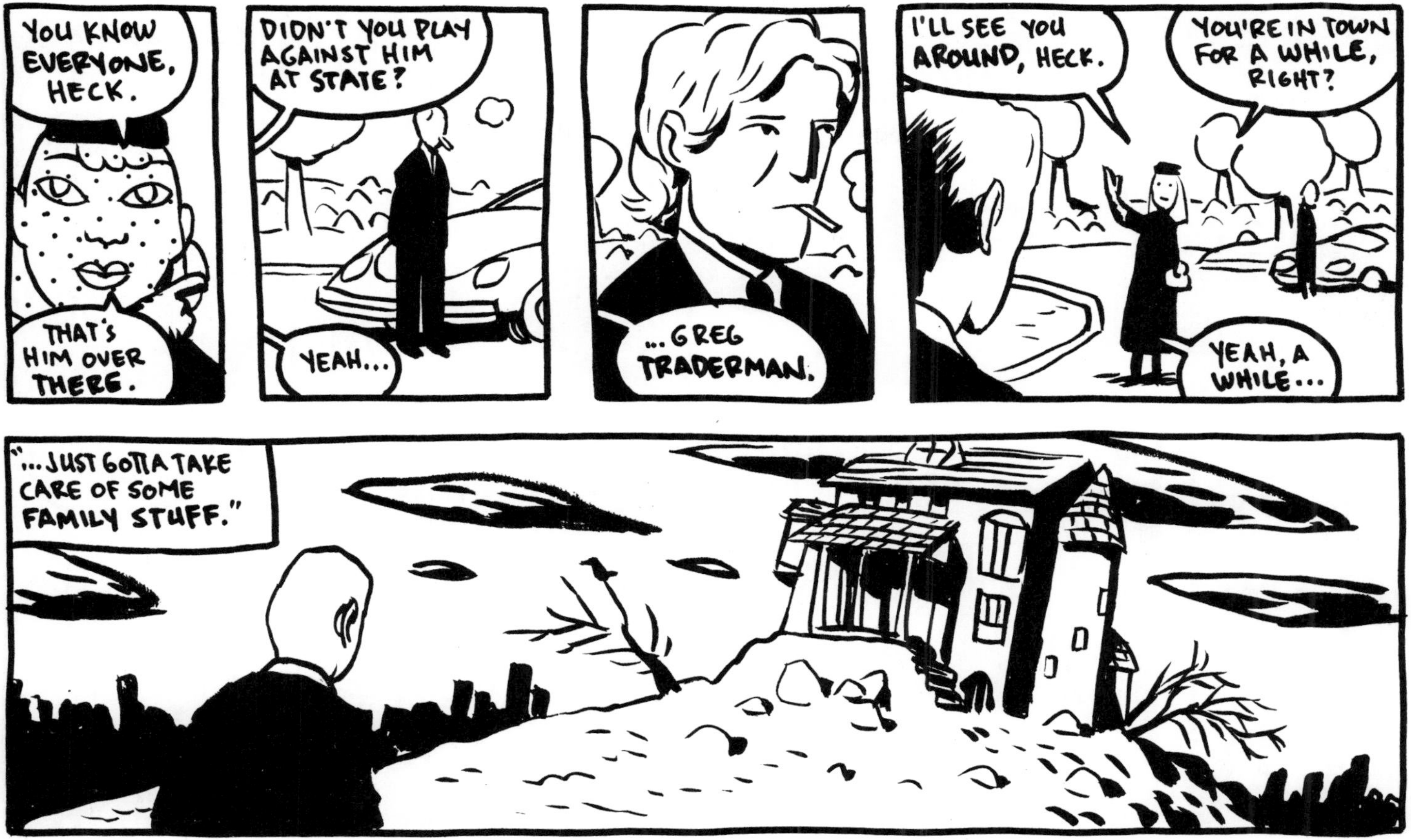
YOU KNOW EVERYONE, HECK.
THAT'S HIM OVER THERE.
DIDN'T YOU PLAY AGAINST HIM AT STATE?
YEAH...
...GREG TRADERMAN.
I'LL SEE YOU AROUND, HECK.
YOU'RE IN TOWN FOR A WHILE, RIGHT?
YEAH, A WHILE...
"...JUST GOTTA TAKE CARE OF SOME FAMILY STUFF."

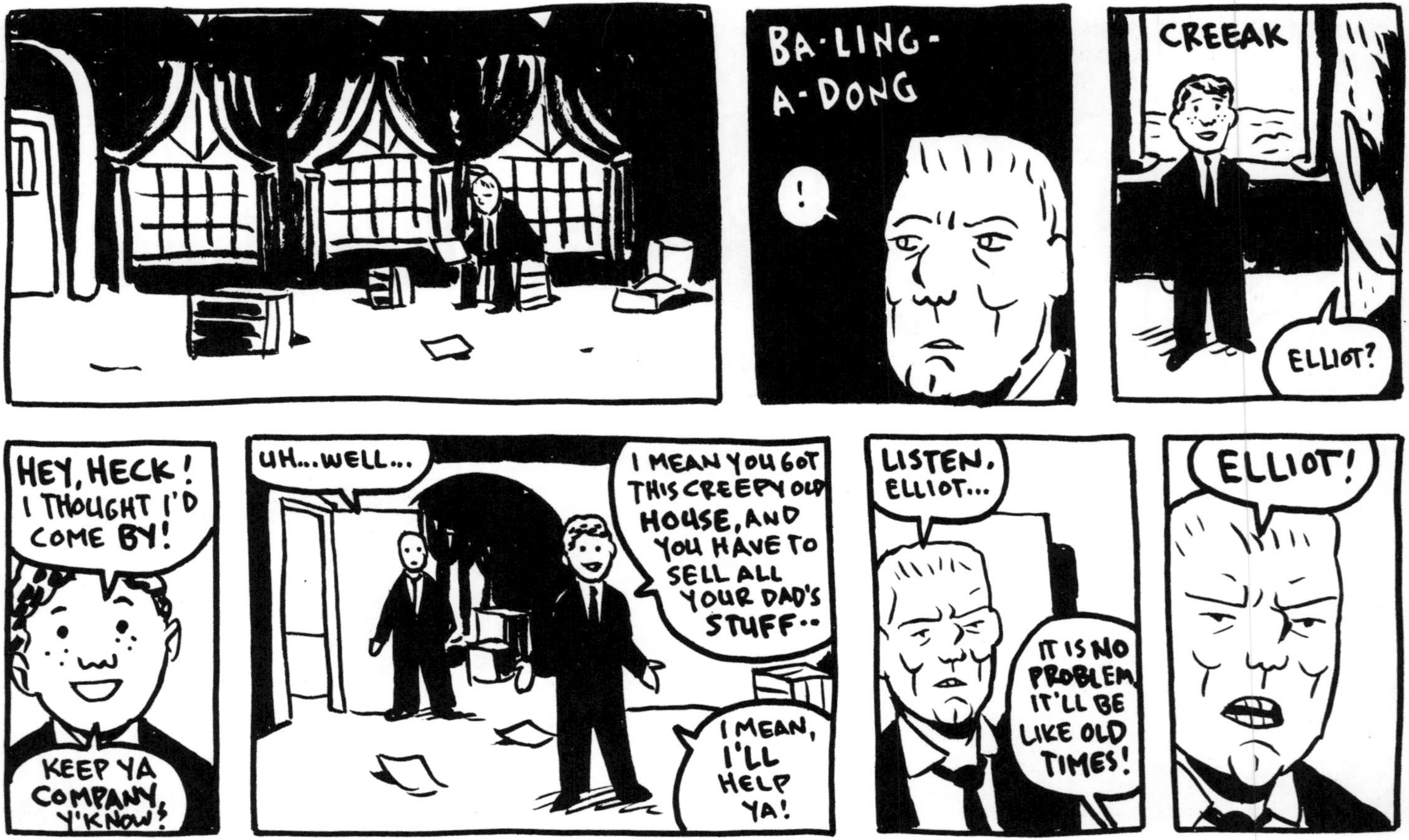
BA-LING-
A-DONG
!
CREEAK
ELLIOT?
HEY, HECK! I THOUGHT I'D COME BY!
KEEP YA COMPANY, Y'KNOW?
UH...WELL...
I MEAN YOU GOT THIS CREEPY OLD HOUSE, AND YOU HAVE TO SELL ALL YOUR DAD'S STUFF..
I MEAN, I'LL HELP YA!
LISTEN, ELLIOT...
IT IS NO PROBLEM. IT'LL BE LIKE OLD TIMES!
ELLIOT!

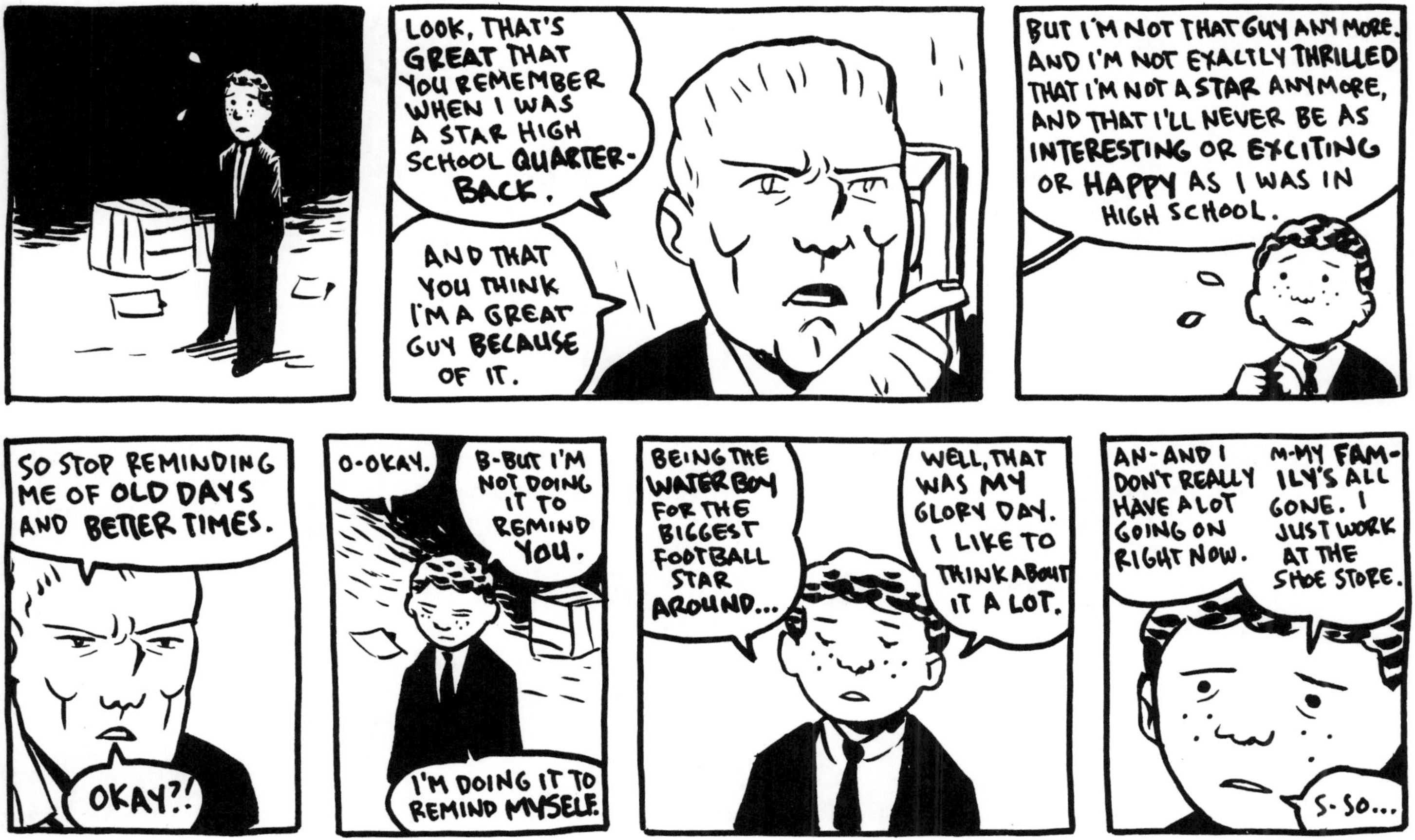
LOOK, THAT'S GREAT THAT YOU REMEMBER WHEN I WAS A STAR HIGH SCHOOL QUARTER-BACK.
AND THAT YOU THINK I'M A GREAT GUY BECAUSE OF IT.
BUT I'M NOT THAT GUY ANY MORE. AND I'M NOT EXACTLY THRILLED THAT I'M NOT A STAR ANYMORE, AND THAT I'LL NEVER BE AS INTERESTING OR EXCITING OR HAPPY AS I WAS IN HIGH SCHOOL.
SO STOP REMINDING ME OF OLD DAYS AND BETTER TIMES.
OKAY?!
O-OKAY.
B-BUT I'M NOT DOING IT TO REMIND YOU.
I'M DOING IT TO REMIND MYSELF.
BEING THE WATER BOY FOR THE BIGGEST FOOTBALL STAR AROUND...
WELL, THAT WAS MY GLORY DAY. I LIKE TO THINK ABOUT IT A LOT.
AN- AND I DON'T REALLY HAVE A LOT GOING ON RIGHT NOW.
M-MY FAMILY'S ALL GONE. I JUST WORK AT THE SHOE STORE.
S-SO...

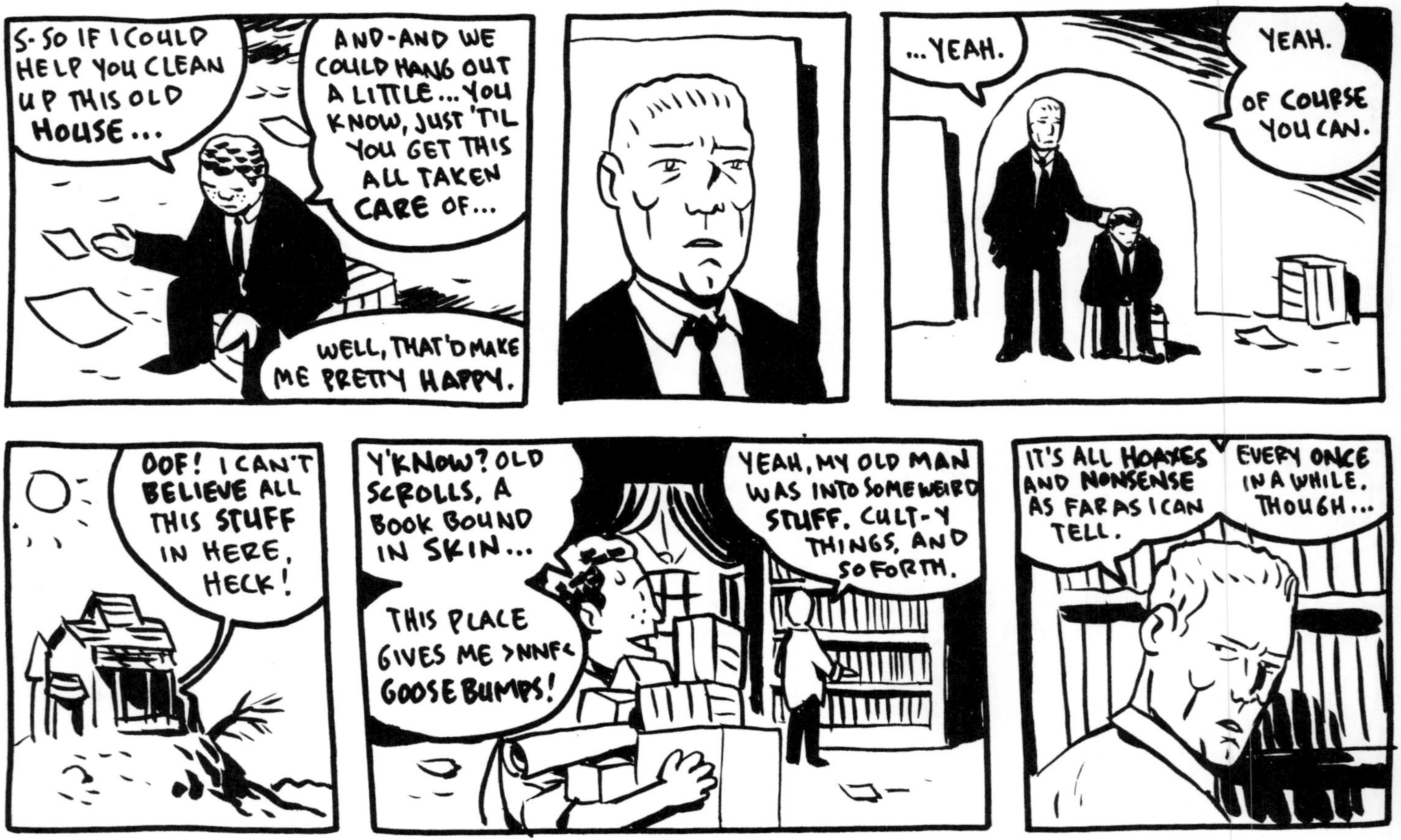
S-SO IF I COULD HELP YOU CLEAN UP THIS OLD HOUSE...
AND-AND WE COULD HANG OUT A LITTLE... YOU KNOW, JUST 'TIL YOU GET THIS ALL TAKEN CARE OF...
WELL, THAT'D MAKE ME PRETTY HAPPY.
...YEAH.
YEAH.
OF COURSE YOU CAN.
OOF! I CAN'T BELIEVE ALL THIS STUFF IN HERE, HECK!
Y'KNOW? OLD SCROLLS, A BOOK BOUND IN SKIN...
THIS PLACE GIVES ME >NNF< GOOSEBUMPS!
YEAH, MY OLD MAN WAS INTO SOME WEIRD STUFF. CULT-Y THINGS, AND SO FORTH.
IT'S ALL HOAXES AND NONSENSE AS FAR AS I CAN TELL.
EVERY ONCE IN A WHILE, THOUGH...

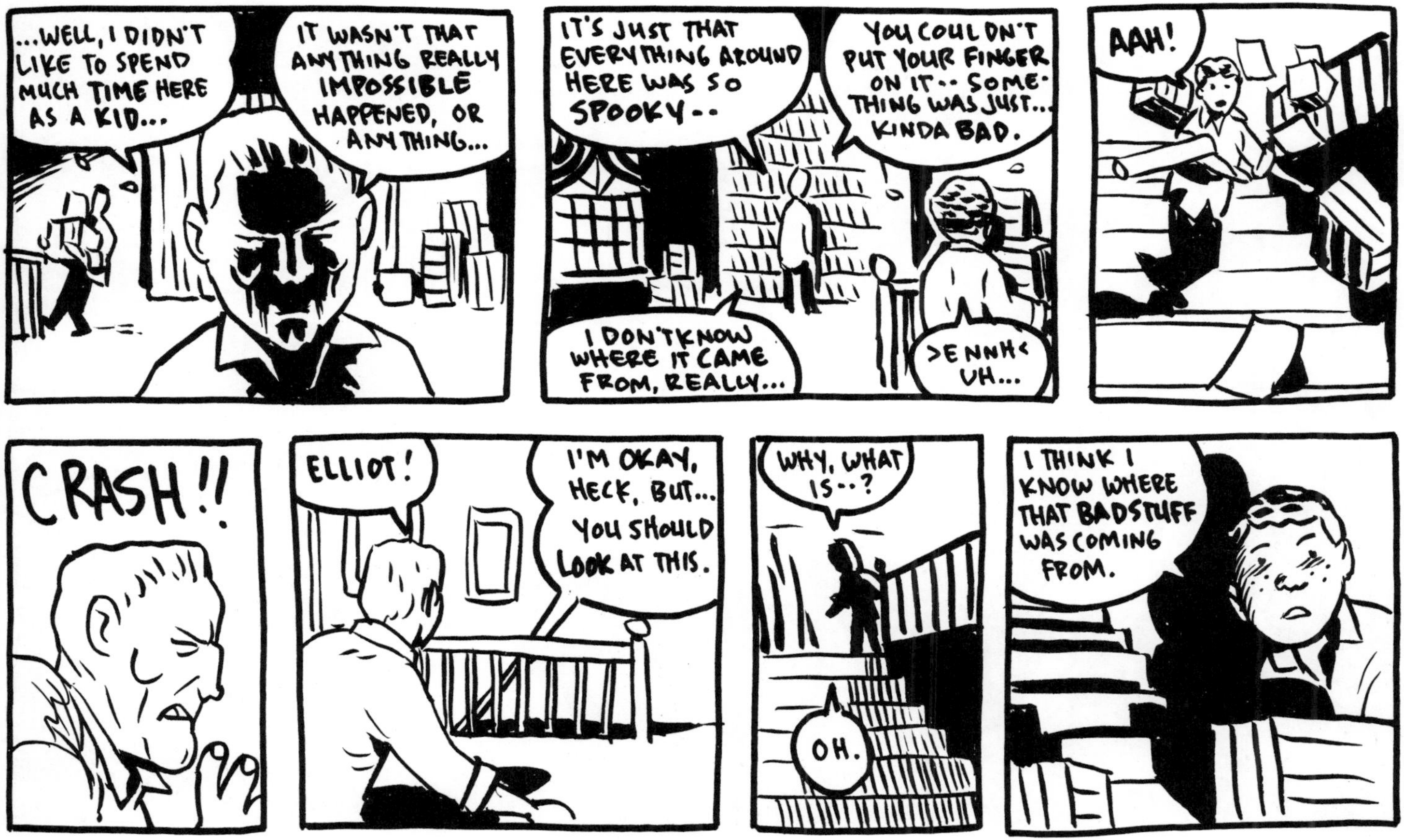
...WELL, I DIDN'T LIKE TO SPEND MUCH TIME HERE AS A KID...
IT WASN'T THAT ANYTHING REALLY IMPOSSIBLE HAPPENED, OR ANYTHING...
IT'S JUST THAT EVERYTHING AROUND HERE WAS SO SPOOKY--
I DON'T KNOW WHERE IT CAME FROM, REALLY...
YOU COULDN'T PUT YOUR FINGER ON IT-- SOMETHING WAS JUST... KINDA BAD.
>ENNH< UH...
AAH!
CRASH!!
ELLIOT!
I'M OKAY, HECK, BUT... YOU SHOULD LOOK AT THIS.
WHY, WHAT IS--?
OH.
I THINK I KNOW WHERE THAT BAD STUFF WAS COMING FROM.

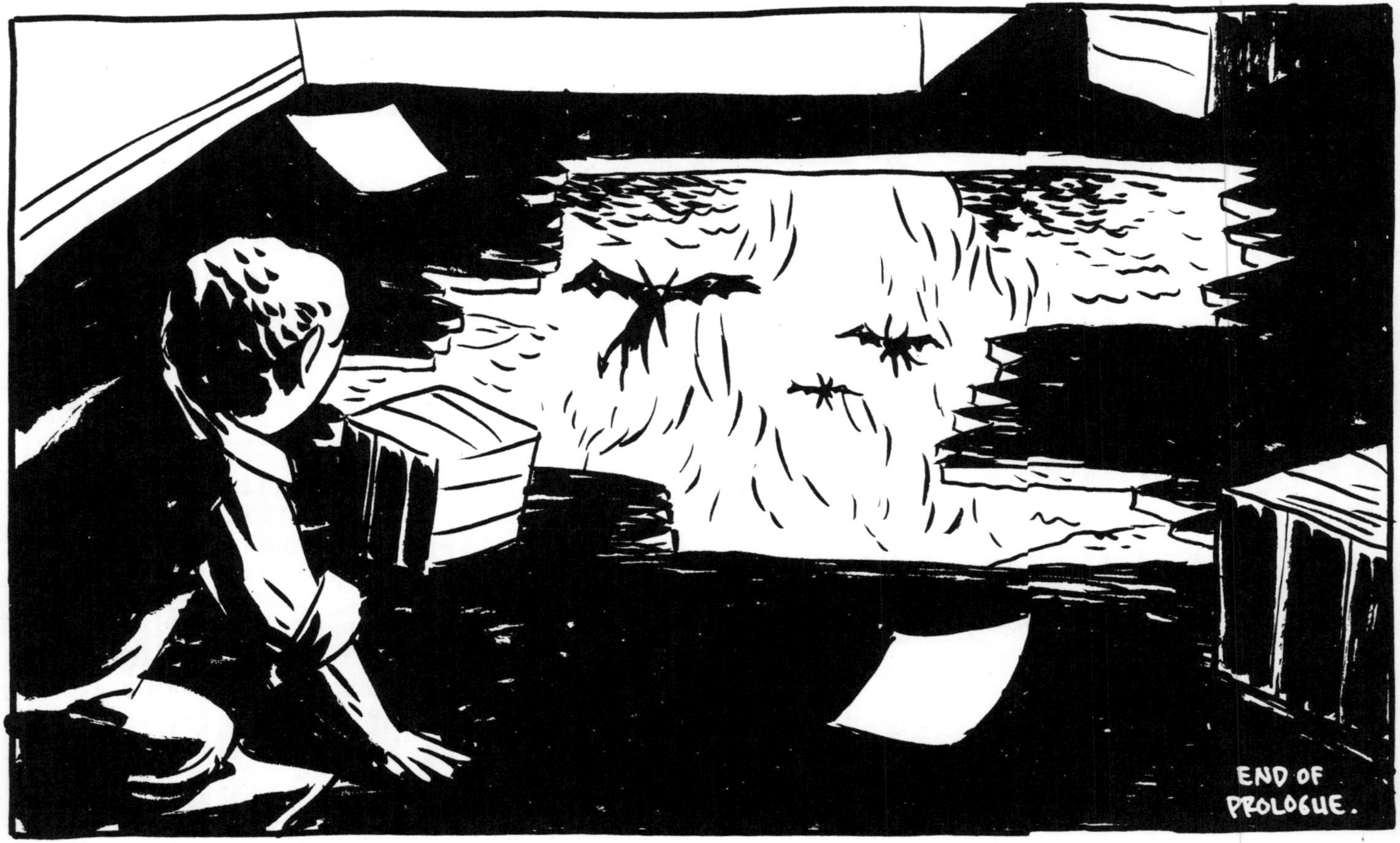
END OF
PROLOGUE.

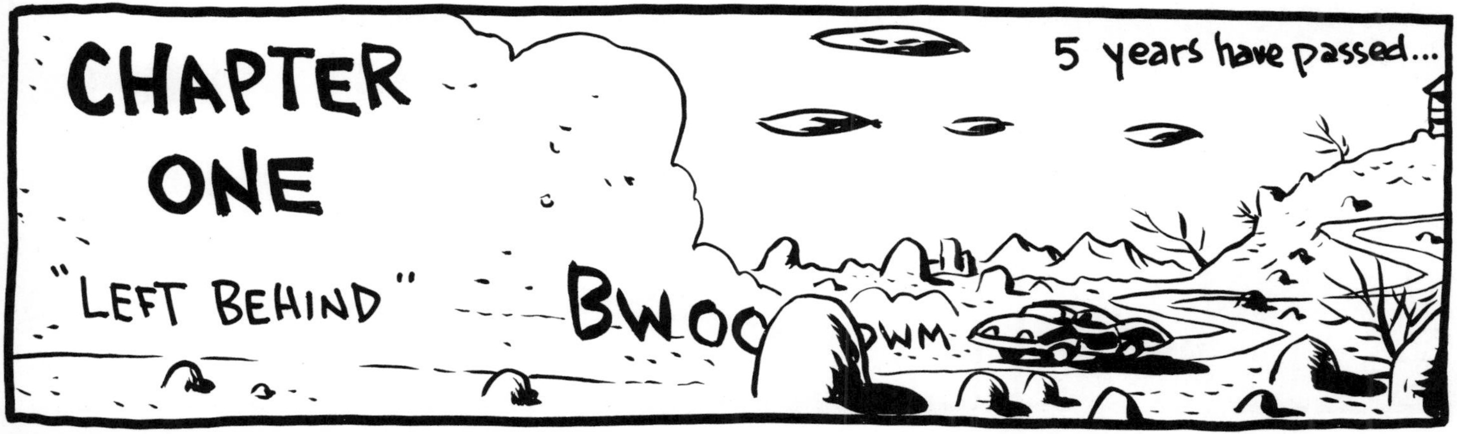
CHAPTER ONE
"LEFT BEHIND"
5 years have passed...
BWOO
WM

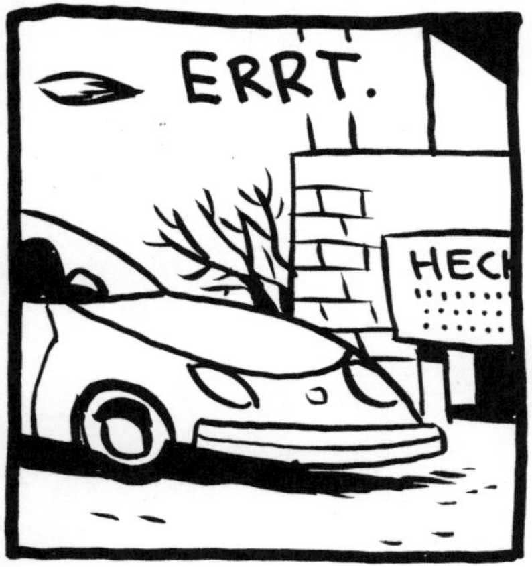
ERRT.
HEC

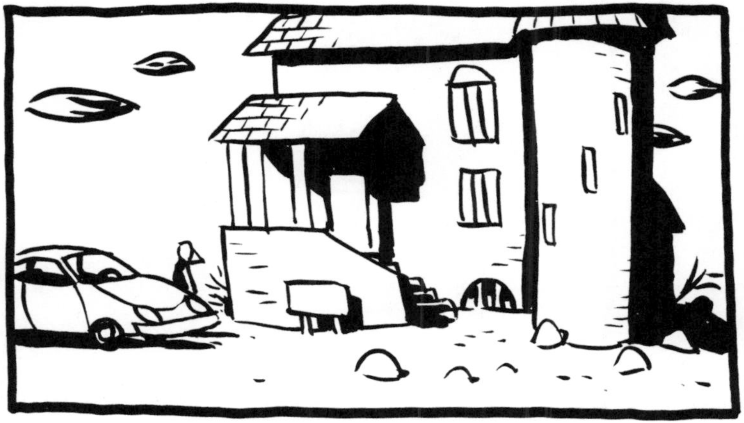

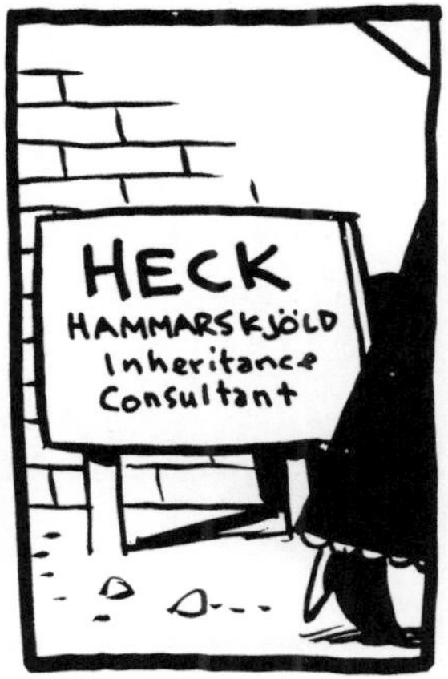
HECK
HAMMARSKJÖLD
Inheritance
Consultant

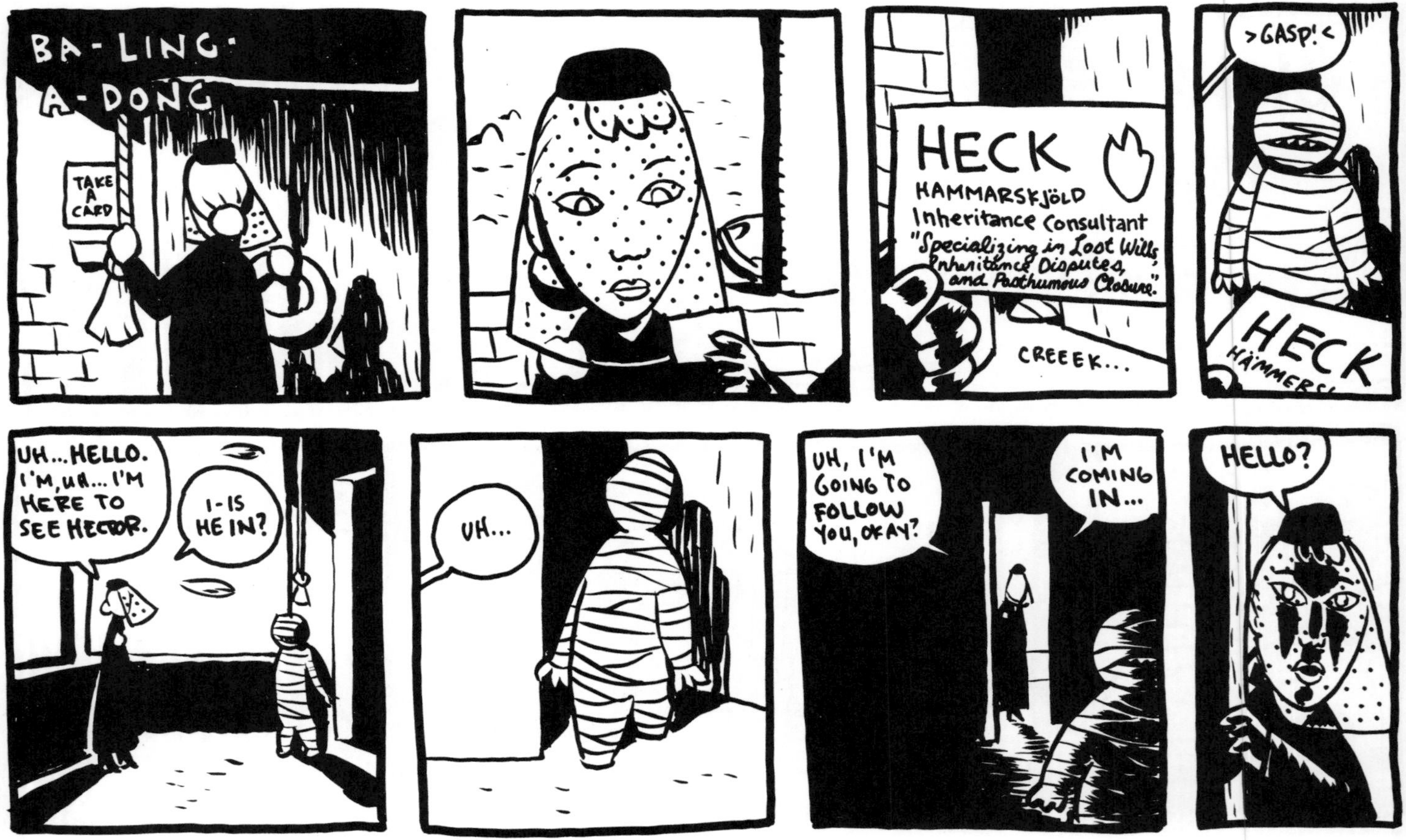
BA-LING-
A-DONG
TAKE A CARD
HECK
HAMMARSKJÖLD
Inheritance Consultant
"Specializing in Lost Wills, Inheritance Disputes, and Posthumous Closure."
CREEEK...
>GASP!<
HECK
UH...HELLO. I'M, UH... I'M HERE TO SEE HECTOR.
I-IS HE IN?
UH...
UH, I'M GOING TO FOLLOW YOU, OKAY?
I'M COMING IN...
HELLO?

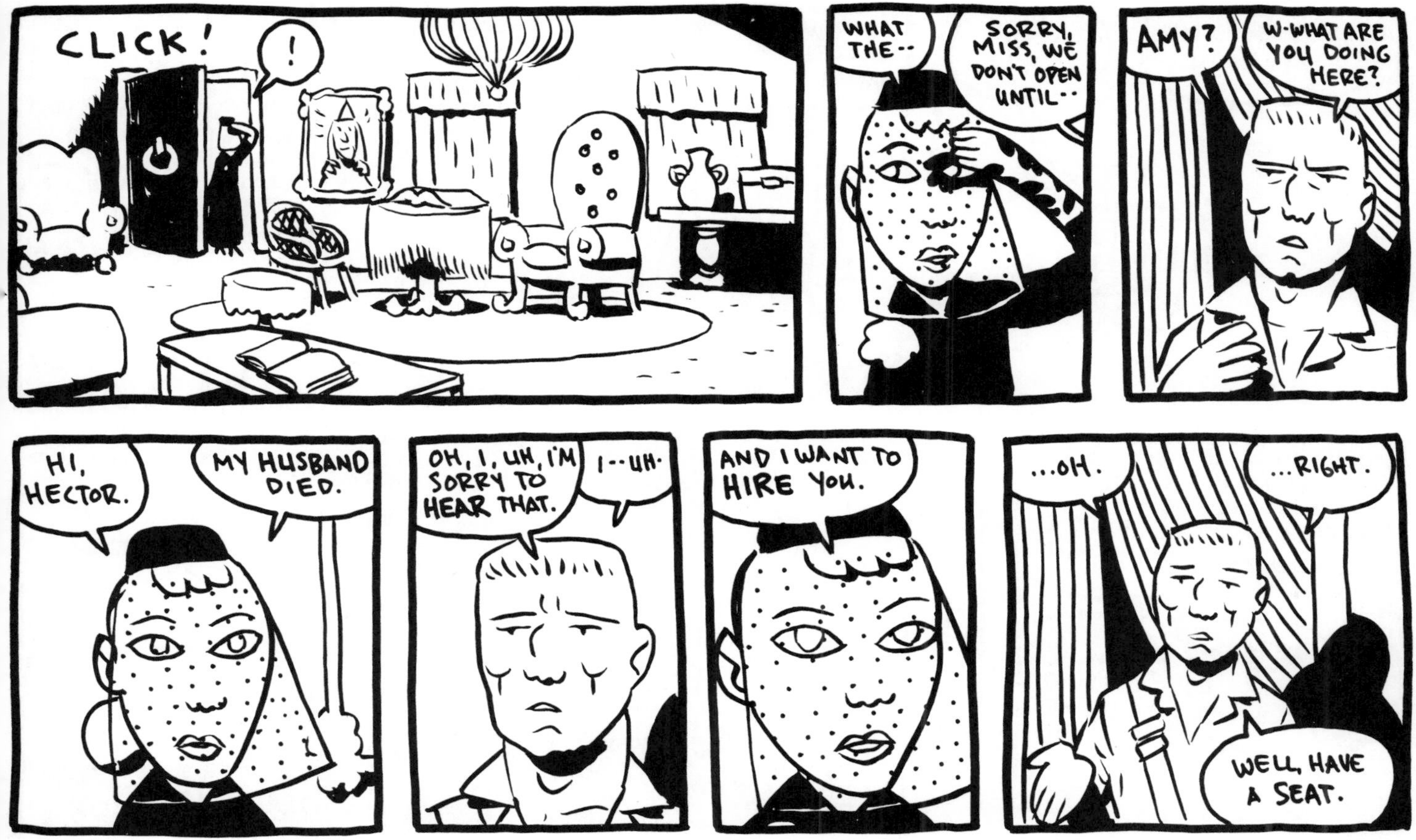
CLICK!
!
WHAT THE--
SORRY, MISS, WE DON'T OPEN UNTIL--
AMY?
W-WHAT ARE YOU DOING HERE?
HI, HECTOR.
MY HUSBAND DIED.
OH, I, UH, I'M SORRY TO HEAR THAT.
I--UH.
AND I WANT TO HIRE YOU.
...OH.
...RIGHT.
WELL, HAVE A SEAT.

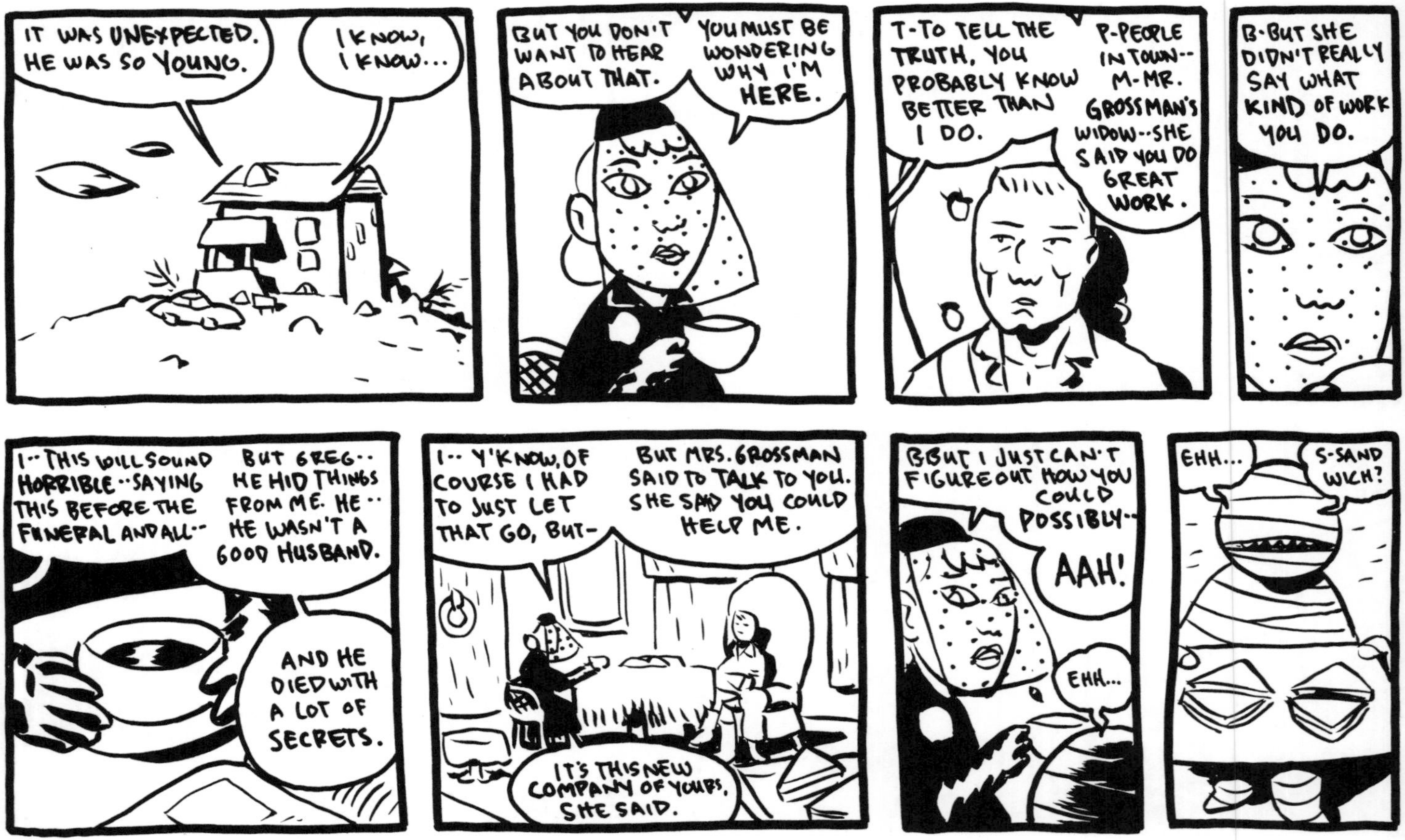
IT WAS UNEXPECTED. HE WAS SO YOUNG.
I KNOW, I KNOW...
BUT YOU DON'T WANT TO HEAR ABOUT THAT.
YOU MUST BE WONDERING WHY I'M HERE.
T-TO TELL THE TRUTH, YOU PROBABLY KNOW BETTER THAN I DO.
P-PEOPLE IN TOWN-- M-MR. GROSSMAN'S WIDOW--SHE SAID YOU DO GREAT WORK.
B-BUT SHE DIDN'T REALLY SAY WHAT KIND OF WORK YOU DO.
I-- THIS WILL SOUND HORRIBLE--SAYING THIS BEFORE THE FUNERAL AND ALL--
BUT GREG-- HE HID THINGS FROM ME. HE-- HE WASN'T A GOOD HUSBAND.
AND HE DIED WITH A LOT OF SECRETS.
I-- Y'KNOW, OF COURSE I HAD TO JUST LET THAT GO, BUT-
BUT MRS. GROSSMAN SAID TO TALK TO YOU. SHE SAID YOU COULD HELP ME.
IT'S THIS NEW COMPANY OF YOURS, SHE SAID.
B-BUT I JUST CAN'T FIGURE OUT HOW YOU COULD POSSIBLY--
AAH!
EHH...
EHH...
S-SANDWICH?

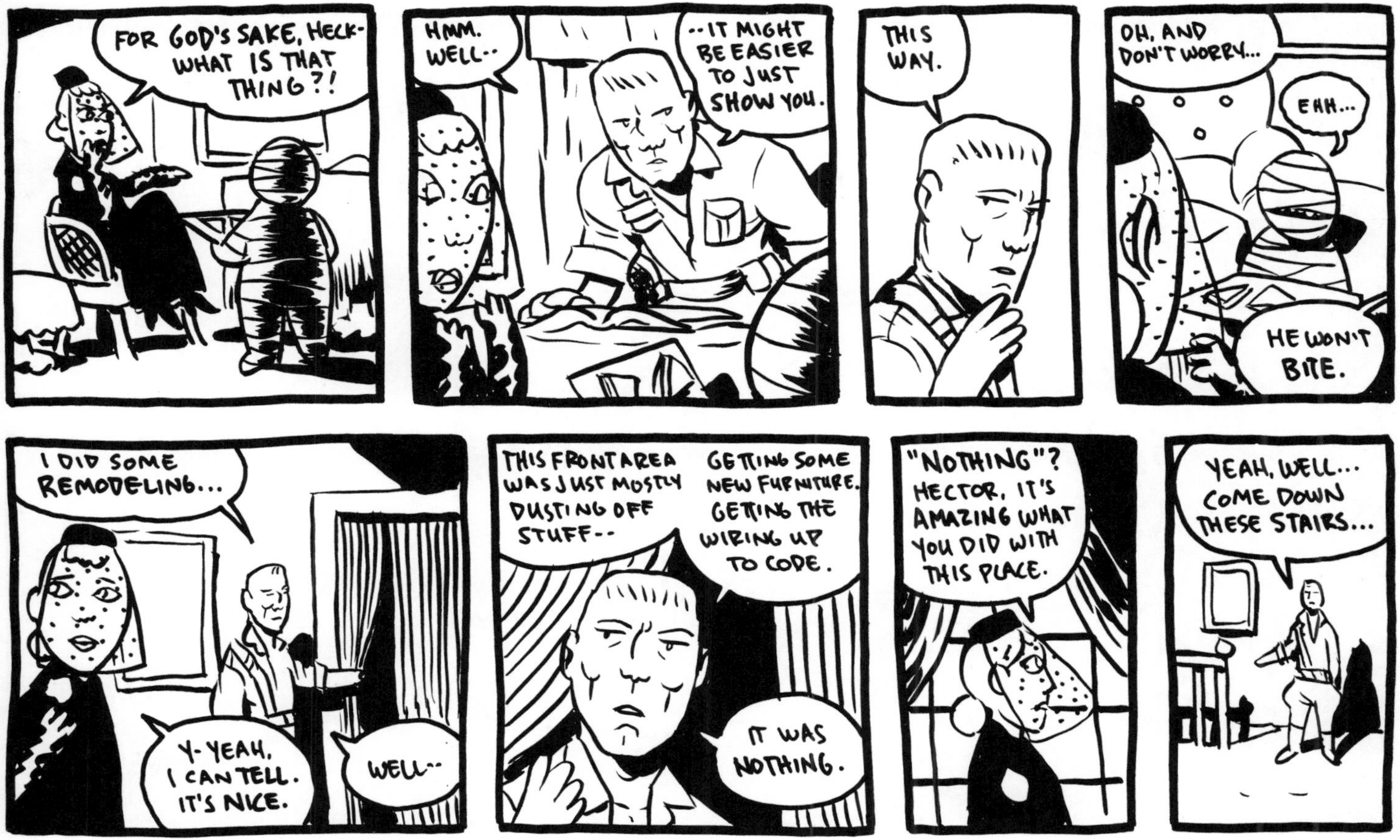
FOR GOD'S SAKE, HECK-WHAT IS THAT THING?!
HMM. WELL--
--IT MIGHT BE EASIER TO JUST SHOW YOU.
THIS WAY.
OH, AND DON'T WORRY...
EHH...
HE WON'T BITE.
I DID SOME REMODELING...
Y-YEAH, I CAN TELL. IT'S NICE.
WELL--
THIS FRONT AREA WAS JUST MOSTLY DUSTING OFF STUFF--
GETTING SOME NEW FURNITURE. GETTING THE WIRING UP TO CODE.
IT WAS NOTHING.
"NOTHING"? HECTOR, IT'S AMAZING WHAT YOU DID WITH THIS PLACE.
YEAH, WELL... COME DOWN THESE STAIRS...

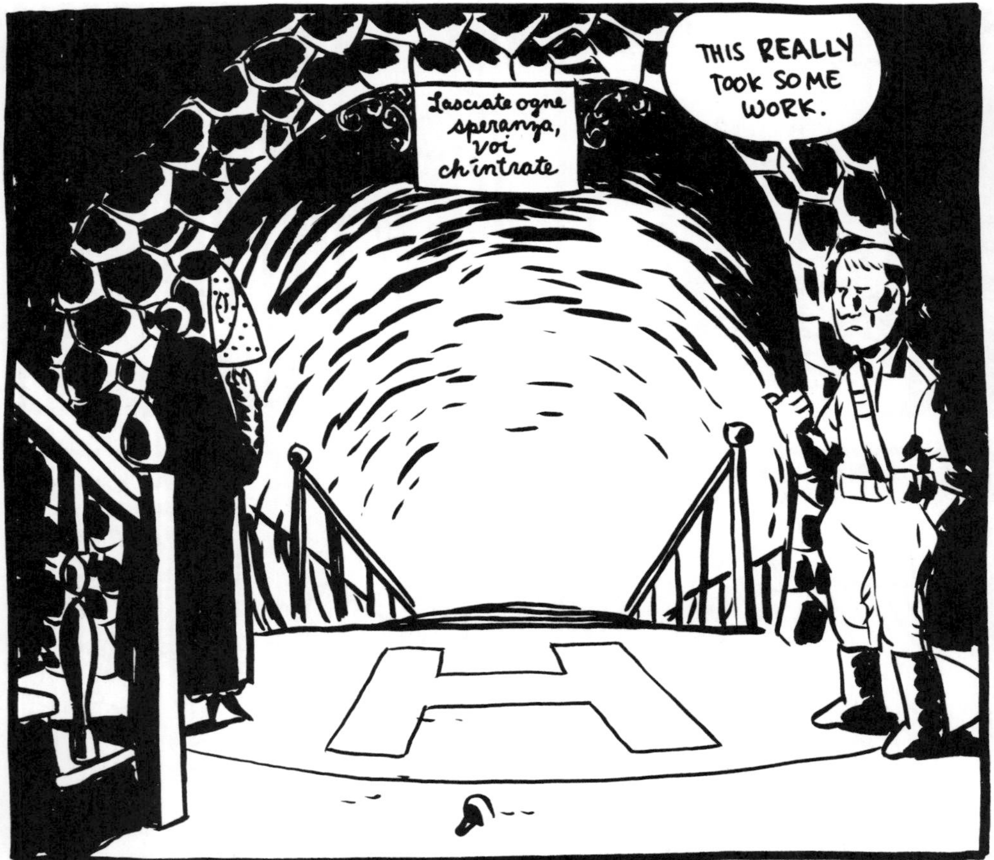
Lasciate ogne speranza, voi ch'intrate
THIS REALLY TOOK SOME WORK.

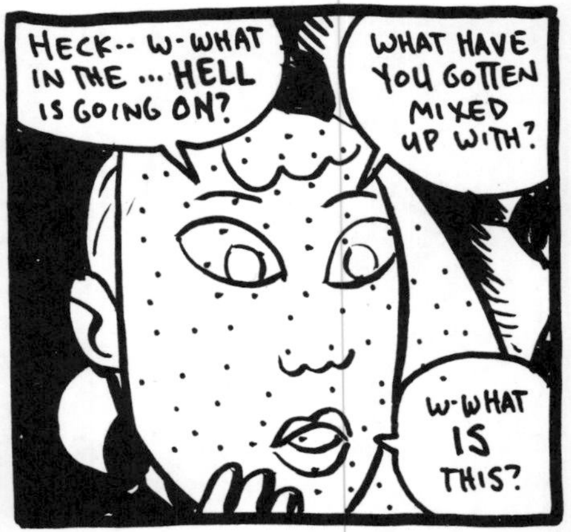
HECK.. W-WHAT IN THE ... HELL IS GOING ON?
WHAT HAVE YOU GOTTEN MIXED UP WITH?
W-WHAT IS THIS?

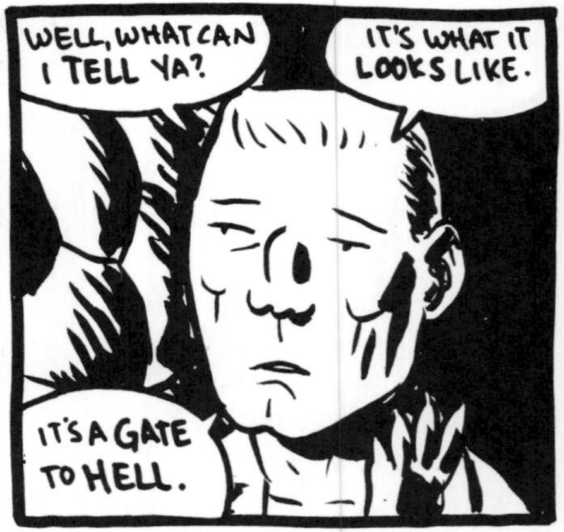
WELL, WHAT CAN I TELL YA?
IT'S WHAT IT LOOKS LIKE.
IT'S A GATE TO HELL.

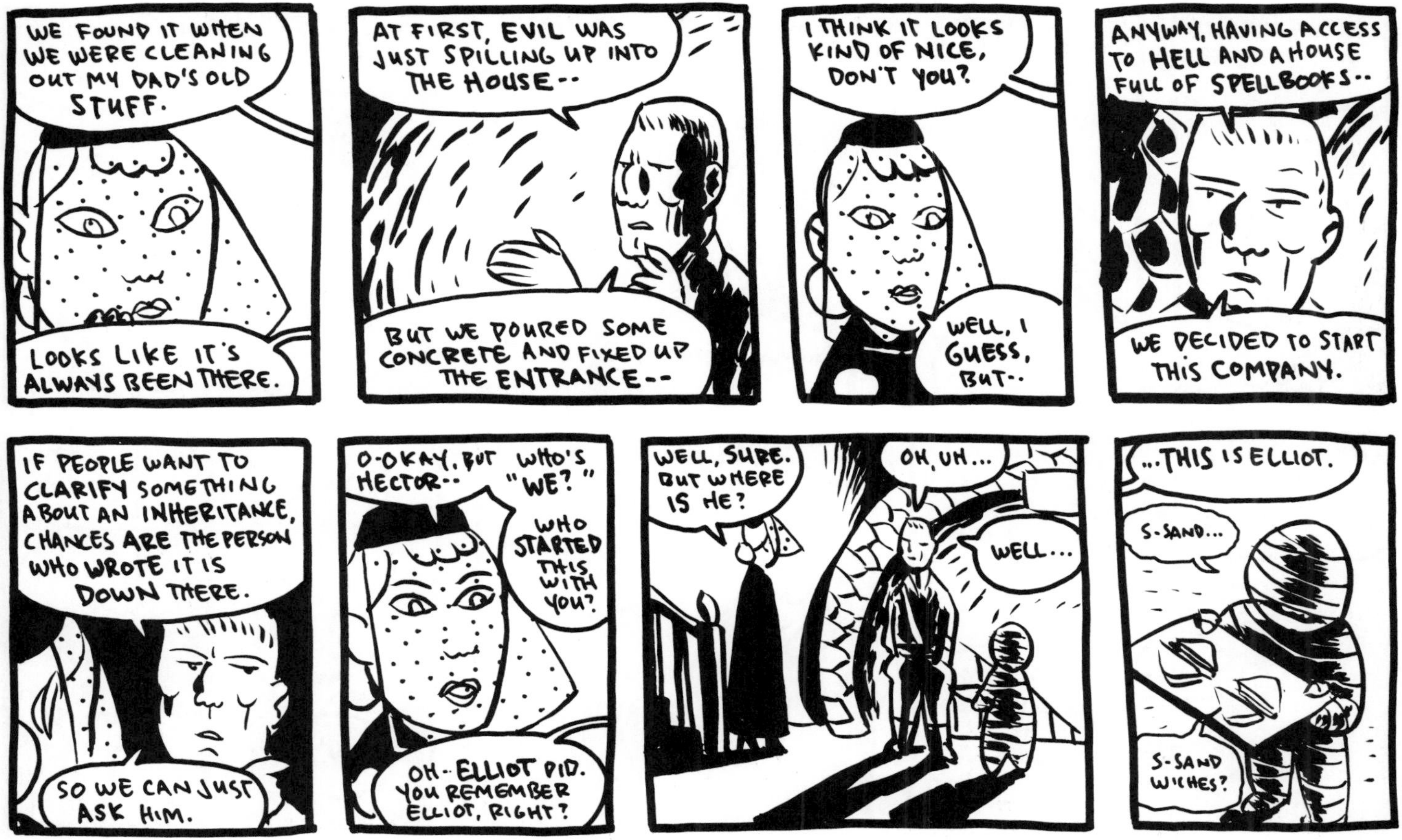
WE FOUND IT WHEN WE WERE CLEANING OUT MY DAD'S OLD STUFF.
LOOKS LIKE IT'S ALWAYS BEEN THERE.
AT FIRST, EVIL WAS JUST SPILLING UP INTO THE HOUSE--
BUT WE POURED SOME CONCRETE AND FIXED UP THE ENTRANCE--
I THINK IT LOOKS KIND OF NICE, DON'T YOU?
WELL, I GUESS, BUT..
ANYWAY, HAVING ACCESS TO HELL AND A HOUSE FULL OF SPELLBOOKS..
WE DECIDED TO START THIS COMPANY.
IF PEOPLE WANT TO CLARIFY SOMETHING ABOUT AN INHERITANCE, CHANCES ARE THE PERSON WHO WROTE IT IS DOWN THERE.
SO WE CAN JUST ASK HIM.
O-OKAY, BUT HECTOR--
WHO'S "WE?"
WHO STARTED THIS WITH YOU?
OH.. ELLIOT DID. YOU REMEMBER ELLIOT, RIGHT?
WELL, SURE. BUT WHERE IS HE?
OH, UH...
WELL...
...THIS IS ELLIOT.
S-SAND...
S-SAND WICHES?

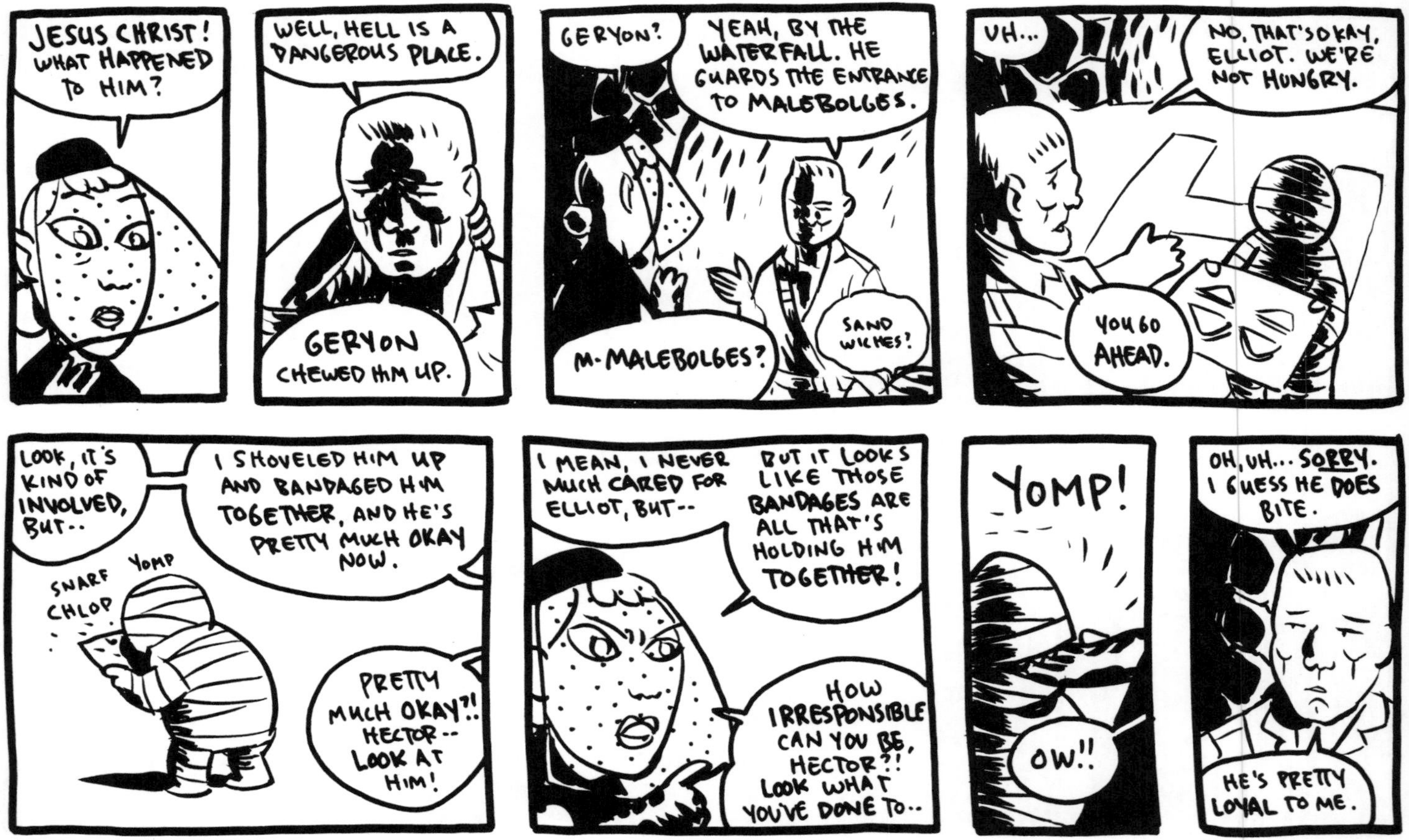
JESUS CHRIST! WHAT HAPPENED TO HIM?
WELL, HELL IS A DANGEROUS PLACE.
GERYON CHEWED HIM UP.
GERYON?
YEAH, BY THE WATERFALL. HE GUARDS THE ENTRANCE TO MALEBOLGES.
M-MALEBOLGES?
SAND WICHES?
UH...
NO, THAT'S OKAY, ELLIOT. WE'RE NOT HUNGRY.
YOU GO AHEAD.
LOOK, IT'S KIND OF INVOLVED, BUT..
I SHOVELED HIM UP AND BANDAGED HIM TOGETHER, AND HE'S PRETTY MUCH OKAY NOW.
SNARF
YOMP
CHLOP
PRETTY MUCH OKAY?!! HECTOR -- LOOK AT HIM!
I MEAN, I NEVER MUCH CARED FOR ELLIOT, BUT--
BUT IT LOOKS LIKE THOSE BANDAGES ARE ALL THAT'S HOLDING HIM TOGETHER!
HOW IRRESPONSIBLE CAN YOU BE, HECTOR?! LOOK WHAT YOU'VE DONE TO..
YOMP!
OW!!
OH, UH... SORRY. I GUESS HE DOES BITE.
HE'S PRETTY LOYAL TO ME.

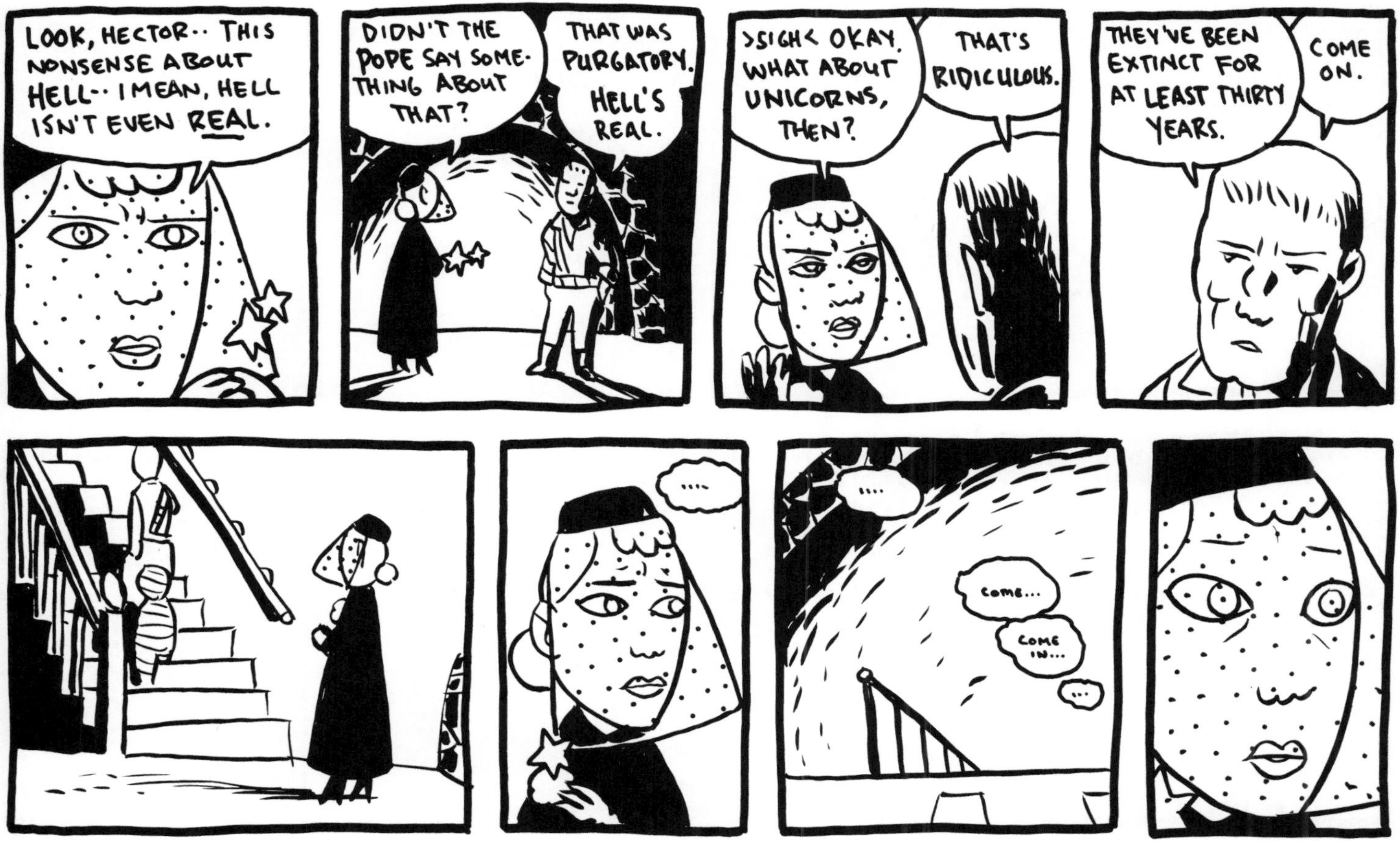
LOOK, HECTOR.. THIS NONSENSE ABOUT HELL.. I MEAN, HELL ISN'T EVEN REAL.
DIDN'T THE POPE SAY SOMETHING ABOUT THAT?
THAT WAS PURGATORY.
HELL'S REAL.
>SIGH< OKAY. WHAT ABOUT UNICORNS, THEN?
THAT'S RIDICULOUS.
THEY'VE BEEN EXTINCT FOR AT LEAST THIRTY YEARS.
COME ON.
....
....
COME...
COME IN...
...

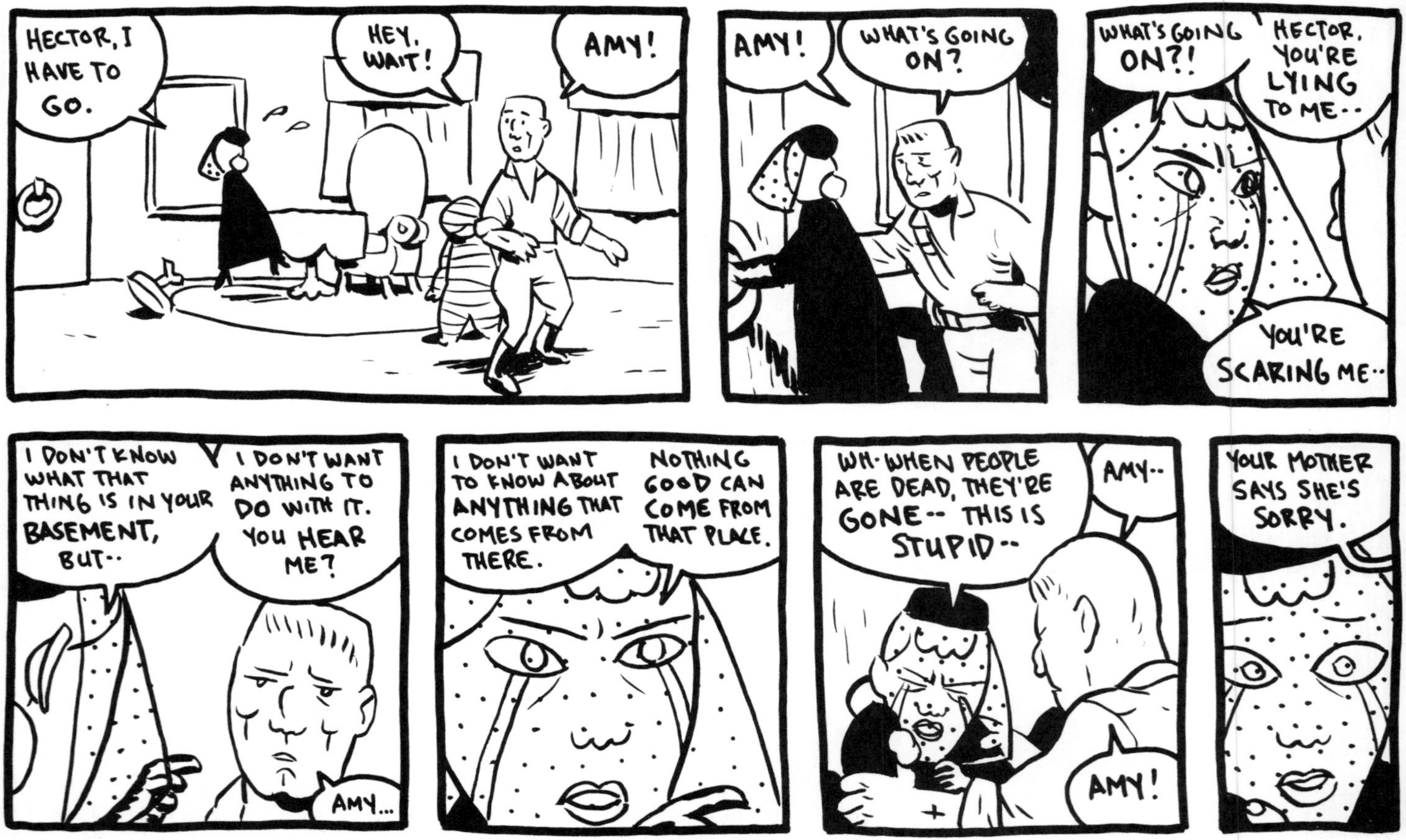
HECTOR, I HAVE TO GO.
HEY, WAIT!
AMY!
AMY!
WHAT'S GOING ON?
WHAT'S GOING ON?!
HECTOR, YOU'RE LYING TO ME--
YOU'RE SCARING ME--
I DON'T KNOW WHAT THAT THING IS IN YOUR BASEMENT, BUT--
I DON'T WANT ANYTHING TO DO WITH IT. YOU HEAR ME?
AMY...
I DON'T WANT TO KNOW ABOUT ANYTHING THAT COMES FROM THERE.
NOTHING GOOD CAN COME FROM THAT PLACE.
WH-WHEN PEOPLE ARE DEAD, THEY'RE GONE-- THIS IS STUPID--
AMY--
AMY!
YOUR MOTHER SAYS SHE'S SORRY.

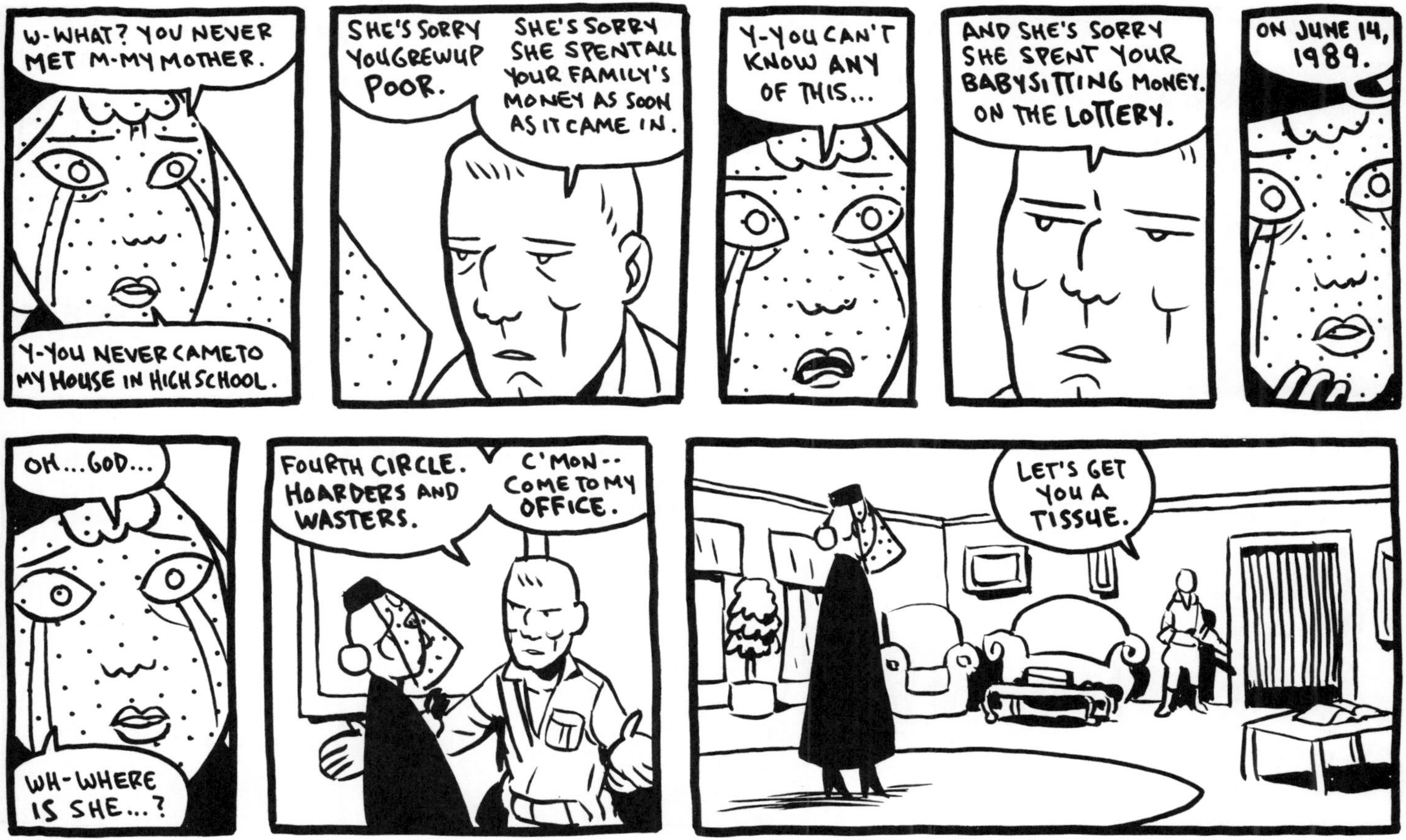
W-WHAT? YOU NEVER MET M-MY MOTHER.
Y-YOU NEVER CAME TO MY HOUSE IN HIGH SCHOOL.
SHE'S SORRY YOU GREW UP POOR.
SHE'S SORRY SHE SPENT ALL YOUR FAMILY'S MONEY AS SOON AS IT CAME IN.
Y-YOU CAN'T KNOW ANY OF THIS...
AND SHE'S SORRY SHE SPENT YOUR BABYSITTING MONEY. ON THE LOTTERY.
ON JUNE 14, 1989.
OH...GOD...
WH-WHERE IS SHE...?
FOURTH CIRCLE. HOARDERS AND WASTERS.
C'MON-- COME TO MY OFFICE.
LET'S GET YOU A TISSUE.

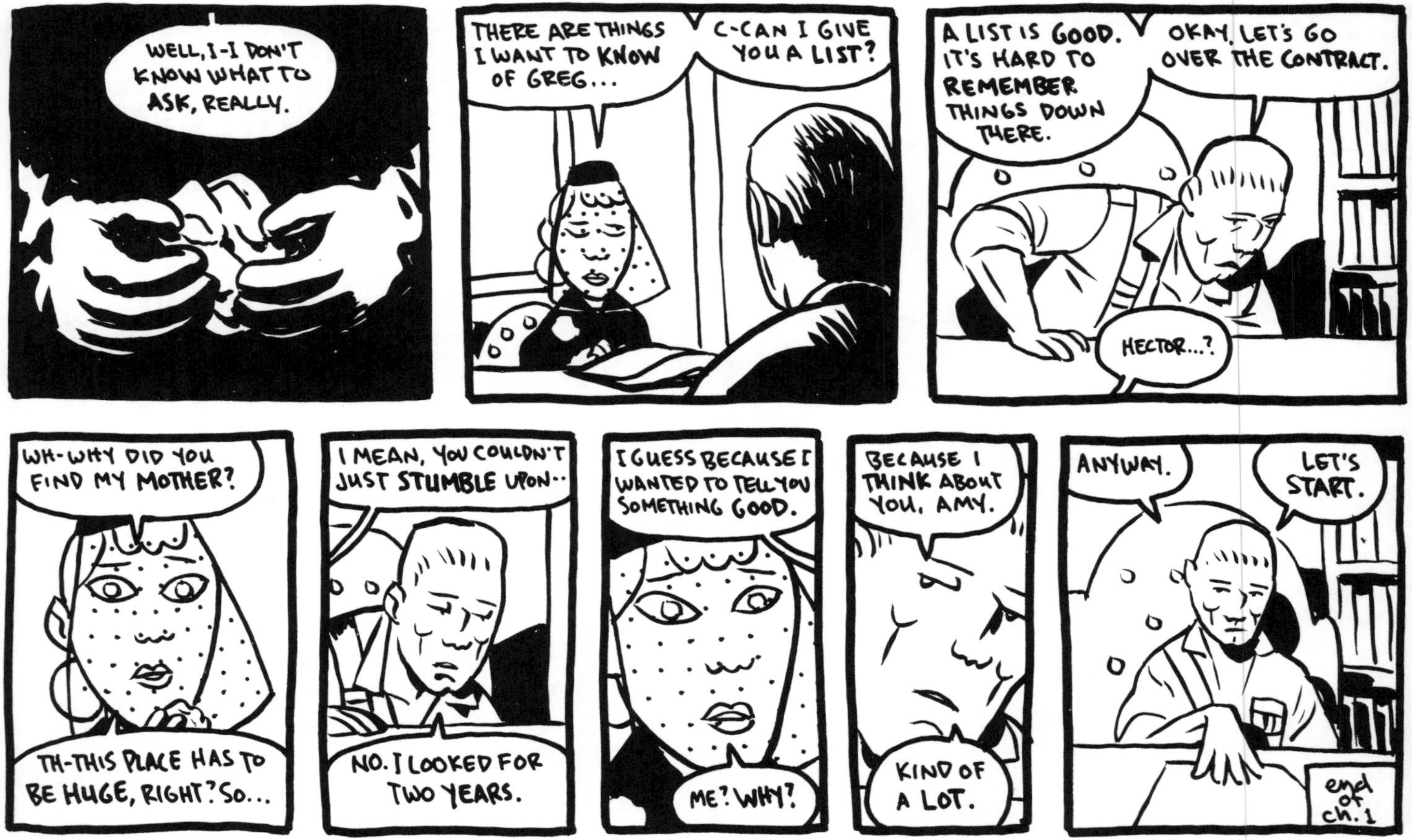
WELL, I-I DON'T KNOW WHAT TO ASK, REALLY.
THERE ARE THINGS I WANT TO KNOW OF GREG...
C-CAN I GIVE YOU A LIST?
A LIST IS GOOD. IT'S HARD TO REMEMBER THINGS DOWN THERE.
OKAY. LET'S GO OVER THE CONTRACT.
HECTOR...?
WH-WHY DID YOU FIND MY MOTHER?
TH-THIS PLACE HAS TO BE HUGE, RIGHT? SO...
I MEAN, YOU COULDN'T JUST STUMBLE UPON..
NO. I LOOKED FOR TWO YEARS.
I GUESS BECAUSE I WANTED TO TELL YOU SOMETHING GOOD.
ME? WHY?
BECAUSE I THINK ABOUT YOU, AMY.
KIND OF A LOT.
ANYWAY.
LET'S START.
end of ch. 1

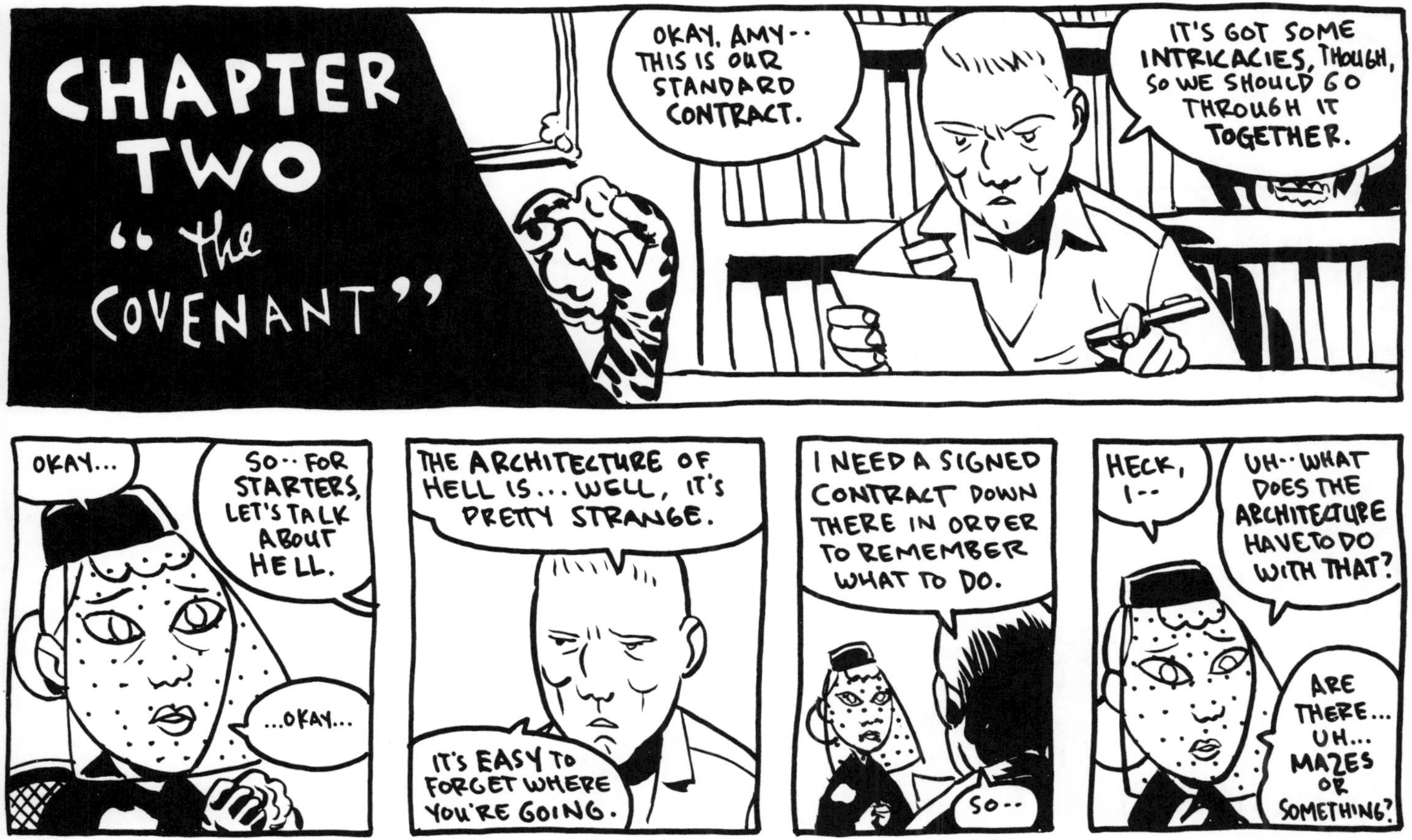
CHAPTER TWO "the COVENANT"
OKAY, AMY.. THIS IS OUR STANDARD CONTRACT.
IT'S GOT SOME INTRICACIES, THOUGH, SO WE SHOULD GO THROUGH IT TOGETHER.
OKAY...
SO.. FOR STARTERS, LET'S TALK ABOUT HELL.
...OKAY...
THE ARCHITECTURE OF HELL IS... WELL, IT'S PRETTY STRANGE.
IT'S EASY TO FORGET WHERE YOU'RE GOING.
I NEED A SIGNED CONTRACT DOWN THERE IN ORDER TO REMEMBER WHAT TO DO.
SO..
HECK, I--
UH.. WHAT DOES THE ARCHITECTURE HAVE TO DO WITH THAT?
ARE THERE... UH... MAZES OR SOMETHING?

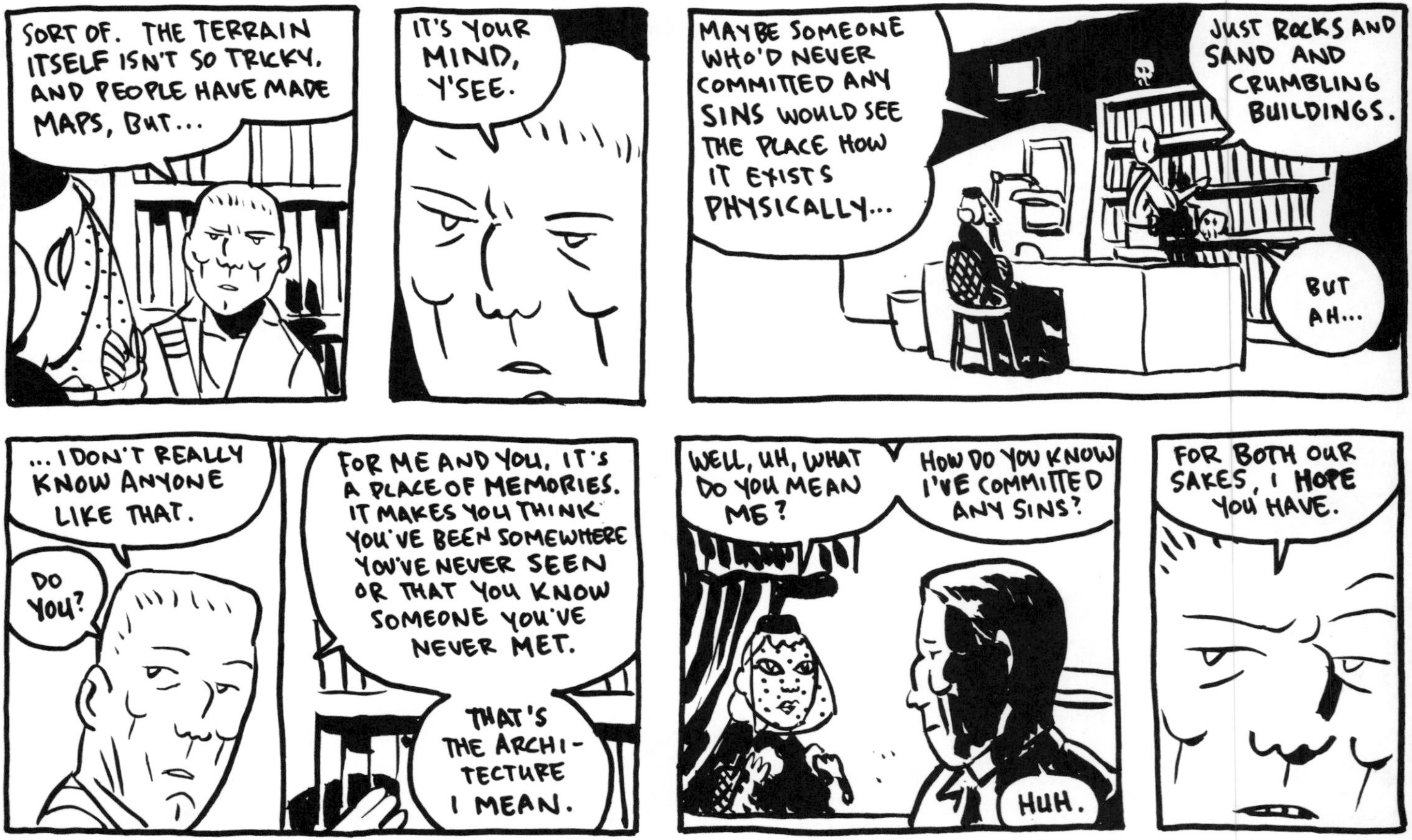
SORT OF. THE TERRAIN ITSELF ISN'T SO TRICKY, AND PEOPLE HAVE MADE MAPS, BUT...
IT'S YOUR MIND, Y'SEE.
MAYBE SOMEONE WHO'D NEVER COMMITTED ANY SINS WOULD SEE THE PLACE HOW IT EXISTS PHYSICALLY...
JUST ROCKS AND SAND AND CRUMBLING BUILDINGS.
BUT AH...
...I DON'T REALLY KNOW ANYONE LIKE THAT.
DO YOU?
FOR ME AND YOU, IT'S A PLACE OF MEMORIES. IT MAKES YOU THINK YOU'VE BEEN SOMEWHERE YOU'VE NEVER SEEN OR THAT YOU KNOW SOMEONE YOU'VE NEVER MET.
THAT'S THE ARCHITECTURE I MEAN.
WELL, UH, WHAT DO YOU MEAN ME?
HOW DO YOU KNOW I'VE COMMITTED ANY SINS?
HUH.
FOR BOTH OUR SAKES, I HOPE YOU HAVE.

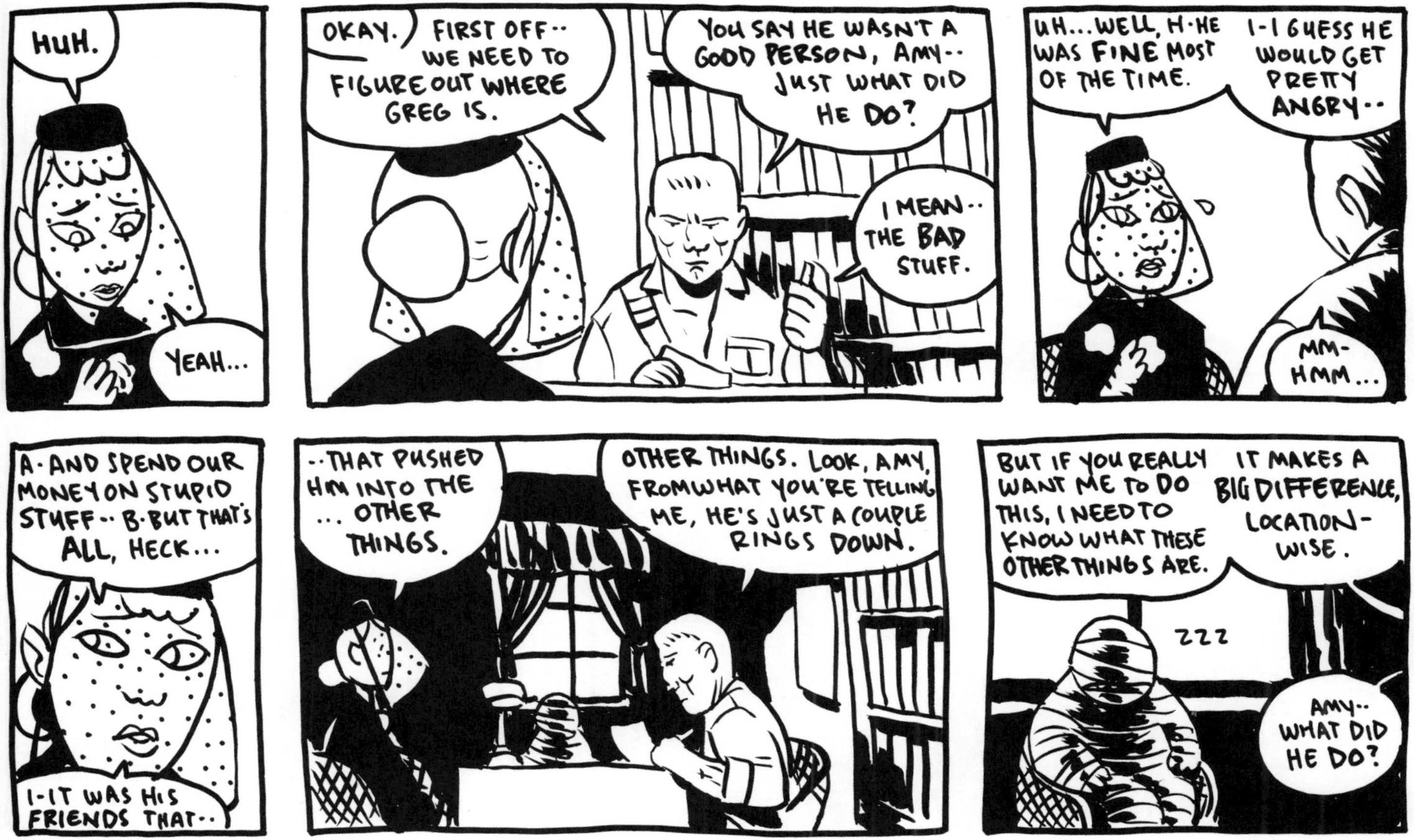
HUH.
YEAH...
OKAY.
FIRST OFF.. WE NEED TO FIGURE OUT WHERE GREG IS.
YOU SAY HE WASN'T A GOOD PERSON, AMY.. JUST WHAT DID HE DO?
I MEAN.. THE BAD STUFF.
UH...WELL, H-HE WAS FINE MOST OF THE TIME.
I-I GUESS HE WOULD GET PRETTY ANGRY..
MM-HMM...
A-AND SPEND OUR MONEY ON STUPID STUFF.. B-BUT THAT'S ALL, HECK...
I-IT WAS HIS FRIENDS THAT..
..THAT PUSHED HIM INTO THE ... OTHER THINGS.
OTHER THINGS. LOOK, AMY, FROM WHAT YOU'RE TELLING ME, HE'S JUST A COUPLE RINGS DOWN.
BUT IF YOU REALLY WANT ME TO DO THIS, I NEED TO KNOW WHAT THESE OTHER THINGS ARE.
IT MAKES A BIG DIFFERENCE, LOCATION-WISE.
ZZZ
AMY.. WHAT DID HE DO?

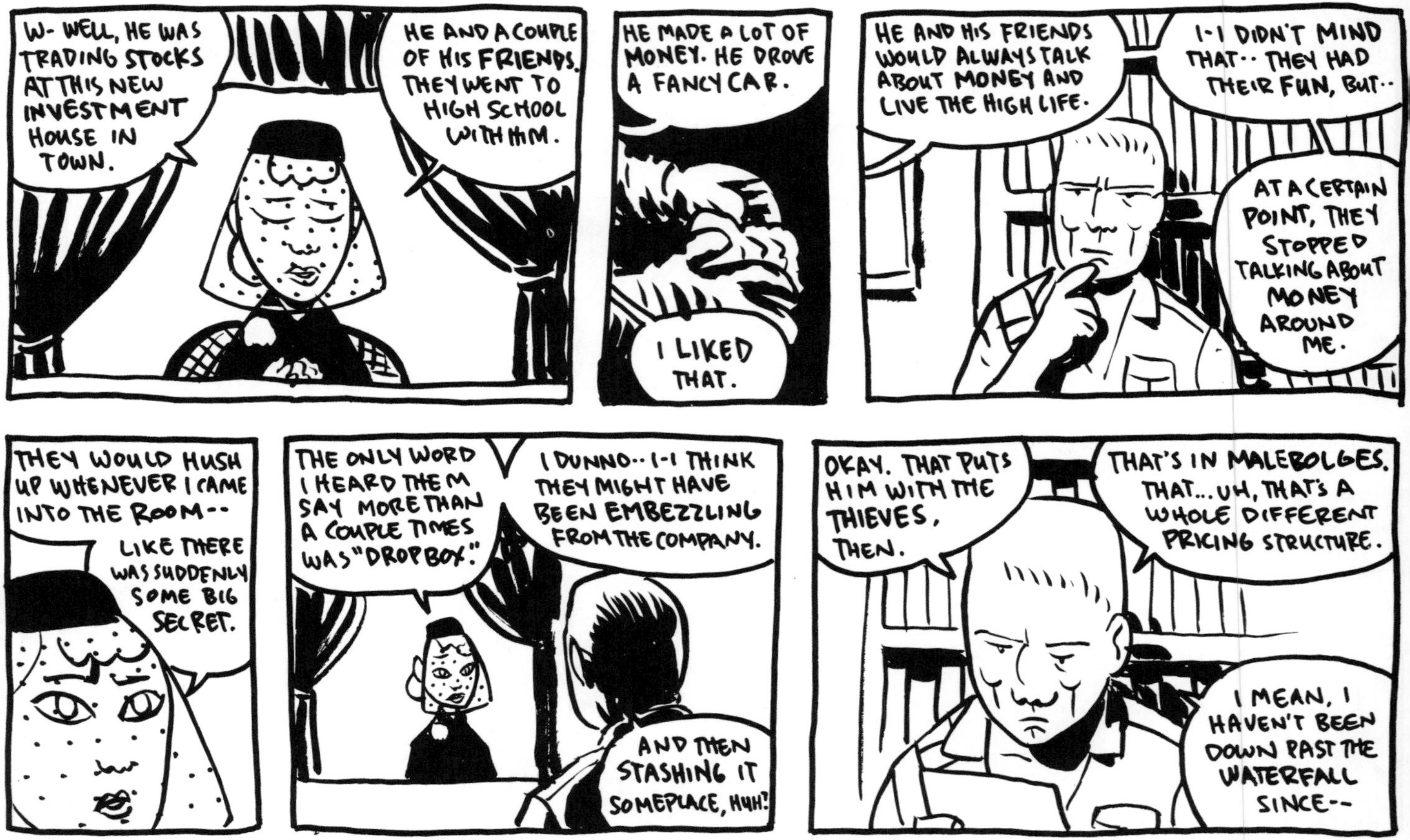
W- WELL, HE WAS TRADING STOCKS AT THIS NEW INVESTMENT HOUSE IN TOWN.
HE AND A COUPLE OF HIS FRIENDS. THEY WENT TO HIGH SCHOOL WITH HIM.
HE MADE A LOT OF MONEY. HE DROVE A FANCY CAR.
I LIKED THAT.
HE AND HIS FRIENDS WOULD ALWAYS TALK ABOUT MONEY AND LIVE THE HIGH LIFE.
I-I DIDN'T MIND THAT·· THEY HAD THEIR FUN, BUT··
AT A CERTAIN POINT, THEY STOPPED TALKING ABOUT MONEY AROUND ME.
THEY WOULD HUSH UP WHENEVER I CAME INTO THE ROOM--
LIKE THERE WAS SUDDENLY SOME BIG SECRET.
THE ONLY WORD I HEARD THEM SAY MORE THAN A COUPLE TIMES WAS "DROPBOX."
I DUNNO·· I-I THINK THEY MIGHT HAVE BEEN EMBEZZLING FROM THE COMPANY.
AND THEN STASHING IT SOMEPLACE, HUH?
OKAY. THAT PUTS HIM WITH THE THIEVES, THEN.
THAT'S IN MALEBOLGES. THAT... UH, THAT'S A WHOLE DIFFERENT PRICING STRUCTURE.
I MEAN, I HAVEN'T BEEN DOWN PAST THE WATERFALL SINCE--

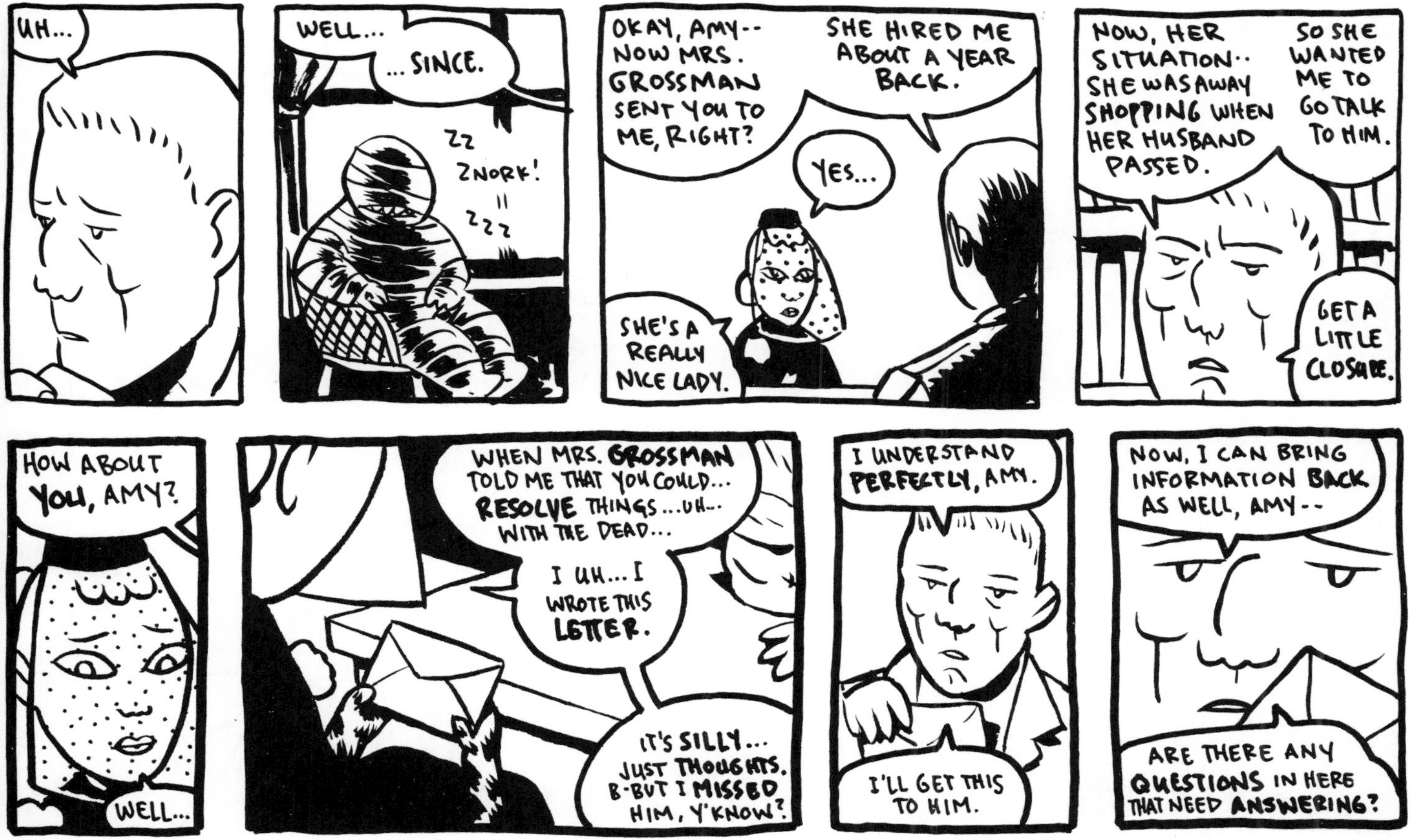
UH...
WELL...
...SINCE.
ZZ
ZNORK!
ZZZ
OKAY, AMY-- NOW MRS. GROSSMAN SENT YOU TO ME, RIGHT?
SHE HIRED ME ABOUT A YEAR BACK.
YES...
SHE'S A REALLY NICE LADY.
NOW, HER SITUATION.. SHE WAS AWAY SHOPPING WHEN HER HUSBAND PASSED.
SO SHE WANTED ME TO GO TALK TO HIM.
GET A LITTLE CLOSURE.
HOW ABOUT YOU, AMY?
WELL...
WHEN MRS. GROSSMAN TOLD ME THAT YOU COULD... RESOLVE THINGS...UH... WITH THE DEAD...
I UH... I WROTE THIS LETTER.
IT'S SILLY... JUST THOUGHTS. B-BUT I MISSED HIM, Y'KNOW?
I UNDERSTAND PERFECTLY, AMY.
I'LL GET THIS TO HIM.
NOW, I CAN BRING INFORMATION BACK AS WELL, AMY--
ARE THERE ANY QUESTIONS IN HERE THAT NEED ANSWERING?

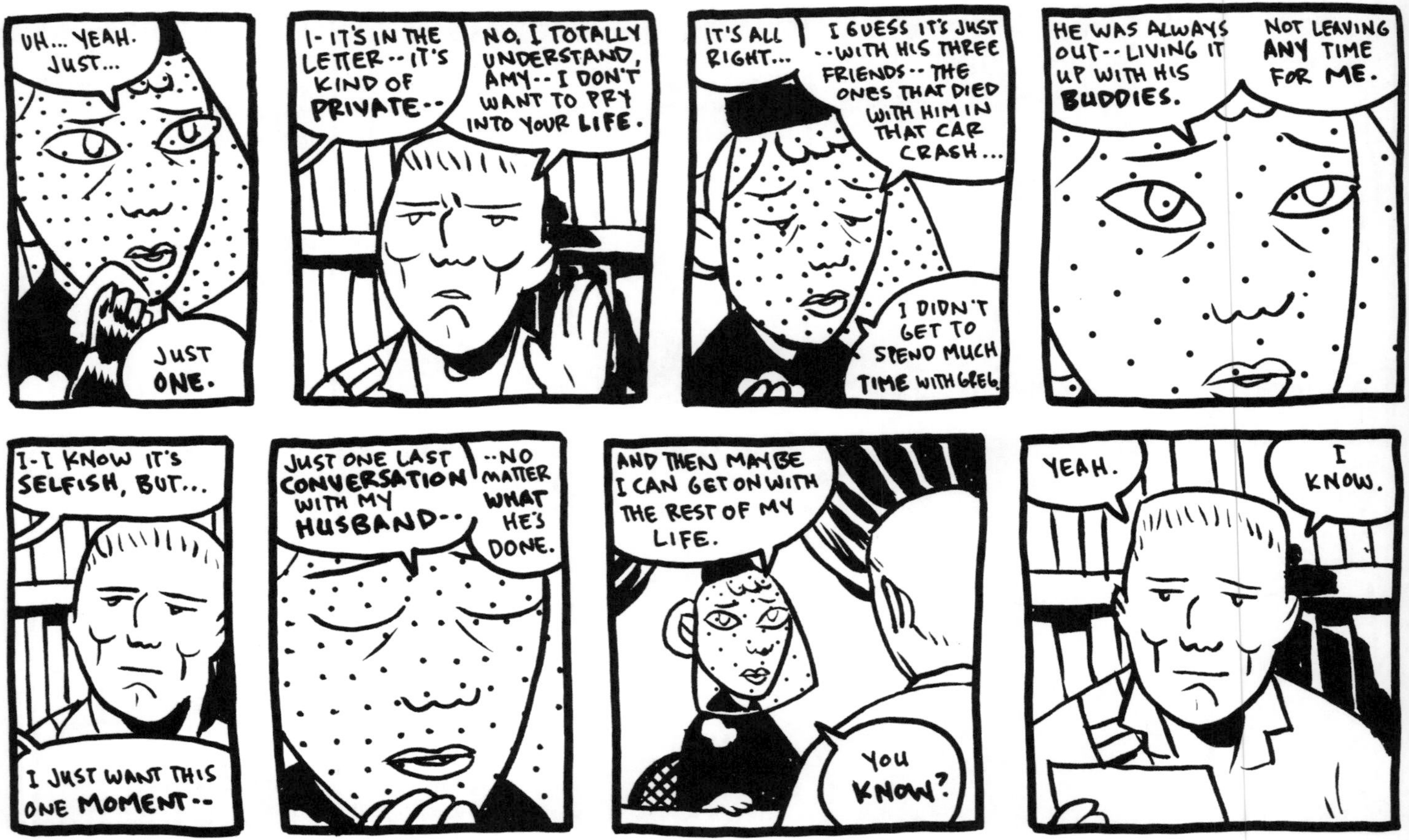

UH... YEAH. JUST...
JUST ONE.
I- IT'S IN THE LETTER -- IT'S KIND OF PRIVATE--
NO, I TOTALLY UNDERSTAND, AMY -- I DON'T WANT TO PRY INTO YOUR LIFE.
IT'S ALL RIGHT...
I GUESS IT'S JUST -- WITH HIS THREE FRIENDS -- THE ONES THAT DIED WITH HIM IN THAT CAR CRASH...
I DIDN'T GET TO SPEND MUCH TIME WITH GREG.
HE WAS ALWAYS OUT -- LIVING IT UP WITH HIS BUDDIES.
NOT LEAVING ANY TIME FOR ME.
I-I KNOW IT'S SELFISH, BUT...
I JUST WANT THIS ONE MOMENT--
JUST ONE LAST CONVERSATION WITH MY HUSBAND--
--NO MATTER WHAT HE'S DONE.
AND THEN MAYBE I CAN GET ON WITH THE REST OF MY LIFE.
YOU KNOW?
YEAH.
I KNOW.

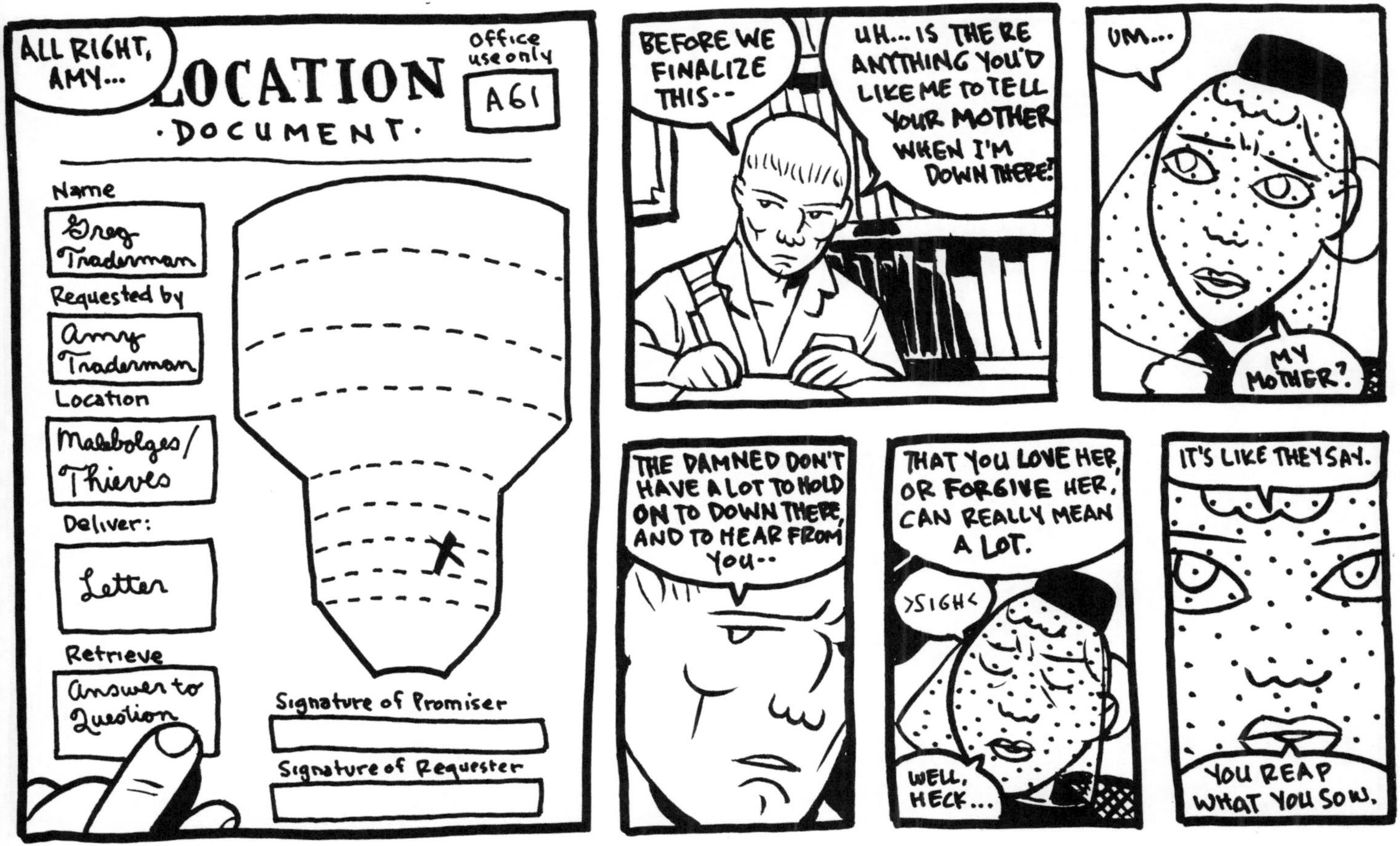
ALL RIGHT, AMY...
LOCATION
·DOCUMENT·
Office use only
A61
Name
Greg Traderman
Requested by
Amy Traderman
Location
Malebolges/ Thieves
Deliver:
Letter
Retrieve
Answer to Question
Signature of Promiser
Signature of Requester
BEFORE WE FINALIZE THIS--
UH... IS THERE ANYTHING YOU'D LIKE ME TO TELL YOUR MOTHER WHEN I'M DOWN THERE?
UM...
MY MOTHER?
THE DAMNED DON'T HAVE A LOT TO HOLD ON TO DOWN THERE, AND TO HEAR FROM YOU--
THAT YOU LOVE HER, OR FORGIVE HER, CAN REALLY MEAN A LOT.
>SIGH<
WELL, HECK...
IT'S LIKE THEY SAY.
YOU REAP WHAT YOU SOW.

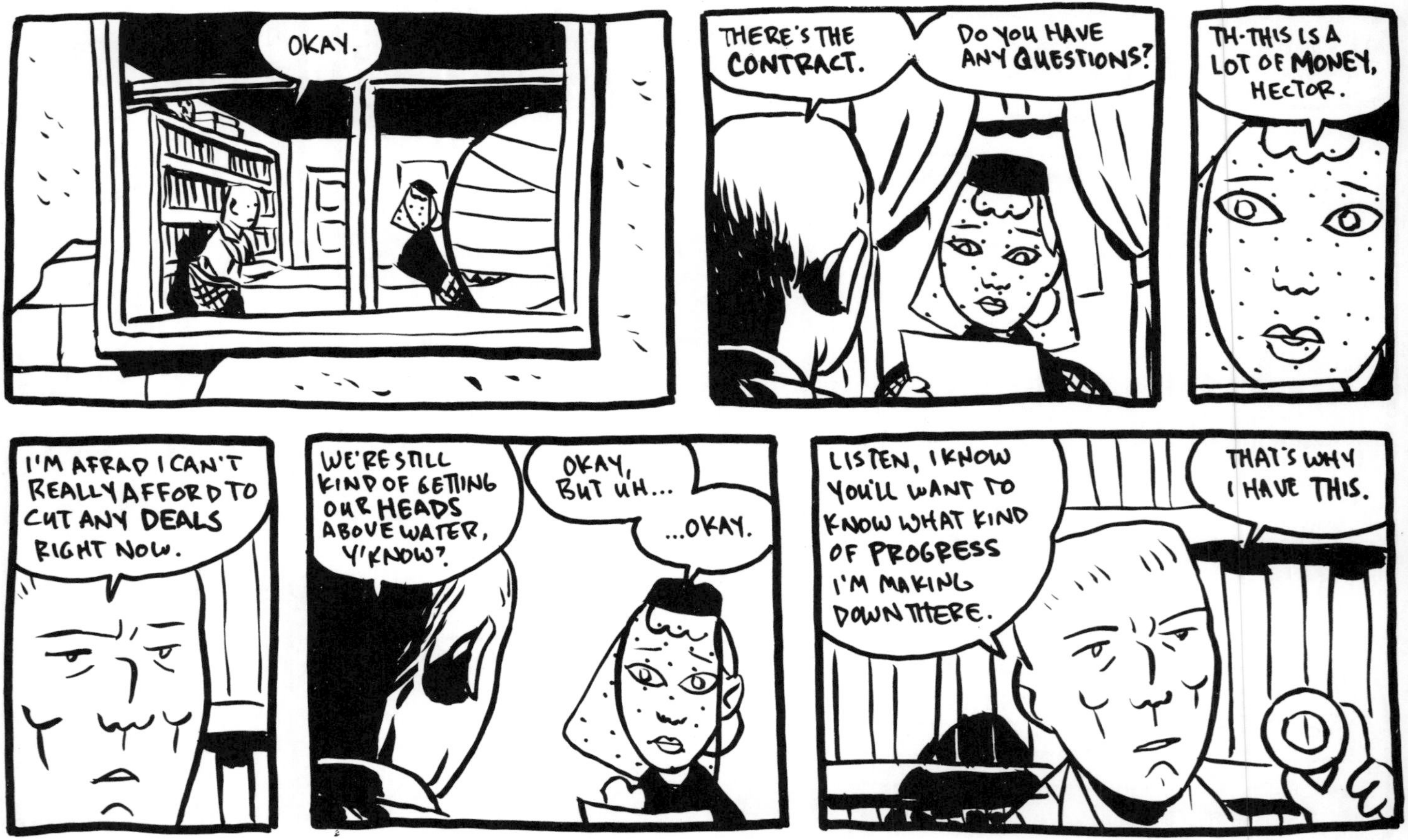
OKAY.
THERE'S THE CONTRACT.
DO YOU HAVE ANY QUESTIONS?
TH-THIS IS A LOT OF MONEY, HECTOR.
I'M AFRAID I CAN'T REALLY AFFORD TO CUT ANY DEALS RIGHT NOW.
WE'RE STILL KIND OF GETTING OUR HEADS ABOVE WATER, Y'KNOW?
OKAY, BUT UH...
...OKAY.
LISTEN, I KNOW YOU'LL WANT TO KNOW WHAT KIND OF PROGRESS I'M MAKING DOWN THERE.
THAT'S WHY I HAVE THIS.

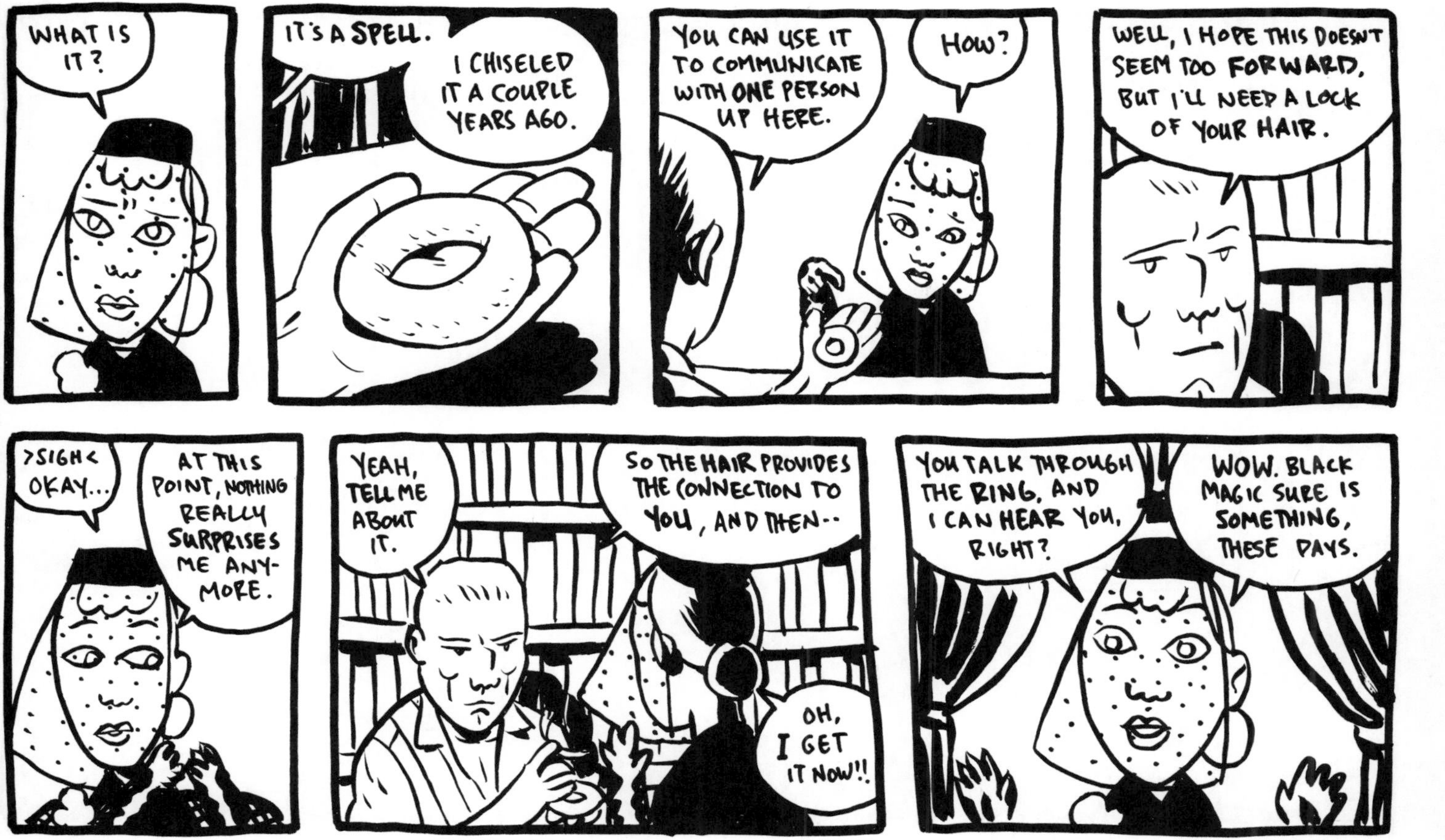
WHAT IS IT?
IT'S A SPELL.
I CHISELED IT A COUPLE YEARS AGO.
YOU CAN USE IT TO COMMUNICATE WITH ONE PERSON UP HERE.
HOW?
WELL, I HOPE THIS DOESN'T SEEM TOO FORWARD, BUT I'LL NEED A LOCK OF YOUR HAIR.
>SIGH< OKAY...
AT THIS POINT, NOTHING REALLY SURPRISES ME ANYMORE.
YEAH, TELL ME ABOUT IT.
SO THE HAIR PROVIDES THE CONNECTION TO YOU, AND THEN--
OH, I GET IT NOW!!
YOU TALK THROUGH THE RING, AND I CAN HEAR YOU, RIGHT?
WOW. BLACK MAGIC SURE IS SOMETHING, THESE DAYS.

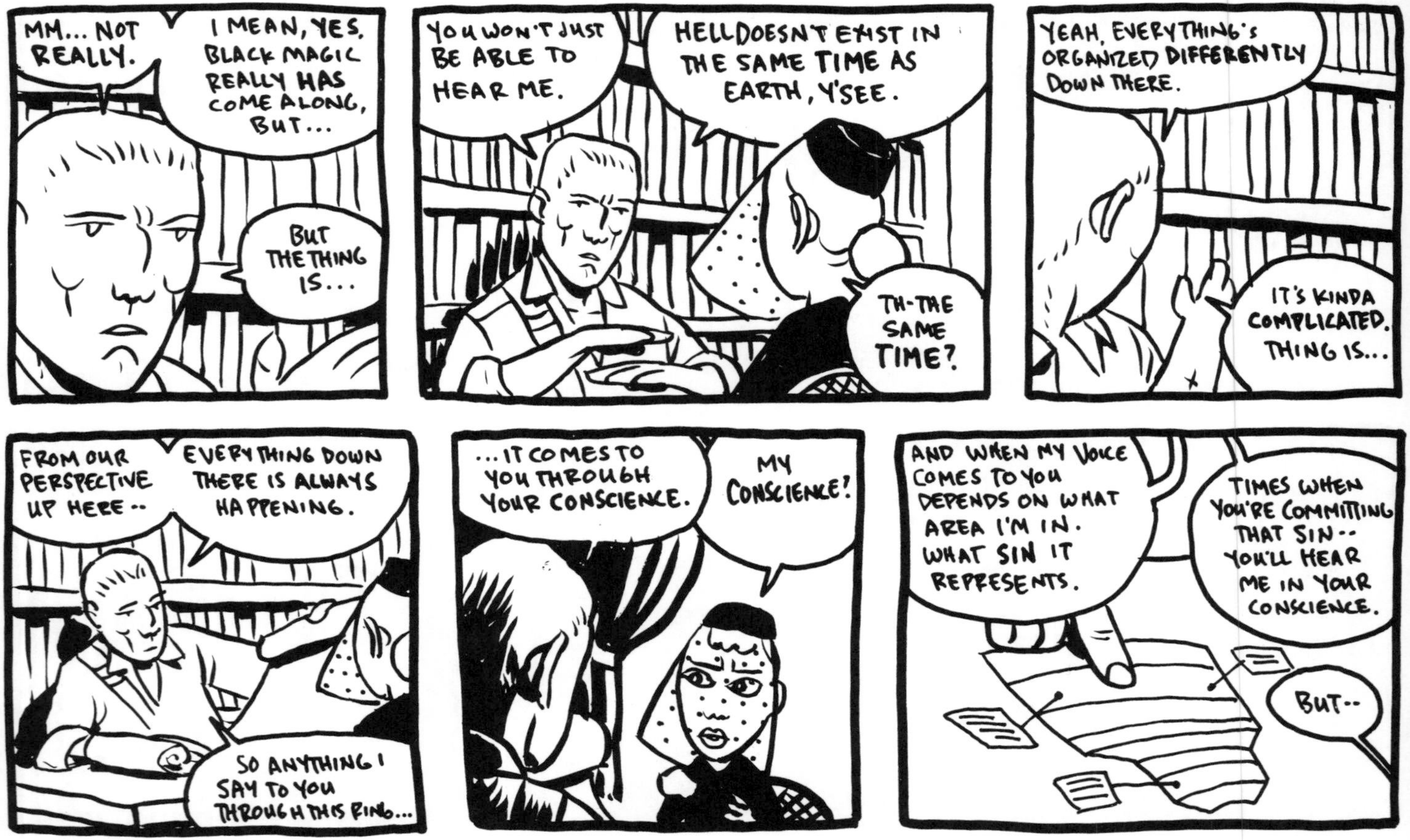
MM... NOT REALLY.
I MEAN, YES, BLACK MAGIC REALLY HAS COME ALONG, BUT...
BUT THE THING IS...
YOU WON'T JUST BE ABLE TO HEAR ME.
HELL DOESN'T EXIST IN THE SAME TIME AS EARTH, Y'SEE.
TH-THE SAME TIME?
YEAH, EVERYTHING'S ORGANIZED DIFFERENTLY DOWN THERE.
IT'S KINDA COMPLICATED. THING IS...
FROM OUR PERSPECTIVE UP HERE--
EVERYTHING DOWN THERE IS ALWAYS HAPPENING.
SO ANYTHING I SAY TO YOU THROUGH THIS RING...
...IT COMES TO YOU THROUGH YOUR CONSCIENCE.
MY CONSCIENCE?
AND WHEN MY VOICE COMES TO YOU DEPENDS ON WHAT AREA I'M IN. WHAT SIN IT REPRESENTS.
TIMES WHEN YOU'RE COMMITTING THAT SIN-- YOU'LL HEAR ME IN YOUR CONSCIENCE.
BUT--

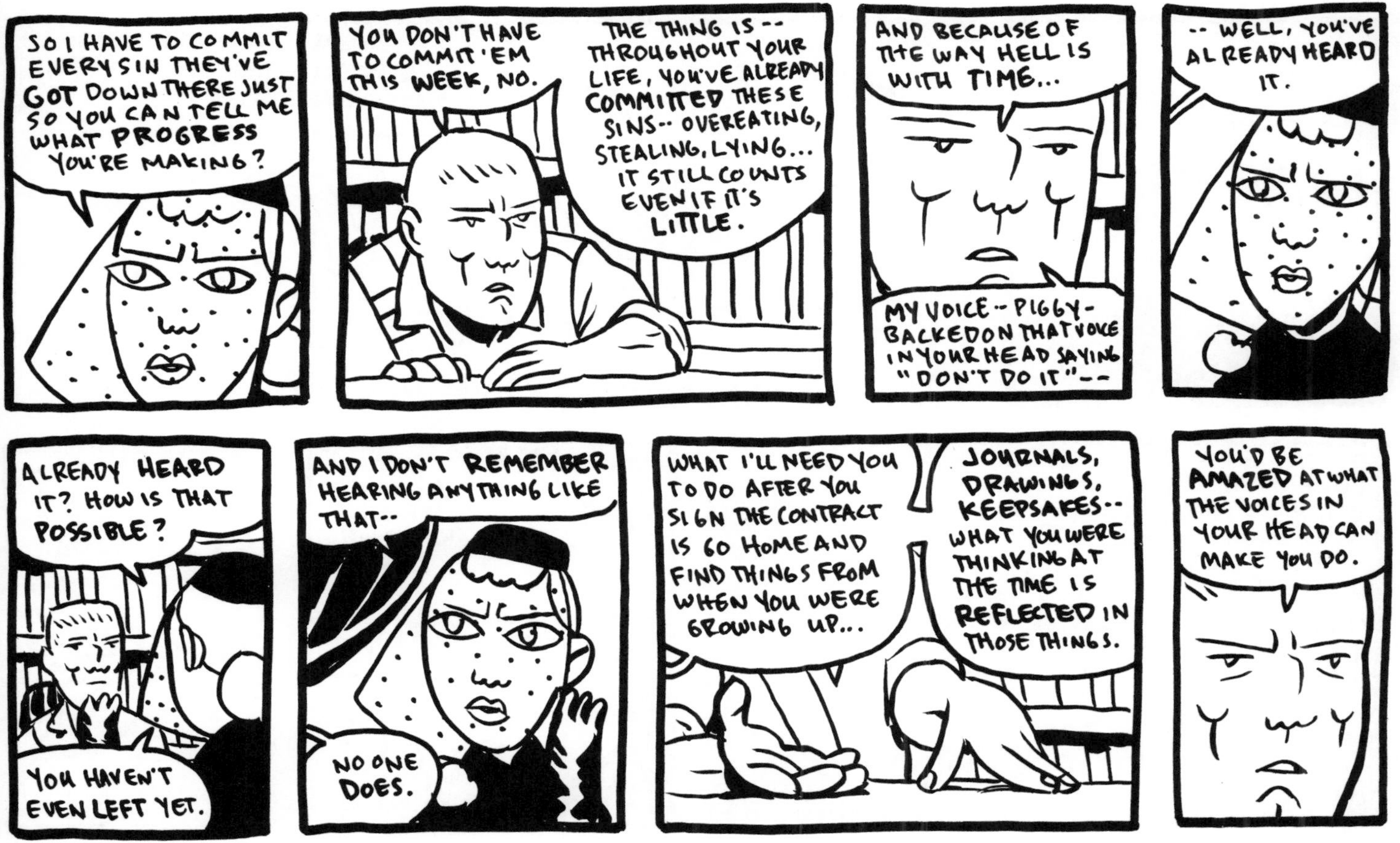
SO I HAVE TO COMMIT EVERY SIN THEY'VE GOT DOWN THERE JUST SO YOU CAN TELL ME WHAT PROGRESS YOU'RE MAKING?
YOU DON'T HAVE TO COMMIT 'EM THIS WEEK, NO.
THE THING IS -- THROUGHOUT YOUR LIFE, YOU'VE ALREADY COMMITTED THESE SINS -- OVEREATING, STEALING, LYING... IT STILL COUNTS EVEN IF IT'S LITTLE.
AND BECAUSE OF THE WAY HELL IS WITH TIME...
MY VOICE -- PIGGY-BACKED ON THAT VOICE IN YOUR HEAD SAYING "DON'T DO IT" --
-- WELL, YOU'VE ALREADY HEARD IT.
ALREADY HEARD IT? HOW IS THAT POSSIBLE?
YOU HAVEN'T EVEN LEFT YET.
AND I DON'T REMEMBER HEARING ANYTHING LIKE THAT --
NO ONE DOES.
WHAT I'LL NEED YOU TO DO AFTER YOU SIGN THE CONTRACT IS GO HOME AND FIND THINGS FROM WHEN YOU WERE GROWING UP...
JOURNALS, DRAWINGS, KEEPSAKES -- WHAT YOU WERE THINKING AT THE TIME IS REFLECTED IN THOSE THINGS.
YOU'D BE AMAZED AT WHAT THE VOICES IN YOUR HEAD CAN MAKE YOU DO.

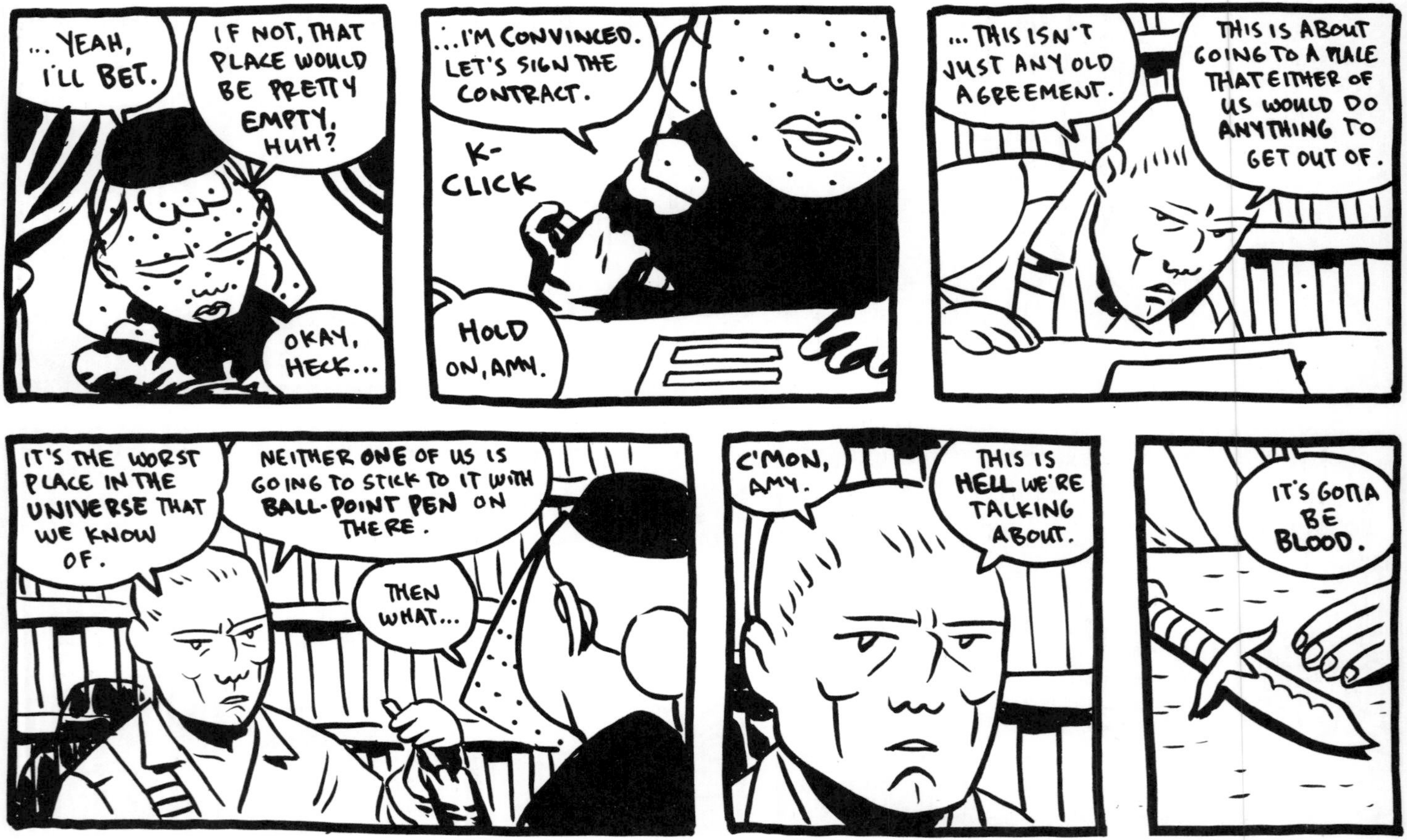
... YEAH, I'LL BET.
IF NOT, THAT PLACE WOULD BE PRETTY EMPTY, HUH?
OKAY, HECK...
...I'M CONVINCED. LET'S SIGN THE CONTRACT.
K-CLICK
HOLD ON, AMY.
... THIS ISN'T JUST ANY OLD AGREEMENT.
THIS IS ABOUT GOING TO A PLACE THAT EITHER OF US WOULD DO ANYTHING TO GET OUT OF.
IT'S THE WORST PLACE IN THE UNIVERSE THAT WE KNOW OF.
NEITHER ONE OF US IS GOING TO STICK TO IT WITH BALL-POINT PEN ON THERE.
THEN WHAT...
C'MON, AMY.
THIS IS HELL WE'RE TALKING ABOUT.
IT'S GONNA BE BLOOD.

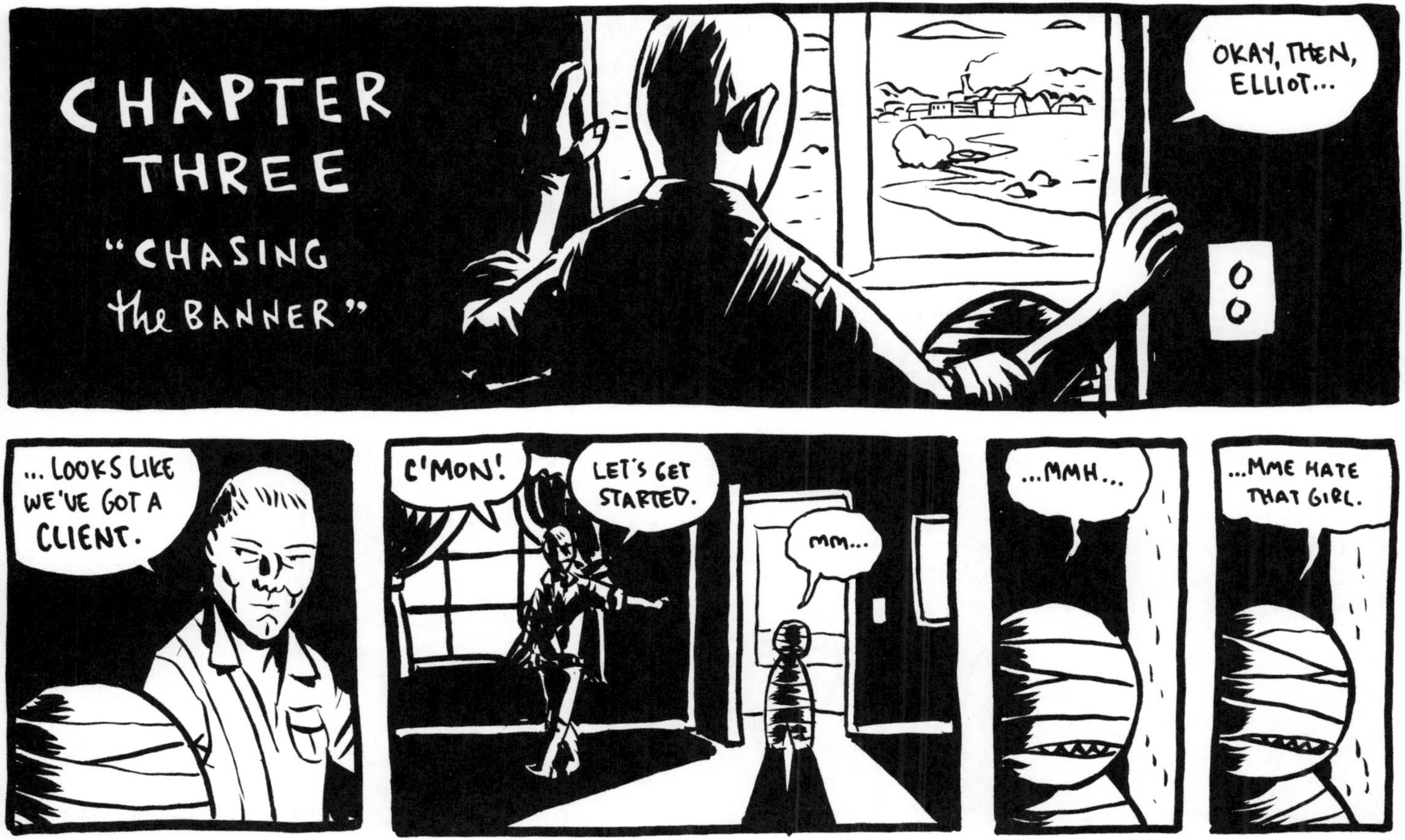
CHAPTER THREE
"CHASING the BANNER"
OKAY, THEN, ELLIOT...
...LOOKS LIKE WE'VE GOT A CLIENT.
C'MON!
LET'S GET STARTED.
MM...
...MMH...
...MME HATE THAT GIRL.

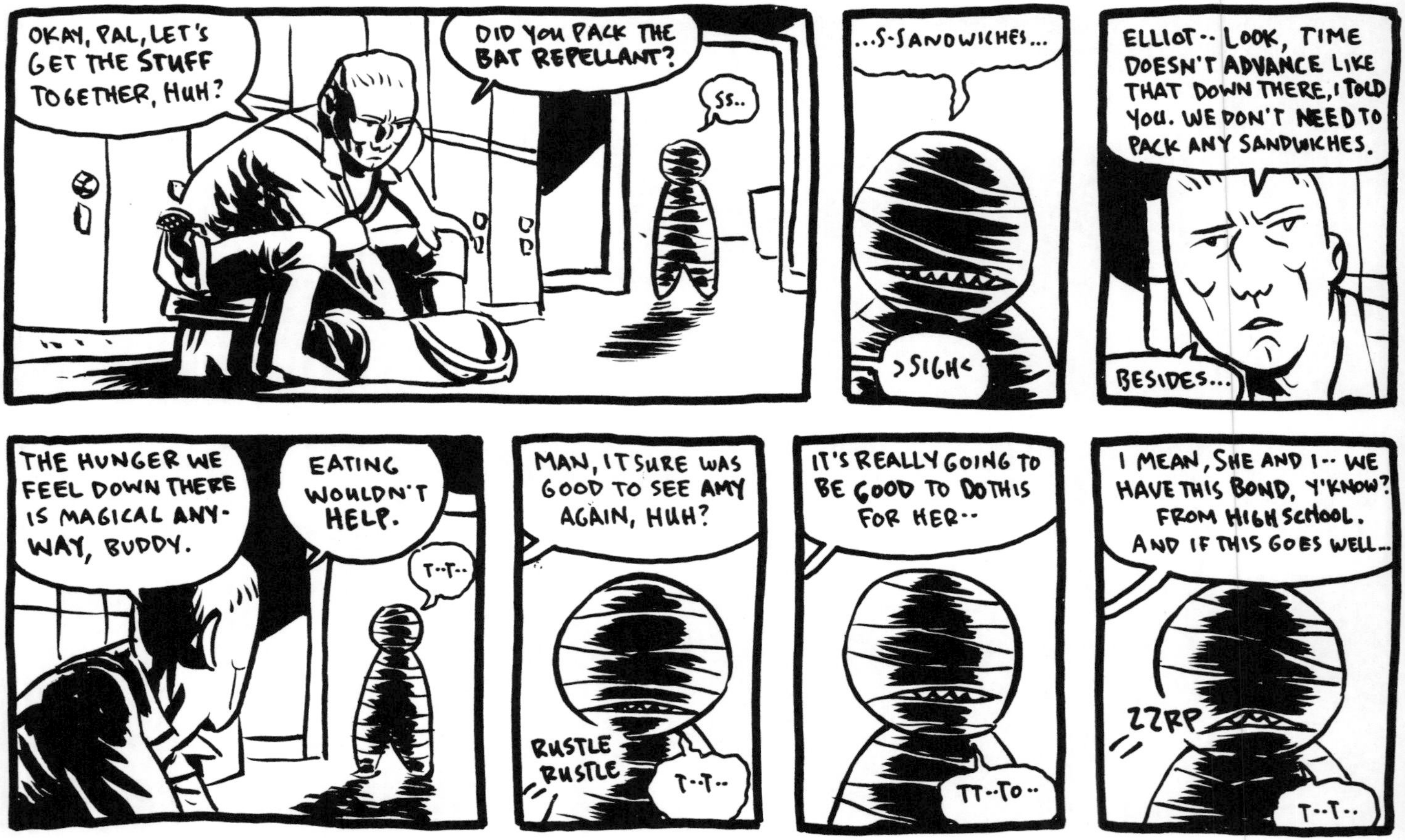
OKAY, PAL, LET'S GET THE STUFF TOGETHER, HUH?
DID YOU PACK THE BAT REPELLANT?
SS..
...S-SANDWICHES...
>SIGH<
ELLIOT-- LOOK, TIME DOESN'T ADVANCE LIKE THAT DOWN THERE, I TOLD YOU. WE DON'T NEED TO PACK ANY SANDWICHES.
BESIDES...
THE HUNGER WE FEEL DOWN THERE IS MAGICAL ANY-WAY, BUDDY.
EATING WOULDN'T HELP.
T--T--
MAN, IT SURE WAS GOOD TO SEE AMY AGAIN, HUH?
RUSTLE RUSTLE
T--T--
IT'S REALLY GOING TO BE GOOD TO DO THIS FOR HER--
TT--TO--
I MEAN, SHE AND I-- WE HAVE THIS BOND, Y'KNOW? FROM HIGH SCHOOL. AND IF THIS GOES WELL...
ZZRP
T--T--

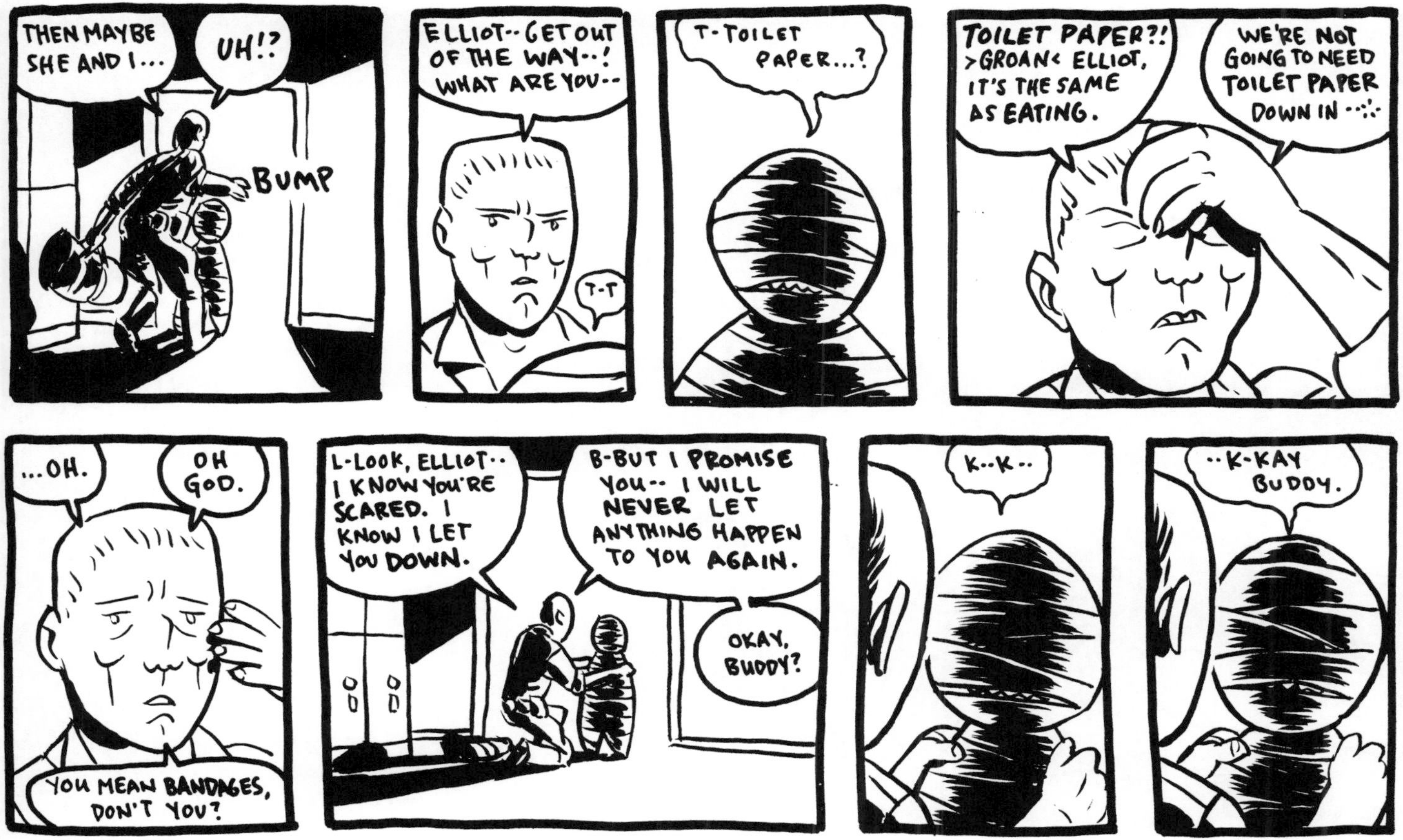
THEN MAYBE SHE AND I...
UH!?
BUMP
ELLIOT.. GET OUT OF THE WAY..! WHAT ARE YOU..
T-T
T-TOILET PAPER...?
TOILET PAPER?! >GROAN< ELLIOT, IT'S THE SAME AS EATING.
WE'RE NOT GOING TO NEED TOILET PAPER DOWN IN ..
...OH.
OH GOD.
YOU MEAN BANDAGES, DON'T YOU?
L-LOOK, ELLIOT.. I KNOW YOU'RE SCARED. I KNOW I LET YOU DOWN.
B-BUT I PROMISE YOU.. I WILL NEVER LET ANYTHING HAPPEN TO YOU AGAIN.
OKAY, BUDDY?
K..K..
..K-KAY BUDDY.

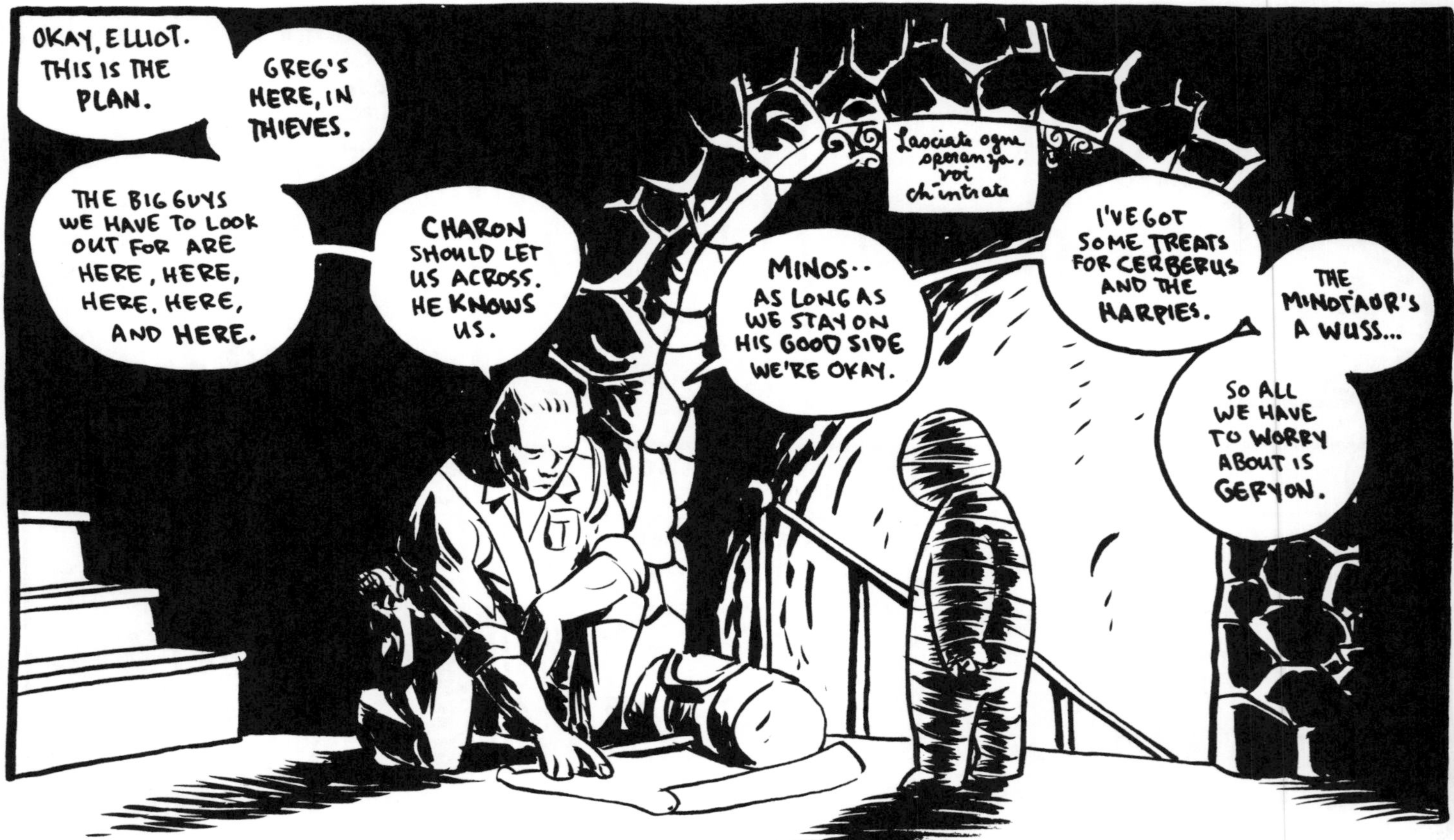
OKAY, ELLIOT. THIS IS THE PLAN.
GREG'S HERE, IN THIEVES.
THE BIG GUYS WE HAVE TO LOOK OUT FOR ARE HERE, HERE, HERE, HERE, AND HERE.
CHARON SHOULD LET US ACROSS. HE KNOWS US.
Lasciate ogne speranza, voi ch'intrate
MINOS.. AS LONG AS WE STAY ON HIS GOOD SIDE WE'RE OKAY.
I'VE GOT SOME TREATS FOR CERBERUS AND THE HARPIES.
THE MINOTAUR'S A WUSS...
SO ALL WE HAVE TO WORRY ABOUT IS GERYON.

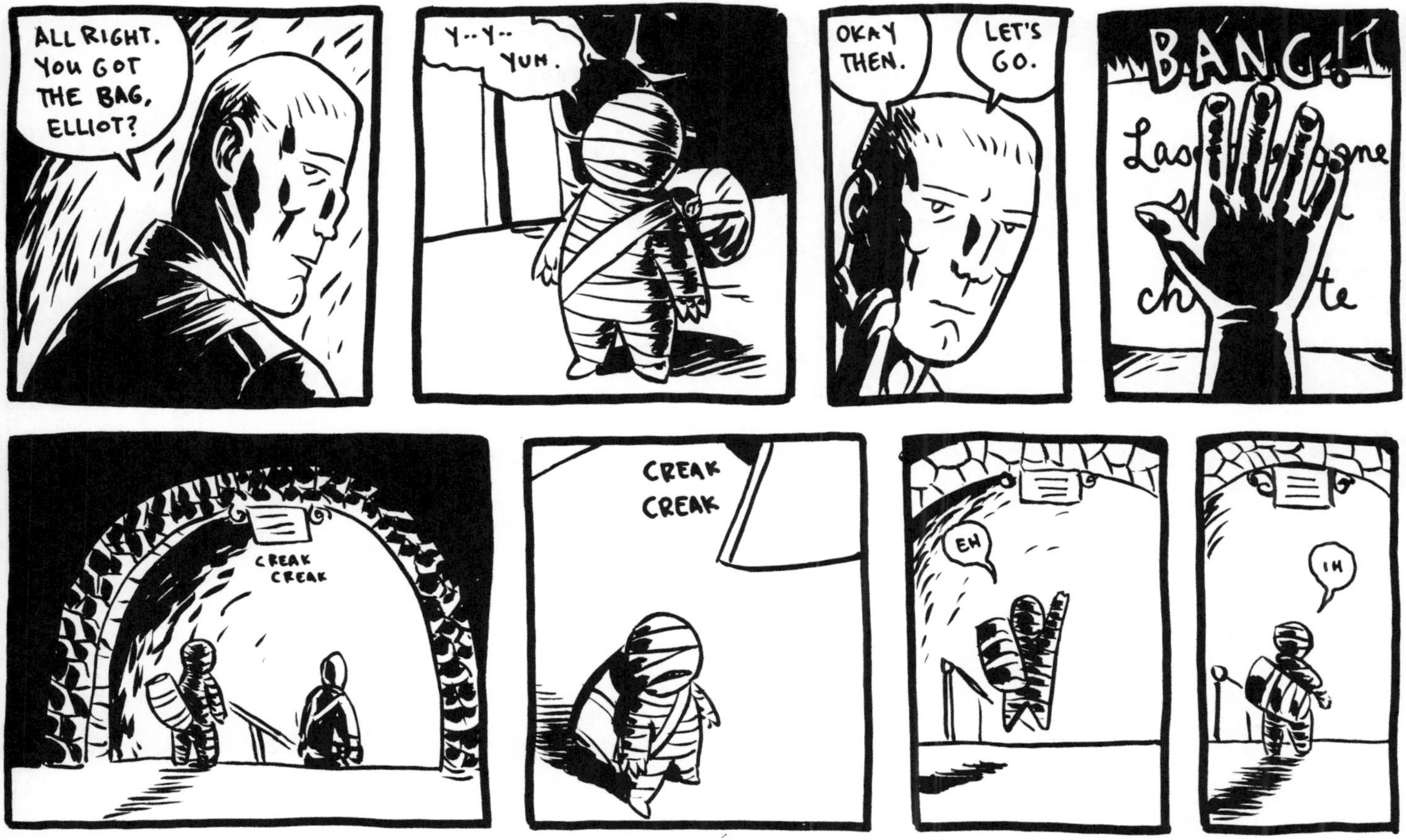
ALL RIGHT. YOU GOT THE BAG, ELLIOT?
Y-- Y-- YUM.
OKAY THEN.
LET'S GO.
BANG!
CREAK CREAK
CREAK CREAK
EH
IH

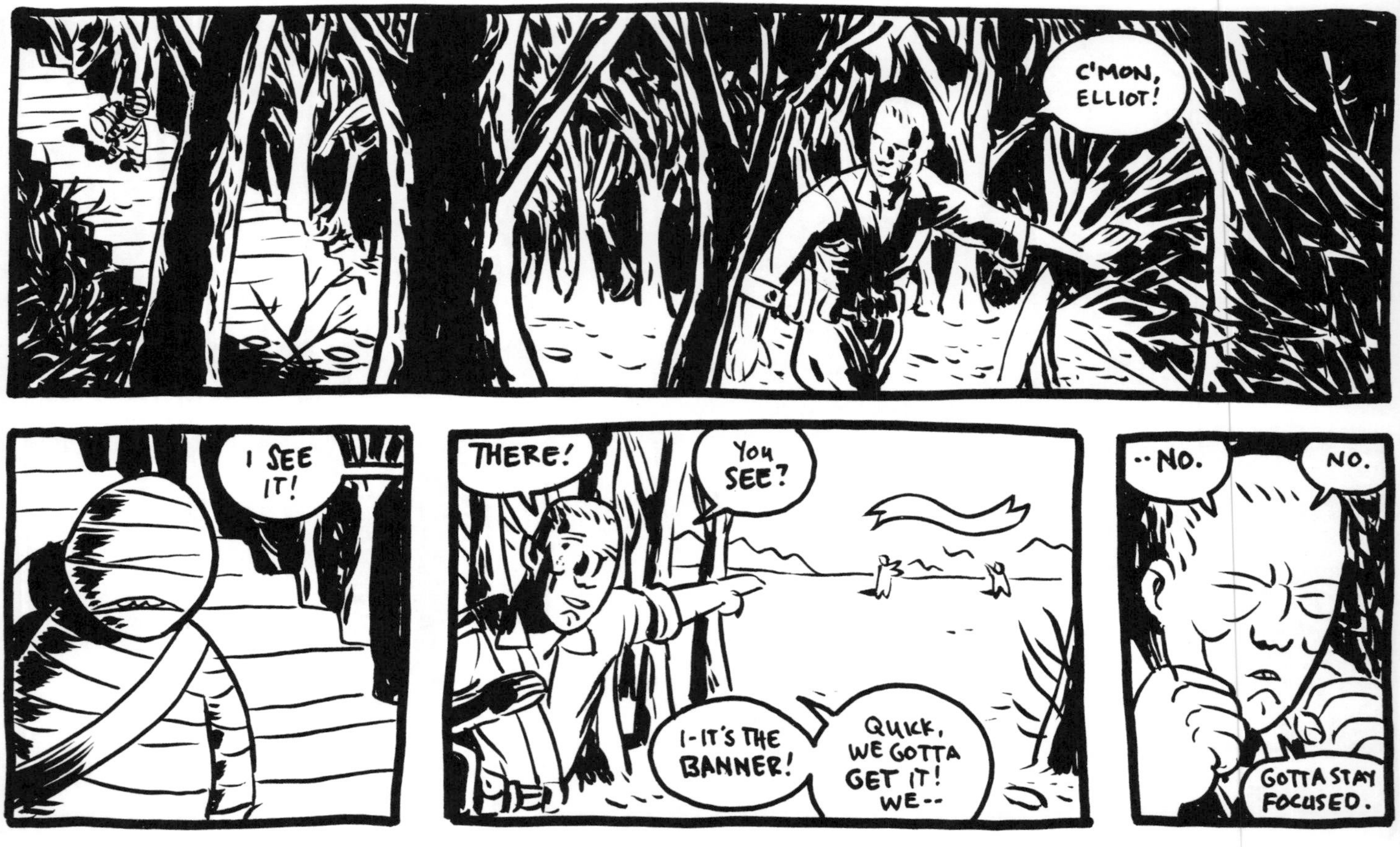
C'MON, ELLIOT!
I SEE IT!
THERE!
YOU SEE?
I-IT'S THE BANNER!
QUICK, WE GOTTA GET IT! WE--
..NO.
NO.
GOTTA STAY FOCUSED.

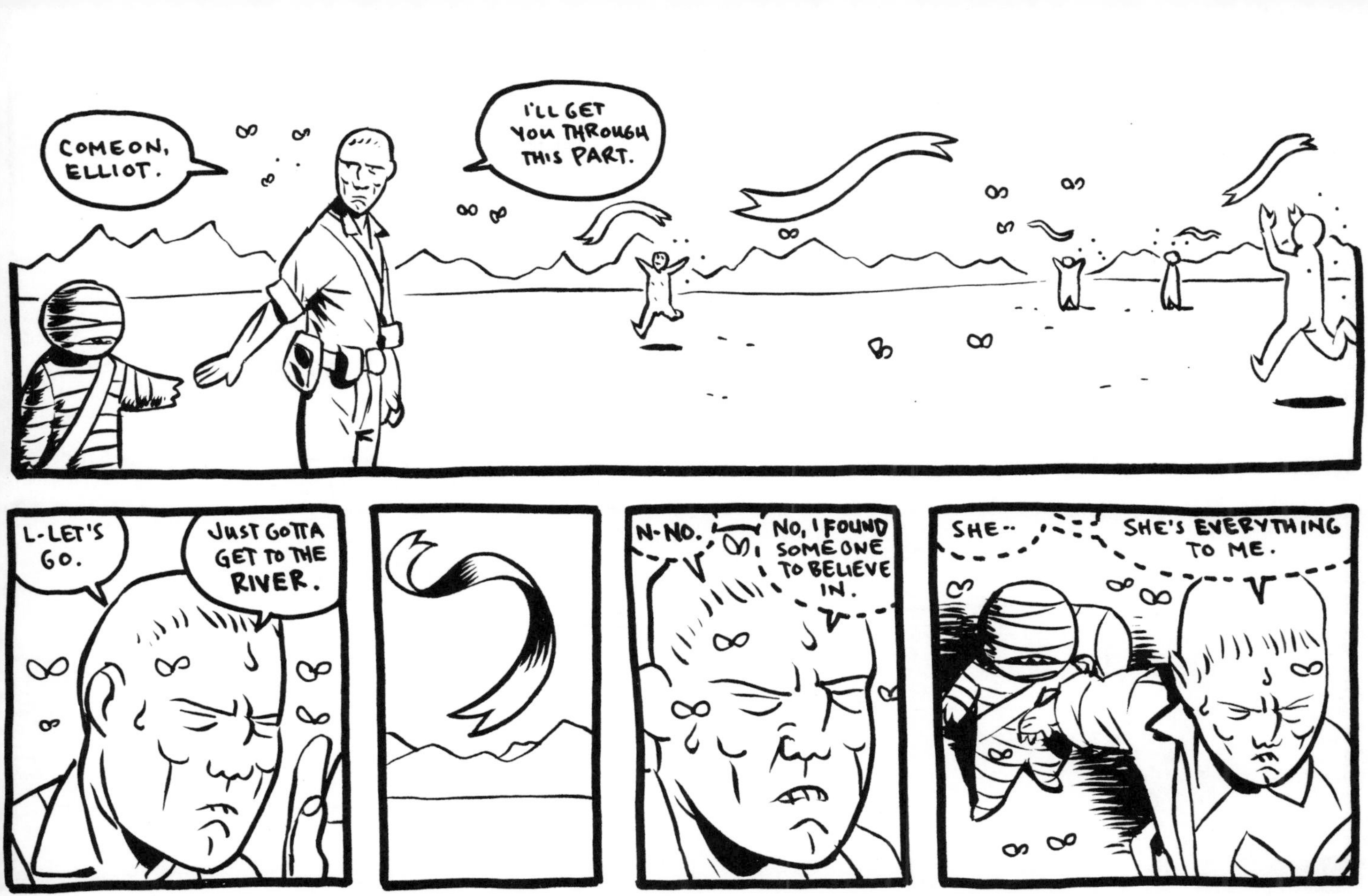
COMEON, ELLIOT.
I'LL GET YOU THROUGH THIS PART.
L-LET'S GO.
JUST GOTTA GET TO THE RIVER.
N-NO.
NO, I FOUND SOMEONE TO BELIEVE IN.
SHE--
SHE'S EVERYTHING TO ME.

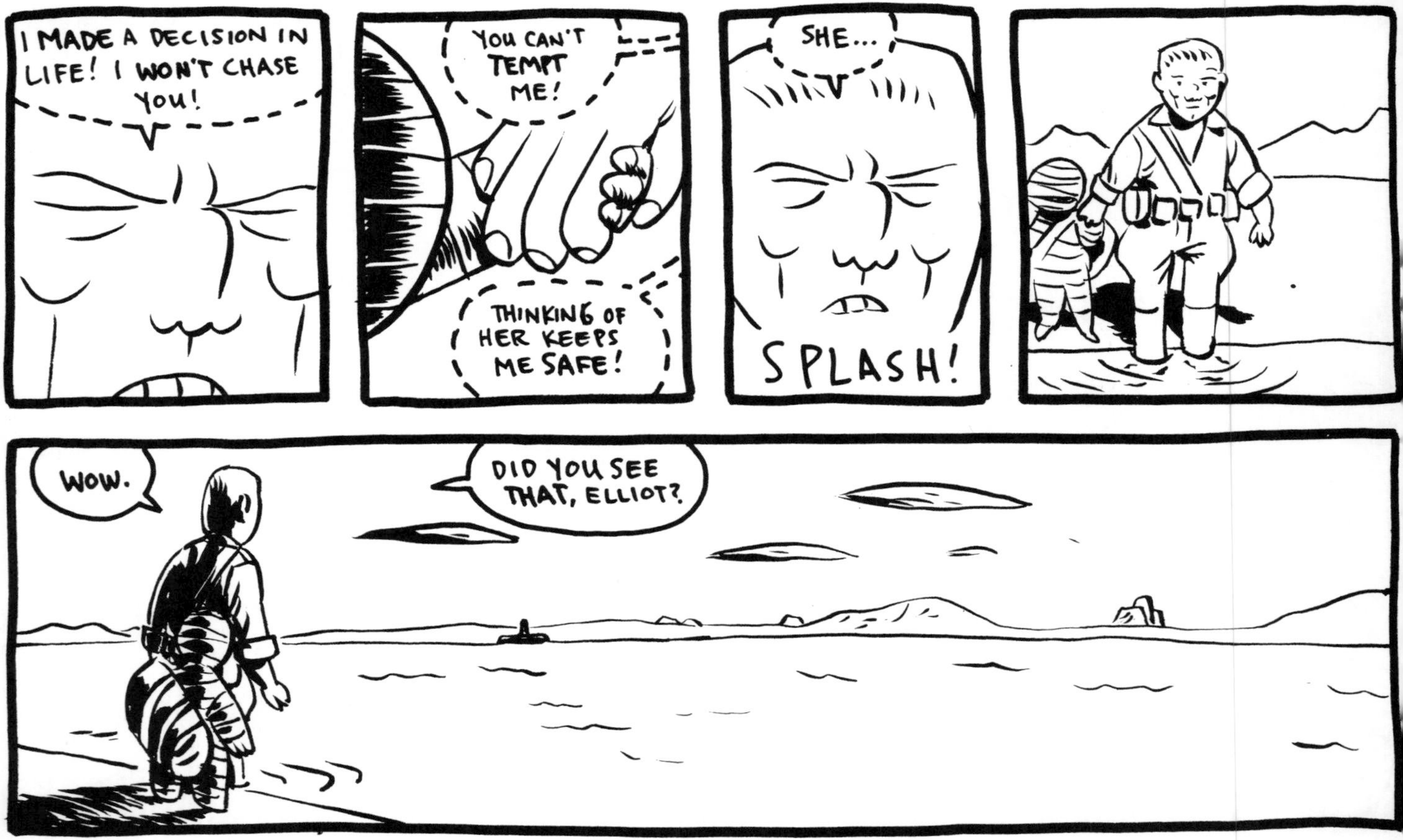
I MADE A DECISION IN LIFE! I WON'T CHASE YOU!
YOU CAN'T TEMPT ME!
THINKING OF HER KEEPS ME SAFE!
SHE...
SPLASH!
WOW.
DID YOU SEE THAT, ELLIOT?

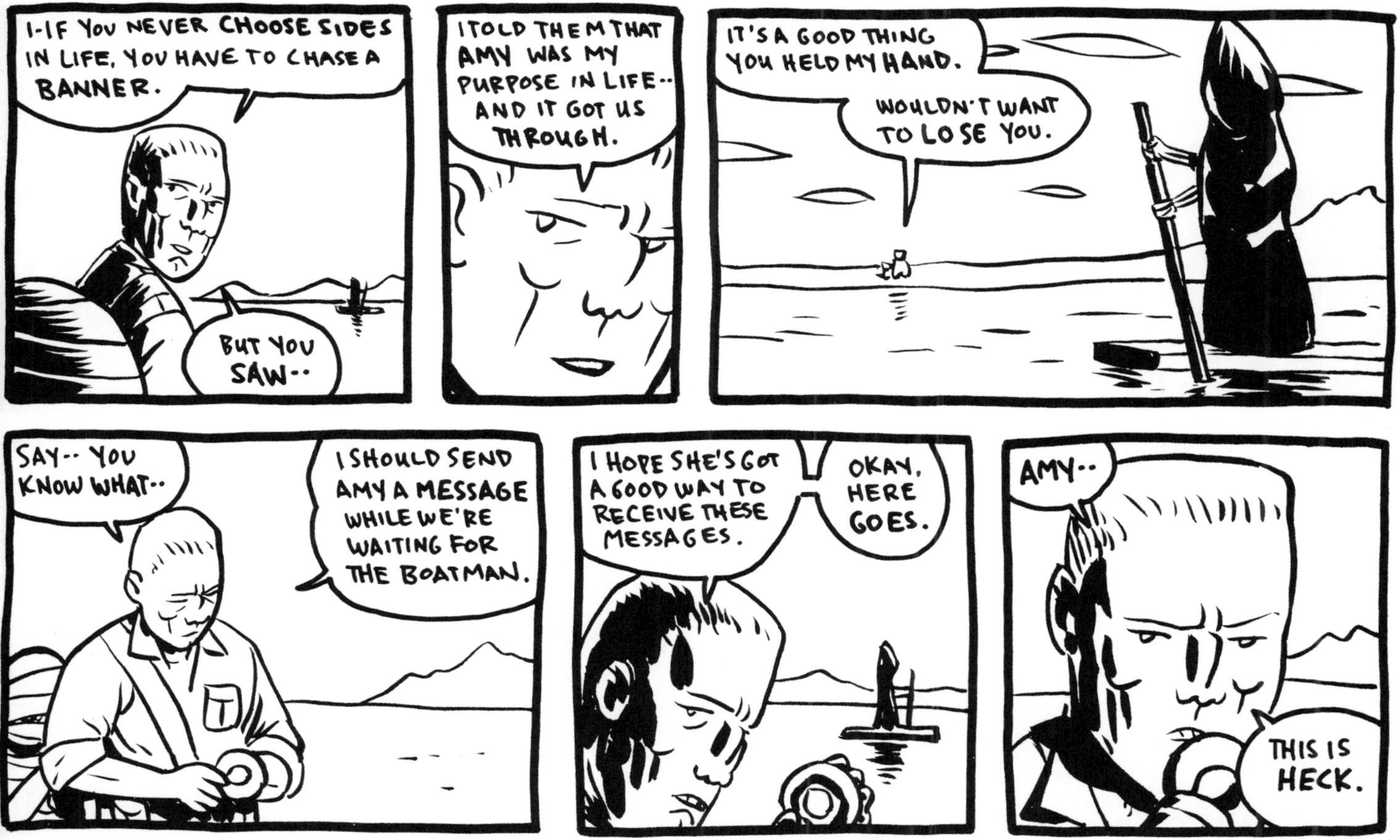
I-IF YOU NEVER CHOOSE SIDES IN LIFE, YOU HAVE TO CHASE A BANNER.
BUT YOU SAW..
I TOLD THEM THAT AMY WAS MY PURPOSE IN LIFE.. AND IT GOT US THROUGH.
IT'S A GOOD THING YOU HELD MY HAND.
WOULDN'T WANT TO LOSE YOU.
SAY.. YOU KNOW WHAT..
I SHOULD SEND AMY A MESSAGE WHILE WE'RE WAITING FOR THE BOATMAN.
I HOPE SHE'S GOT A GOOD WAY TO RECEIVE THESE MESSAGES.
OKAY, HERE GOES.
AMY..
THIS IS HECK.

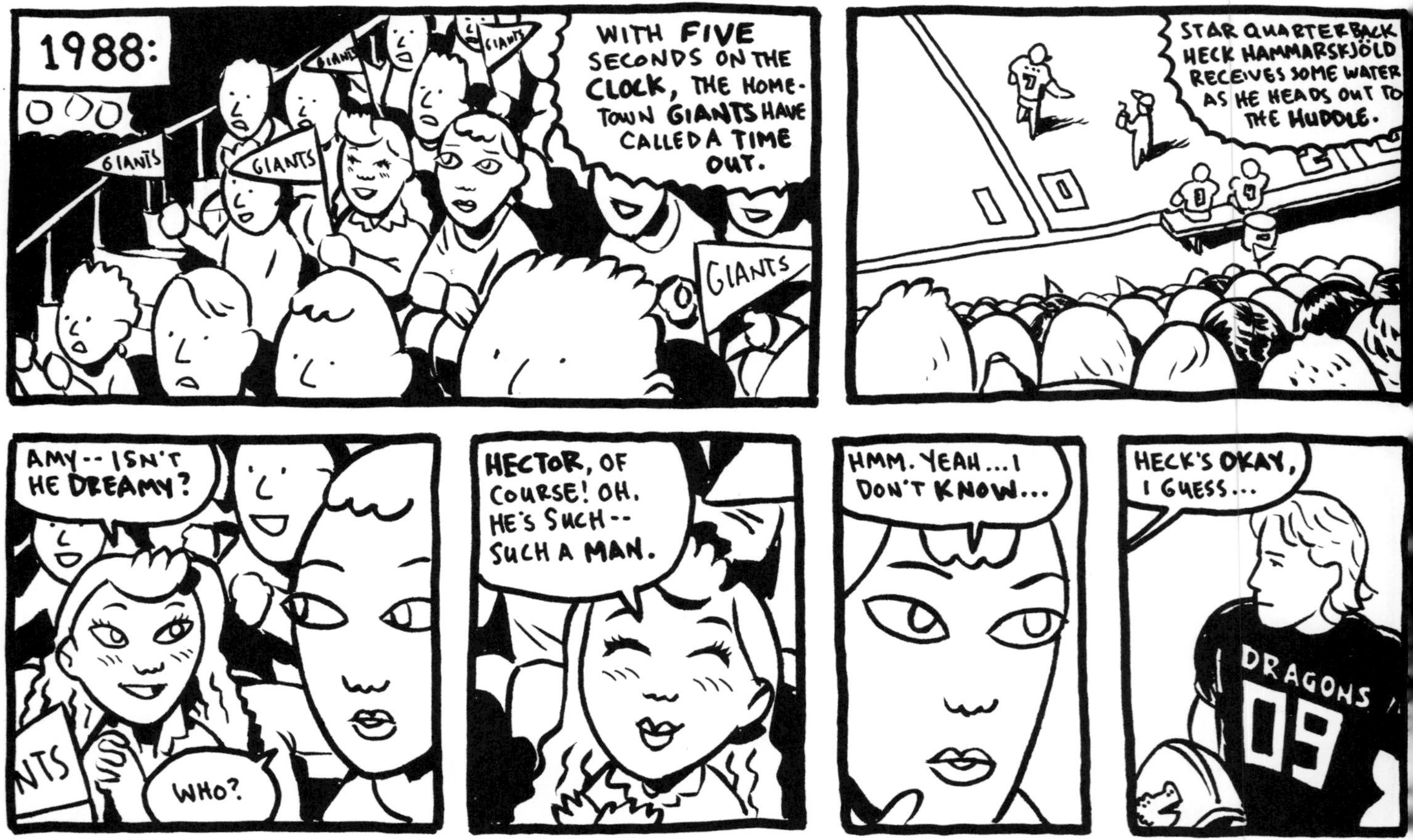
1988:
GIANTS
GIANTS
GIANTS
GIANTS
GIANTS
GIANTS
WITH FIVE SECONDS ON THE CLOCK, THE HOME-TOWN GIANTS HAVE CALLED A TIME OUT.
STAR QUARTERBACK HECK HAMMARSKJÖLD RECEIVES SOME WATER AS HE HEADS OUT TO THE HUDDLE.
AMY -- ISN'T HE DREAMY?
WHO?
NTS
HECTOR, OF COURSE! OH, HE'S SUCH -- SUCH A MAN.
HMM. YEAH... I DON'T KNOW...
HECK'S OKAY, I GUESS...
DRAGONS
09

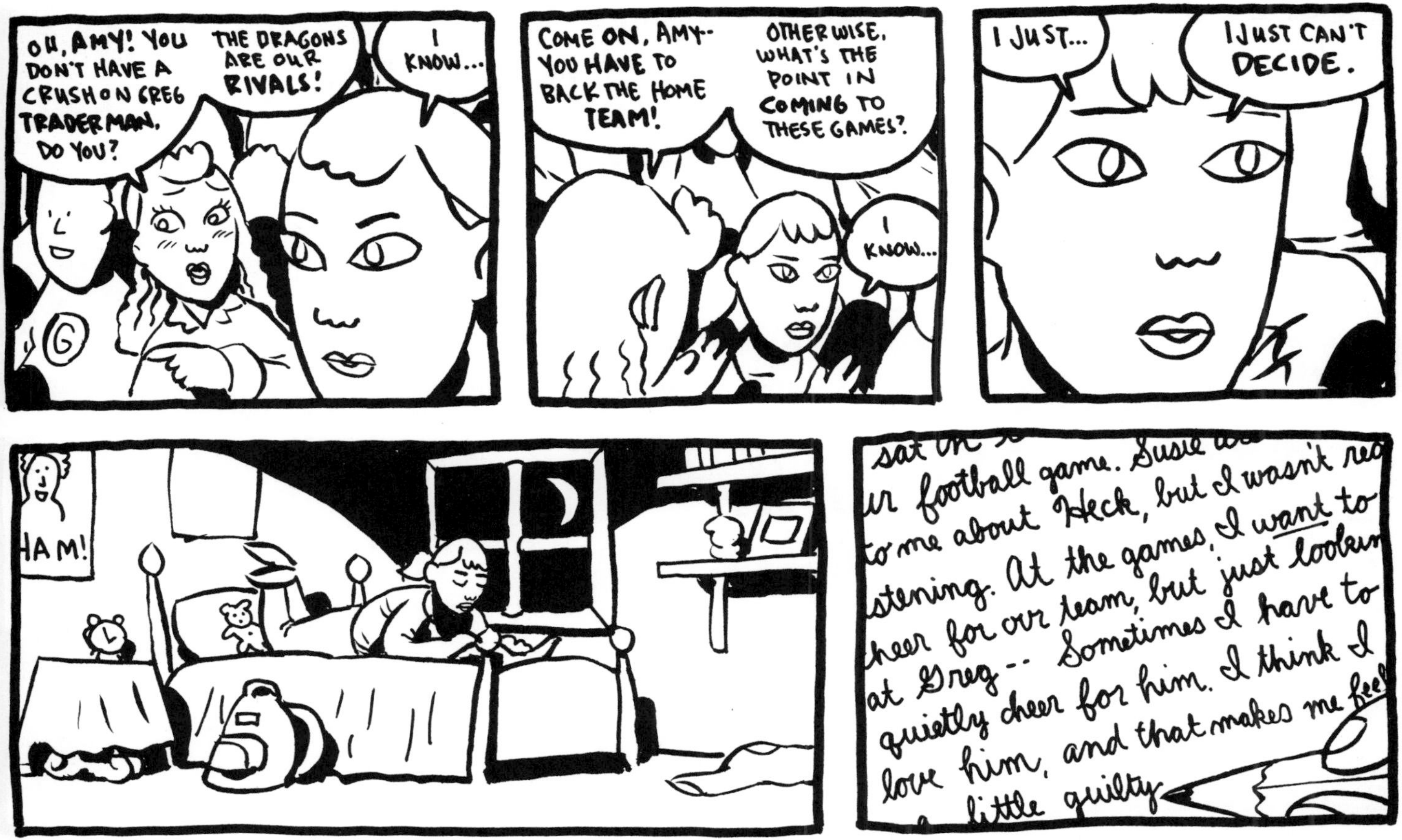
OH, AMY! YOU DON'T HAVE A CRUSH ON GREG TRADERMAN. DO YOU?
THE DRAGONS ARE OUR RIVALS!
I KNOW...
COME ON, AMY-- YOU HAVE TO BACK THE HOME TEAM!
OTHERWISE, WHAT'S THE POINT IN COMING TO THESE GAMES?
I KNOW...
I JUST...
I JUST CAN'T DECIDE.
HAM!
sat in
ur football game. Susie
to me about Heck, but I wasn't
stening. At the games, I want to
heer for our team, but just lookin
at Greg -- Sometimes I have to
quietly cheer for him. I think I
love him, and that makes me feel
little guilty

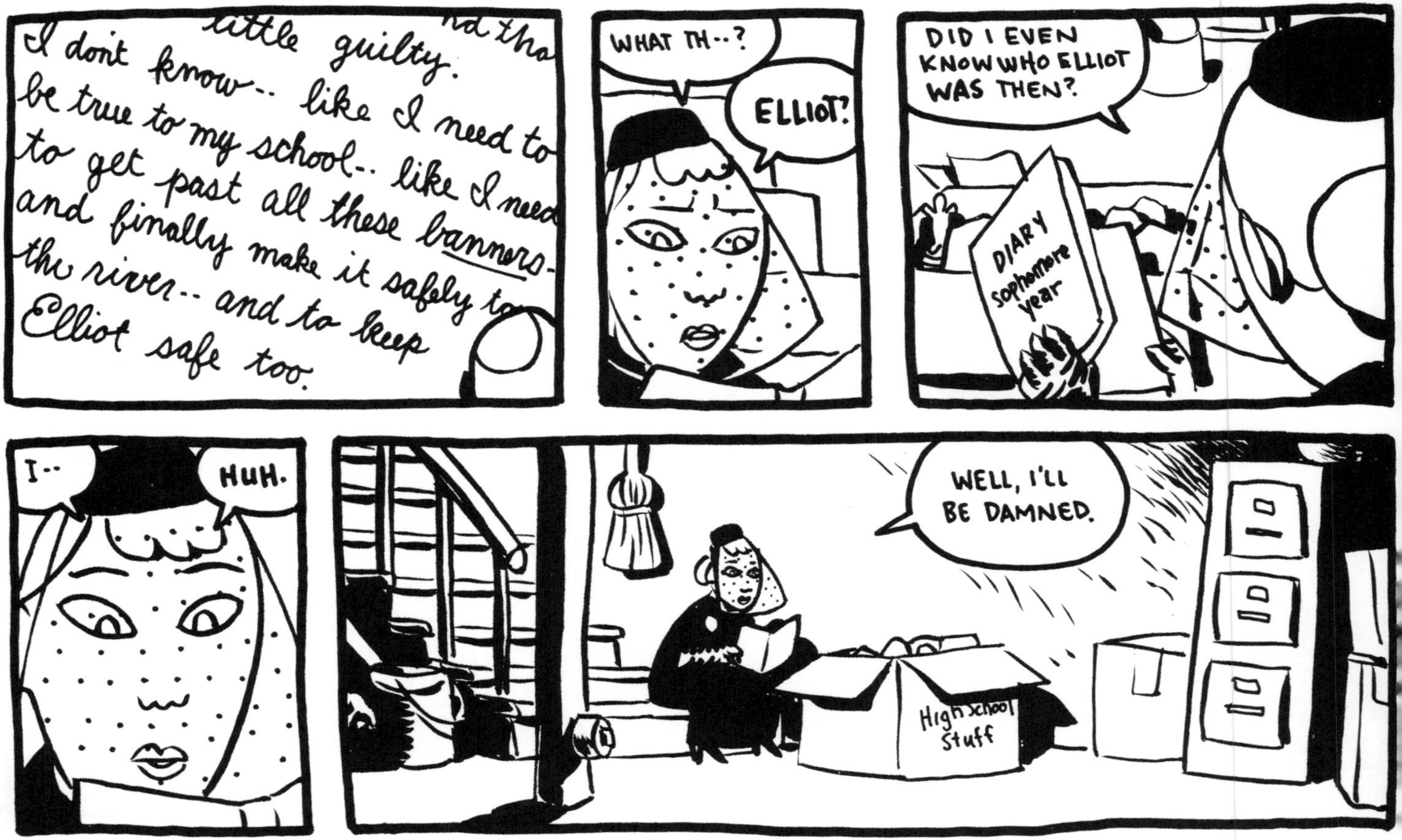
little guilty.
nd tha
I don't know-- like I need to
be true to my school-- like I need
to get past all these banners-
and finally make it safely to
the river-- and to keep
Elliot safe too.
WHAT TH--?
ELLIOT?
DID I EVEN KNOW WHO ELLIOT WAS THEN?
DIARY sophomore year
I--
HUH.
WELL, I'LL BE DAMNED.
High School Stuff

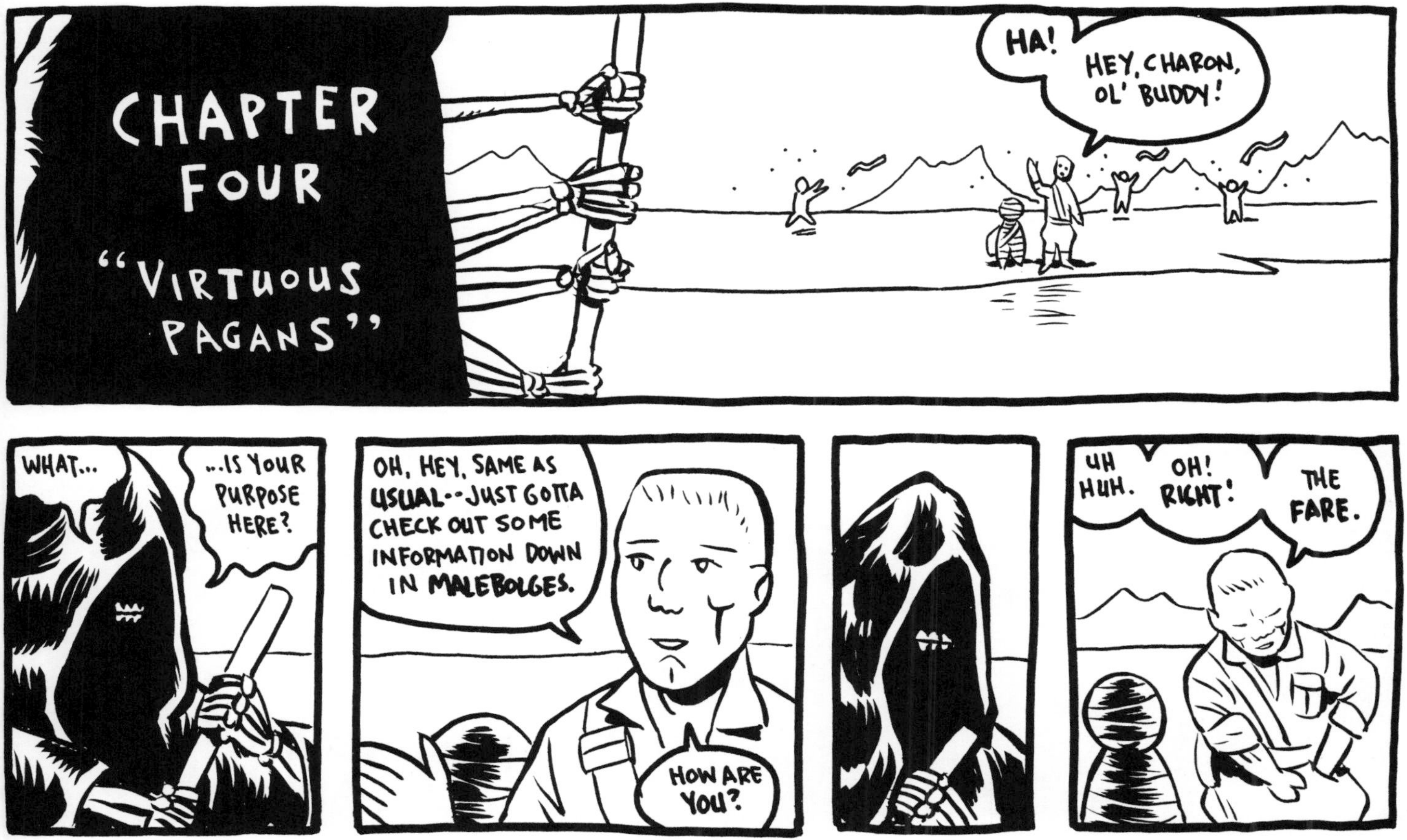
CHAPTER FOUR
"VIRTUOUS PAGANS"
HA!
HEY, CHARON, OL' BUDDY!
WHAT...
...IS YOUR PURPOSE HERE?
OH, HEY, SAME AS USUAL--JUST GOTTA CHECK OUT SOME INFORMATION DOWN IN MALEBOLGES.
HOW ARE YOU?
UH HUH.
OH! RIGHT!
THE FARE.

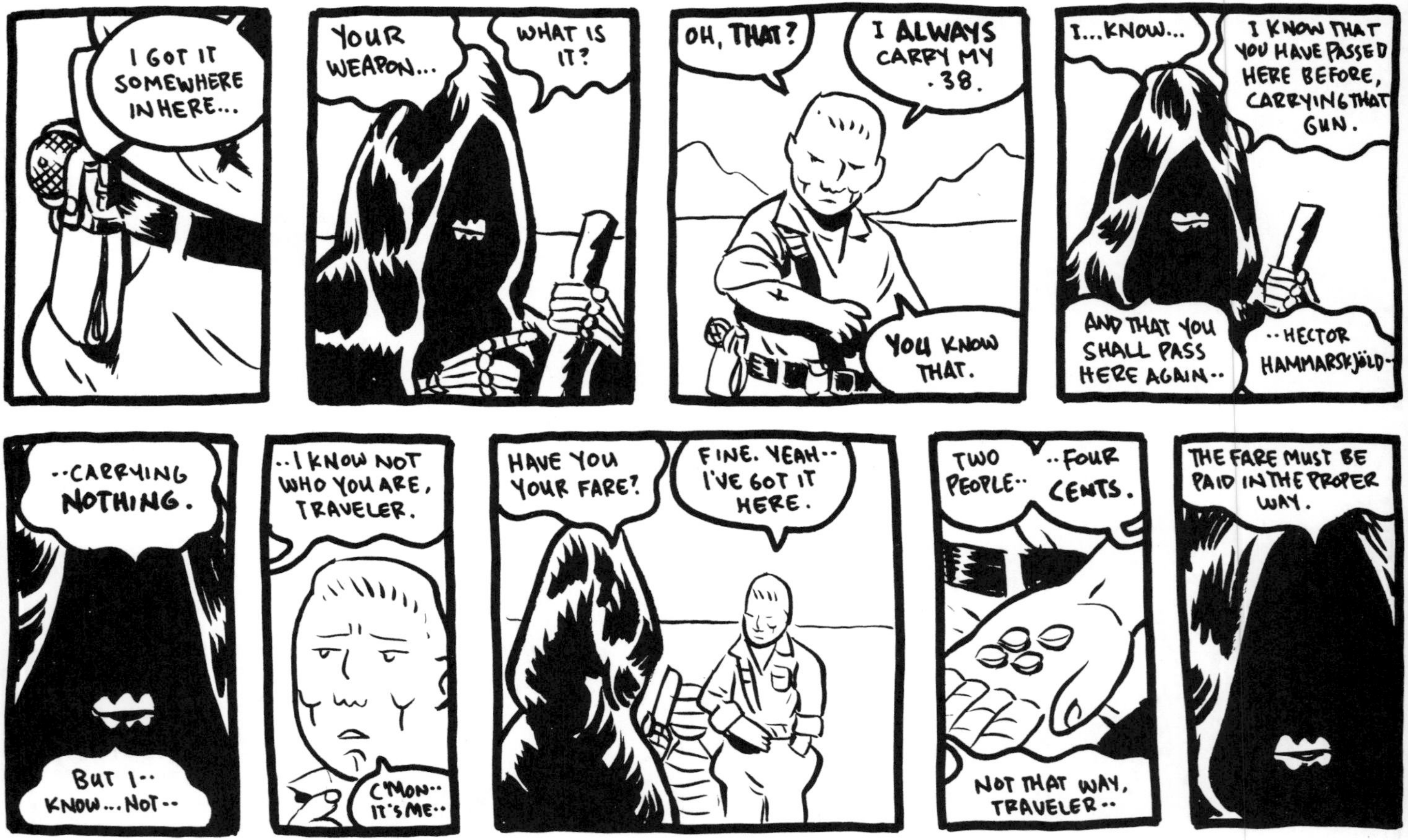
I GOT IT SOMEWHERE IN HERE...
YOUR WEAPON...
WHAT IS IT?
OH, THAT?
I ALWAYS CARRY MY .38.
YOU KNOW THAT.
I... KNOW...
I KNOW THAT YOU HAVE PASSED HERE BEFORE, CARRYING THAT GUN.
AND THAT YOU SHALL PASS HERE AGAIN--
--HECTOR HAMMARSKJÖLD--
--CARRYING NOTHING.
BUT I-- KNOW... NOT--
--I KNOW NOT WHO YOU ARE, TRAVELER.
C'MON-- IT'S ME--
HAVE YOU YOUR FARE?
FINE. YEAH-- I'VE GOT IT HERE.
TWO PEOPLE--
--FOUR CENTS.
NOT THAT WAY, TRAVELER--
THE FARE MUST BE PAID IN THE PROPER WAY.

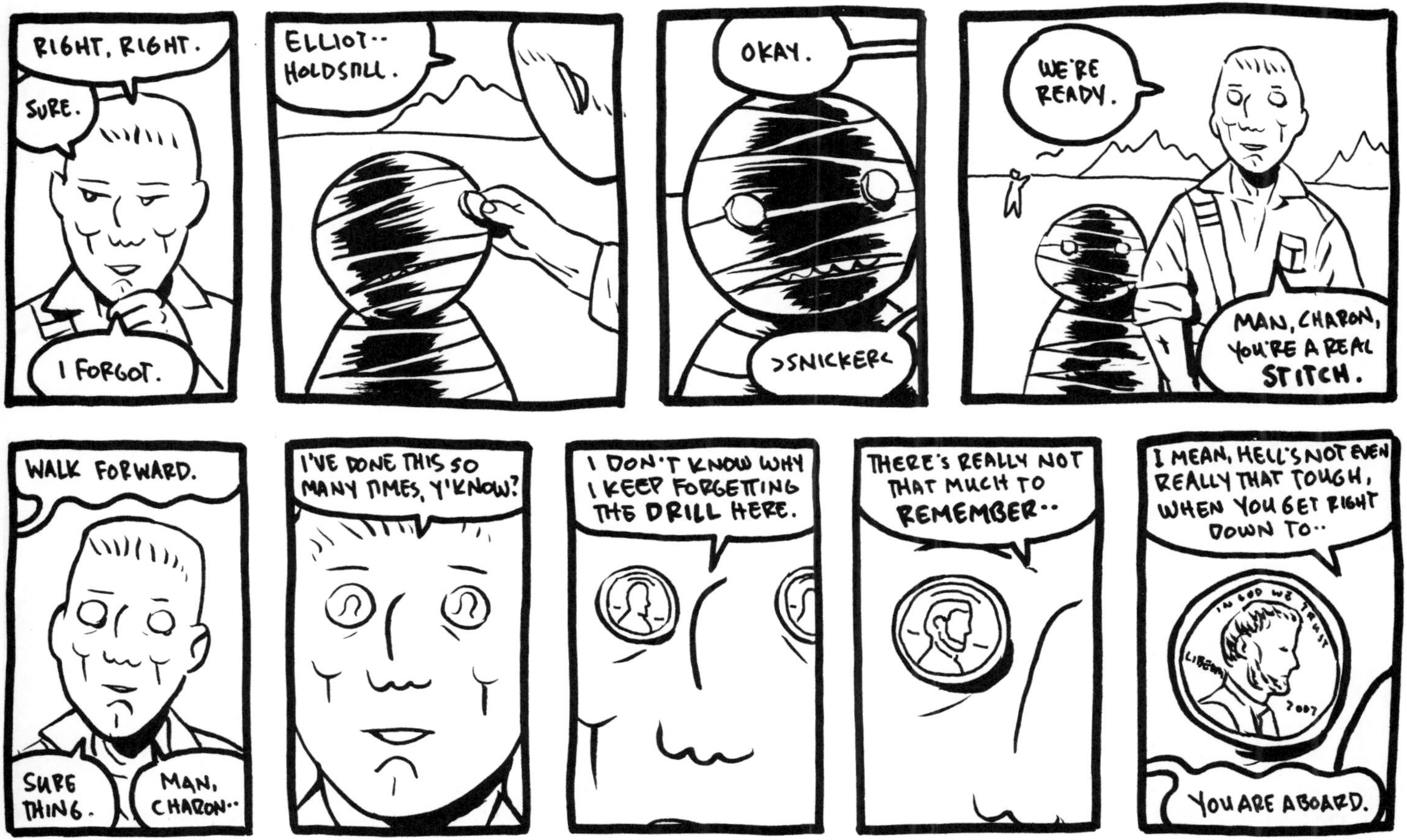

RIGHT, RIGHT.
SURE.
I FORGOT.
ELLIOT.. HOLD STILL.
OKAY.
>SNICKER<
WE'RE READY.
MAN, CHARON, YOU'RE A REAL STITCH.
WALK FORWARD.
SURE THING.
MAN, CHARON..
I'VE DONE THIS SO MANY TIMES, Y'KNOW?
I DON'T KNOW WHY I KEEP FORGETTING THE DRILL HERE.
THERE'S REALLY NOT THAT MUCH TO REMEMBER..
I MEAN, HELL'S NOT EVEN REALLY THAT TOUGH, WHEN YOU GET RIGHT DOWN TO..
YOU ARE ABOARD.

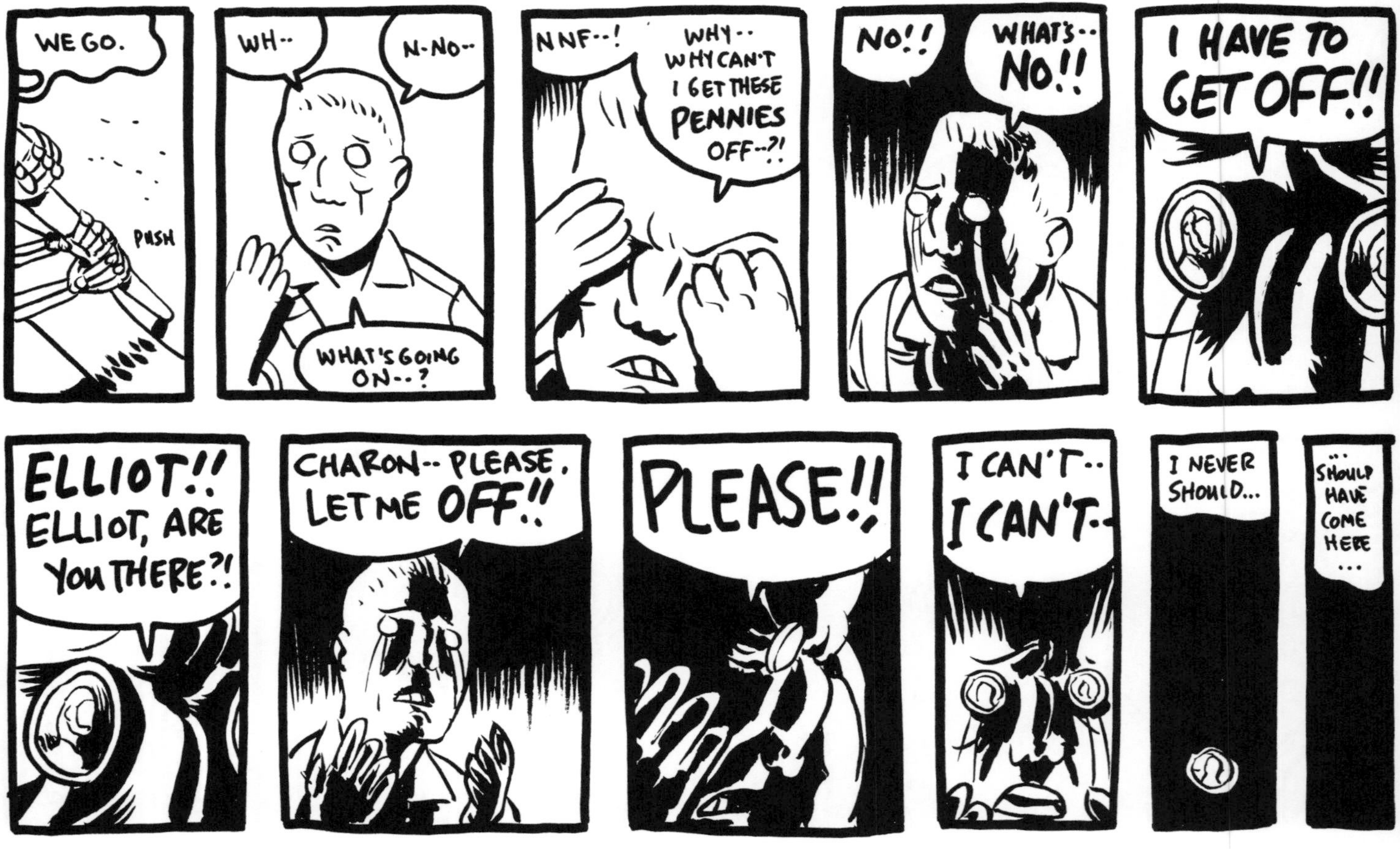
WE GO.
PUSH
WH--
N-NO--
WHAT'S GOING ON--?
NNF--!
WHY-- WHY CAN'T I GET THESE PENNIES OFF--?!
NO!!
WHAT'S-- NO!!
I HAVE TO GET OFF!!
ELLIOT!! ELLIOT, ARE YOU THERE?!
CHARON-- PLEASE, LET ME OFF!!
PLEASE!!
I CAN'T-- I CAN'T--
I NEVER SHOULD...
...SHOULD HAVE COME HERE
...

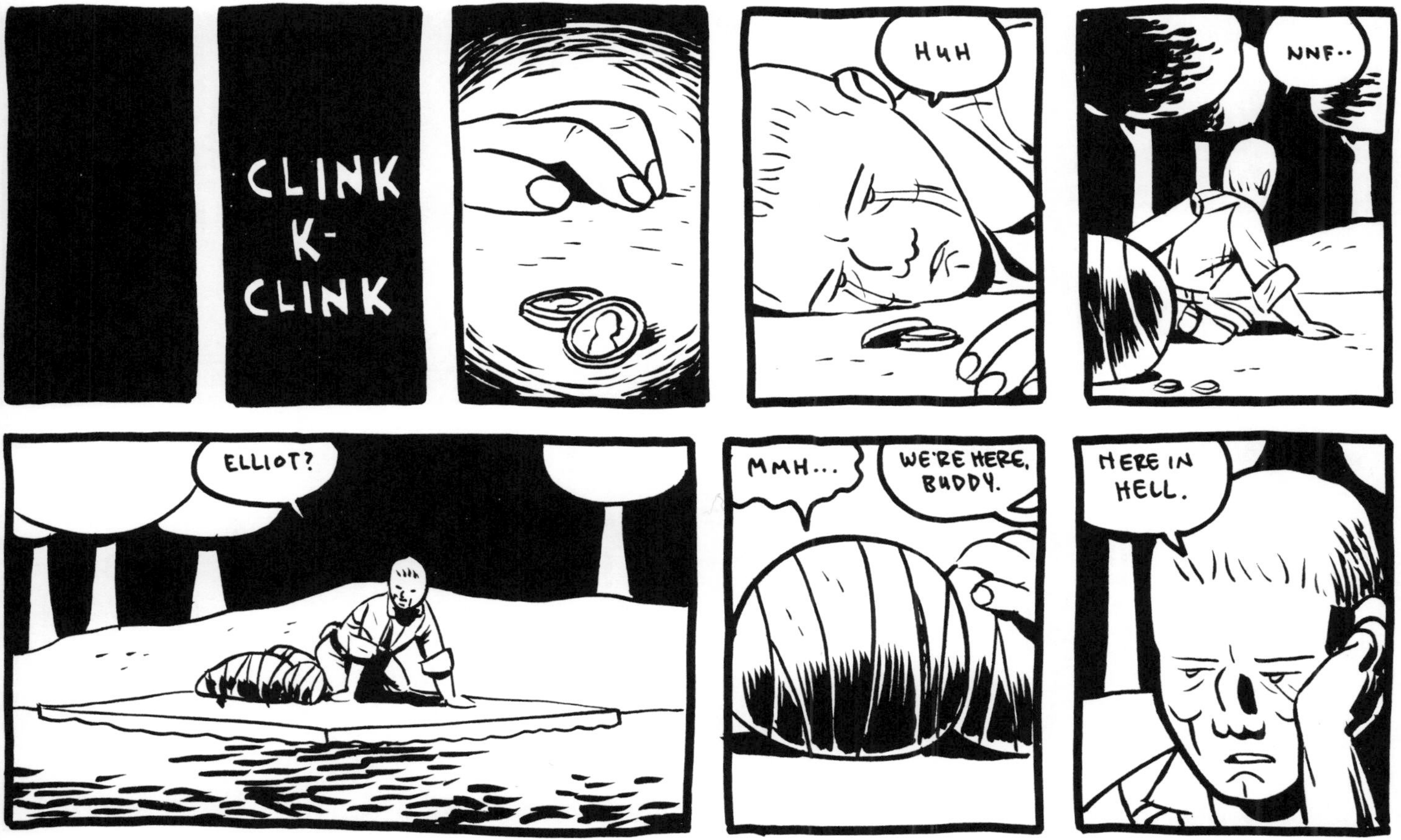
CLINK K- CLINK
HUH
NNF..
ELLIOT?
MMH...
WE'RE HERE, BUDDY.
HERE IN HELL.

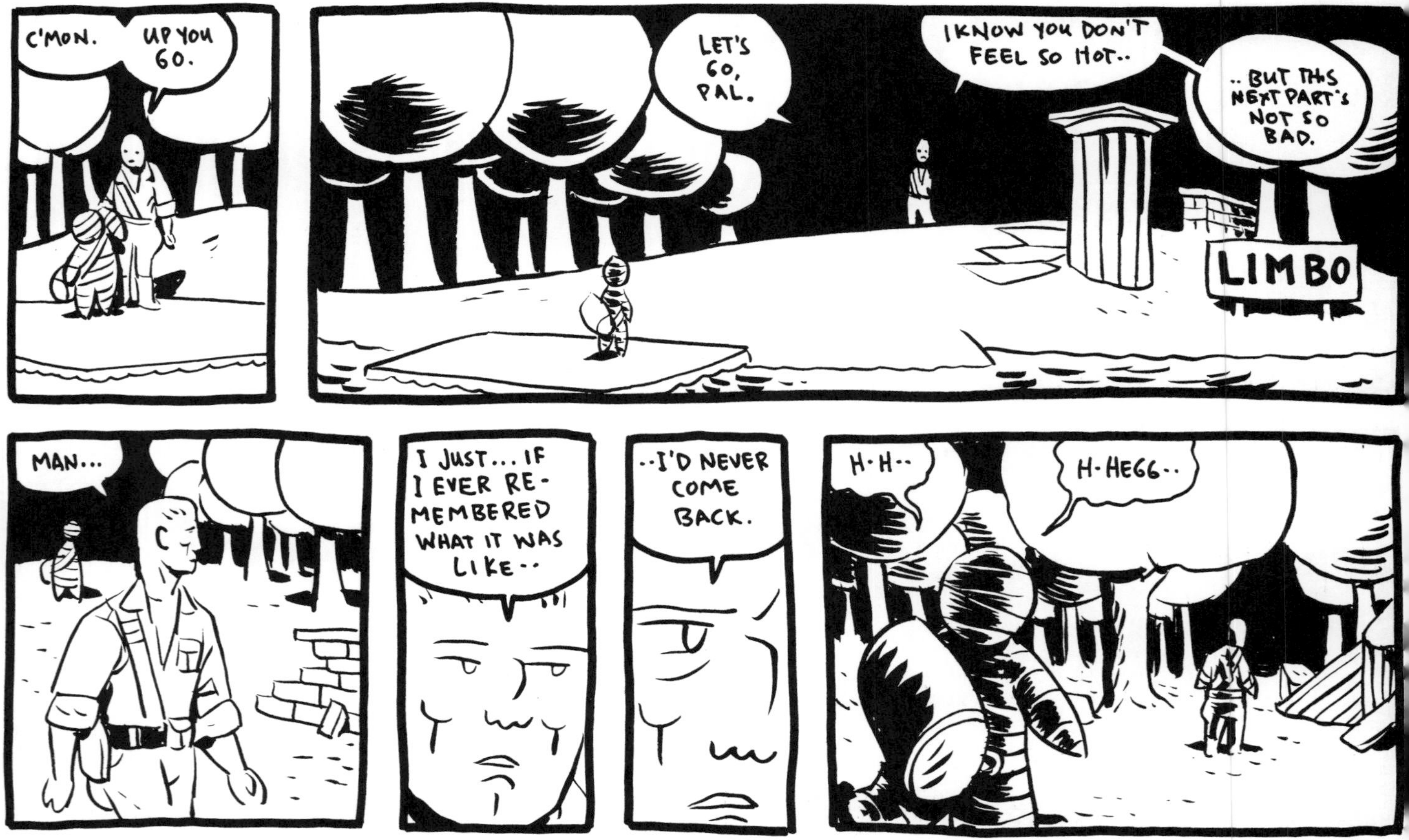
C'MON.
UP YOU GO.
LET'S GO, PAL.
I KNOW YOU DON'T FEEL SO HOT..
.. BUT THIS NEXT PART'S NOT SO BAD.
LIMBO
MAN...
I JUST... IF I EVER RE-MEMBERED WHAT IT WAS LIKE..
..I'D NEVER COME BACK.
H-H..
H-HEGG..

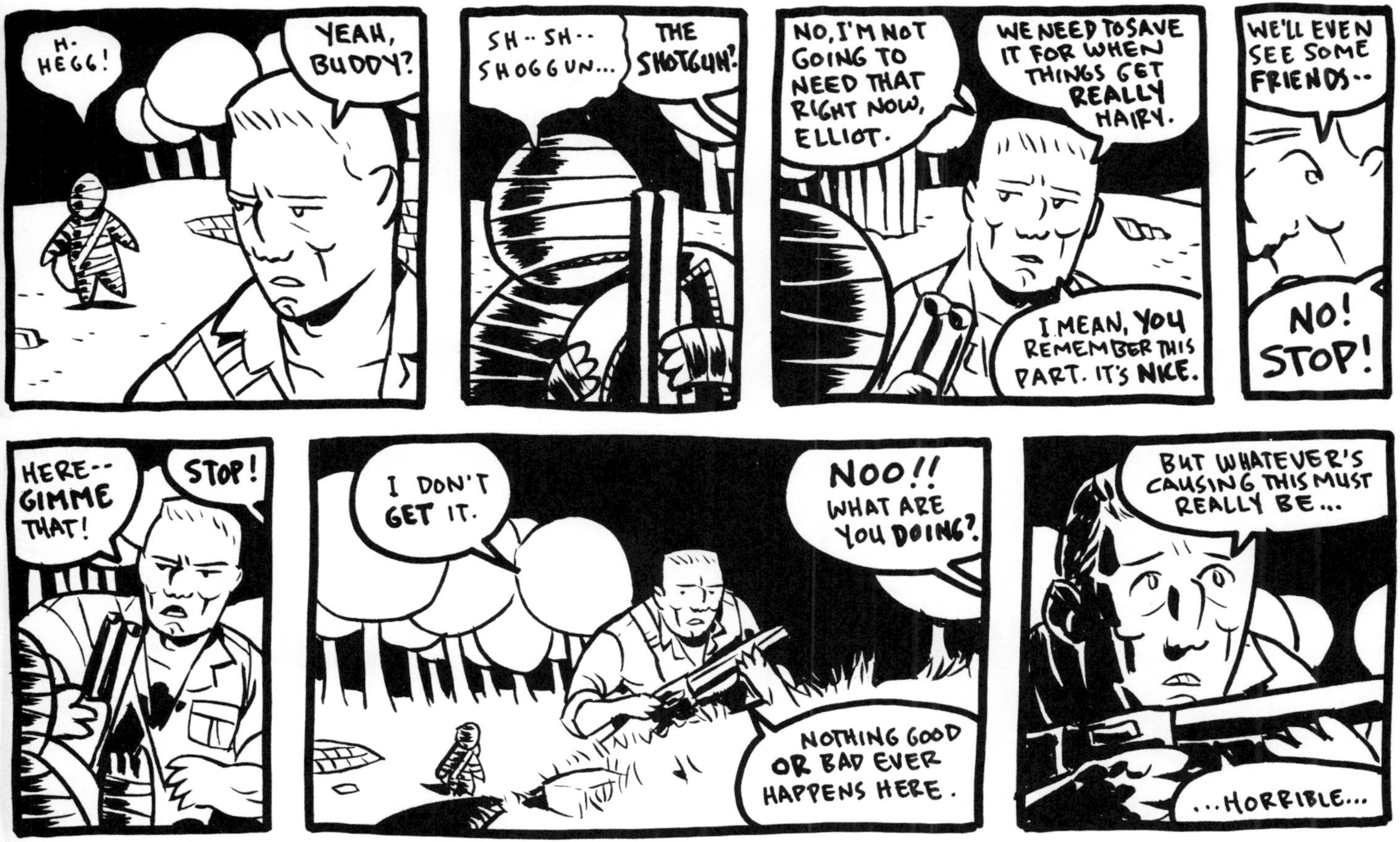
H-HEGG!
YEAH, BUDDY?
SH-- SH-- SHOGGUN...
THE SHOTGUN?
NO, I'M NOT GOING TO NEED THAT RIGHT NOW, ELLIOT.
WE NEED TO SAVE IT FOR WHEN THINGS GET REALLY HAIRY.
I MEAN, YOU REMEMBER THIS PART. IT'S NICE.
WE'LL EVEN SEE SOME FRIENDS--
NO! STOP!
HERE-- GIMME THAT!
STOP!
I DON'T GET IT.
NOO!! WHAT ARE YOU DOING?
NOTHING GOOD OR BAD EVER HAPPENS HERE.
BUT WHATEVER'S CAUSING THIS MUST REALLY BE...
...HORRIBLE...

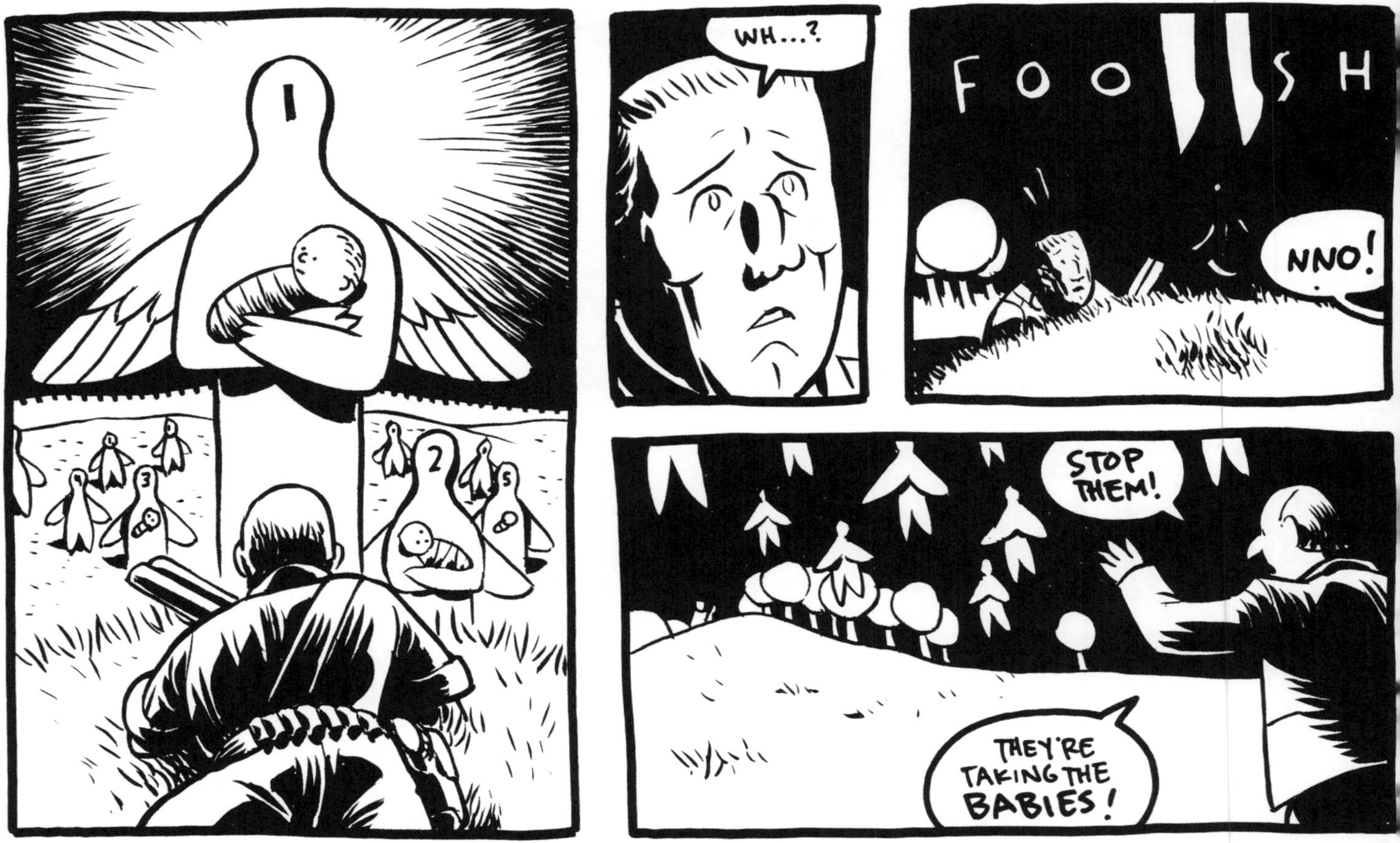
WH...?
FOO SH
NNO!
STOP THEM!
THEY'RE TAKING THE BABIES!

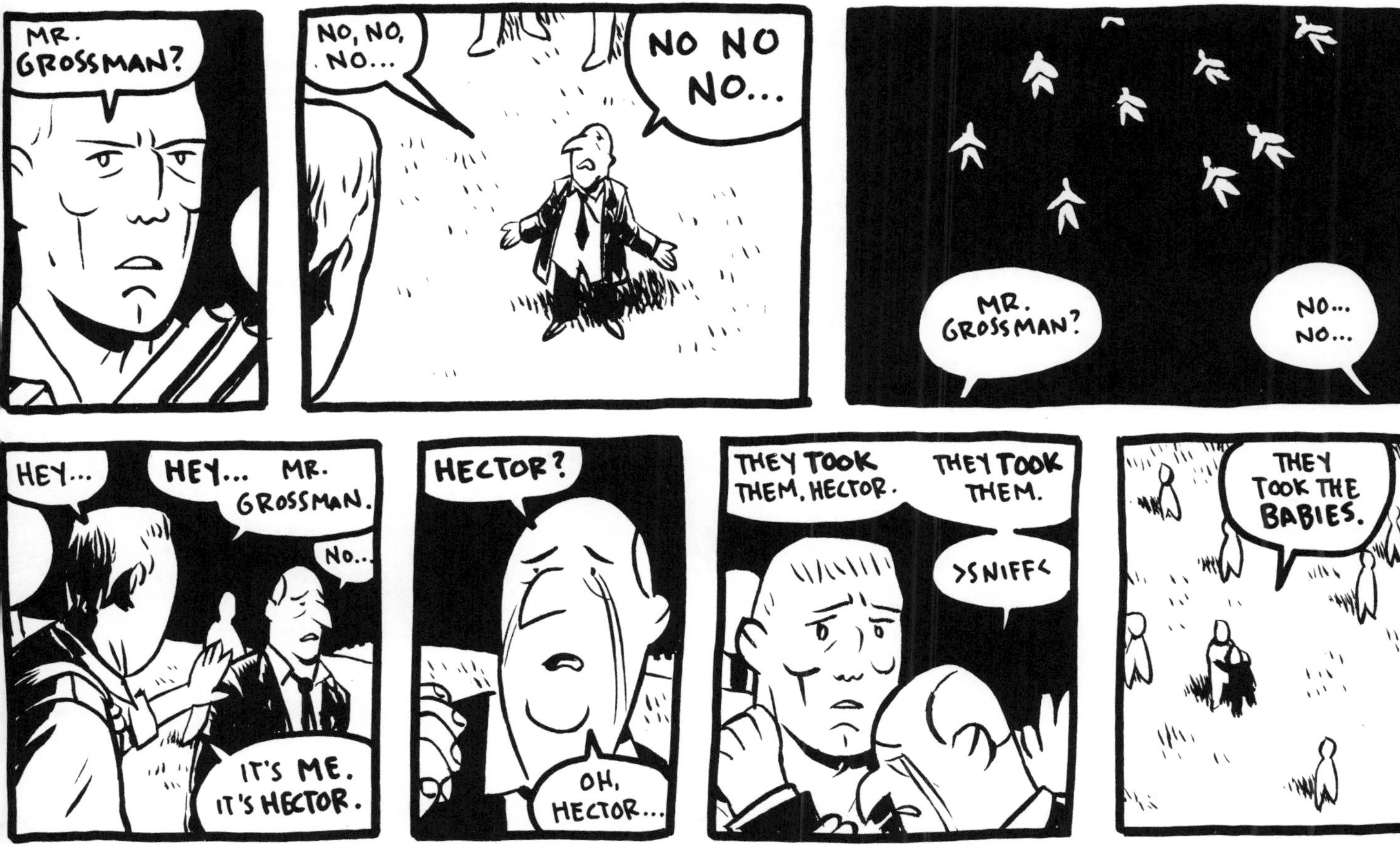
MR. GROSSMAN?
NO, NO, NO...
NO NO NO...
MR. GROSSMAN?
NO... NO...
HEY...
HEY... MR. GROSSMAN.
NO...
IT'S ME. IT'S HECTOR.
HECTOR?
OH, HECTOR...
THEY TOOK THEM, HECTOR.
THEY TOOK THEM.
>SNIFF<
THEY TOOK THE BABIES.

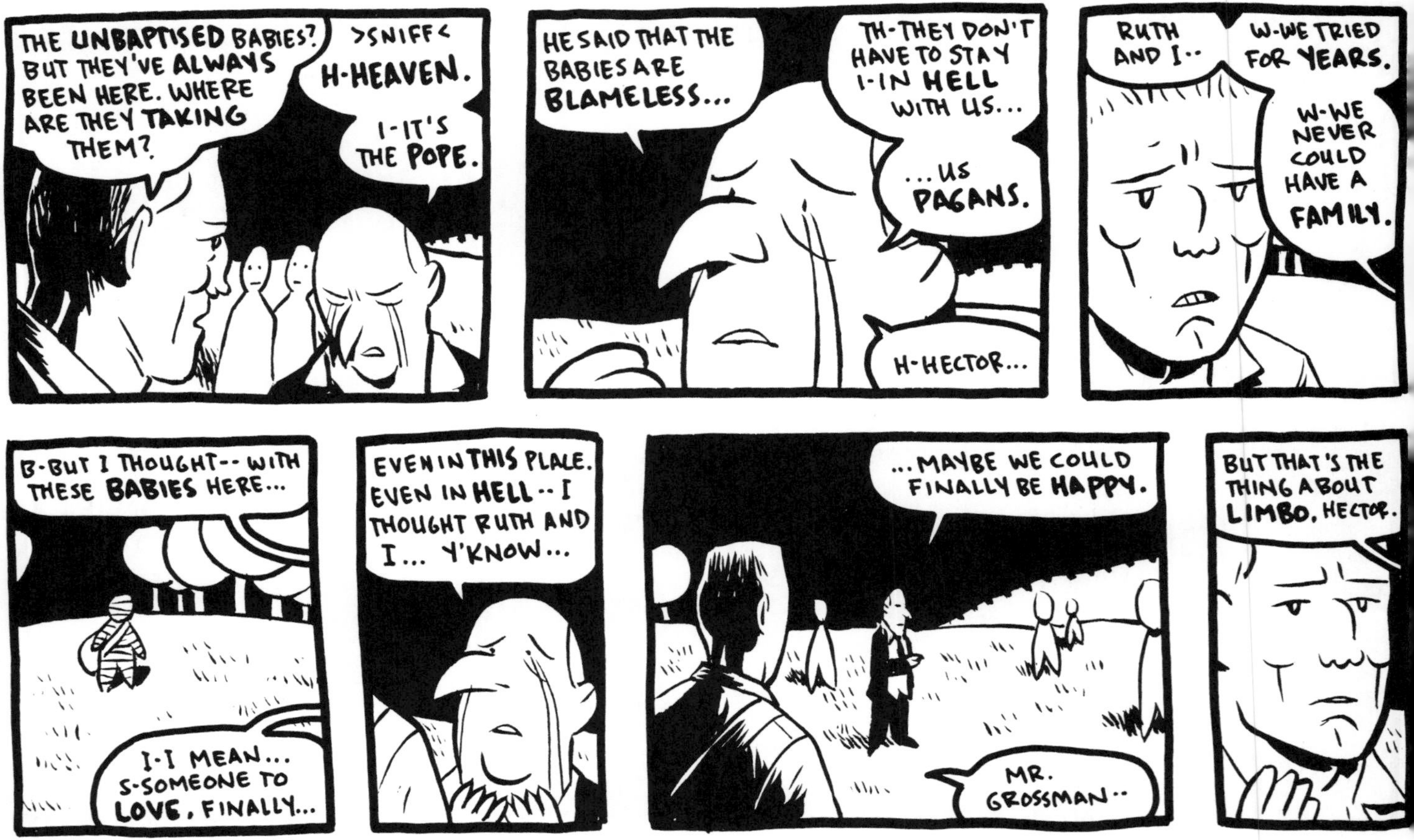
THE UNBAPTISED BABIES? BUT THEY'VE ALWAYS BEEN HERE. WHERE ARE THEY TAKING THEM?
>SNIFF<
H-HEAVEN.
I-IT'S THE POPE.
HE SAID THAT THE BABIES ARE BLAMELESS...
TH-THEY DON'T HAVE TO STAY I-IN HELL WITH US...
...US PAGANS.
H-HECTOR...
RUTH AND I..
W-WE TRIED FOR YEARS.
W-WE NEVER COULD HAVE A FAMILY.
B-BUT I THOUGHT-- WITH THESE BABIES HERE...
I-I MEAN... S-SOMEONE TO LOVE, FINALLY...
EVEN IN THIS PLACE. EVEN IN HELL.. I THOUGHT RUTH AND I... Y'KNOW...
...MAYBE WE COULD FINALLY BE HAPPY.
MR. GROSSMAN..
BUT THAT'S THE THING ABOUT LIMBO, HECTOR.

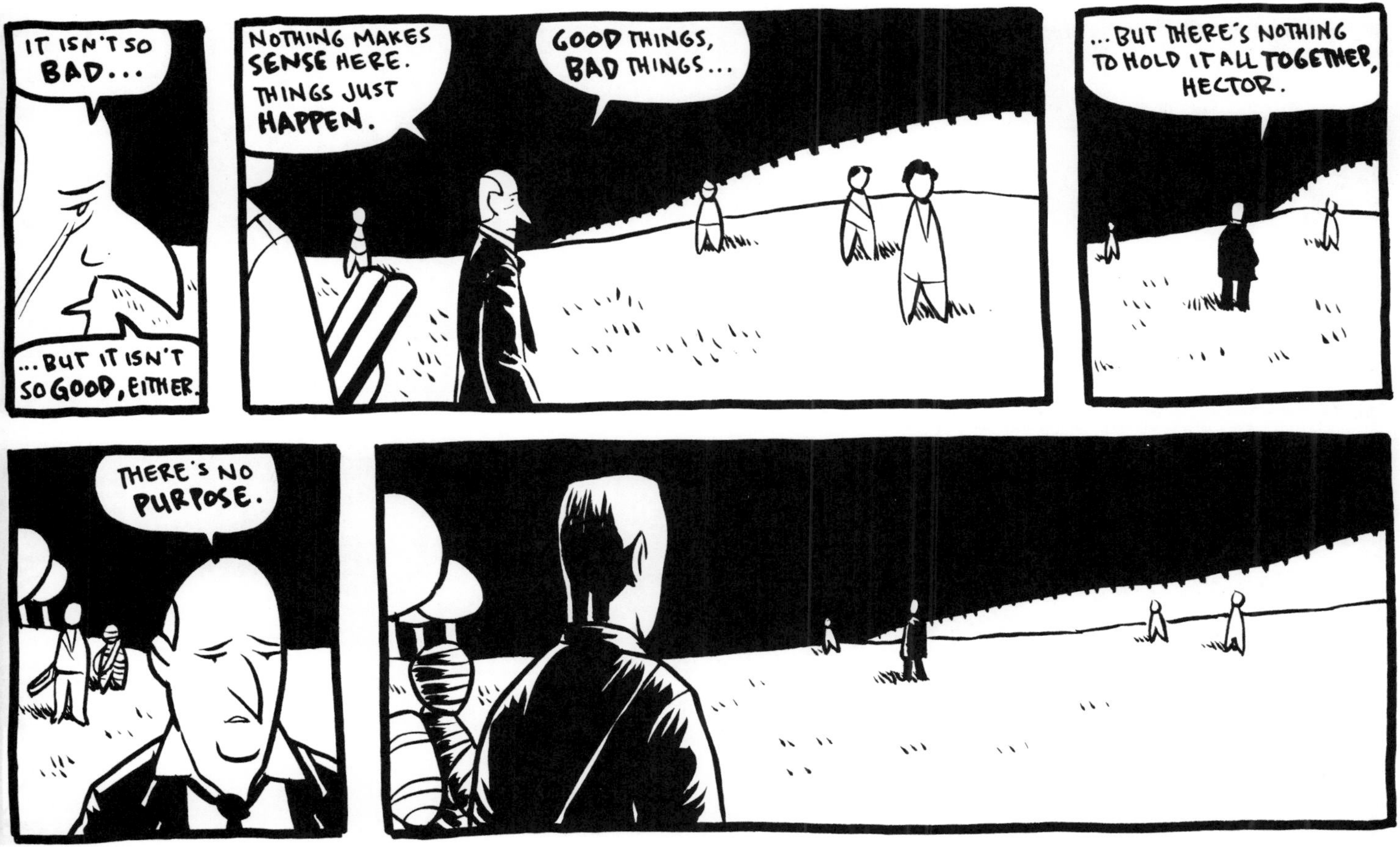
IT ISN'T SO BAD...
...BUT IT ISN'T SO GOOD, EITHER.
NOTHING MAKES SENSE HERE. THINGS JUST HAPPEN.
GOOD THINGS, BAD THINGS...
...BUT THERE'S NOTHING TO HOLD IT ALL TOGETHER, HECTOR.
THERE'S NO PURPOSE.

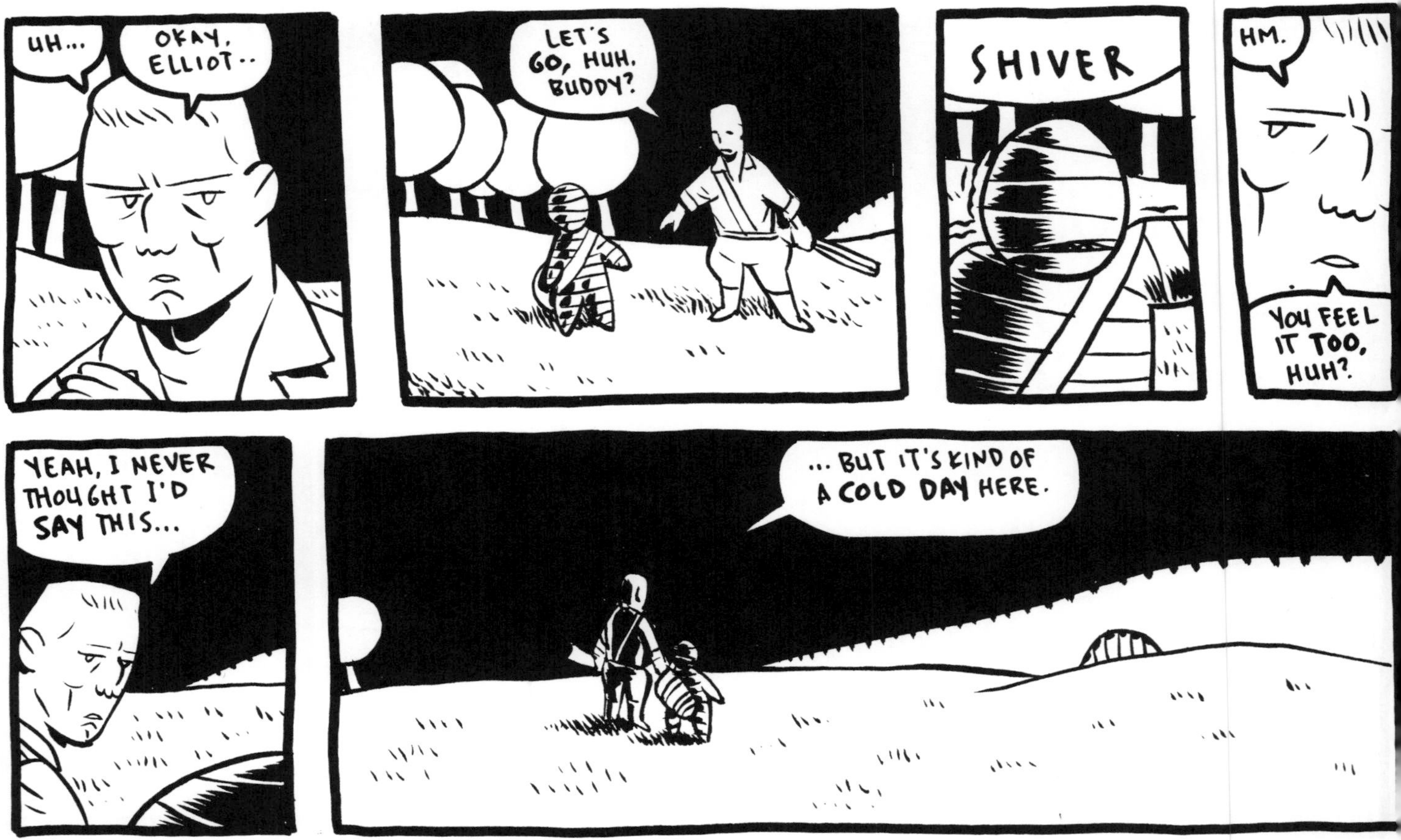
UH...
OKAY, ELLIOT..
LET'S GO, HUH, BUDDY?
SHIVER
HM.
YOU FEEL IT TOO, HUH?
YEAH, I NEVER THOUGHT I'D SAY THIS...
... BUT IT'S KIND OF A COLD DAY HERE.

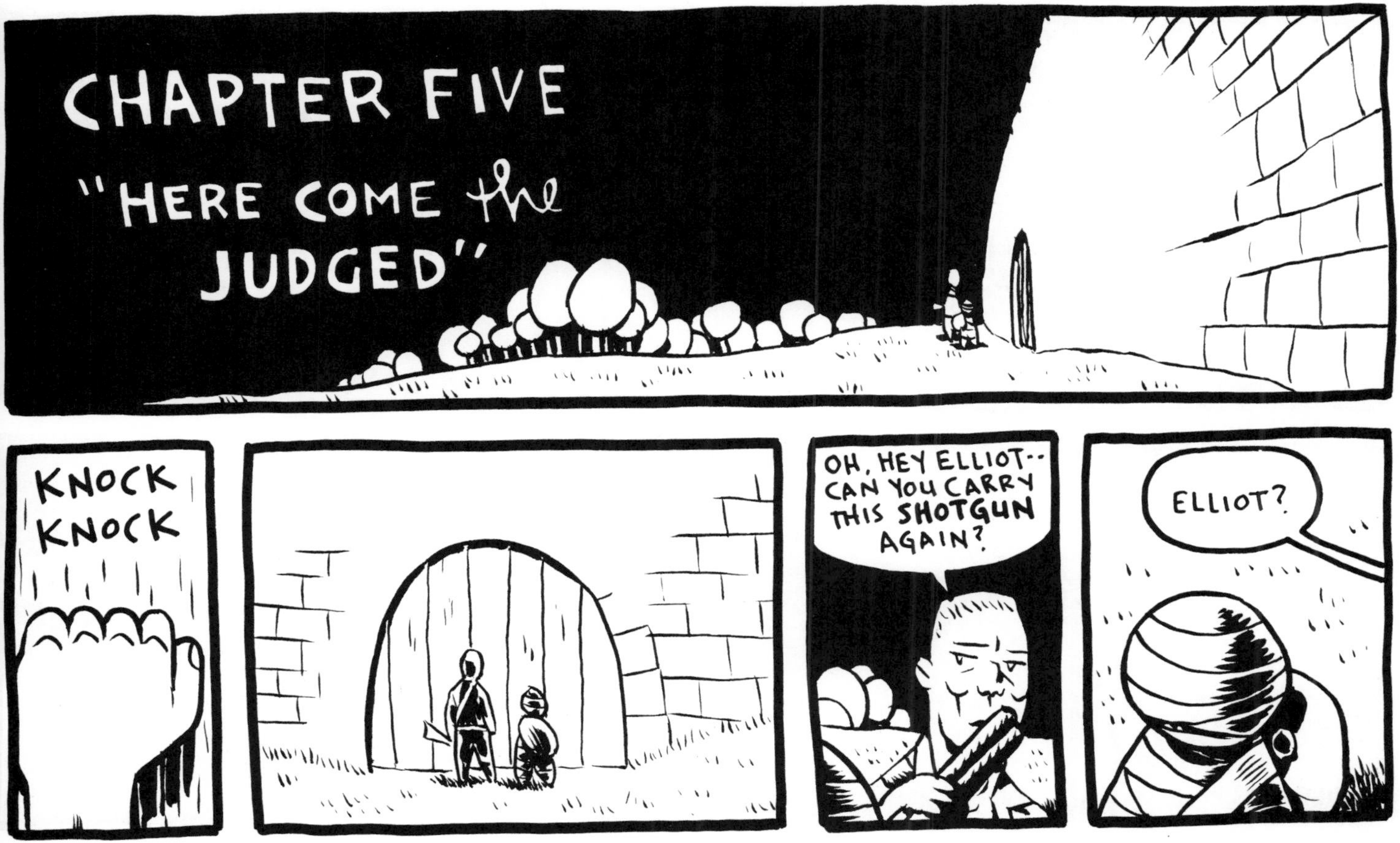
CHAPTER FIVE
"HERE COME the JUDGED"
KNOCK KNOCK
OH, HEY ELLIOT-- CAN YOU CARRY THIS SHOTGUN AGAIN?
ELLIOT?

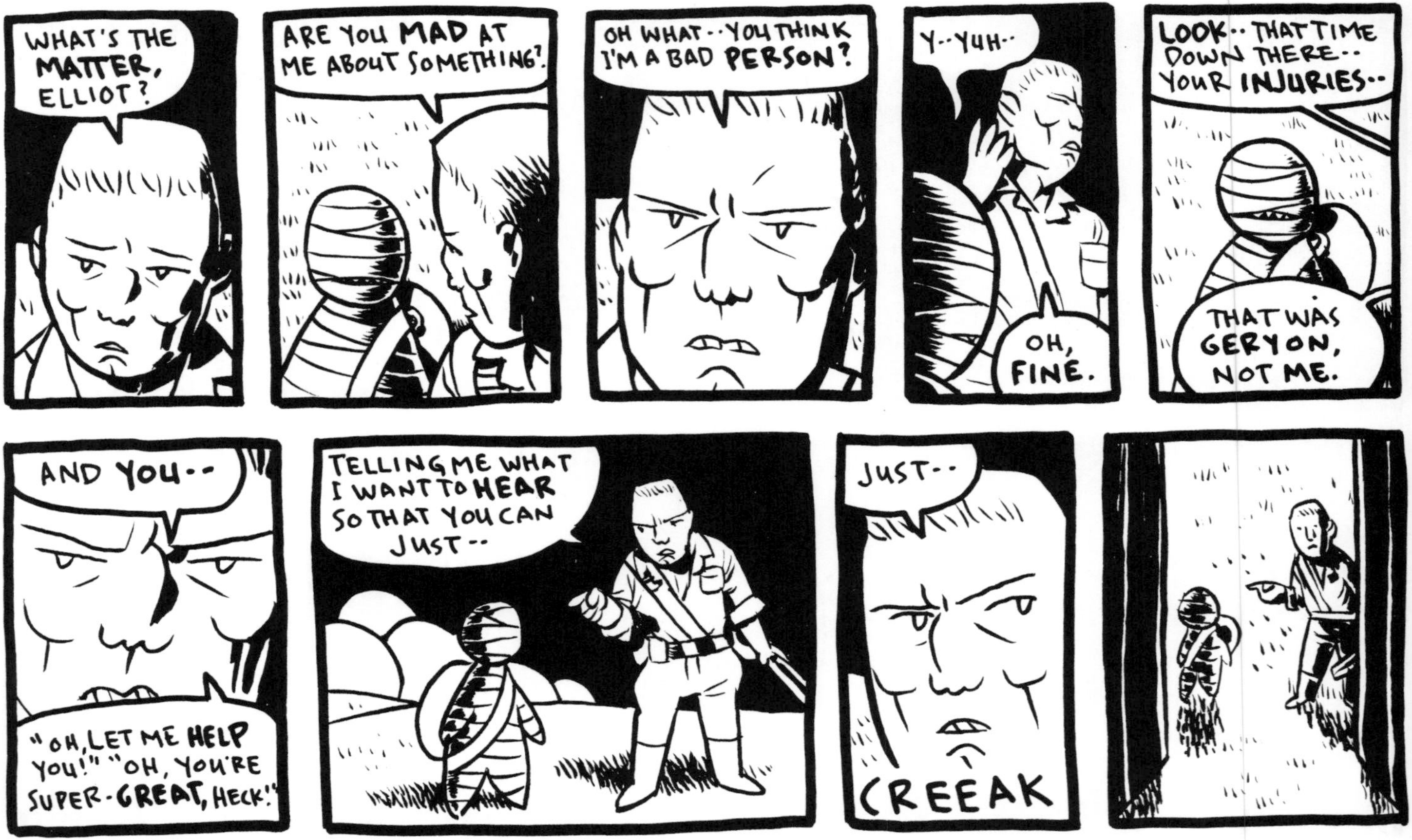
WHAT'S THE MATTER, ELLIOT?
ARE YOU MAD AT ME ABOUT SOMETHING?
OH WHAT-- YOU THINK I'M A BAD PERSON?
Y-- YUH--
OH, FINE.
LOOK-- THAT TIME DOWN THERE-- YOUR INJURIES--
THAT WAS GERYON, NOT ME.
AND YOU--
"OH, LET ME HELP YOU!" "OH, YOU'RE SUPER-GREAT, HECK!"
TELLING ME WHAT I WANT TO HEAR SO THAT YOU CAN JUST--
JUST--
CREEAK

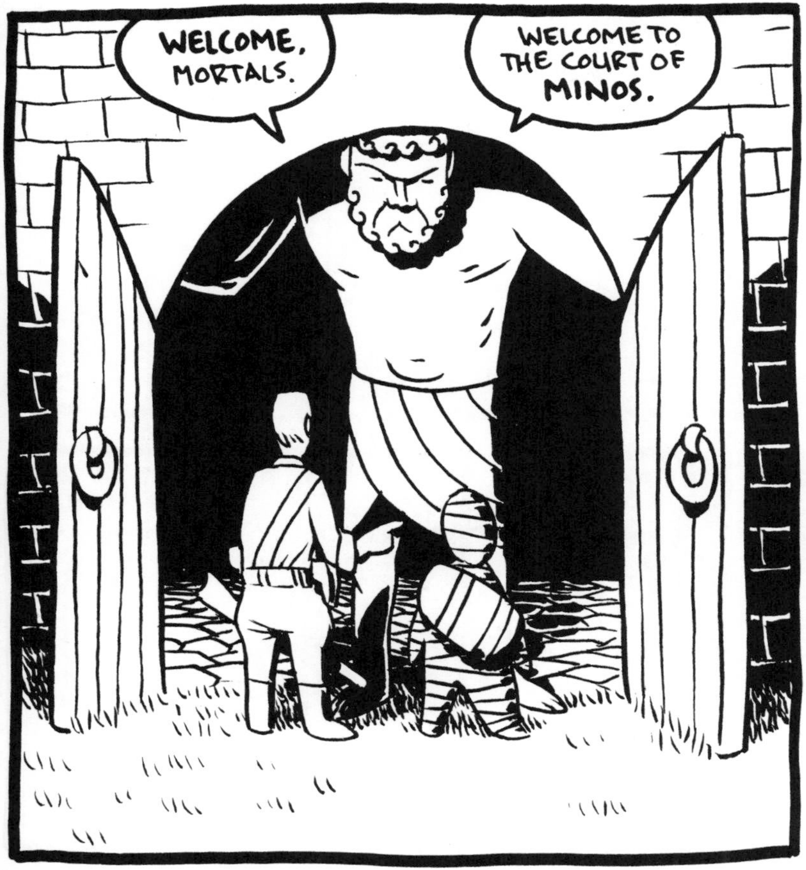
WELCOME, MORTALS.
WELCOME TO THE COURT OF MINOS.

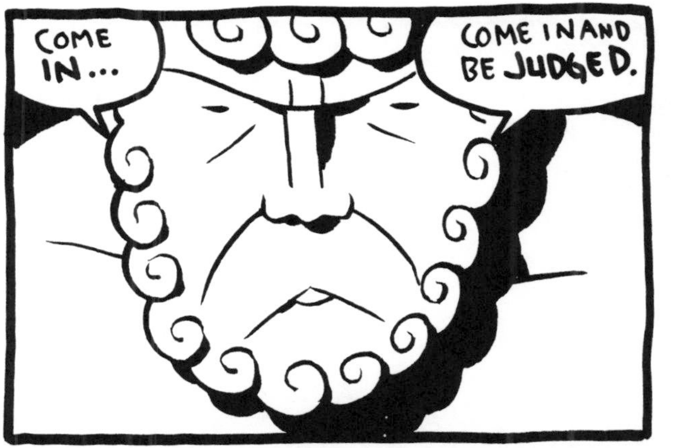
COME IN...
COME IN AND BE JUDGED.

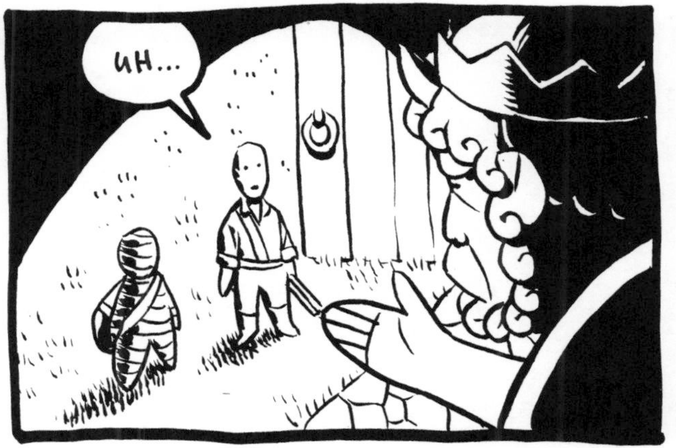
UH...

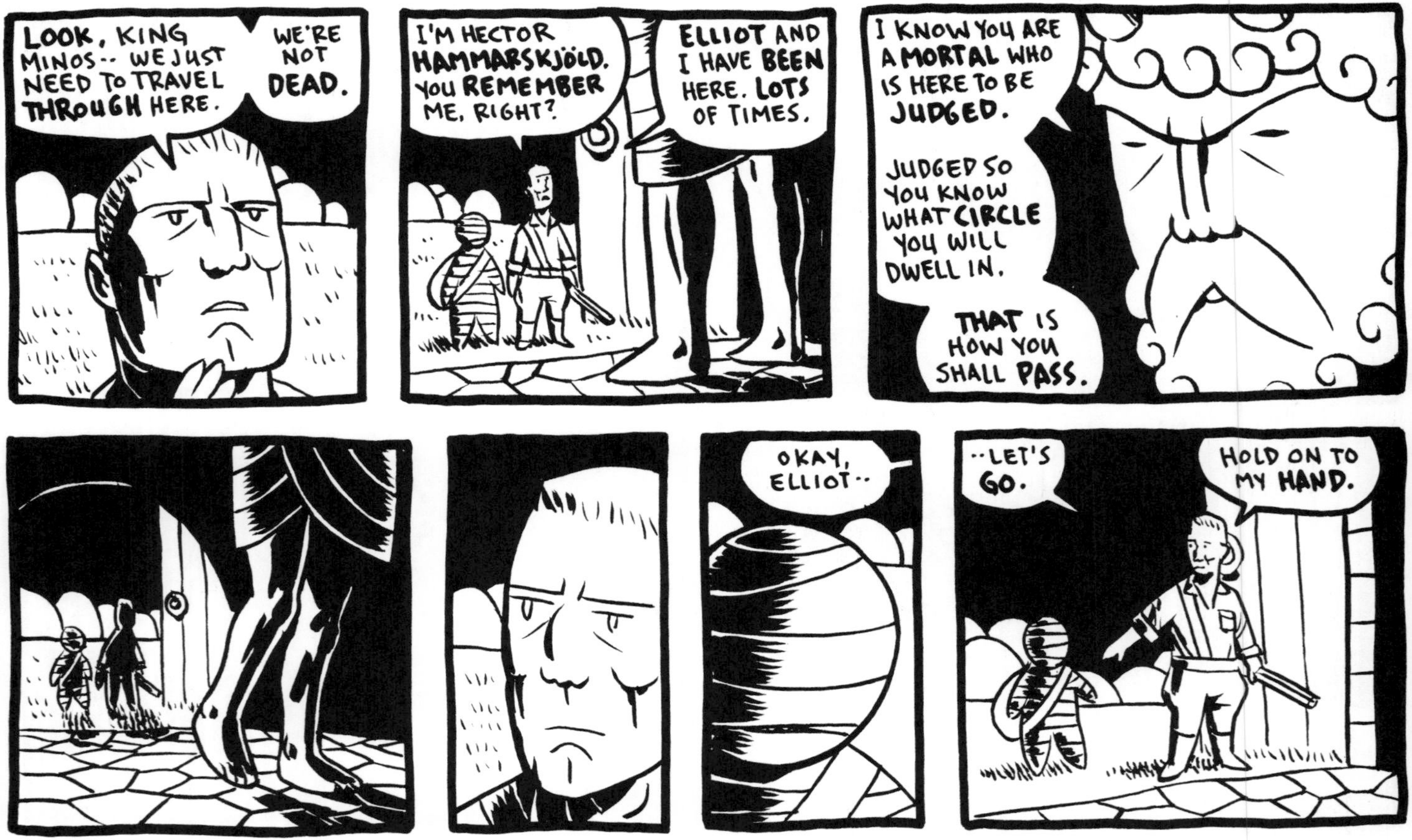
LOOK, KING MINOS-- WE JUST NEED TO TRAVEL THROUGH HERE.
WE'RE NOT DEAD.
I'M HECTOR HAMMARSKJÖLD. YOU REMEMBER ME, RIGHT?
ELLIOT AND I HAVE BEEN HERE. LOTS OF TIMES.
I KNOW YOU ARE A MORTAL WHO IS HERE TO BE JUDGED.
JUDGED SO YOU KNOW WHAT CIRCLE YOU WILL DWELL IN.
THAT IS HOW YOU SHALL PASS.
OKAY, ELLIOT--
--LET'S GO.
HOLD ON TO MY HAND.

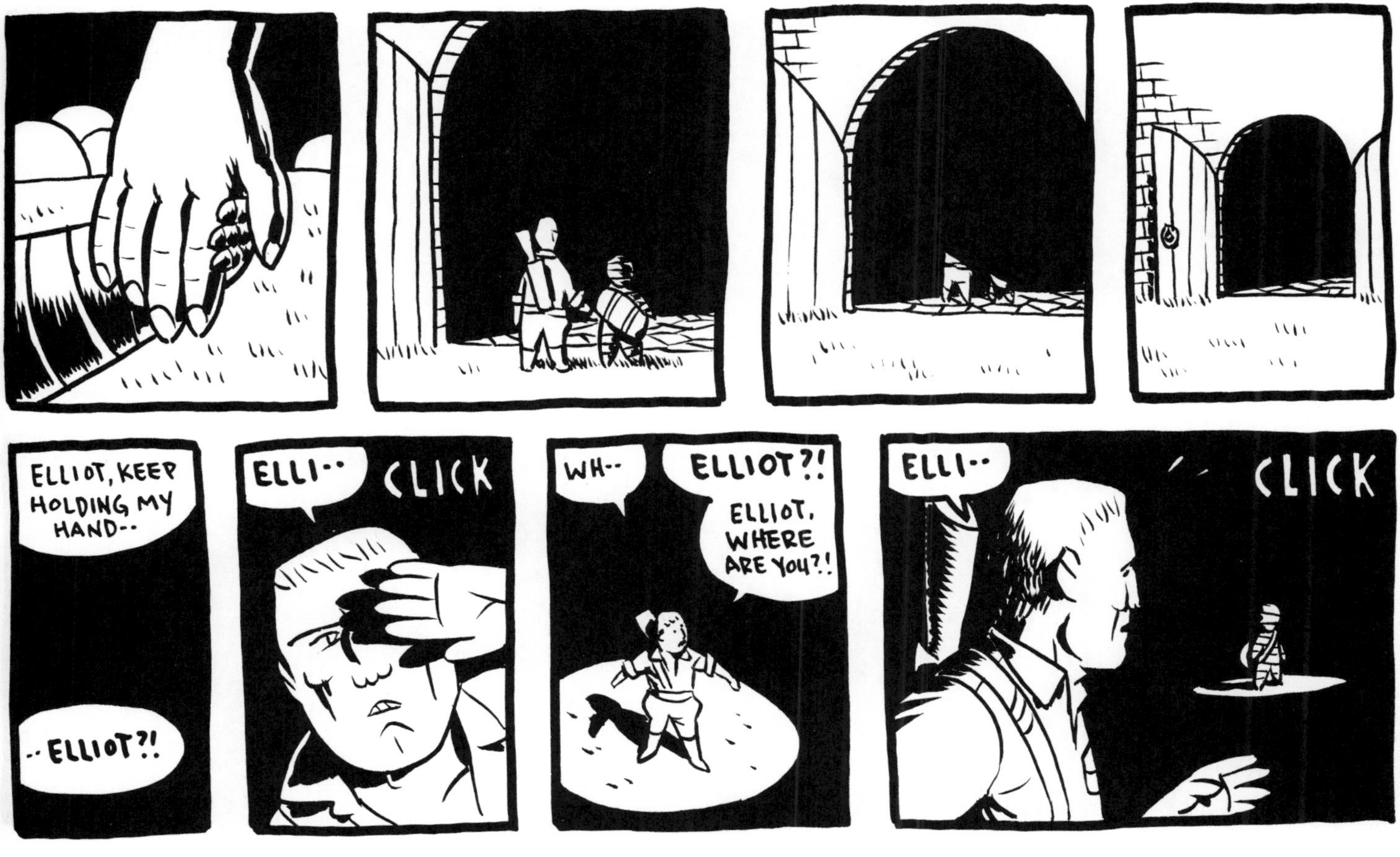
ELLIOT, KEEP HOLDING MY HAND--
--ELLIOT?!
ELLI--
CLICK
WH--
ELLIOT?!
ELLIOT, WHERE ARE YOU?!
ELLI--
CLICK

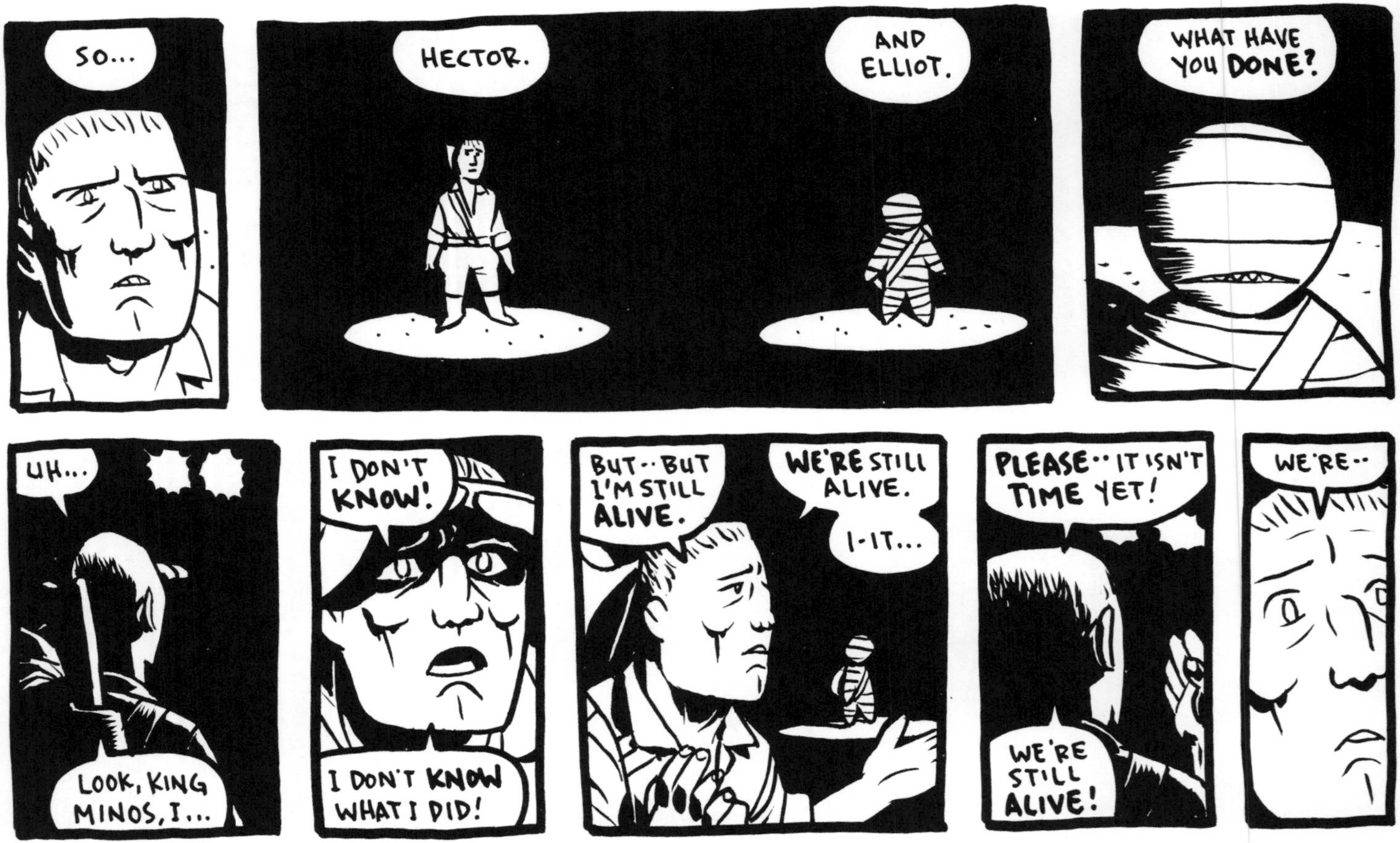
SO...
HECTOR.
AND ELLIOT.
WHAT HAVE YOU DONE?
UH...
LOOK, KING MINOS, I...
I DON'T KNOW!
I DON'T KNOW WHAT I DID!
BUT.. BUT I'M STILL ALIVE.
WE'RE STILL ALIVE.
I-IT...
PLEASE.. IT ISN'T TIME YET!
WE'RE STILL ALIVE!
WE'RE..

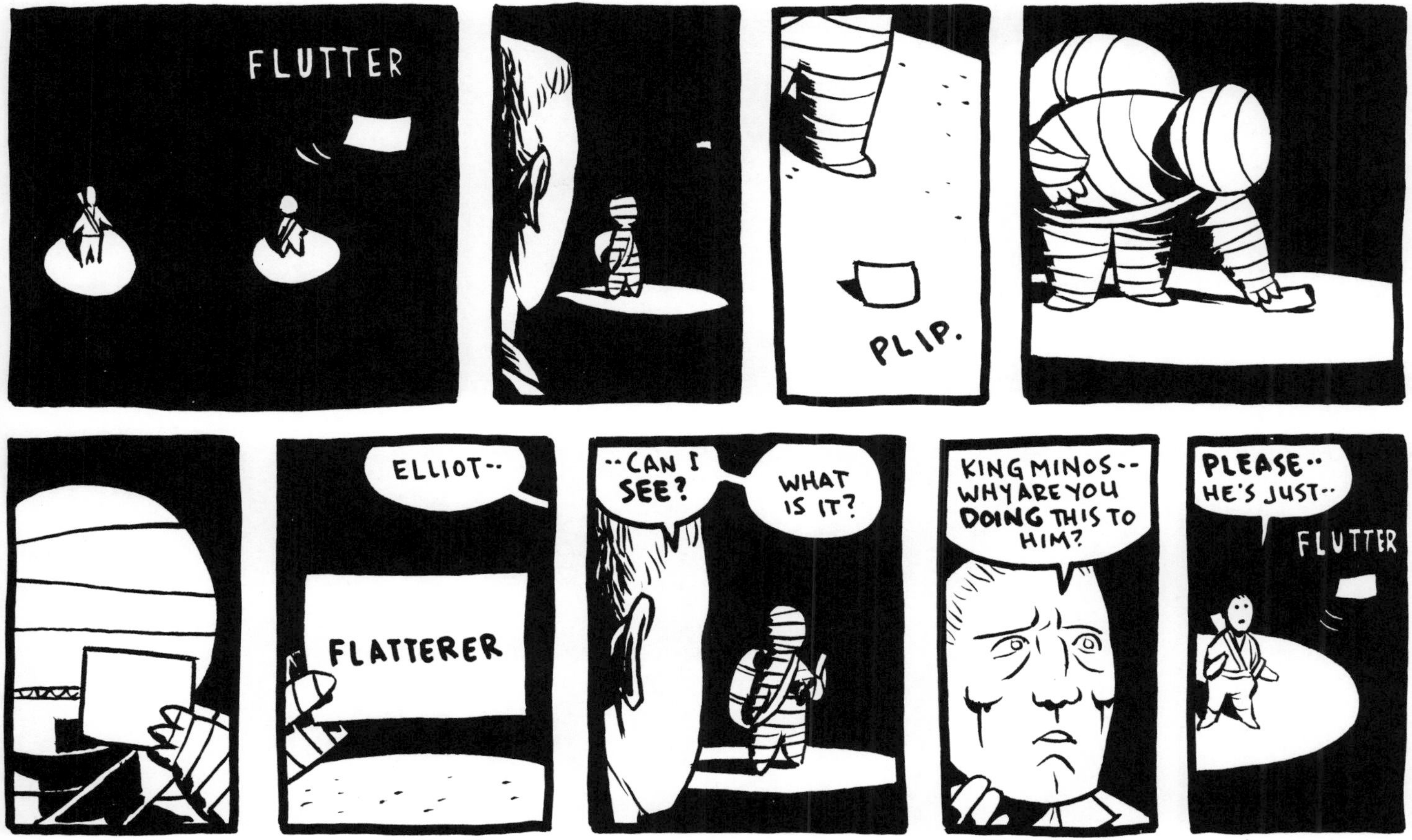
FLUTTER
PLIP.
ELLIOT--
FLATTERER
--CAN I SEE?
WHAT IS IT?
KING MINOS-- WHY ARE YOU DOING THIS TO HIM?
PLEASE-- HE'S JUST--
FLUTTER

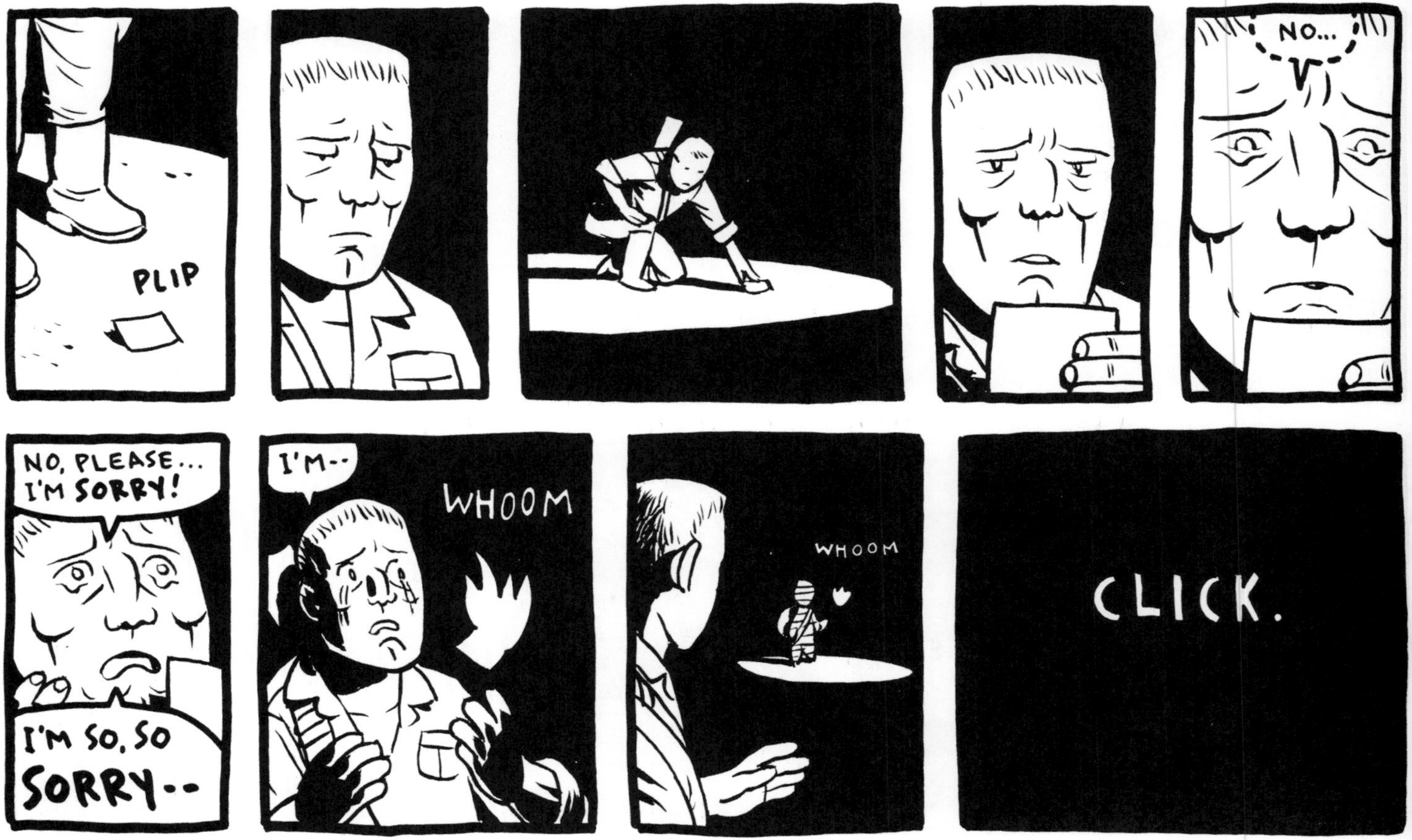
PLIP
NO...
NO, PLEASE... I'M SORRY!
I'M SO, SO SORRY--
I'M--
WHOOM
WHOOM
CLICK.

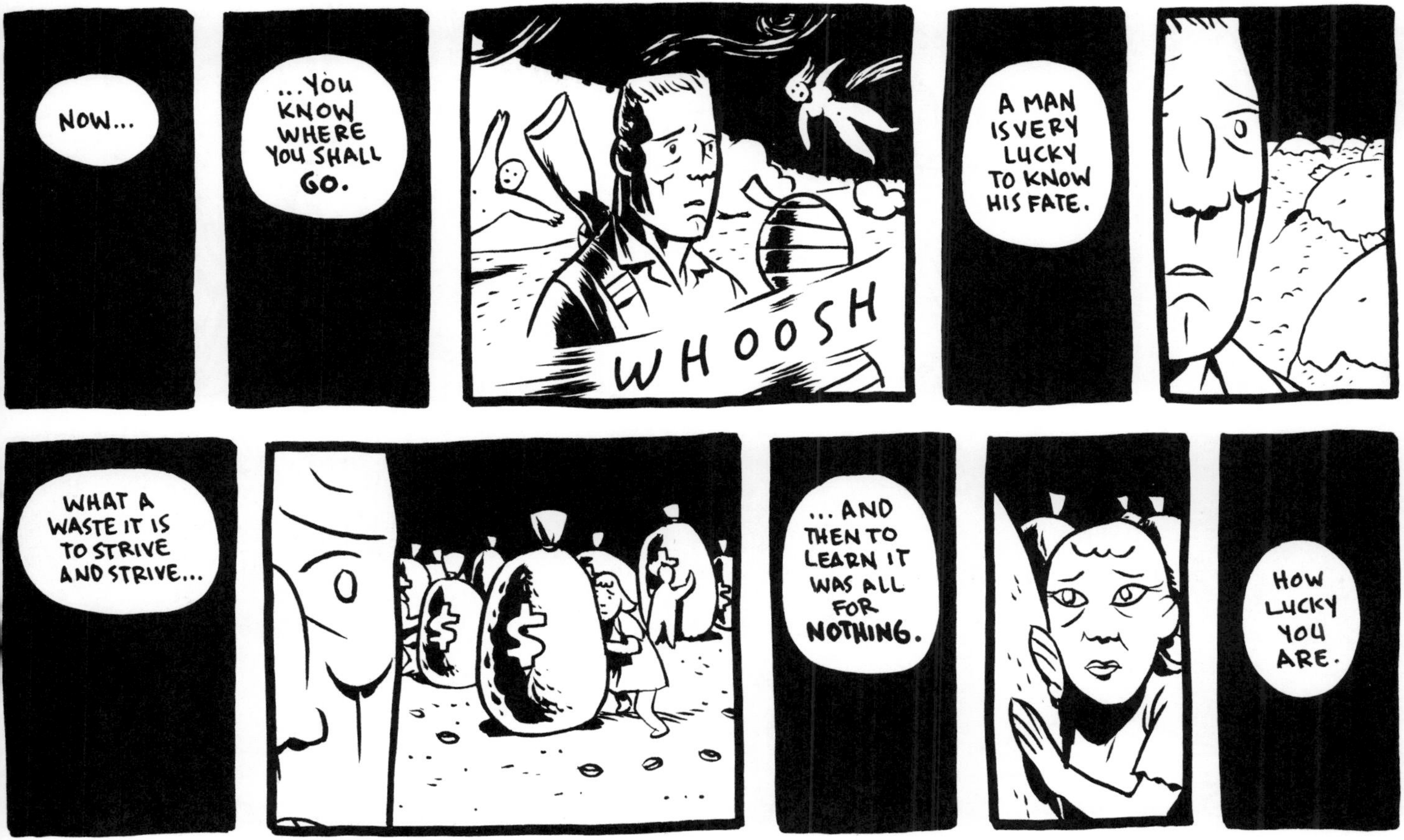
NOW...
...YOU KNOW WHERE YOU SHALL GO.
WHOOSH
A MAN IS VERY LUCKY TO KNOW HIS FATE.
WHAT A WASTE IT IS TO STRIVE AND STRIVE...
...AND THEN TO LEARN IT WAS ALL FOR NOTHING.
HOW LUCKY YOU ARE.

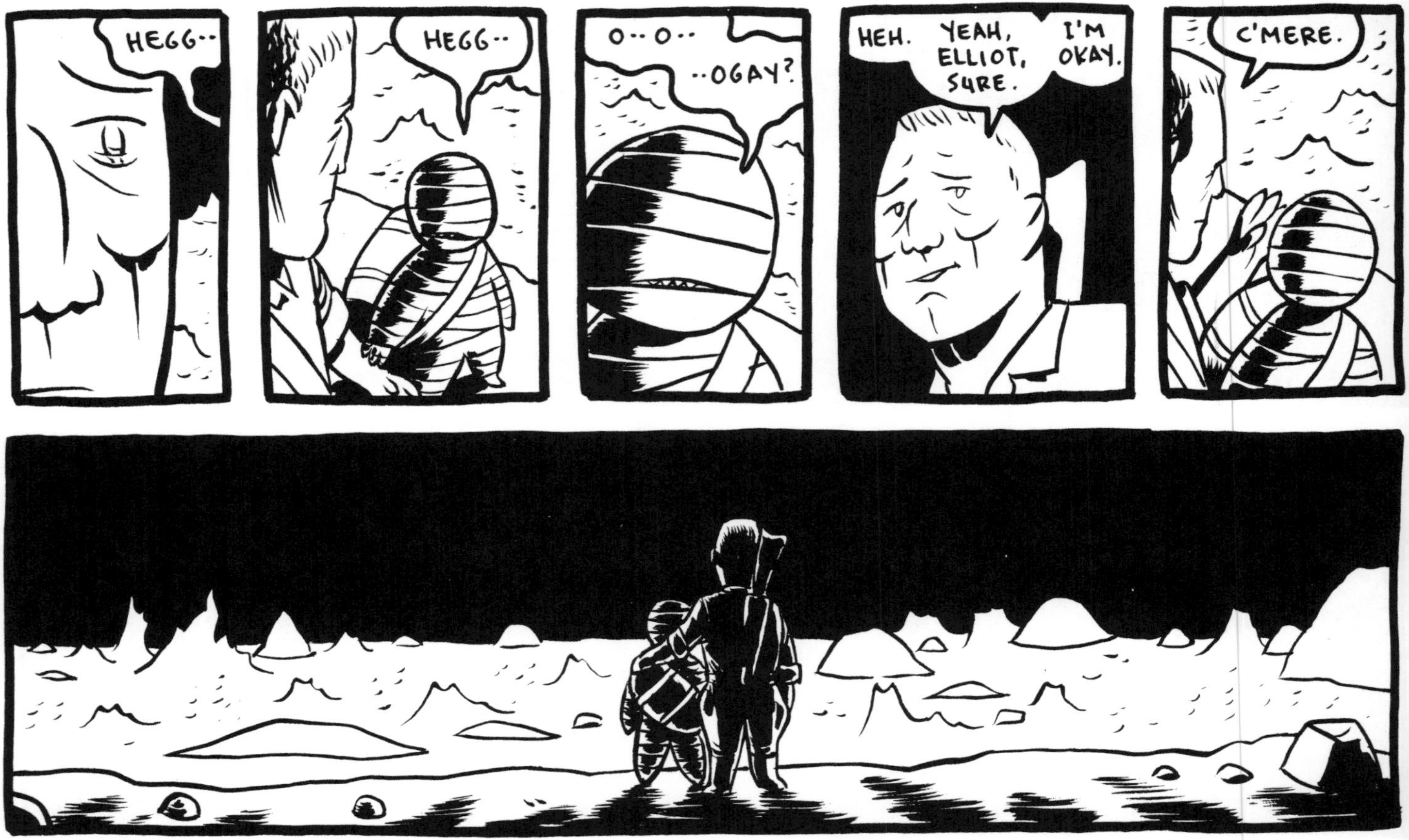
HEGG..
HEGG..
O..O..
..OGAY?
HEH.
YEAH, ELLIOT, SURE.
I'M OKAY.
C'MERE.

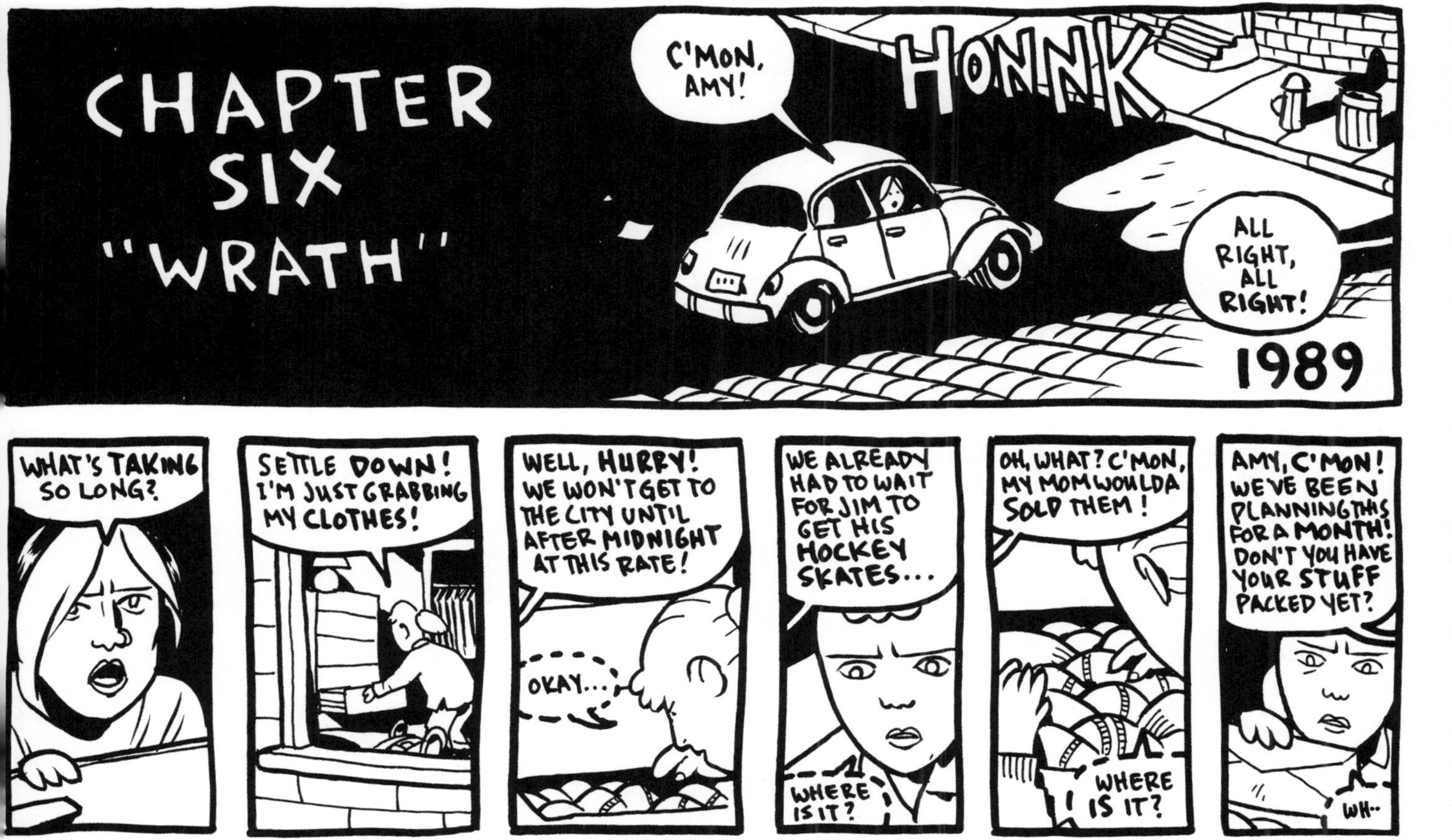
CHAPTER SIX "WRATH"
C'MON, AMY!
HONNK
ALL RIGHT, ALL RIGHT!
1989
WHAT'S TAKING SO LONG?
SETTLE DOWN! I'M JUST GRABBING MY CLOTHES!
WELL, HURRY! WE WON'T GET TO THE CITY UNTIL AFTER MIDNIGHT AT THIS RATE!
OKAY...
WE ALREADY HAD TO WAIT FOR JIM TO GET HIS HOCKEY SKATES...
WHERE IS IT?
OH, WHAT? C'MON, MY MOM WOULDA SOLD THEM!
WHERE IS IT?
AMY, C'MON! WE'VE BEEN PLANNING THIS FOR A MONTH! DON'T YOU HAVE YOUR STUFF PACKED YET?
WH..

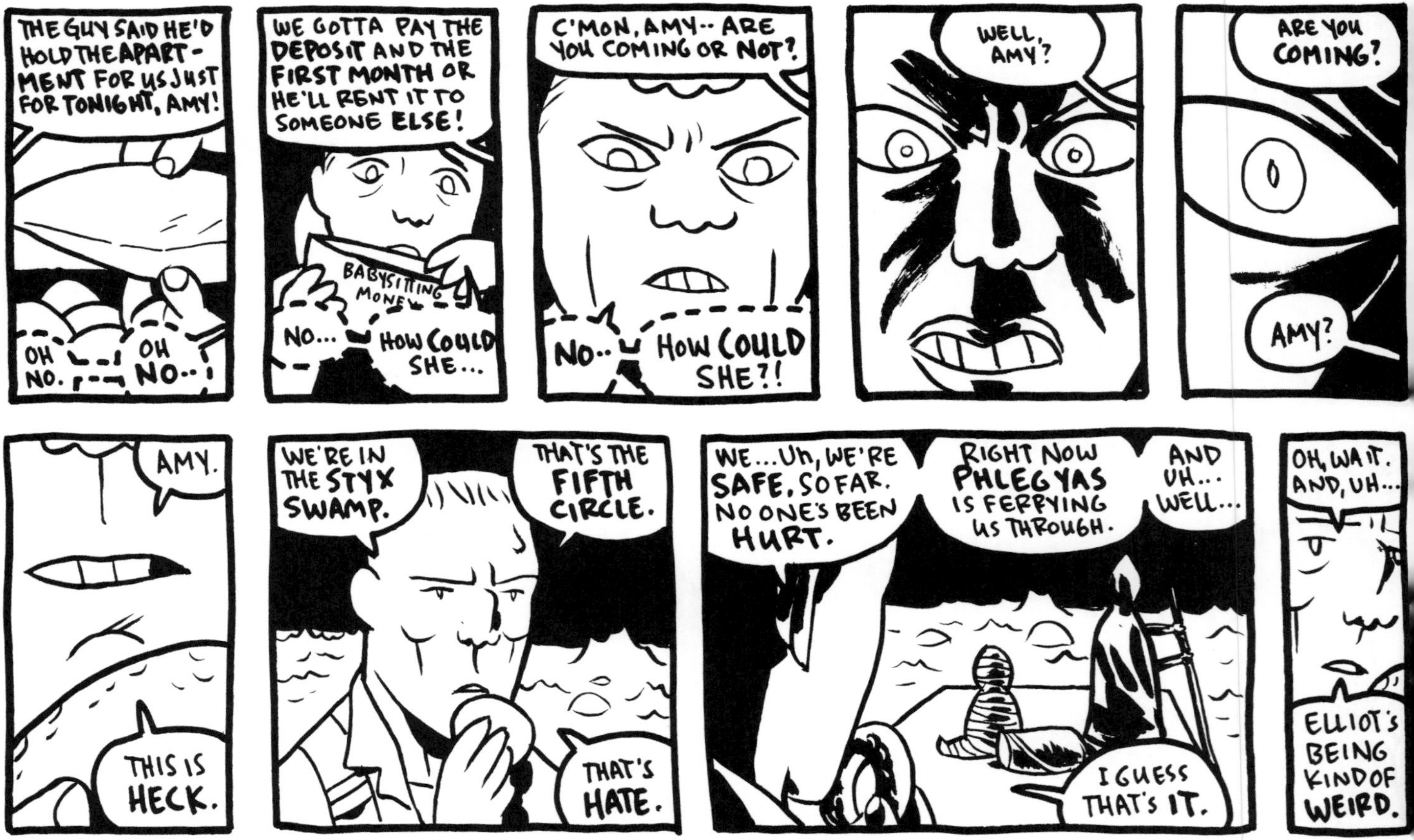
THE GUY SAID HE'D HOLD THE APARTMENT FOR US JUST FOR TONIGHT, AMY!
OH NO.
OH NO..
WE GOTTA PAY THE DEPOSIT AND THE FIRST MONTH OR HE'LL RENT IT TO SOMEONE ELSE!
BABYSITTING MONEY
NO...
HOW COULD SHE...
C'MON, AMY.. ARE YOU COMING OR NOT?
NO..
HOW COULD SHE?!
WELL, AMY?
ARE YOU COMING?
AMY?
AMY.
THIS IS HECK.
WE'RE IN THE STYX SWAMP.
THAT'S THE FIFTH CIRCLE.
THAT'S HATE.
WE...UH, WE'RE SAFE, SO FAR. NO ONE'S BEEN HURT.
RIGHT NOW PHLEGYAS IS FERRYING US THROUGH.
AND UH... WELL...
I GUESS THAT'S IT.
OH, WAIT. AND, UH...
ELLIOT'S BEING KIND OF WEIRD.

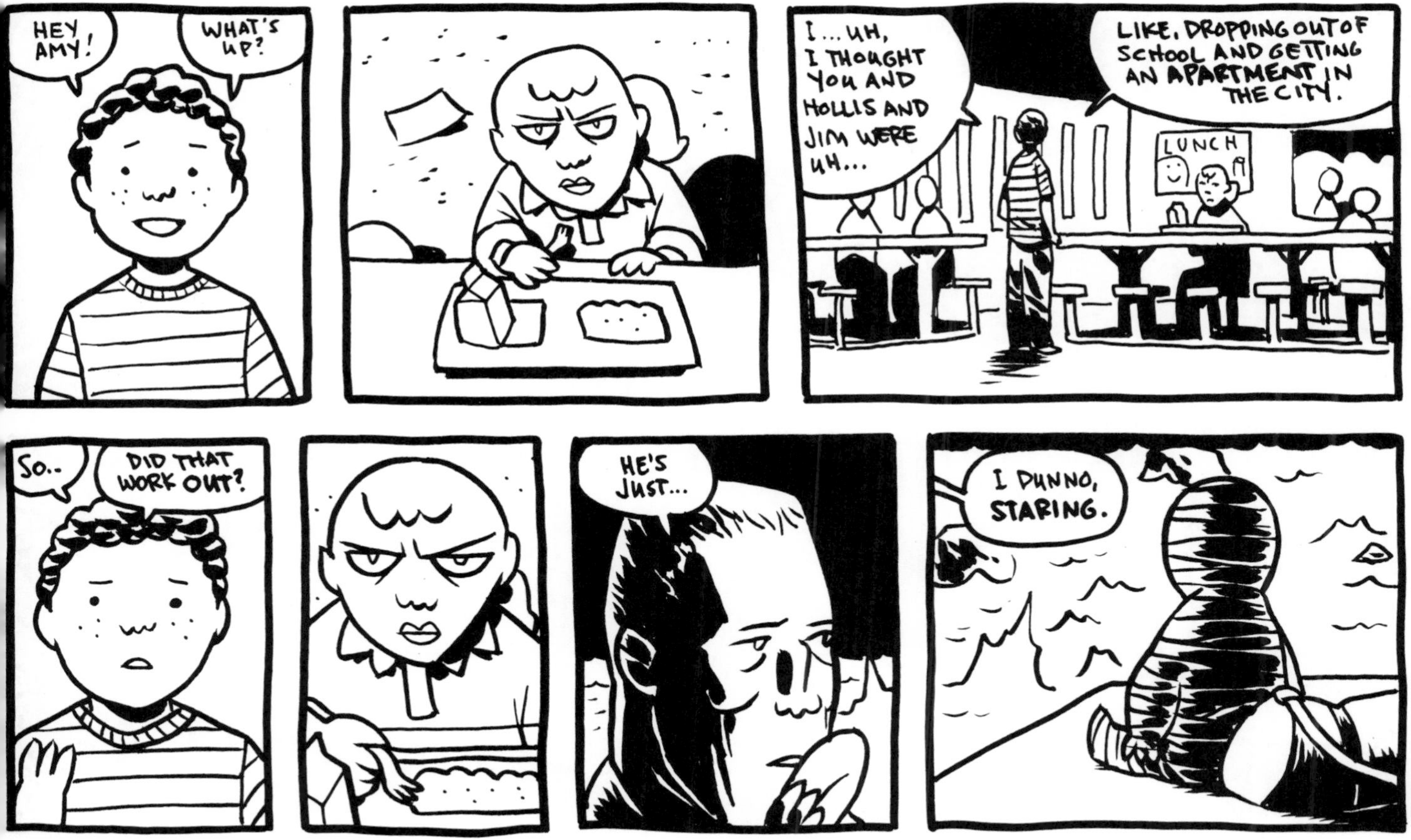
HEY AMY!
WHAT'S UP?
I... UH, I THOUGHT YOU AND HOLLIS AND JIM WERE UH...
LIKE, DROPPING OUT OF SCHOOL AND GETTING AN APARTMENT IN THE CITY.
LUNCH
SO..
DID THAT WORK OUT?
HE'S JUST...
I DUNNO, STARING.

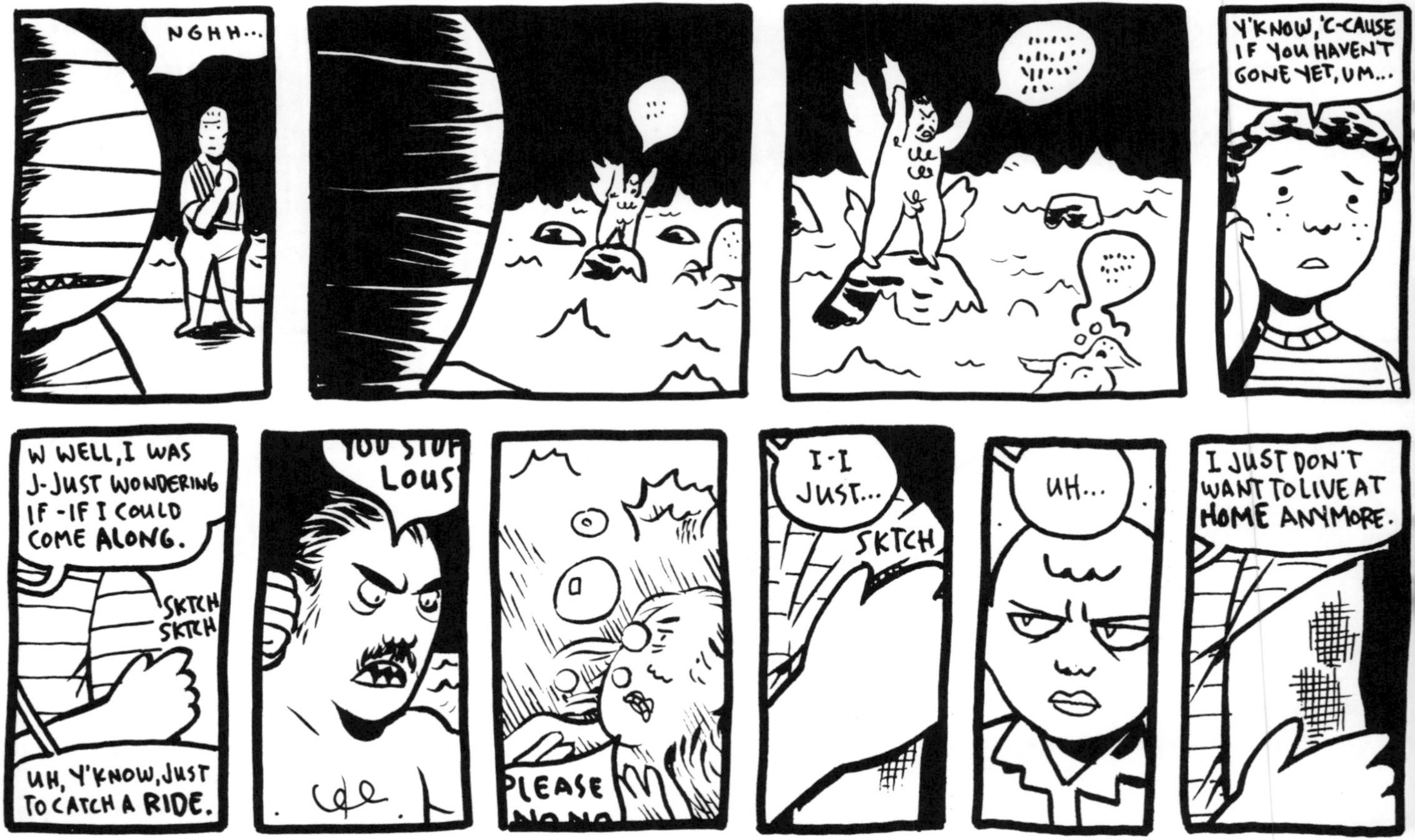
NGHH...
Y'KNOW, 'C-CAUSE IF YOU HAVEN'T GONE YET, UM...
W WELL, I WAS J-JUST WONDERING IF -IF I COULD COME ALONG.
SKTCH SKTCH
UH, Y'KNOW, JUST TO CATCH A RIDE.
PLEASE
I-I JUST...
SKTCH
UH...
I JUST DON'T WANT TO LIVE AT HOME ANYMORE.

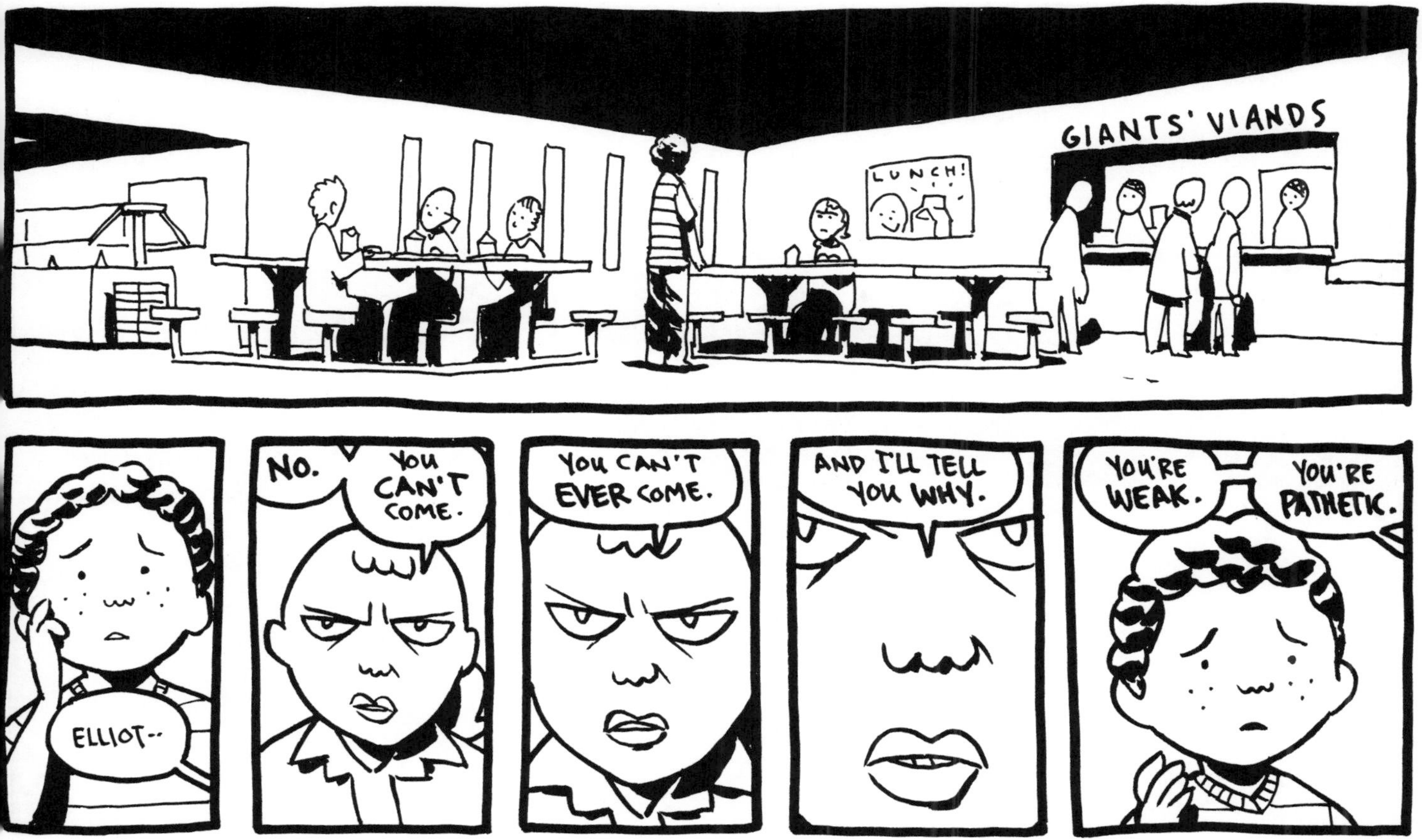
GIANTS' VIANDS
LUNCH!
ELLIOT--
NO.
YOU CAN'T COME.
YOU CAN'T EVER COME.
AND I'LL TELL YOU WHY.
YOU'RE WEAK.
YOU'RE PATHETIC.

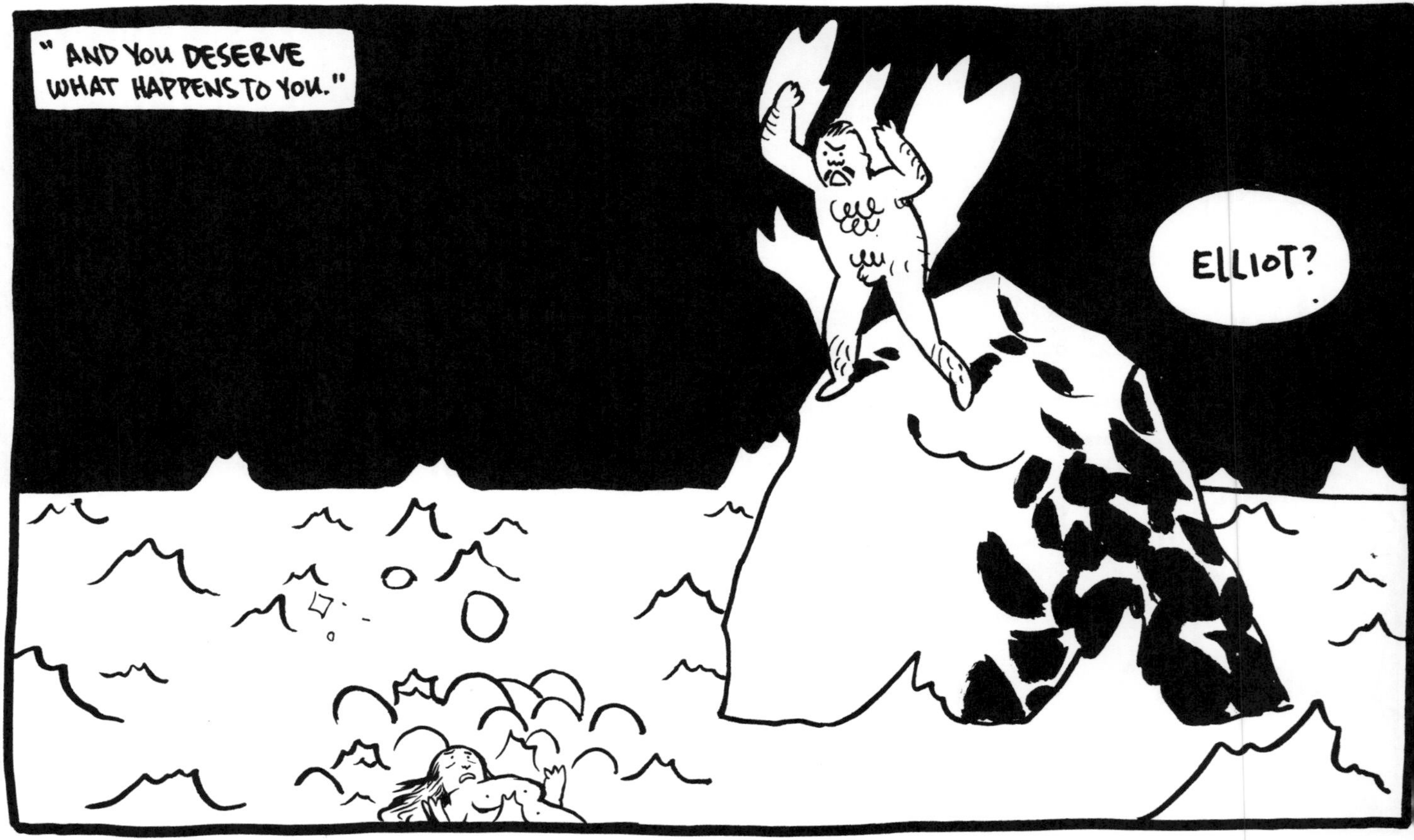
"AND YOU DESERVE WHAT HAPPENS TO YOU."
ELLIOT?

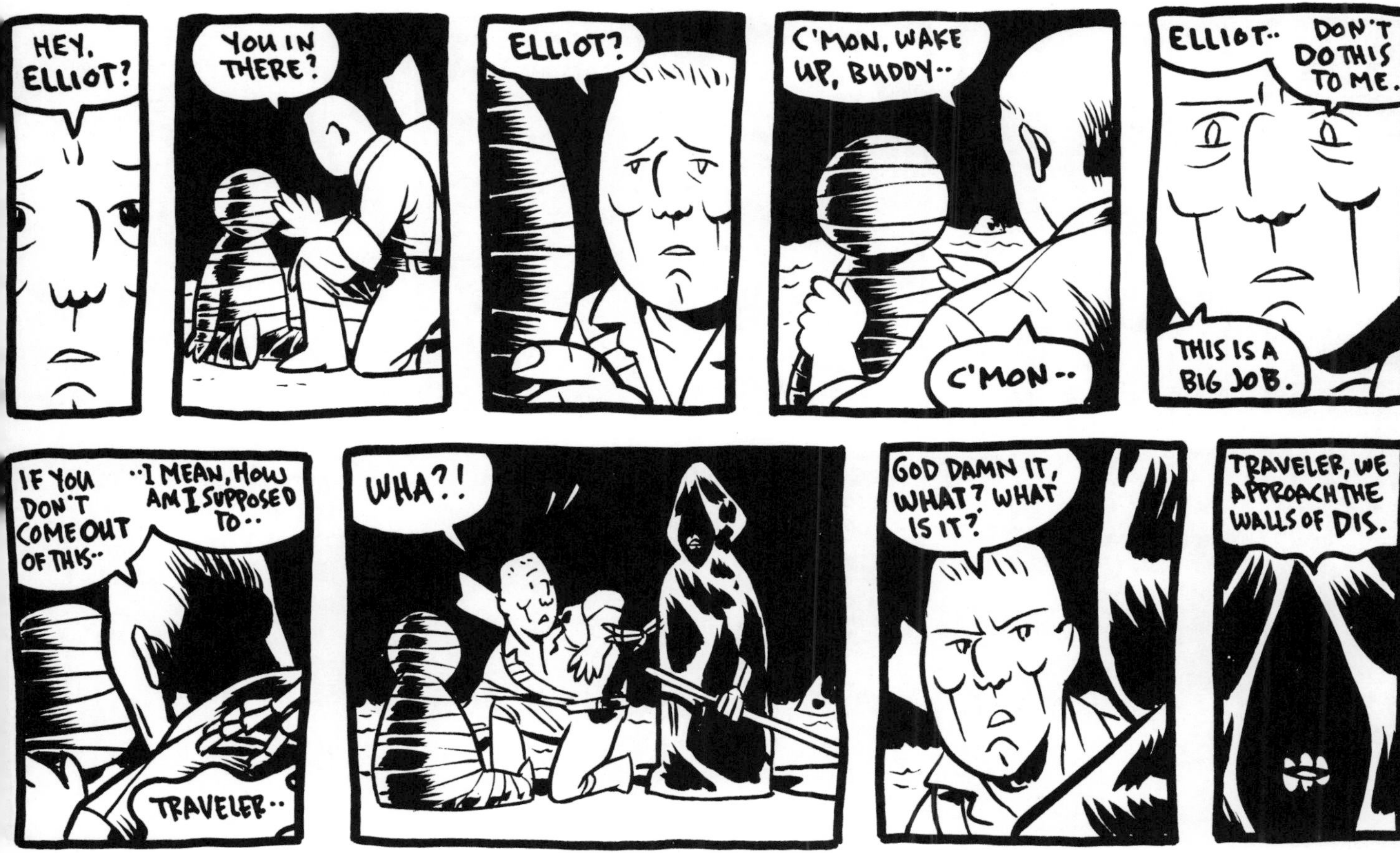
HEY, ELLIOT?
YOU IN THERE?
ELLIOT?
C'MON, WAKE UP, BUDDY..
C'MON..
ELLIOT.. DON'T DO THIS TO ME.
THIS IS A BIG JOB.
IF YOU DON'T COME OUT OF THIS..
..I MEAN, HOW AM I SUPPOSED TO..
TRAVELER..
WHA?!
GOD DAMN IT, WHAT? WHAT IS IT?
TRAVELER, WE APPROACH THE WALLS OF DIS.

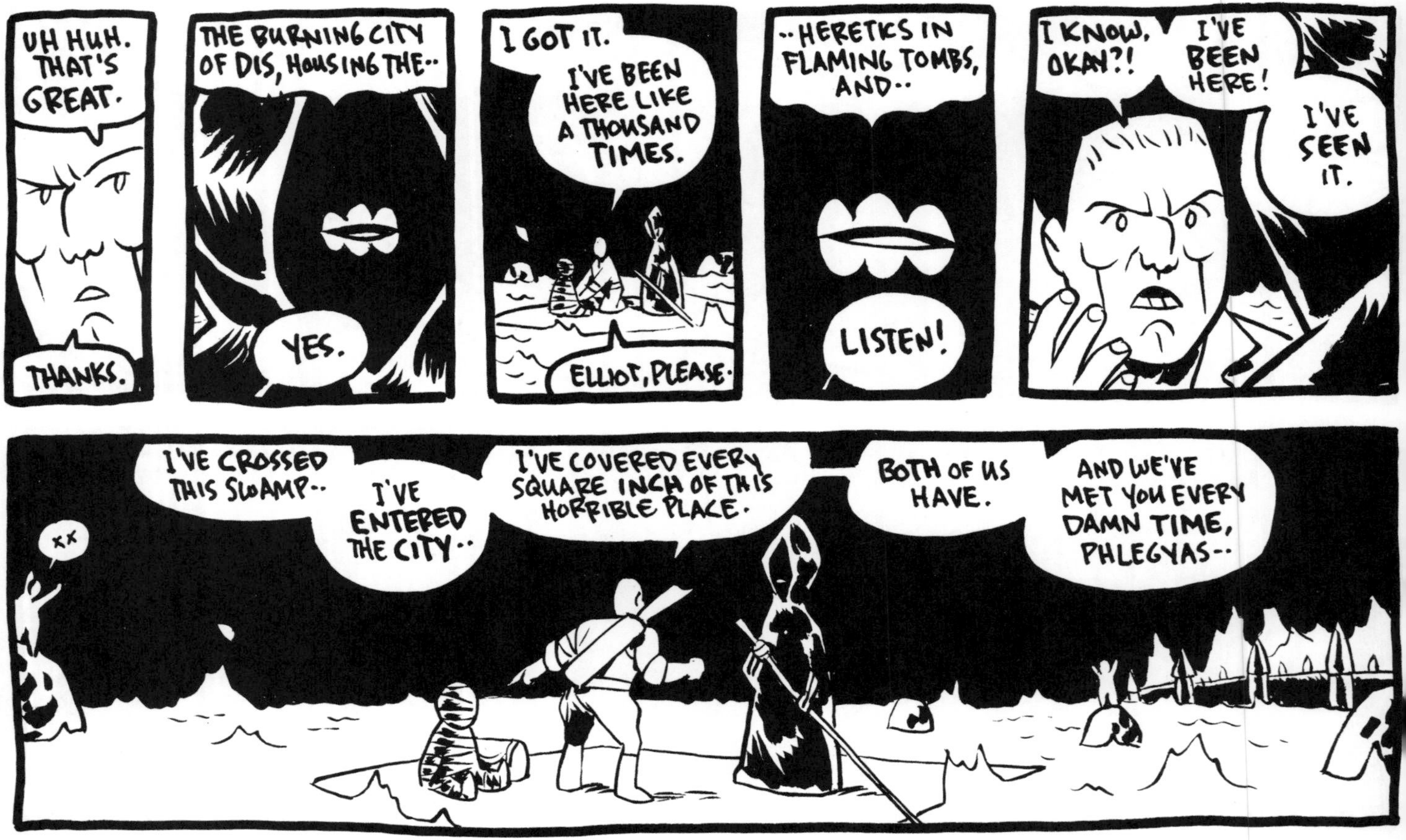
UH HUH. THAT'S GREAT.
THANKS.
THE BURNING CITY OF DIS, HOUSING THE..
YES.
I GOT IT.
I'VE BEEN HERE LIKE A THOUSAND TIMES.
ELLIOT, PLEASE.
..HERETICS IN FLAMING TOMBS, AND..
LISTEN!
I KNOW, OKAY?!
I'VE BEEN HERE!
I'VE SEEN IT.
I'VE CROSSED THIS SWAMP..
I'VE ENTERED THE CITY..
I'VE COVERED EVERY SQUARE INCH OF THIS HORRIBLE PLACE.
BOTH OF US HAVE.
AND WE'VE MET YOU EVERY DAMN TIME, PHLEGYAS..

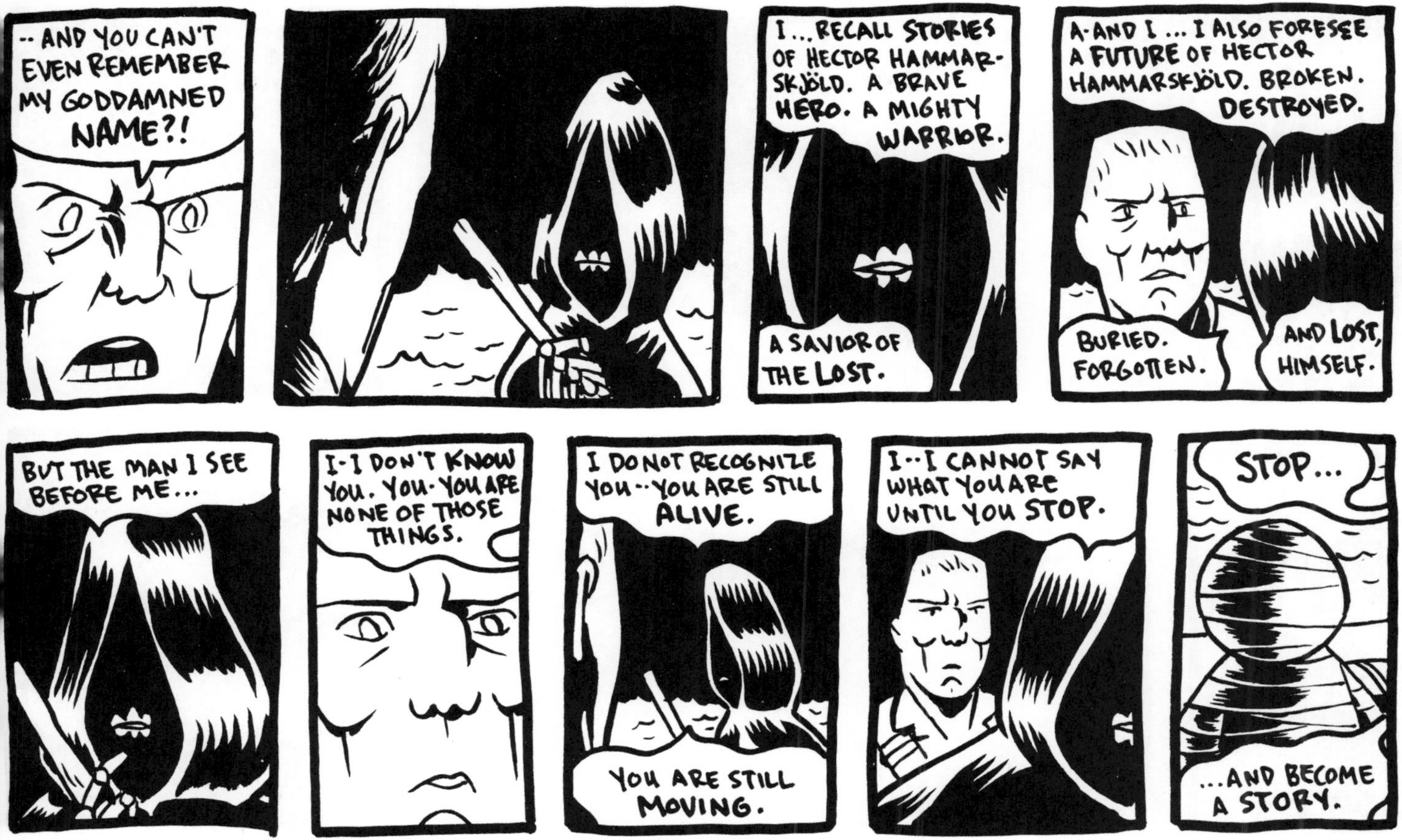
-- AND YOU CAN'T EVEN REMEMBER MY GODDAMNED NAME?!
I... RECALL STORIES OF HECTOR HAMMARSKJÖLD. A BRAVE HERO. A MIGHTY WARRIOR.
A SAVIOR OF THE LOST.
A-AND I ... I ALSO FORESEE A FUTURE OF HECTOR HAMMARSKJÖLD. BROKEN. DESTROYED.
BURIED. FORGOTTEN.
AND LOST, HIMSELF.
BUT THE MAN I SEE BEFORE ME...
I-I DON'T KNOW YOU. YOU- YOU ARE NONE OF THOSE THINGS.
I DO NOT RECOGNIZE YOU-- YOU ARE STILL ALIVE.
YOU ARE STILL MOVING.
I-- I CANNOT SAY WHAT YOU ARE UNTIL YOU STOP.
STOP...
...AND BECOME A STORY.

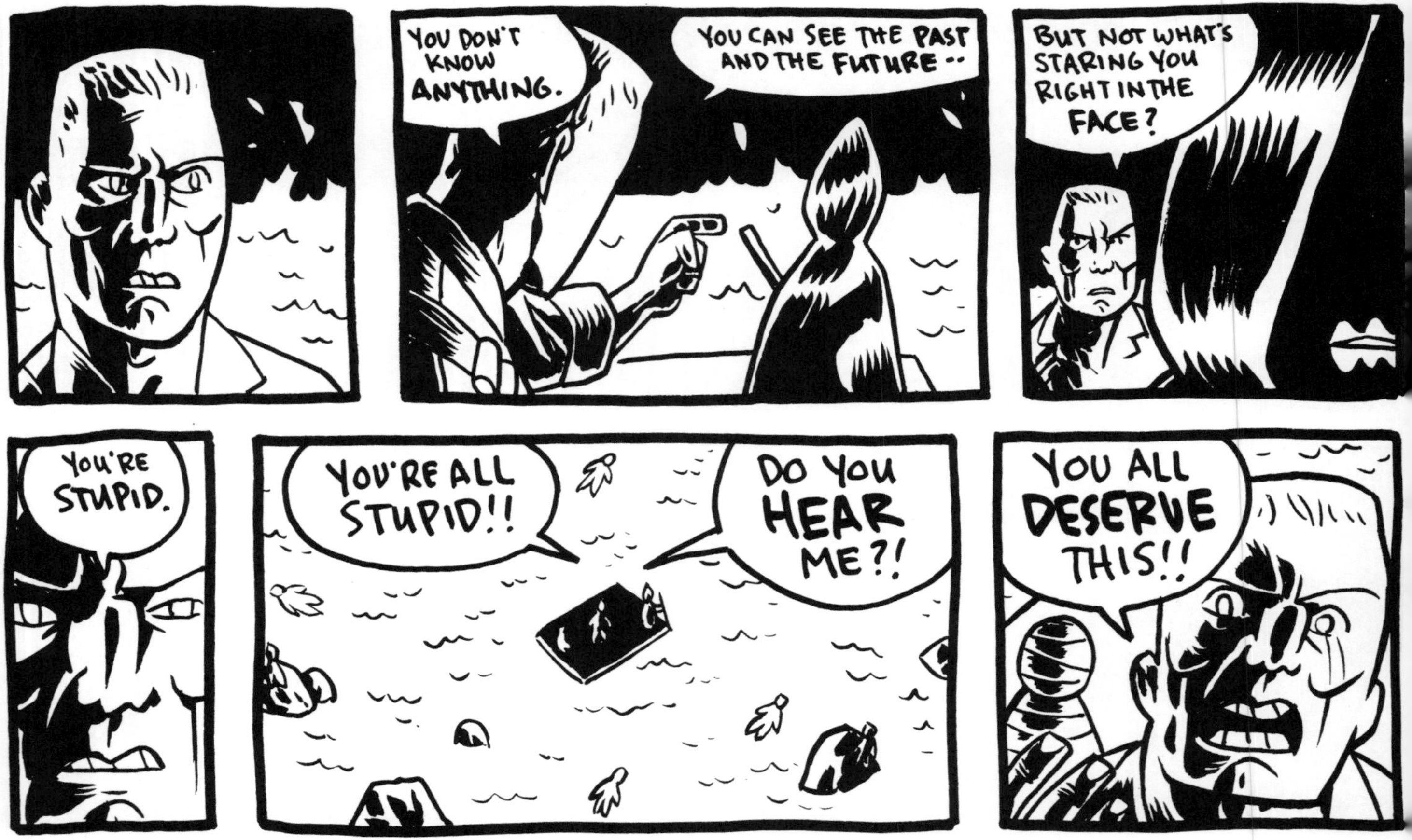
YOU DON'T KNOW ANYTHING.
YOU CAN SEE THE PAST AND THE FUTURE --
BUT NOT WHAT'S STARING YOU RIGHT IN THE FACE?
YOU'RE STUPID.
YOU'RE ALL STUPID!!
DO YOU HEAR ME?!
YOU ALL DESERVE THIS!!

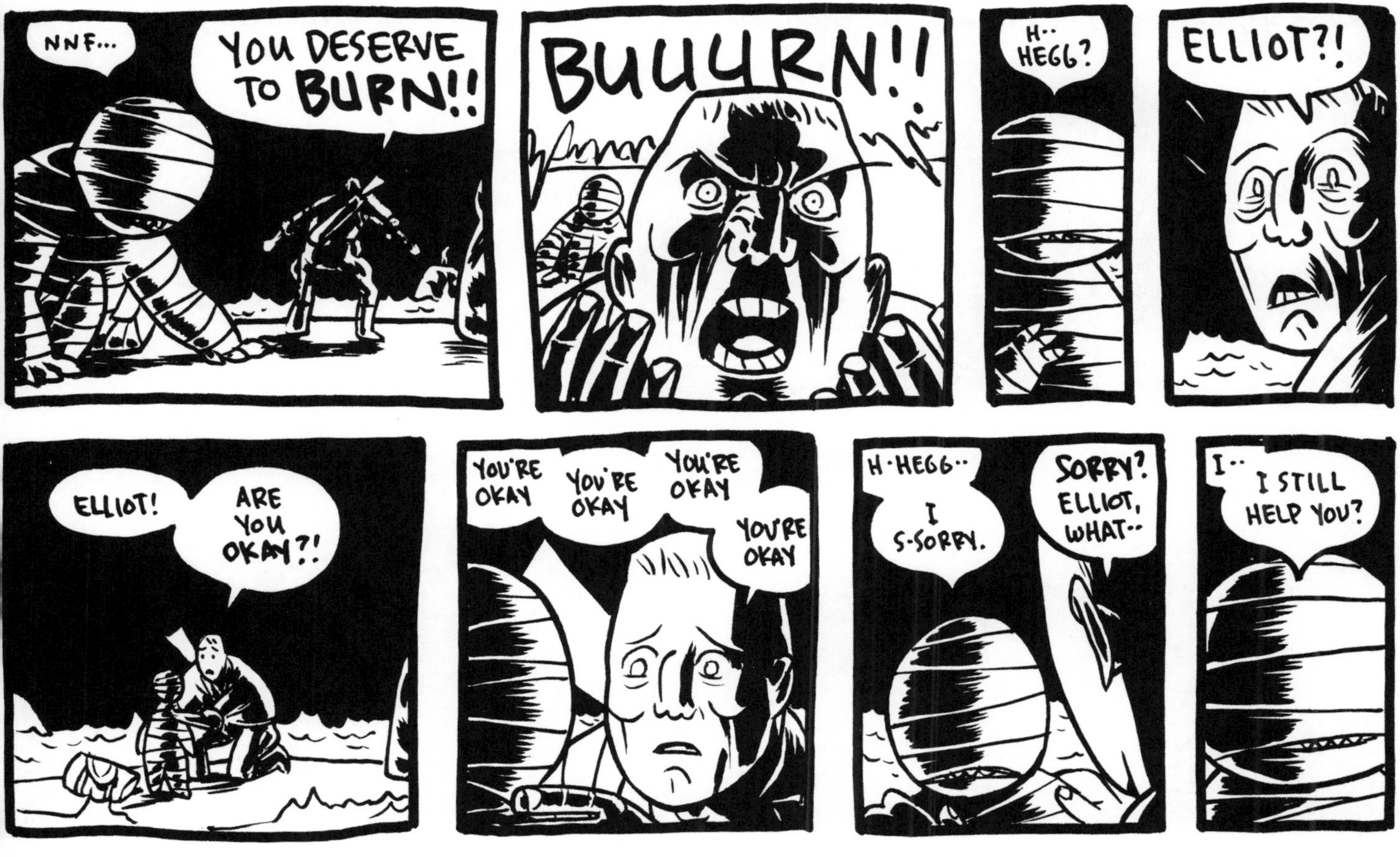
NNF...
YOU DESERVE TO BURN!!
BUUURN!!
H.. HEGG?
ELLIOT?!
ELLIOT!
ARE YOU OKAY?!
YOU'RE OKAY
YOU'RE OKAY
YOU'RE OKAY
YOU'RE OKAY
H-HEGG..
I S-SORRY.
SORRY? ELLIOT, WHAT..
I..
I STILL HELP YOU?

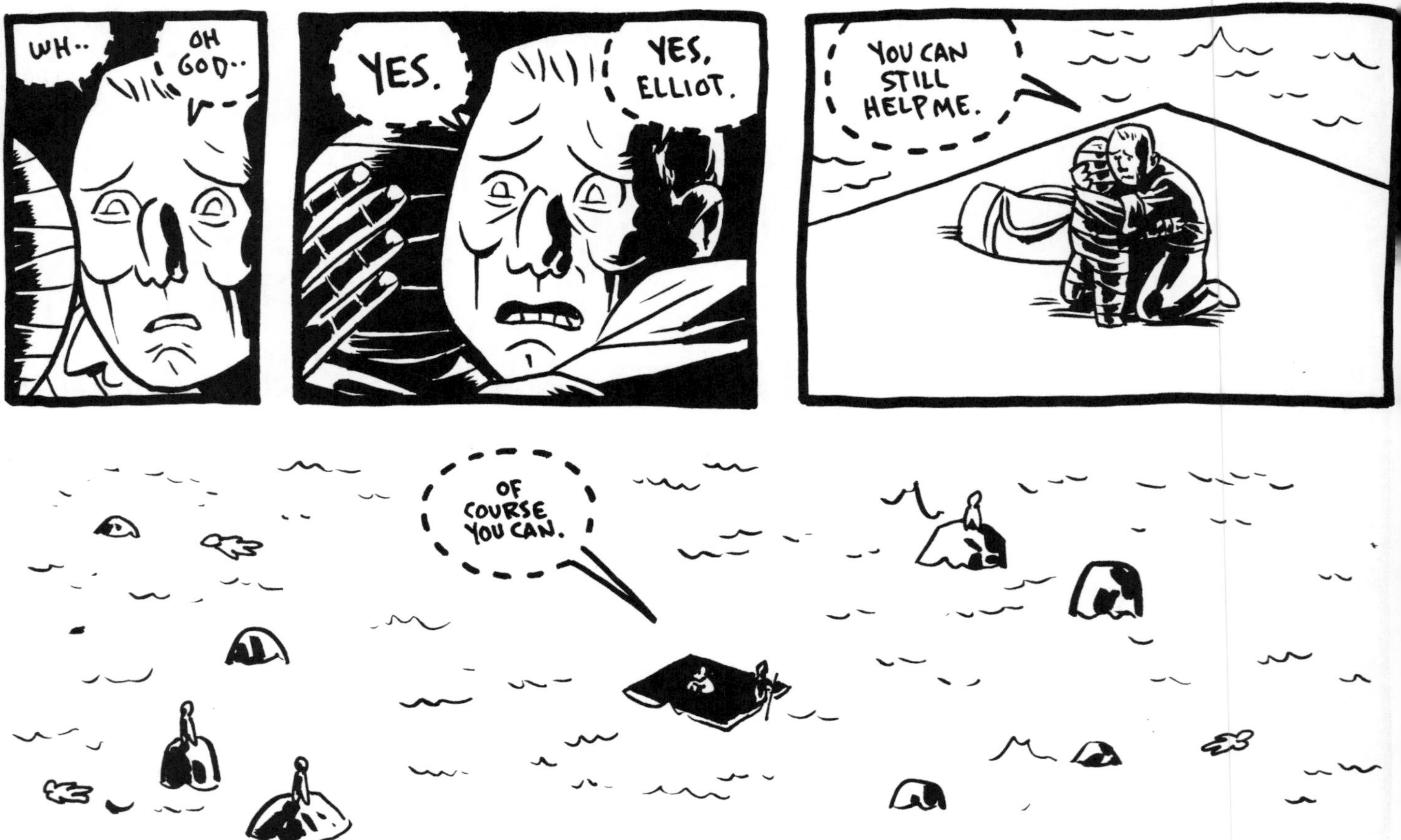
WH..
OH GOD..
YES.
YES, ELLIOT.
YOU CAN STILL HELP ME.
OF COURSE YOU CAN.

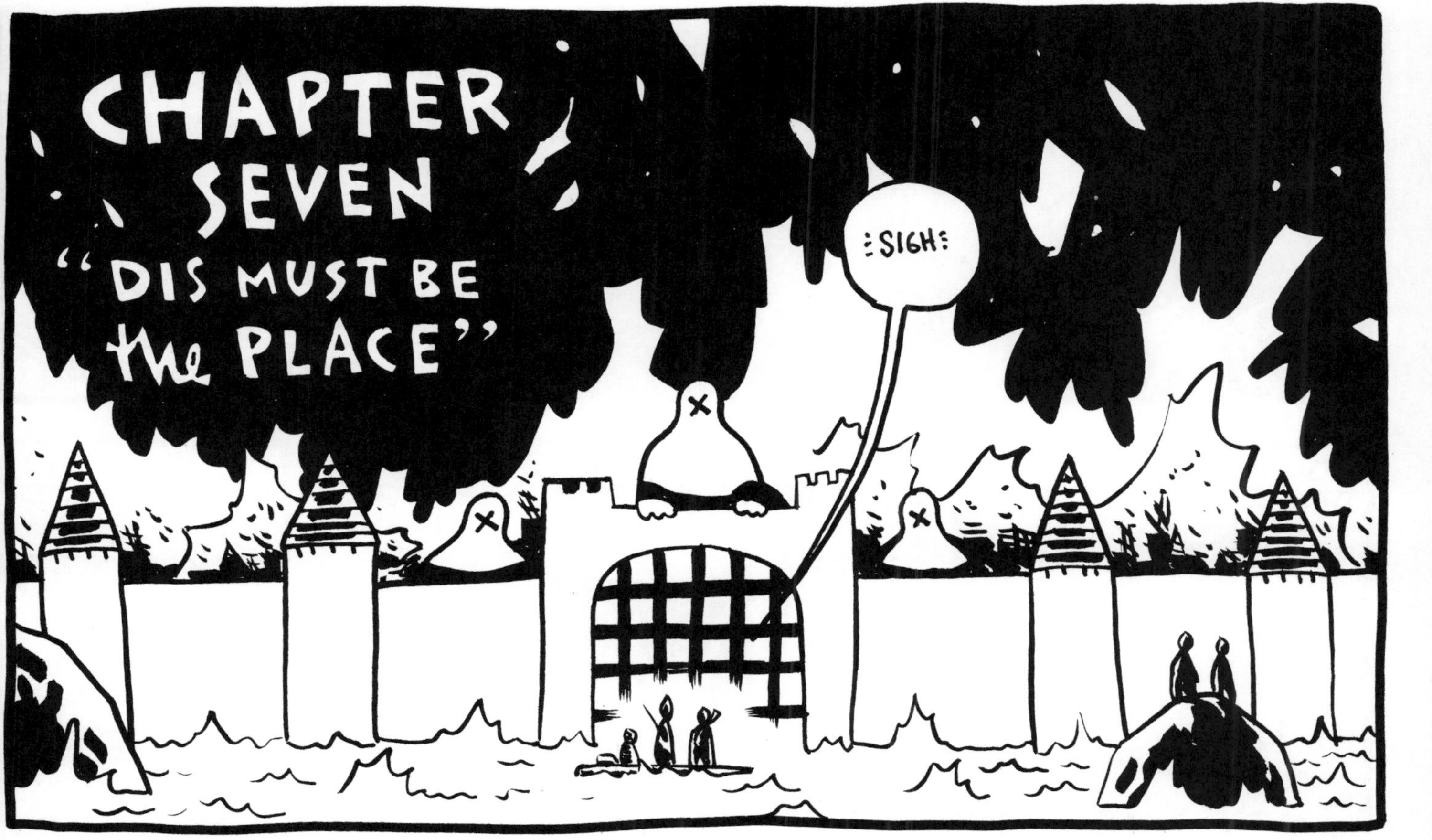
CHAPTER SEVEN "DIS MUST BE the PLACE"
SIGH

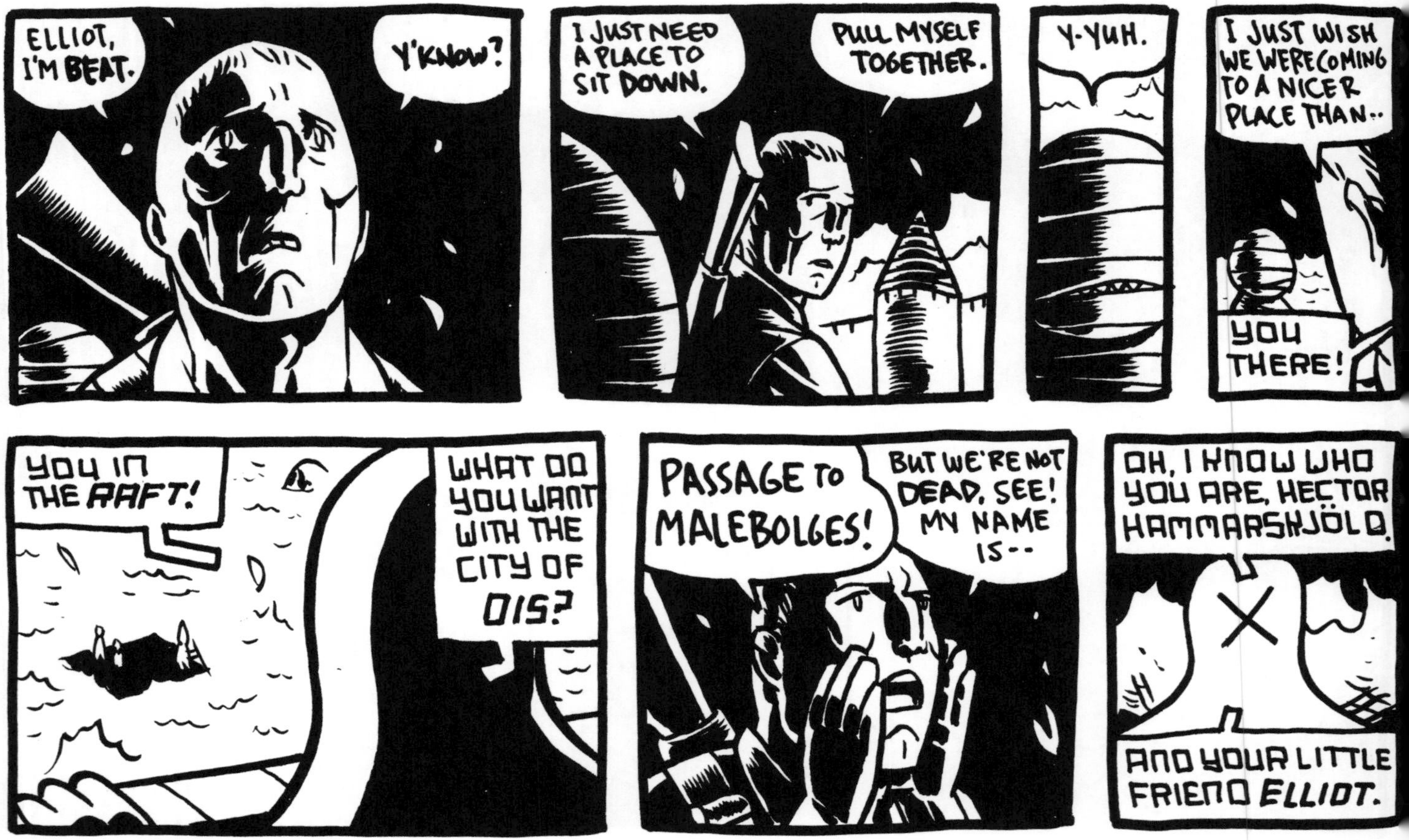
ELLIOT, I'M BEAT.
Y'KNOW?
I JUST NEED A PLACE TO SIT DOWN.
PULL MYSELF TOGETHER.
Y-YUH.
I JUST WISH WE WERE COMING TO A NICER PLACE THAN..
YOU THERE!
YOU IN THE RAFT!
WHAT DO YOU WANT WITH THE CITY OF DIS?
PASSAGE TO MALEBOLGES!
BUT WE'RE NOT DEAD, SEE! MY NAME IS--
OH, I KNOW WHO YOU ARE, HECTOR HAMMARSHJÖLD.
AND YOUR LITTLE FRIEND ELLIOT.

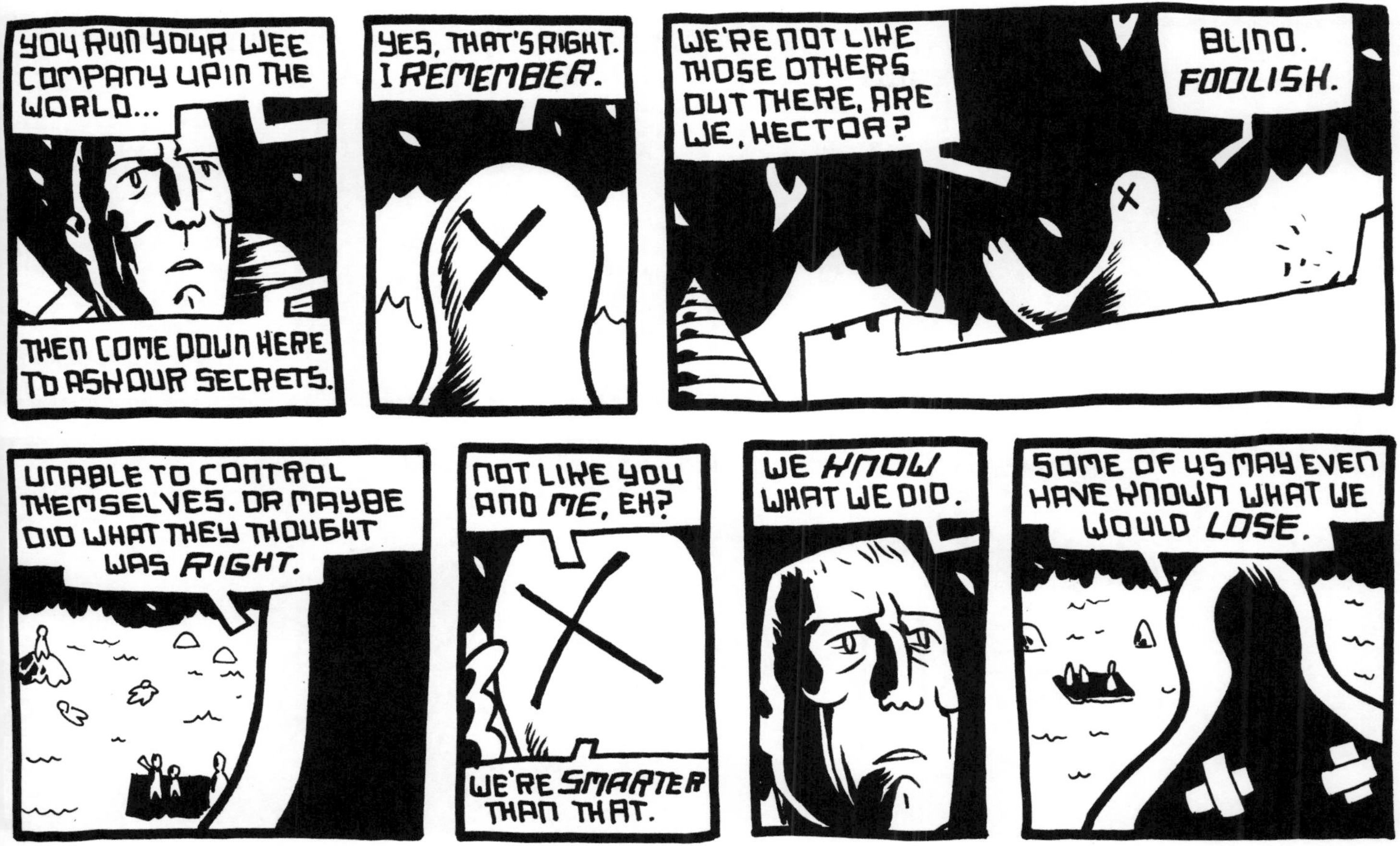
YOU RUN YOUR WEE COMPANY UP IN THE WORLD...
THEN COME DOWN HERE TO ASK OUR SECRETS.
YES, THAT'S RIGHT. I *REMEMBER*.
WE'RE NOT LIKE THOSE OTHERS OUT THERE, ARE WE, HECTOR?
BLIND. *FOOLISH*.
UNABLE TO CONTROL THEMSELVES. OR MAYBE DID WHAT THEY THOUGHT WAS *RIGHT*.
NOT LIKE YOU AND *ME*, EH?
WE'RE *SMARTER* THAN THAT.
WE *KNOW* WHAT WE DID.
SOME OF US MAY EVEN HAVE KNOWN WHAT WE WOULD *LOSE*.

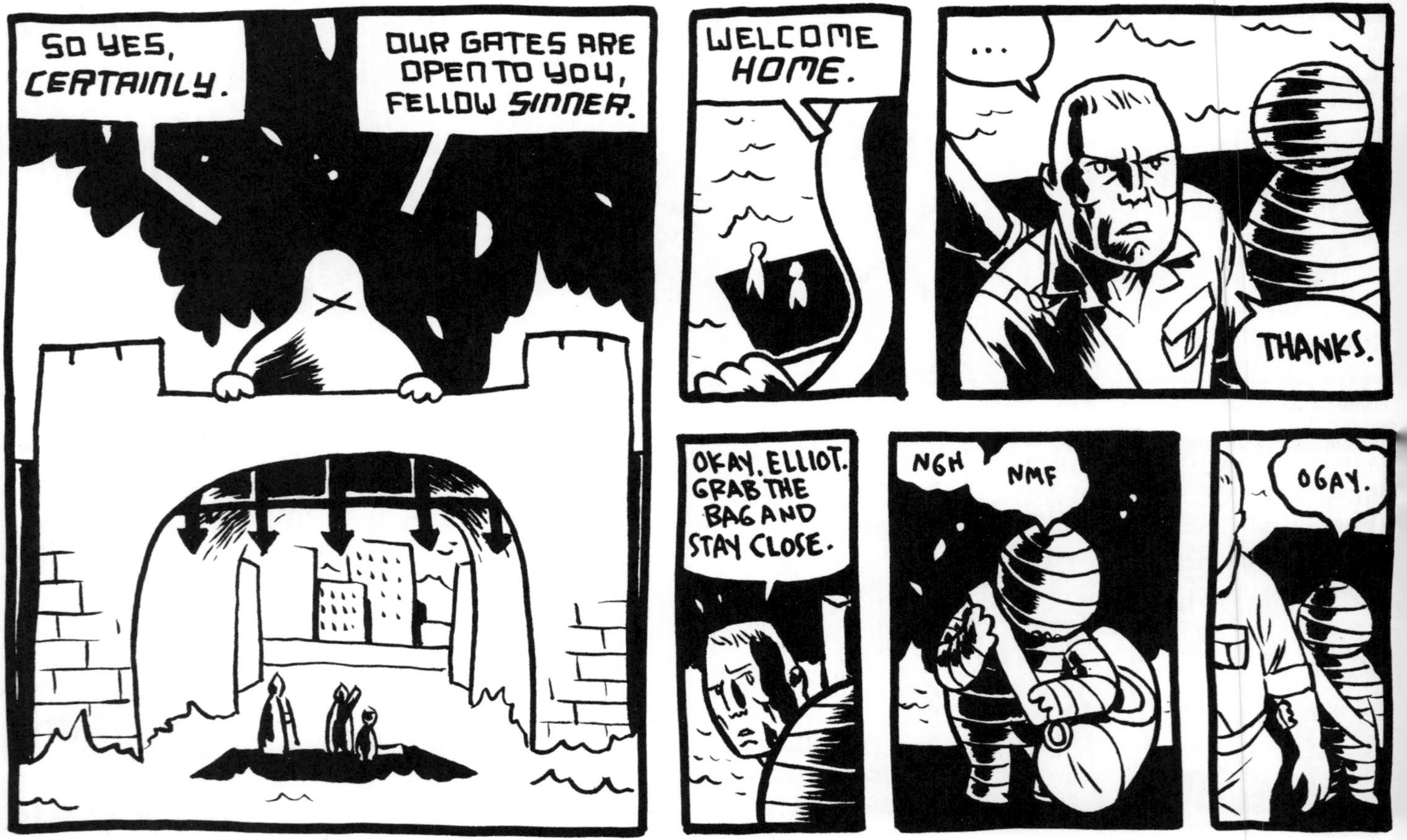
SO YES, CERTAINLY.
OUR GATES ARE OPEN TO YOU, FELLOW SINNER.
WELCOME HOME.
...
THANKS.
OKAY, ELLIOT. GRAB THE BAG AND STAY CLOSE.
NGH
NMF
OGAY.

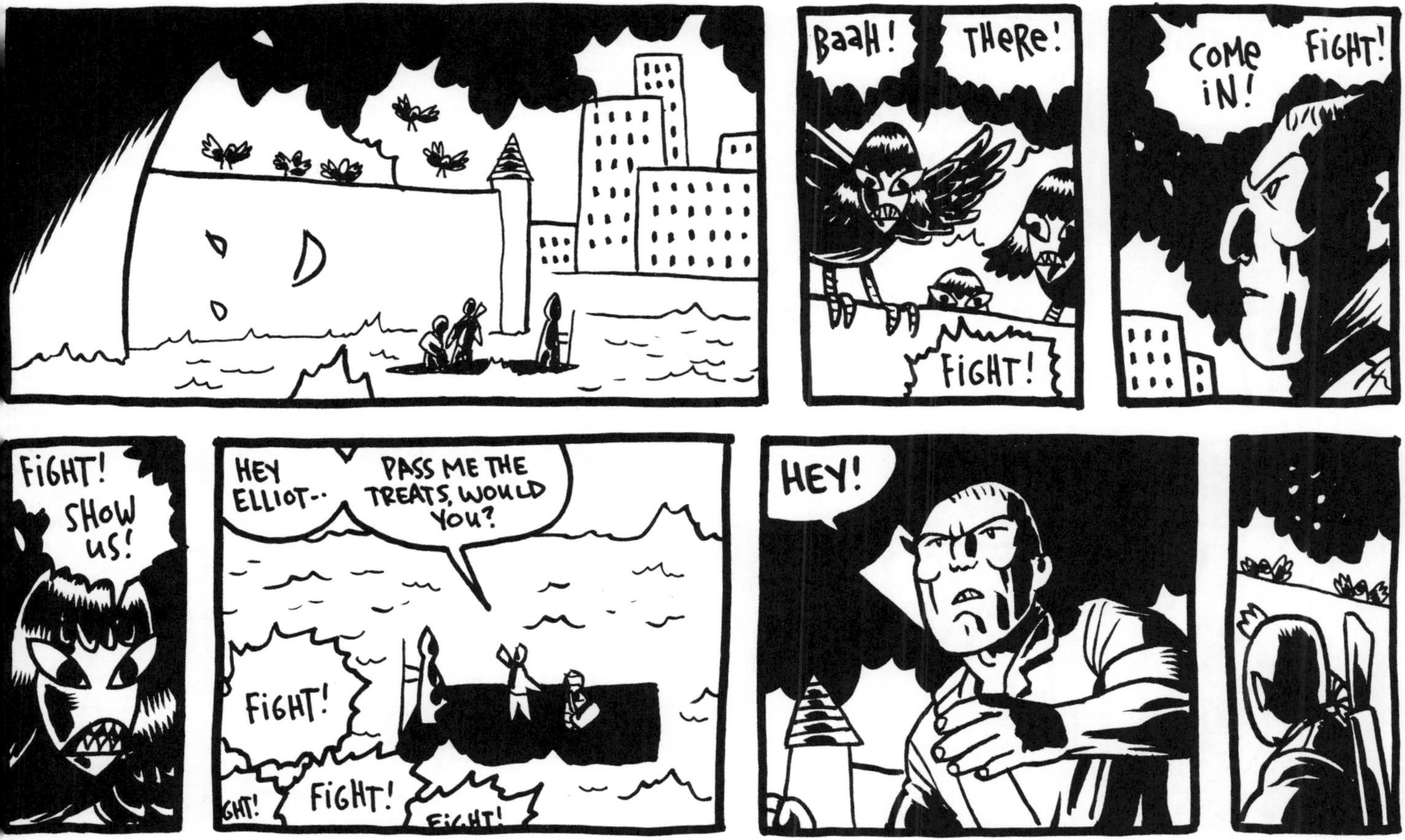
BaaH!
THere!
FIGHT!
COMe iN!
FIGHT!
FiGHT!
SHOW US!
HEY ELLIOT-.
PASS ME THE TREATS, WOULD YOU?
FiGHT!
GHT!
FiGHT!
HEY!

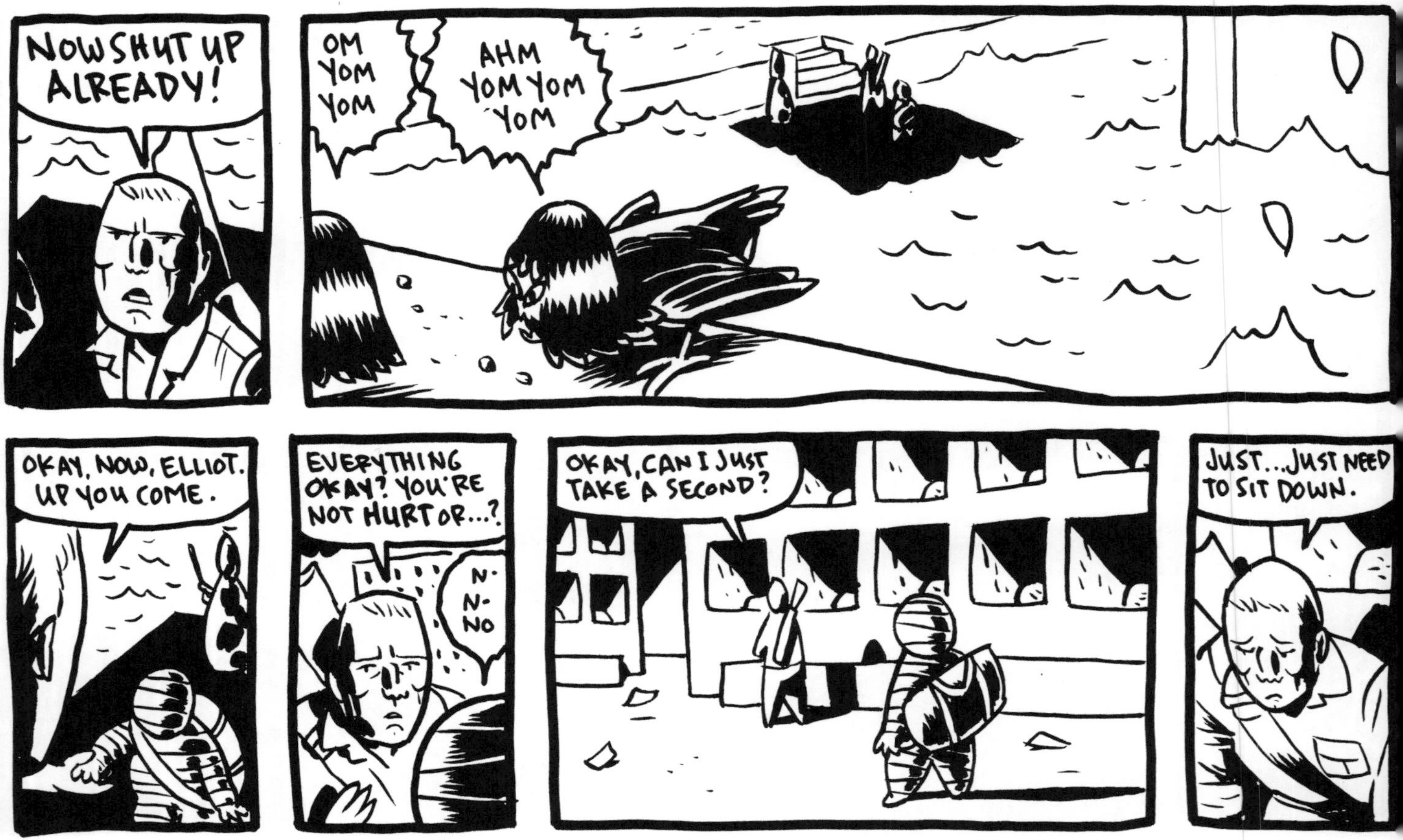
NOW SHUT UP ALREADY!
OM YOM YOM
AHM YOM YOM YOM
OKAY, NOW, ELLIOT. UP YOU COME.
EVERYTHING OKAY? YOU'RE NOT HURT OR...?
N- N- NO
OKAY, CAN I JUST TAKE A SECOND?
JUST...JUST NEED TO SIT DOWN.

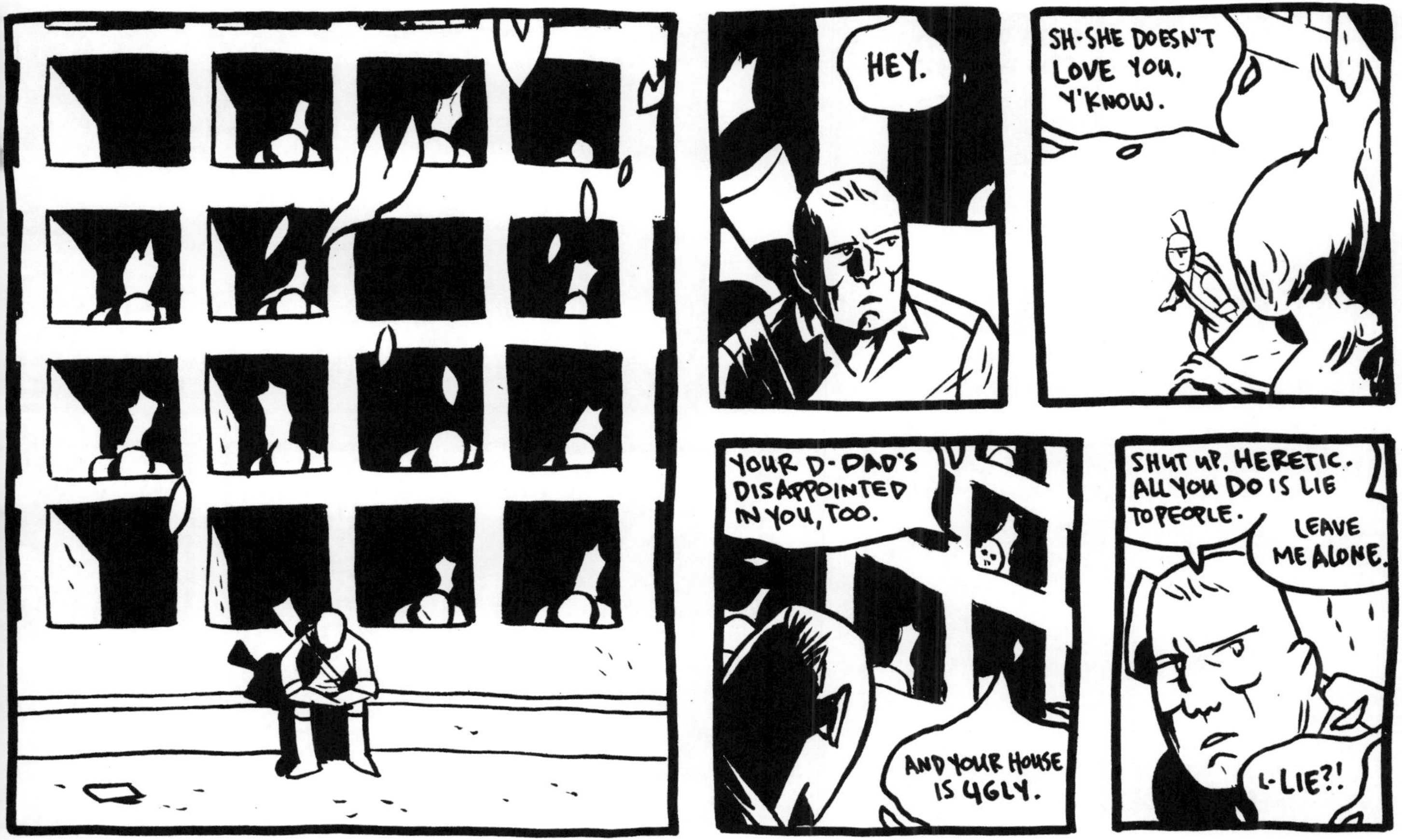
HEY.
SH-SHE DOESN'T LOVE YOU, Y'KNOW.
YOUR D-DAD'S DISAPPOINTED IN YOU, TOO.
AND YOUR HOUSE IS UGLY.
SHUT UP, HERETIC. ALL YOU DO IS LIE TO PEOPLE.
LEAVE ME ALONE.
L-LIE?!

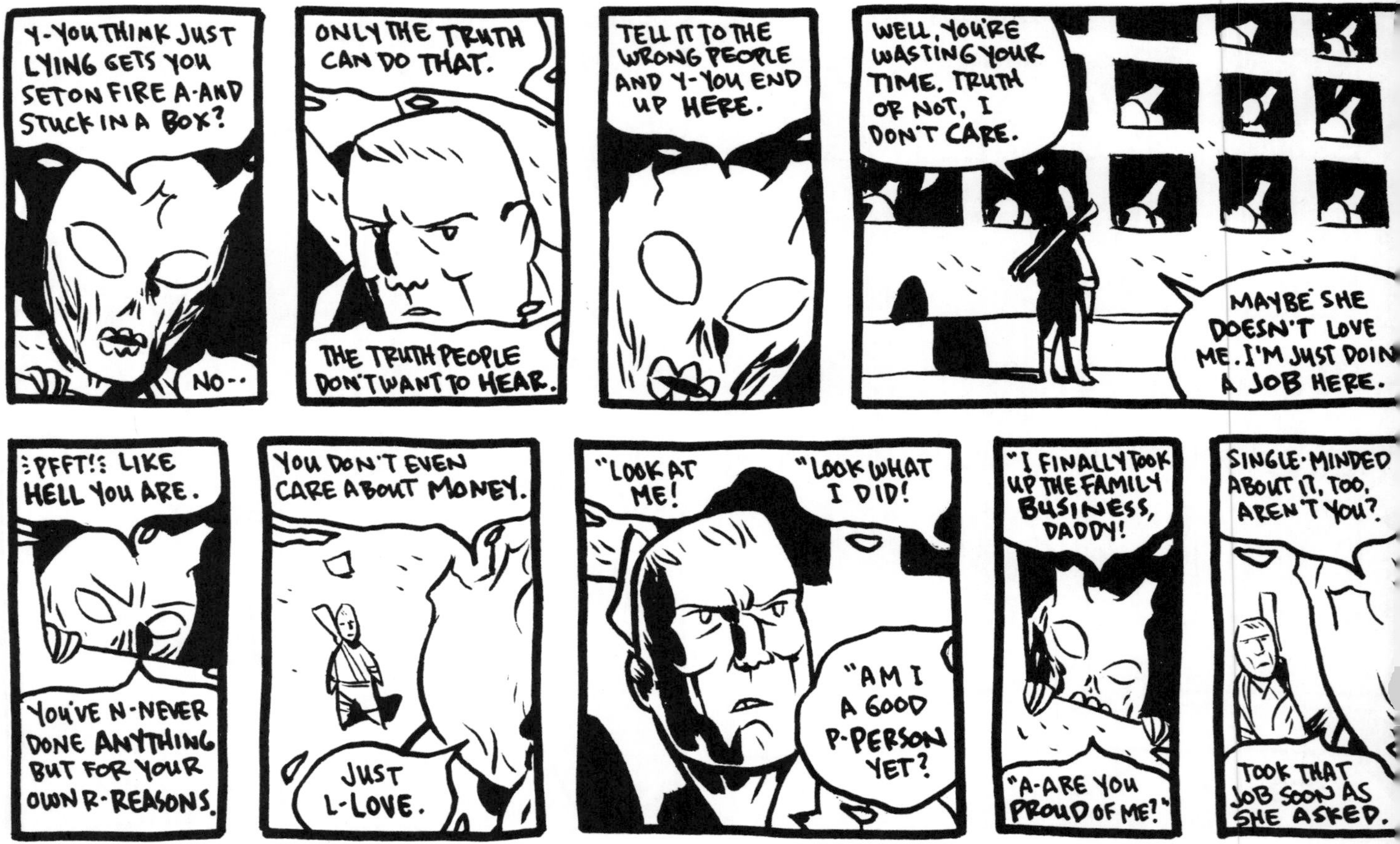
Y-YOU THINK JUST LYING GETS YOU SET ON FIRE A-AND STUCK IN A BOX?
NO--
ONLY THE TRUTH CAN DO THAT.
THE TRUTH PEOPLE DON'T WANT TO HEAR.
TELL IT TO THE WRONG PEOPLE AND Y-YOU END UP HERE.
WELL, YOU'RE WASTING YOUR TIME. TRUTH OR NOT, I DON'T CARE.
MAYBE SHE DOESN'T LOVE ME. I'M JUST DOIN A JOB HERE.
PFFT! LIKE HELL YOU ARE.
YOU'VE N-NEVER DONE ANYTHING BUT FOR YOUR OWN R-REASONS.
YOU DON'T EVEN CARE ABOUT MONEY.
JUST L-LOVE.
"LOOK AT ME!
"LOOK WHAT I DID!
"AM I A GOOD P-PERSON YET?
"I FINALLY TOOK UP THE FAMILY BUSINESS, DADDY!
"A-ARE YOU PROUD OF ME?"
SINGLE-MINDED ABOUT IT, TOO, AREN'T YOU?
TOOK THAT JOB SOON AS SHE ASKED.

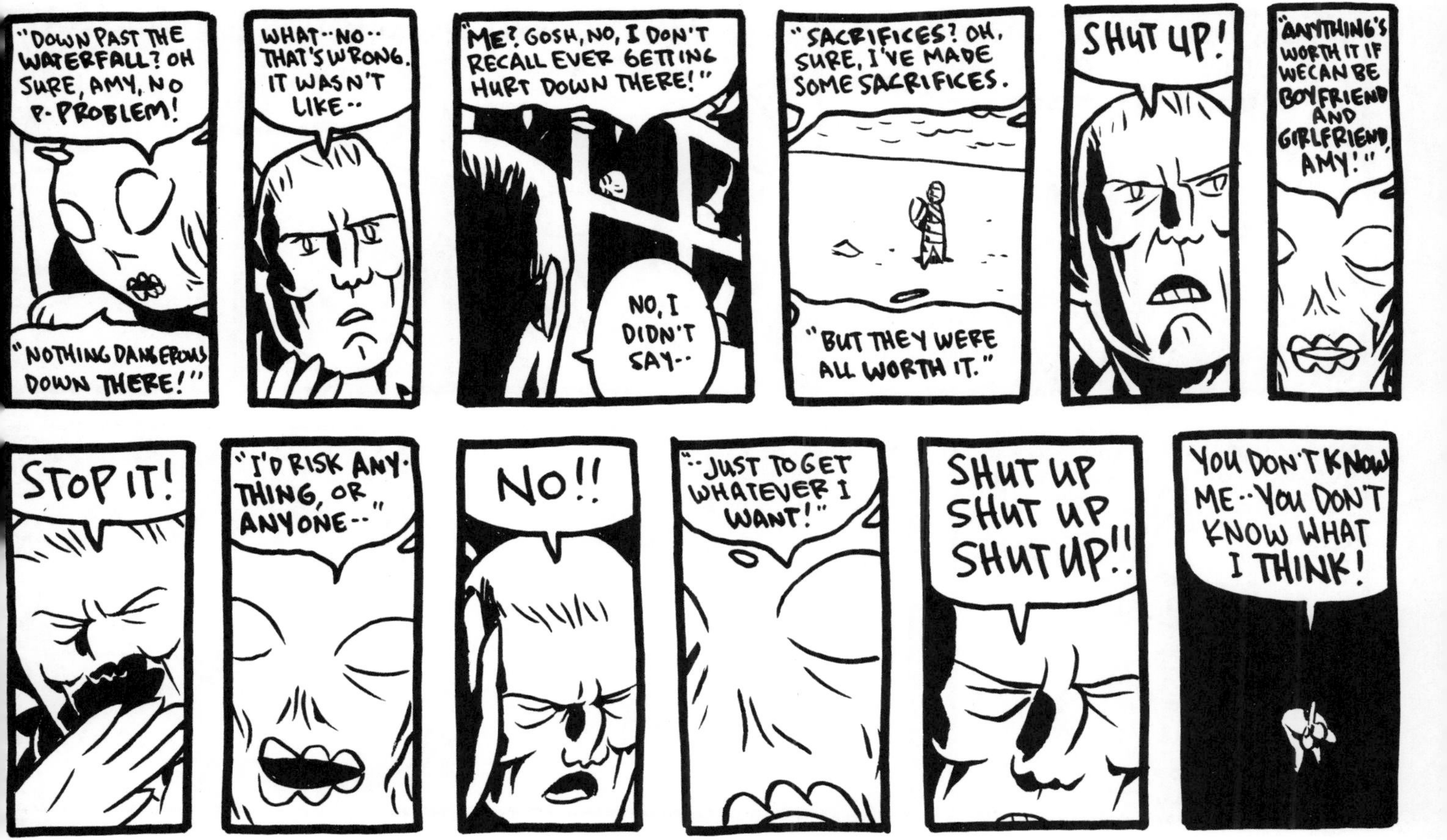
"DOWN PAST THE WATERFALL? OH SURE, AMY, NO P-PROBLEM!
"NOTHING DANGEROUS DOWN THERE!"
WHAT--NO-- THAT'S WRONG. IT WASN'T LIKE--
"ME? GOSH, NO, I DON'T RECALL EVER GETTING HURT DOWN THERE!"
NO, I DIDN'T SAY--
"SACRIFICES? OH, SURE, I'VE MADE SOME SACRIFICES.
"BUT THEY WERE ALL WORTH IT."
SHUT UP!
"ANYTHING'S WORTH IT IF WE CAN BE BOYFRIEND AND GIRLFRIEND, AMY!"
STOP IT!
"I'D RISK ANY-THING, OR ANYONE--"
NO!!
"--JUST TO GET WHATEVER I WANT!"
SHUT UP SHUT UP SHUT UP!!
YOU DON'T KNOW ME--YOU DON'T KNOW WHAT I THINK!

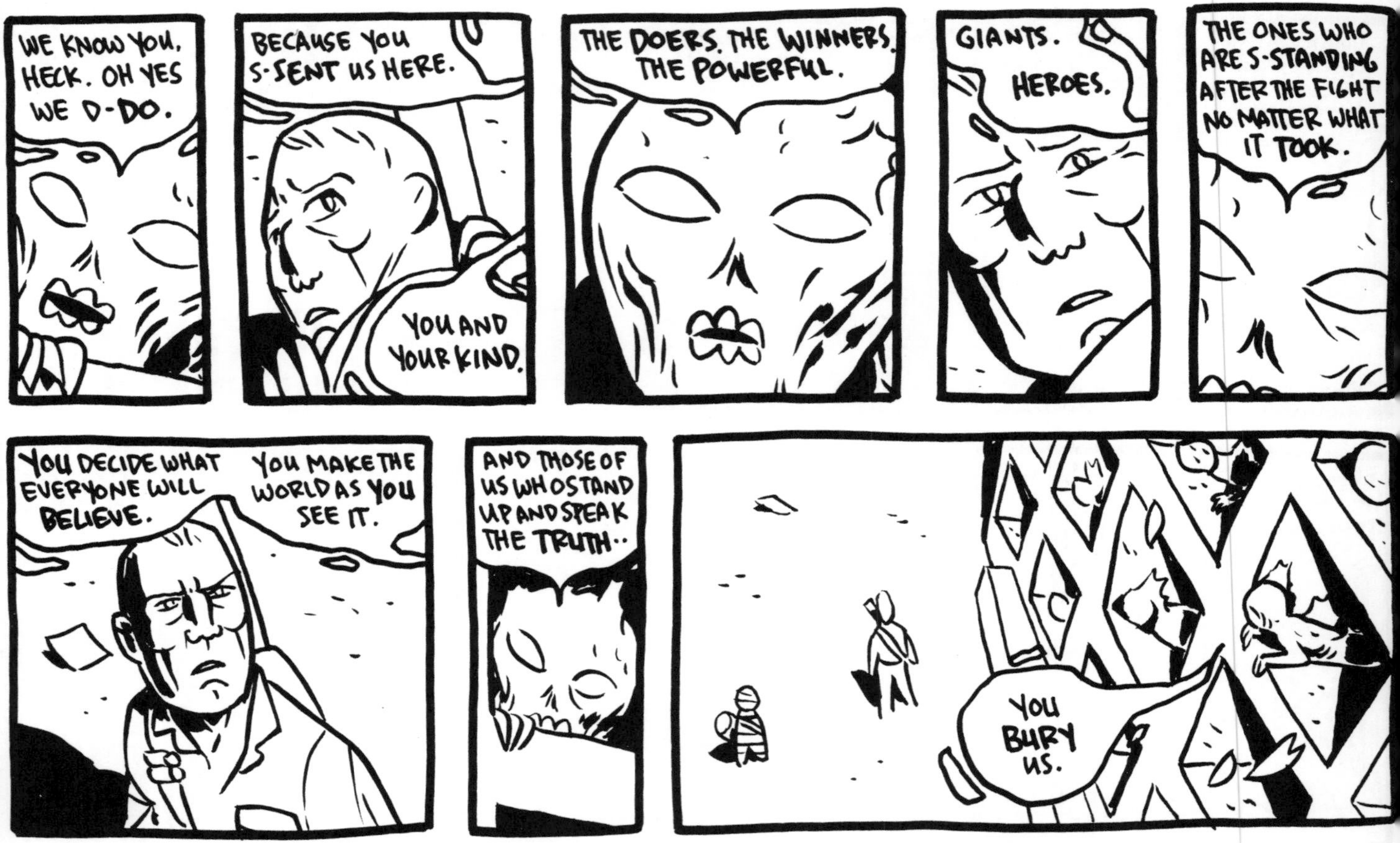
WE KNOW YOU, HECK. OH YES WE D-DO.
BECAUSE YOU S-SENT US HERE.
YOU AND YOUR KIND.
THE DOERS. THE WINNERS. THE POWERFUL.
GIANTS.
HEROES.
THE ONES WHO ARE S-STANDING AFTER THE FIGHT NO MATTER WHAT IT TOOK.
YOU DECIDE WHAT EVERYONE WILL BELIEVE.
YOU MAKE THE WORLD AS YOU SEE IT.
AND THOSE OF US WHO STAND UP AND SPEAK THE TRUTH..
YOU BURY US.

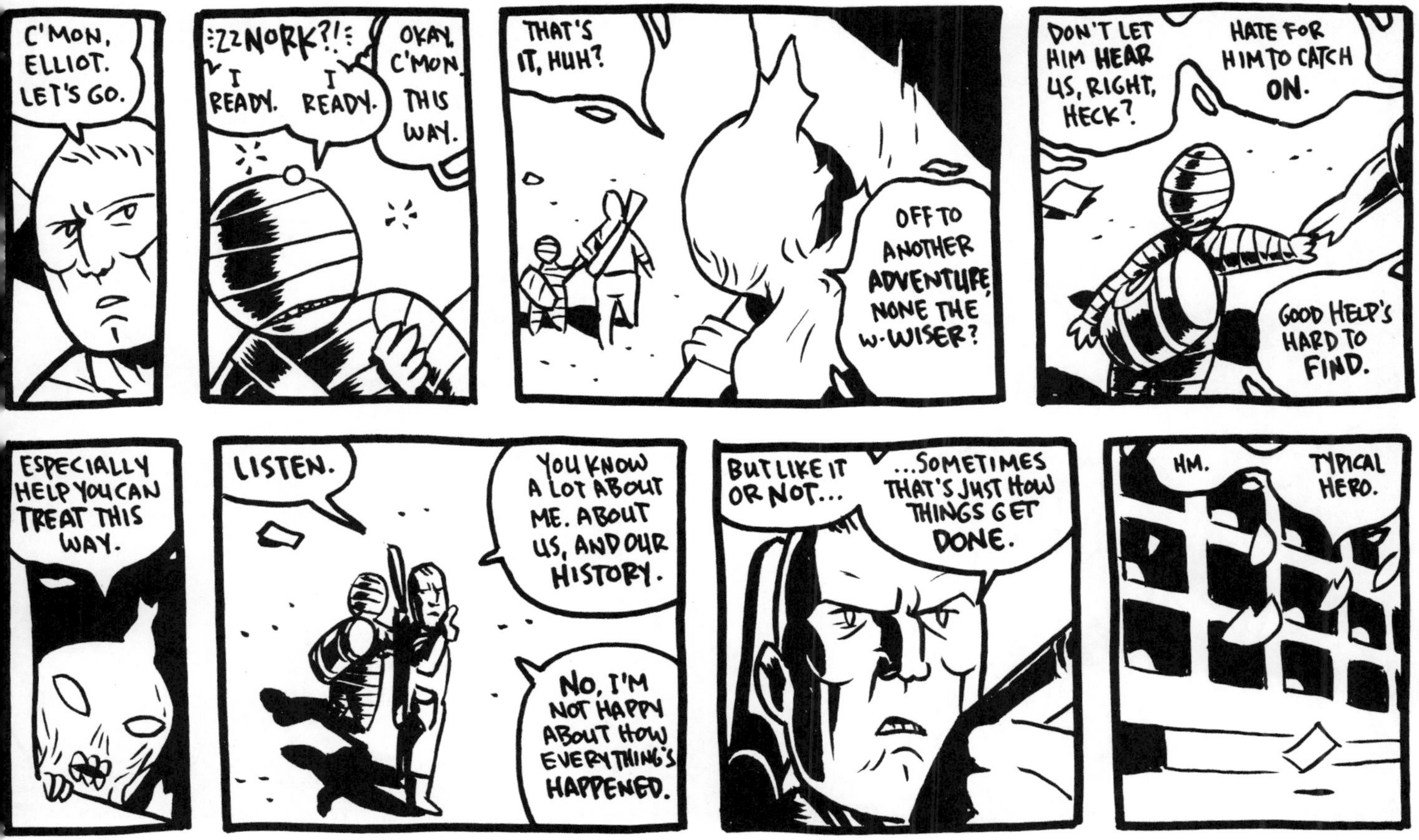
C'MON, ELLIOT. LET'S GO.
ZZNORK?!
I READY. I READY.
OKAY. C'MON. THIS WAY.
THAT'S IT, HUH?
OFF TO ANOTHER ADVENTURE, NONE THE W-WISER?
DON'T LET HIM HEAR US, RIGHT, HECK?
HATE FOR HIM TO CATCH ON.
GOOD HELP'S HARD TO FIND.
ESPECIALLY HELP YOU CAN TREAT THIS WAY.
LISTEN.
YOU KNOW A LOT ABOUT ME. ABOUT US, AND OUR HISTORY.
NO, I'M NOT HAPPY ABOUT HOW EVERYTHING'S HAPPENED.
BUT LIKE IT OR NOT...
...SOMETIMES THAT'S JUST HOW THINGS GET DONE.
HM.
TYPICAL HERO.

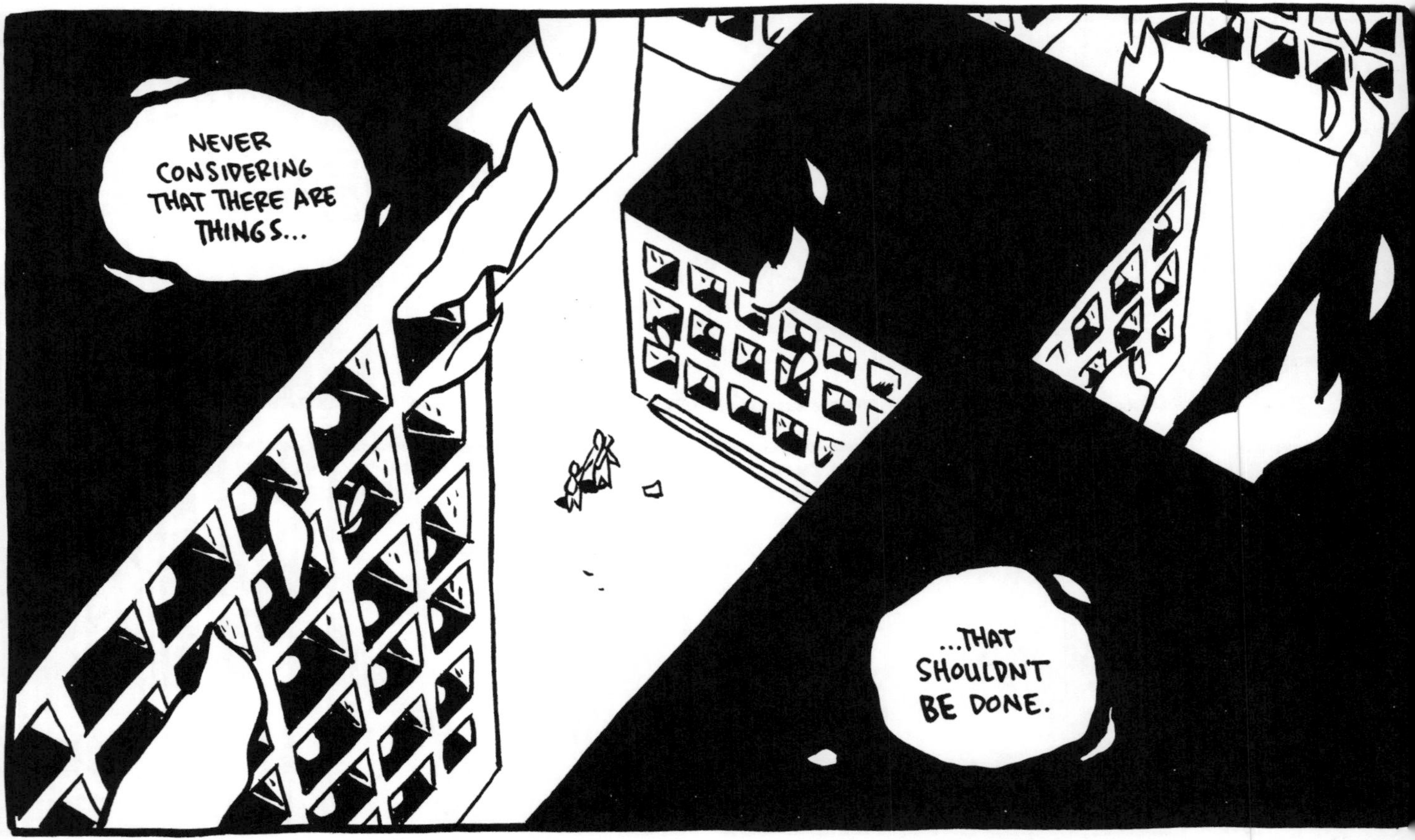
NEVER CONSIDERING THAT THERE ARE THINGS...
...THAT SHOULDN'T BE DONE.

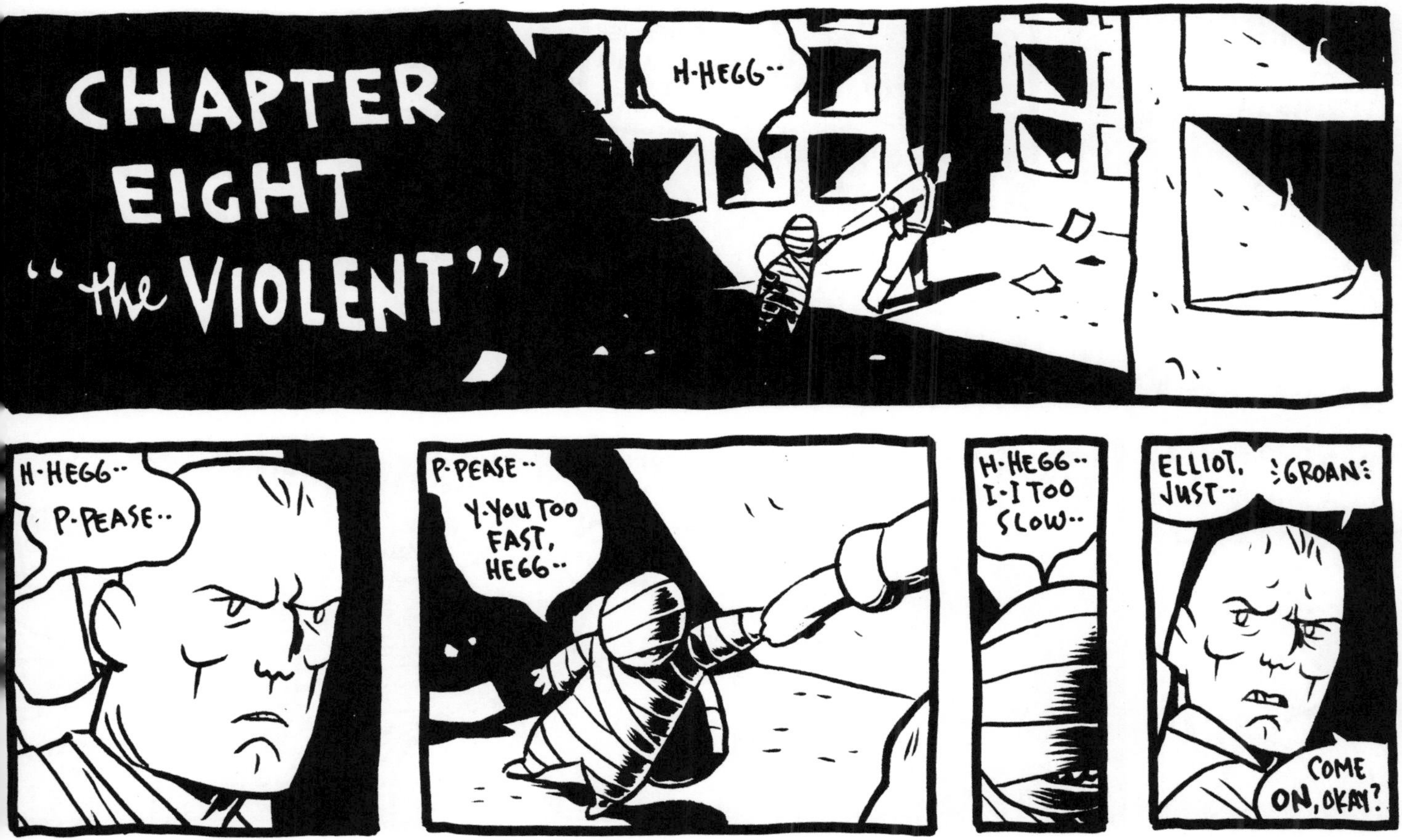
CHAPTER EIGHT
"the VIOLENT"
H-HEGG..
H-HEGG..
P-PEASE..
P-PEASE..
Y-YOU TOO FAST, HEGG..
H-HEGG.. I-I TOO SLOW..
ELLIOT, JUST..
GROAN
COME ON, OKAY?

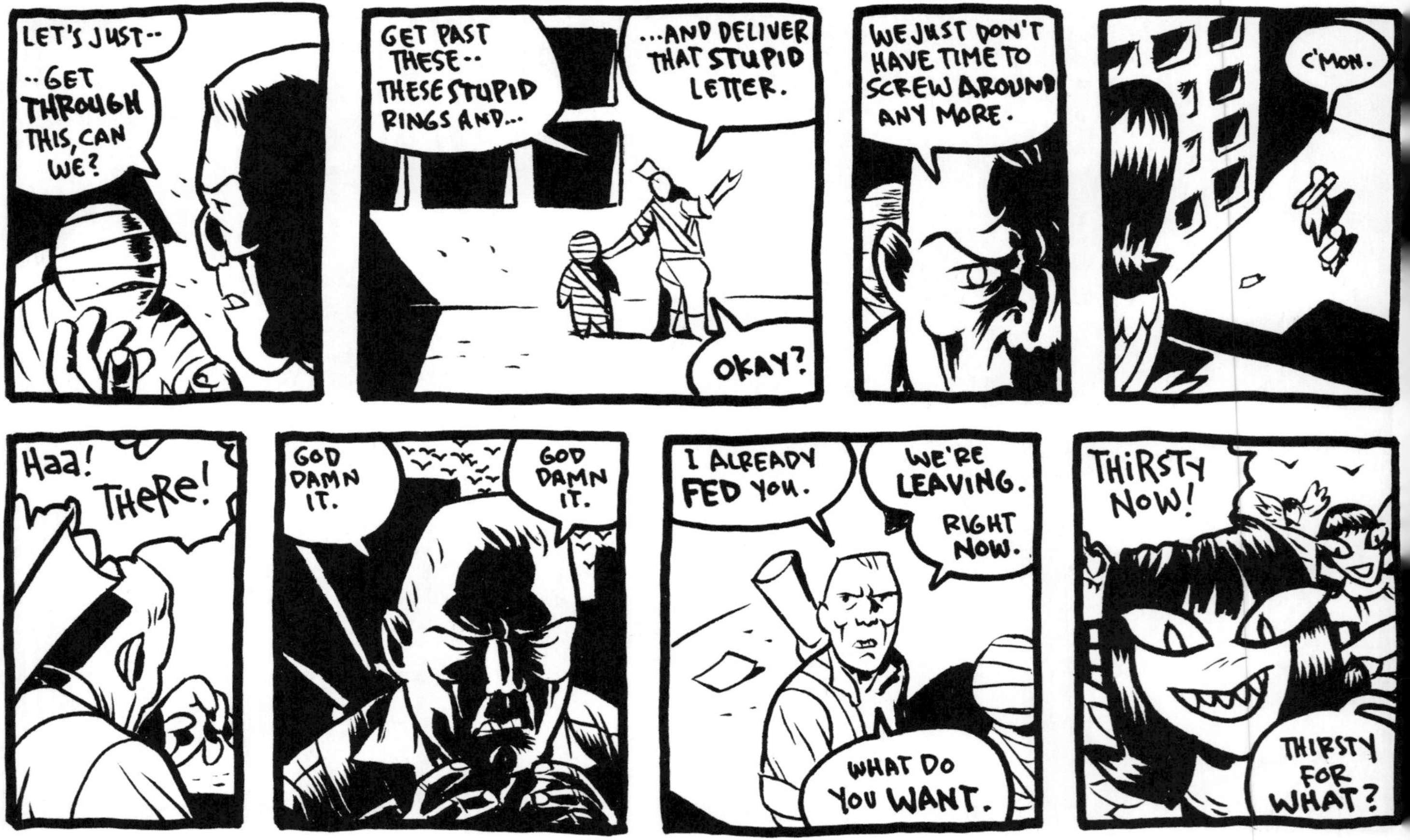
LET'S JUST--
--GET THROUGH THIS, CAN WE?
GET PAST THESE-- THESE STUPID RINGS AND...
...AND DELIVER THAT STUPID LETTER.
OKAY?
WE JUST DON'T HAVE TIME TO SCREW AROUND ANY MORE.
C'MON.
Haa! THERE!
GOD DAMN IT.
GOD DAMN IT.
I ALREADY FED YOU.
WE'RE LEAVING.
RIGHT NOW.
WHAT DO YOU WANT.
THIRSTY NOW!
THIRSTY FOR WHAT?

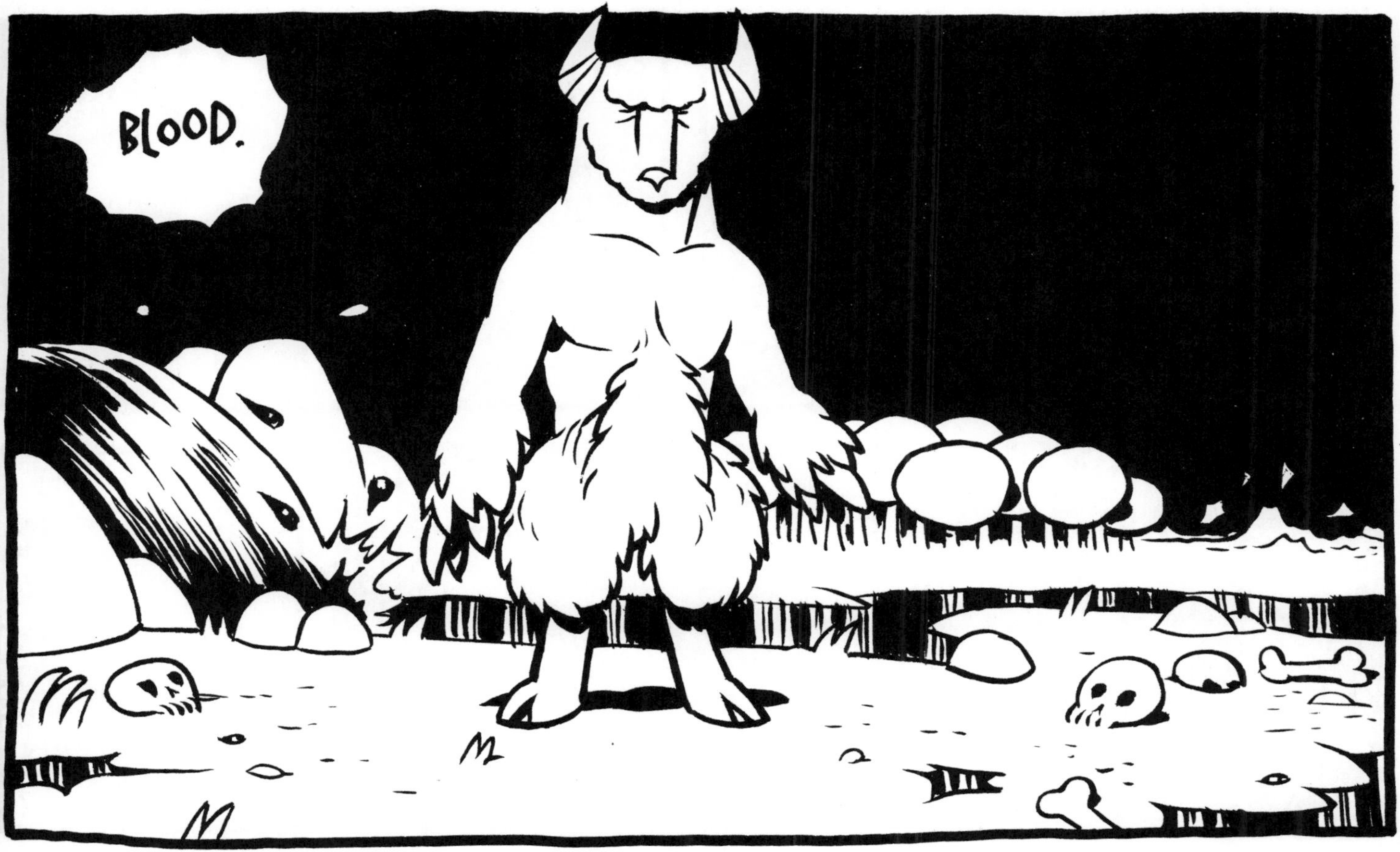
BLOOD.

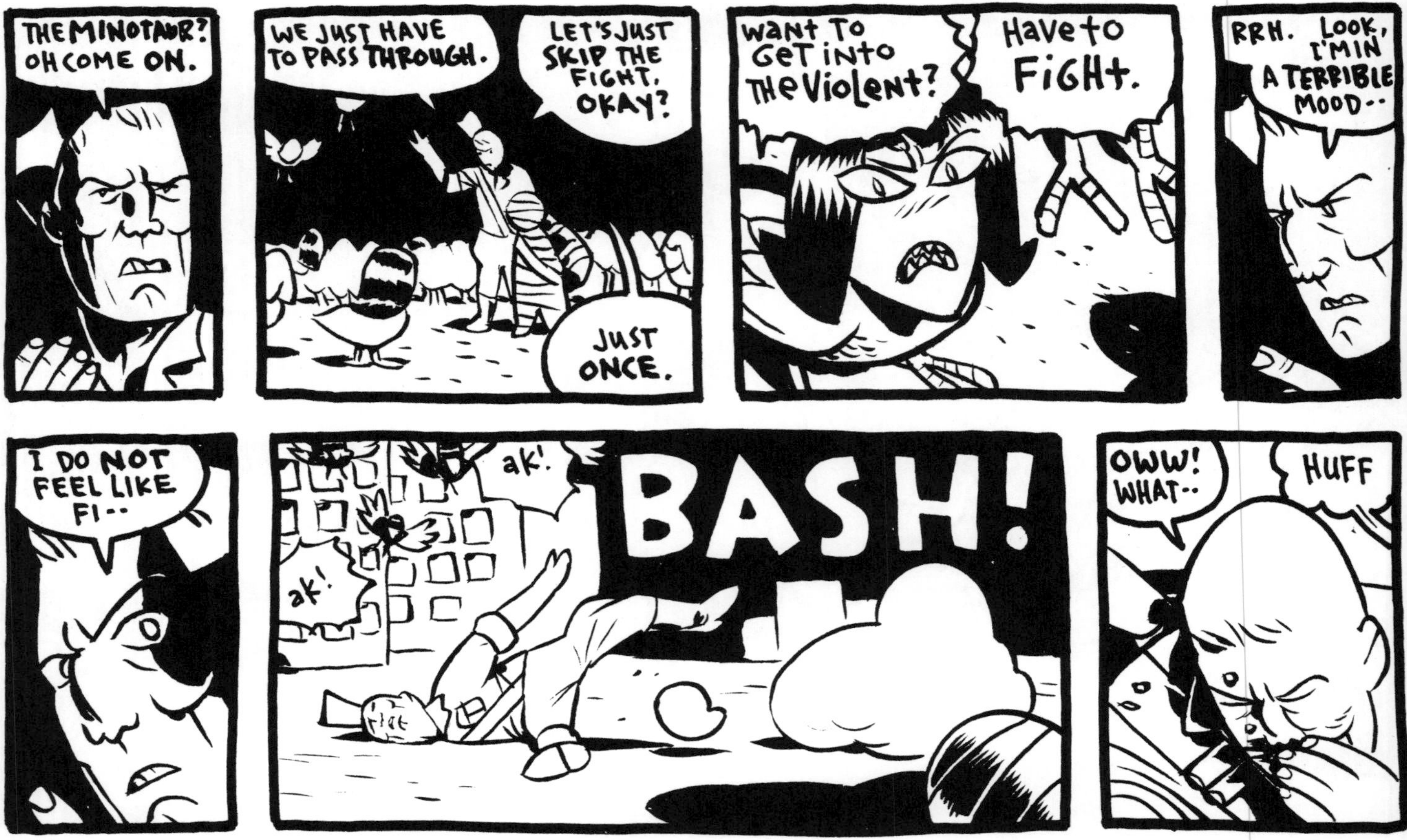
THE MINOTAUR? OH COME ON.
WE JUST HAVE TO PASS THROUGH.
LET'S JUST SKIP THE FIGHT, OKAY?
JUST ONCE.
WANT TO GET INTO THE VIOLENT?
HAVE TO FIGHT.
RRH. LOOK, I'M IN A TERRIBLE MOOD--
I DO NOT FEEL LIKE FI--
AK!
AK!
BASH!
OWW! WHAT--
HUFF

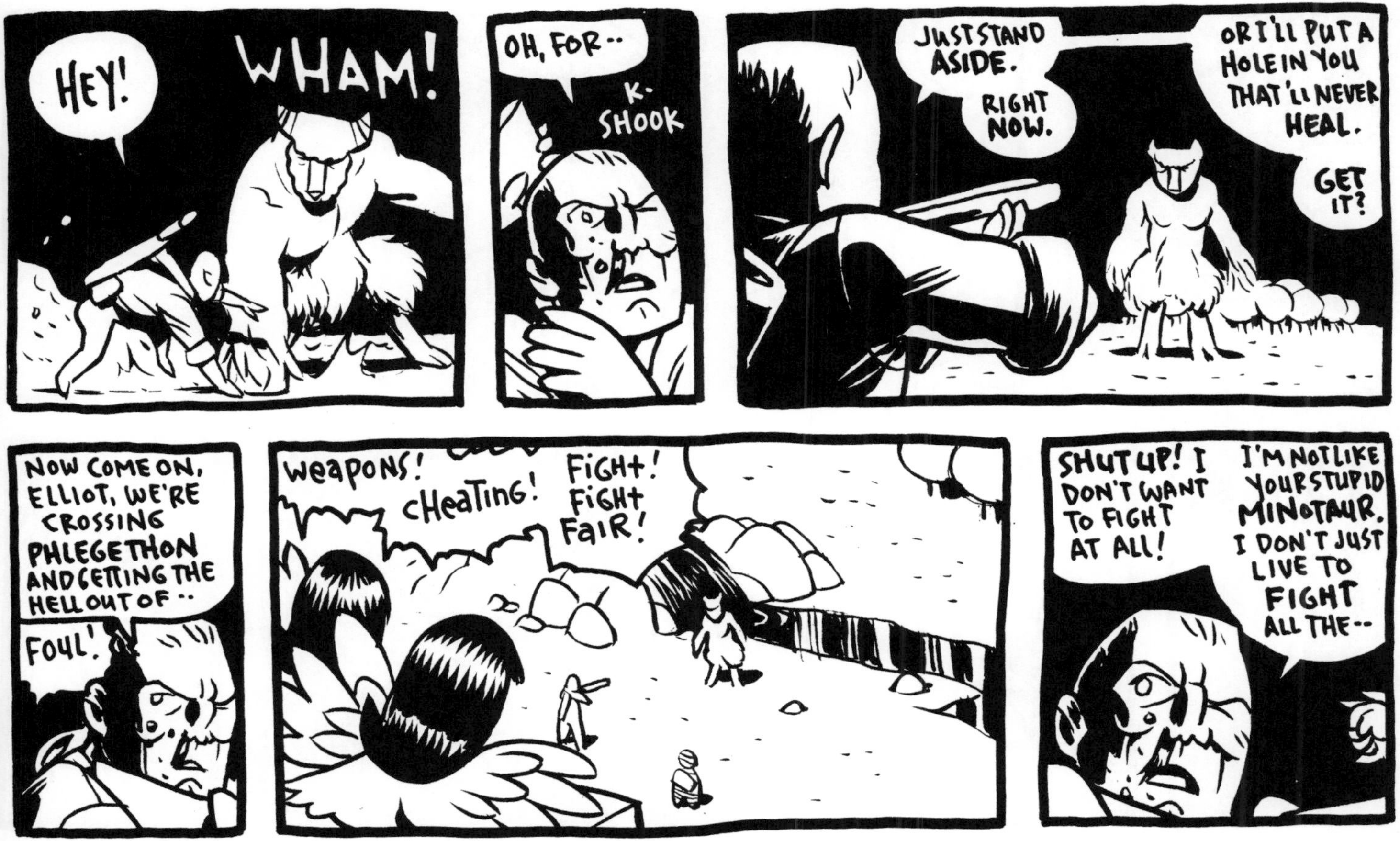
HEY!
WHAM!
OH, FOR--
K-SHOOK
JUST STAND ASIDE.
RIGHT NOW.
OR I'LL PUT A HOLE IN YOU THAT'LL NEVER HEAL.
GET IT?
NOW COME ON, ELLIOT, WE'RE CROSSING PHLEGETHON AND GETTING THE HELL OUT OF--
FOUL!
WEAPONS!
CHEATING!
FIGHT! FIGHT FAIR!
SHUT UP! I DON'T WANT TO FIGHT AT ALL!
I'M NOT LIKE YOUR STUPID MINOTAUR. I DON'T JUST LIVE TO FIGHT ALL THE--

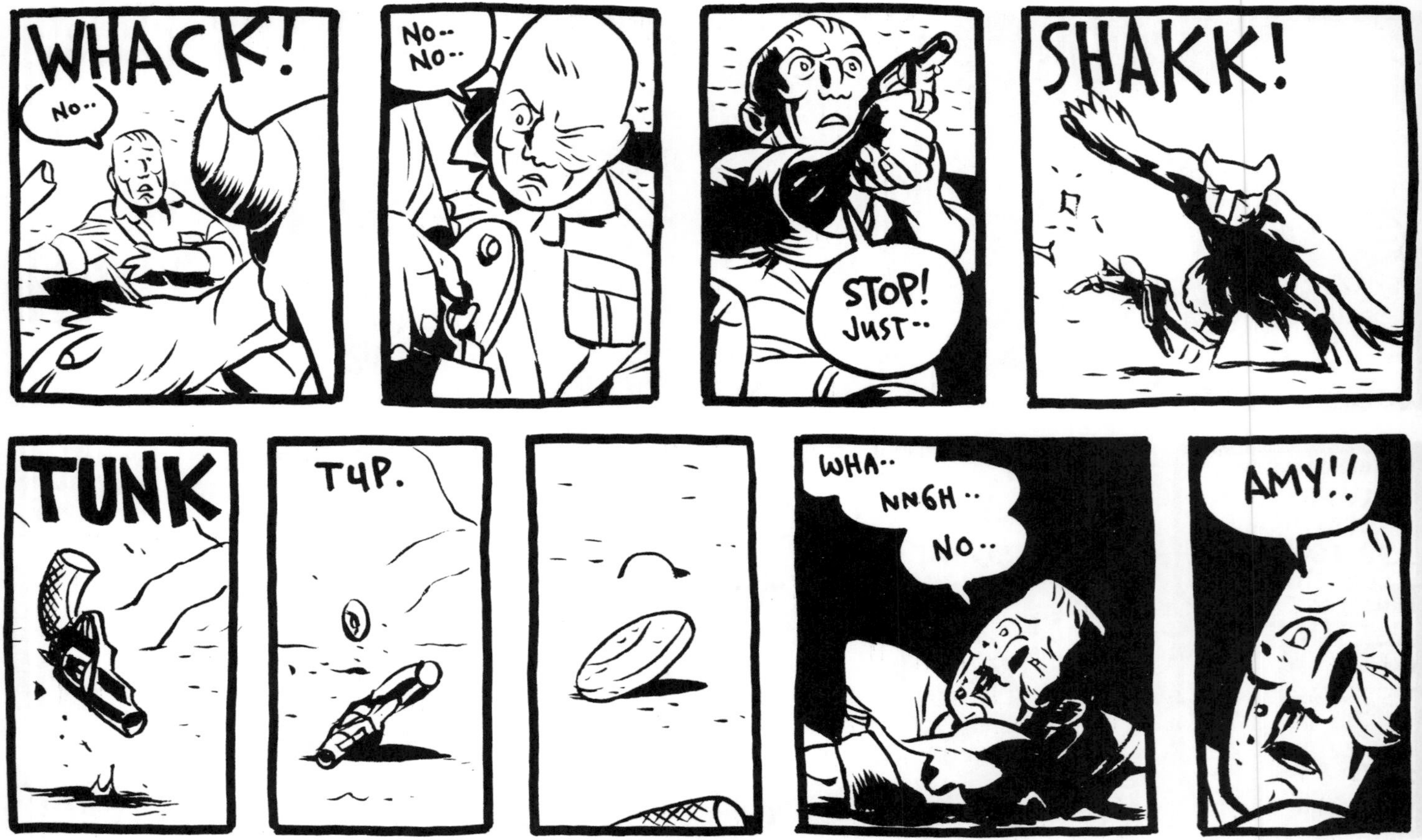
WHACK!
NO..
NO..
NO..
STOP!
JUST..
SHAKK!
TUNK
TUP.
WHA..
NNGH..
NO..
AMY!!

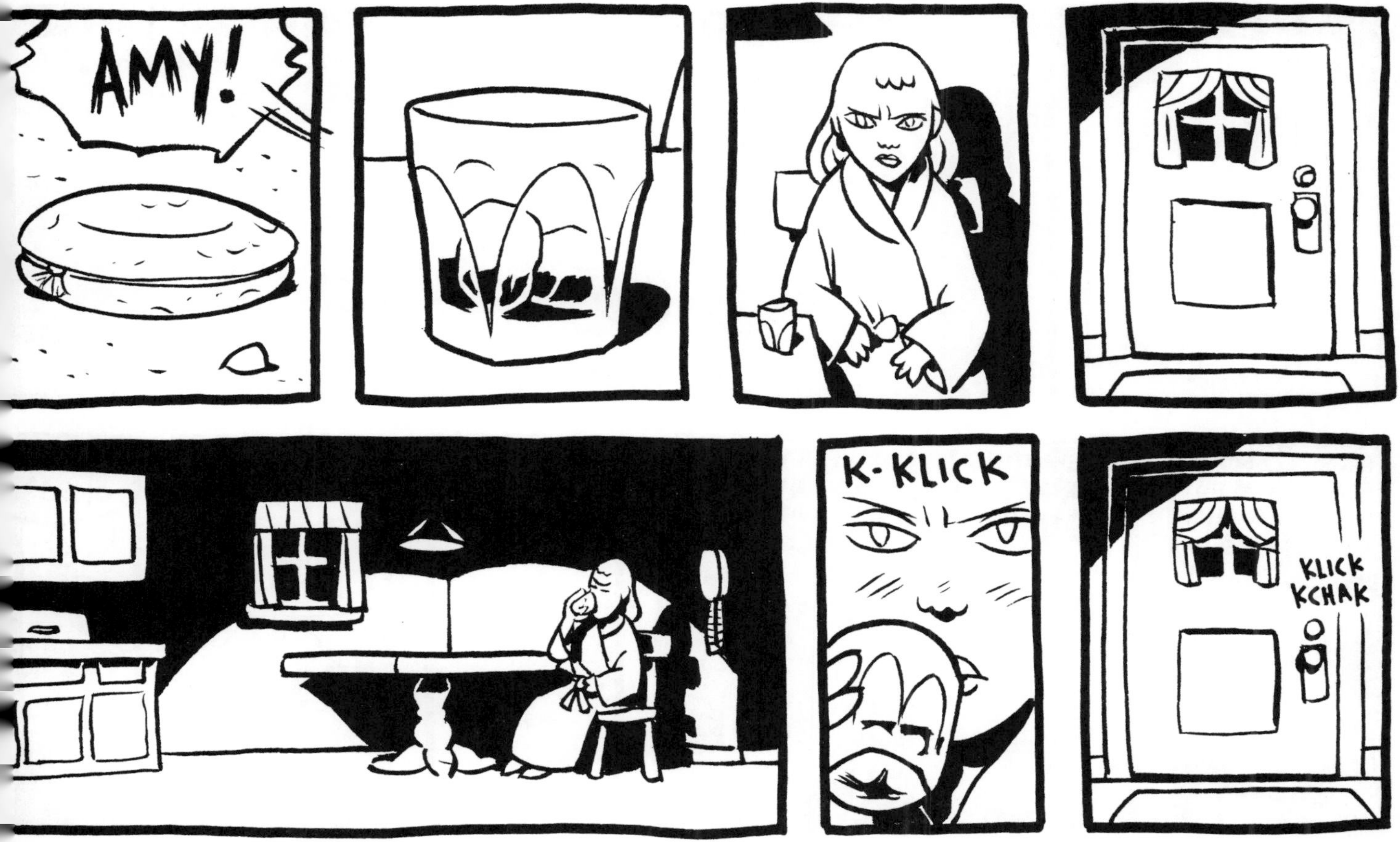
AMY!
K-KLICK
KLICK
KCHAK

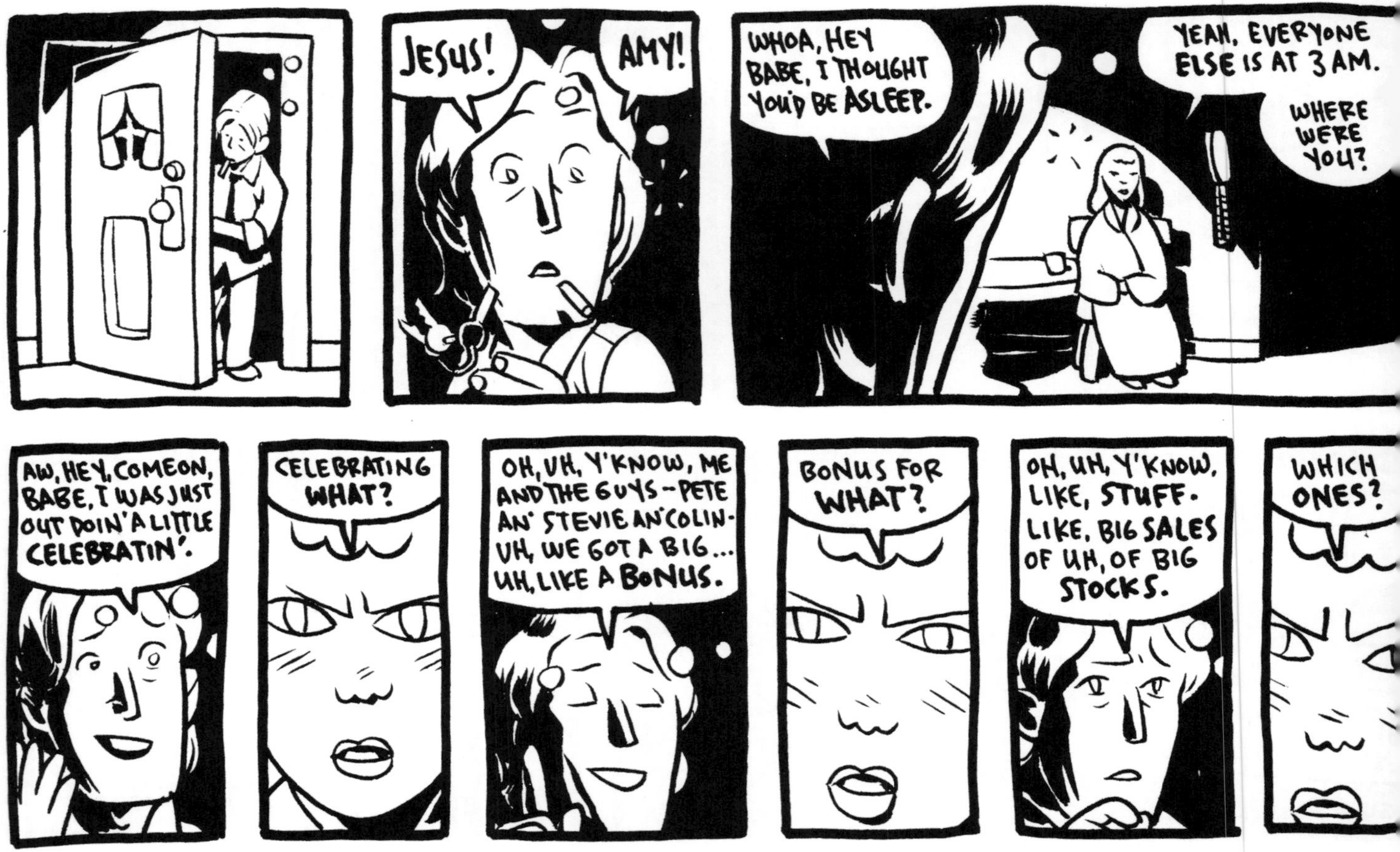
JESUS!
AMY!
WHOA, HEY BABE, I THOUGHT YOU'D BE ASLEEP.
YEAH, EVERYONE ELSE IS AT 3 AM.
WHERE WERE YOU?
AW, HEY, COMEON, BABE, I WAS JUST OUT DOIN' A LITTLE CELEBRATIN'.
CELEBRATING WHAT?
OH, UH, Y'KNOW, ME AND THE GUYS -- PETE AN' STEVIE AN' COLIN-- UH, WE GOT A BIG... UH, LIKE A BONUS.
BONUS FOR WHAT?
OH, UH, Y'KNOW, LIKE, STUFF. LIKE, BIG SALES OF UH, OF BIG STOCKS.
WHICH ONES?

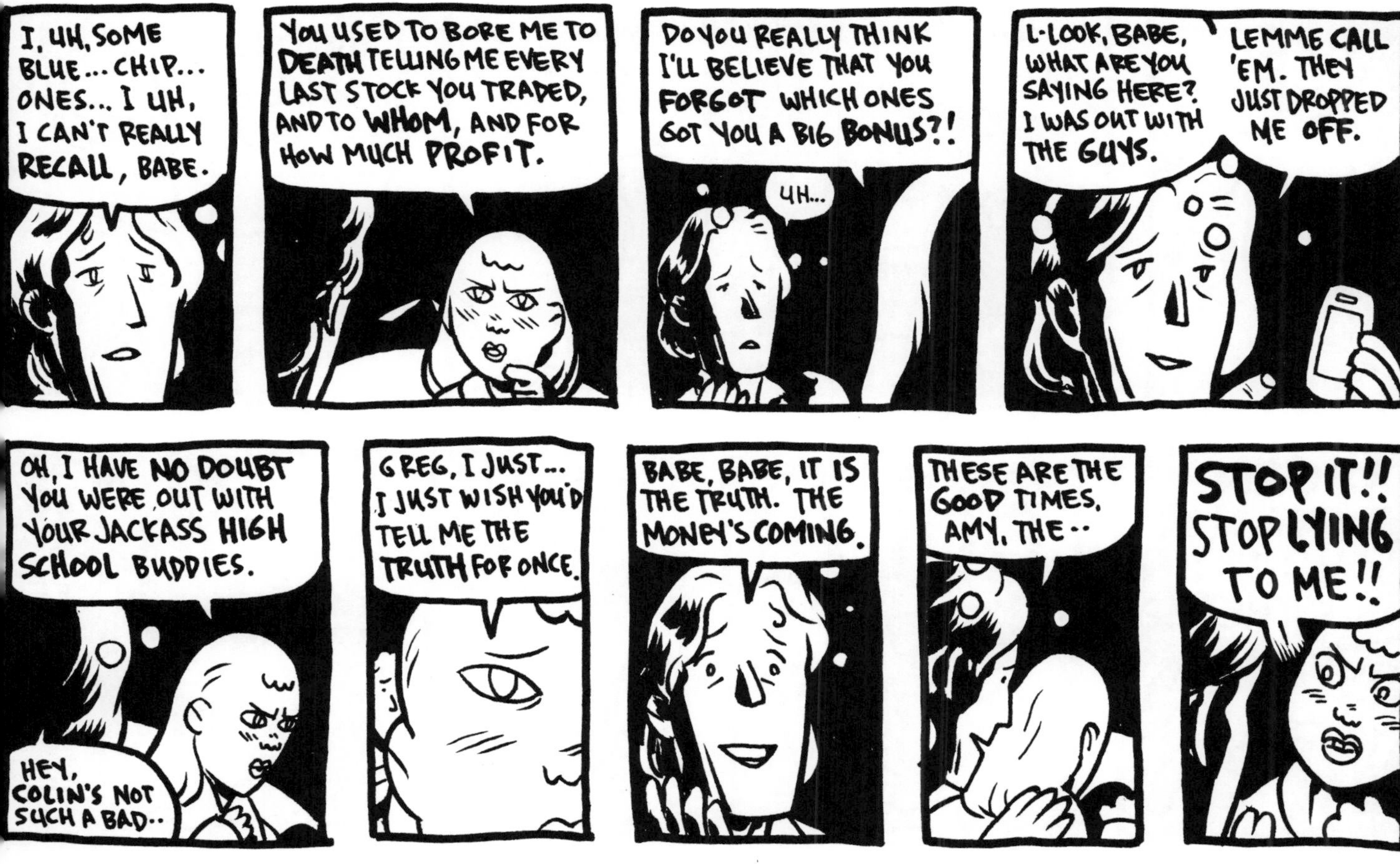
I, UH, SOME BLUE... CHIP... ONES... I UH, I CAN'T REALLY RECALL, BABE.
YOU USED TO BORE ME TO DEATH TELLING ME EVERY LAST STOCK YOU TRADED, AND TO WHOM, AND FOR HOW MUCH PROFIT.
DO YOU REALLY THINK I'LL BELIEVE THAT YOU FORGOT WHICH ONES GOT YOU A BIG BONUS?!
UH...
L-LOOK, BABE, WHAT ARE YOU SAYING HERE? I WAS OUT WITH THE GUYS.
LEMME CALL 'EM. THEY JUST DROPPED ME OFF.
OH, I HAVE NO DOUBT YOU WERE OUT WITH YOUR JACKASS HIGH SCHOOL BUDDIES.
HEY, COLIN'S NOT SUCH A BAD..
GREG, I JUST... I JUST WISH YOU'D TELL ME THE TRUTH FOR ONCE.
BABE, BABE, IT IS THE TRUTH. THE MONEY'S COMING.
THESE ARE THE GOOD TIMES, AMY, THE..
STOP IT!! STOP LYING TO ME!!

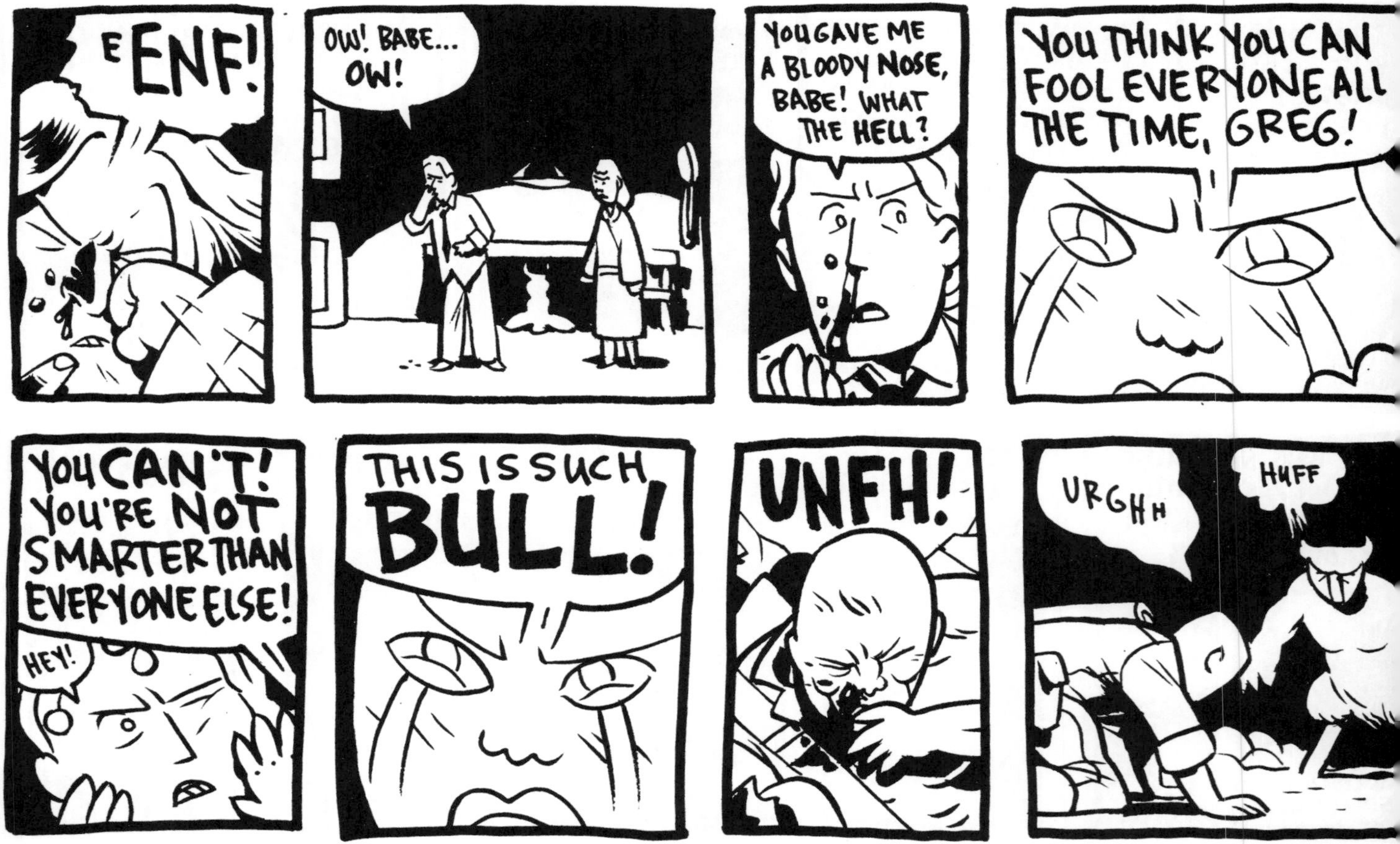
EENF!
OW! BABE... OW!
YOU GAVE ME A BLOODY NOSE, BABE! WHAT THE HELL?
YOU THINK YOU CAN FOOL EVERYONE ALL THE TIME, GREG!
YOU CAN'T! YOU'RE NOT SMARTER THAN EVERYONE ELSE!
HEY!
THIS IS SUCH BULL!
UNFH!
URGHH
HUFF

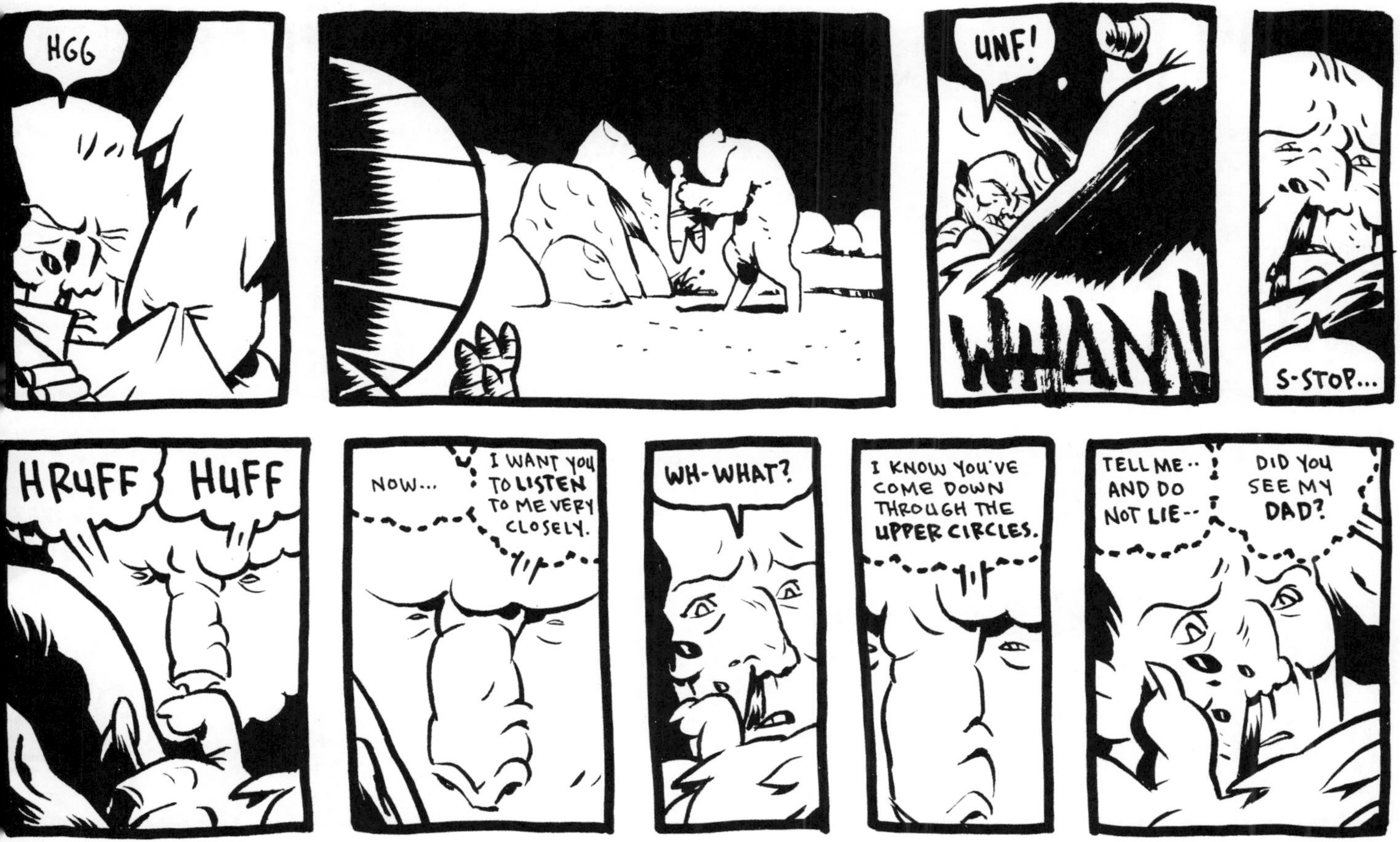
HGG
UNF!
WHAM!
S-STOP...
HRUFF
HUFF
NOW...
I WANT YOU TO LISTEN TO ME VERY CLOSELY.
WH-WHAT?
I KNOW YOU'VE COME DOWN THROUGH THE UPPER CIRCLES.
TELL ME.. AND DO NOT LIE--
DID YOU SEE MY DAD?

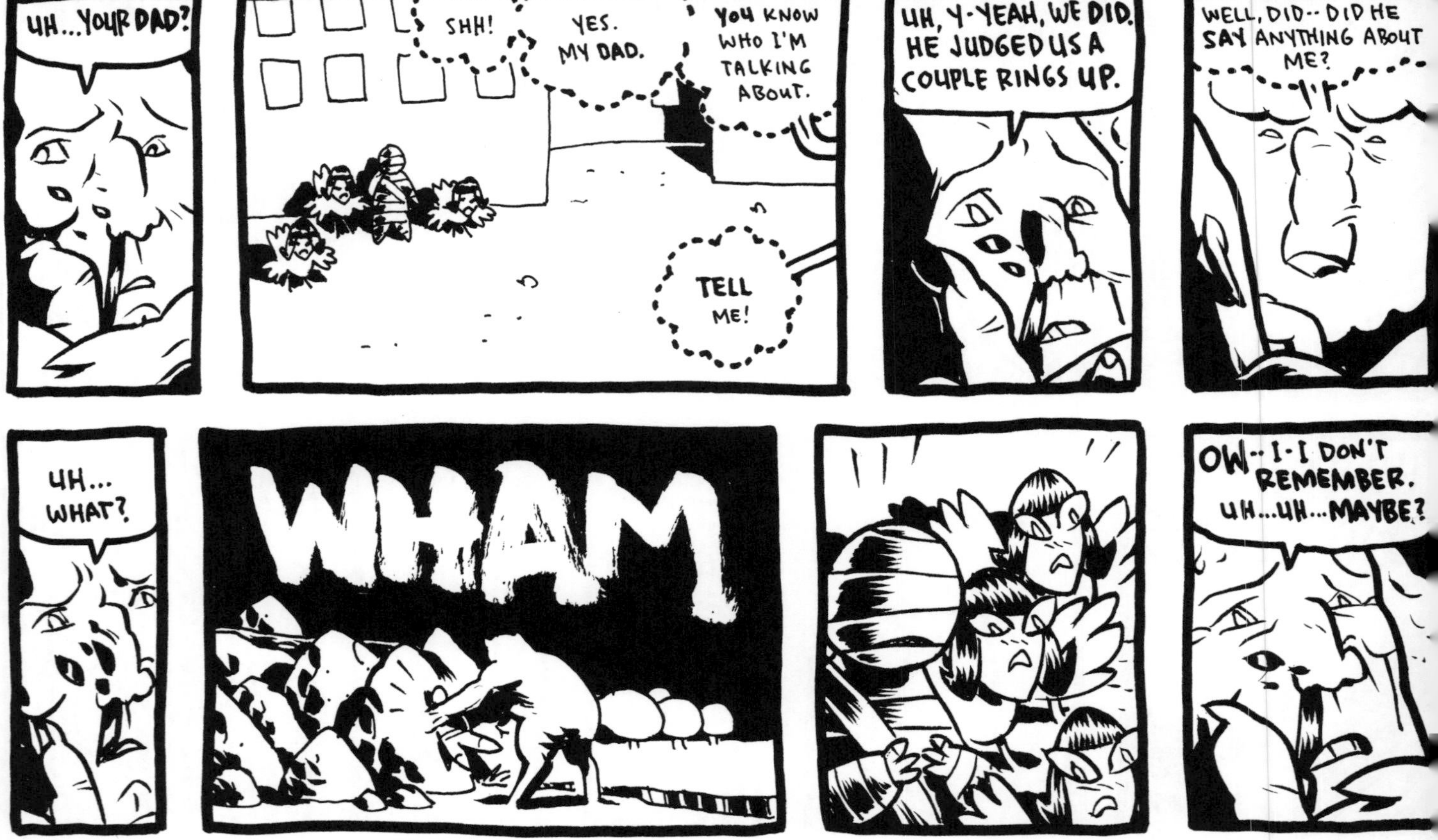
UH...YOUR DAD?
SHH!
YES. MY DAD.
YOU KNOW WHO I'M TALKING ABOUT.
TELL ME!
UH, Y-YEAH, WE DID. HE JUDGED US A COUPLE RINGS UP.
WELL, DID-- DID HE SAY ANYTHING ABOUT ME?
UH... WHAT?
WHAM
OW-- I-I DON'T REMEMBER. UH...UH...MAYBE?

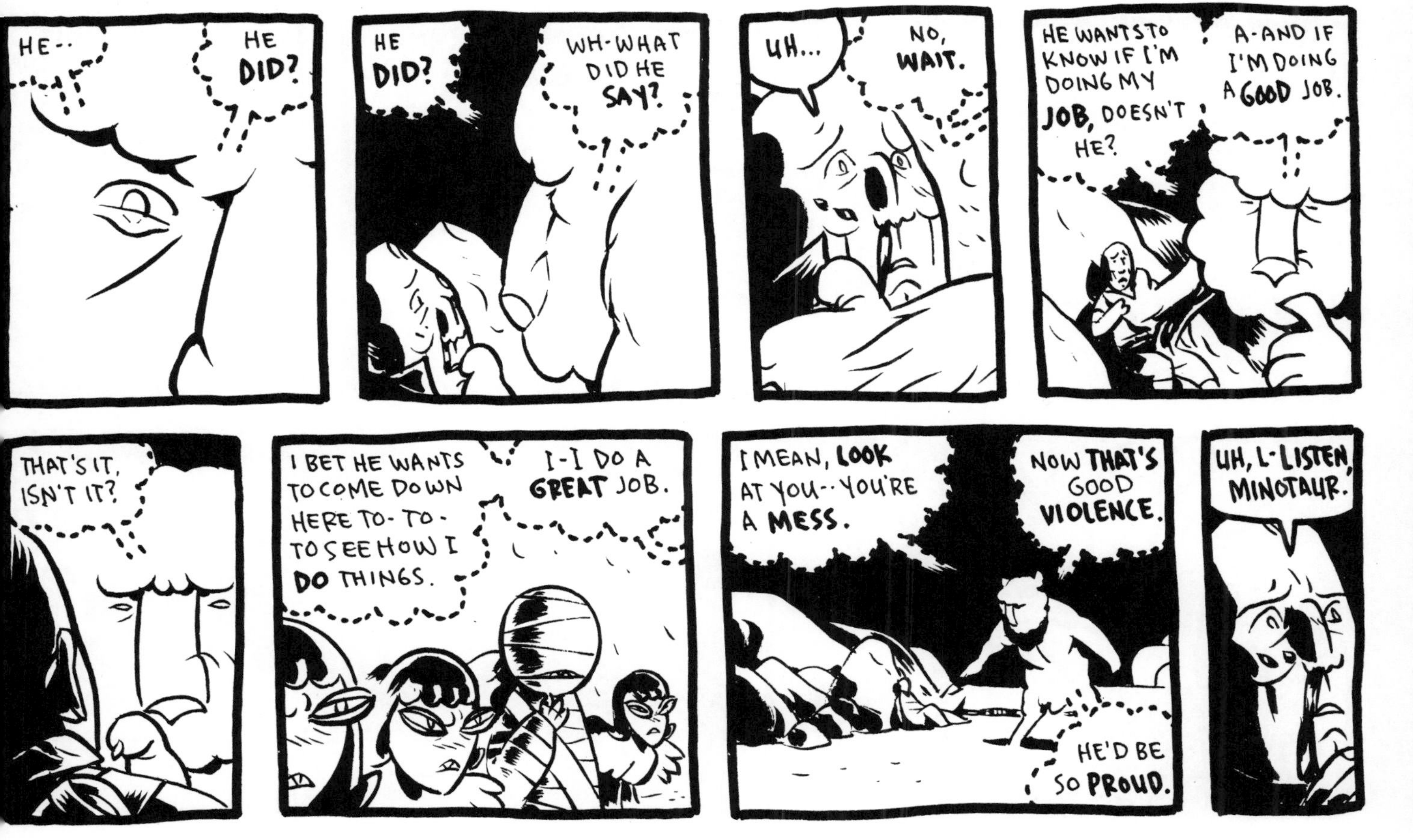
HE--
HE DID?
HE DID?
WH-WHAT DID HE SAY?
UH...
NO, WAIT.
HE WANTS TO KNOW IF I'M DOING MY JOB, DOESN'T HE?
A-AND IF I'M DOING A GOOD JOB.
THAT'S IT, ISN'T IT?
I BET HE WANTS TO COME DOWN HERE TO- TO- TO SEE HOW I DO THINGS.
I-I DO A GREAT JOB.
I MEAN, LOOK AT YOU-- YOU'RE A MESS.
NOW THAT'S GOOD VIOLENCE.
HE'D BE SO PROUD.
UH, L-LISTEN, MINOTAUR.

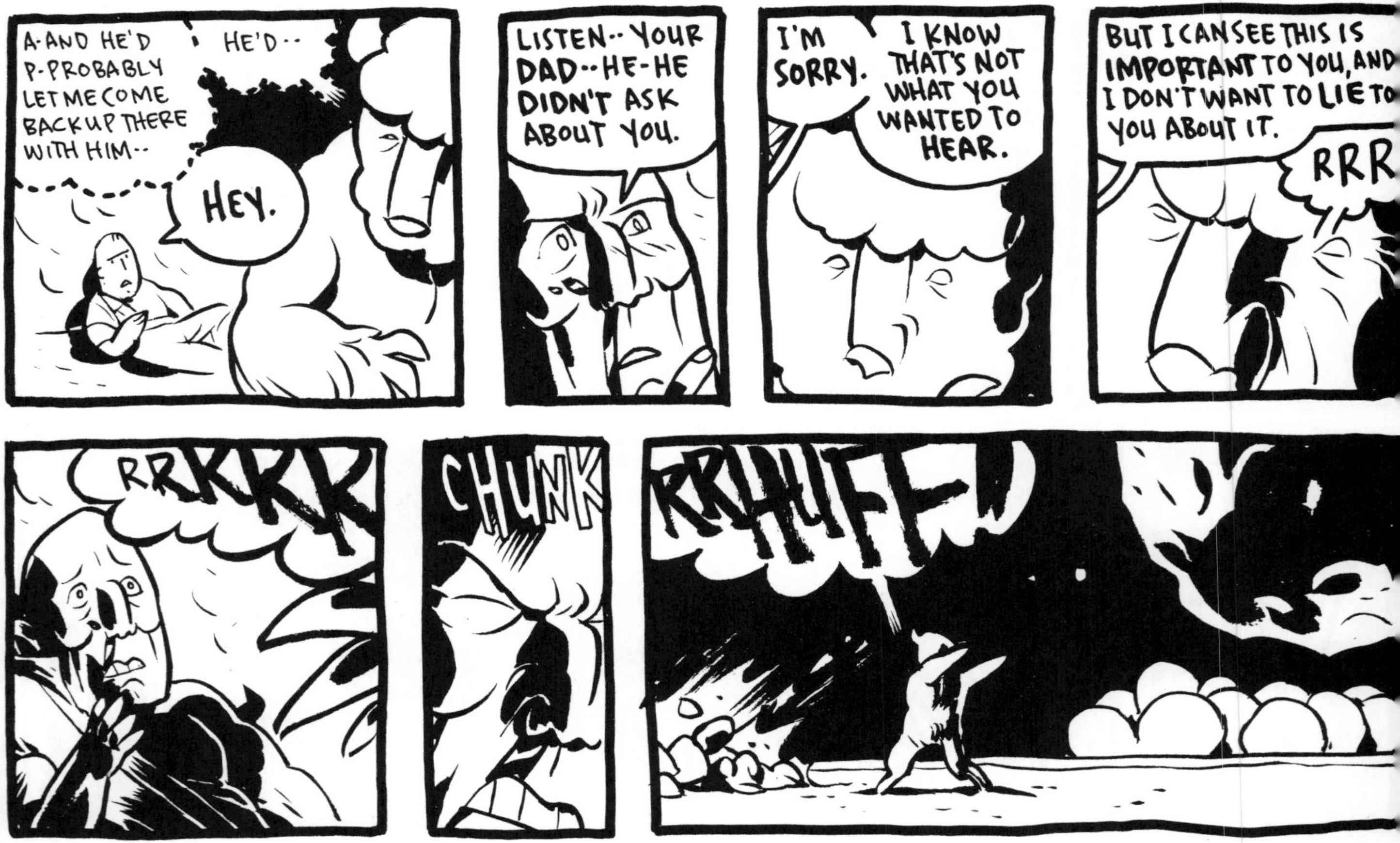
A-AND HE'D P-PROBABLY LET ME COME BACK UP THERE WITH HIM--
HE'D--
HEY.
LISTEN-- YOUR DAD--HE-HE DIDN'T ASK ABOUT YOU.
I'M SORRY.
I KNOW THAT'S NOT WHAT YOU WANTED TO HEAR.
BUT I CAN SEE THIS IS IMPORTANT TO YOU, AND I DON'T WANT TO LIE TO YOU ABOUT IT.
RRR
RRKKRR
CHUNK
RRHUFF

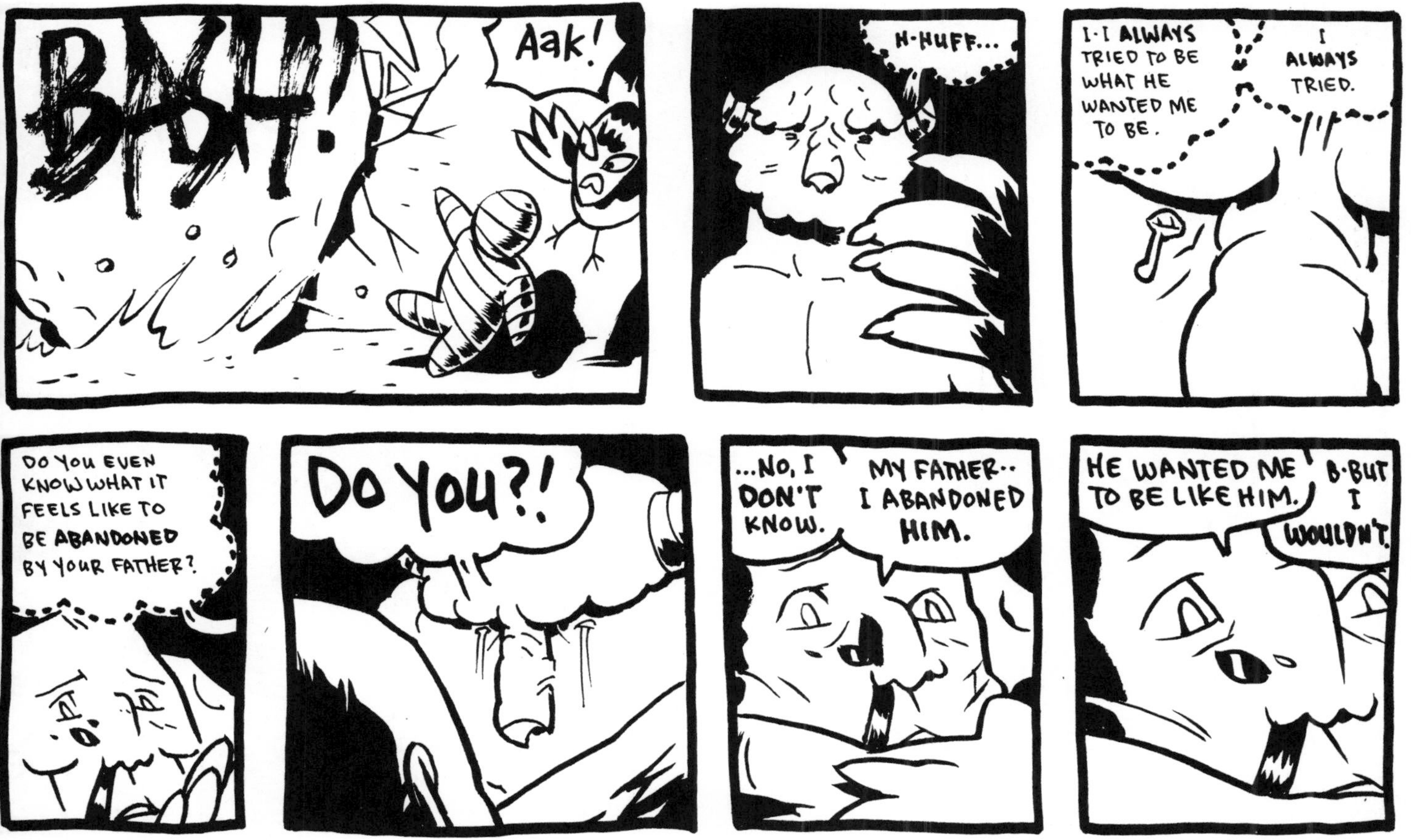
BASH!
Aak!
H-HUFF...
I-I ALWAYS TRIED TO BE WHAT HE WANTED ME TO BE.
I ALWAYS TRIED.
DO YOU EVEN KNOW WHAT IT FEELS LIKE TO BE ABANDONED BY YOUR FATHER?
DO YOU?!
...NO, I DON'T KNOW.
MY FATHER.. I ABANDONED HIM.
HE WANTED ME TO BE LIKE HIM.
B-BUT I WOULDN'T.

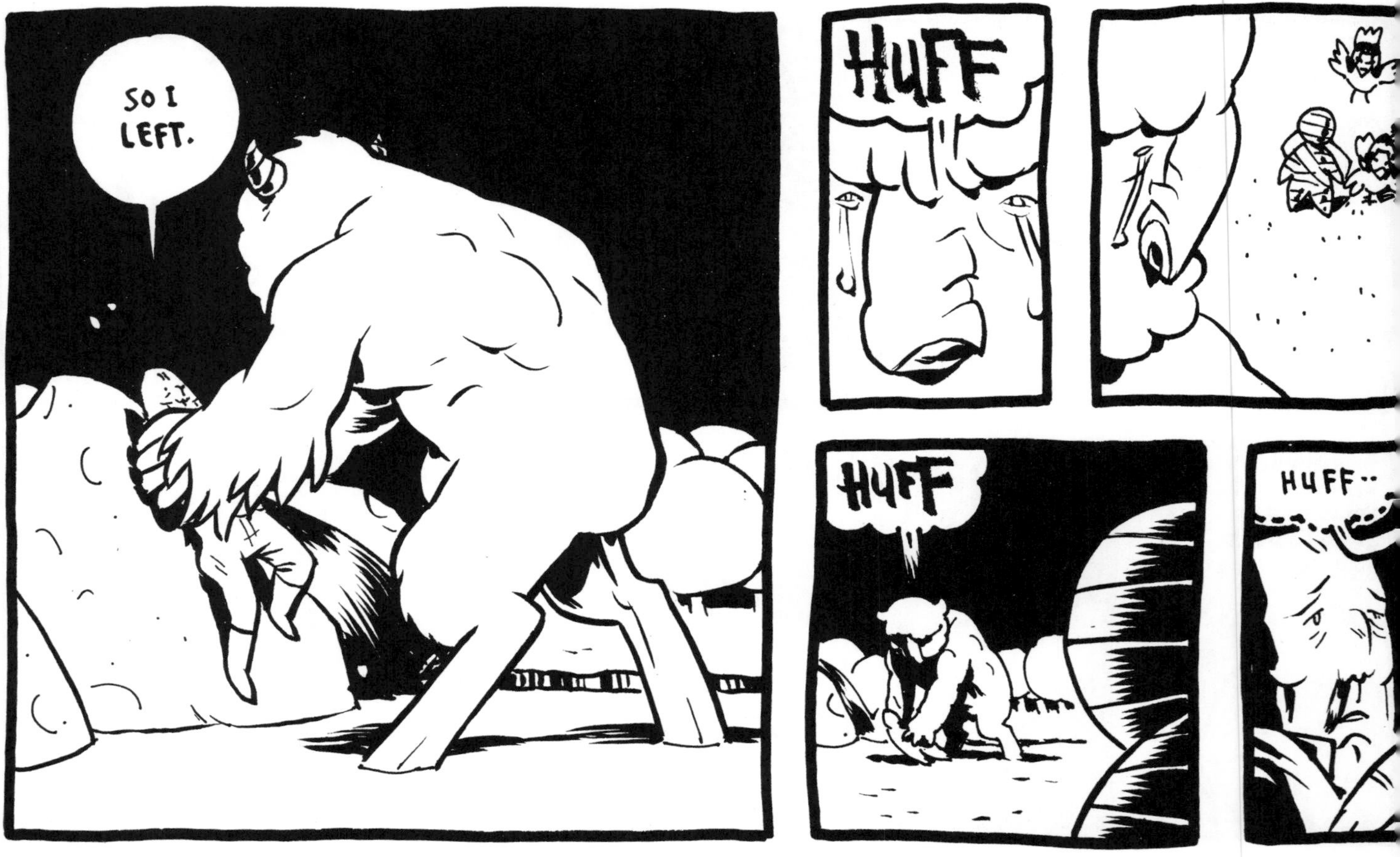
SO I LEFT.
HUFF
HUFF
HUFF..

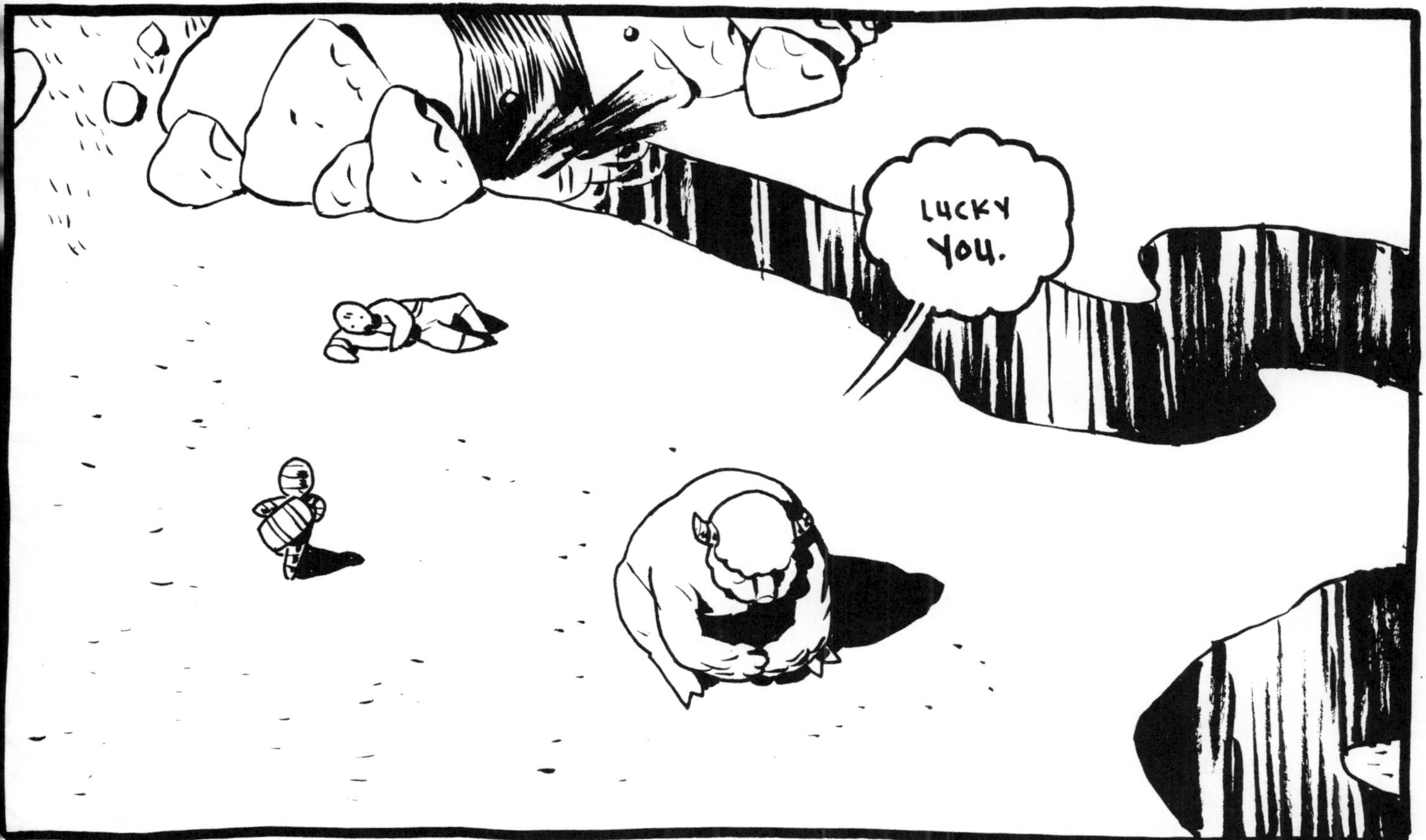
LUCKY YOU.

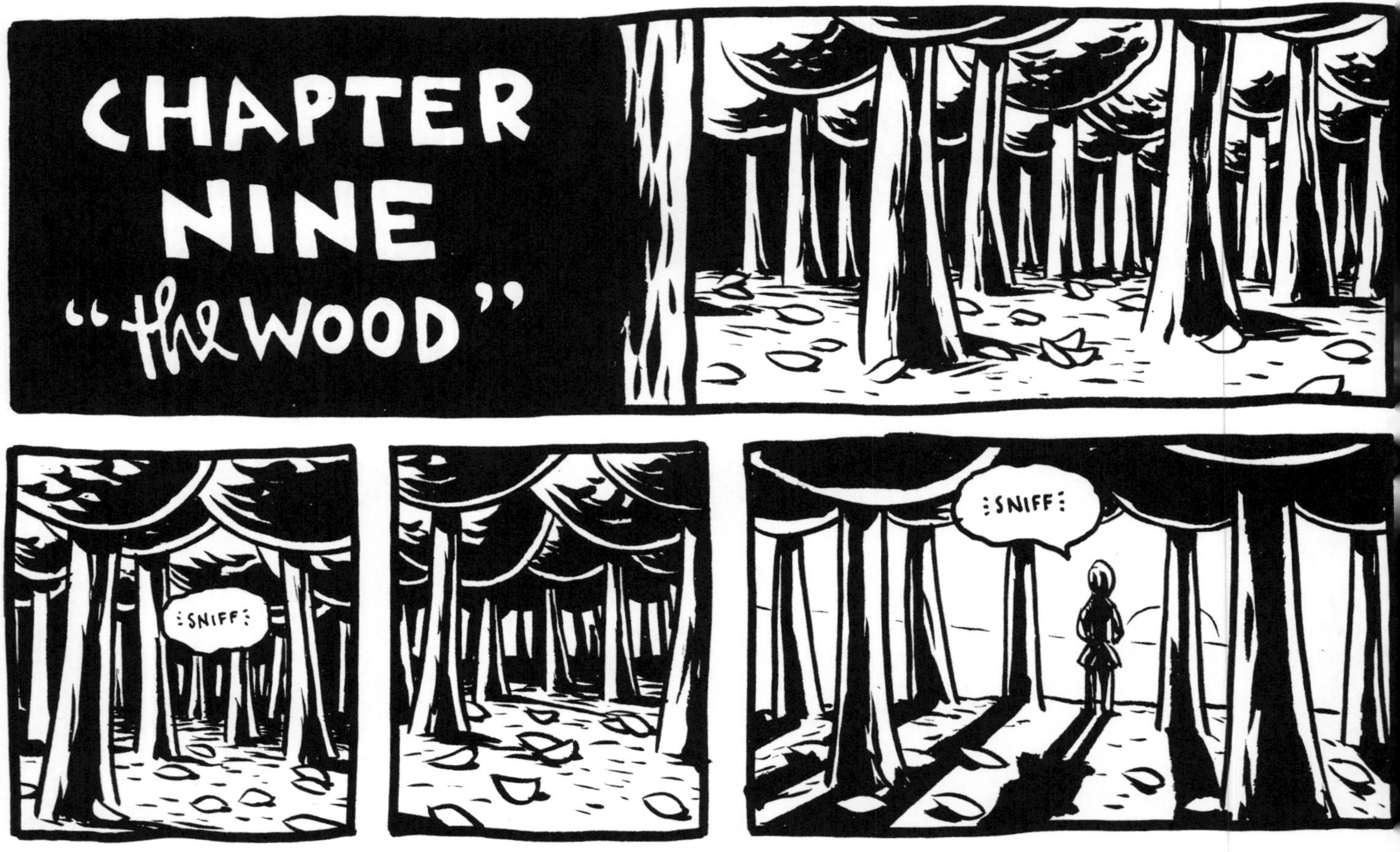
CHAPTER NINE "the WOOD"
SNIFF
SNIFF

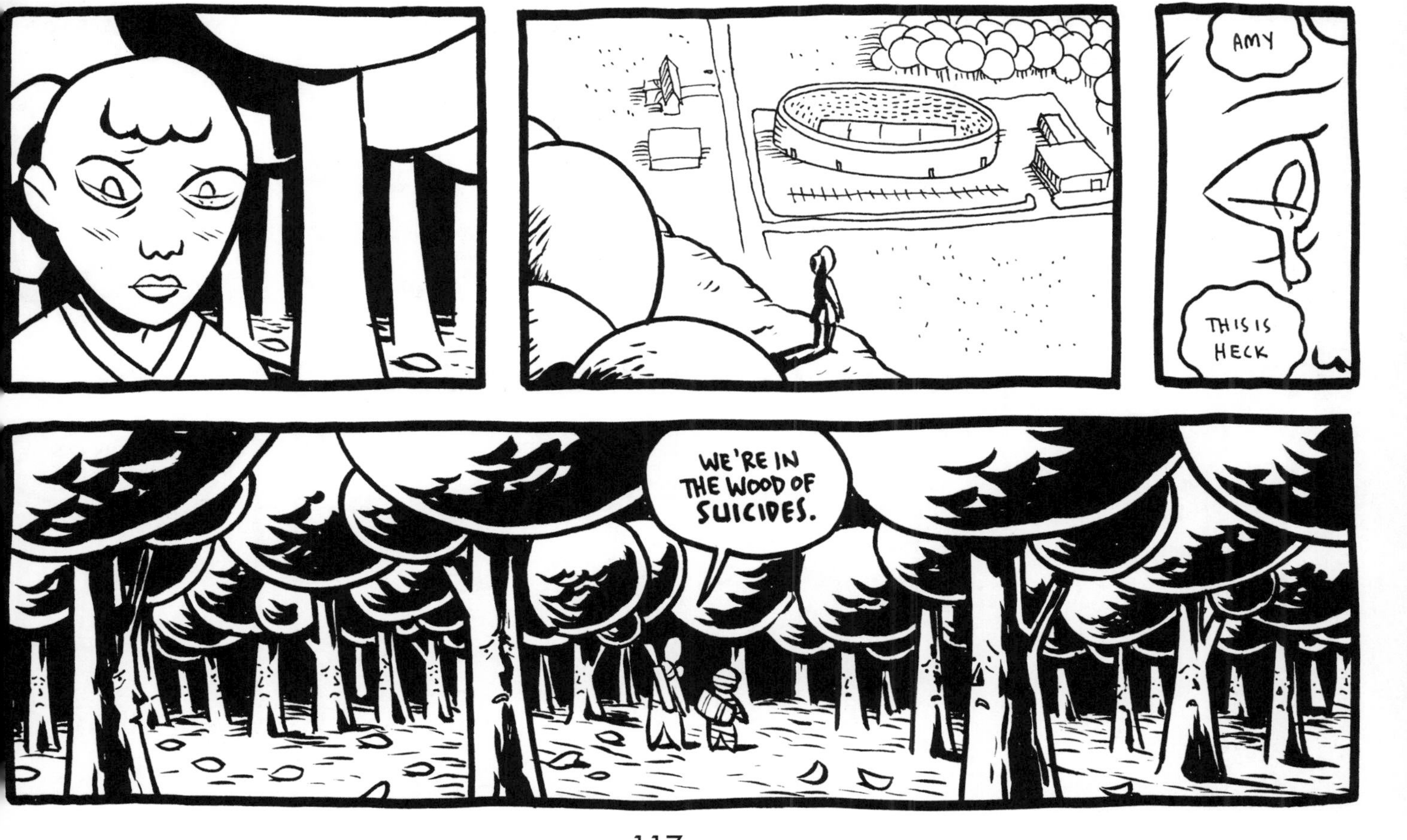
AMY
THIS IS HECK
WE'RE IN THE WOOD OF SUICIDES.

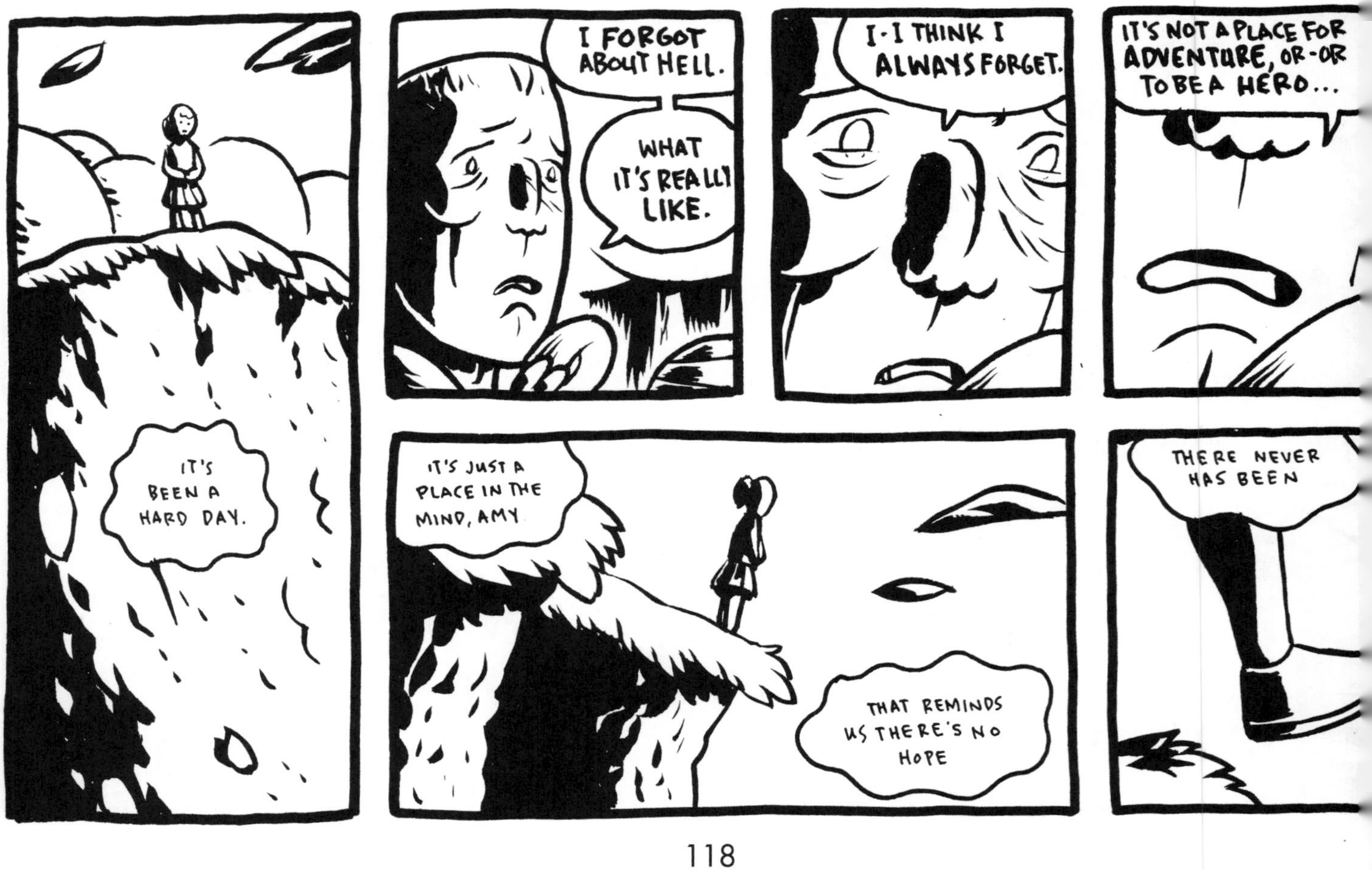
IT'S BEEN A HARD DAY.
I FORGOT ABOUT HELL.
WHAT IT'S REALLY LIKE.
I-I THINK I ALWAYS FORGET.
IT'S NOT A PLACE FOR ADVENTURE, OR-OR TO BE A HERO...
IT'S JUST A PLACE IN THE MIND, AMY
THAT REMINDS US THERE'S NO HOPE
THERE NEVER HAS BEEN

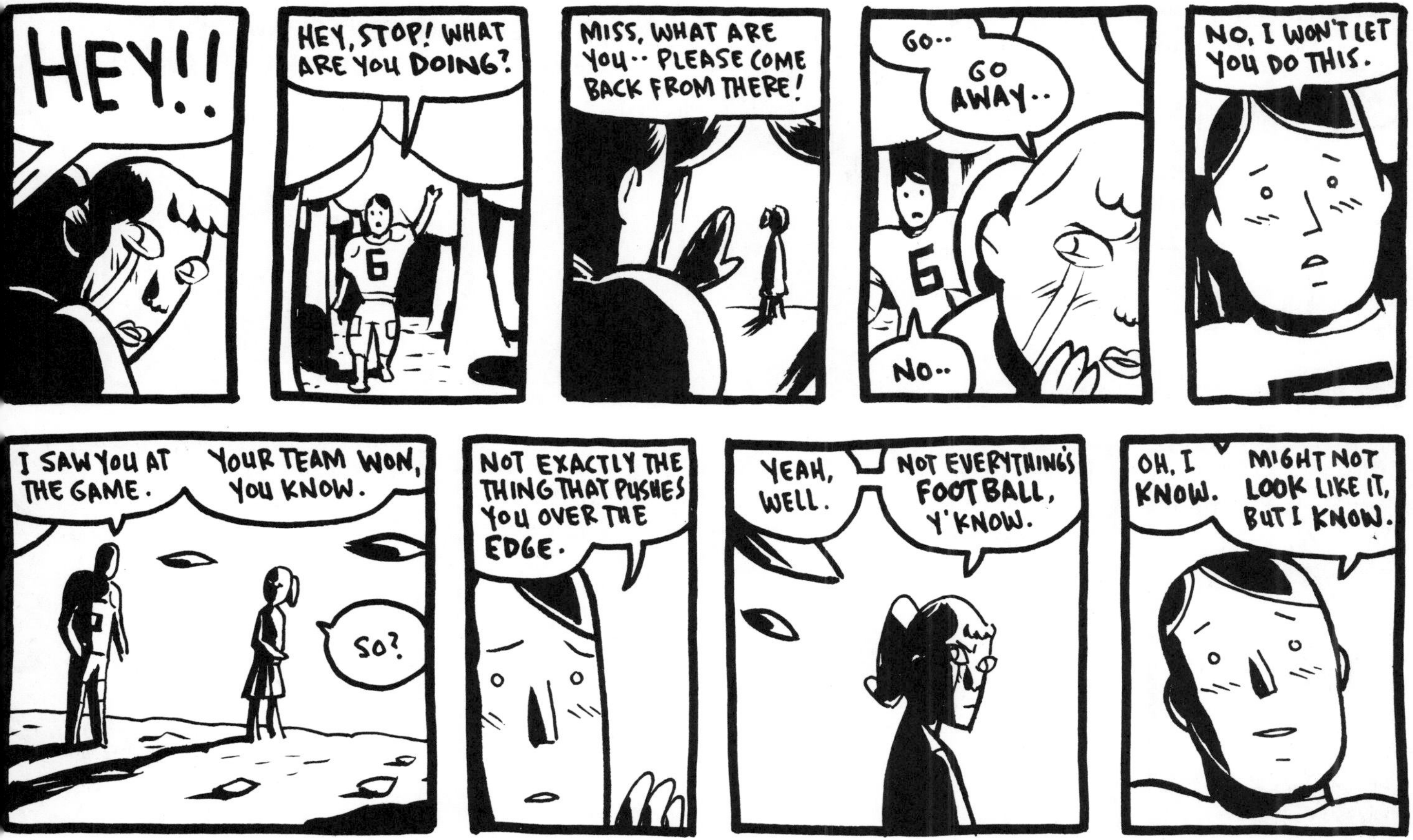
HEY!!
HEY, STOP! WHAT ARE YOU DOING?
MISS, WHAT ARE YOU.. PLEASE COME BACK FROM THERE!
GO..
GO AWAY..
NO..
NO, I WON'T LET YOU DO THIS.
I SAW YOU AT THE GAME.
YOUR TEAM WON, YOU KNOW.
SO?
NOT EXACTLY THE THING THAT PUSHES YOU OVER THE EDGE.
YEAH, WELL.
NOT EVERYTHING'S FOOTBALL, Y'KNOW.
OH, I KNOW.
MIGHT NOT LOOK LIKE IT, BUT I KNOW.

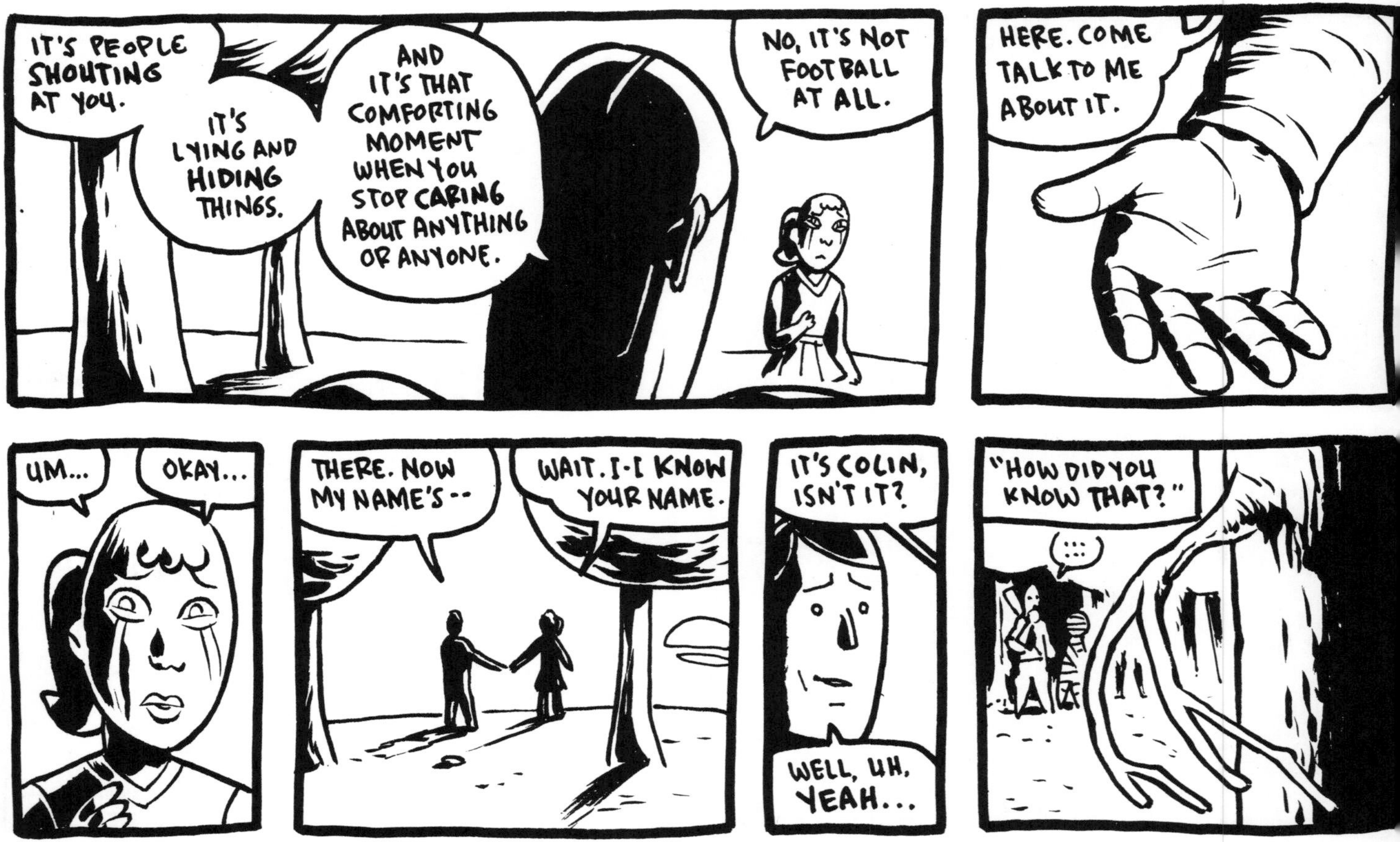
IT'S PEOPLE SHOUTING AT YOU.
IT'S LYING AND HIDING THINGS.
AND IT'S THAT COMFORTING MOMENT WHEN YOU STOP CARING ABOUT ANYTHING OR ANYONE.
NO, IT'S NOT FOOTBALL AT ALL.
HERE. COME TALK TO ME ABOUT IT.
UM...
OKAY...
THERE. NOW MY NAME'S --
WAIT. I-I KNOW YOUR NAME.
IT'S COLIN, ISN'T IT?
WELL, UH, YEAH...
"HOW DID YOU KNOW THAT?"
...

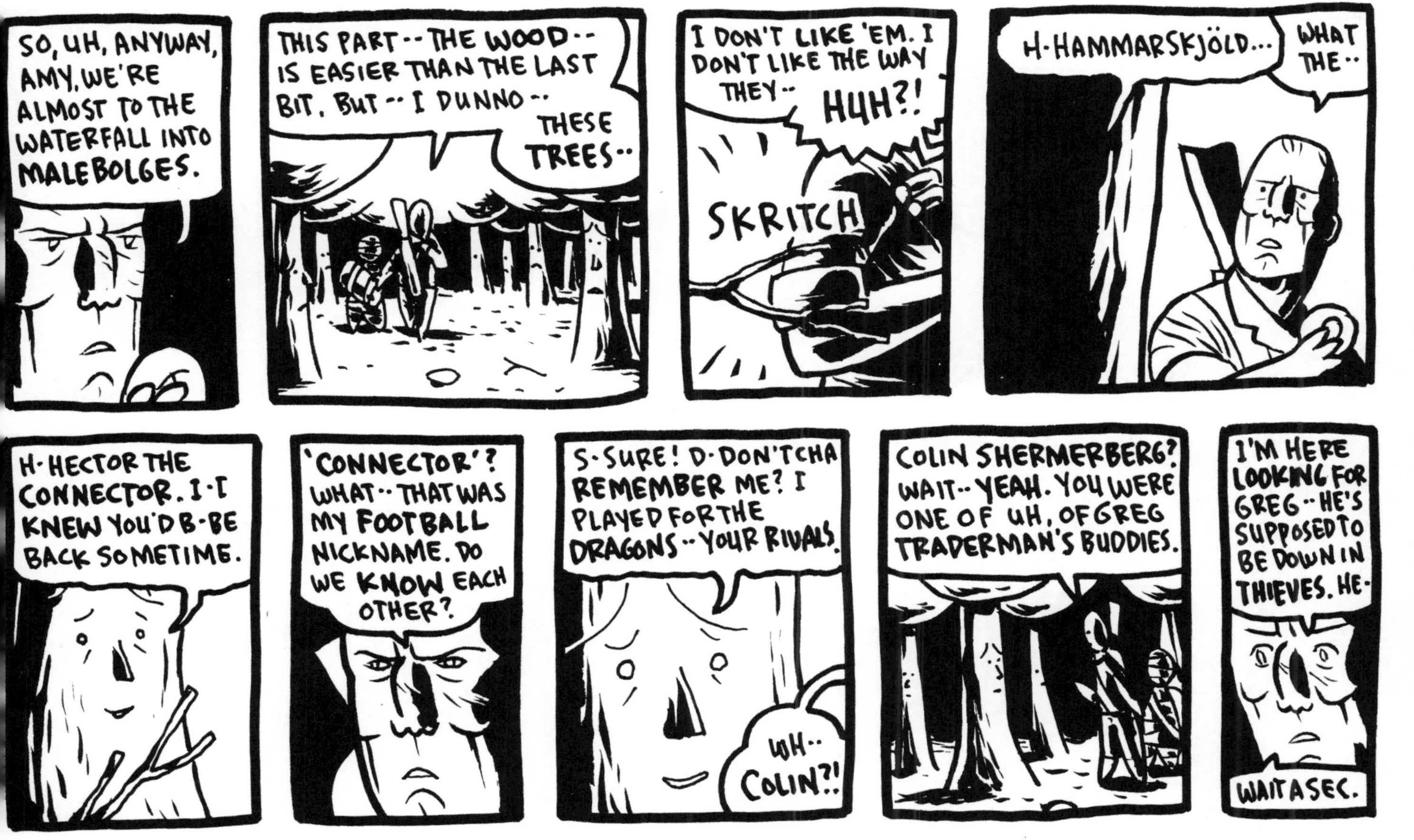

SO, UH, ANYWAY, AMY, WE'RE ALMOST TO THE WATERFALL INTO MALEBOLGES.
THIS PART -- THE WOOD -- IS EASIER THAN THE LAST BIT. BUT -- I DUNNO --
THESE TREES --
I DON'T LIKE 'EM. I DON'T LIKE THE WAY THEY --
HUH?!
SKRITCH
H-HAMMARSKJÖLD...
WHAT THE --
H-HECTOR THE CONNECTOR. I-I KNEW YOU'D B-BE BACK SOMETIME.
'CONNECTOR'? WHAT -- THAT WAS MY FOOTBALL NICKNAME. DO WE KNOW EACH OTHER?
S-SURE! D-DON'TCHA REMEMBER ME? I PLAYED FOR THE DRAGONS -- YOUR RIVALS.
WH -- COLIN?!
COLIN SHERMERBERG? WAIT -- YEAH. YOU WERE ONE OF UH, OF GREG TRADERMAN'S BUDDIES.
I'M HERE LOOKING FOR GREG -- HE'S SUPPOSED TO BE DOWN IN THIEVES. HE-
WAIT A SEC.

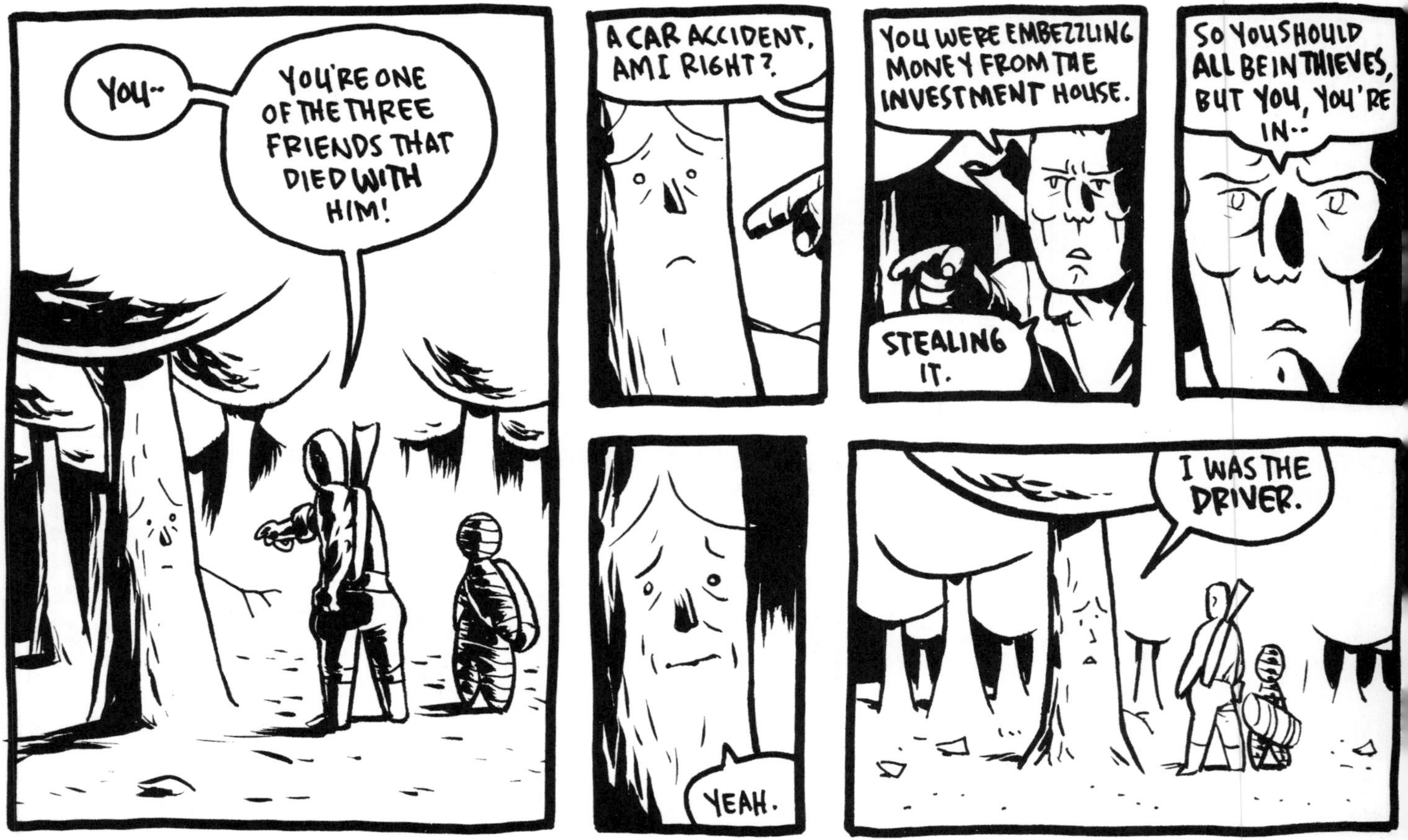
You--
You're one of the three friends that died with him!
A car accident, am I right?
You were embezzling money from the investment house.
Stealing it.
So you should all be in thieves, but you, you're in--
Yeah.
I was the driver.

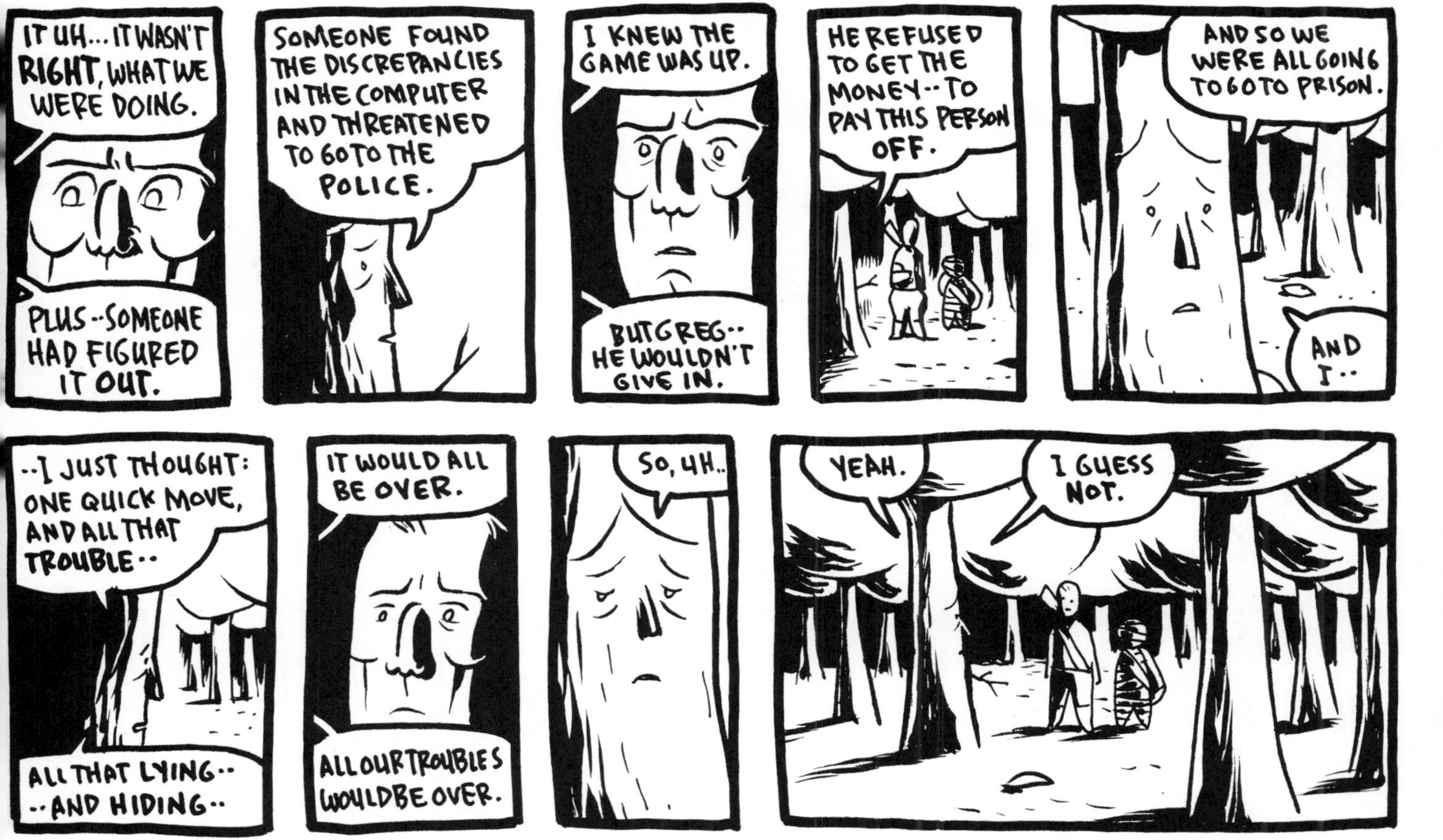
IT UH... IT WASN'T RIGHT, WHAT WE WERE DOING.
PLUS--SOMEONE HAD FIGURED IT OUT.
SOMEONE FOUND THE DISCREPANCIES IN THE COMPUTER AND THREATENED TO GO TO THE POLICE.
I KNEW THE GAME WAS UP.
BUT GREG-- HE WOULDN'T GIVE IN.
HE REFUSED TO GET THE MONEY--TO PAY THIS PERSON OFF.
AND SO WE WERE ALL GOING TO GO TO PRISON.
AND I--
--I JUST THOUGHT: ONE QUICK MOVE, AND ALL THAT TROUBLE--
ALL THAT LYING--
--AND HIDING--
IT WOULD ALL BE OVER.
ALL OUR TROUBLES WOULD BE OVER.
SO, UH..
YEAH.
I GUESS NOT.

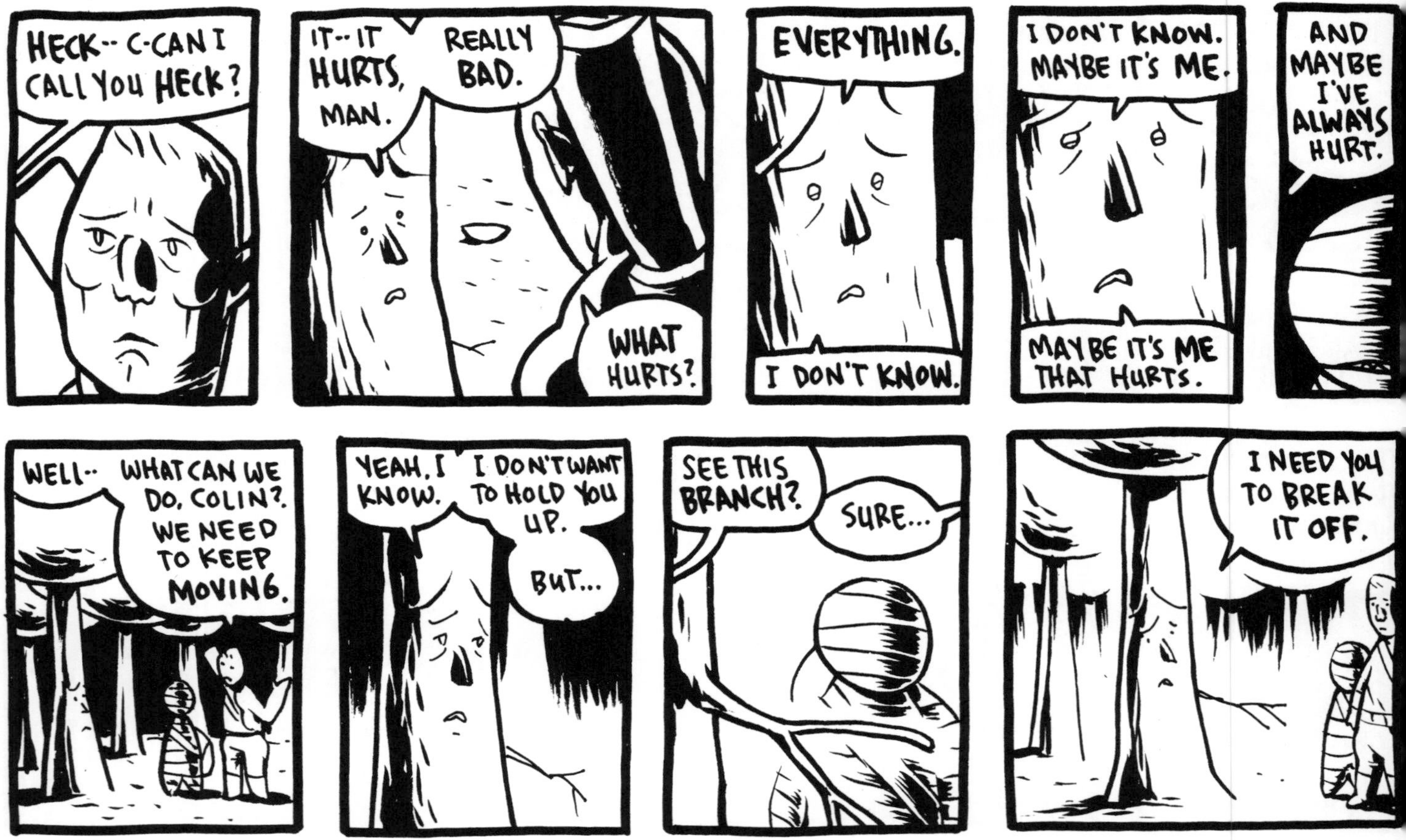
HECK-- C-CAN I CALL YOU HECK?
IT-- IT HURTS, MAN.
REALLY BAD.
WHAT HURTS?
EVERYTHING.
I DON'T KNOW.
I DON'T KNOW. MAYBE IT'S ME.
MAYBE IT'S ME THAT HURTS.
AND MAYBE I'VE ALWAYS HURT.
WELL--
WHAT CAN WE DO, COLIN?. WE NEED TO KEEP MOVING.
YEAH, I KNOW.
I DON'T WANT TO HOLD YOU UP.
BUT...
SEE THIS BRANCH?
SURE...
I NEED YOU TO BREAK IT OFF.

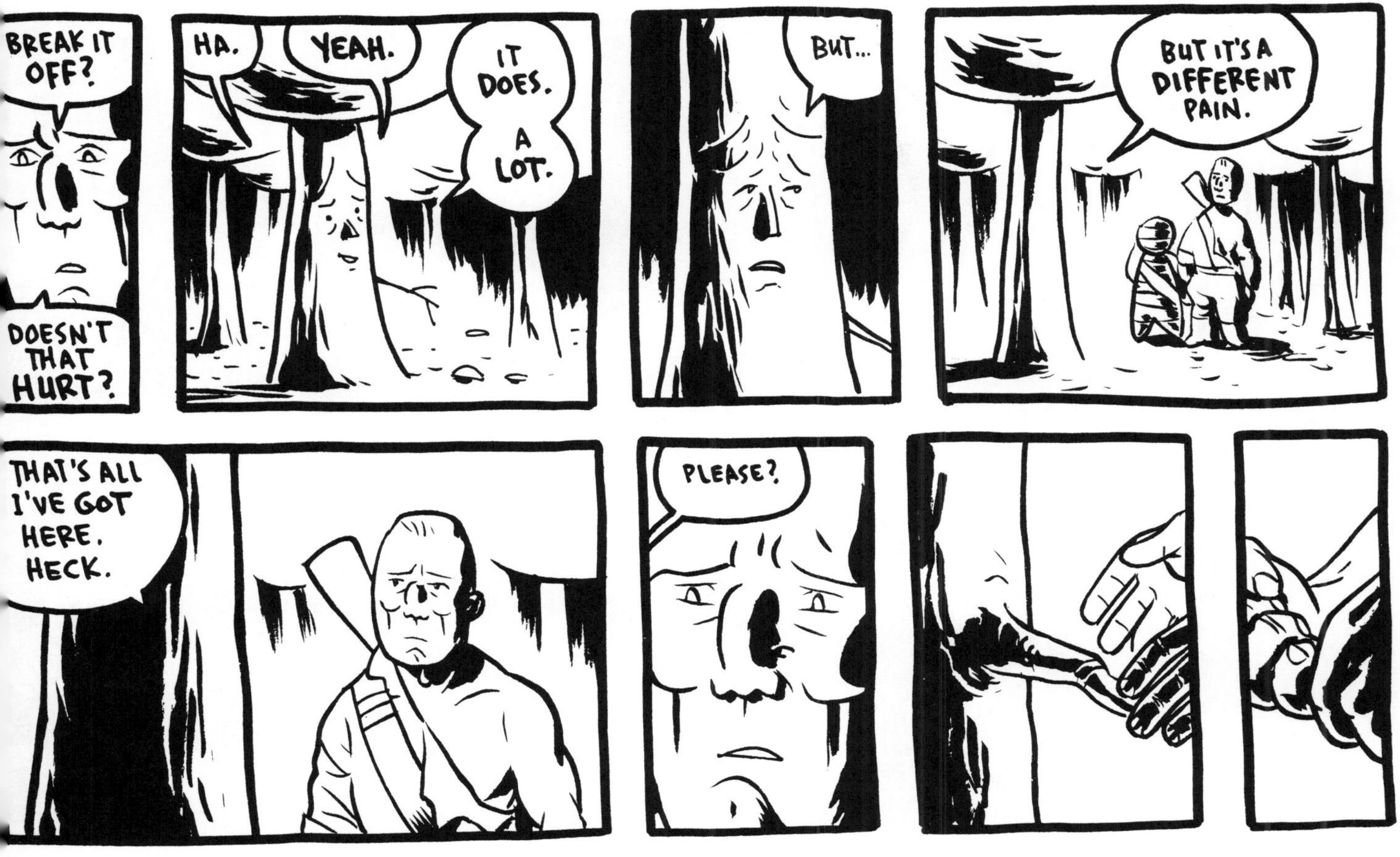
BREAK IT OFF?
DOESN'T THAT HURT?
HA.
YEAH.
IT DOES.
A LOT.
BUT...
BUT IT'S A DIFFERENT PAIN.
THAT'S ALL I'VE GOT HERE. HECK.
PLEASE?

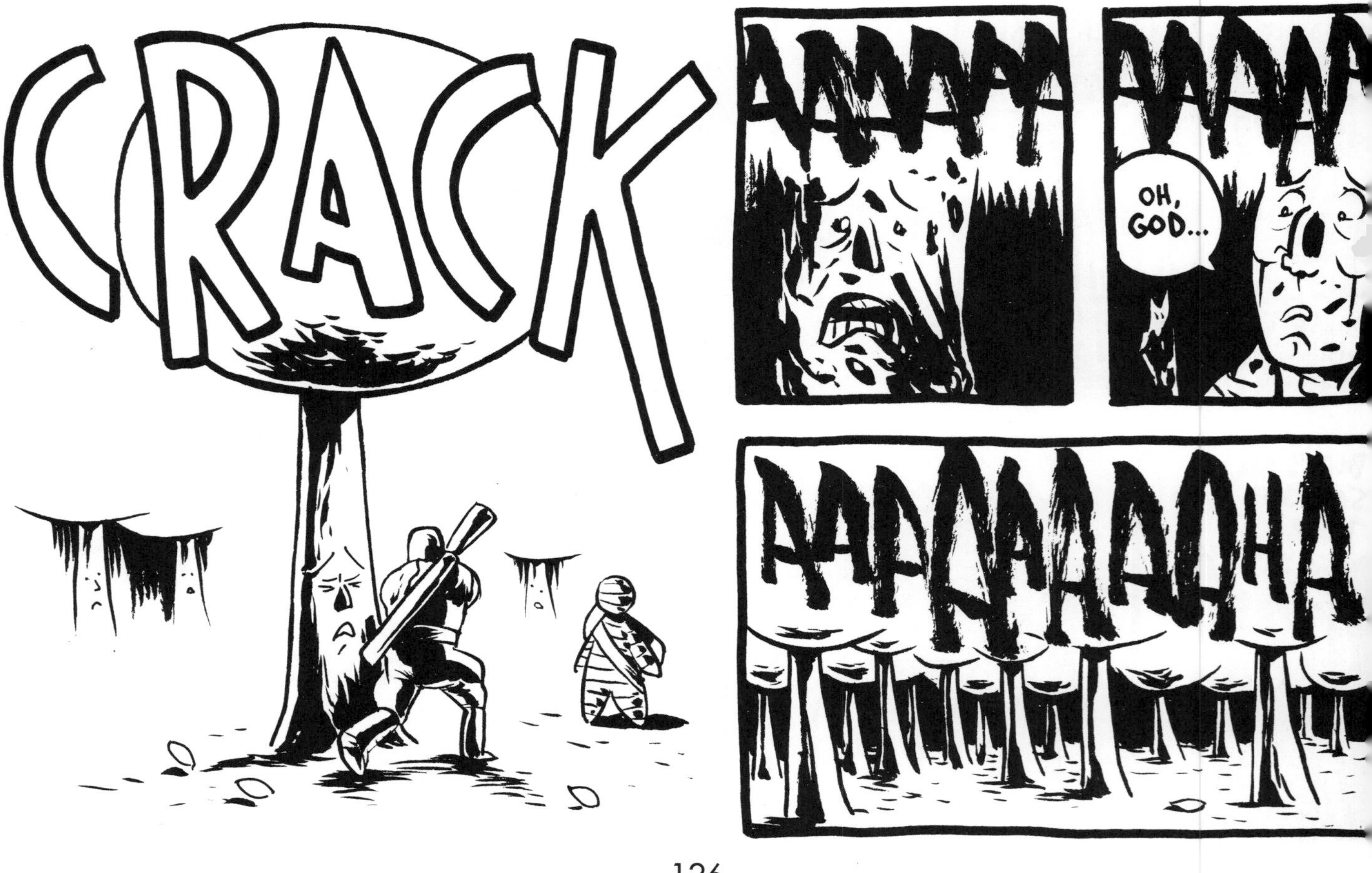
CRACK
OH, GOD...

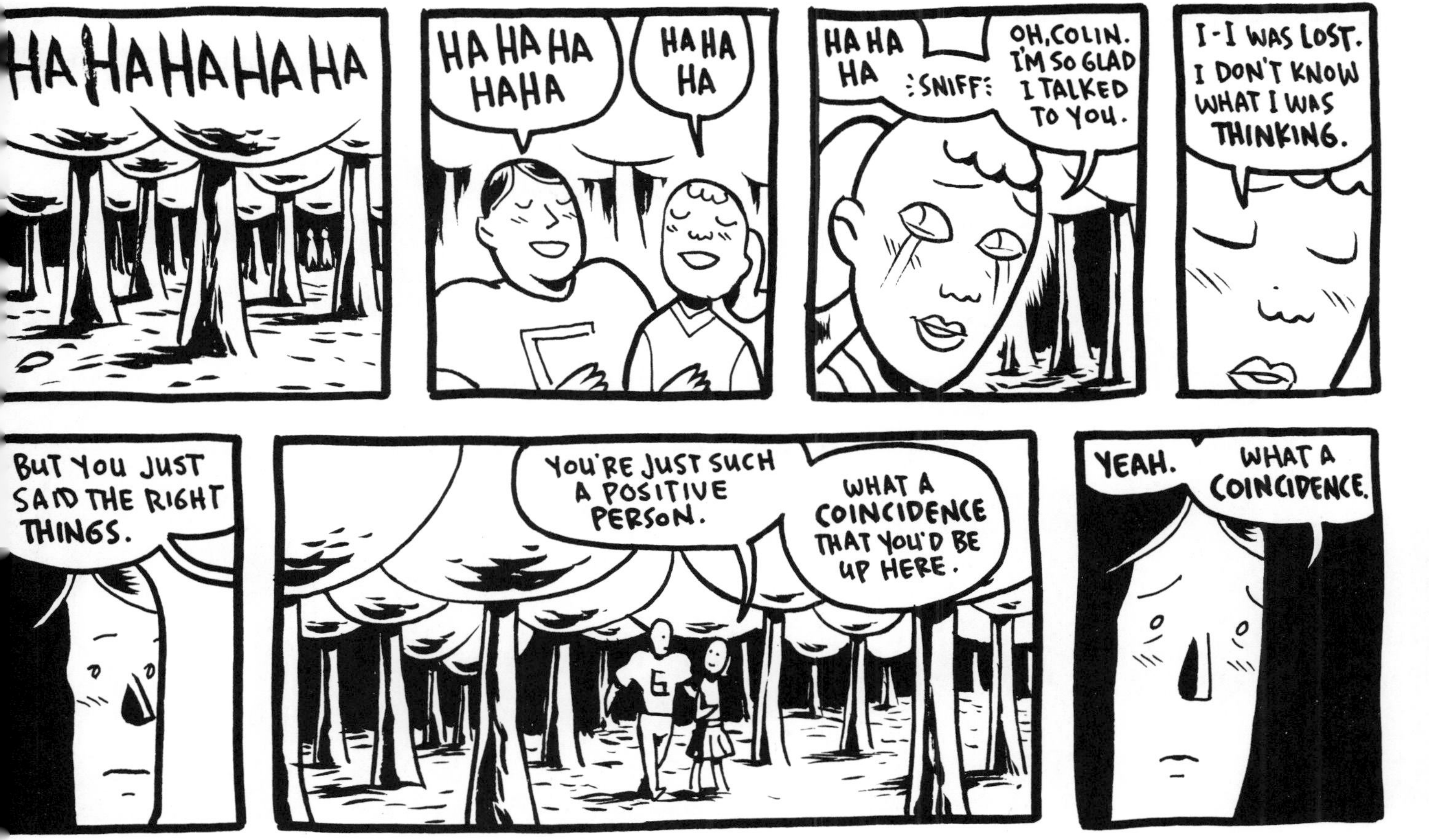
HA HA HA HA HA HA HA
HA HA HA HA HA
HA HA HA
HA HA HA
:SNIFF:
OH, COLIN. I'M SO GLAD I TALKED TO YOU.
I-I WAS LOST. I DON'T KNOW WHAT I WAS THINKING.
BUT YOU JUST SAID THE RIGHT THINGS.
YOU'RE JUST SUCH A POSITIVE PERSON.
WHAT A COINCIDENCE THAT YOU'D BE UP HERE.
YEAH.
WHAT A COINCIDENCE.

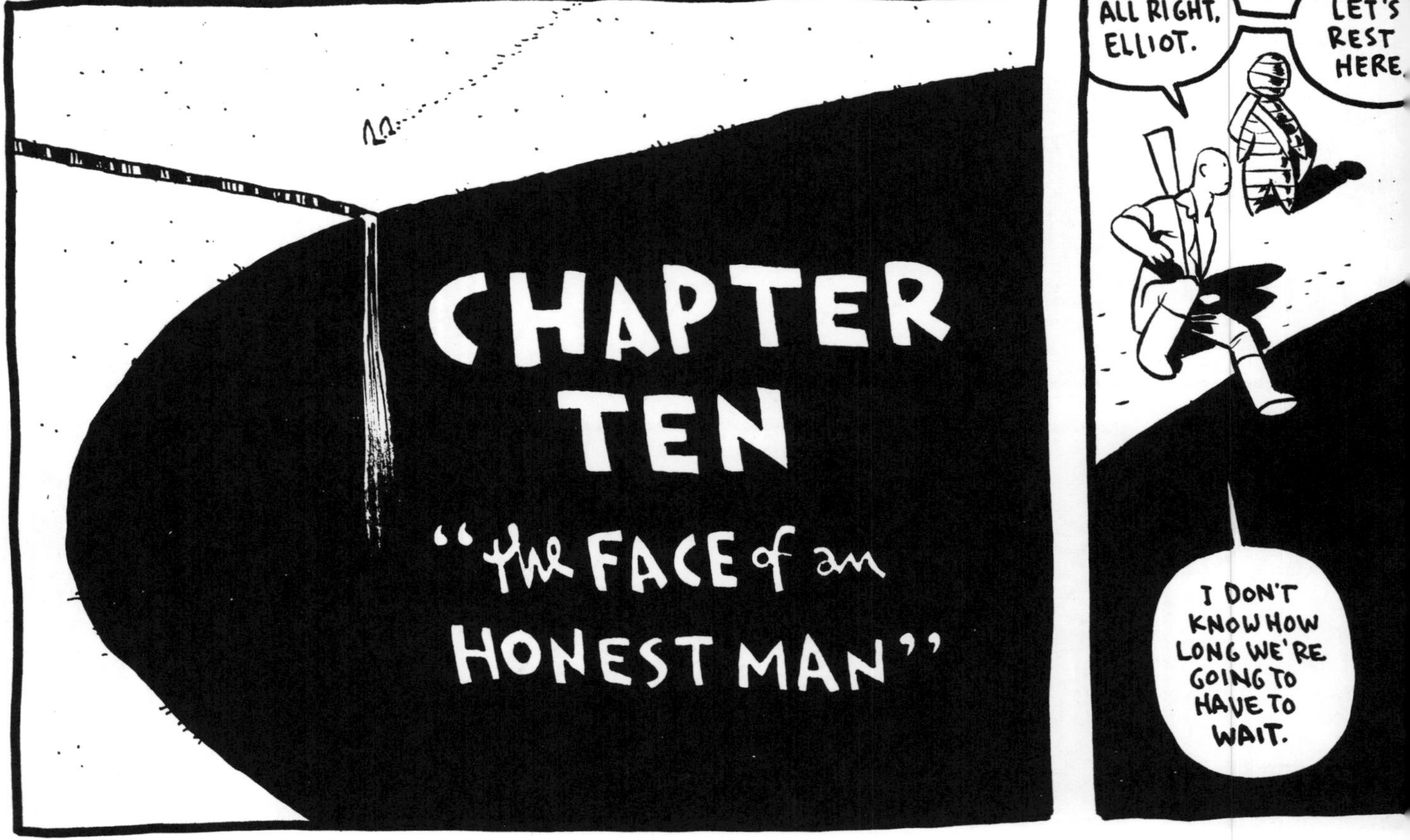
CHAPTER TEN
"the FACE of an HONEST MAN"
ALL RIGHT, ELLIOT.
LET'S REST HERE.
I DON'T KNOW HOW LONG WE'RE GOING TO HAVE TO WAIT.

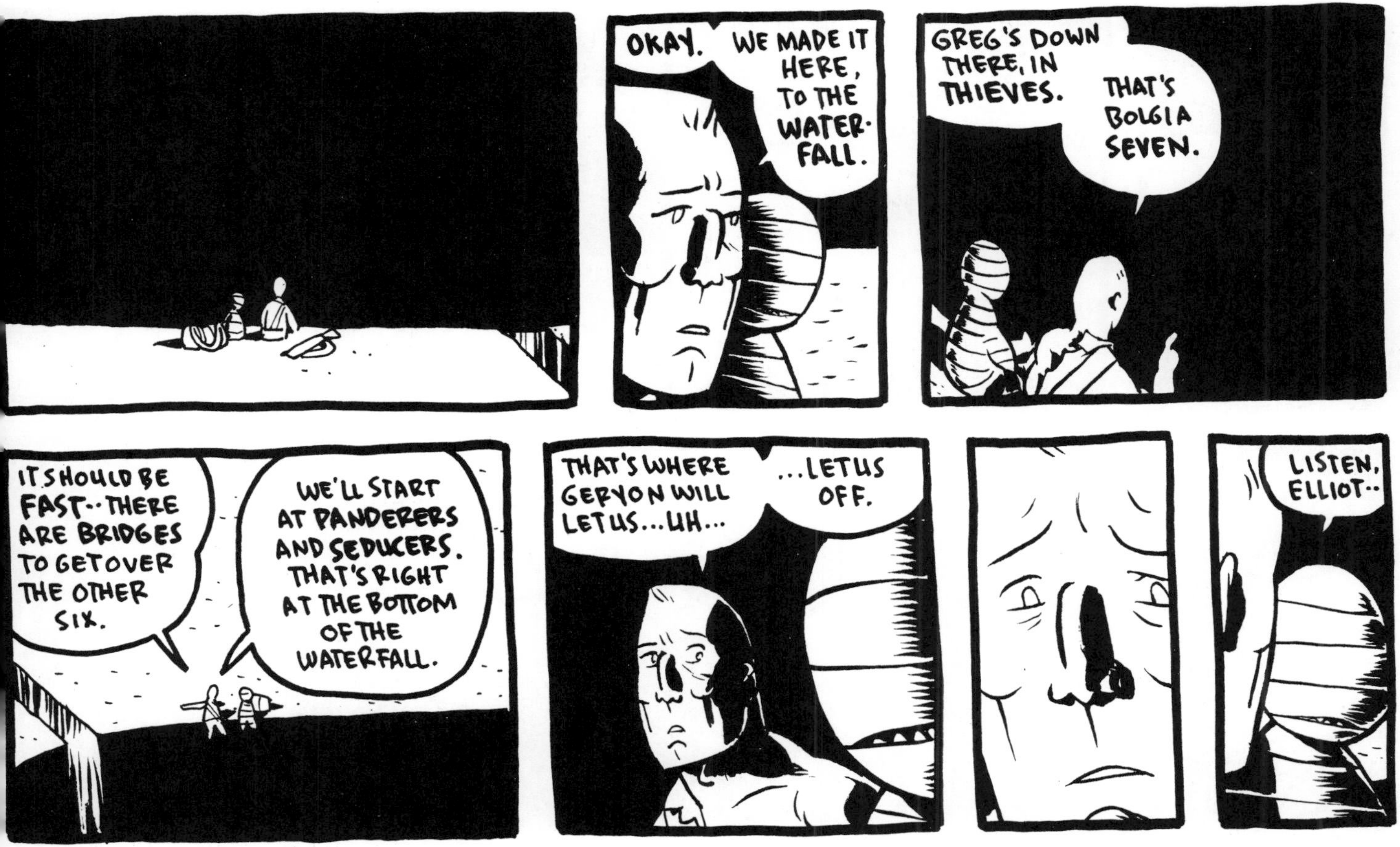
OKAY.
WE MADE IT HERE, TO THE WATER-FALL.
GREG'S DOWN THERE, IN THIEVES.
THAT'S BOLGIA SEVEN.
IT SHOULD BE FAST-- THERE ARE BRIDGES TO GET OVER THE OTHER SIX.
WE'LL START AT PANDERERS AND SEDUCERS. THAT'S RIGHT AT THE BOTTOM OF THE WATERFALL.
THAT'S WHERE GERYON WILL LET US... UH...
...LET US OFF.
LISTEN, ELLIOT--

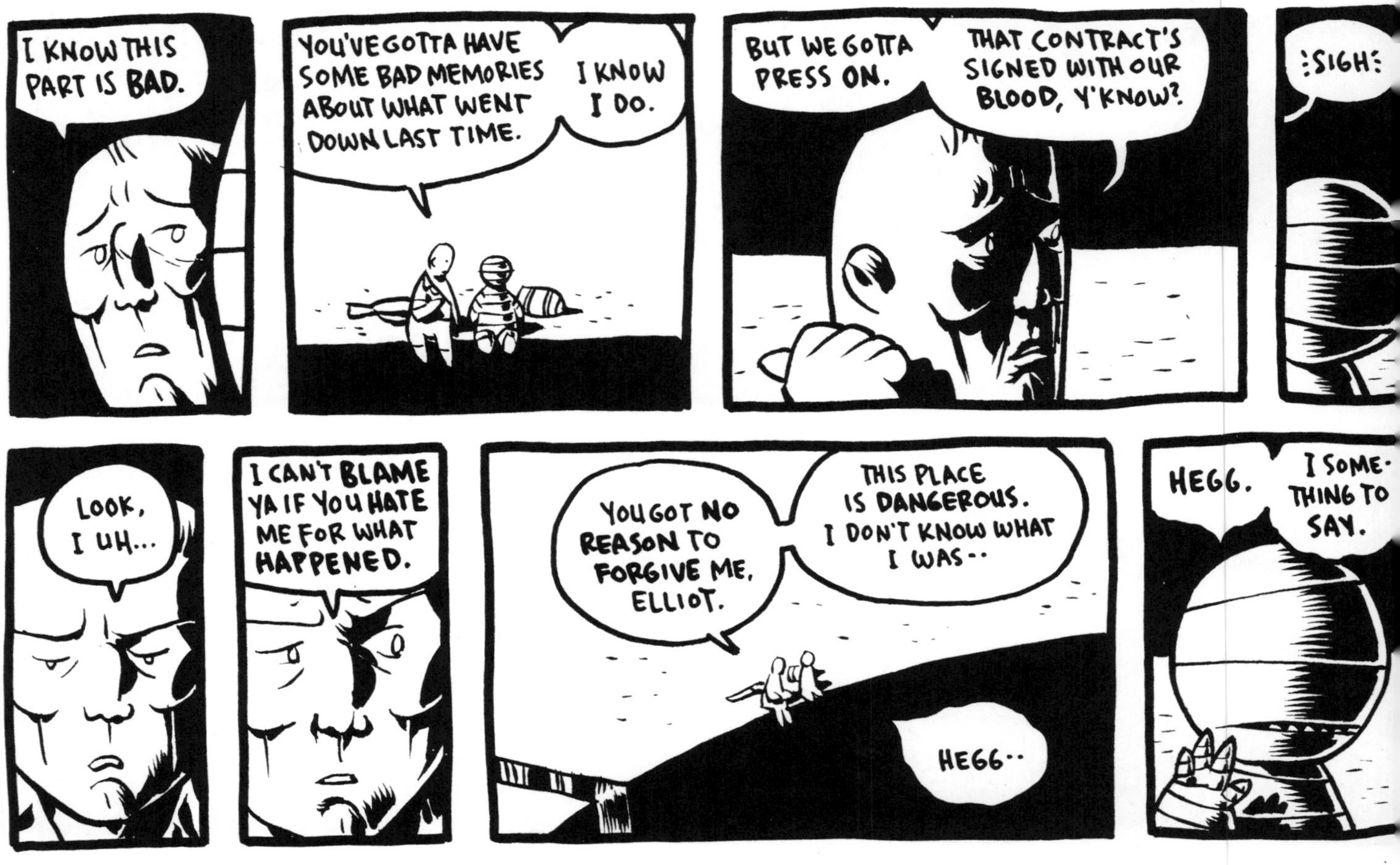

I KNOW THIS PART IS BAD.
YOU'VE GOTTA HAVE SOME BAD MEMORIES ABOUT WHAT WENT DOWN LAST TIME.
I KNOW I DO.
BUT WE GOTTA PRESS ON.
THAT CONTRACT'S SIGNED WITH OUR BLOOD, Y'KNOW?
SIGH
LOOK, I UH...
I CAN'T BLAME YA IF YOU HATE ME FOR WHAT HAPPENED.
YOU GOT NO REASON TO FORGIVE ME, ELLIOT.
THIS PLACE IS DANGEROUS. I DON'T KNOW WHAT I WAS--
HEGG--
HEGG.
I SOME-THING TO SAY.

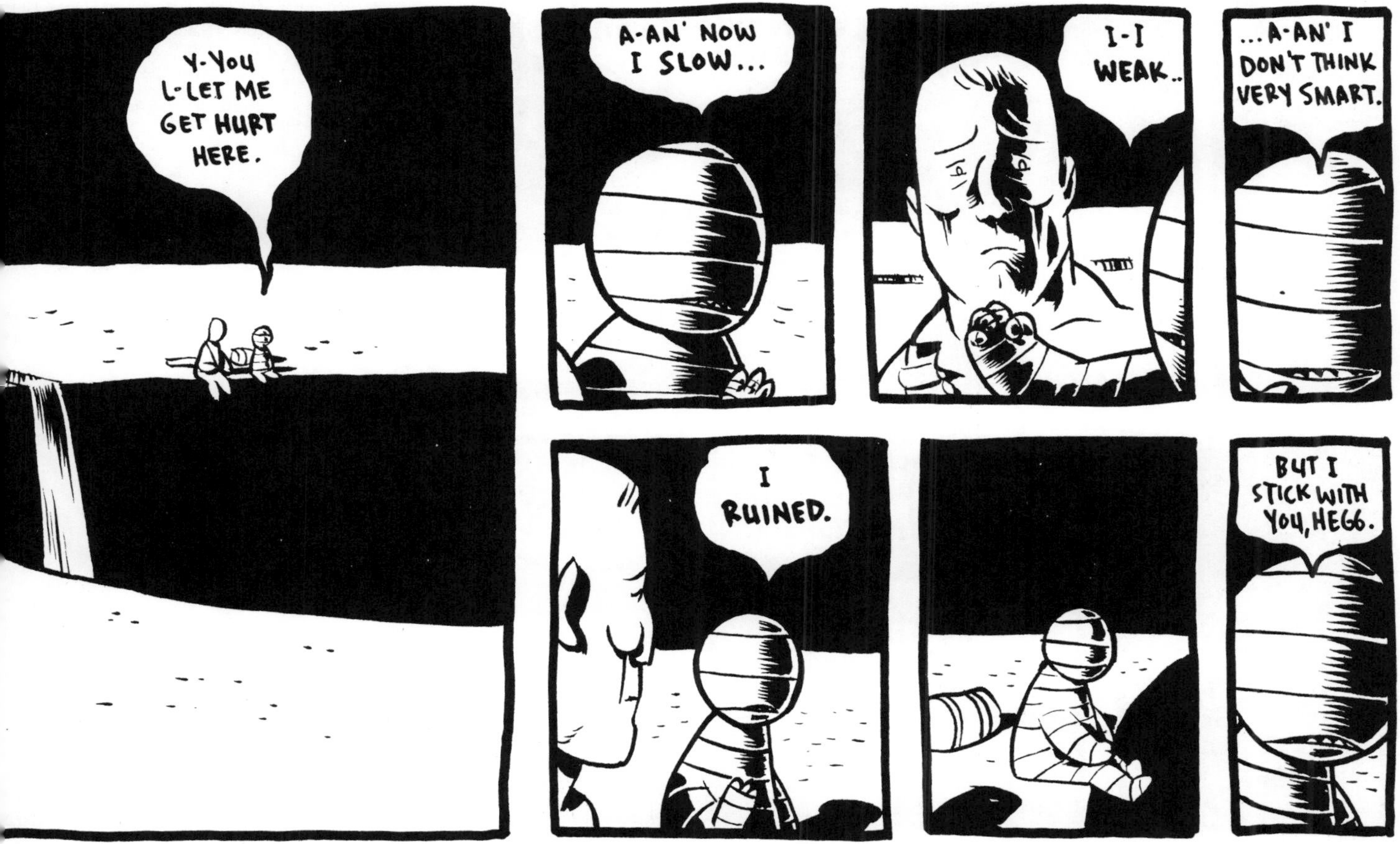
Y-YOU L-LET ME GET HURT HERE.
A-AN' NOW I SLOW...
I-I WEAK..
...A-AN' I DON'T THINK VERY SMART.
I RUINED.
BUT I STICK WITH YOU, HEGG.

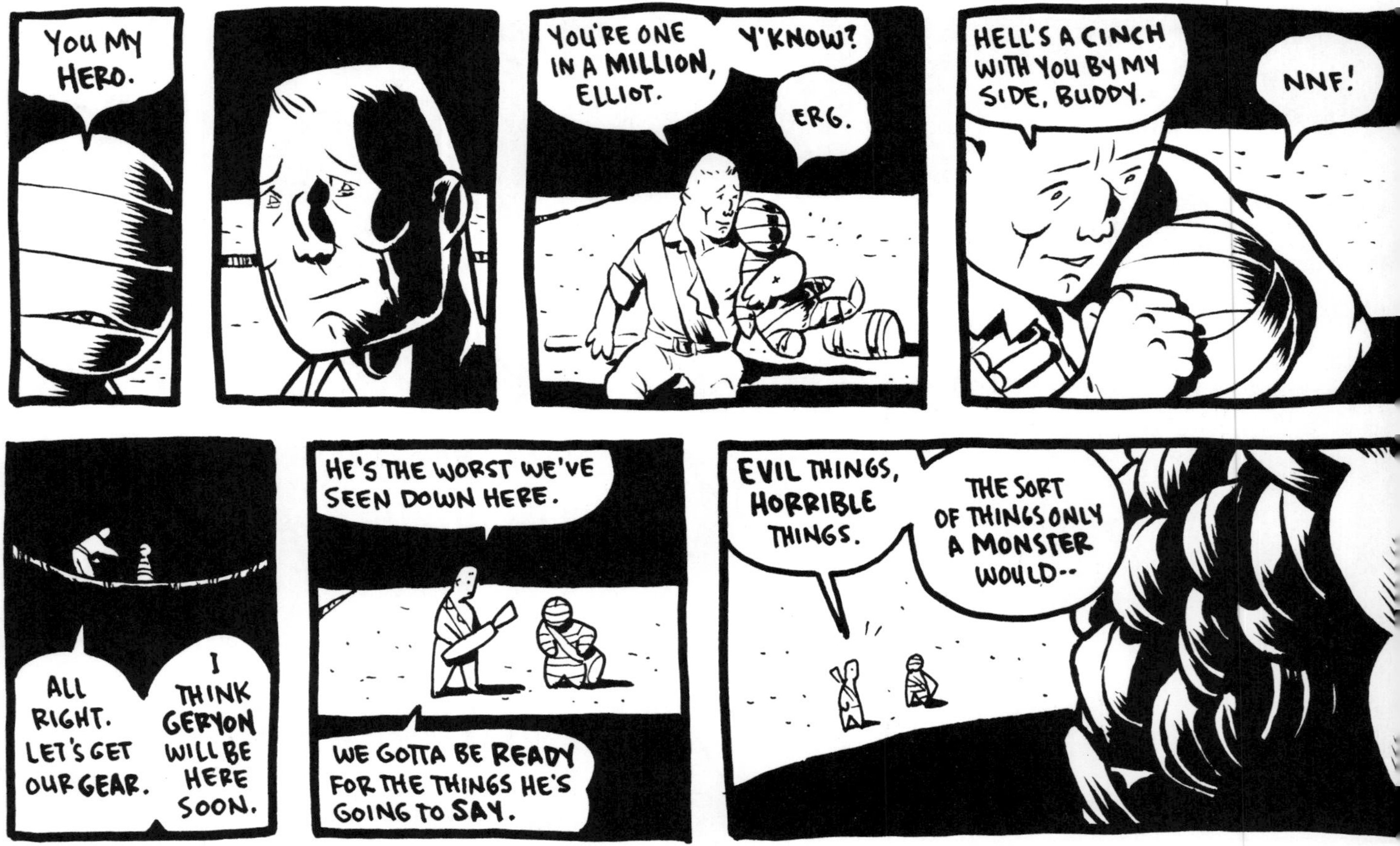

YOU MY HERO.
YOU'RE ONE IN A MILLION, ELLIOT.
Y'KNOW?
ERG.
HELL'S A CINCH WITH YOU BY MY SIDE, BUDDY.
NNF!
ALL RIGHT. LET'S GET OUR GEAR.
I THINK GERYON WILL BE HERE SOON.
HE'S THE WORST WE'VE SEEN DOWN HERE.
WE GOTTA BE READY FOR THE THINGS HE'S GOING TO SAY.
EVIL THINGS, HORRIBLE THINGS.
THE SORT OF THINGS ONLY A MONSTER WOULD--

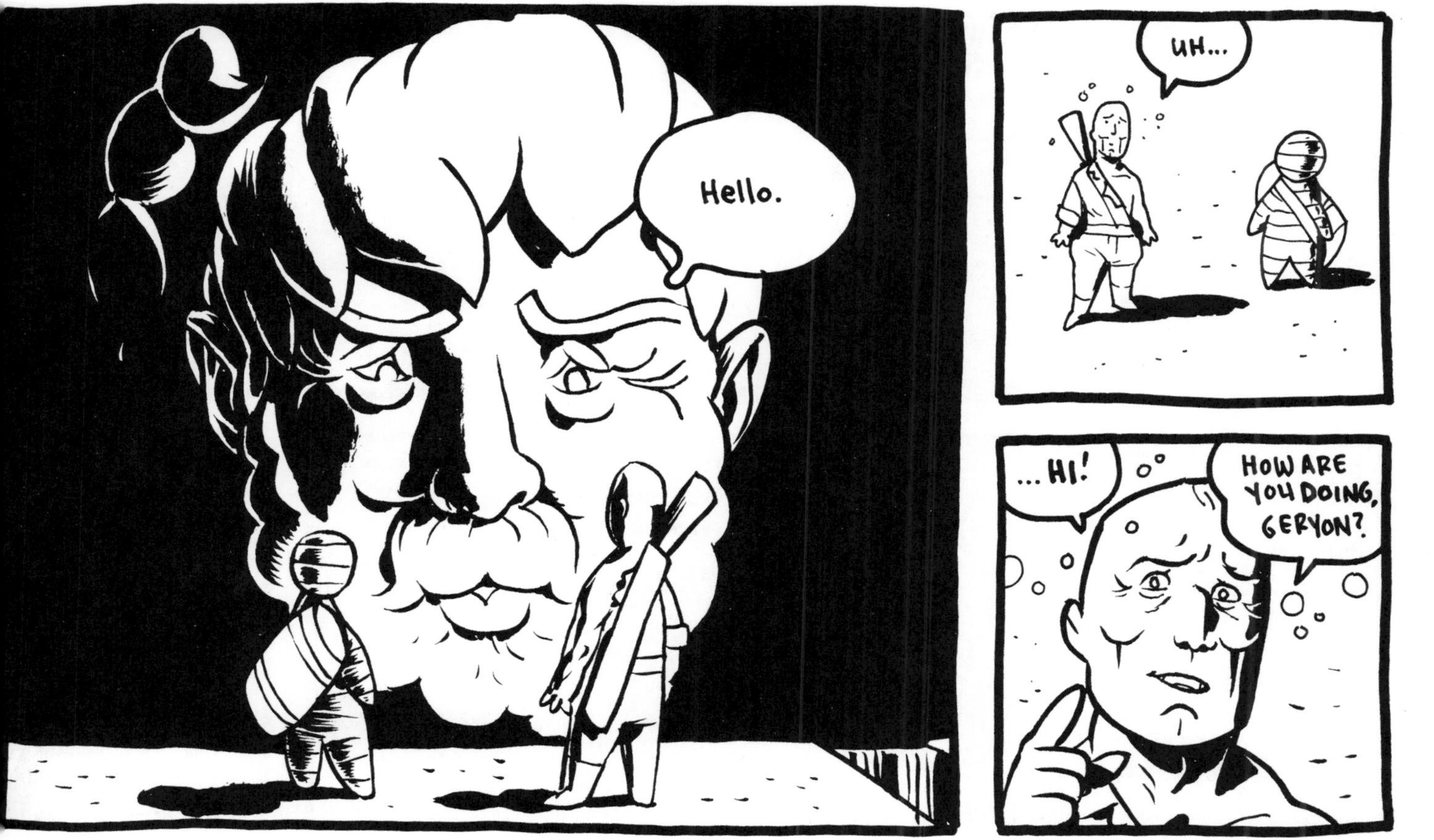
Hello.
UH...
...HI!
HOW ARE YOU DOING, GERYON?

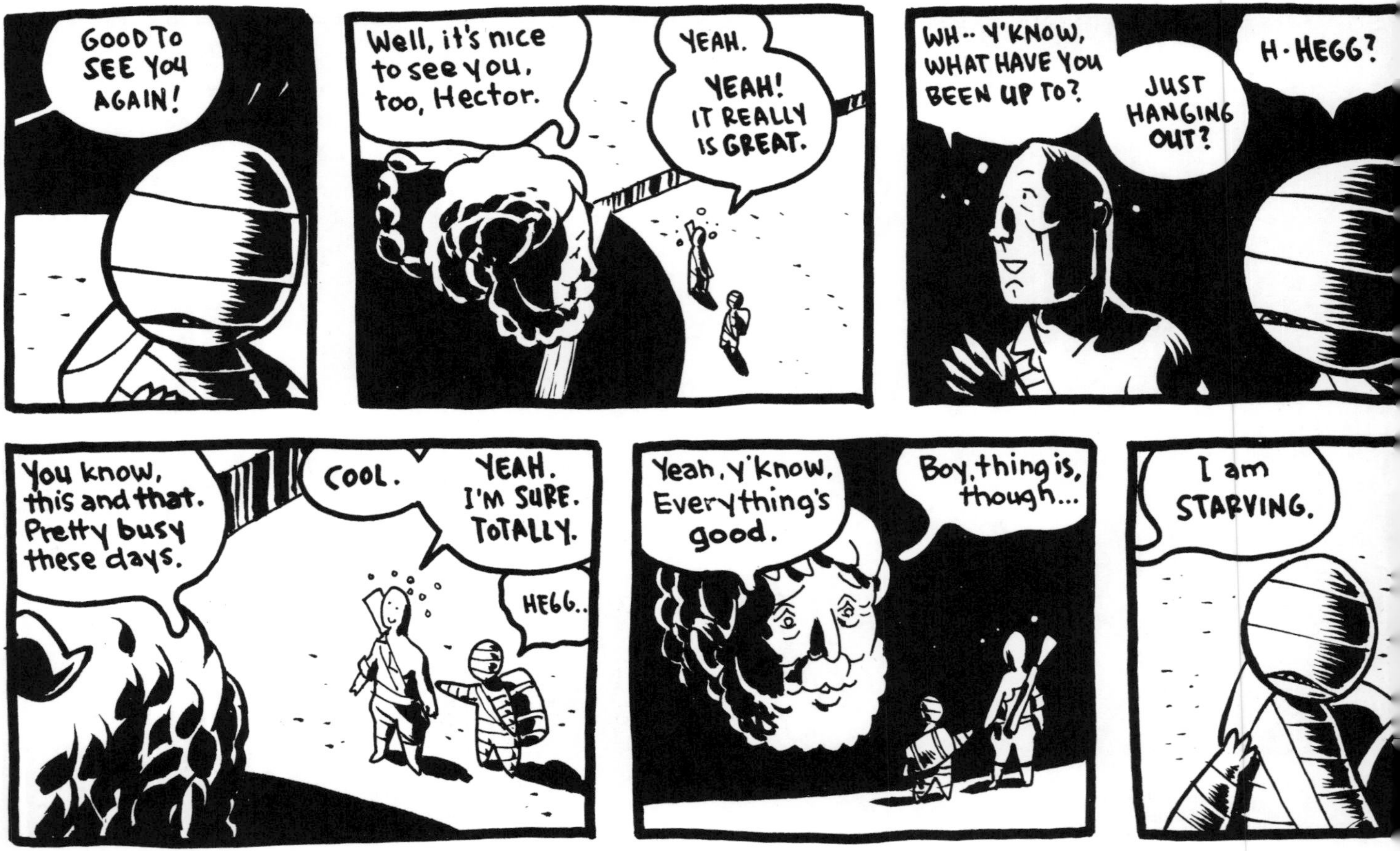
GOOD TO SEE YOU AGAIN!
Well, it's nice to see you, too, Hector.
YEAH.
YEAH! IT REALLY IS GREAT.
WH.. Y'KNOW, WHAT HAVE YOU BEEN UP TO?
JUST HANGING OUT?
H-HEGG?
You know, this and that. Pretty busy these days.
COOL.
YEAH. I'M SURE. TOTALLY.
HEGG..
Yeah, y'know, Everything's good.
Boy, thing is, though...
I am STARVING.

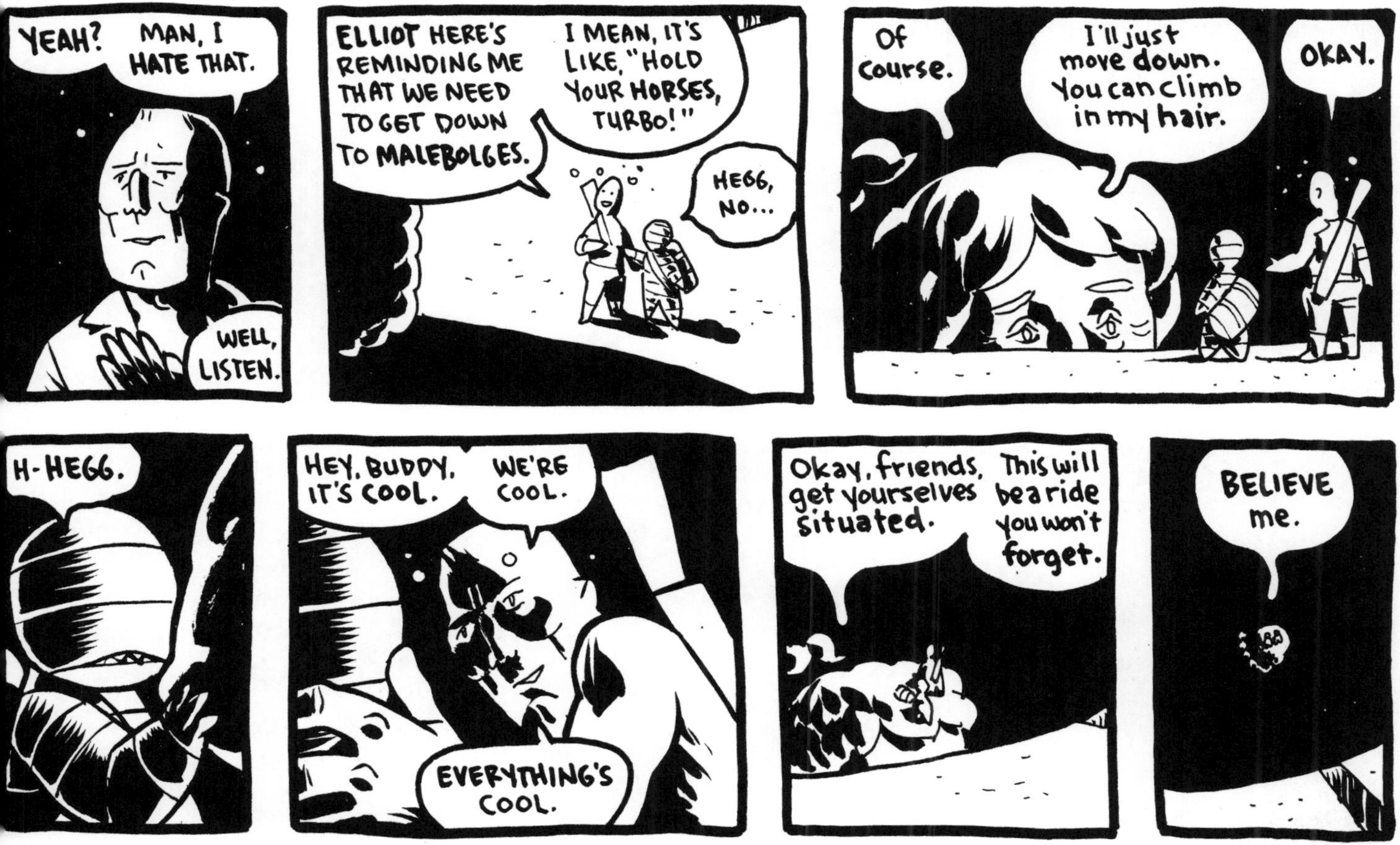
YEAH?
MAN, I HATE THAT.
WELL, LISTEN.
ELLIOT HERE'S REMINDING ME THAT WE NEED TO GET DOWN TO MALEBOLGES.
I MEAN, IT'S LIKE, "HOLD YOUR HORSES, TURBO!"
HEGG, NO...
Of course.
I'll just move down. You can climb in my hair.
OKAY.
H-HEGG.
HEY, BUDDY, IT'S COOL.
WE'RE COOL.
EVERYTHING'S COOL.
Okay, friends, get yourselves situated.
This will be a ride you won't forget.
BELIEVE me.

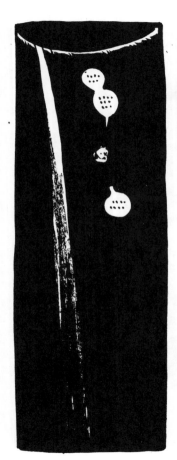

HA HA HA! OH MAN, GERYON, YOU CRACK ME UP!

Y'KNOW, THANKS AGAIN FOR FERRYING US DOWN HERE. You're A PAL.

Oh no, not at ALL.

Now Hector, it's so good to SEE you. Tell me what you've been UP to lately.

Any GIRLFRIENDS in the picture? HA HA! WELL...

...YEAH. THERE IS A GIRL I'M INTERESTED IN. I MEAN, SHE'S REALLY NICE -- I'VE KNOWN HER SINCE HIGH SCHOOL. WELL, I MEAN..

I GUESS I DIDN'T REALLY KNOW HER THAT WELL BACK THEN.

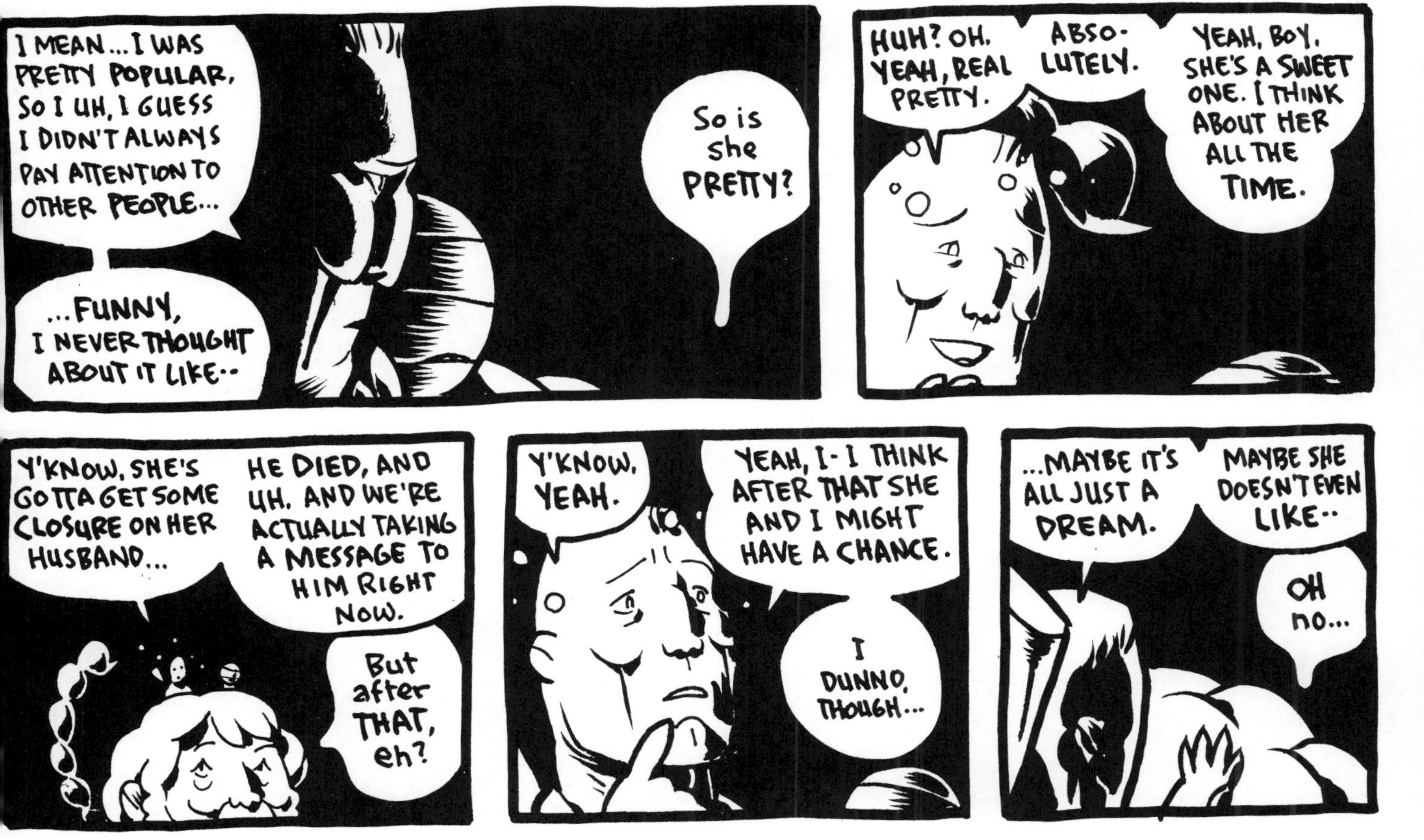

I MEAN... I WAS PRETTY POPULAR, SO I UH, I GUESS I DIDN'T ALWAYS PAY ATTENTION TO OTHER PEOPLE...
...FUNNY, I NEVER THOUGHT ABOUT IT LIKE--
So is she PRETTY?
HUH? OH. YEAH, REAL PRETTY.
ABSO-LUTELY.
YEAH, BOY. SHE'S A SWEET ONE. I THINK ABOUT HER ALL THE TIME.
Y'KNOW, SHE'S GOTTA GET SOME CLOSURE ON HER HUSBAND...
HE DIED, AND UH, AND WE'RE ACTUALLY TAKING A MESSAGE TO HIM RIGHT NOW.
But after THAT, eh?
Y'KNOW, YEAH.
YEAH, I- I THINK AFTER THAT SHE AND I MIGHT HAVE A CHANCE.
I DUNNO, THOUGH...
...MAYBE IT'S ALL JUST A DREAM.
MAYBE SHE DOESN'T EVEN LIKE--
OH no...

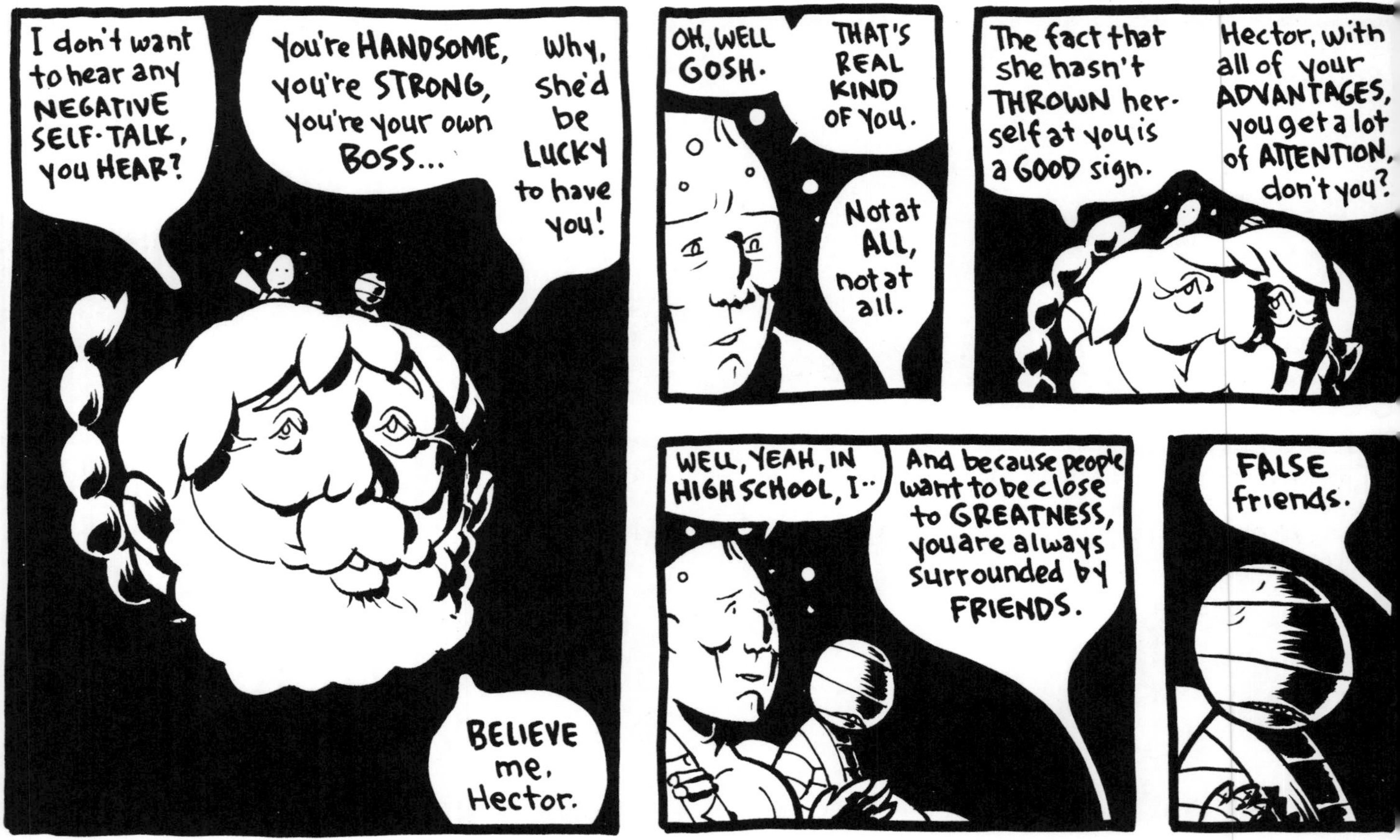

I don't want to hear any NEGATIVE SELF-TALK, you HEAR?
You're HANDSOME, you're STRONG, you're your own BOSS...
Why, she'd be LUCKY to have you!
BELIEVE me, Hector.
OH, WELL GOSH.
THAT'S REAL KIND OF YOU.
Not at ALL, not at all.
The fact that she hasn't THROWN herself at you is a GOOD sign.
Hector, with all of your ADVANTAGES, you get a lot of ATTENTION, don't you?
WELL, YEAH, IN HIGH SCHOOL, I..
And because people want to be close to GREATNESS, you are always surrounded by FRIENDS.
FALSE friends.

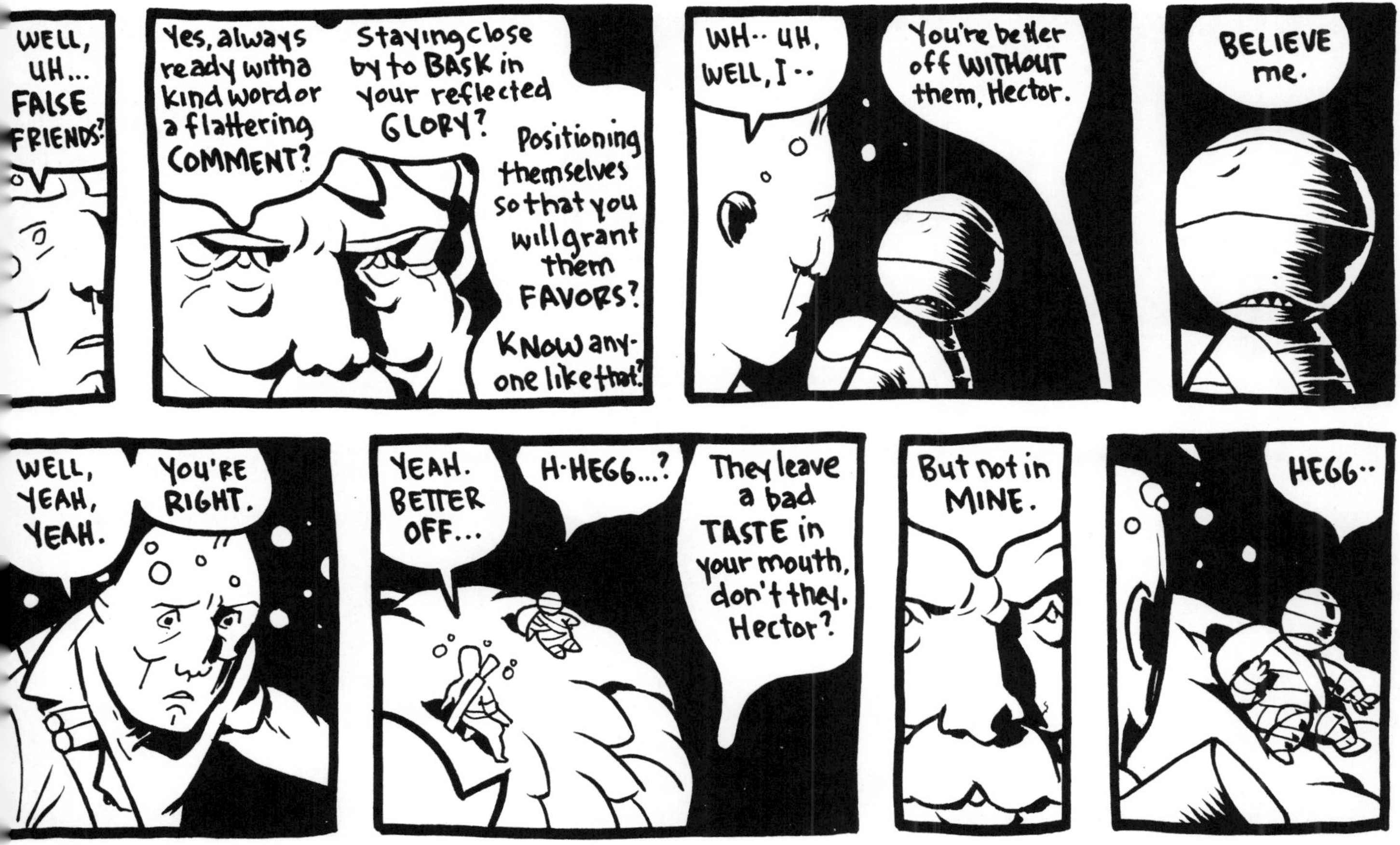
WELL, UH... FALSE FRIENDS?
Yes, always ready with a kind word or a flattering COMMENT?
Staying close by to BASK in your reflected GLORY?
Positioning themselves so that you will grant them FAVORS?
KNOW anyone like that?
WH.. UH, WELL, I..
You're better off WITHOUT them, Hector.
BELIEVE me.
WELL, YEAH, YEAH.
YOU'RE RIGHT.
YEAH. BETTER OFF...
H-HEGG...?
They leave a bad TASTE in your mouth, don't they, Hector?
But not in MINE.
HEGG..

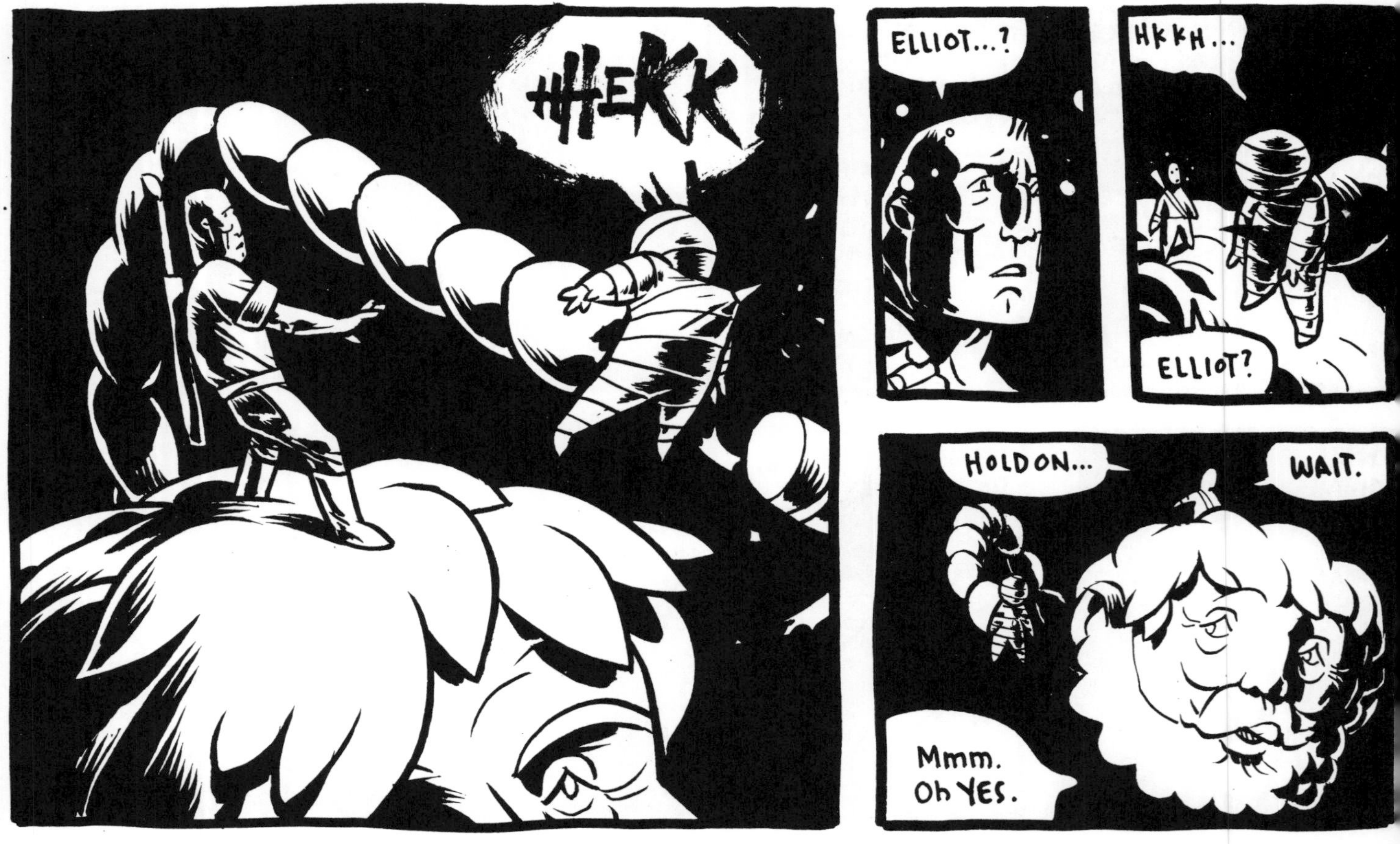
HHERKK
ELLIOT...?
HKKH...
ELLIOT?
HOLD ON...
WAIT.
Mmm.
Oh YES.

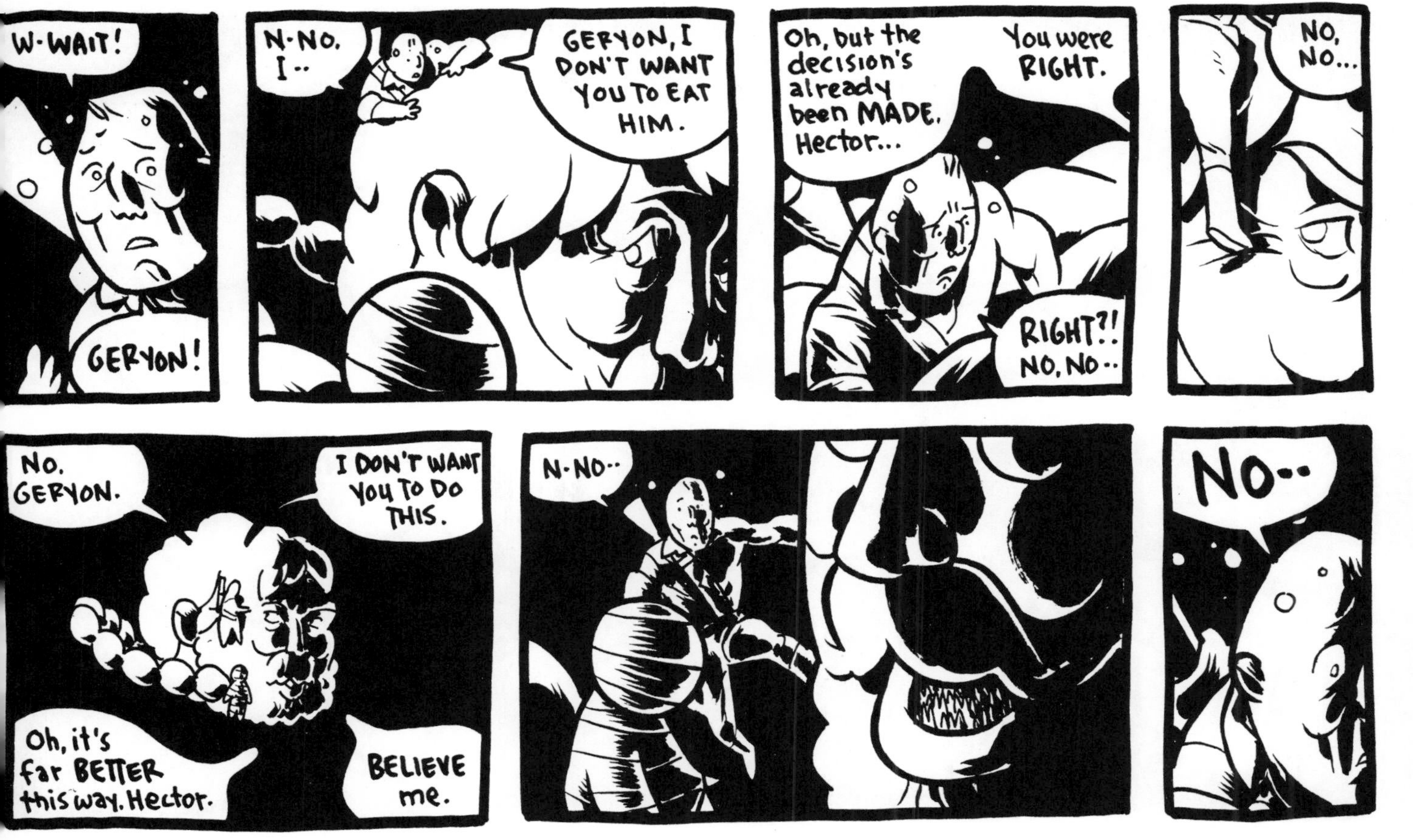
W-WAIT!
GERYON!
N-NO. I..
GERYON, I DON'T WANT YOU TO EAT HIM.
Oh, but the decision's already been MADE. Hector...
You were RIGHT.
RIGHT?! NO, NO..
NO, NO...
No. GERYON.
I DON'T WANT YOU TO DO THIS.
Oh, it's far BETTER this way. Hector.
BELIEVE me.
N-NO..
NO..

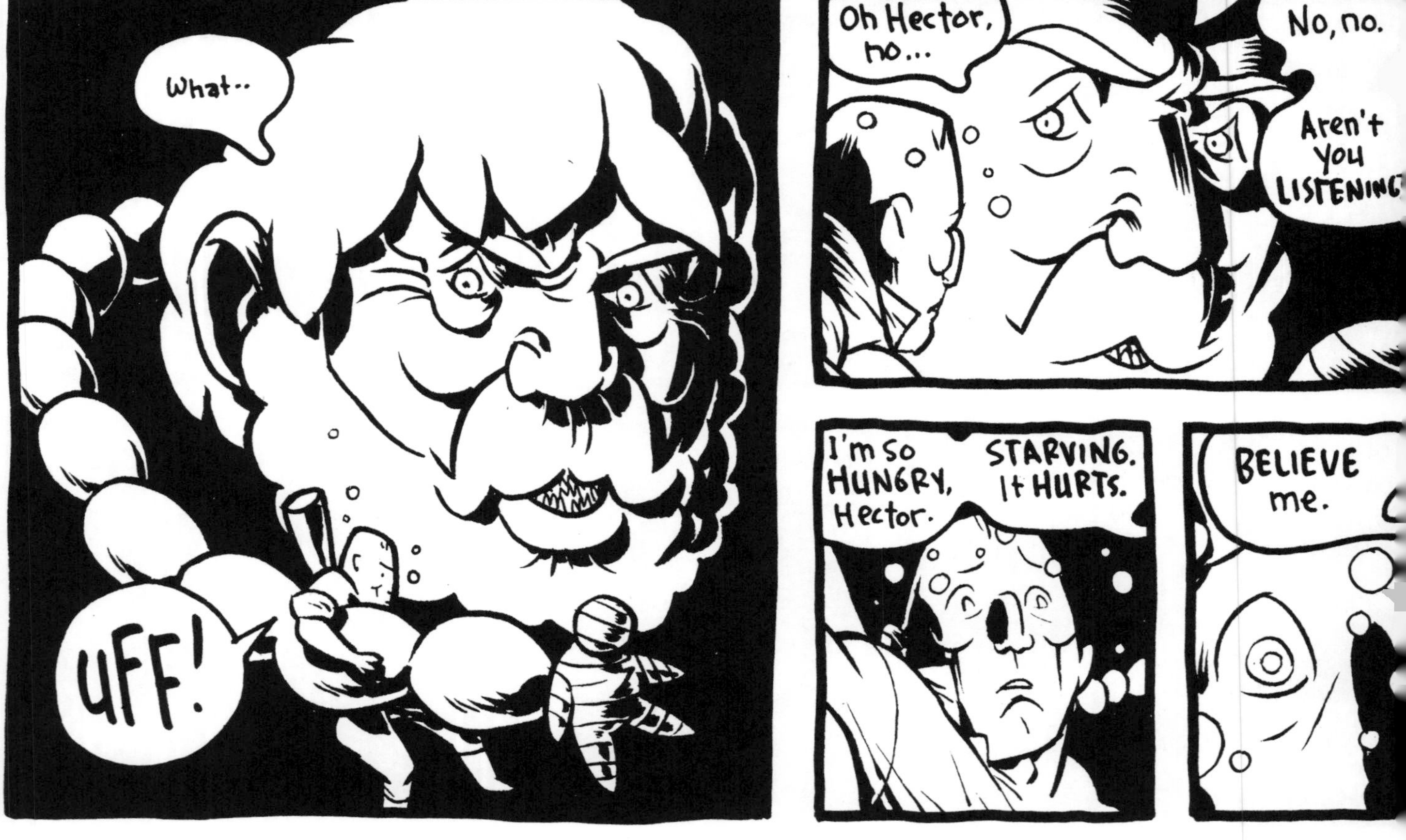

What..
UFF!
Oh Hector, no...
No, no.
Aren't you LISTENING
I'm so HUNGRY, Hector.
STARVING. It HURTS.
BELIEVE me.

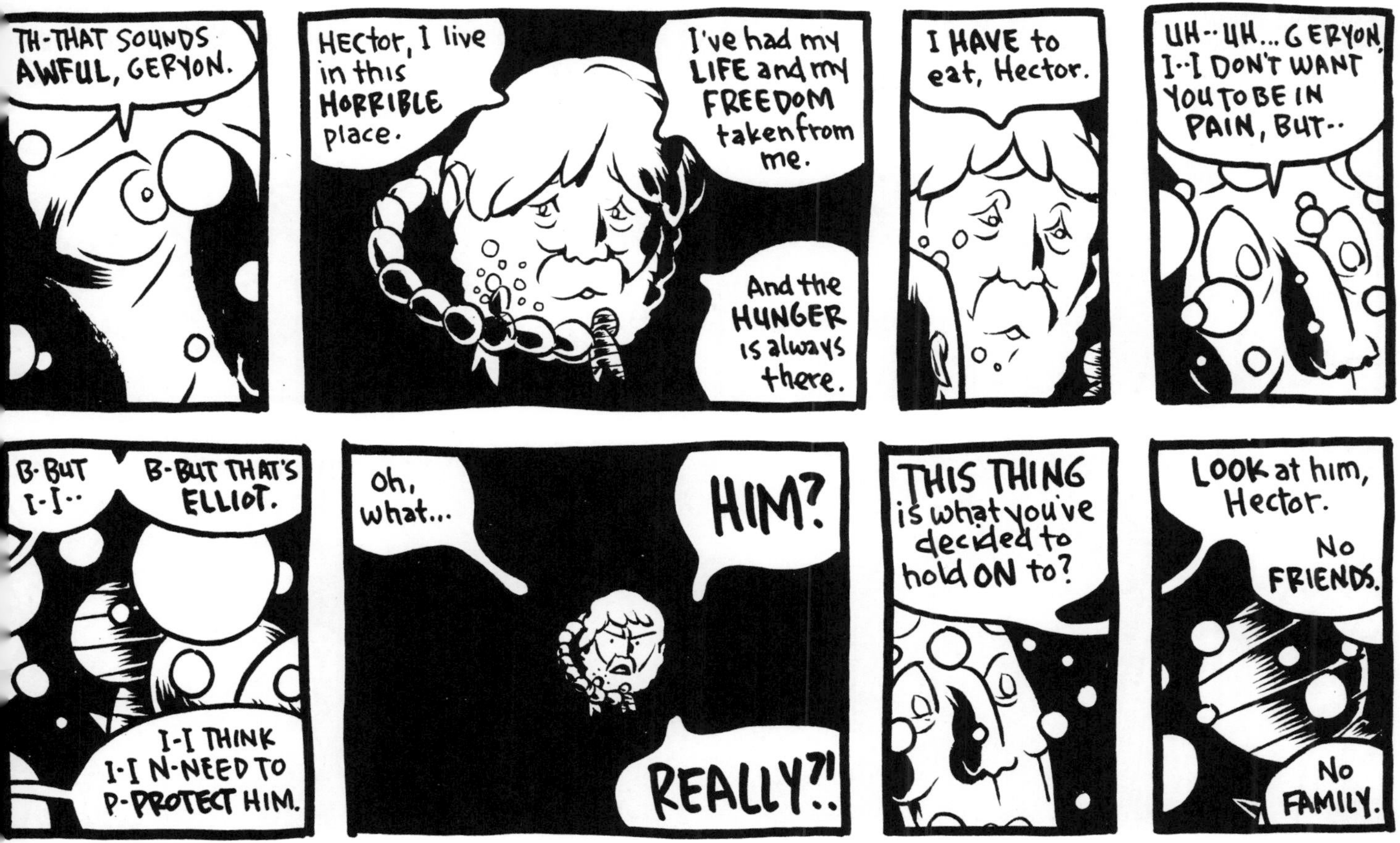
TH-THAT SOUNDS AWFUL, GERYON.
HECtor, I live in this HORRIBLE place.
I've had my LIFE and my FREEDOM taken from me.
And the HUNGER is always there.
I HAVE to eat, Hector.
UH-- UH... GERYON, I--I DON'T WANT YOU TO BE IN PAIN, BUT--
B-BUT I-I--
B-BUT THAT'S ELLIOT.
I-I THINK I-I N-NEED TO P-PROTECT HIM.
Oh, what...
HIM?
REALLY?!
THIS THING is what you've decided to hold ON to?
LOOK at him, Hector.
No FRIENDS.
No FAMILY.

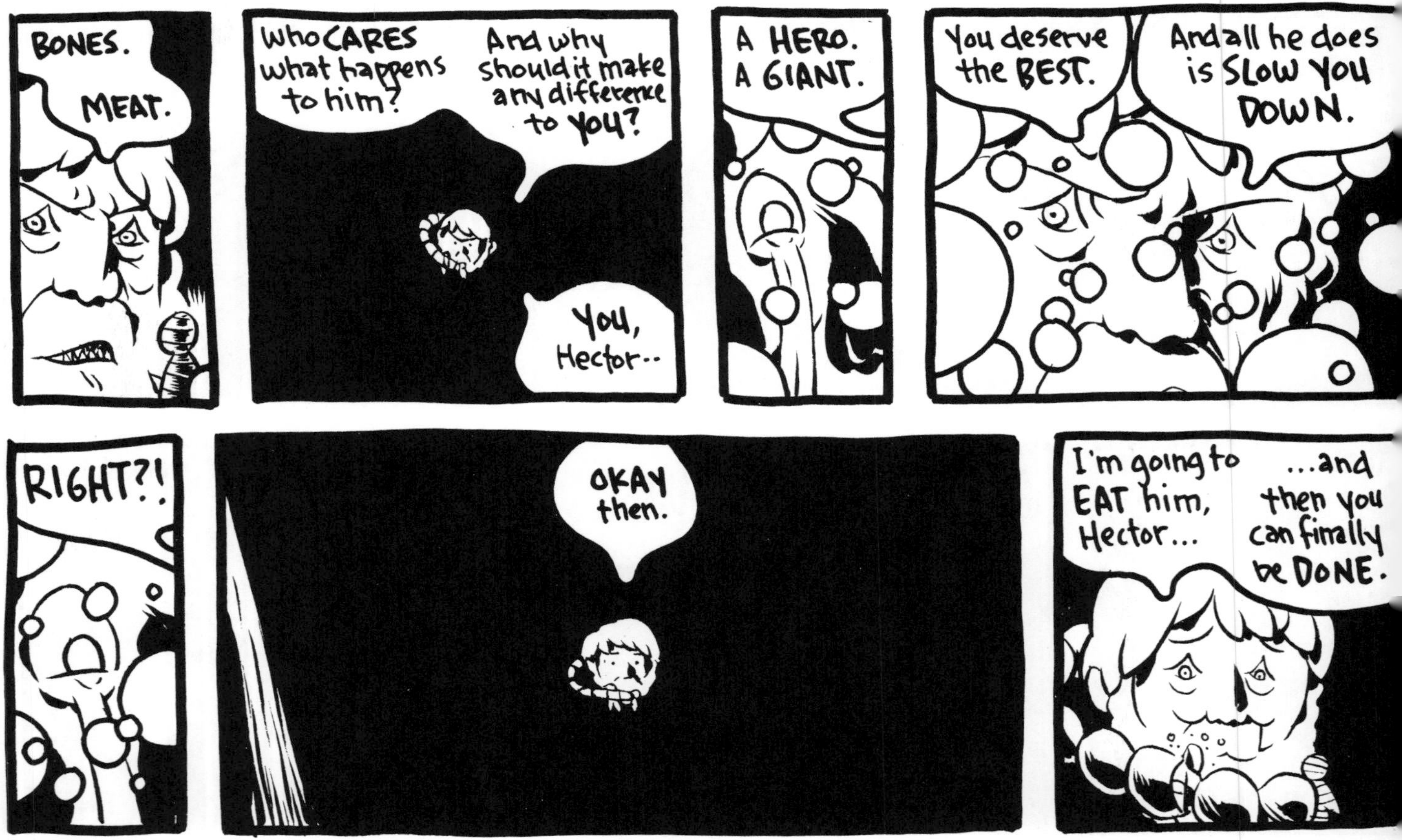
BONES.
MEAT.
Who CARES what happens to him?
And why should it make any difference to YOU?
You, Hector..
A HERO. A GIANT.
You deserve the BEST.
And all he does is SLOW YOU DOWN.
RIGHT?!
OKAY then.
I'm going to EAT him, Hector...
...and then you can finally be DONE.

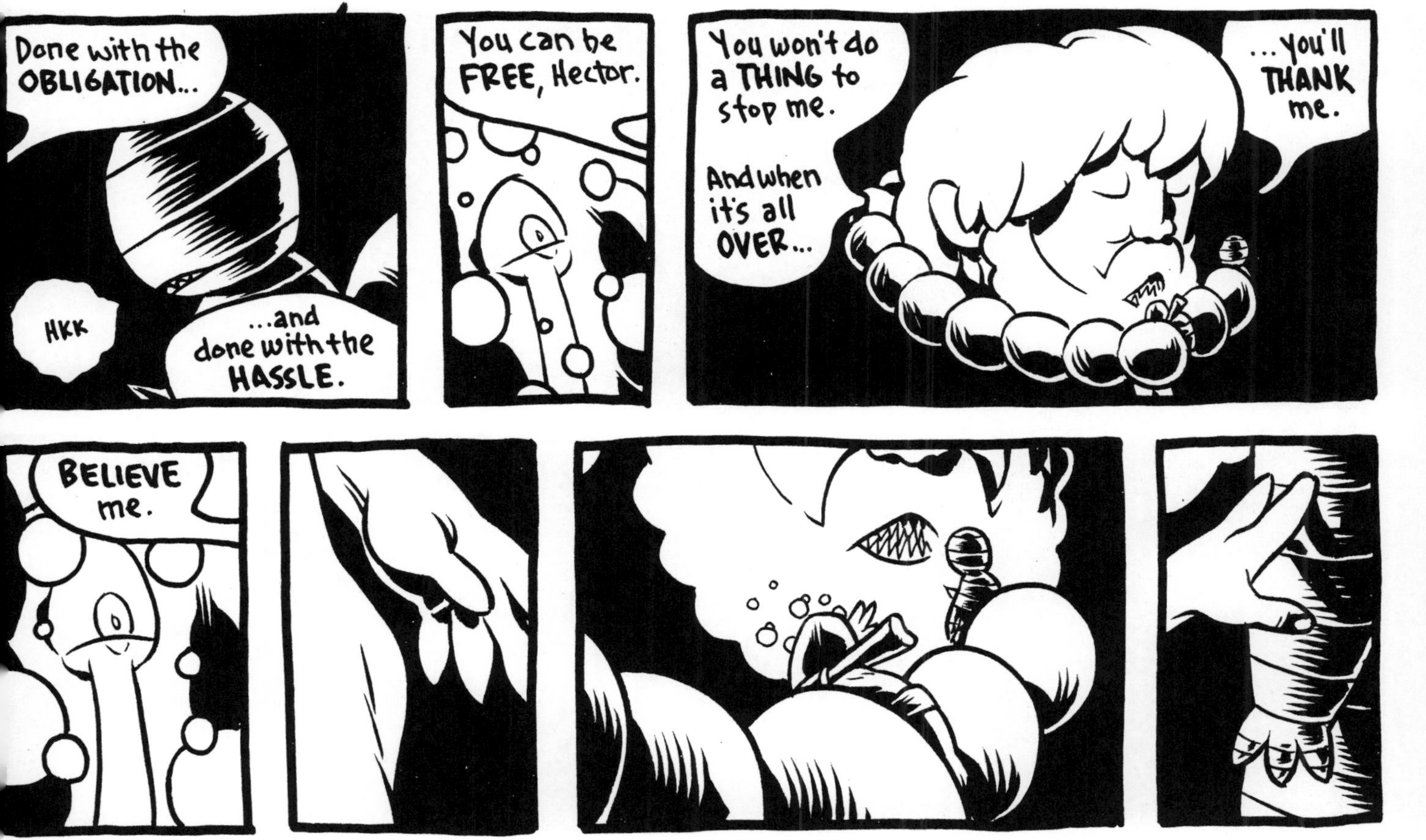
Done with the OBLIGATION...
HKK
...and done with the HASSLE.
You can be FREE, Hector.
You won't do a THING to stop me.
And when it's all OVER...
...you'll THANK me.
BELIEVE me.

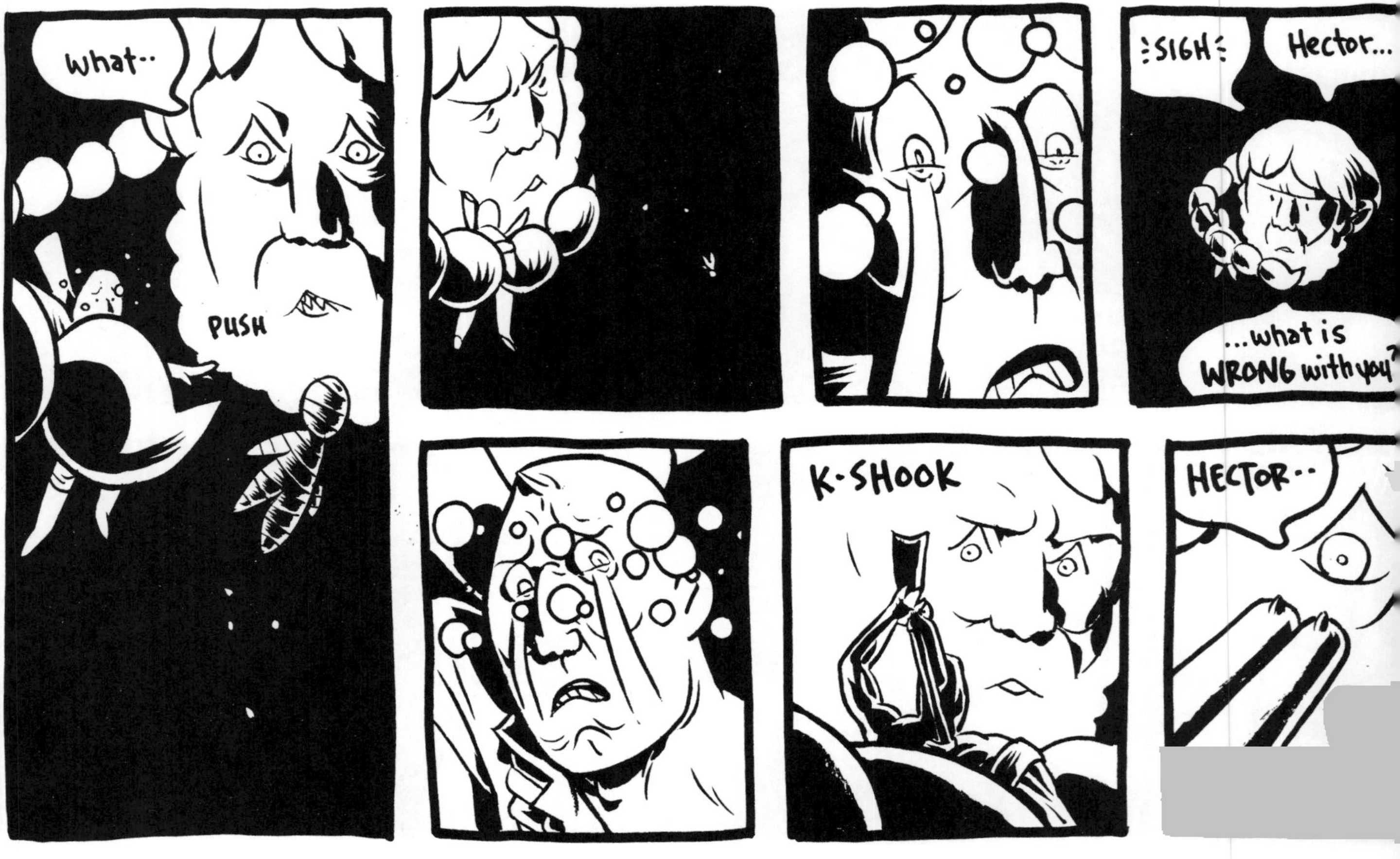
what..
PUSH
SIGH
Hector...
...what is WRONG with you?
K-SHOOK
HECTOR..

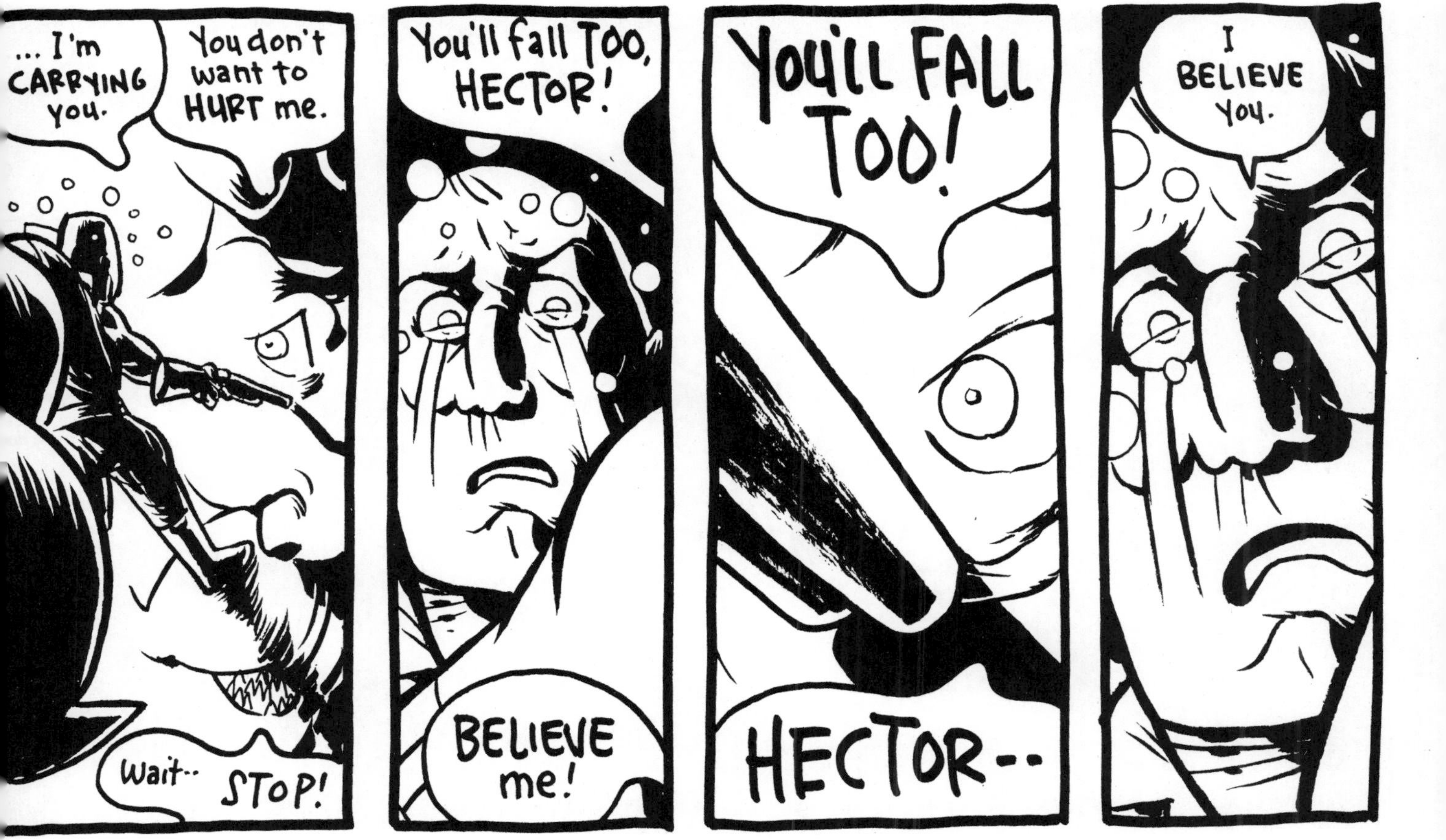
... I'm CARRYING you.
You don't want to HURT me.
Wait.. STOP!
You'll fall TOO, HECTOR!
BELIEVE me!
YOU'LL FALL TOO!
HECTOR--
I BELIEVE YOU.

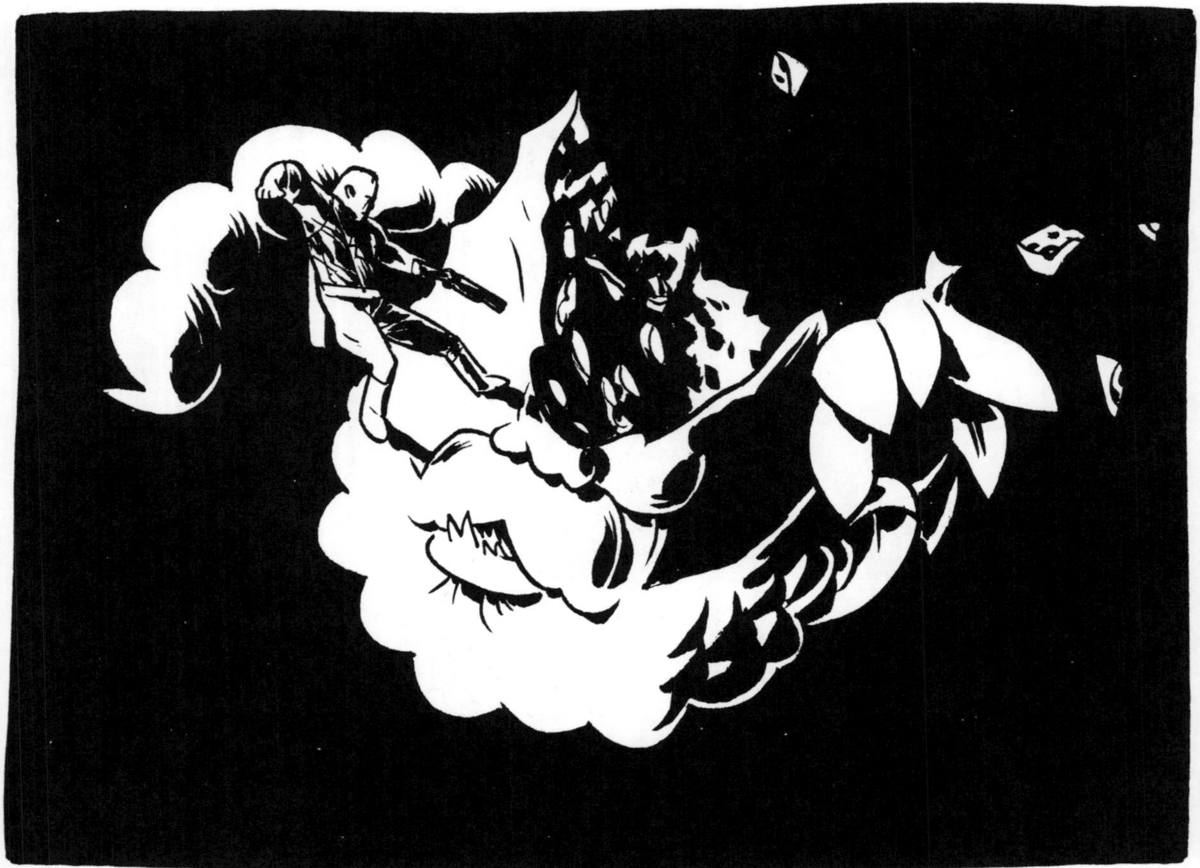
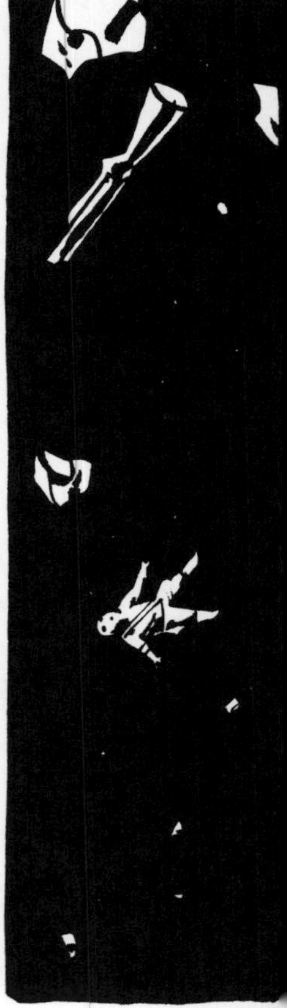

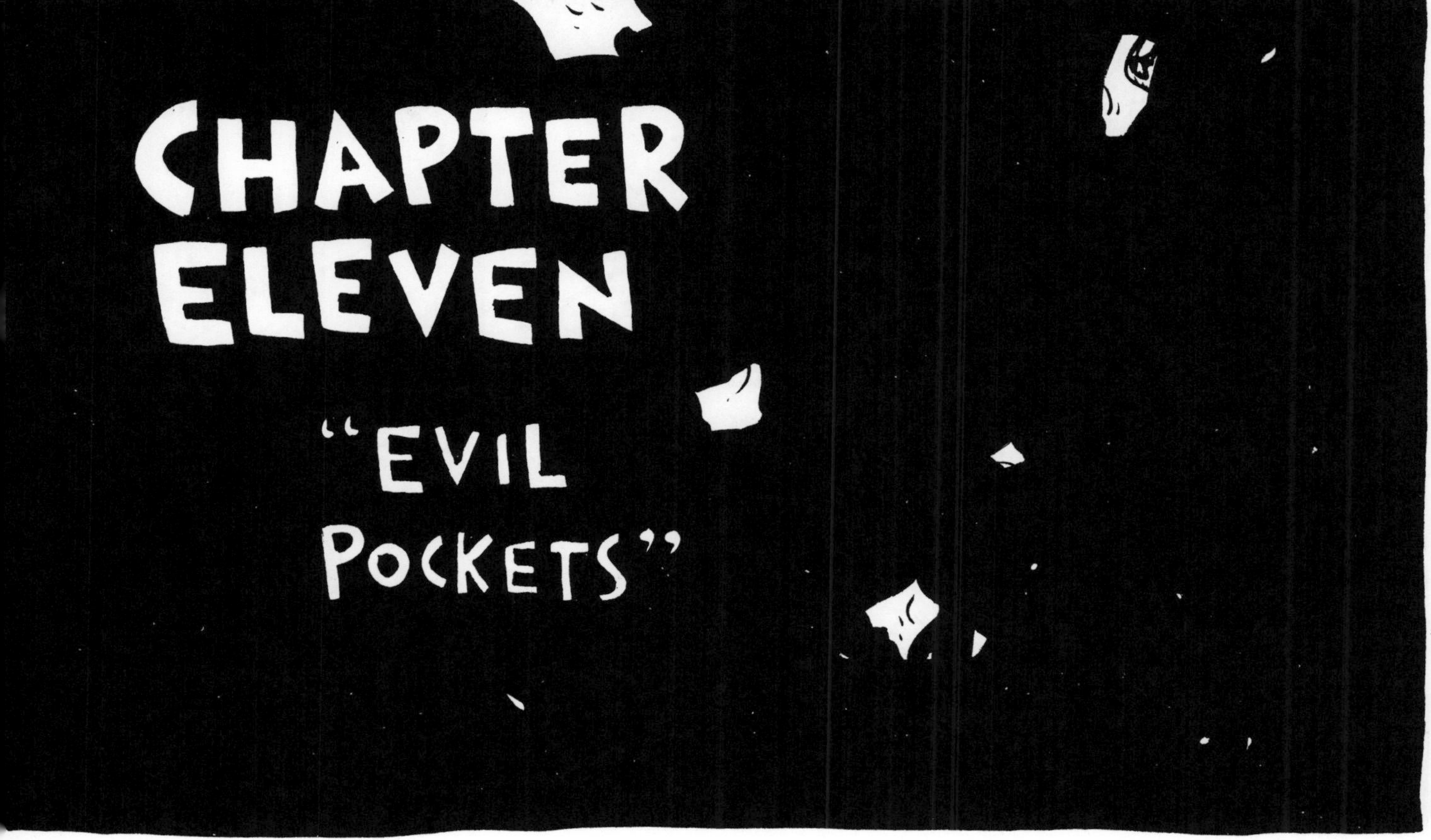
CHAPTER ELEVEN
"EVIL POCKETS"

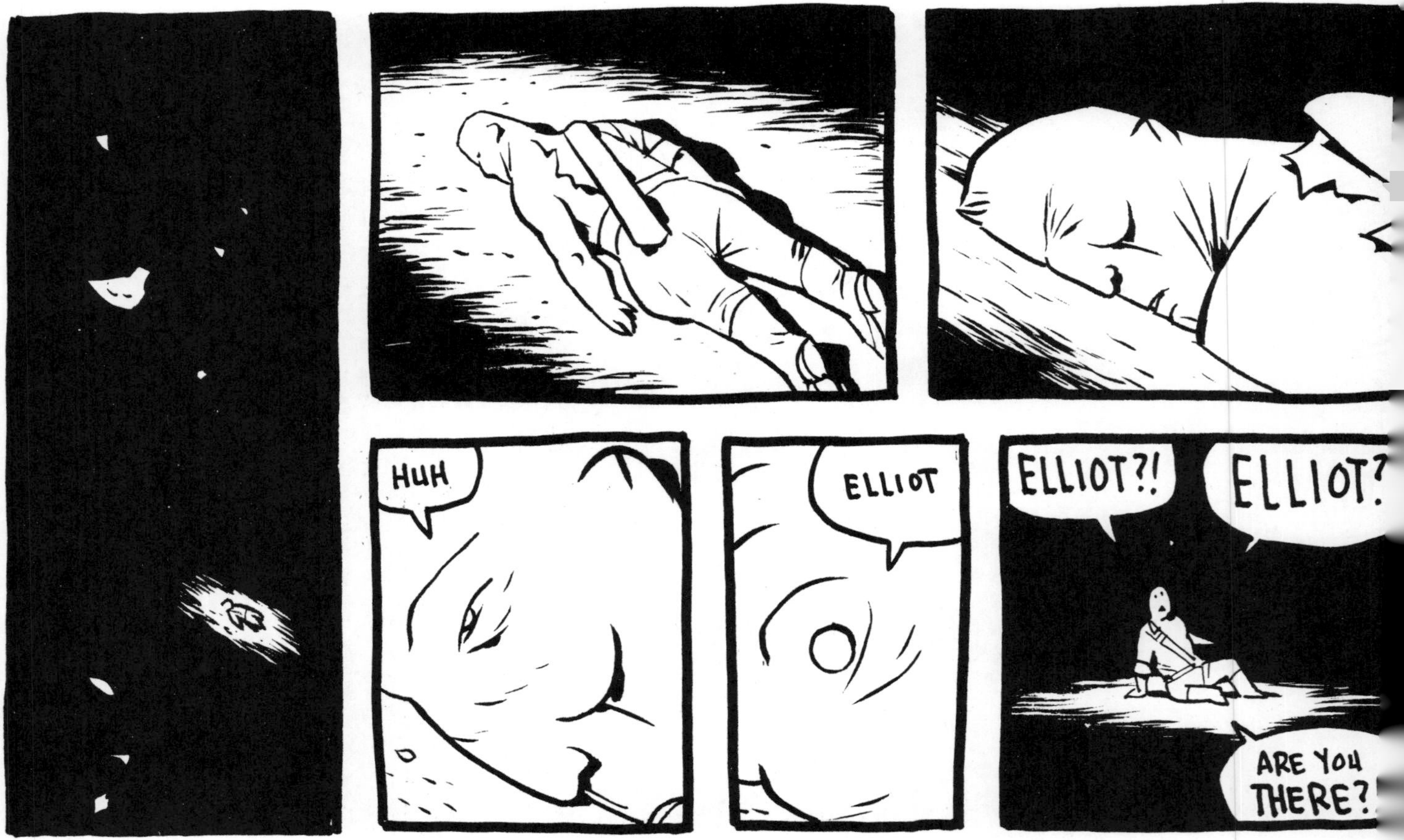

HUH
ELLIOT
ELLIOT?!
ELLIOT?
ARE YOU THERE?

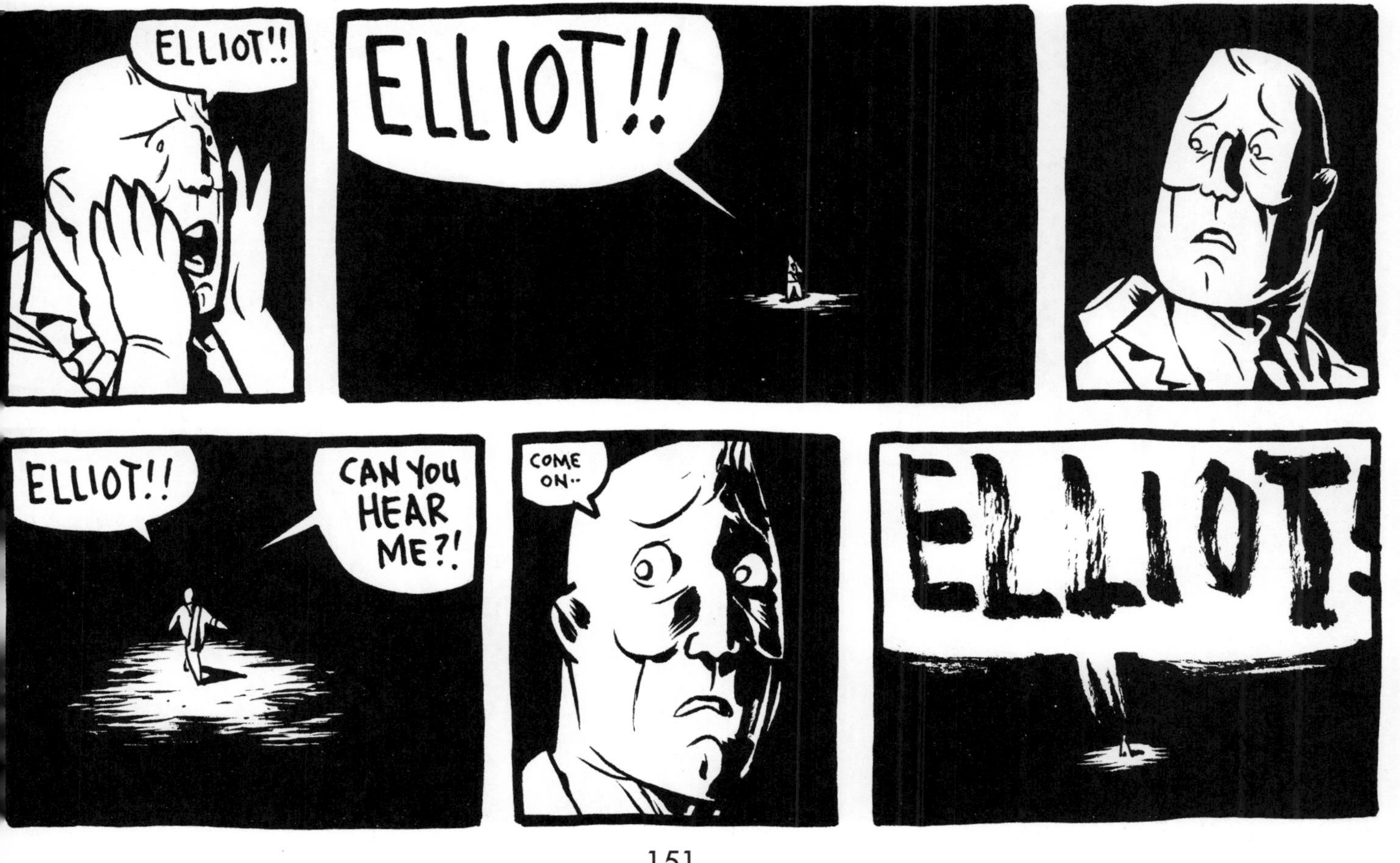
ELLIOT!!
ELLIOT!!
ELLIOT!!
CAN YOU HEAR ME?!
COME ON..

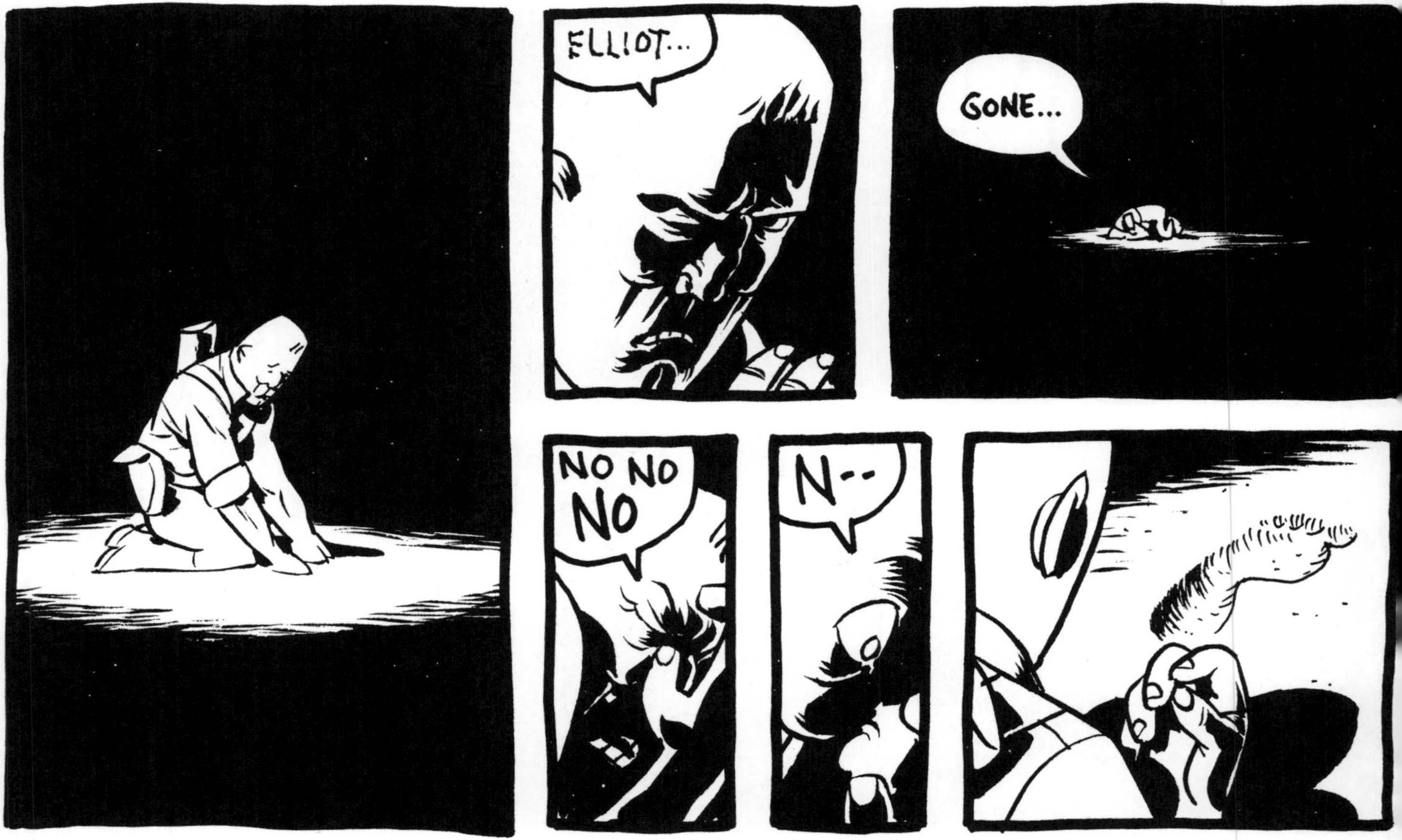
ELLIOT...
GONE...
NO NO NO
N--

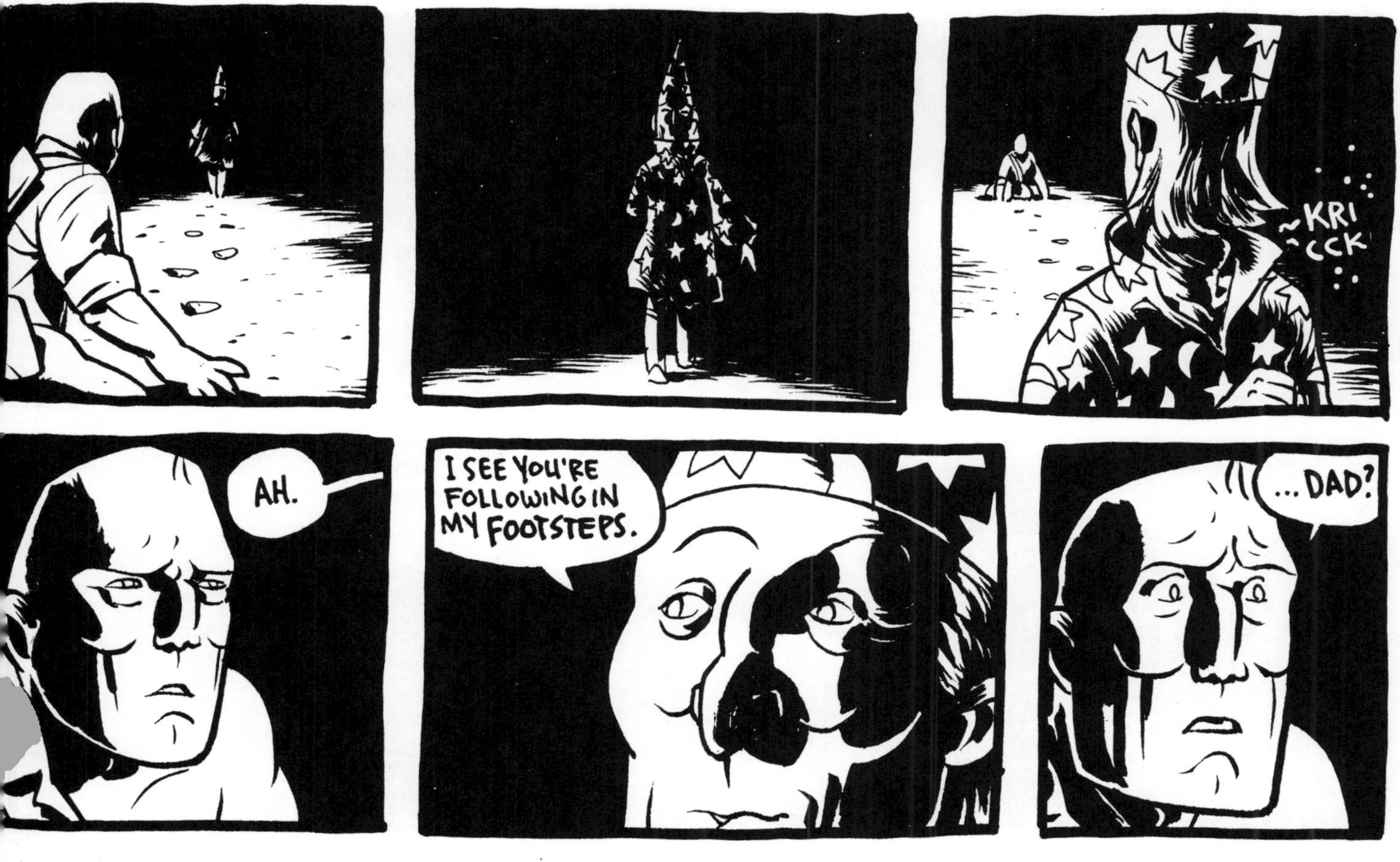
KRI
CCK
AH.
I SEE YOU'RE FOLLOWING IN MY FOOTSTEPS.
...DAD?

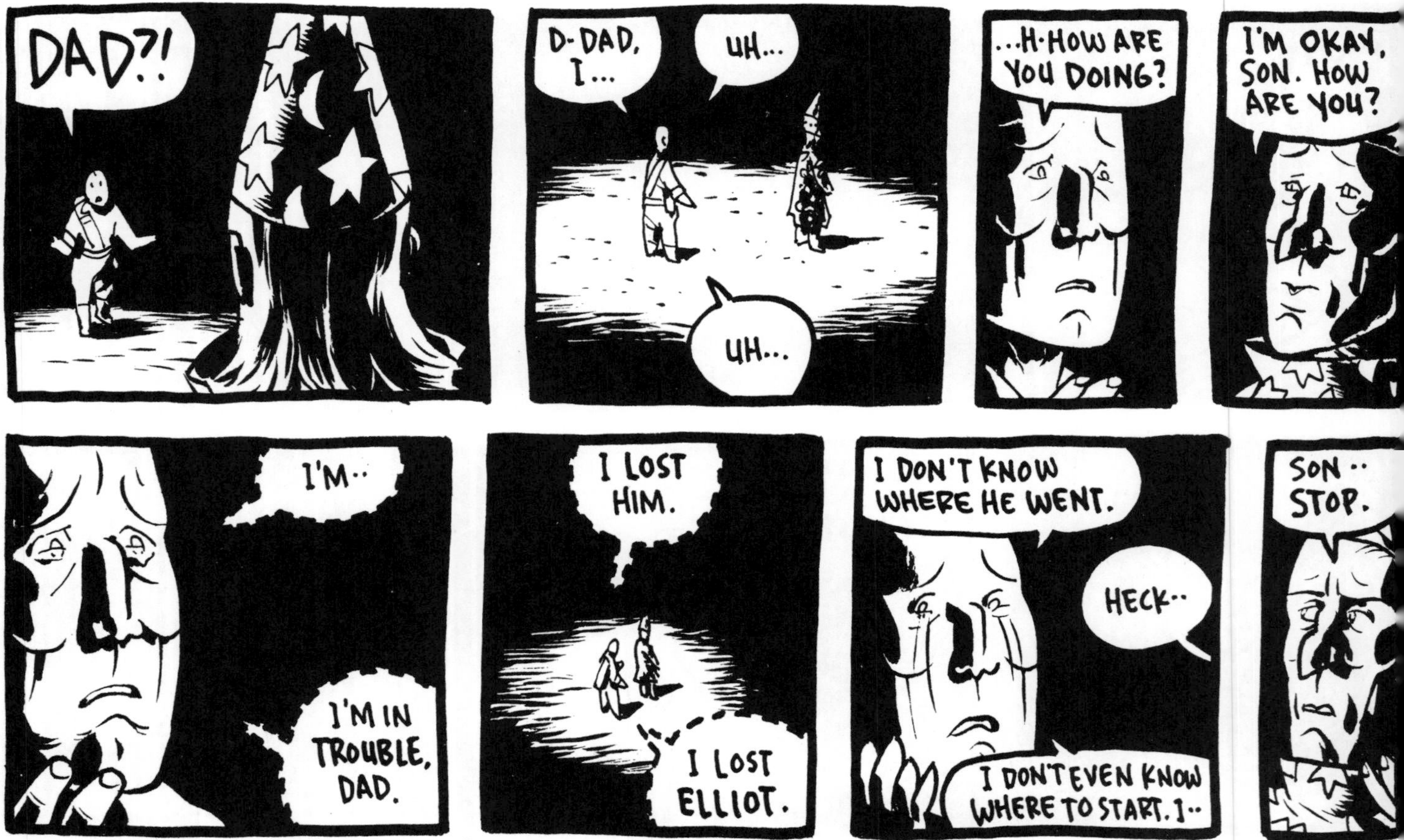
DAD?!
D-DAD, I...
UH...
UH...
...H-HOW ARE YOU DOING?
I'M OKAY, SON. HOW ARE YOU?
I'M..
I'M IN TROUBLE, DAD.
I LOST HIM.
I LOST ELLIOT.
I DON'T KNOW WHERE HE WENT.
HECK..
I DON'T EVEN KNOW WHERE TO START. I..
SON.. STOP.

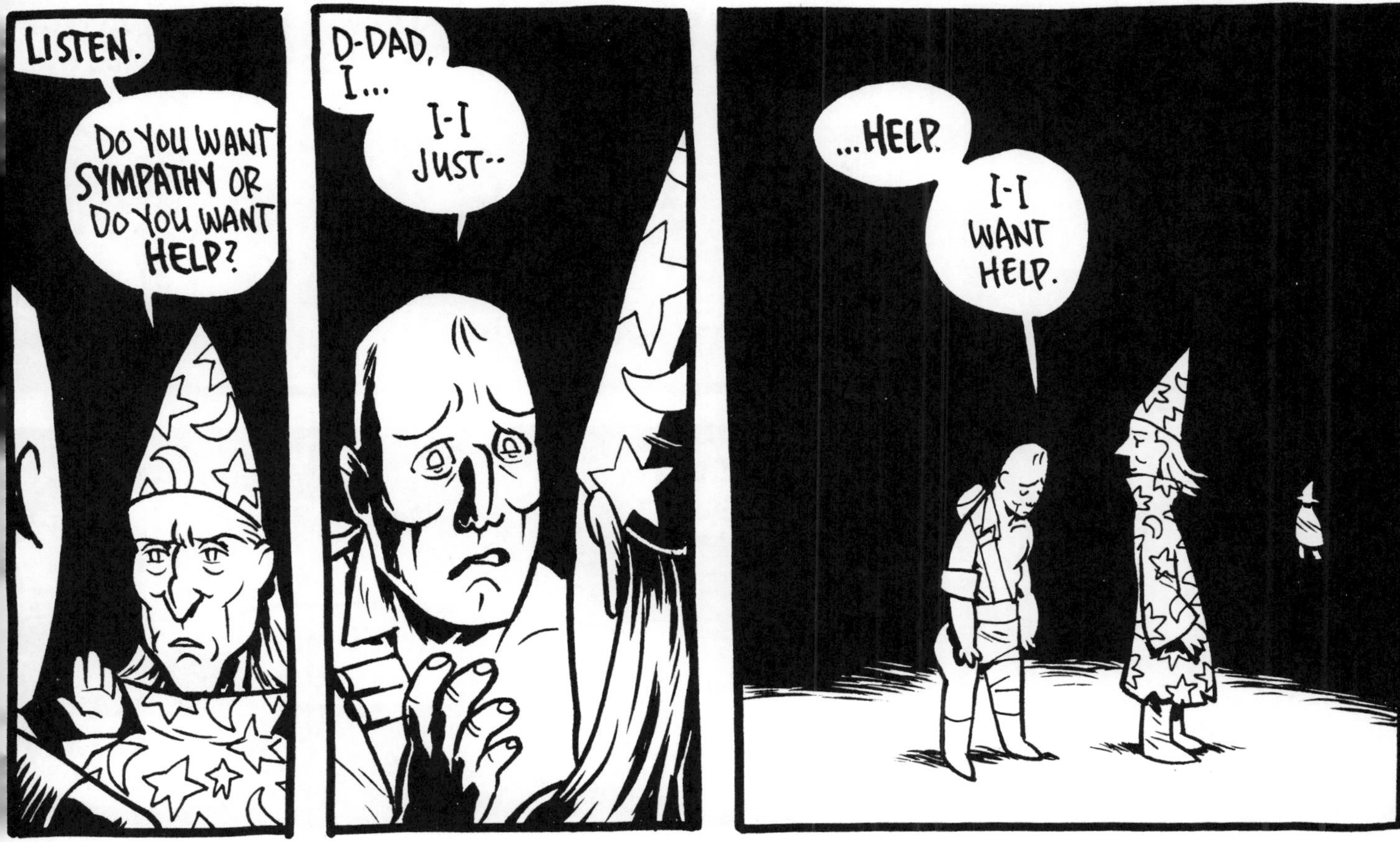
LISTEN.
DO YOU WANT SYMPATHY OR DO YOU WANT HELP?
D-DAD, I...
I-I JUST--
...HELP.
I-I WANT HELP.

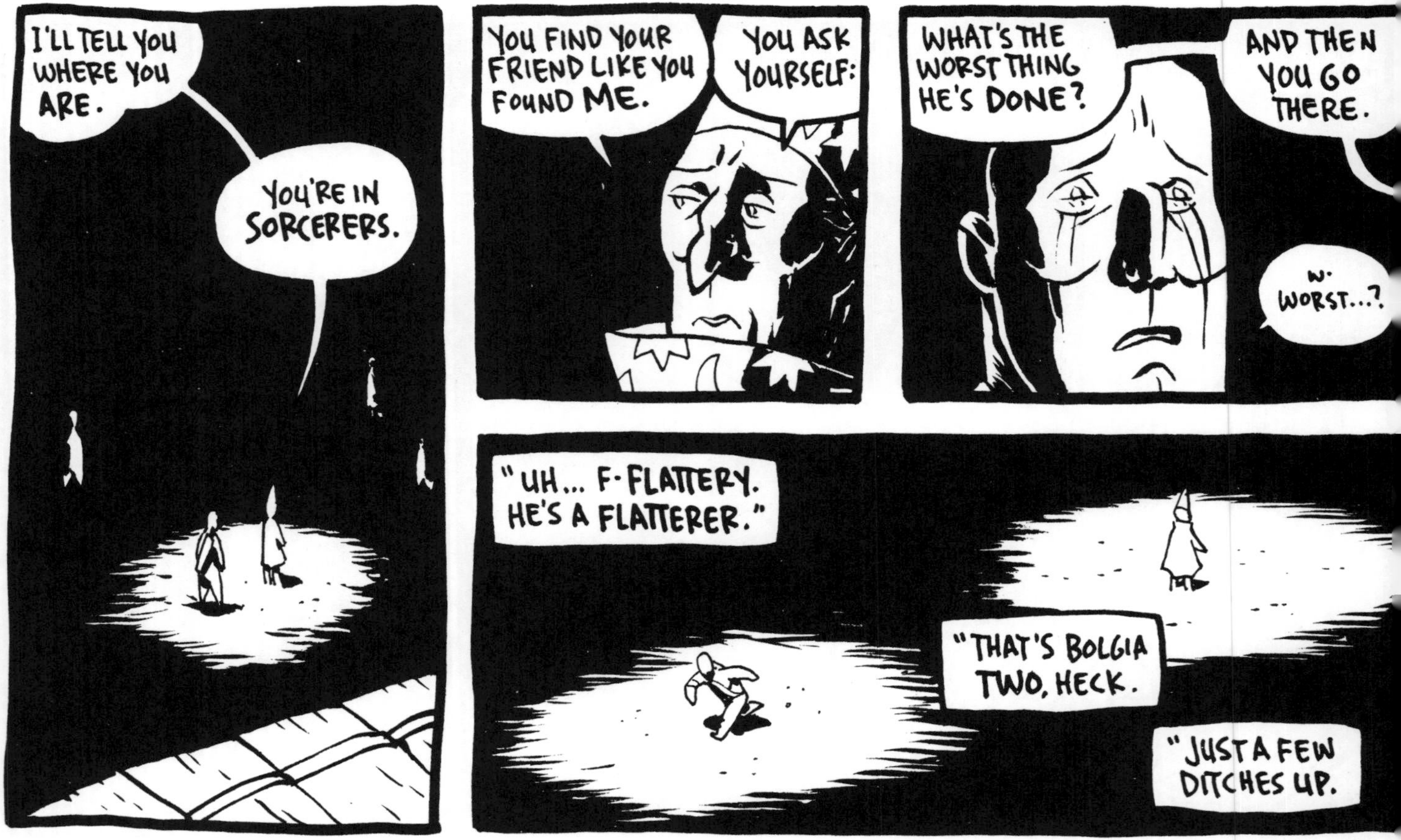
I'LL TELL YOU WHERE YOU ARE.
YOU'RE IN SORCERERS.
YOU FIND YOUR FRIEND LIKE YOU FOUND ME.
YOU ASK YOURSELF:
WHAT'S THE WORST THING HE'S DONE?
AND THEN YOU GO THERE.
W. WORST...?
"UH... F-FLATTERY. HE'S A FLATTERER."
"THAT'S BOLGIA TWO, HECK.
"JUST A FEW DITCHES UP.

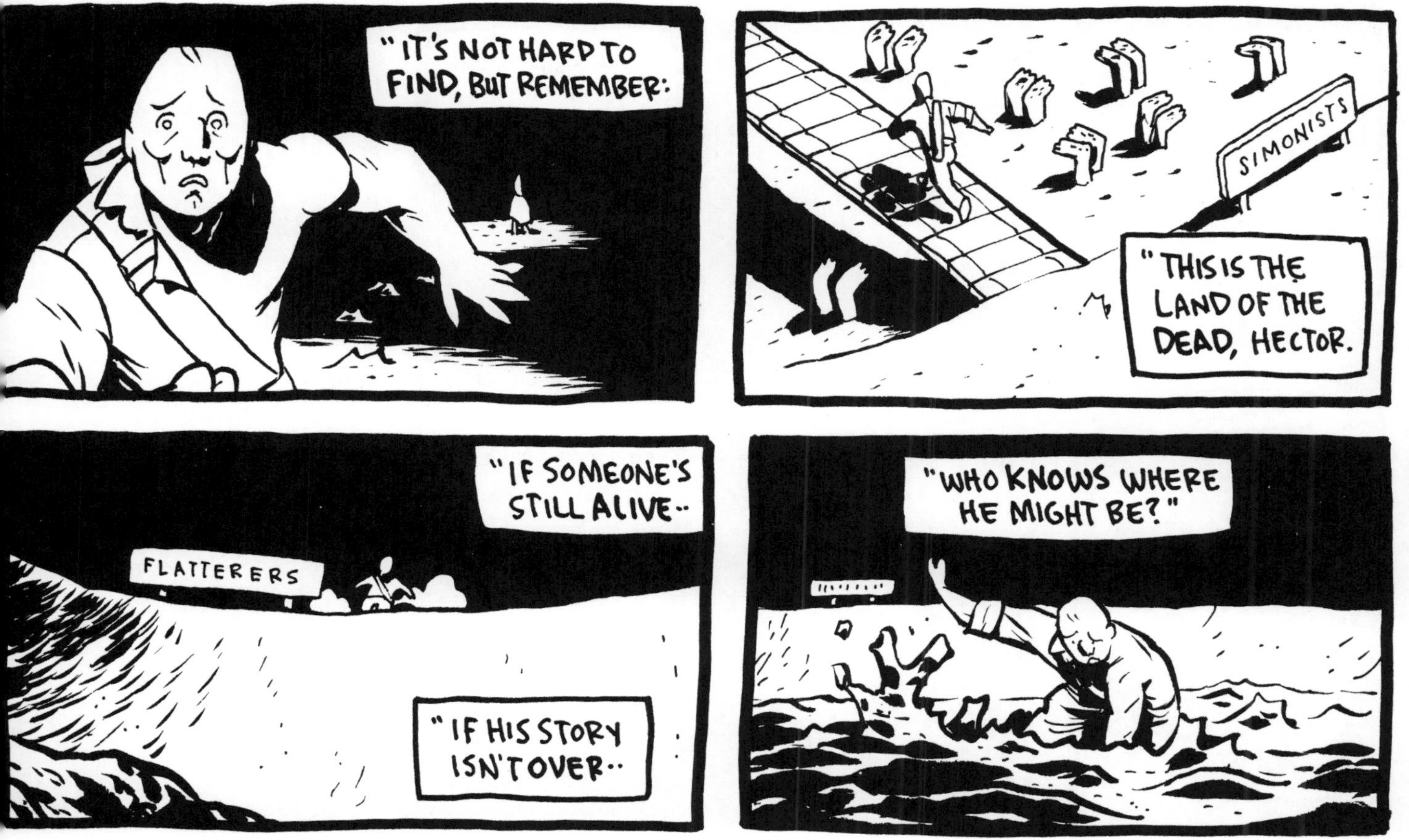
"IT'S NOT HARD TO FIND, BUT REMEMBER:
SIMONISTS
"THIS IS THE LAND OF THE DEAD, HECTOR.
"IF SOMEONE'S STILL ALIVE..
FLATTERERS
"IF HIS STORY ISN'T OVER..
"WHO KNOWS WHERE HE MIGHT BE?"

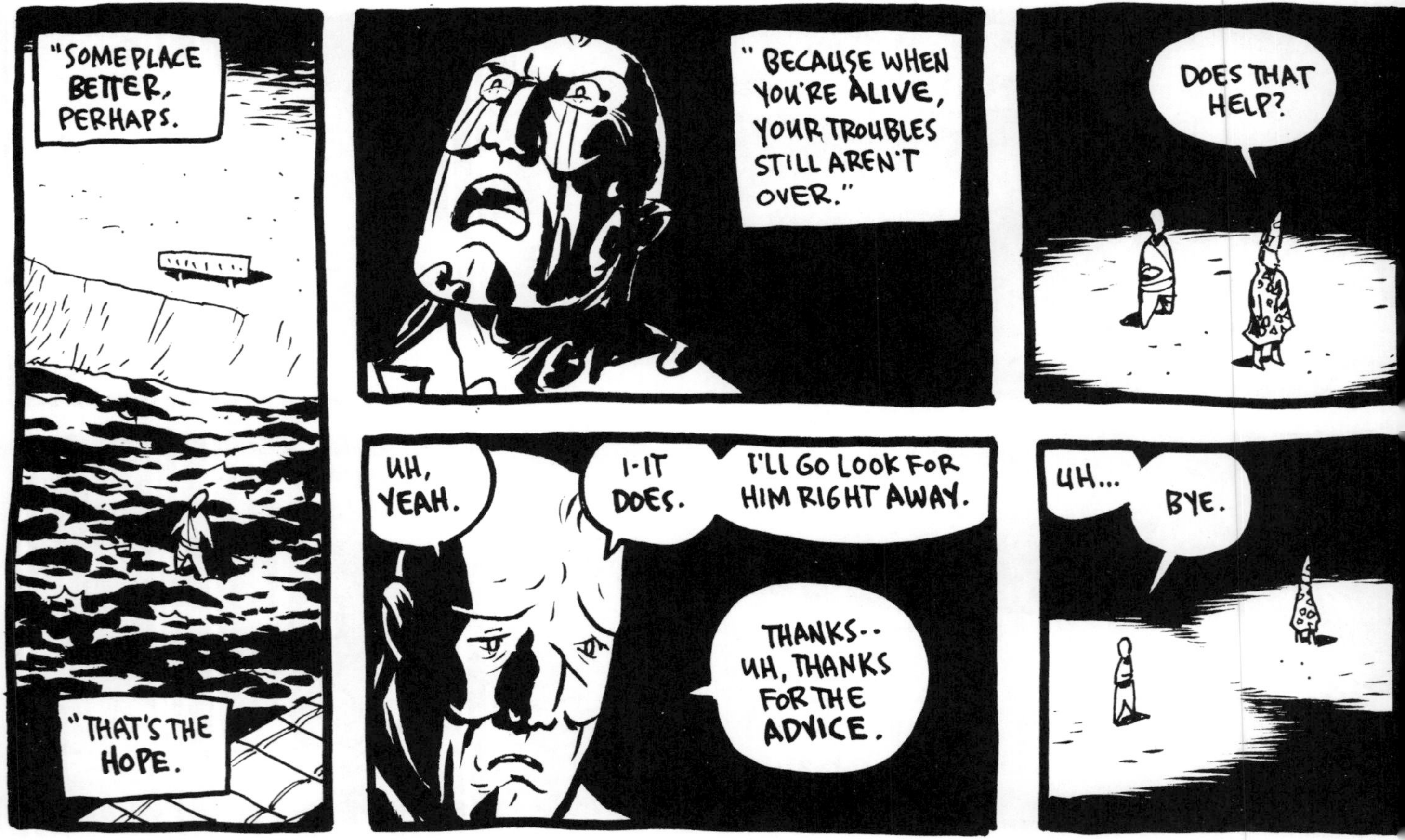
"SOMEPLACE BETTER, PERHAPS.
"THAT'S THE HOPE.
"BECAUSE WHEN YOU'RE ALIVE, YOUR TROUBLES STILL AREN'T OVER."
UH, YEAH.
I-IT DOES.
I'LL GO LOOK FOR HIM RIGHT AWAY.
THANKS.. UH, THANKS FOR THE ADVICE.
DOES THAT HELP?
UH...
BYE.

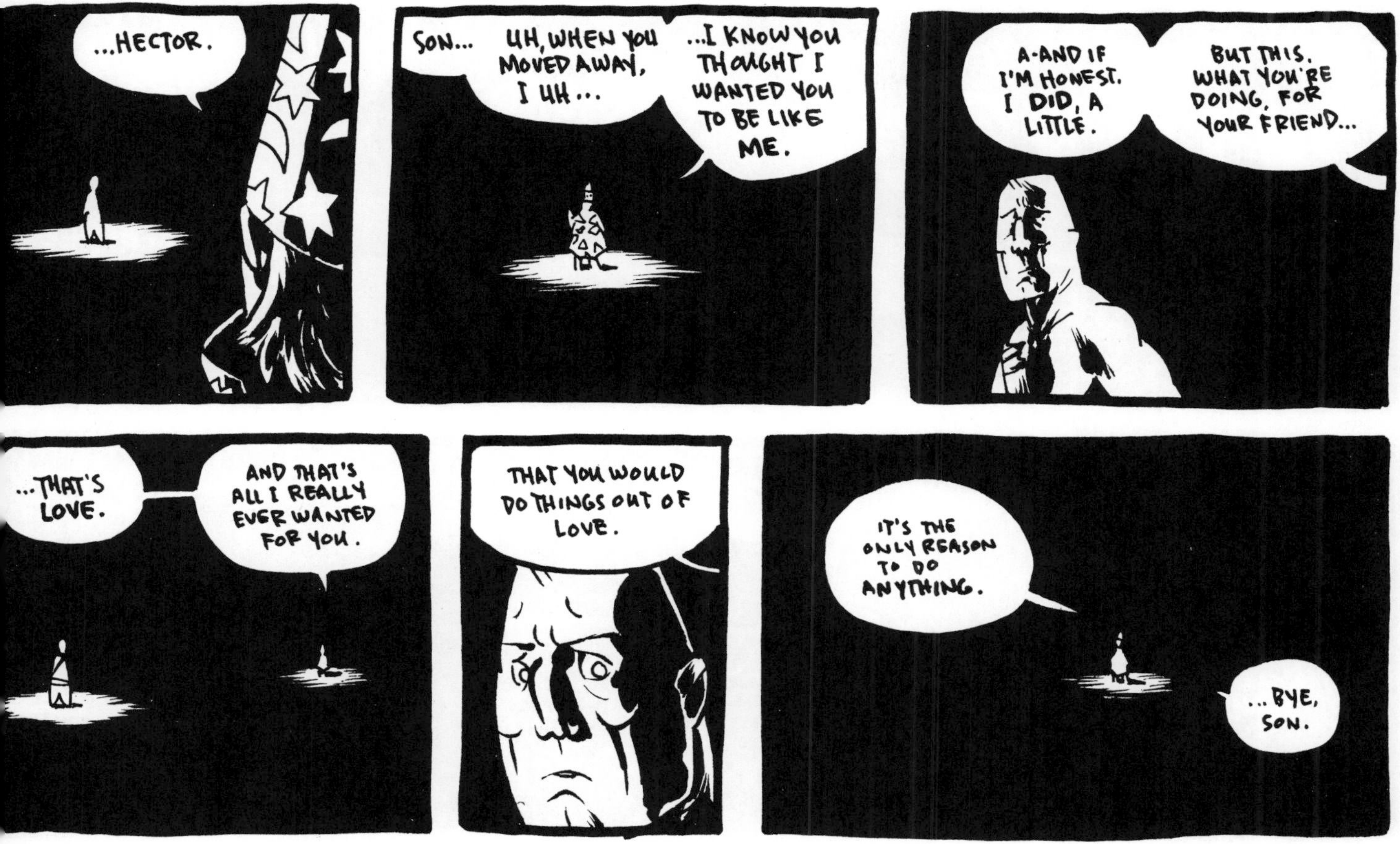
...HECTOR.
SON...
UH, WHEN YOU MOVED AWAY, I UH...
...I KNOW YOU THOUGHT I WANTED YOU TO BE LIKE ME.
A-AND IF I'M HONEST, I DID, A LITTLE.
BUT THIS, WHAT YOU'RE DOING, FOR YOUR FRIEND...
...THAT'S LOVE.
AND THAT'S ALL I REALLY EVER WANTED FOR YOU.
THAT YOU WOULD DO THINGS OUT OF LOVE.
IT'S THE ONLY REASON TO DO ANYTHING.
...BYE, SON.

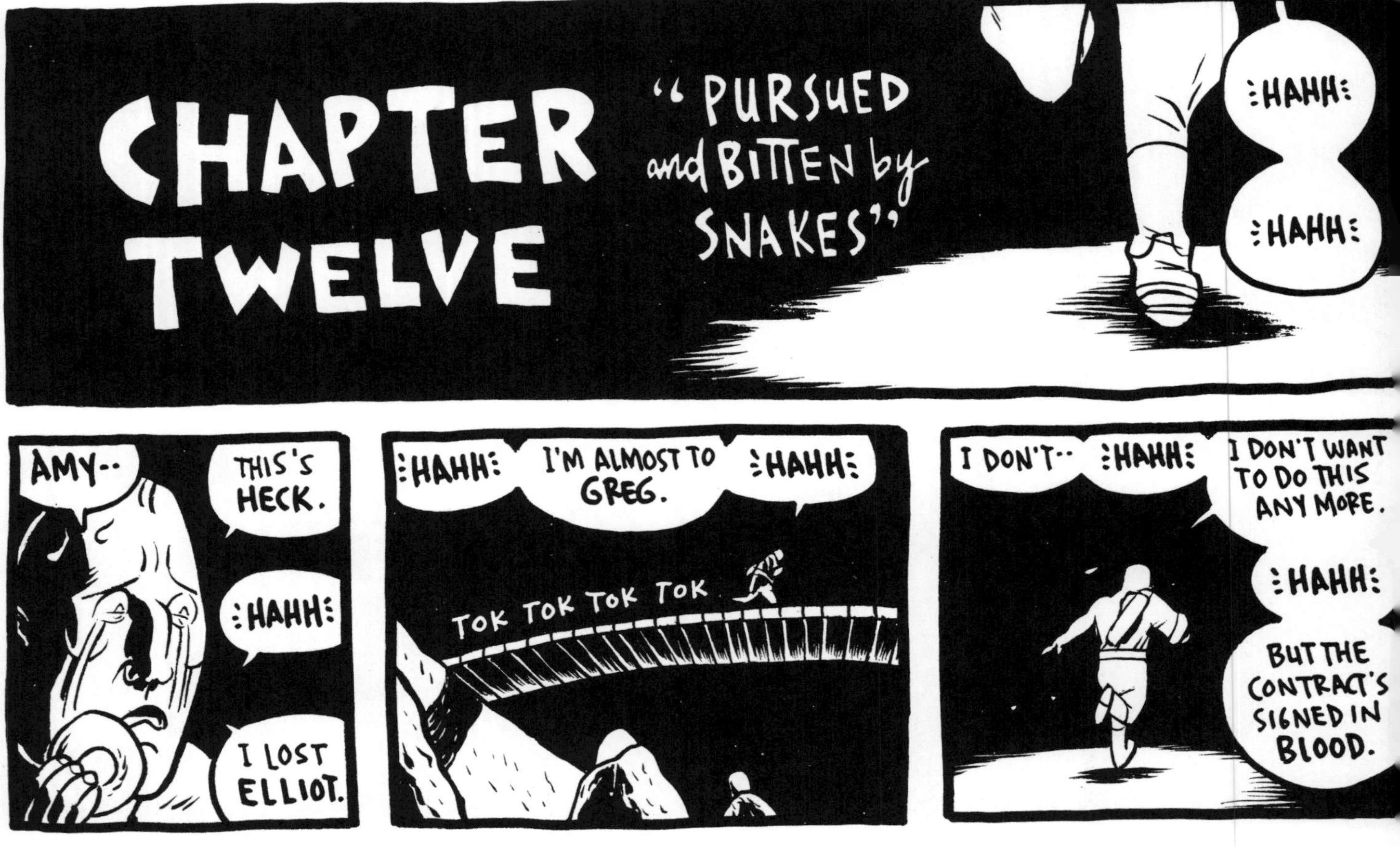
CHAPTER TWELVE
"PURSUED and BITTEN by SNAKES"
HAHH
HAHH
AMY..
THIS'S HECK.
HAHH
I LOST ELLIOT.
HAHH
I'M ALMOST TO GREG.
HAHH
TOK TOK TOK TOK
I DON'T..
HAHH
I DON'T WANT TO DO THIS ANY MORE.
HAHH
BUT THE CONTRACT'S SIGNED IN BLOOD.

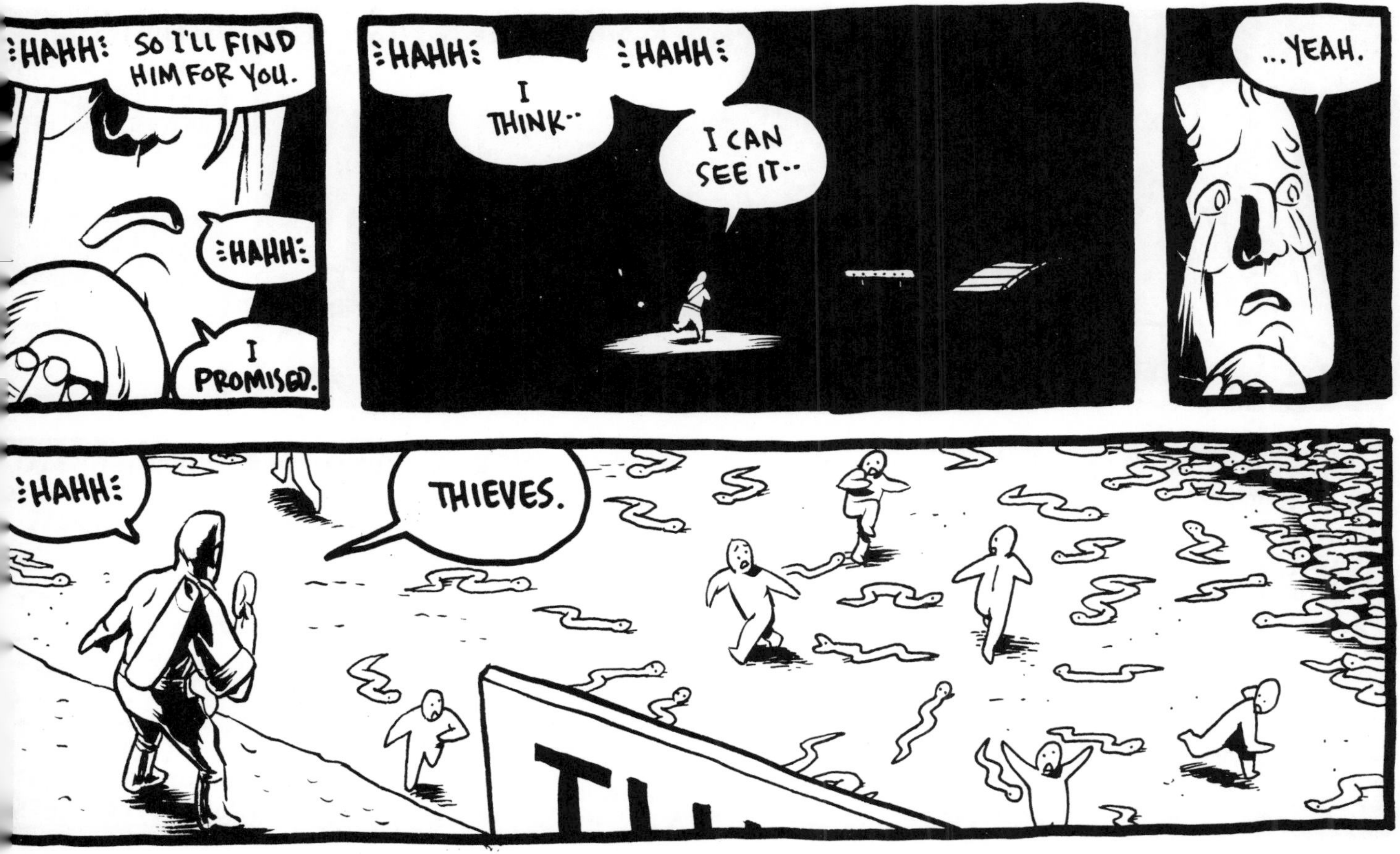
HAHH
SO I'LL FIND HIM FOR YOU.
HAHH
I PROMISED.
HAHH
I THINK..
HAHH
I CAN SEE IT..
...YEAH.
HAHH
THIEVES.

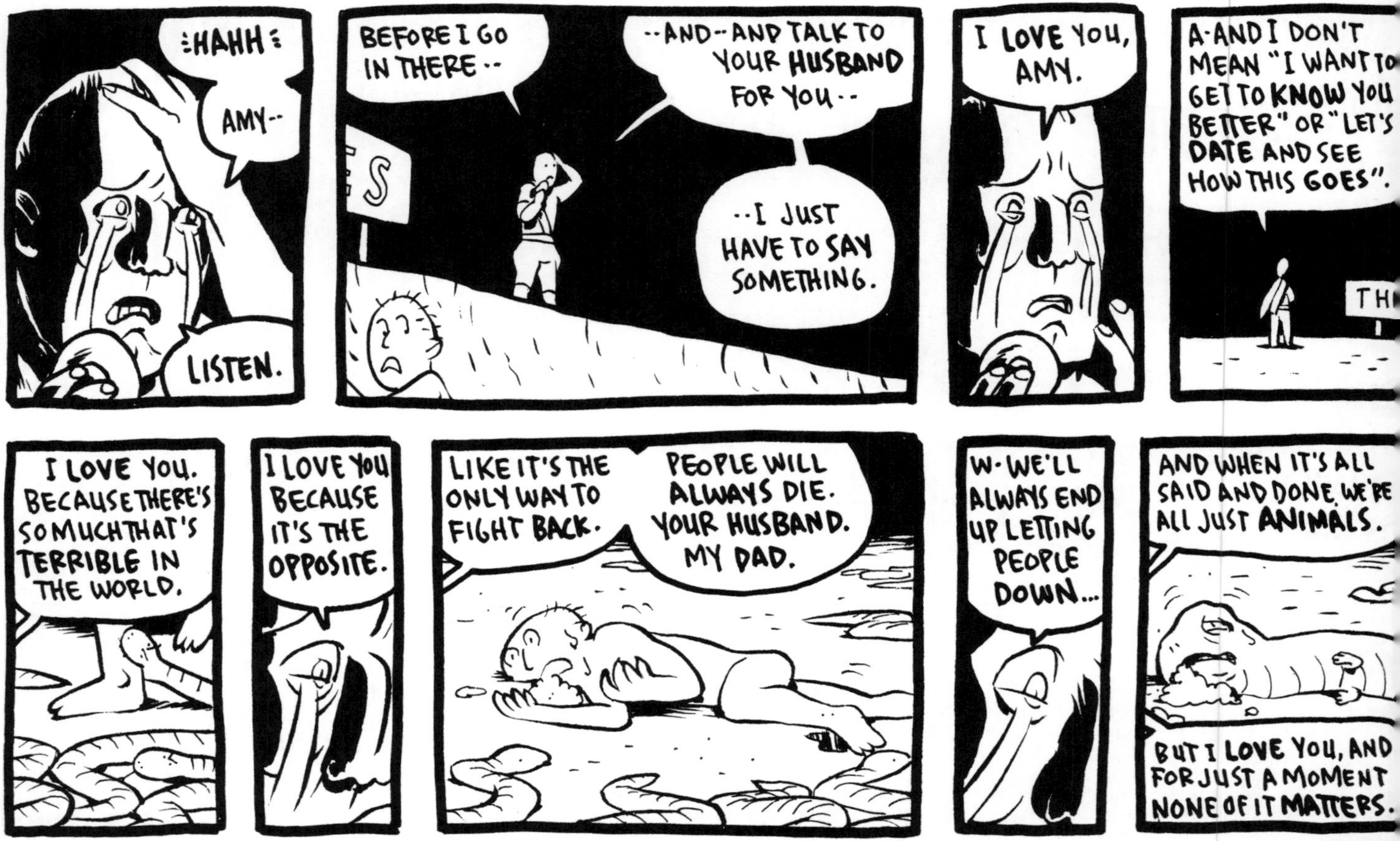
HAHH
AMY--
LISTEN.
BEFORE I GO IN THERE--
--AND--AND TALK TO YOUR HUSBAND FOR YOU--
--I JUST HAVE TO SAY SOMETHING.
ES
I LOVE YOU, AMY.
A-AND I DON'T MEAN "I WANT TO GET TO KNOW YOU BETTER" OR "LET'S DATE AND SEE HOW THIS GOES".
TH
I LOVE YOU. BECAUSE THERE'S SO MUCH THAT'S TERRIBLE IN THE WORLD.
I LOVE YOU BECAUSE IT'S THE OPPOSITE.
LIKE IT'S THE ONLY WAY TO FIGHT BACK.
PEOPLE WILL ALWAYS DIE. YOUR HUSBAND. MY DAD.
W-WE'LL ALWAYS END UP LETTING PEOPLE DOWN...
AND WHEN IT'S ALL SAID AND DONE, WE'RE ALL JUST ANIMALS.
BUT I LOVE YOU, AND FOR JUST A MOMENT NONE OF IT MATTERS.

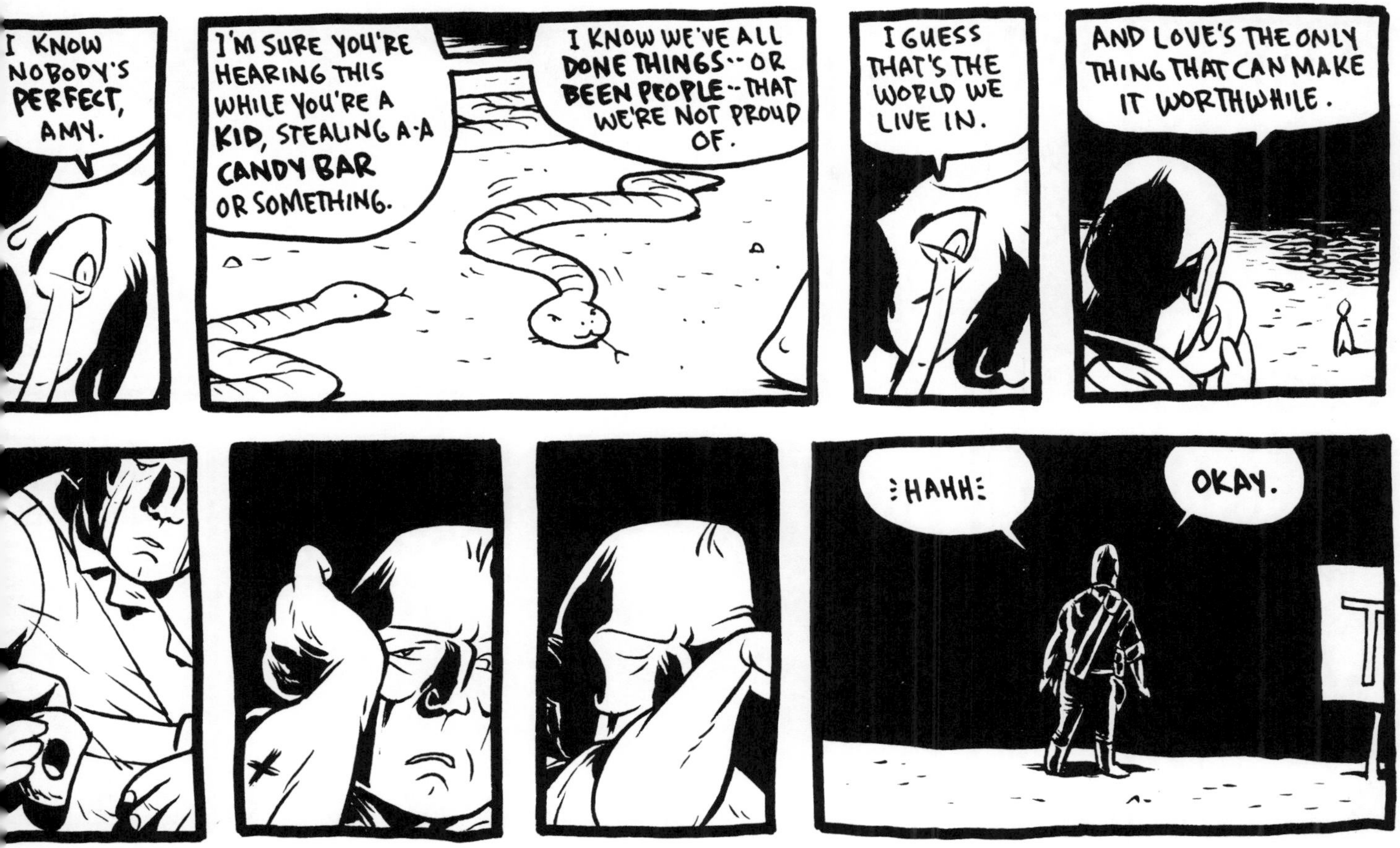

I KNOW NOBODY'S PERFECT, AMY.
I'M SURE YOU'RE HEARING THIS WHILE YOU'RE A KID, STEALING A-A CANDY BAR OR SOMETHING.
I KNOW WE'VE ALL DONE THINGS--OR BEEN PEOPLE--THAT WE'RE NOT PROUD OF.
I GUESS THAT'S THE WORLD WE LIVE IN.
AND LOVE'S THE ONLY THING THAT CAN MAKE IT WORTHWHILE.
HAHH
OKAY.

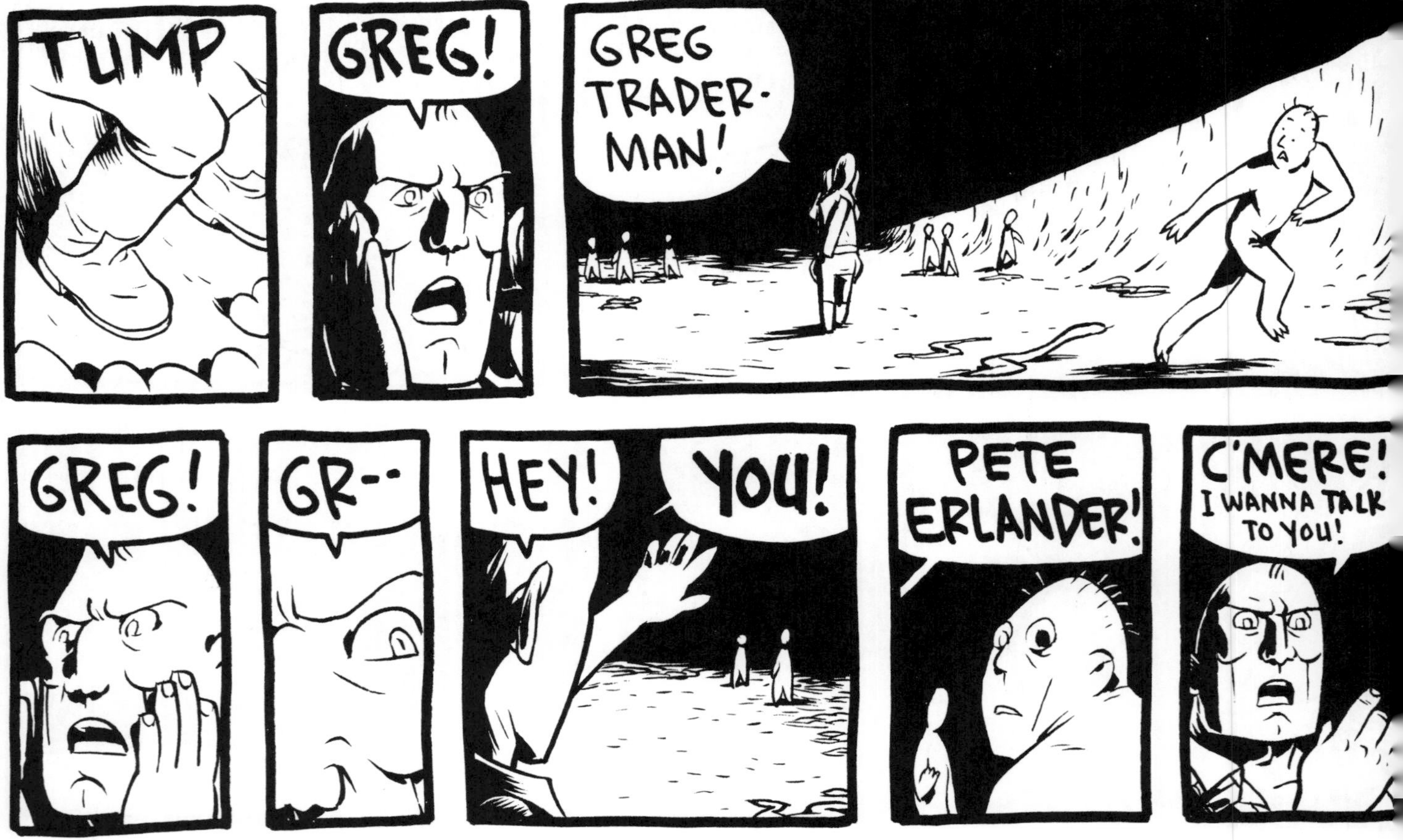
TUMP
GREG!
GREG TRADER-MAN!
GREG!
GR--
HEY!
YOU!
PETE ERLANDER!
C'MERE! I WANNA TALK TO YOU!

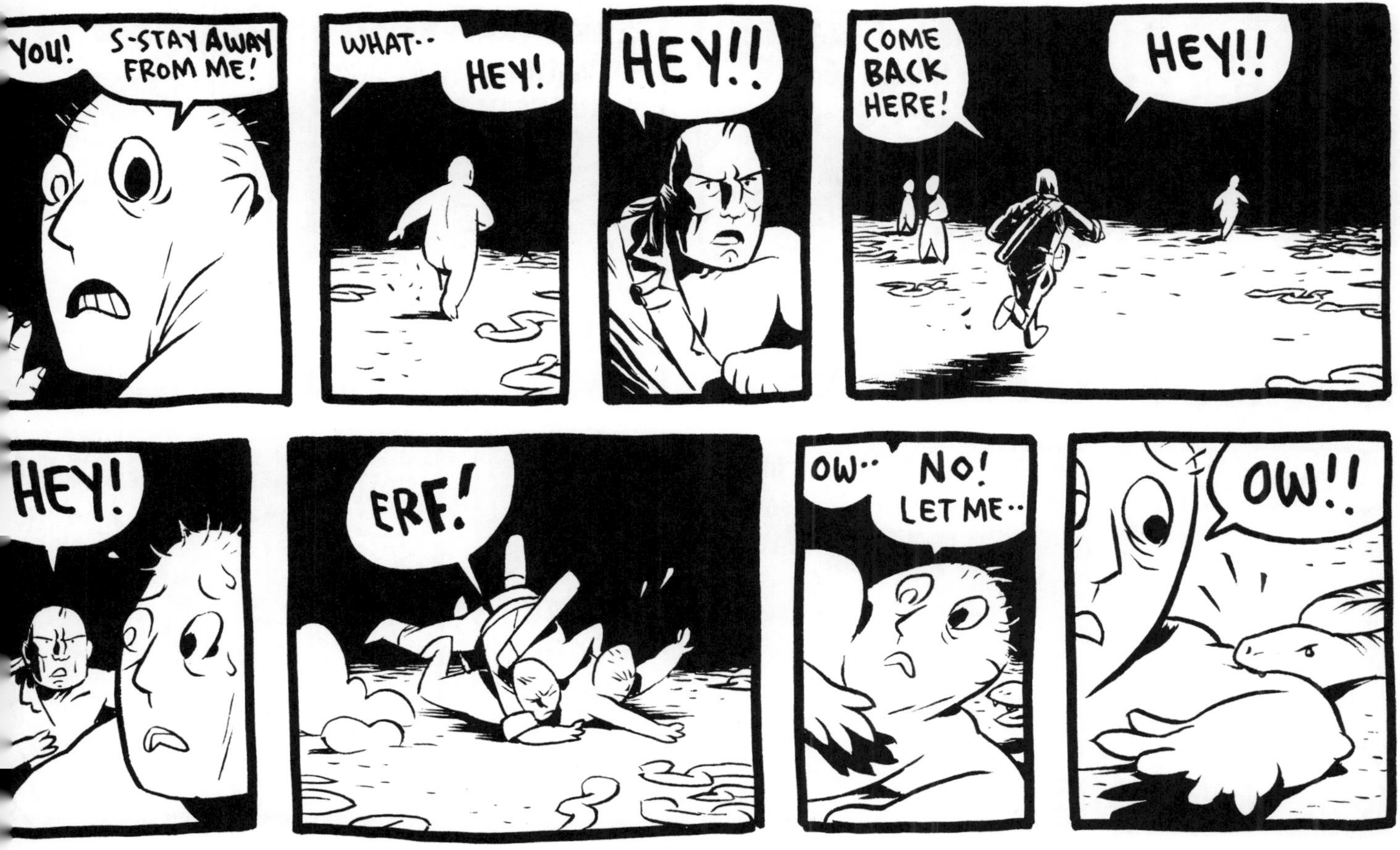
YOU!
S-STAY AWAY FROM ME!
WHAT..
HEY!
HEY!!
COME BACK HERE!
HEY!!
HEY!
ERF!
OW..
NO! LET ME..
OW!!

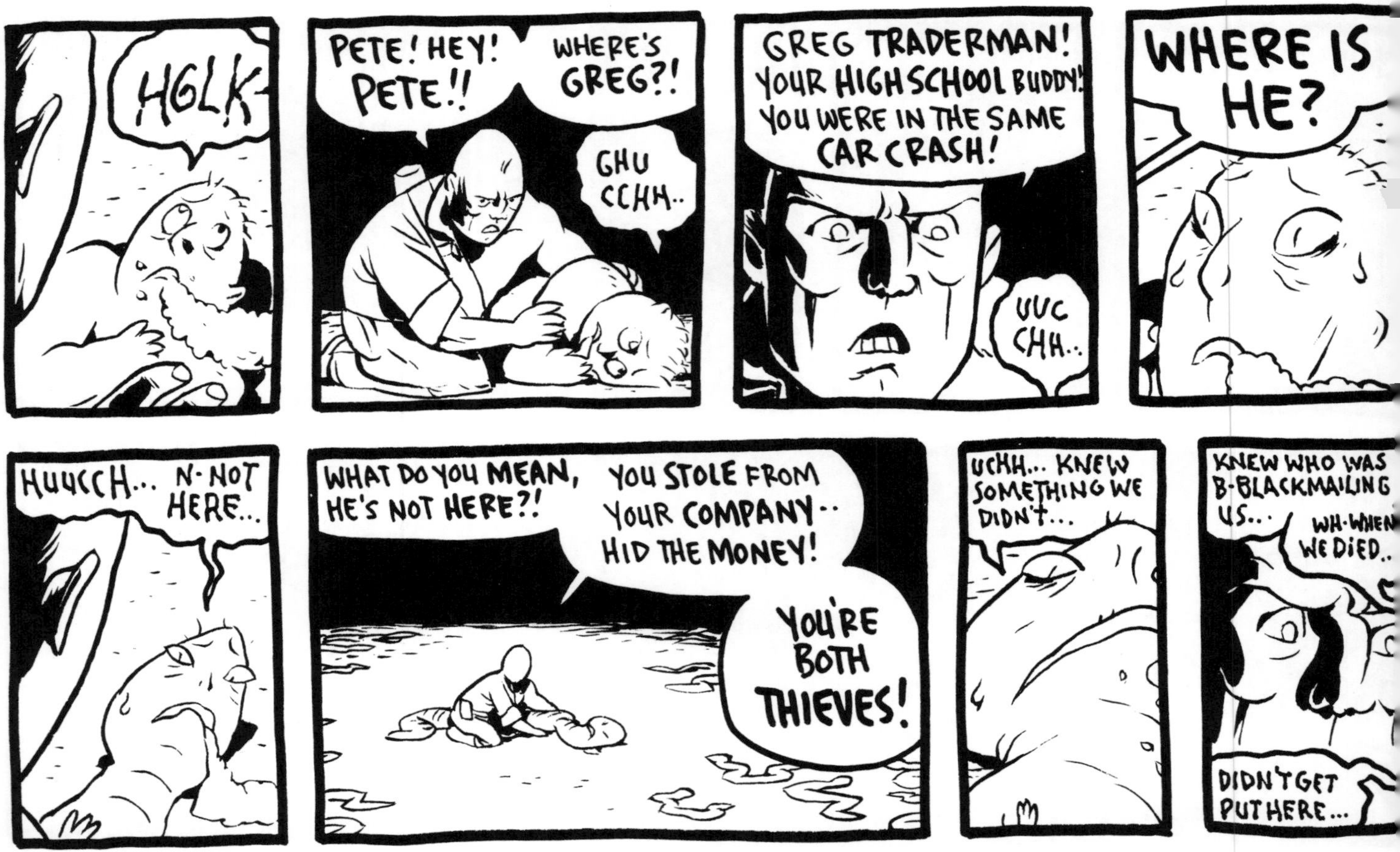
HGLK
PETE! HEY! PETE!!
WHERE'S GREG?!
GHU CCHH..
GREG TRADERMAN! YOUR HIGH SCHOOL BUDDY! YOU WERE IN THE SAME CAR CRASH!
UUC CHH..
WHERE IS HE?
HUUCCH... N-NOT HERE...
WHAT DO YOU MEAN, HE'S NOT HERE?!
YOU STOLE FROM YOUR COMPANY.. HID THE MONEY!
YOU'RE BOTH THIEVES!
UCHH... KNEW SOMETHING WE DIDN'T...
KNEW WHO WAS B-BLACKMAILING US...
WH-WHEN WE DIED..
DIDN'T GET PUT HERE...

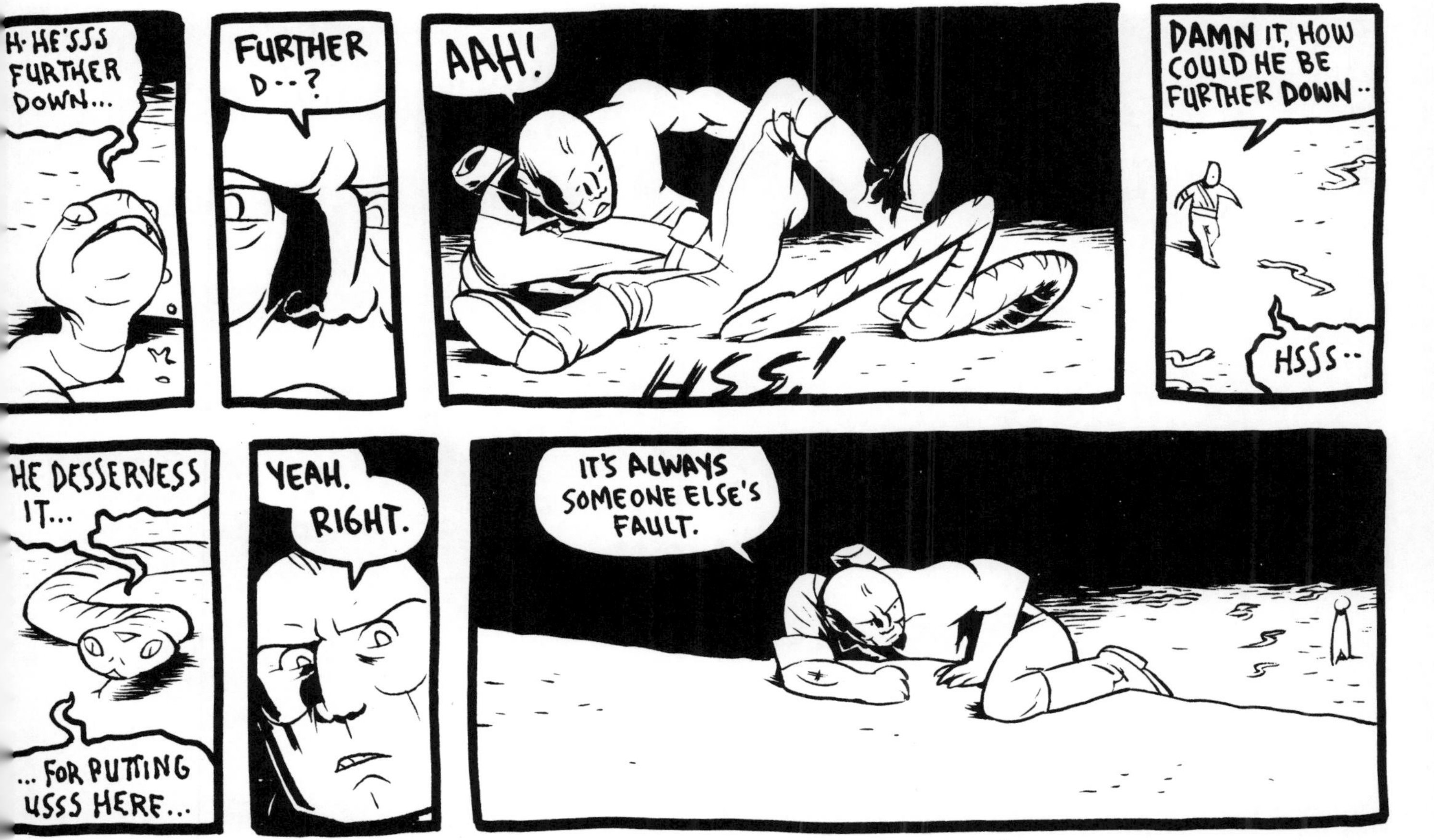
H-HE'SSS FURTHER DOWN...
FURTHER D--?
AAH!
HSSS!
DAMN IT, HOW COULD HE BE FURTHER DOWN..
HSSS..
HE DESSERVESS IT...
... FOR PUTTING USSS HERE...
YEAH.
RIGHT.
IT'S ALWAYS SOMEONE ELSE'S FAULT.

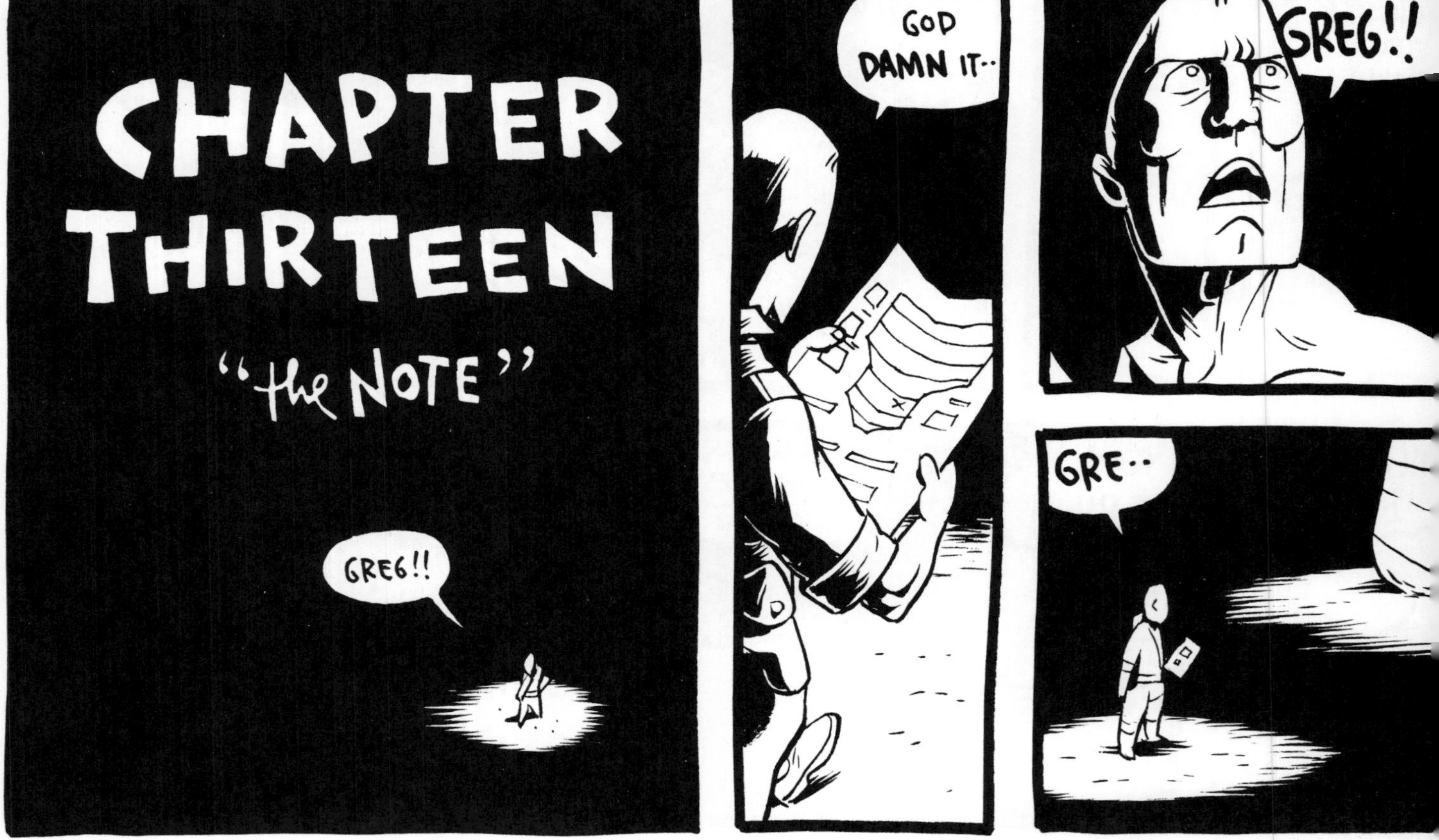
CHAPTER THIRTEEN
"the NOTE"
GREG!!
GOD DAMN IT..
GREG!!
GRE..

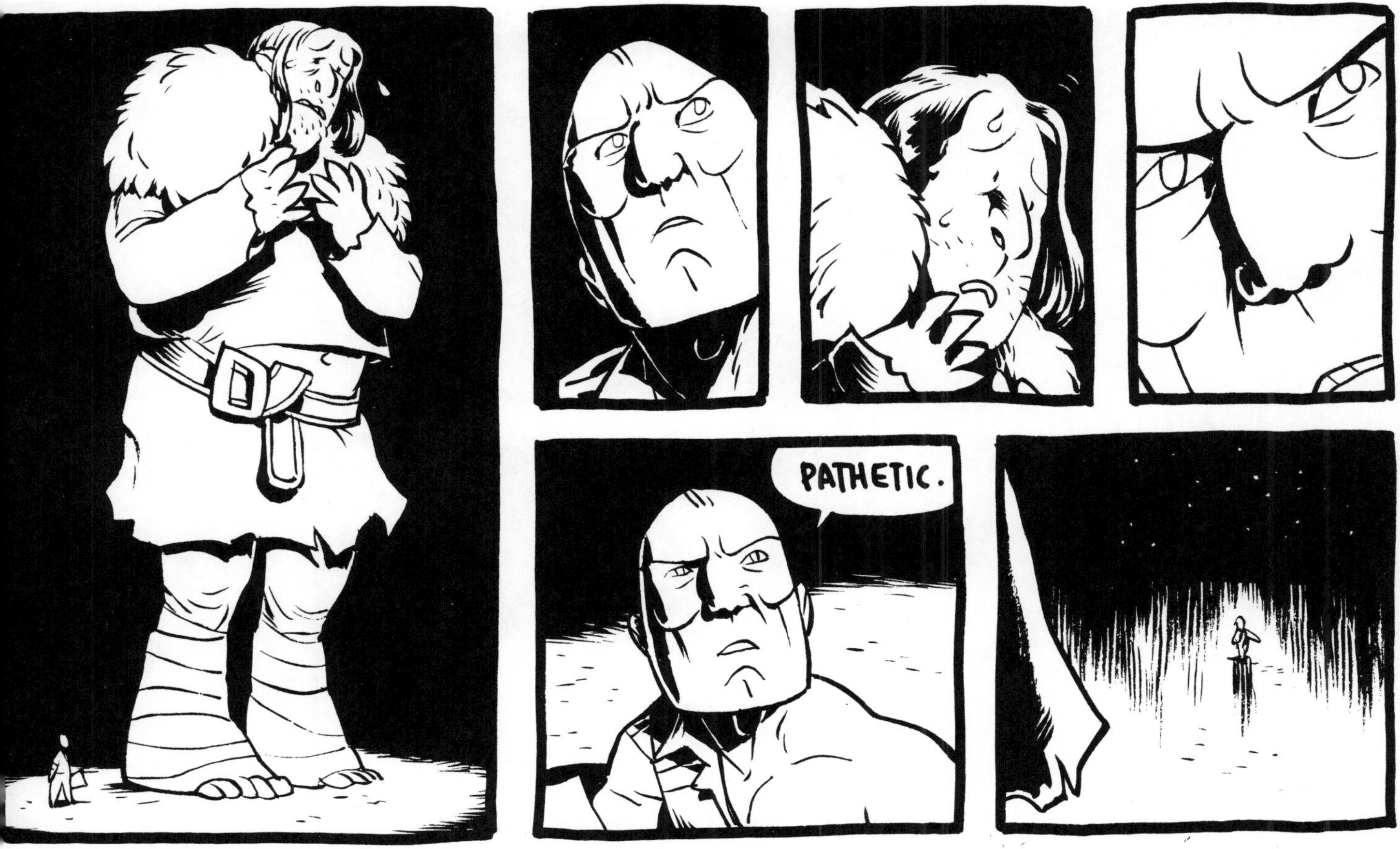
PATHETIC.

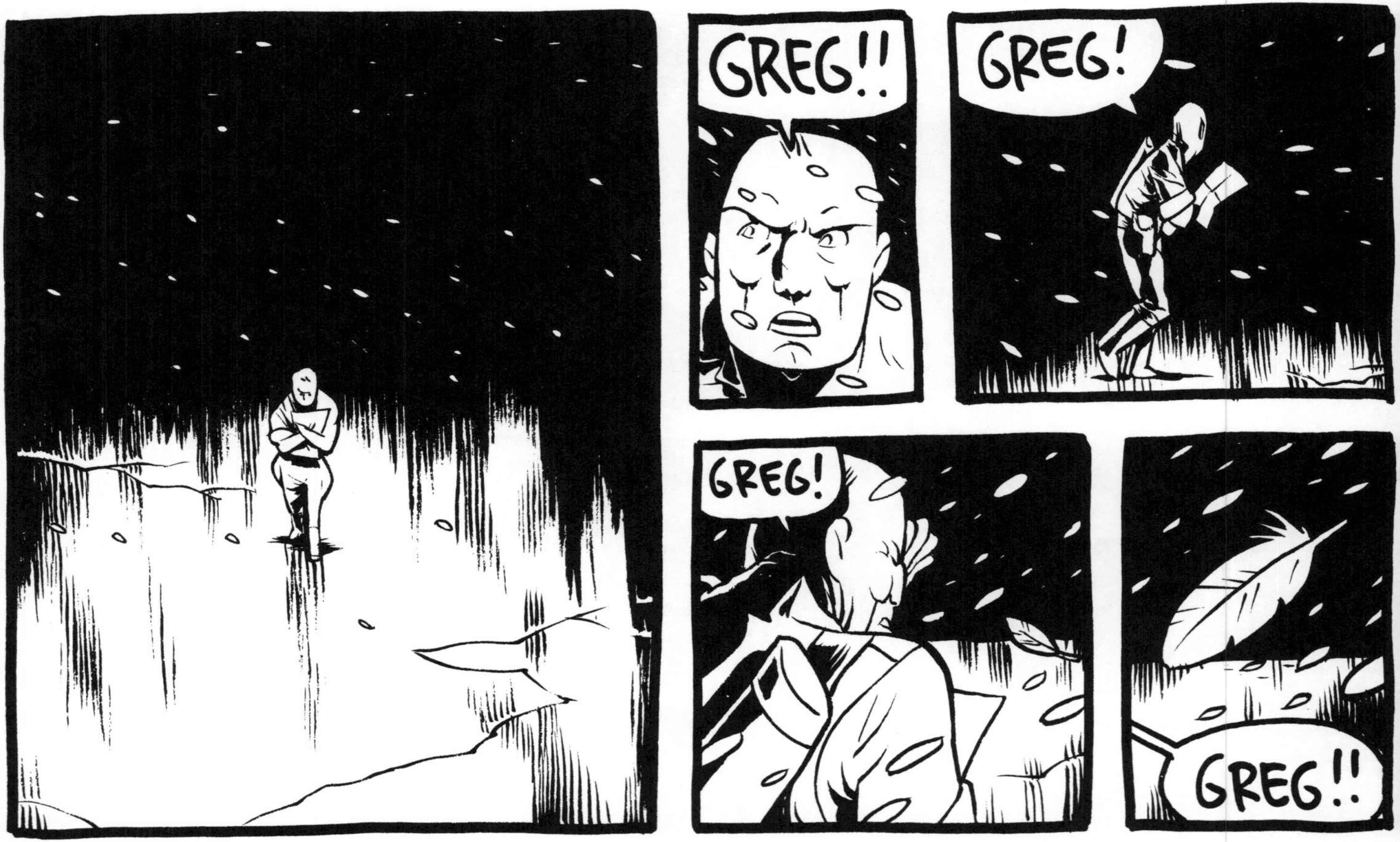
GREG!!
GREG!
GREG!
GREG!!

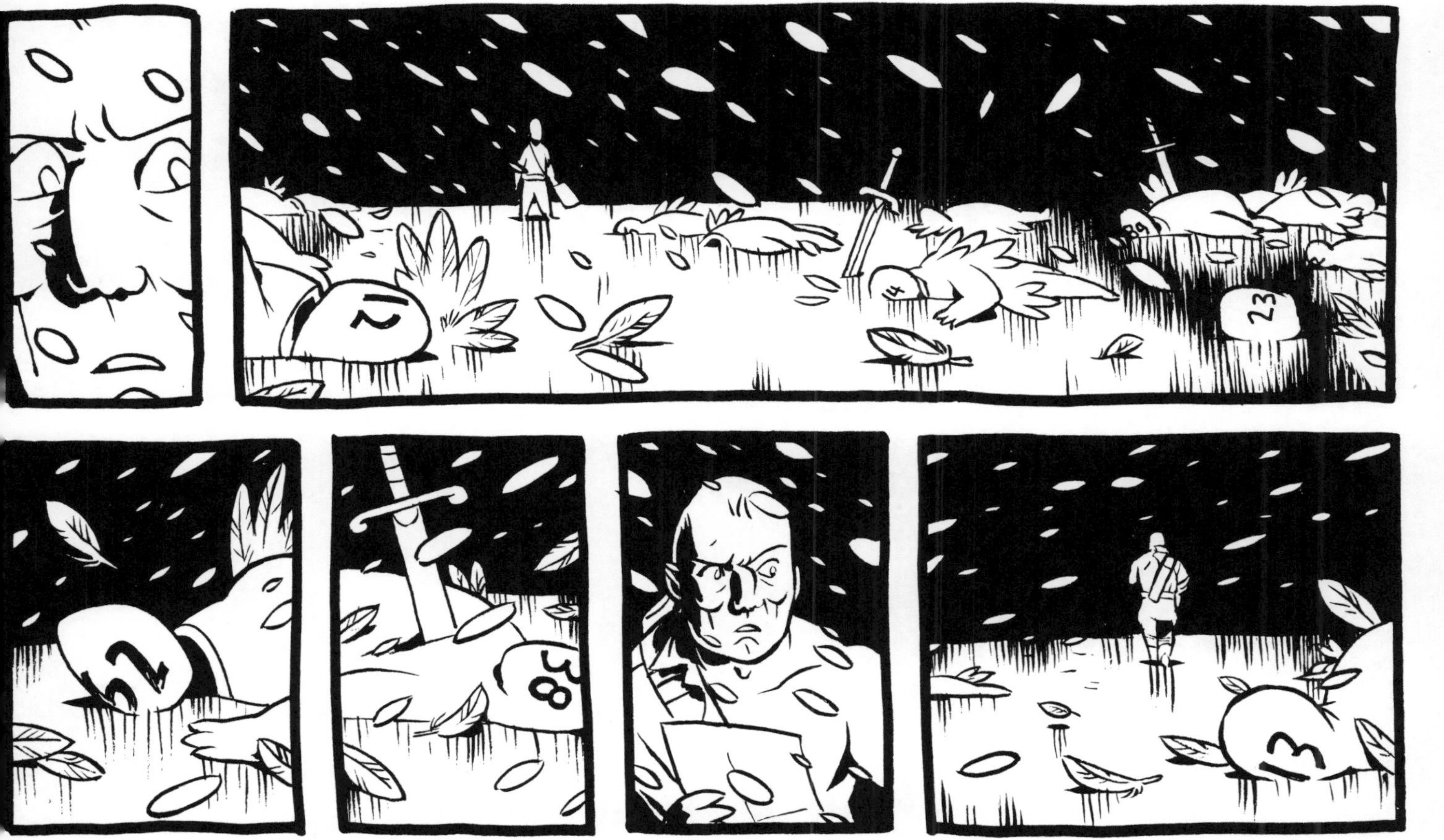

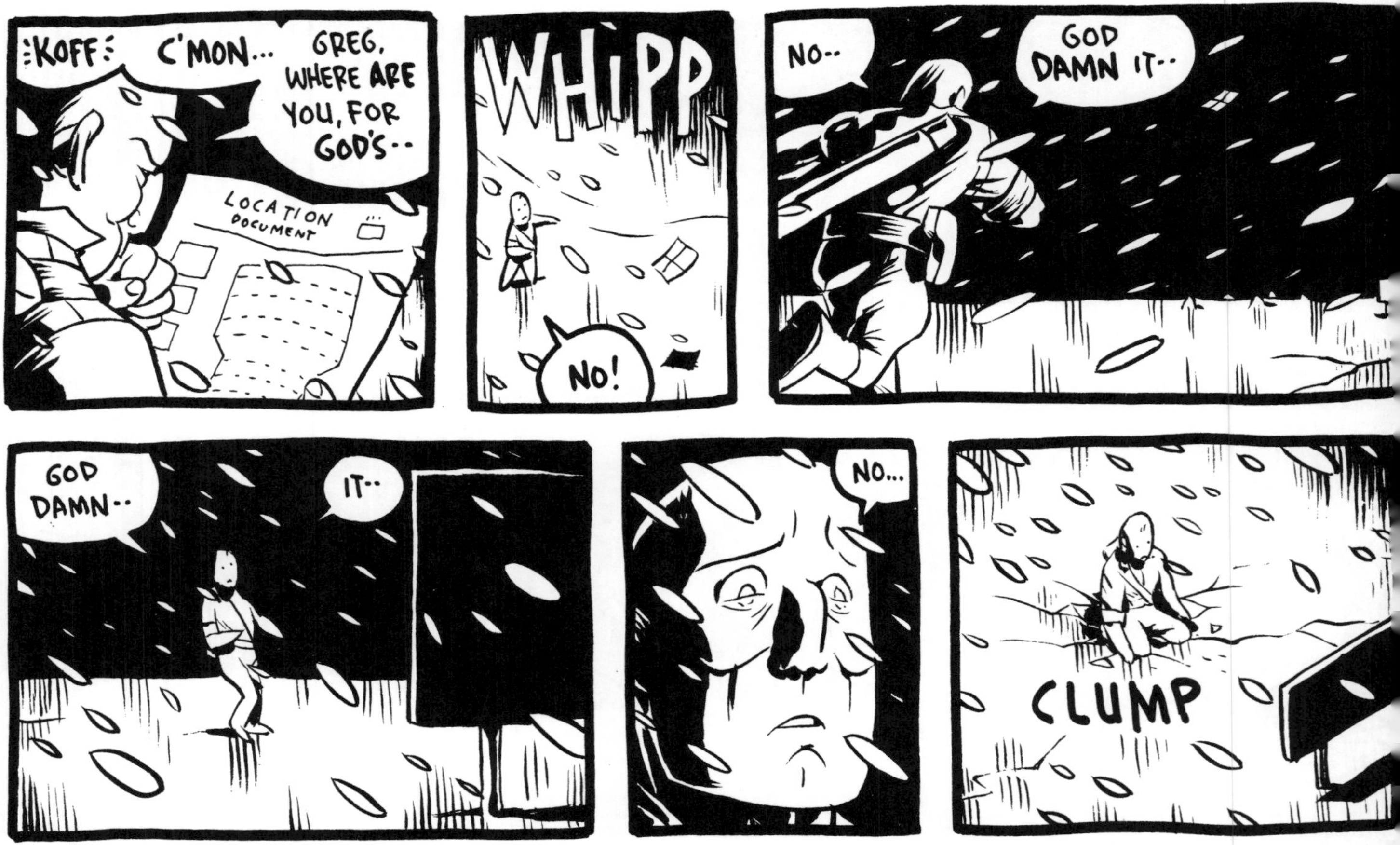

KOFF
C'MON...
GREG, WHERE ARE YOU, FOR GOD'S..
LOCATION DOCUMENT
WHIPP
NO!
NO..
GOD DAMN IT..
GOD DAMN..
IT..
NO...
CLUMP

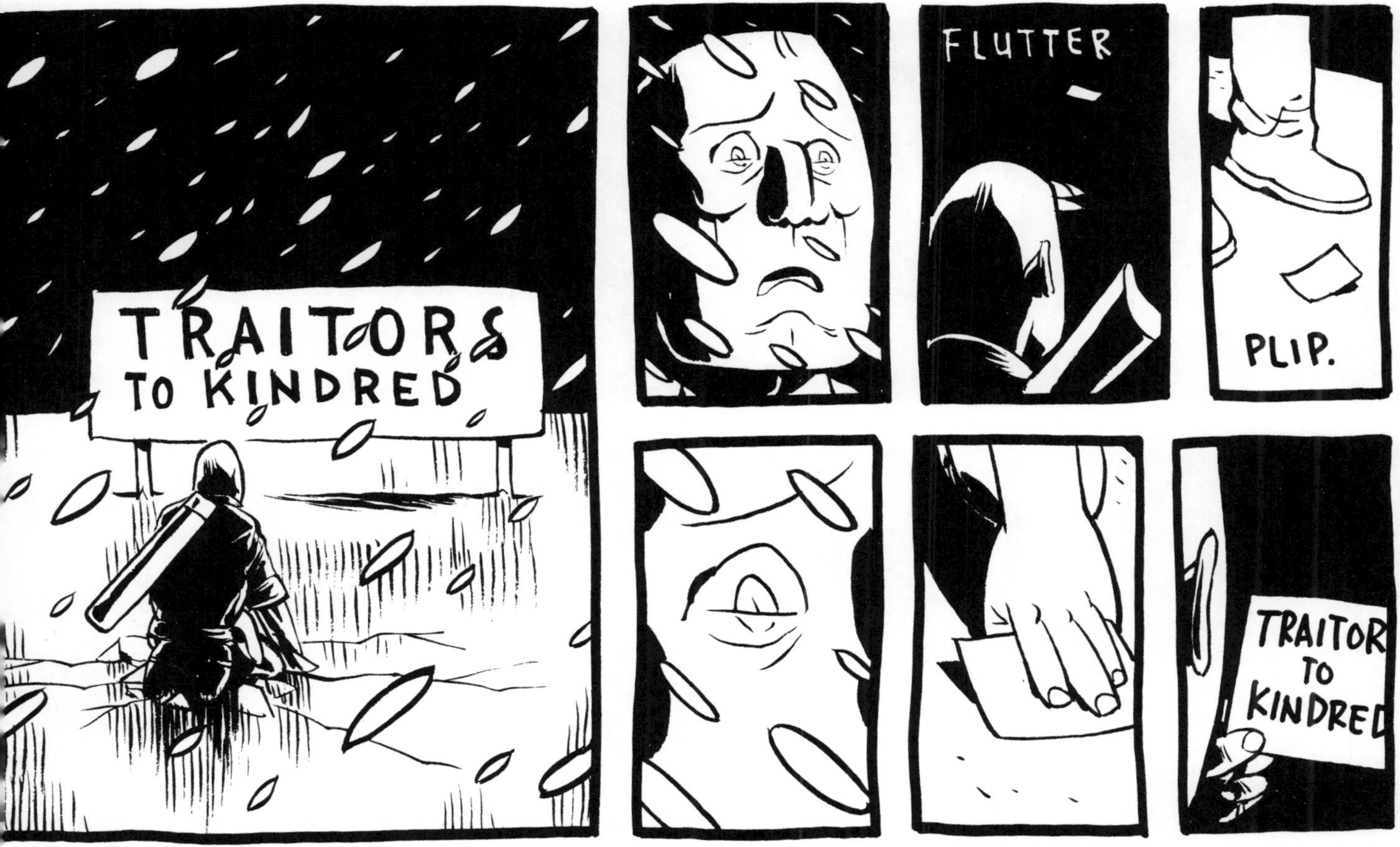
TRAITORS TO KINDRED
FLUTTER
PLIP.
TRAITOR TO KINDRED

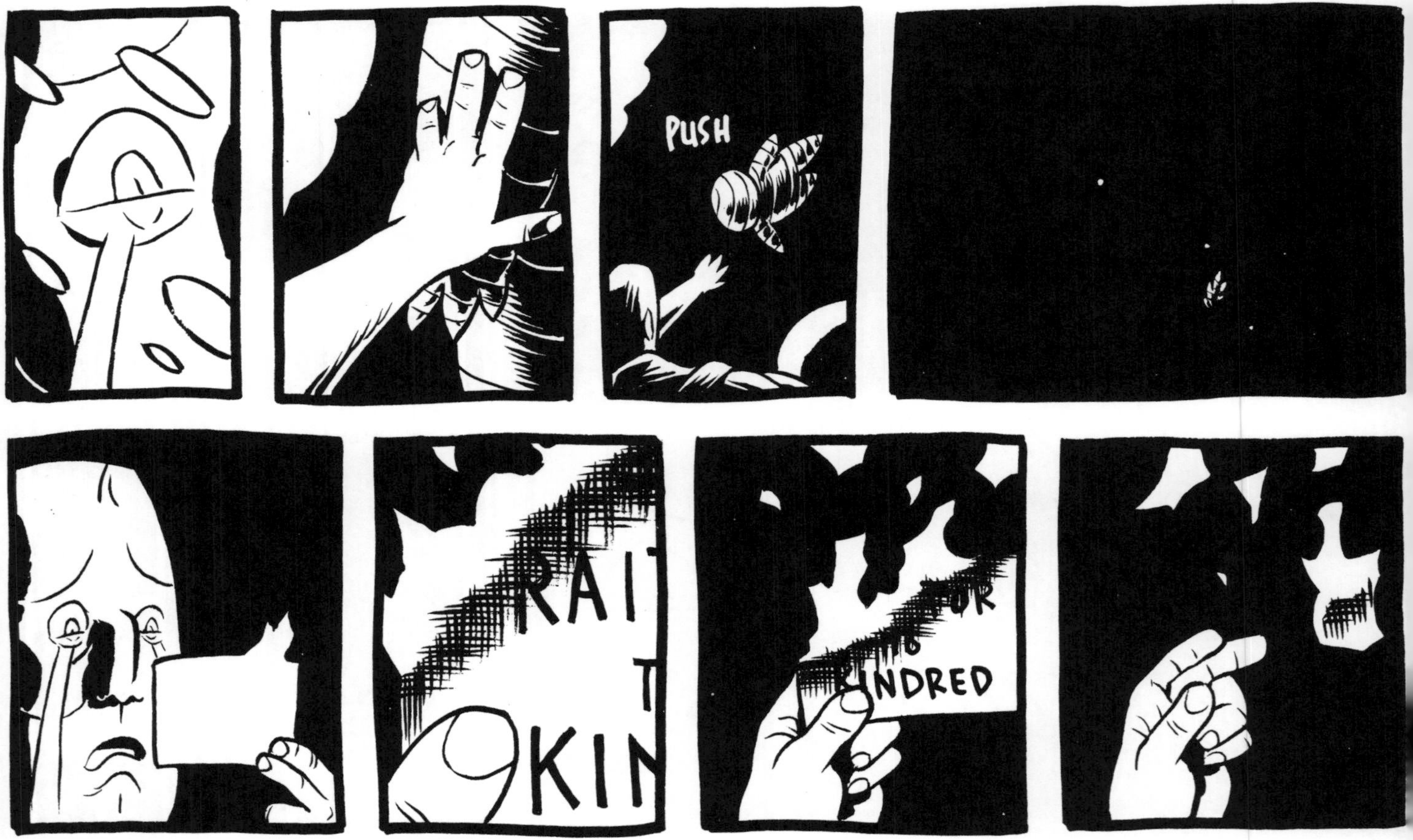
PUSH
RAI
T
KIN
OR
KINDRED

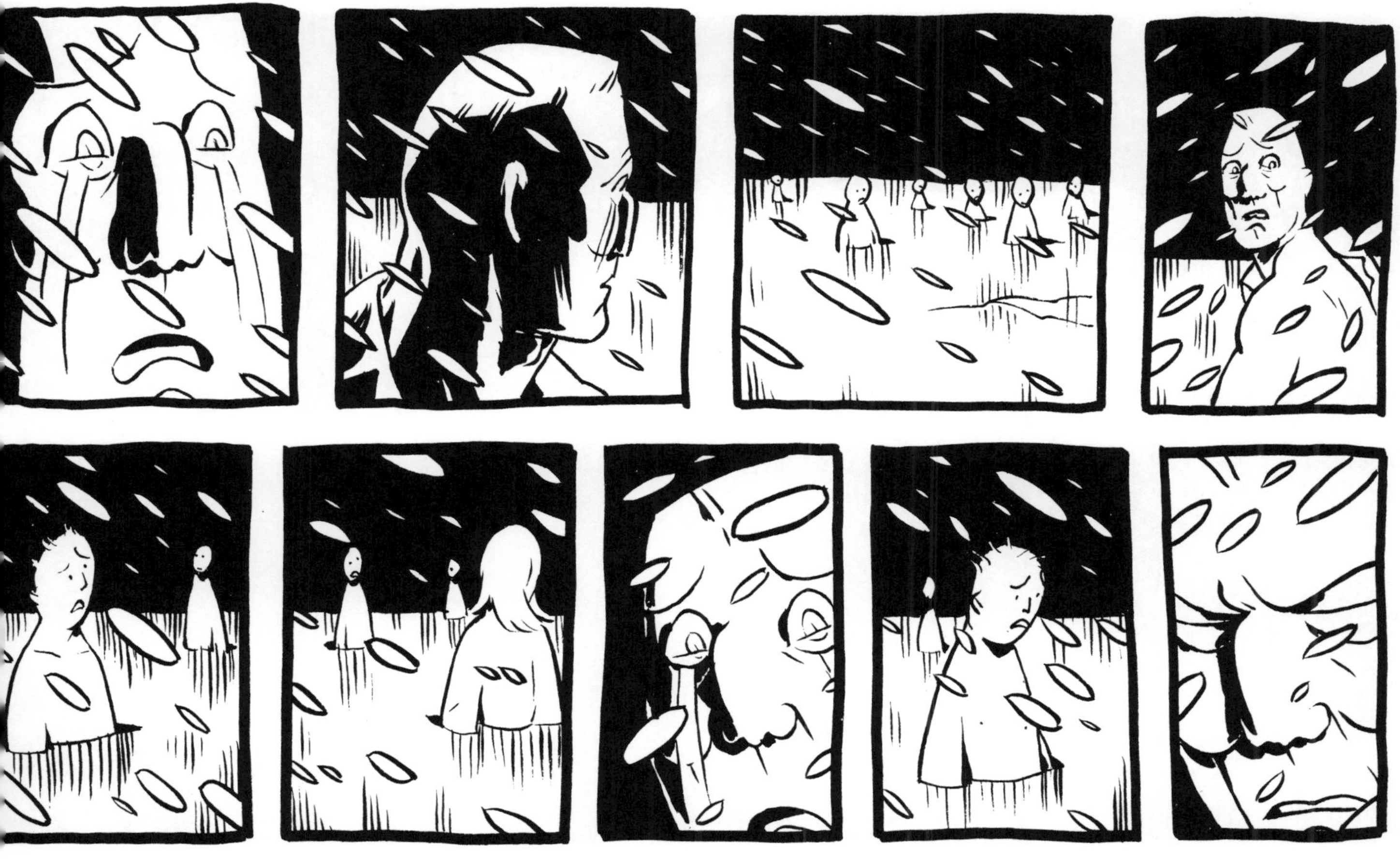

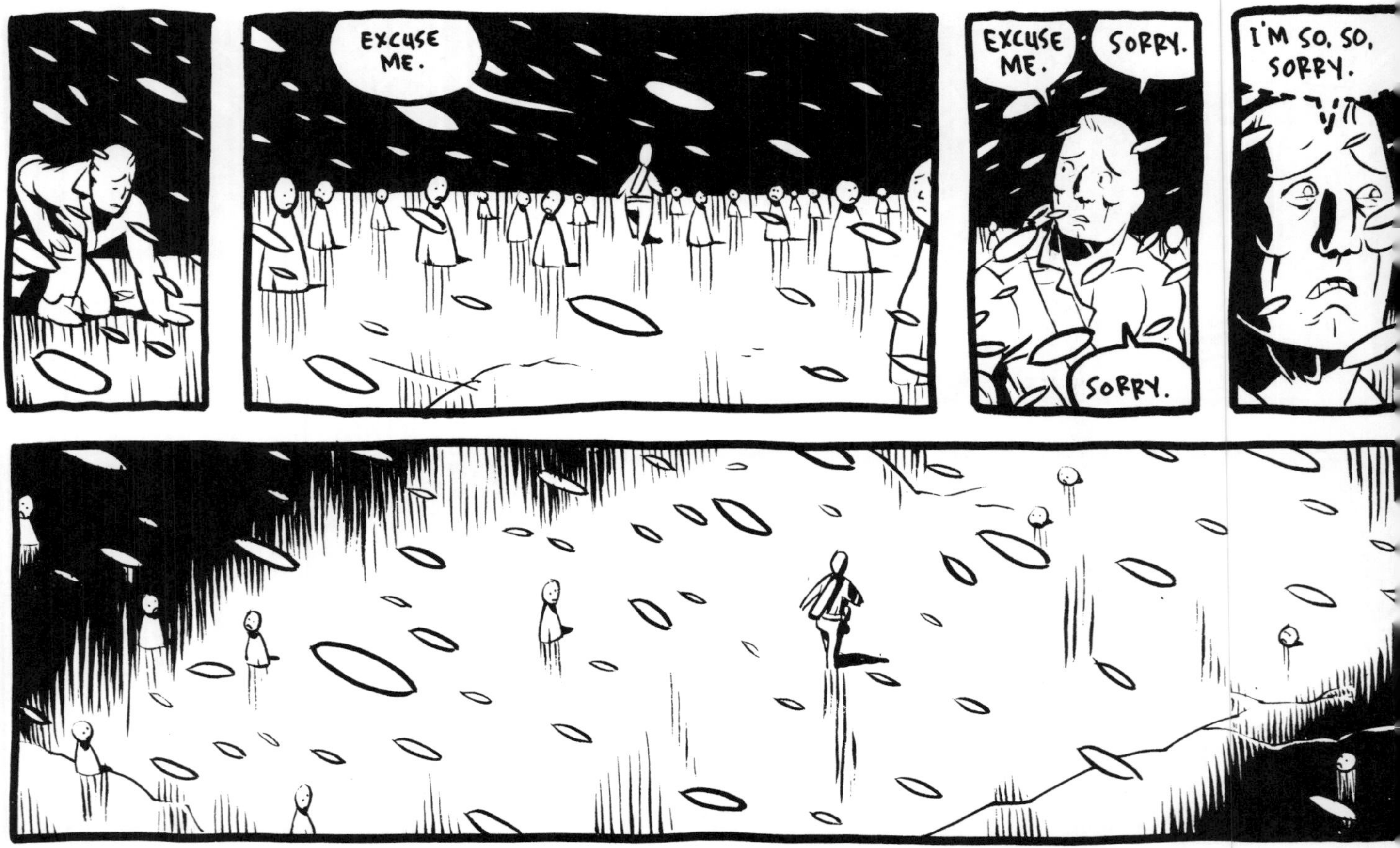
EXCUSE ME.
EXCUSE ME.
SORRY.
SORRY.
I'M SO, SO, SORRY.

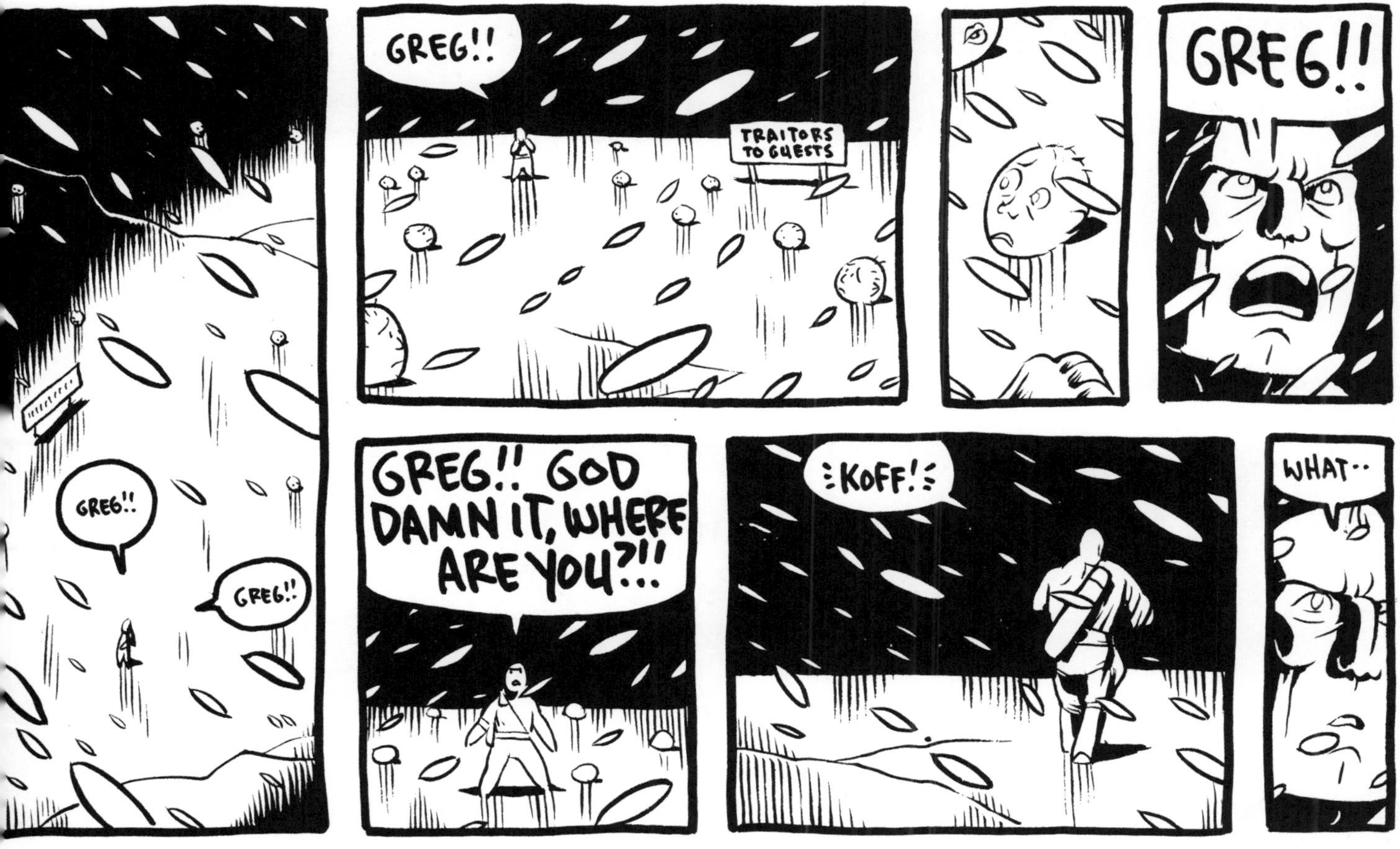
GREG!!
GREG!!
GREG!!
TRAITORS TO GUESTS
GREG!!
GREG!! GOD DAMN IT, WHERE ARE YOU?!!
KOFF!
WHAT..

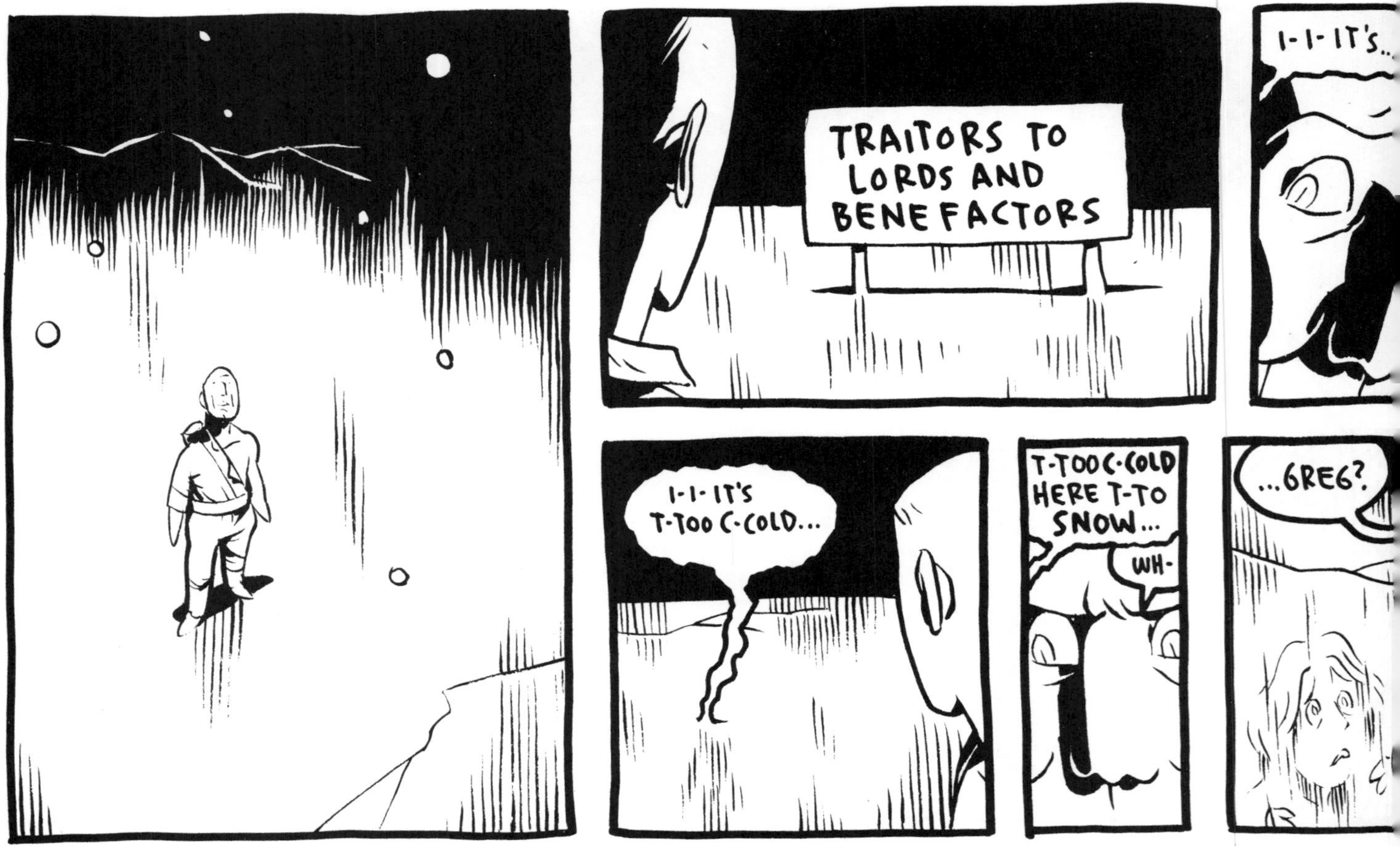
TRAITORS TO
LORDS AND
BENE FACTORS
I-I-IT'S...
I-I-IT'S
T-TOO C-COLD...
T-TOO C-COLD
HERE T-TO
SNOW...
WH-
...GREG?

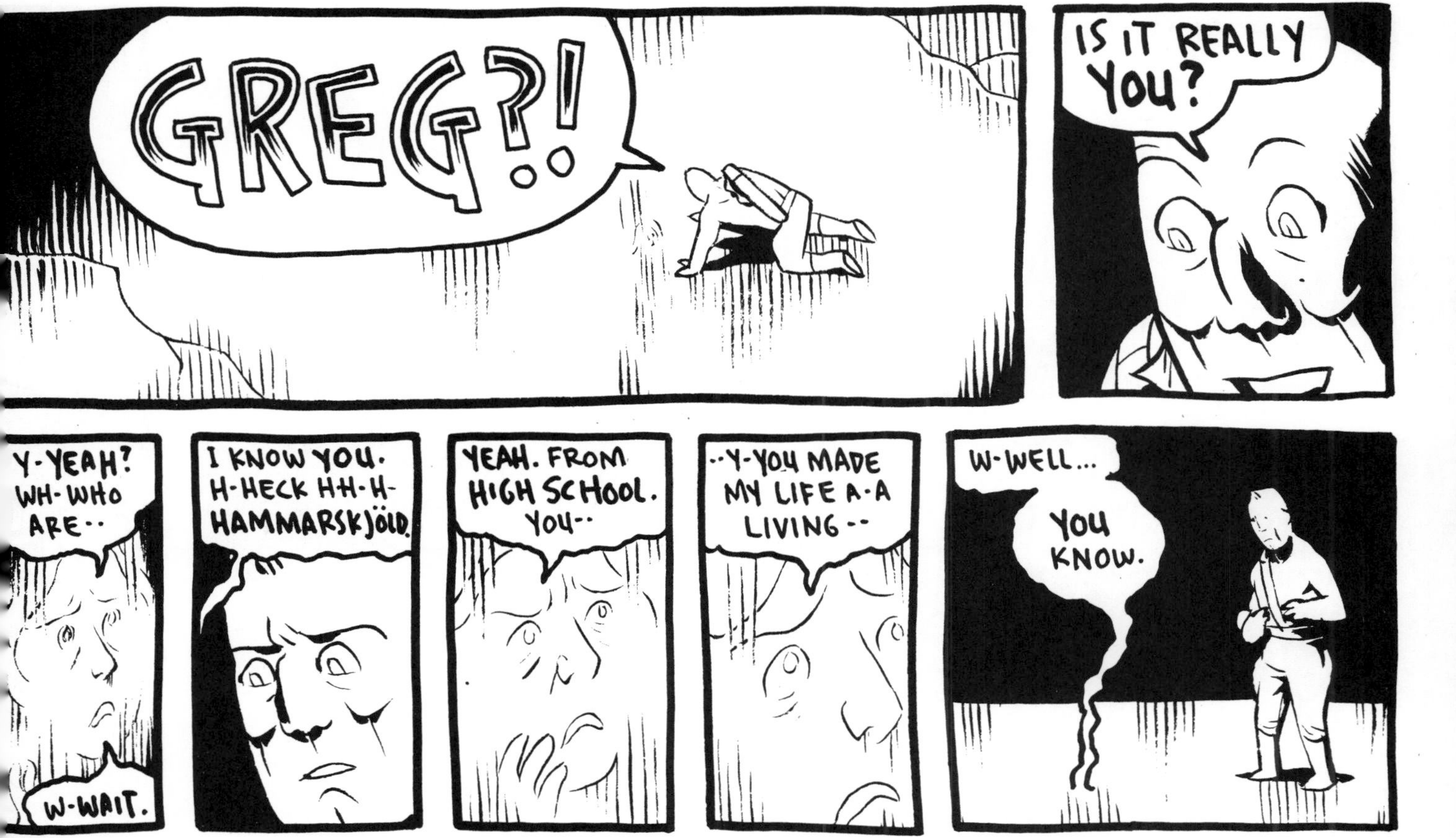
GREG?!
IS IT REALLY YOU?
Y-YEAH? WH-WHO ARE--
W-WAIT.
I KNOW YOU. H-HECK HH-H-HAMMARSKJÖLD.
YEAH. FROM HIGH SCHOOL. YOU--
--Y-YOU MADE MY LIFE A-A LIVING--
W-WELL...
YOU KNOW.

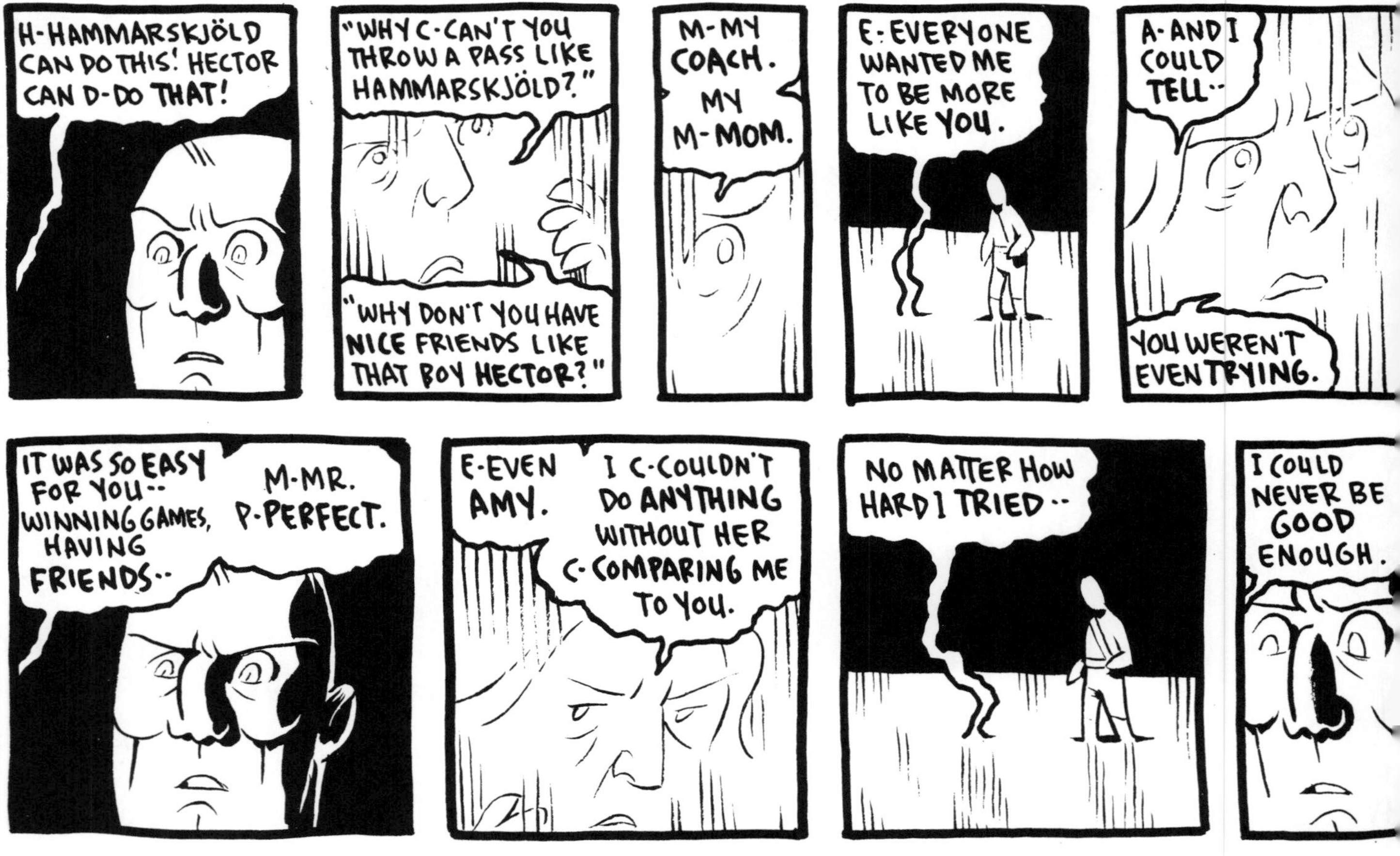
H-HAMMARSKJÖLD CAN DO THIS! HECTOR CAN D-DO THAT!
"WHY C-CAN'T YOU THROW A PASS LIKE HAMMARSKJÖLD?"
"WHY DON'T YOU HAVE NICE FRIENDS LIKE THAT BOY HECTOR?"
M-MY COACH.
MY M-MOM.
E-EVERYONE WANTED ME TO BE MORE LIKE YOU.
A-AND I COULD TELL--
YOU WEREN'T EVEN TRYING.
IT WAS SO EASY FOR YOU-- WINNING GAMES, HAVING FRIENDS--
M-MR. P-PERFECT.
E-EVEN AMY.
I C-COULDN'T DO ANYTHING WITHOUT HER C-COMPARING ME TO YOU.
NO MATTER HOW HARD I TRIED--
I COULD NEVER BE GOOD ENOUGH.

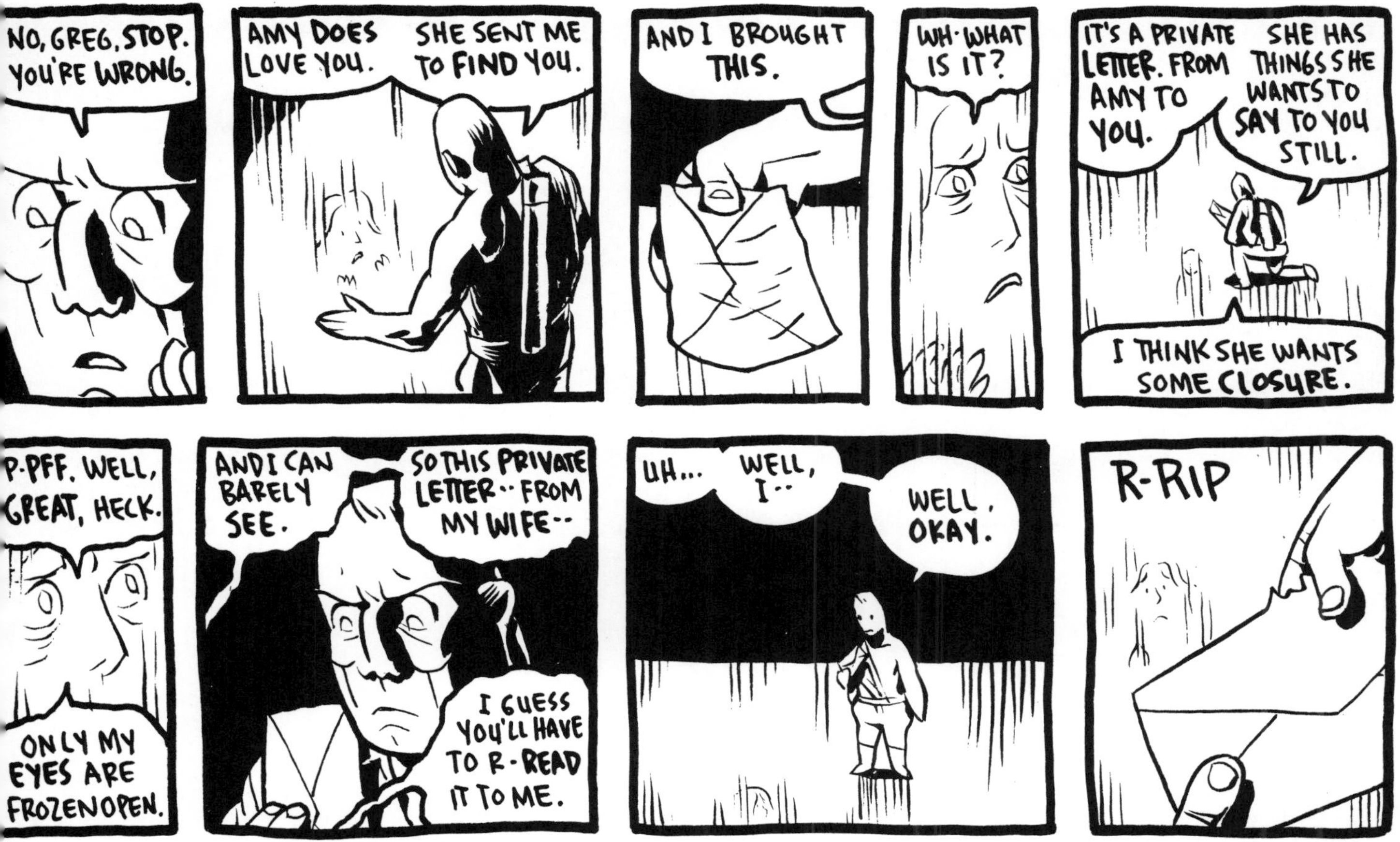
NO, GREG, STOP. YOU'RE WRONG.
AMY DOES LOVE YOU.
SHE SENT ME TO FIND YOU.
AND I BROUGHT THIS.
WH-WHAT IS IT?
IT'S A PRIVATE LETTER. FROM AMY TO YOU.
SHE HAS THINGS SHE WANTS TO SAY TO YOU STILL.
I THINK SHE WANTS SOME CLOSURE.
P-PFF. WELL, GREAT, HECK.
ONLY MY EYES ARE FROZEN OPEN.
AND I CAN BARELY SEE.
SO THIS PRIVATE LETTER-- FROM MY WIFE--
I GUESS YOU'LL HAVE TO R-READ IT TO ME.
UH...
WELL, I--
WELL, OKAY.
R-RIP

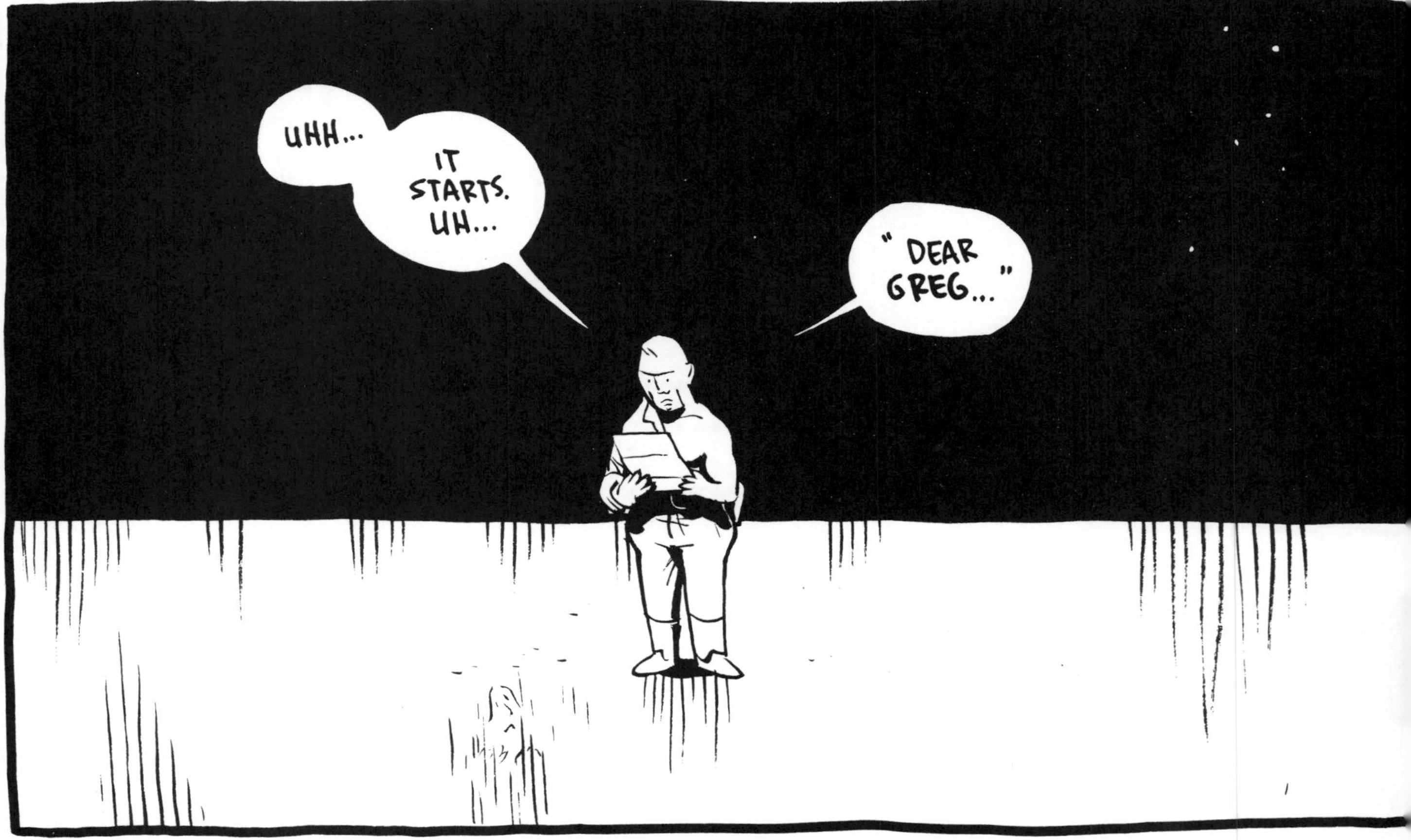
UHH...
IT STARTS. UH...
"DEAR GREG..."

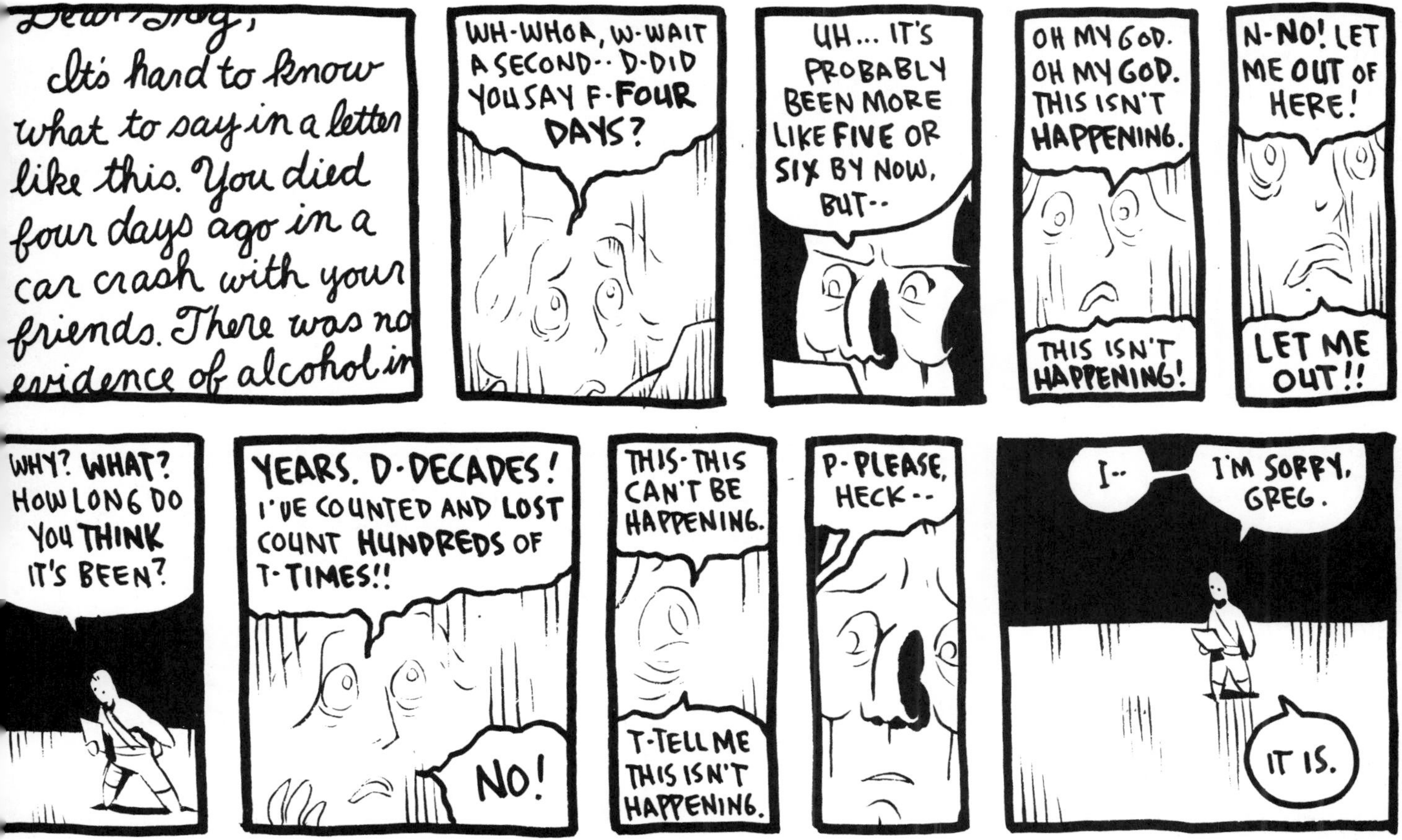
It's hard to know what to say in a letter like this. You died four days ago in a car crash with your friends. There was no evidence of alcohol in
WH-WHOA, W-WAIT A SECOND-- D-DID YOU SAY F-FOUR DAYS?
UH... IT'S PROBABLY BEEN MORE LIKE FIVE OR SIX BY NOW, BUT--
OH MY GOD. OH MY GOD. THIS ISN'T HAPPENING.
THIS ISN'T HAPPENING!
N-NO! LET ME OUT OF HERE!
LET ME OUT!!
WHY? WHAT? HOW LONG DO YOU THINK IT'S BEEN?
YEARS. D-DECADES! I'VE COUNTED AND LOST COUNT HUNDREDS OF T-TIMES!!
NO!
THIS-THIS CAN'T BE HAPPENING.
T-TELL ME THIS ISN'T HAPPENING.
P-PLEASE, HECK--
I--
I'M SORRY, GREG.
IT IS.

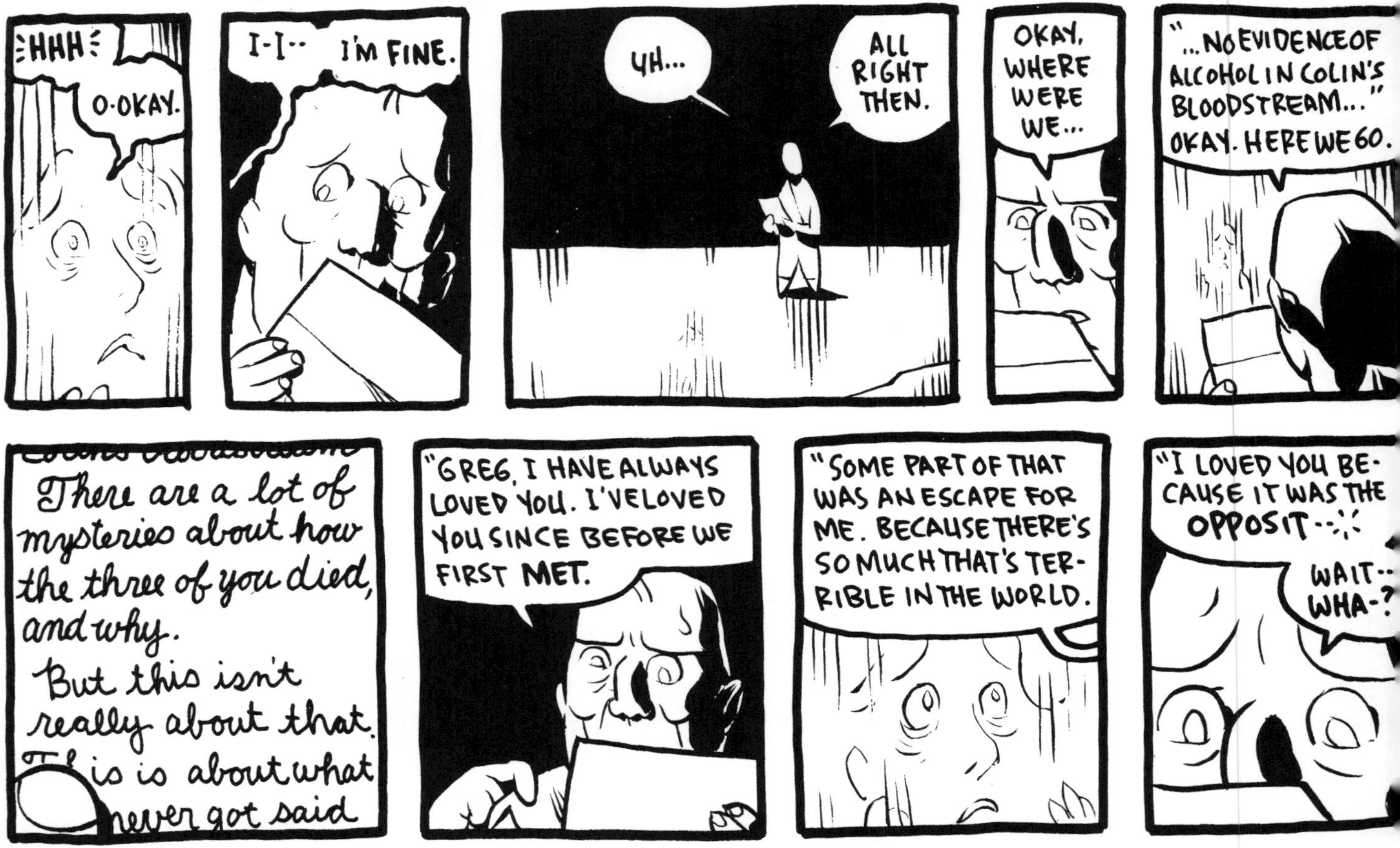
HHH
O-OKAY.
I-I·· I'M FINE.
UH...
ALL RIGHT THEN.
OKAY, WHERE WERE WE...
"...NO EVIDENCE OF ALCOHOL IN COLIN'S BLOODSTREAM..." OKAY. HERE WE GO.
There are a lot of mysteries about how the three of you died, and why.
But this isn't really about that.
This is about what never got said
"GREG, I HAVE ALWAYS LOVED YOU. I'VE LOVED YOU SINCE BEFORE WE FIRST MET.
"SOME PART OF THAT WAS AN ESCAPE FOR ME. BECAUSE THERE'S SO MUCH THAT'S TERRIBLE IN THE WORLD.
"I LOVED YOU BECAUSE IT WAS THE OPPOSIT··
WAIT-- WHA-?

because it was the opposite. Like it was the only way to fight back.

People will always die, we'll always let people down and when it's all said and done, we're all just animals. But I loved you, and just a moment, none of it matt

WHAT IN THE HELL--

WH-WHAT'S THE MATTER WITH YOU? WHY'D YOU STOP?

THIS-- THESE ARE MY WORDS! I SAID THESE THINGS TO AMY, BUT--

WH-WHAT?

YOU T-TOLD MY WIFE YOU'RE IN LOVE WITH HER?

I'VE ONLY B-BEEN DEAD FOR FOUR DAYS! WHAT THE HELL IS WRONG WITH--

NO, IT'S NOT THAT. IT'S WHERE I SAID IT TO HER--

I WAS IN THIEVES-- I-- HOLD ON A SEC--

moment, none of it matt

But love could only sustain us for so long and eventually it all does matter again. Things like houses. Things like possessions. Things like money. Things that made you start stealing from your company.

"A GOOD START, GREG...

...BUT YOU DIDN'T THINK BIG ENOUGH.

... UH...

I-IT...

"IT TOOK ME TO TAKE IT TO THE NEXT LEVEL.

"I FIGURED OUT THE LOOPHOLE.

"I SAW IT IN THE COMPUTERS.

"THE TAKE WAS NINE TIMES WHAT YOU'D MANAGED.

"AND NO ONE SUSPECTED A THING.

'ALL THANKS TO ME.

"AND WHAT WAS MY THANKS, GREG?

"YOU LIED ABOUT IT.

"YOU HID IT FROM ME.

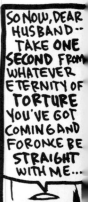

SO NOW, DEAR HUSBAND-- TAKE ONE SECOND FROM WHATEVER ETERNITY OF TORTURE YOU'VE GOT COMING AND FOR ONCE BE STRAIGHT WITH ME...

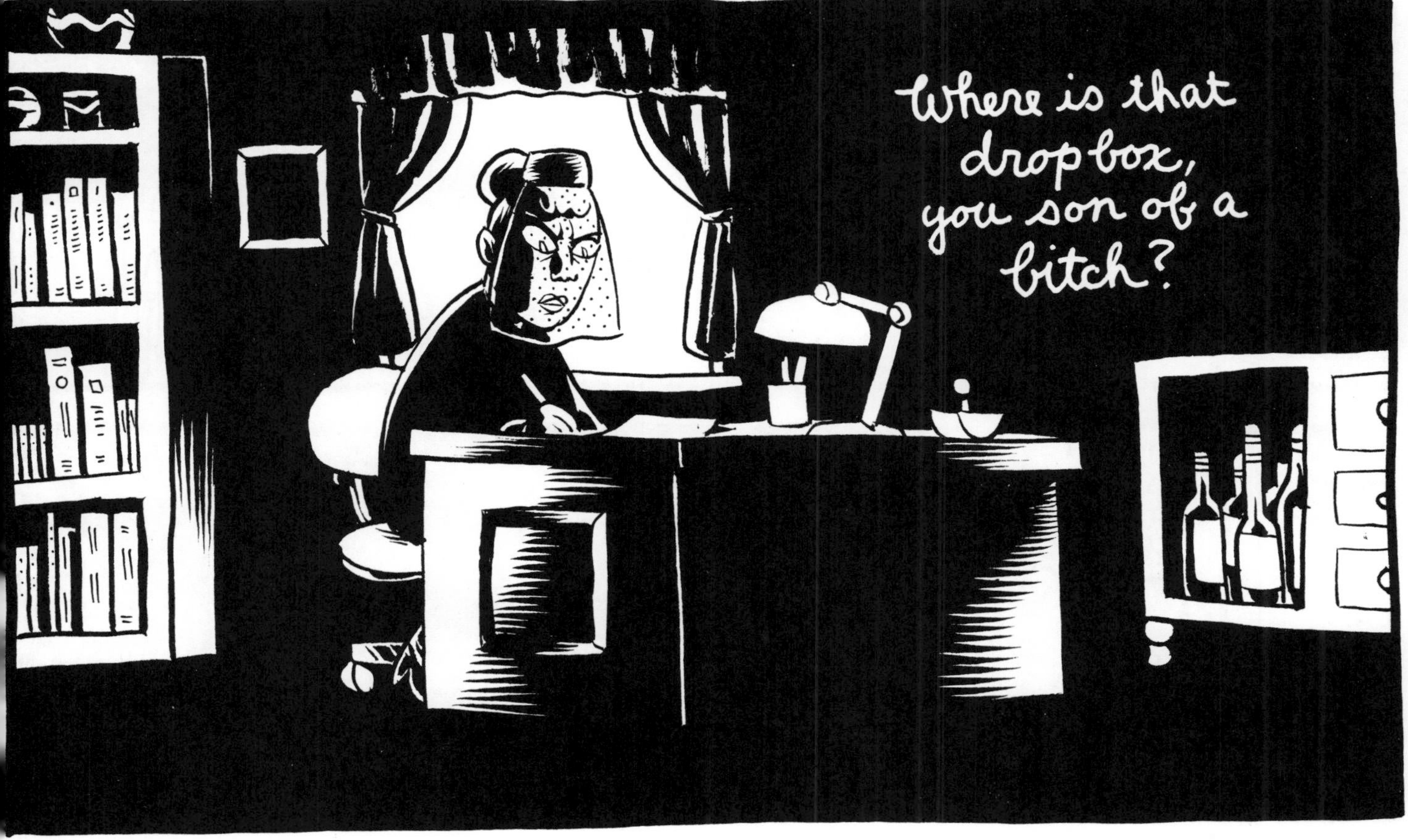
Where is that drop box, you son of a bitch?

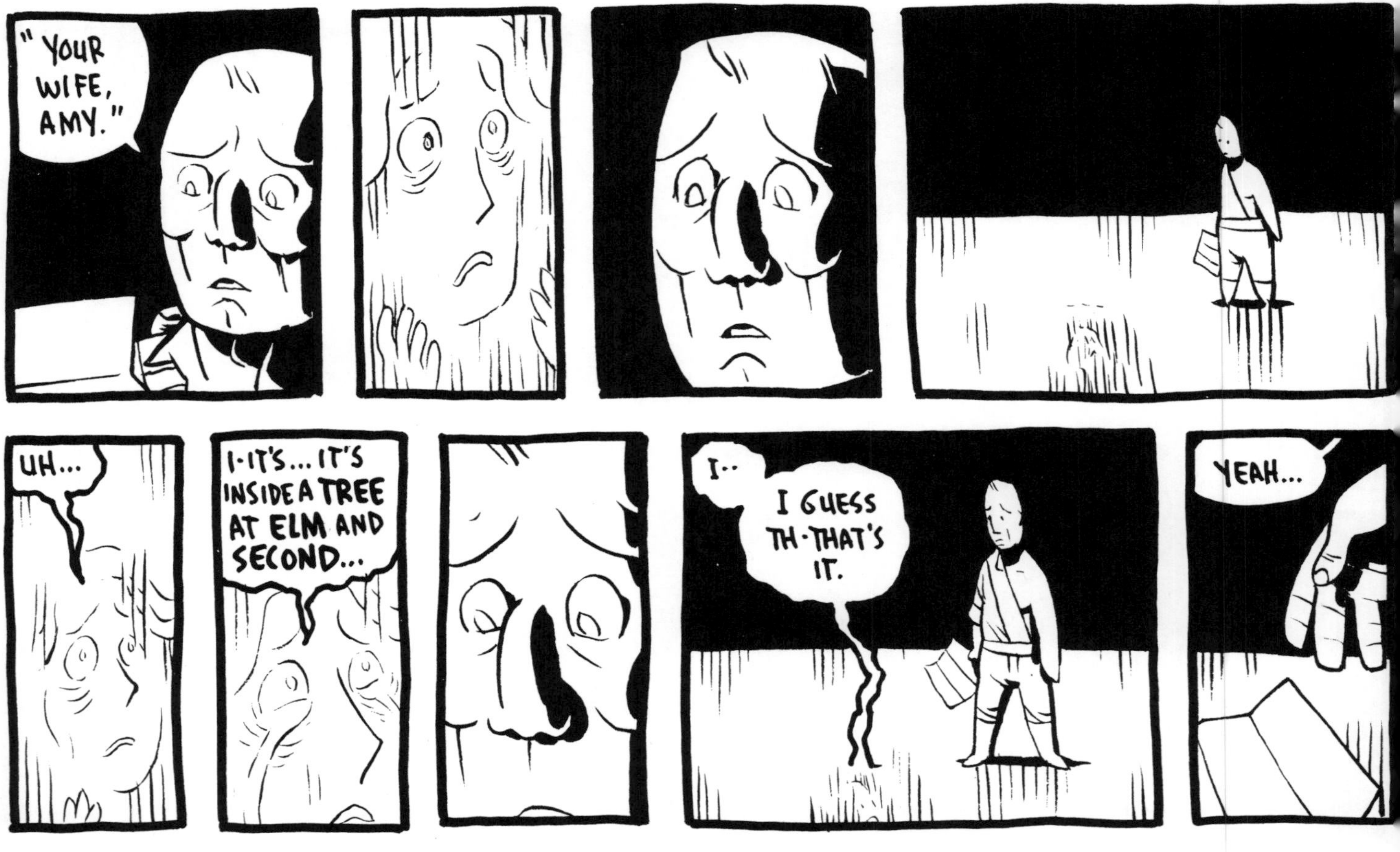
"YOUR WIFE, AMY."
UH...
I-IT'S... IT'S INSIDE A TREE AT ELM AND SECOND...
I..
I GUESS TH-THAT'S IT.
YEAH...

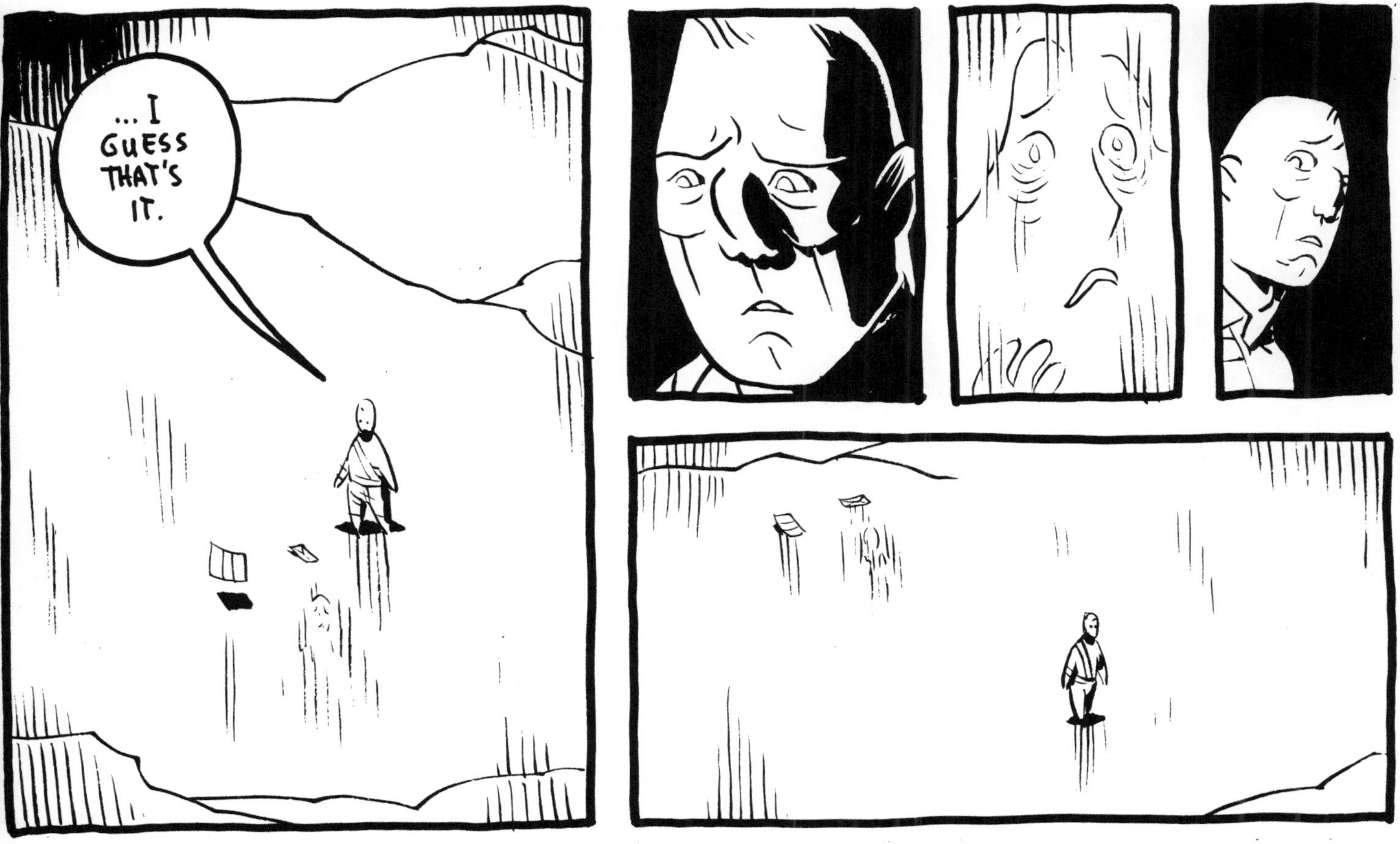
...I GUESS THAT'S IT.

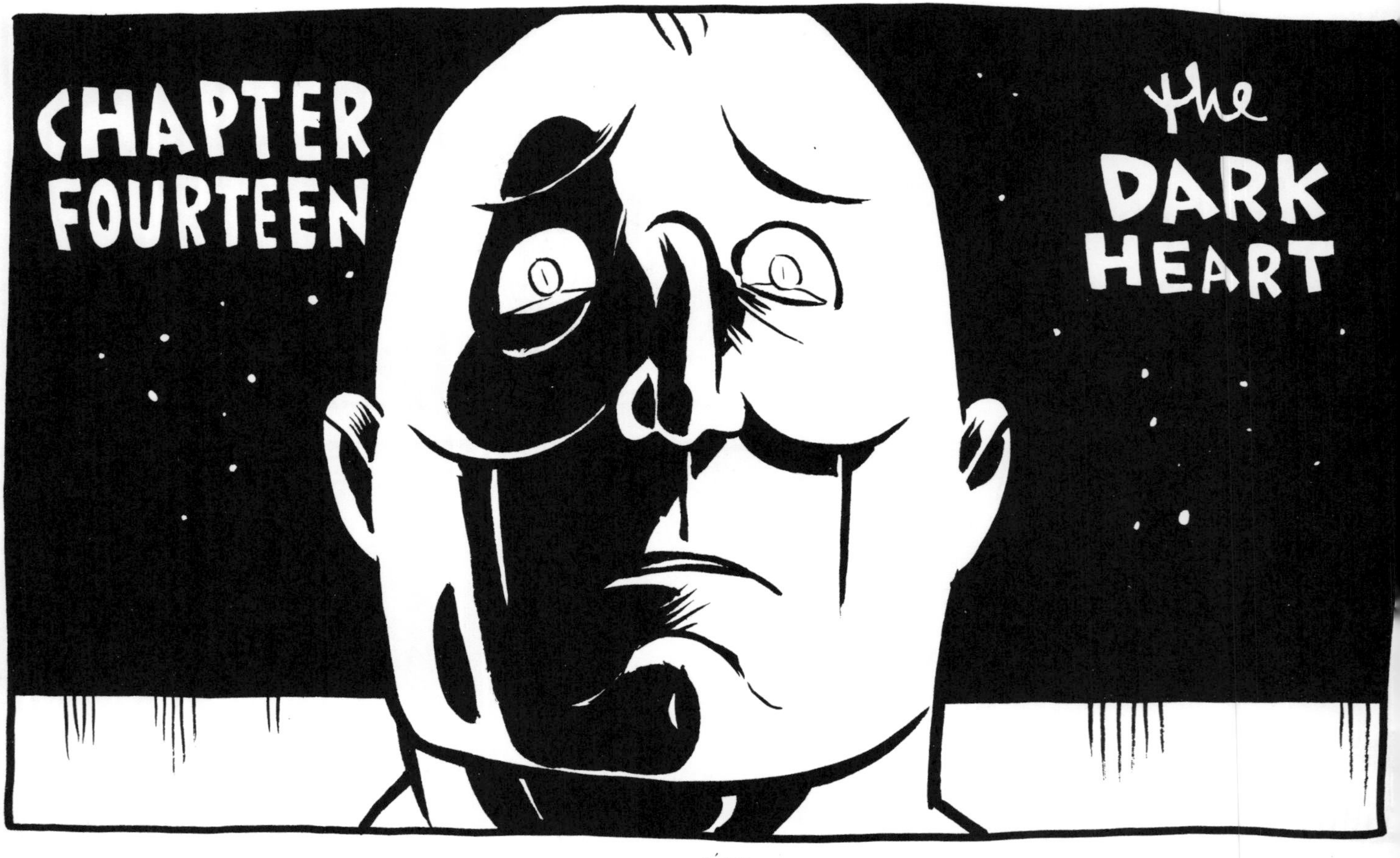
CHAPTER FOURTEEN
the DARK HEART

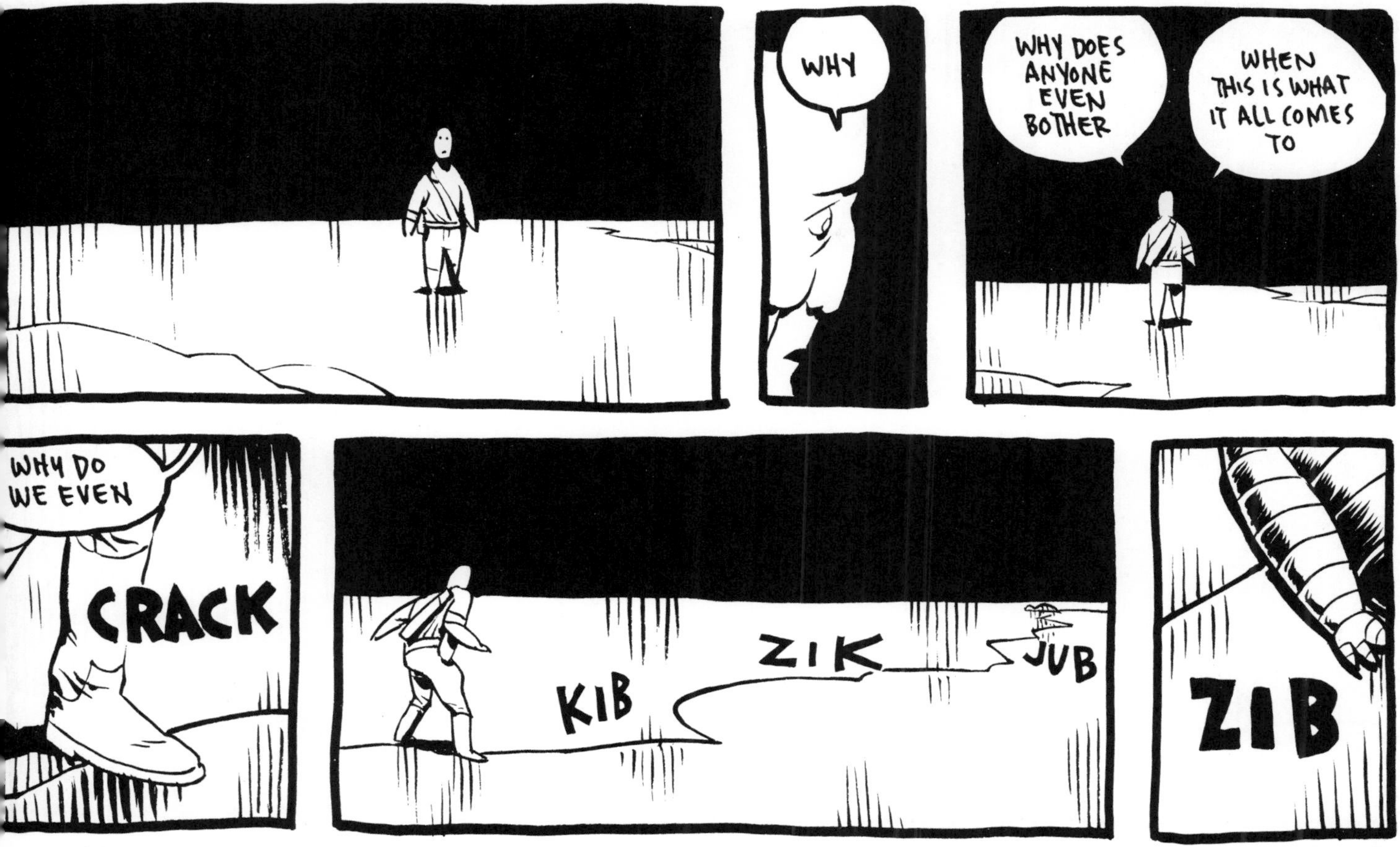
WHY
WHY DOES ANYONE EVEN BOTHER
WHEN THIS IS WHAT IT ALL COMES TO
WHY DO WE EVEN
CRACK
KIB
ZIK
JUB
ZIB

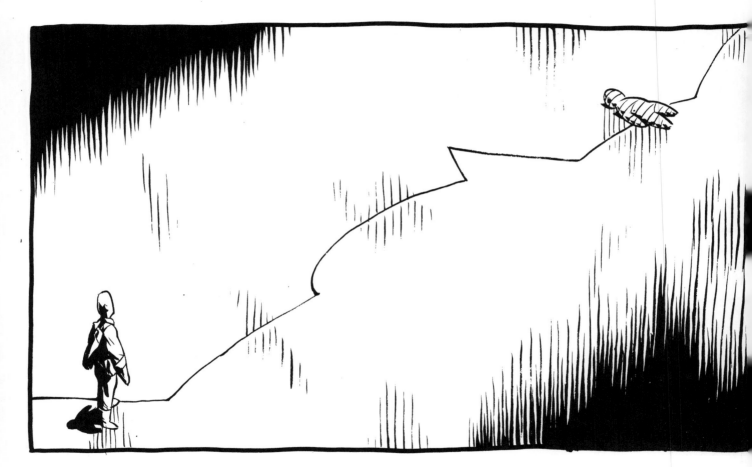

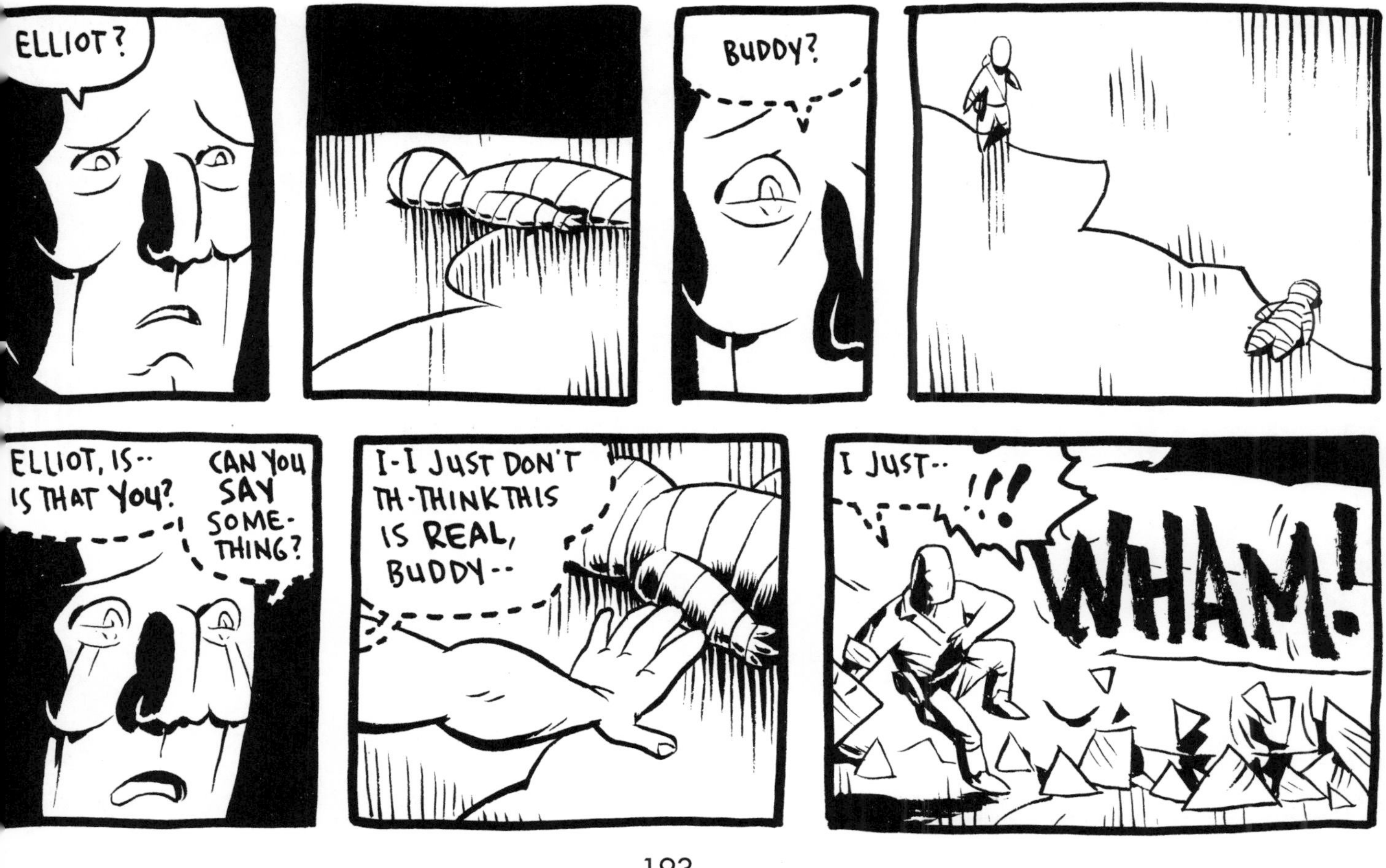
ELLIOT?
BUDDY?
ELLIOT, IS--
IS THAT YOU?
CAN YOU SAY SOME-THING?
I-I JUST DON'T TH-THINK THIS IS REAL, BUDDY--
I JUST--
!!!
WHAM!

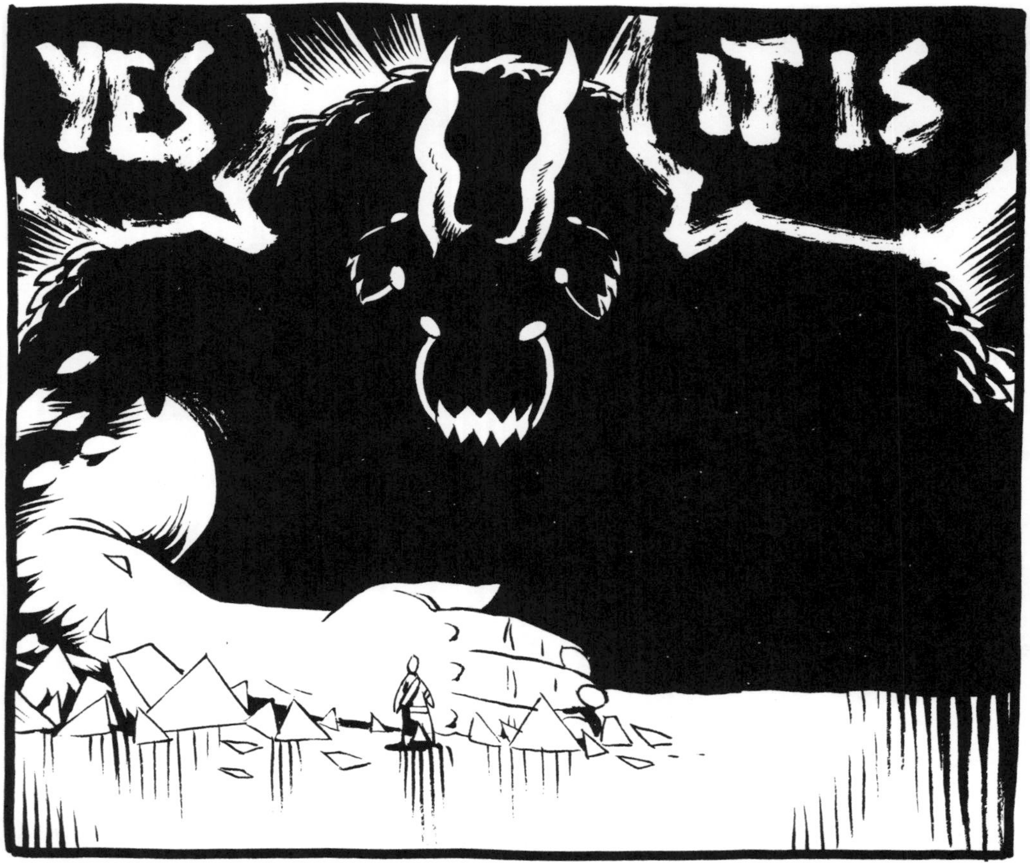
YES
IT IS

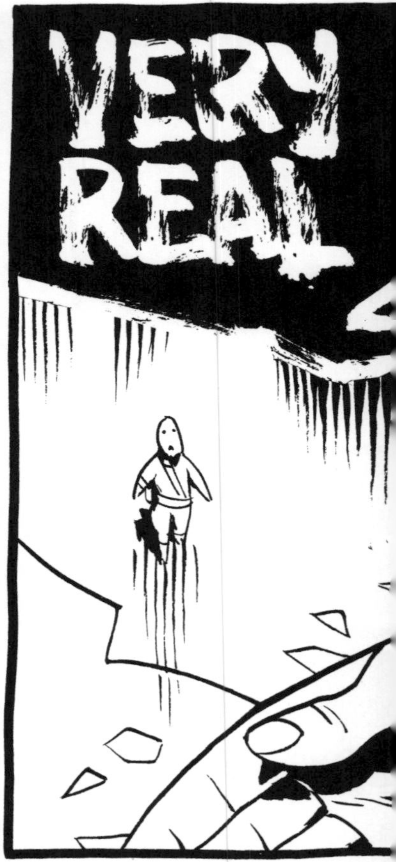
VERY
REAL

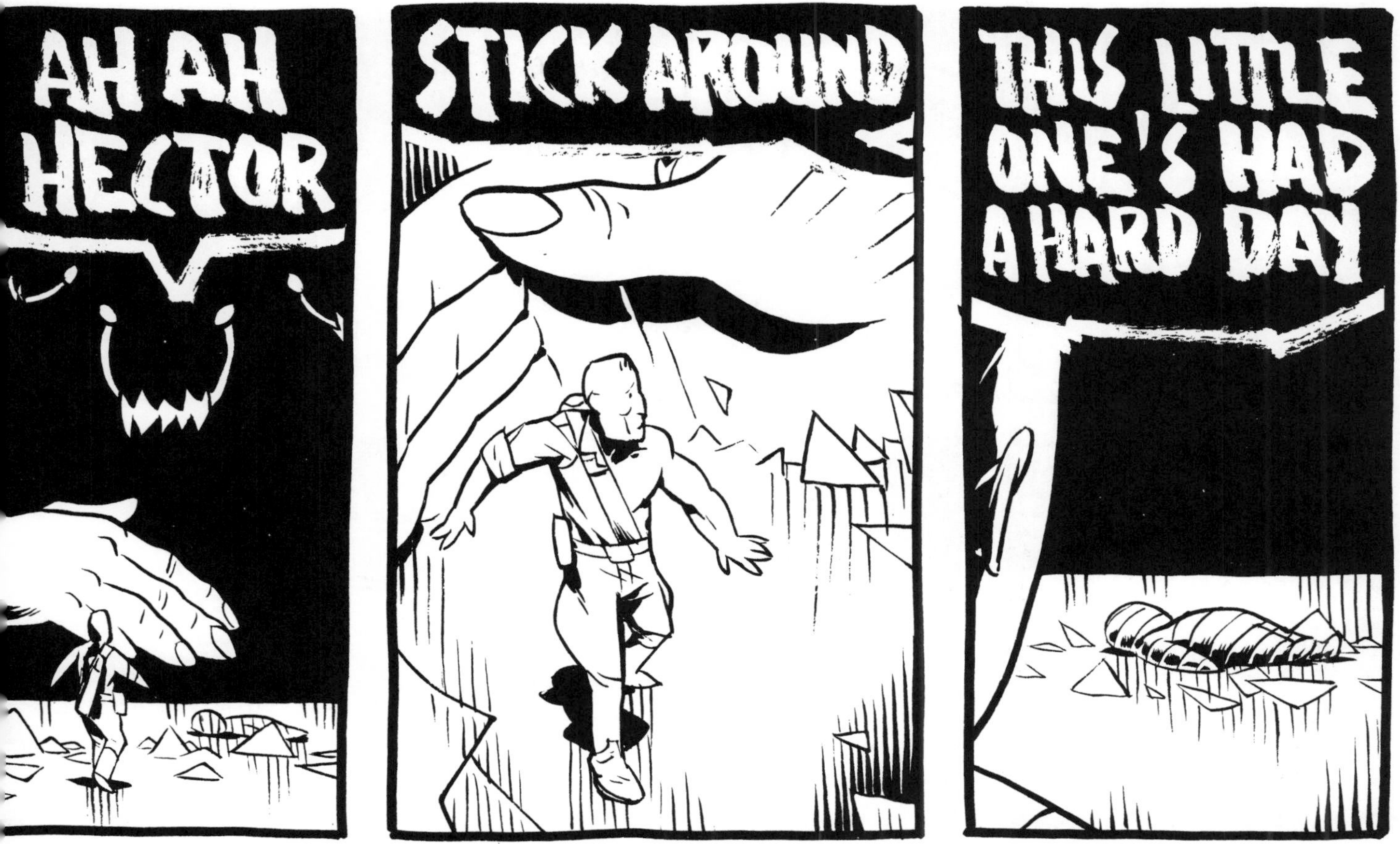
AH AH HECTOR
STICK AROUND
THIS LITTLE ONE'S HAD A HARD DAY

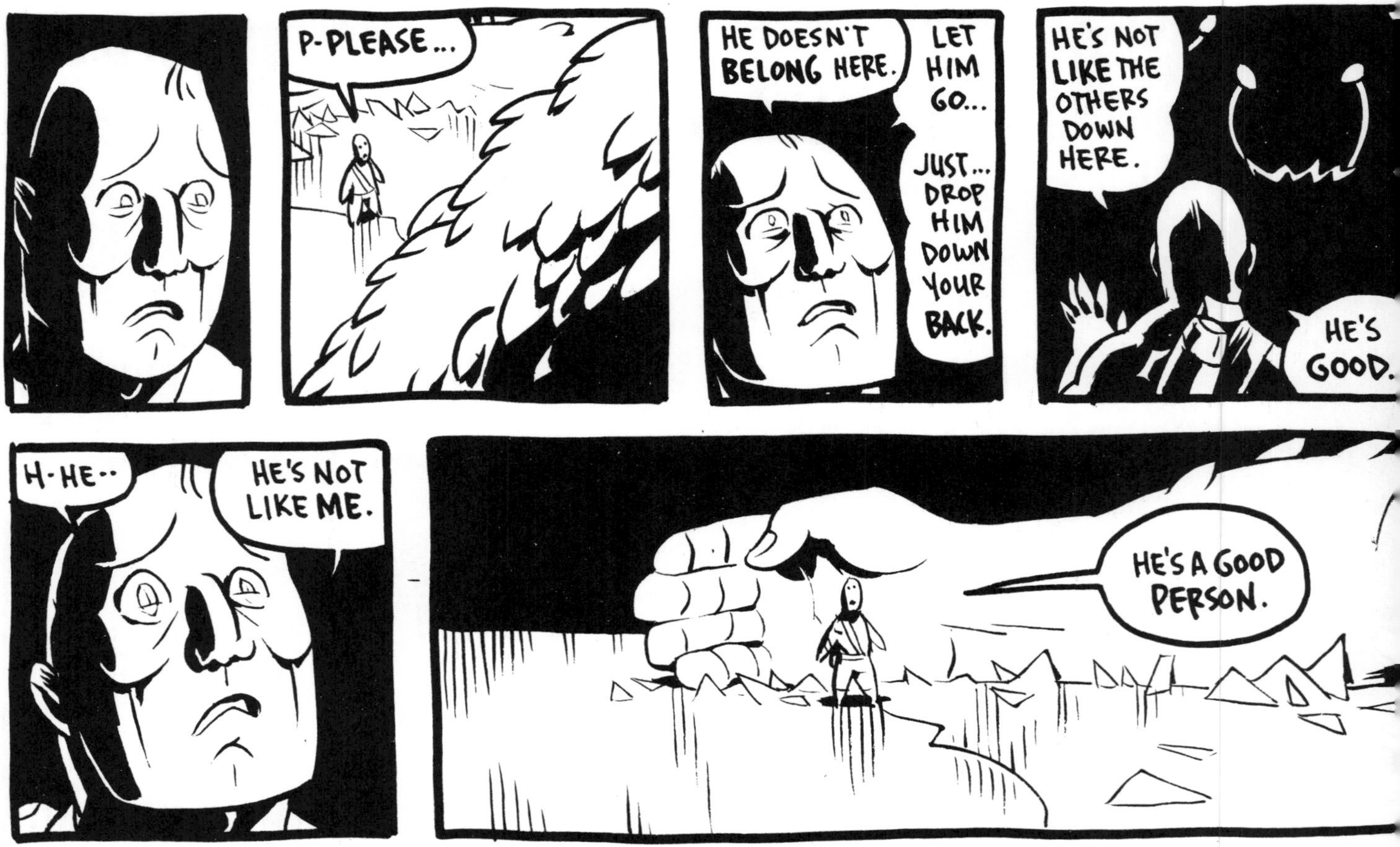

P-PLEASE...
HE DOESN'T BELONG HERE.
LET HIM GO...
JUST... DROP HIM DOWN YOUR BACK.
HE'S NOT LIKE THE OTHERS DOWN HERE.
HE'S GOOD.
H-HE..
HE'S NOT LIKE ME.
HE'S A GOOD PERSON.

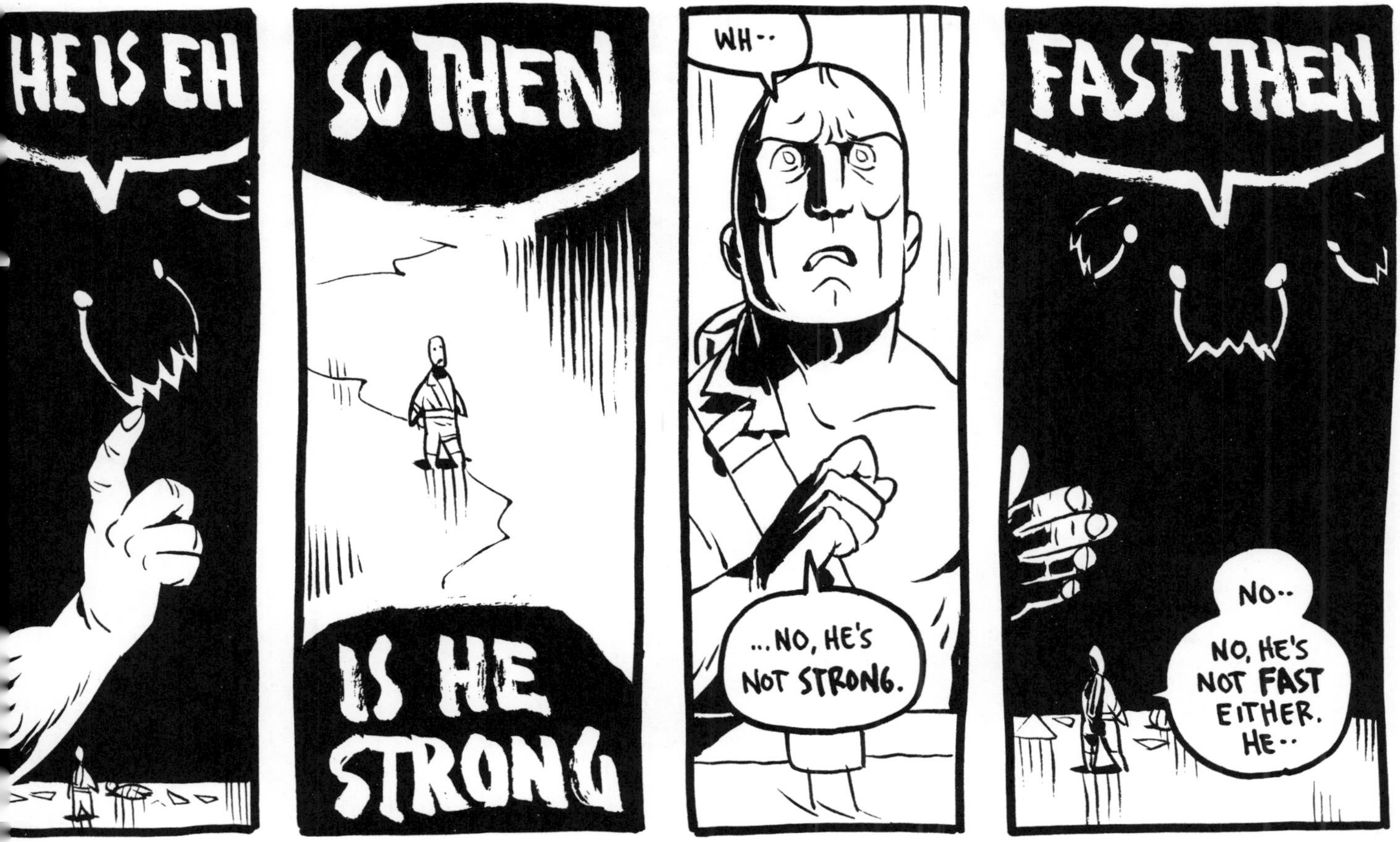
HE IS EH
SO THEN
IS HE STRONG
WH--
...NO, HE'S NOT STRONG.
FAST THEN
NO--
NO, HE'S NOT FAST EITHER. HE--

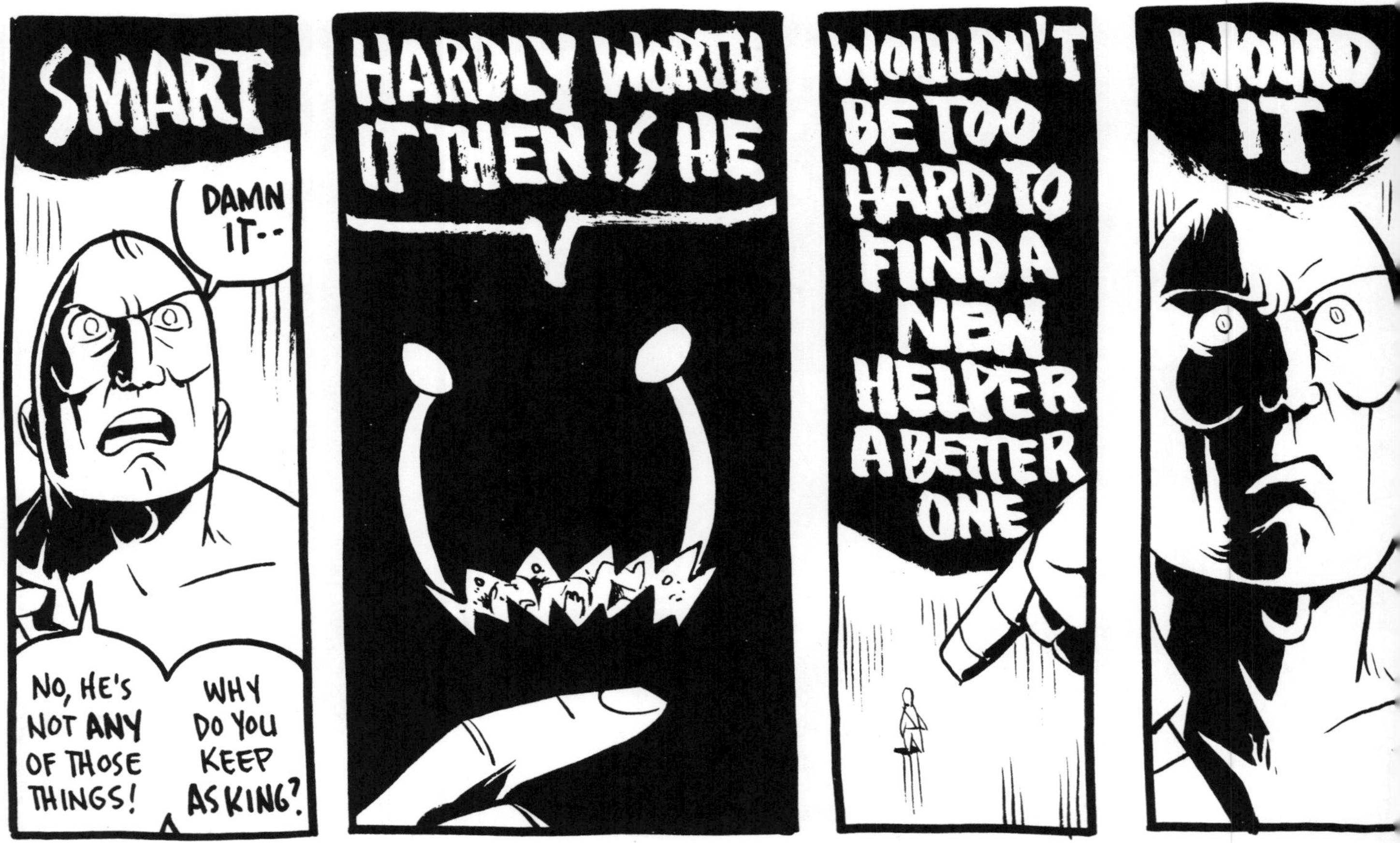
SMART
DAMN IT--
NO, HE'S NOT ANY OF THOSE THINGS!
WHY DO YOU KEEP ASKING?
HARDLY WORTH IT THEN IS HE
WOULDN'T BE TOO HARD TO FIND A NEW HELPER A BETTER ONE
WOULD IT

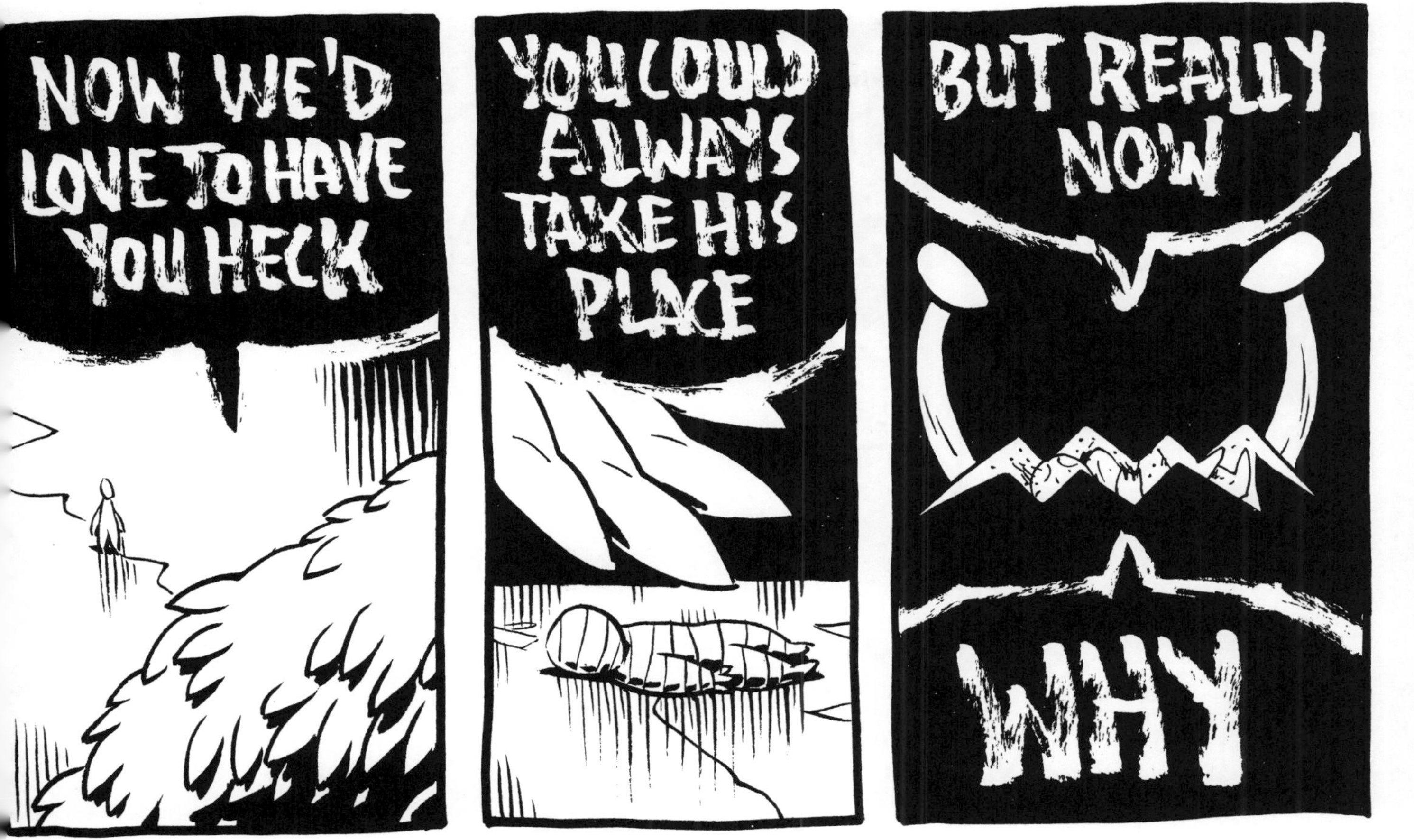
NOW WE'D LOVE TO HAVE YOU HECK
YOU COULD ALWAYS TAKE HIS PLACE
BUT REALLY NOW
WHY

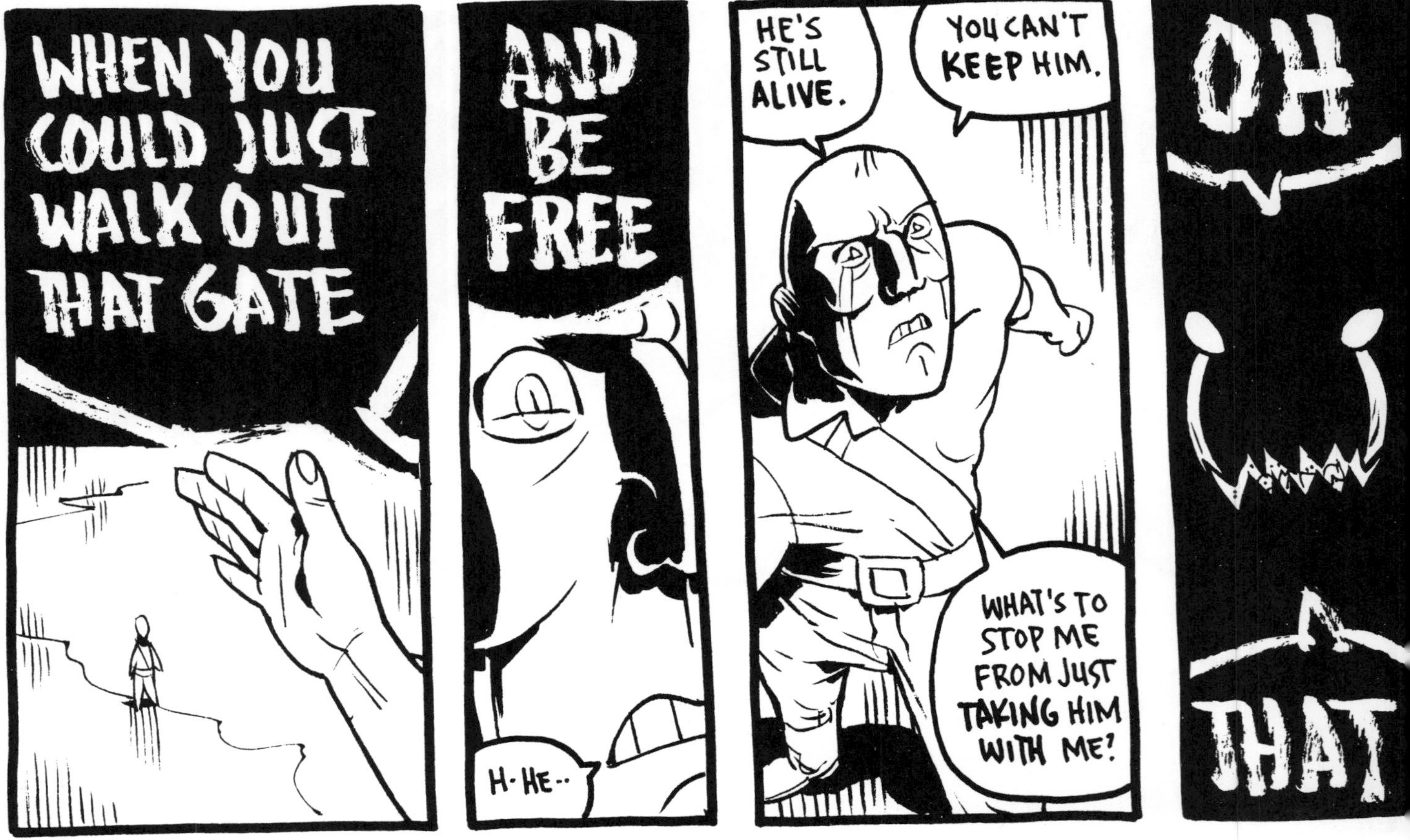
WHEN YOU COULD JUST WALK OUT THAT GATE
AND BE FREE
H- HE--
HE'S STILL ALIVE.
YOU CAN'T KEEP HIM.
WHAT'S TO STOP ME FROM JUST TAKING HIM WITH ME?
OH
THAT

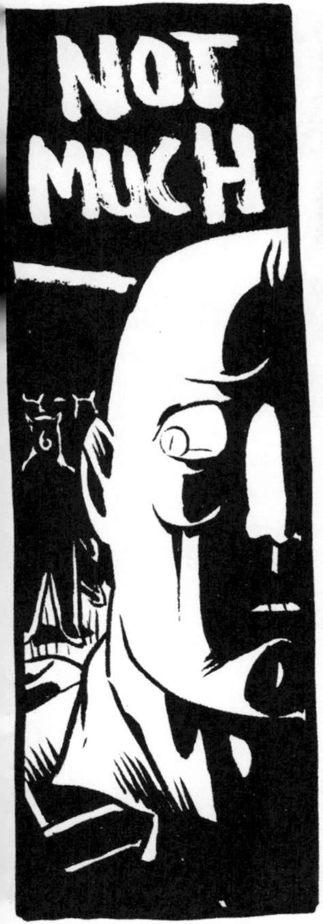
NOT MUCH

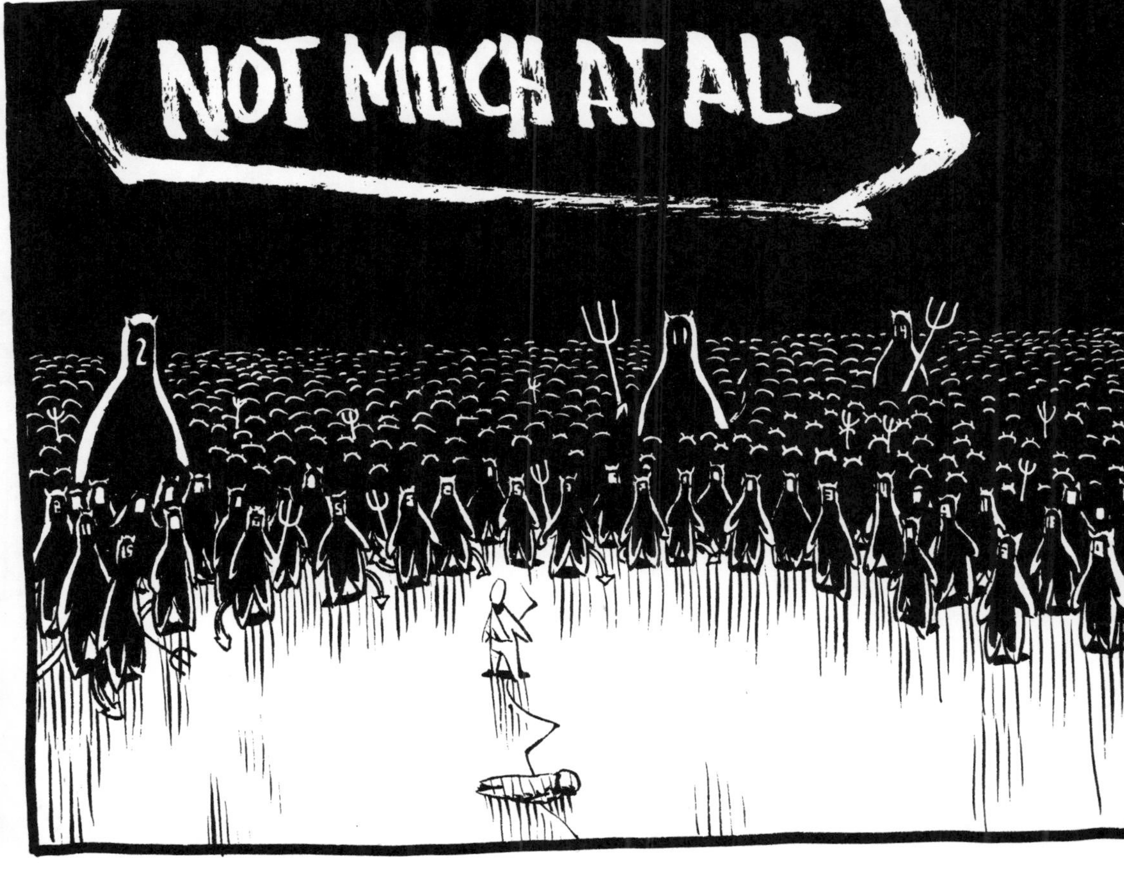
NOT MUCH AT ALL

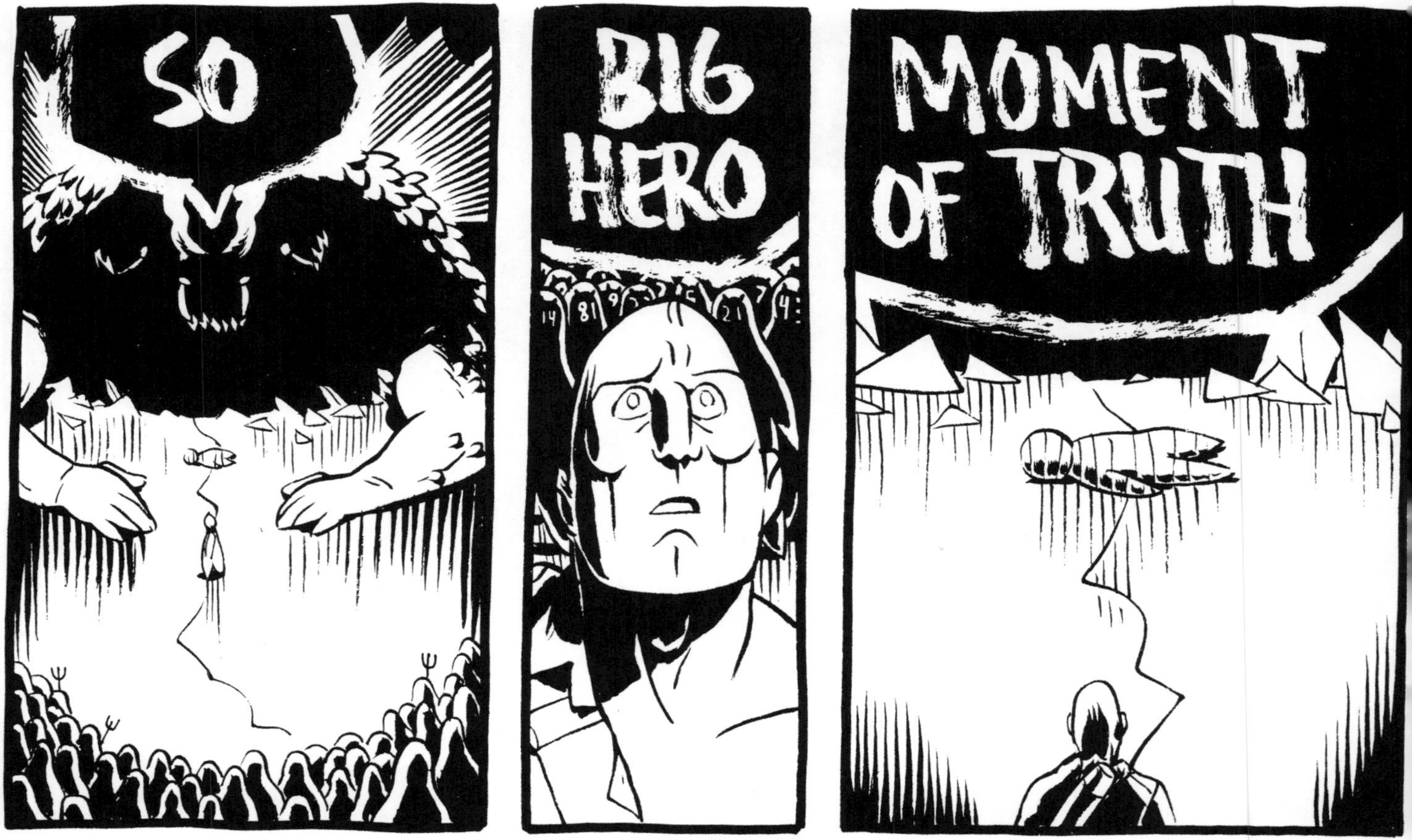
SO
BIG HERO
MOMENT OF TRUTH

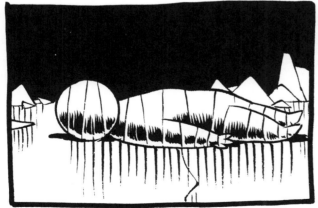

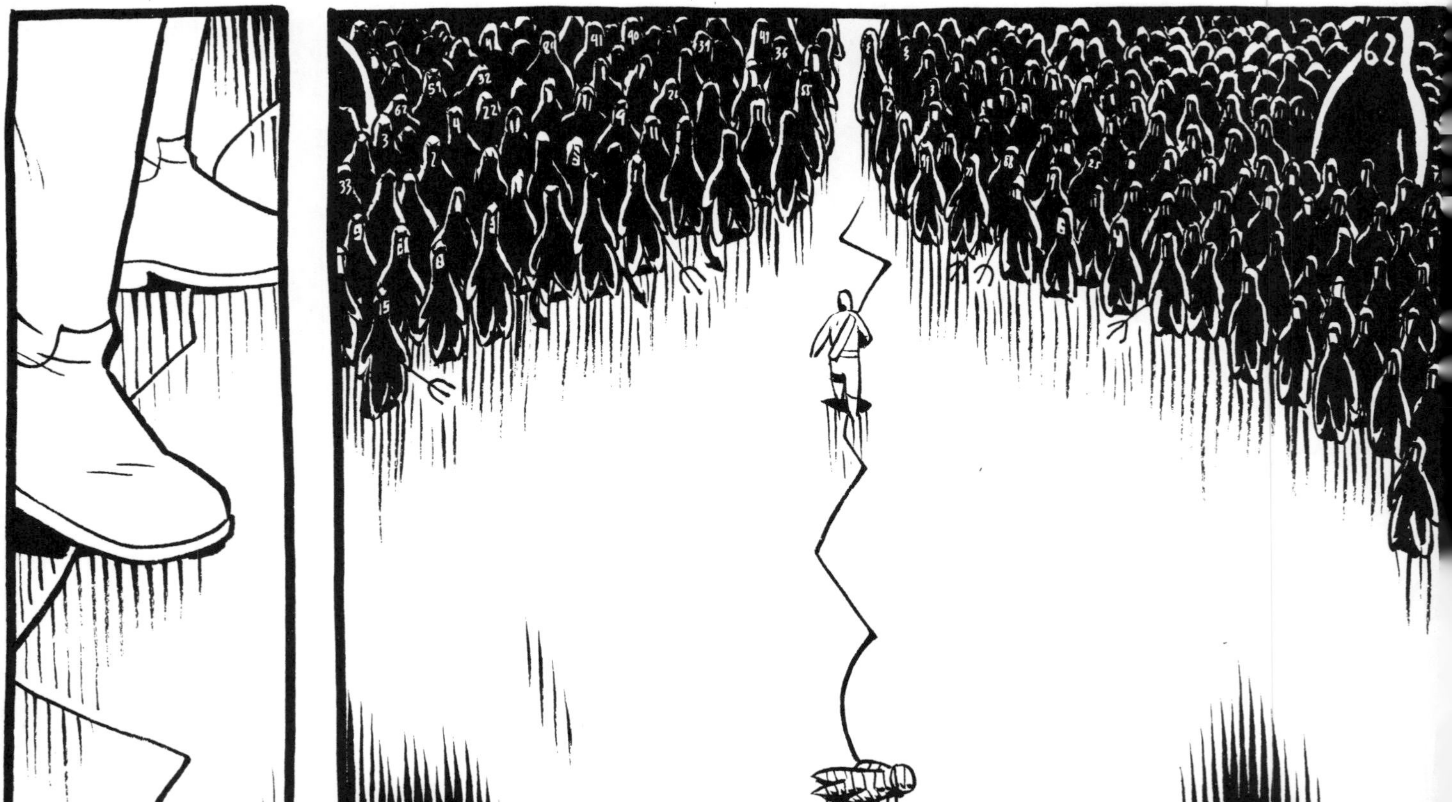

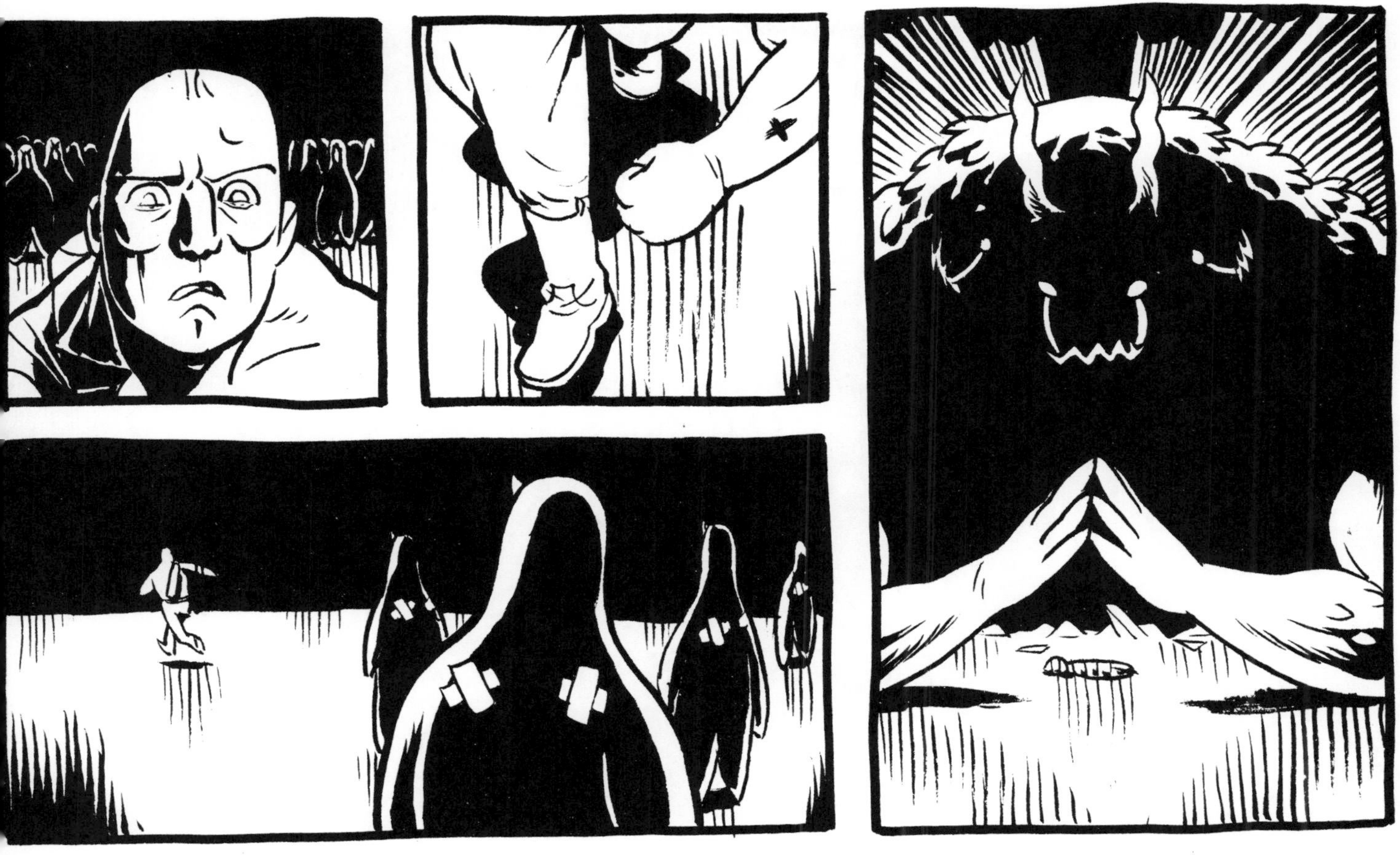

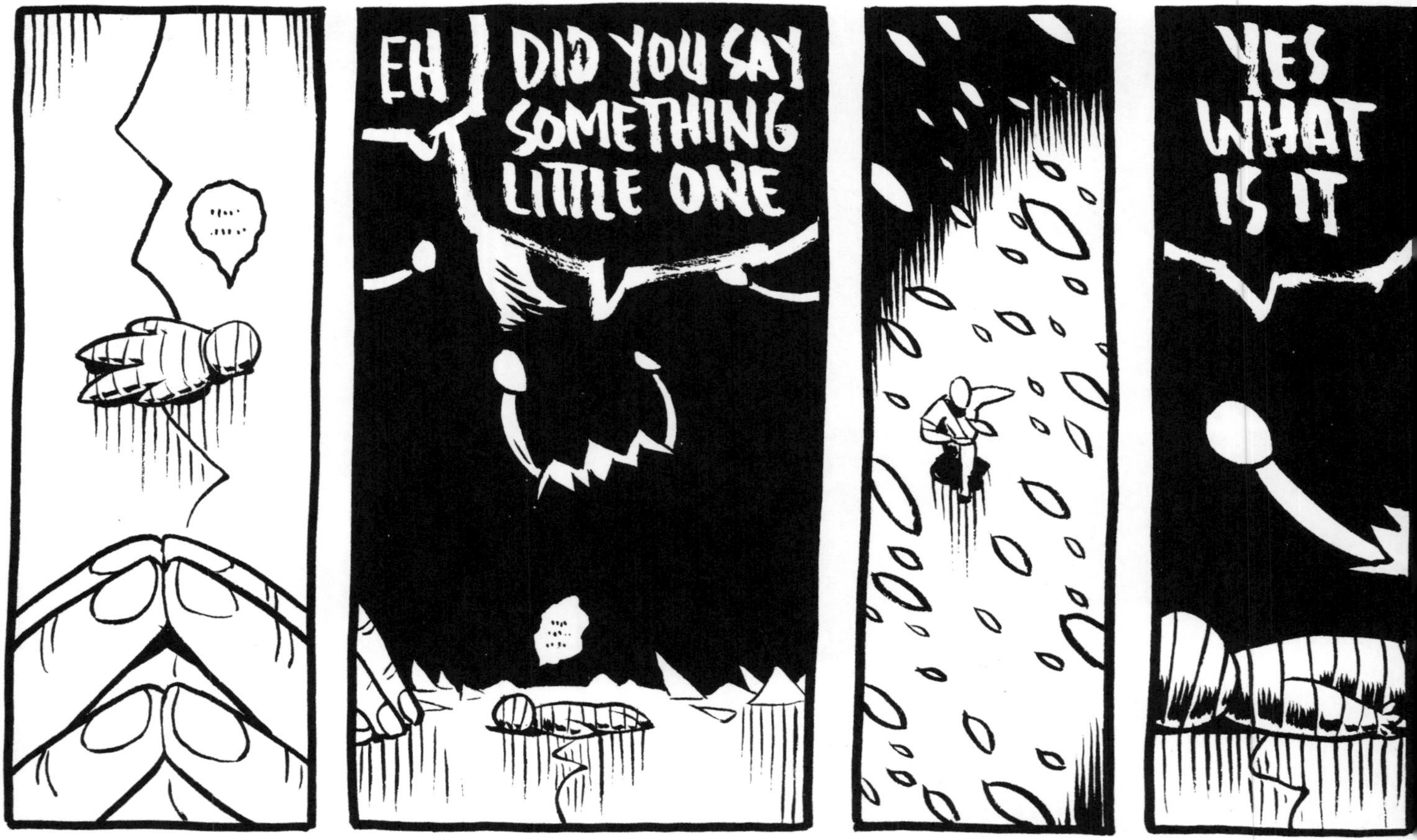
EH
DID YOU SAY SOMETHING LITTLE ONE
YES WHAT IS IT

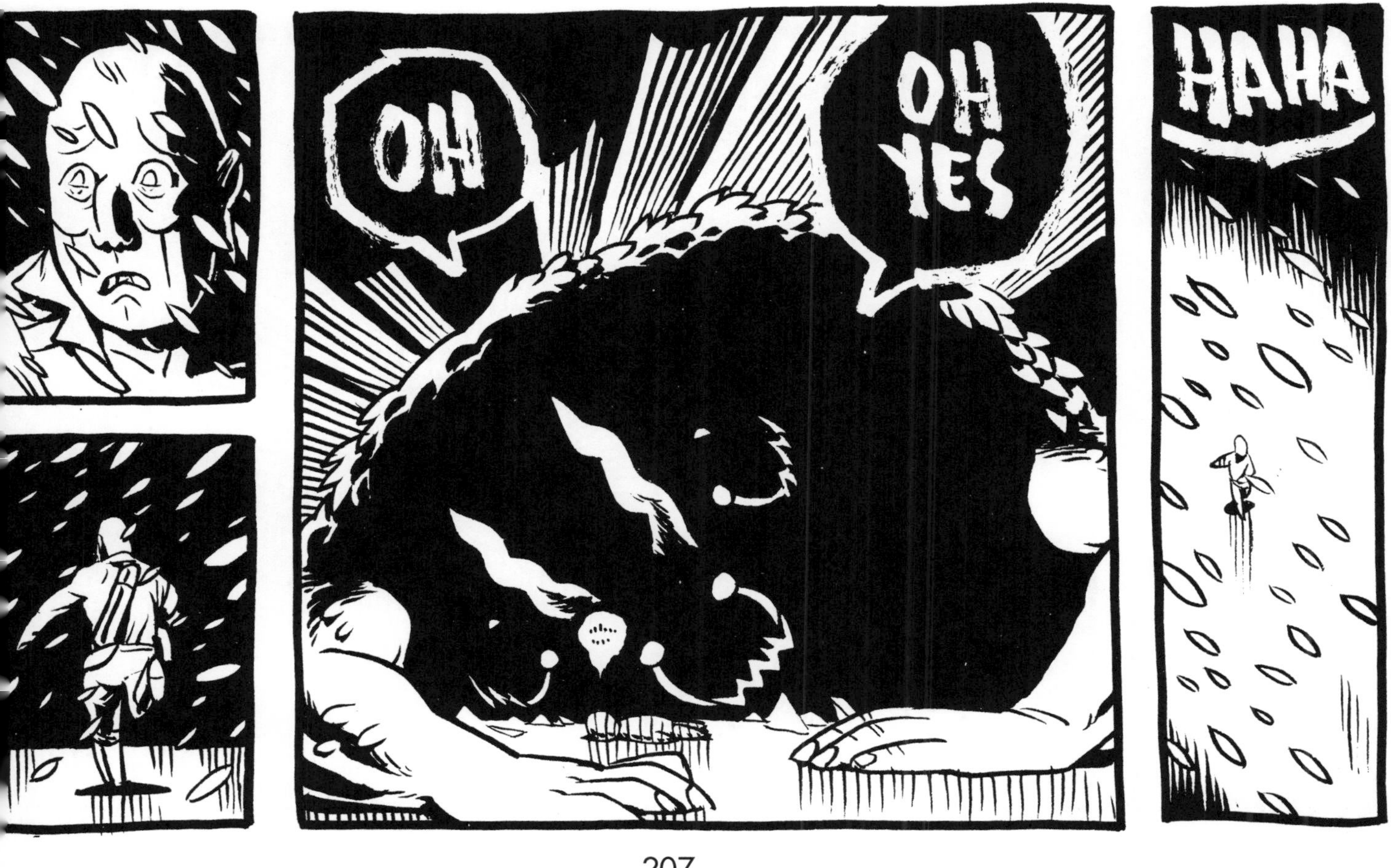
OH
OH YES
HAHA

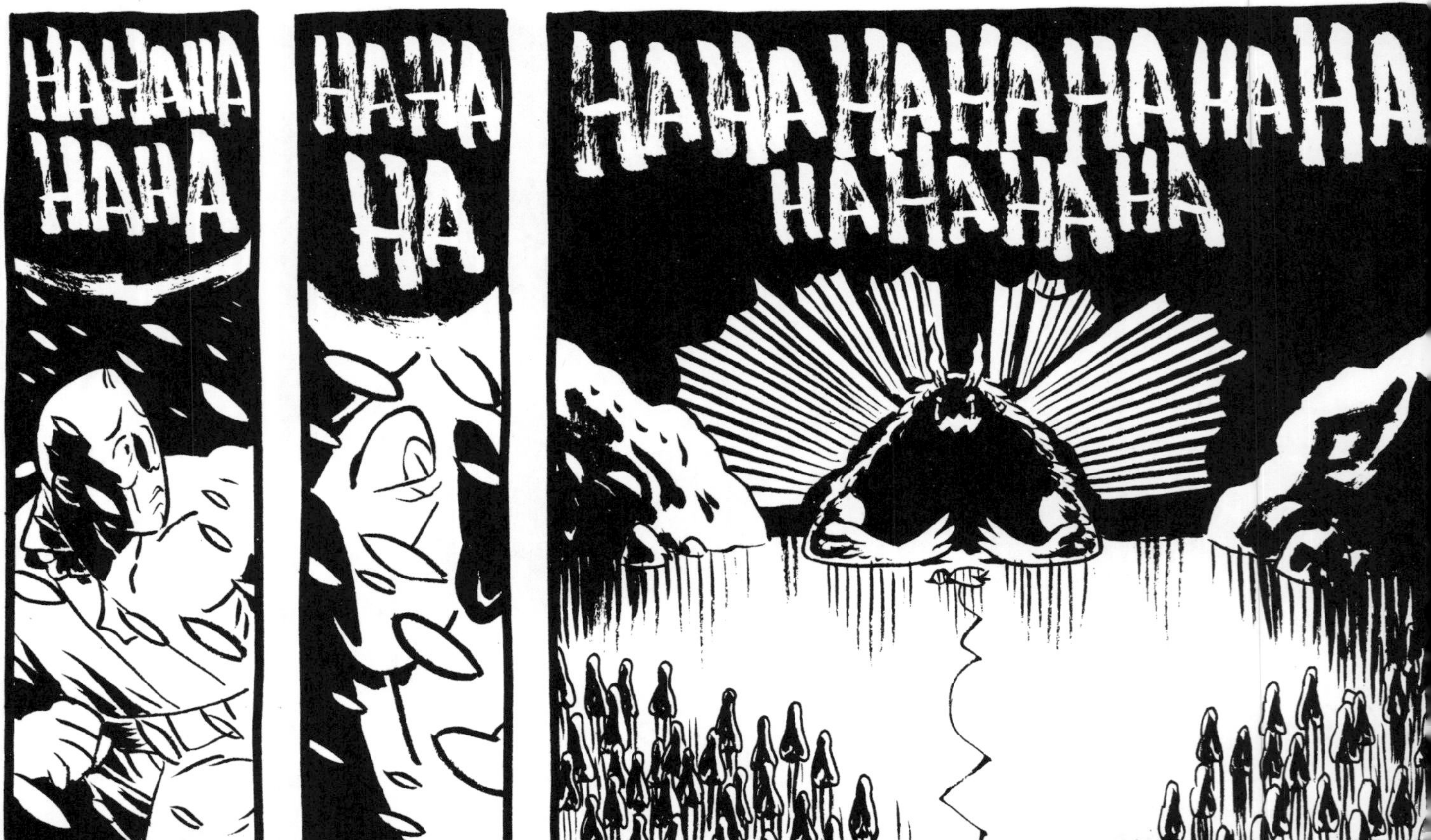
HAHAHA
HAHA
HAHA
HA
HAHAHAHAHAHAHAHA
HAHAHAHA

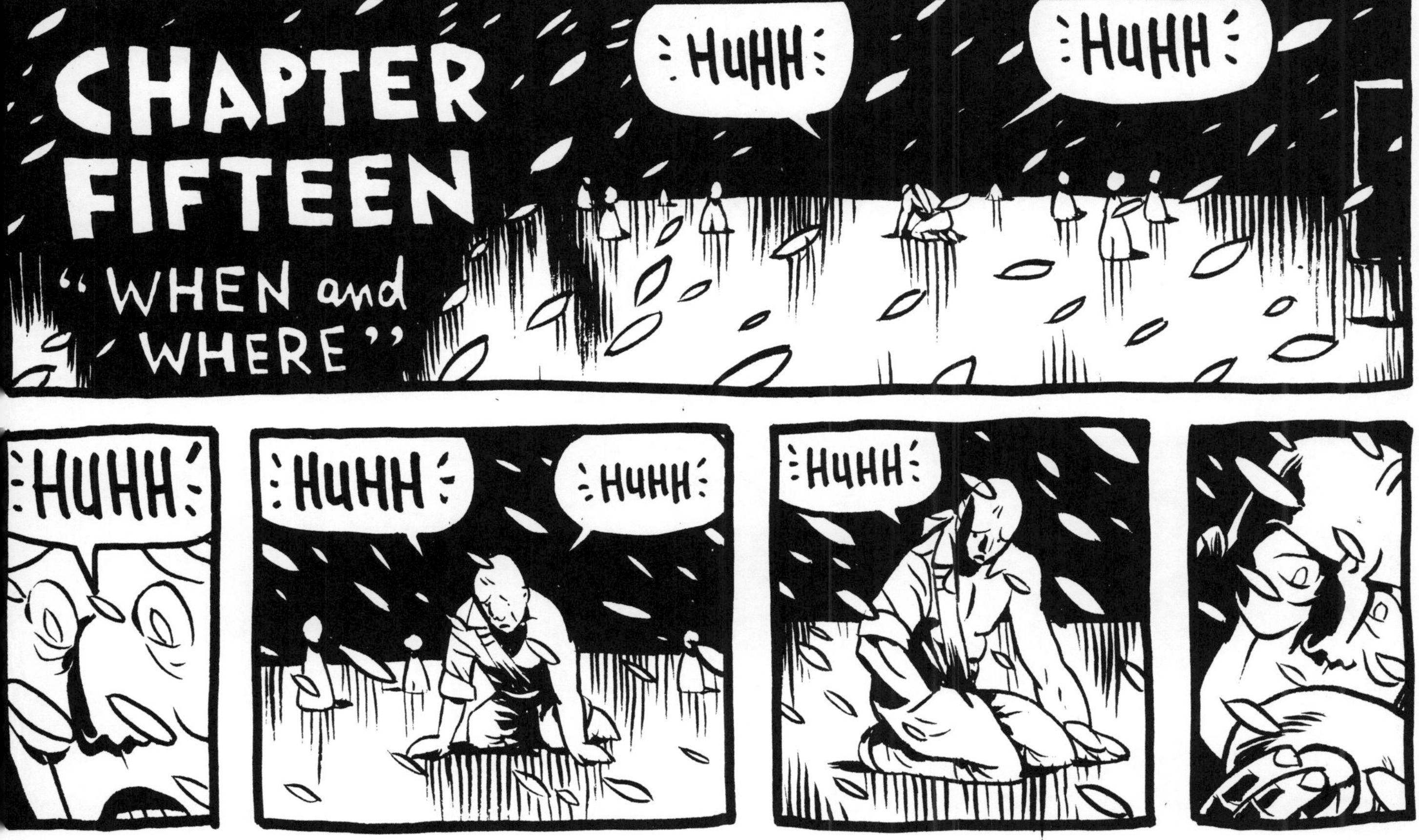
CHAPTER FIFTEEN
"WHEN and WHERE"
HUHH
HUHH
HUHH
HUHH
HUHH
HUHH

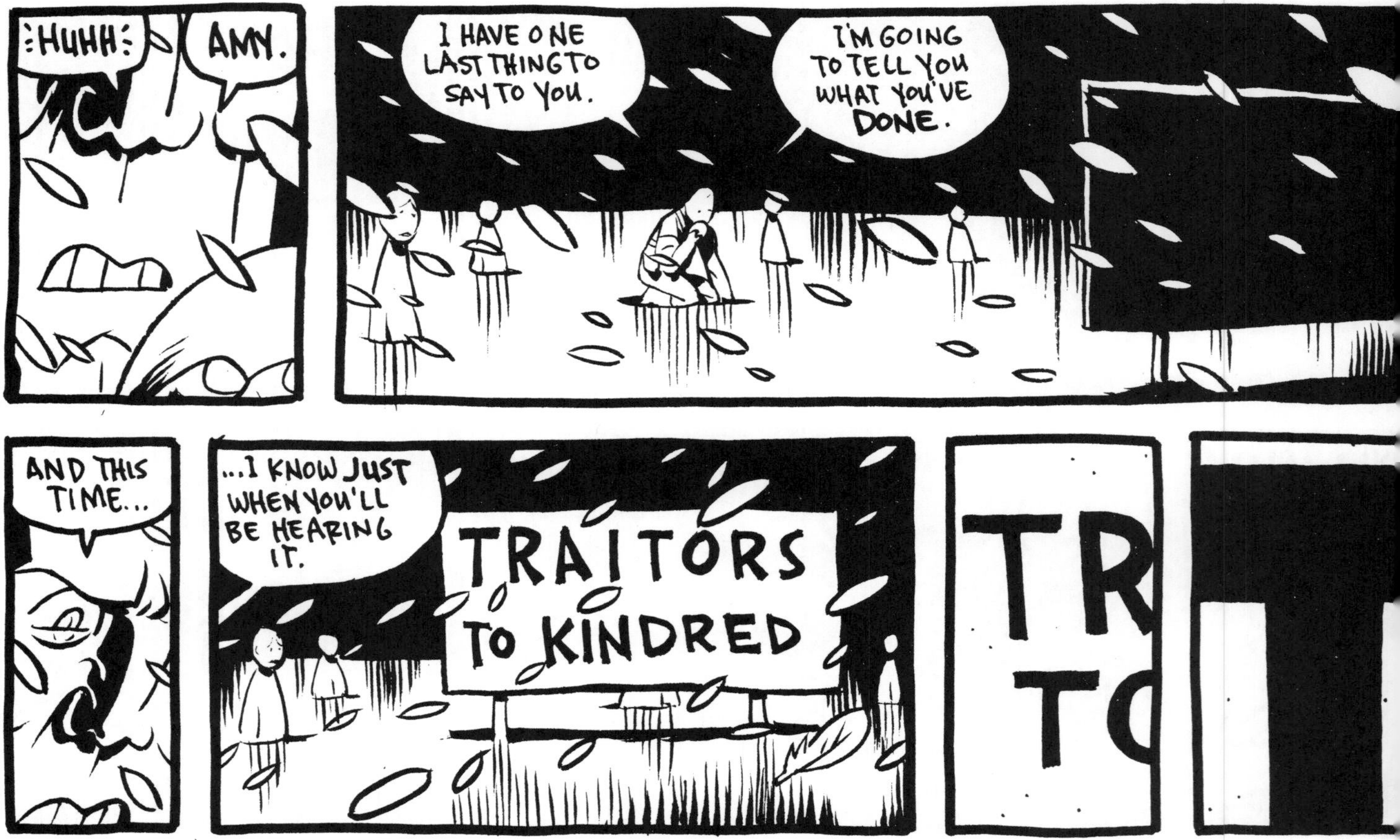
HUHH
AMY.
I HAVE ONE LAST THING TO SAY TO YOU.
I'M GOING TO TELL YOU WHAT YOU'VE DONE.
AND THIS TIME...
...I KNOW JUST WHEN YOU'LL BE HEARING IT.
TRAITORS TO KINDRED
TR TO

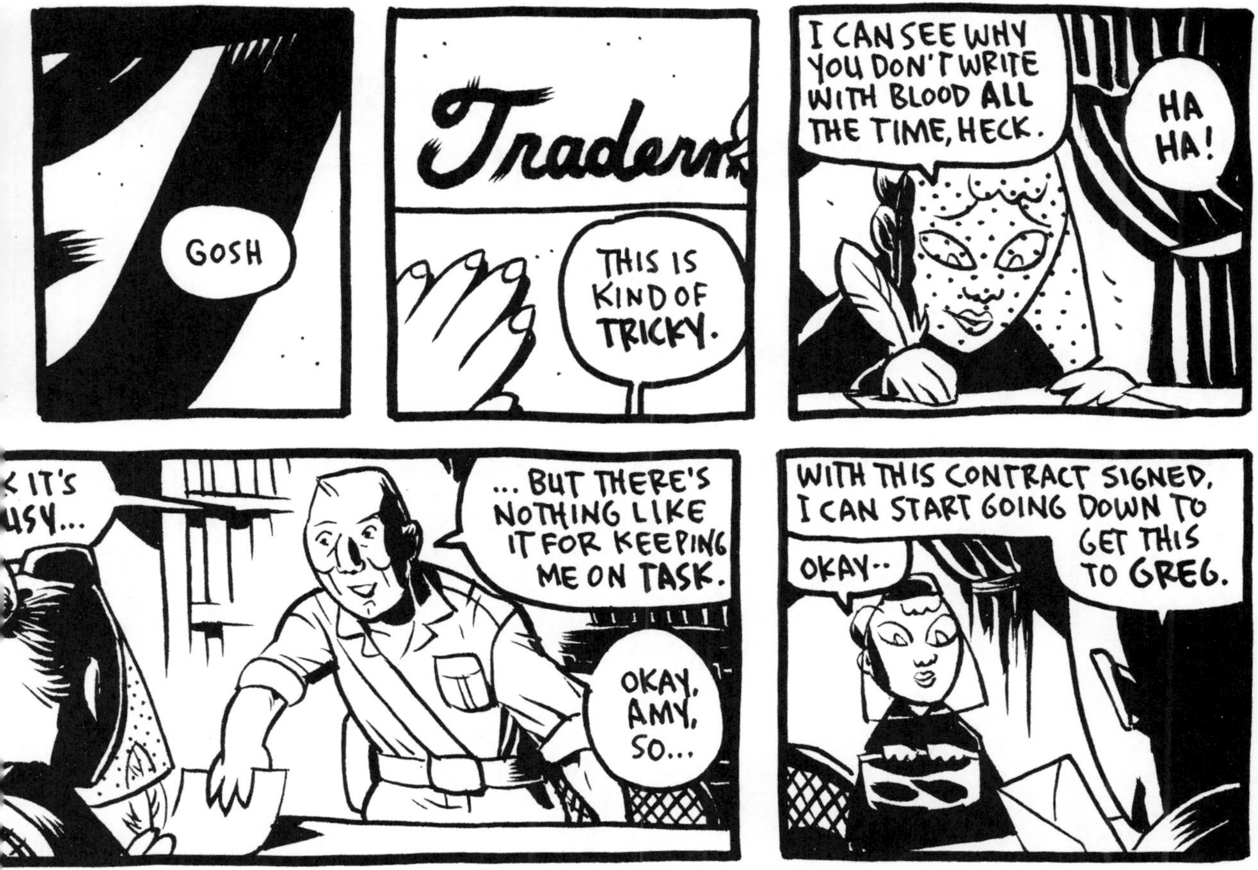
GOSH
Tradern
THIS IS KIND OF TRICKY.
I CAN SEE WHY YOU DON'T WRITE WITH BLOOD ALL THE TIME, HECK.
HA HA!
IT'S
... BUT THERE'S NOTHING LIKE IT FOR KEEPING ME ON TASK.
OKAY, AMY, SO...
WITH THIS CONTRACT SIGNED, I CAN START GOING DOWN TO GET THIS TO GREG.
OKAY..

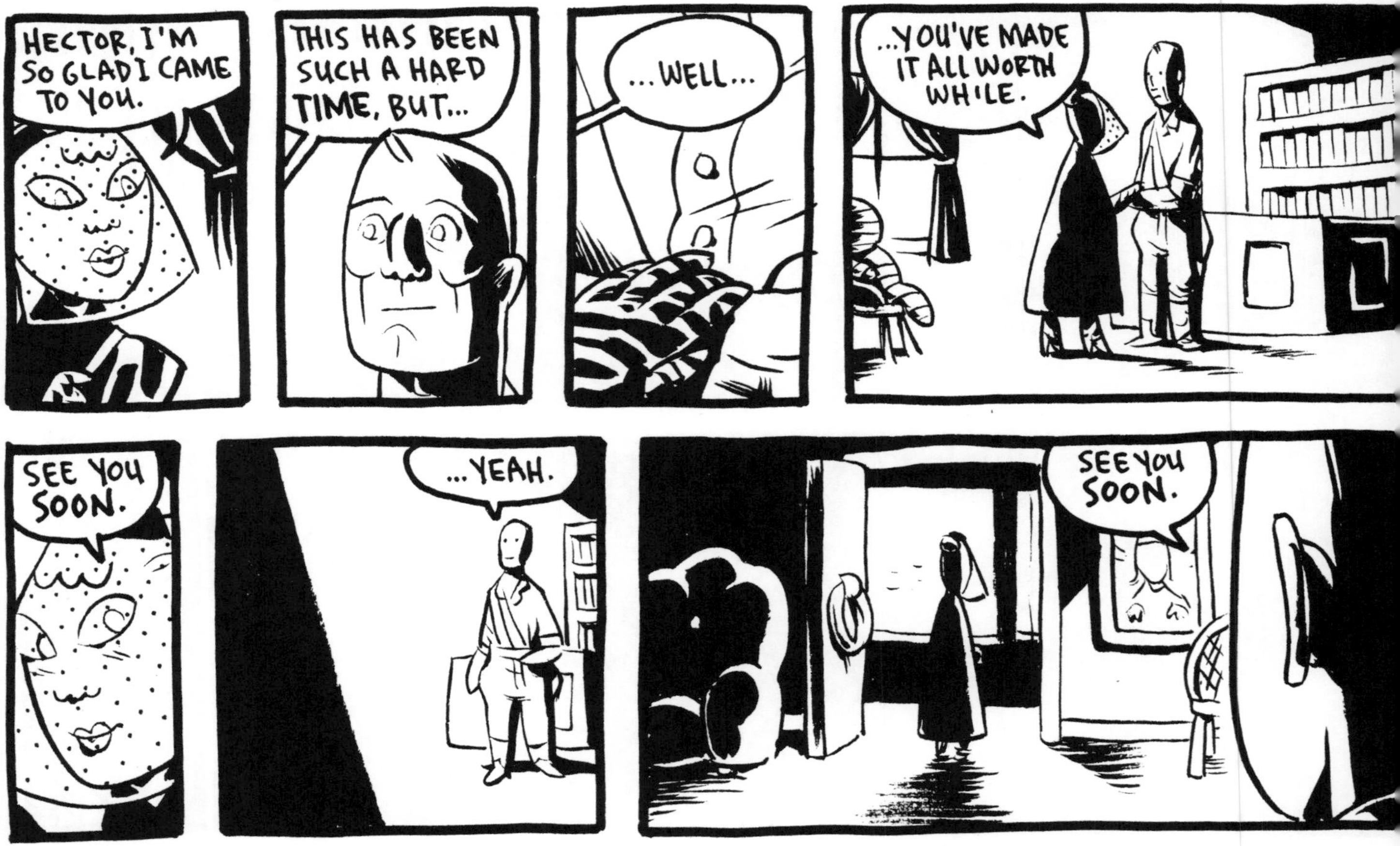
HECTOR, I'M SO GLAD I CAME TO YOU.
THIS HAS BEEN SUCH A HARD TIME, BUT...
...WELL...
...YOU'VE MADE IT ALL WORTH WHILE.
SEE YOU SOON.
...YEAH.
SEE YOU SOON.

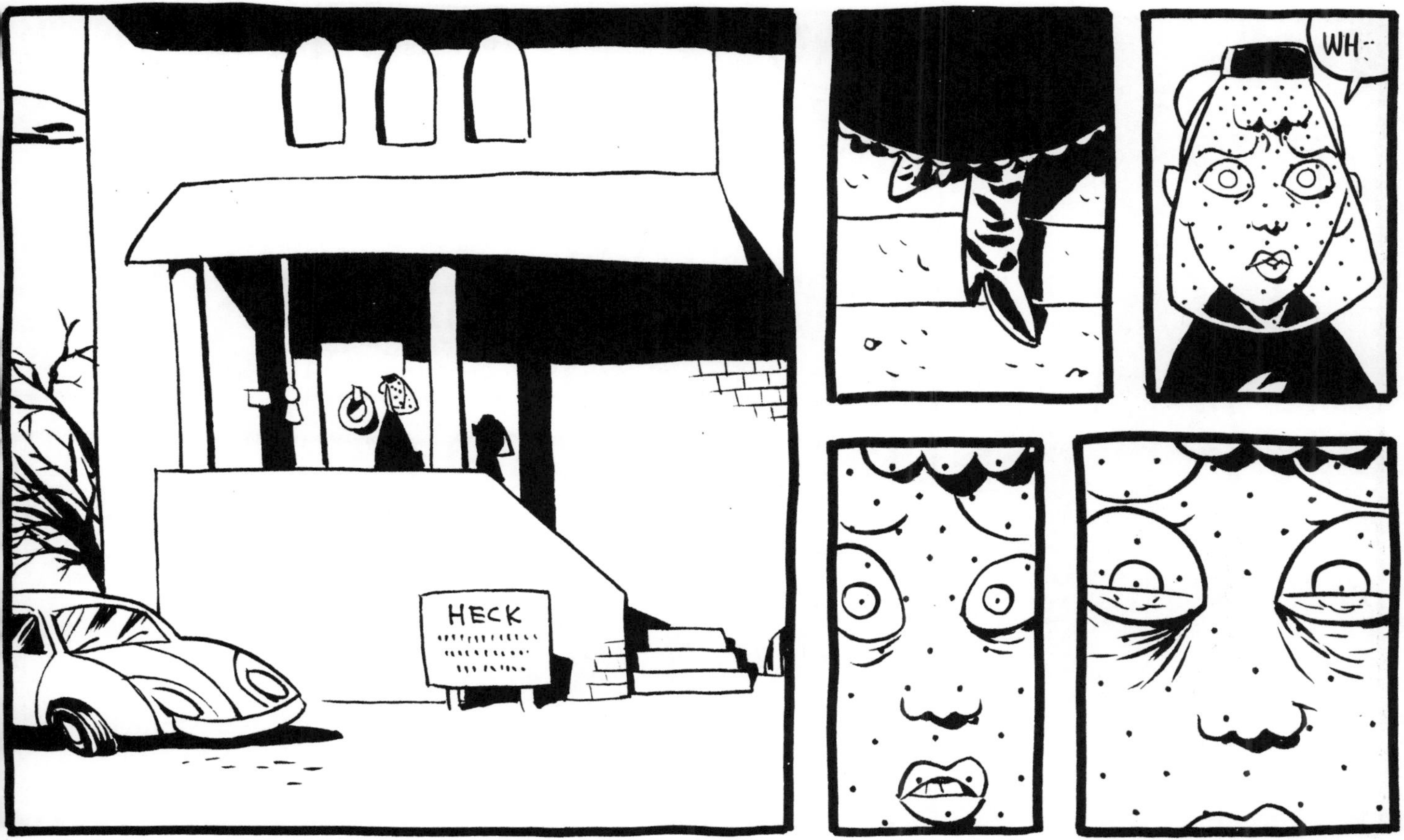

HECK
WH--

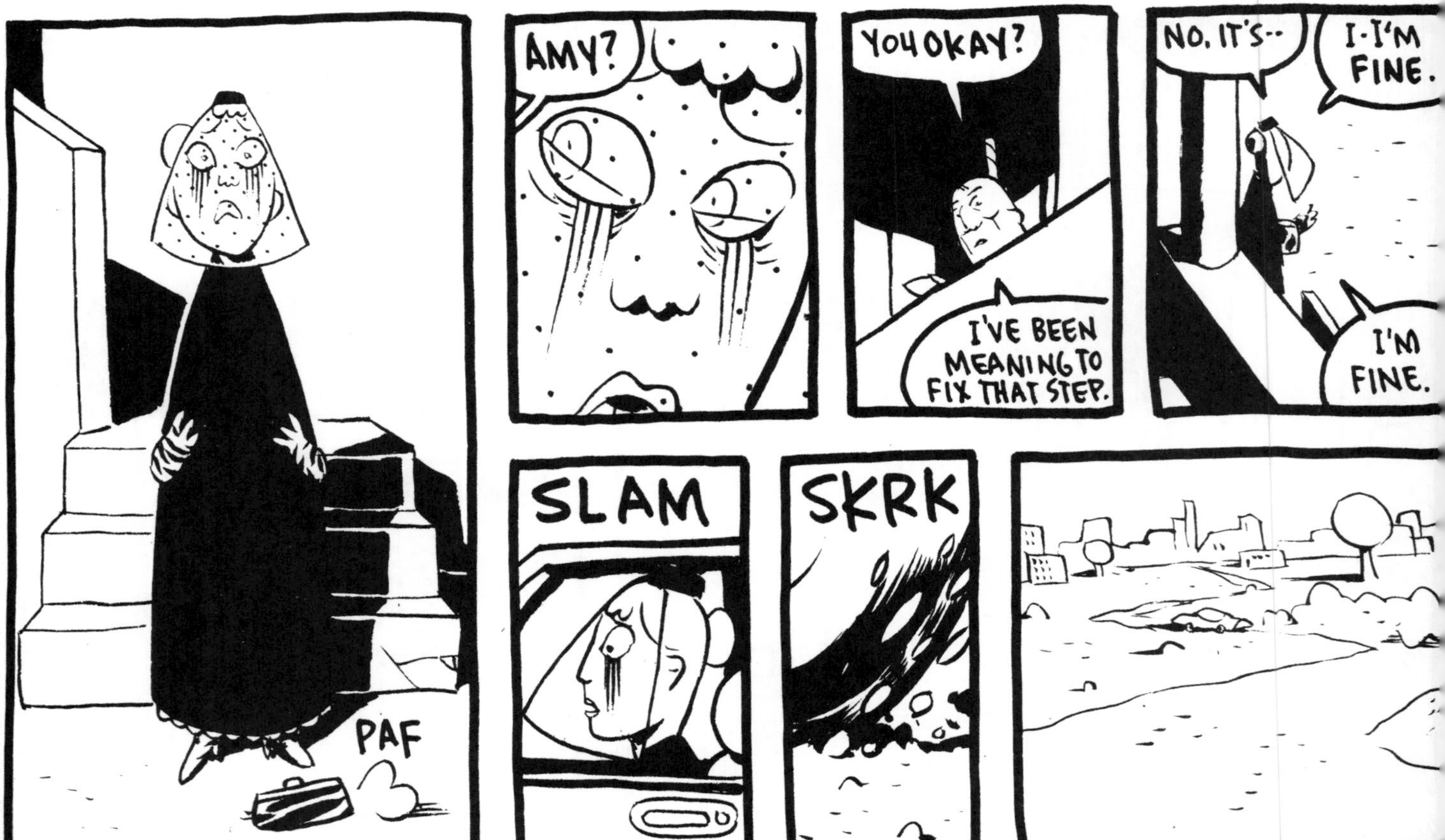
PAF
AMY?
YOU OKAY?
I'VE BEEN MEANING TO FIX THAT STEP.
NO, IT'S--
I-I'M FINE.
I'M FINE.
SLAM
SKRK

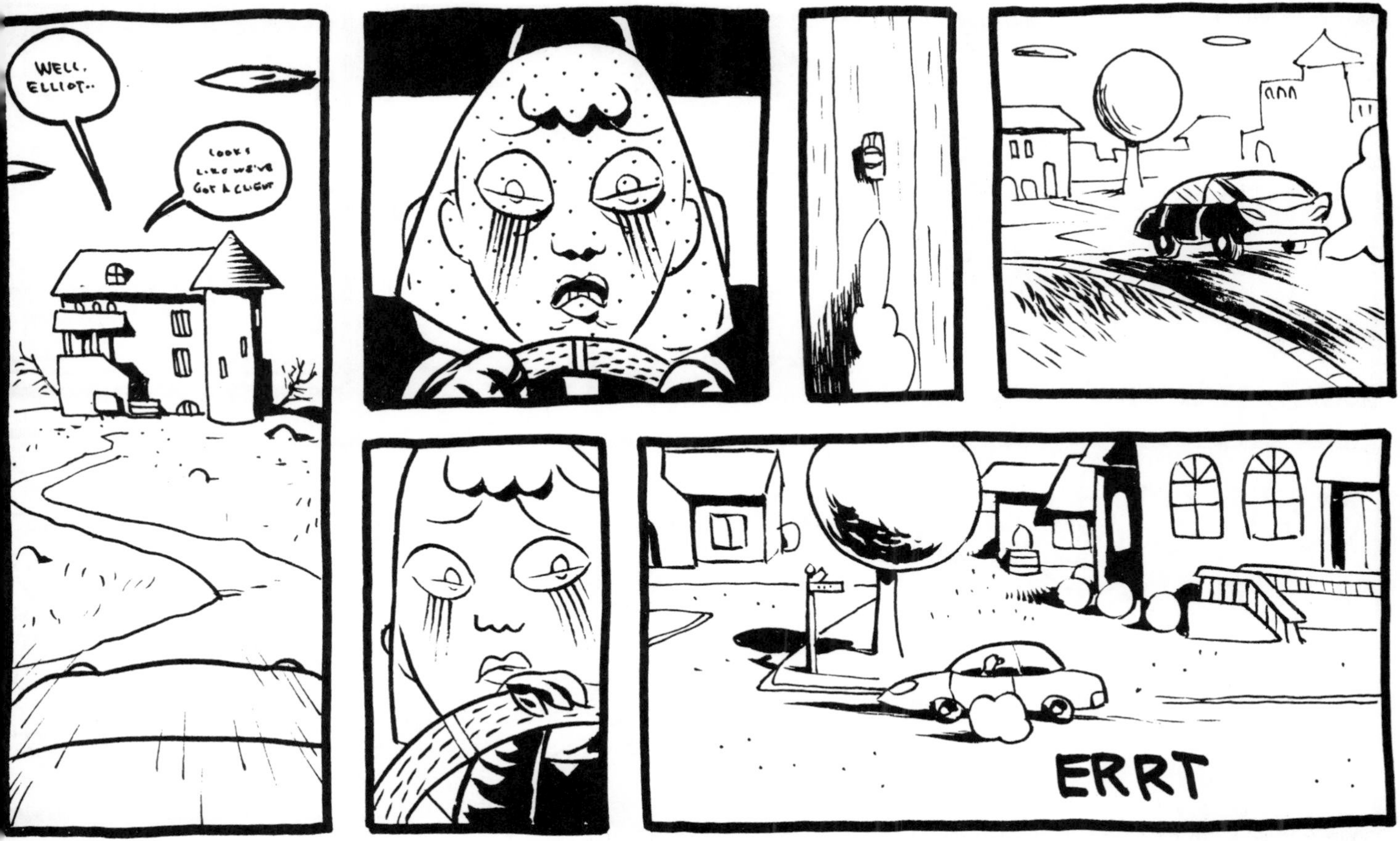
WELL, ELLIOT..
LOOKS LIKE WE'VE GOT A CLIENT
ERRT

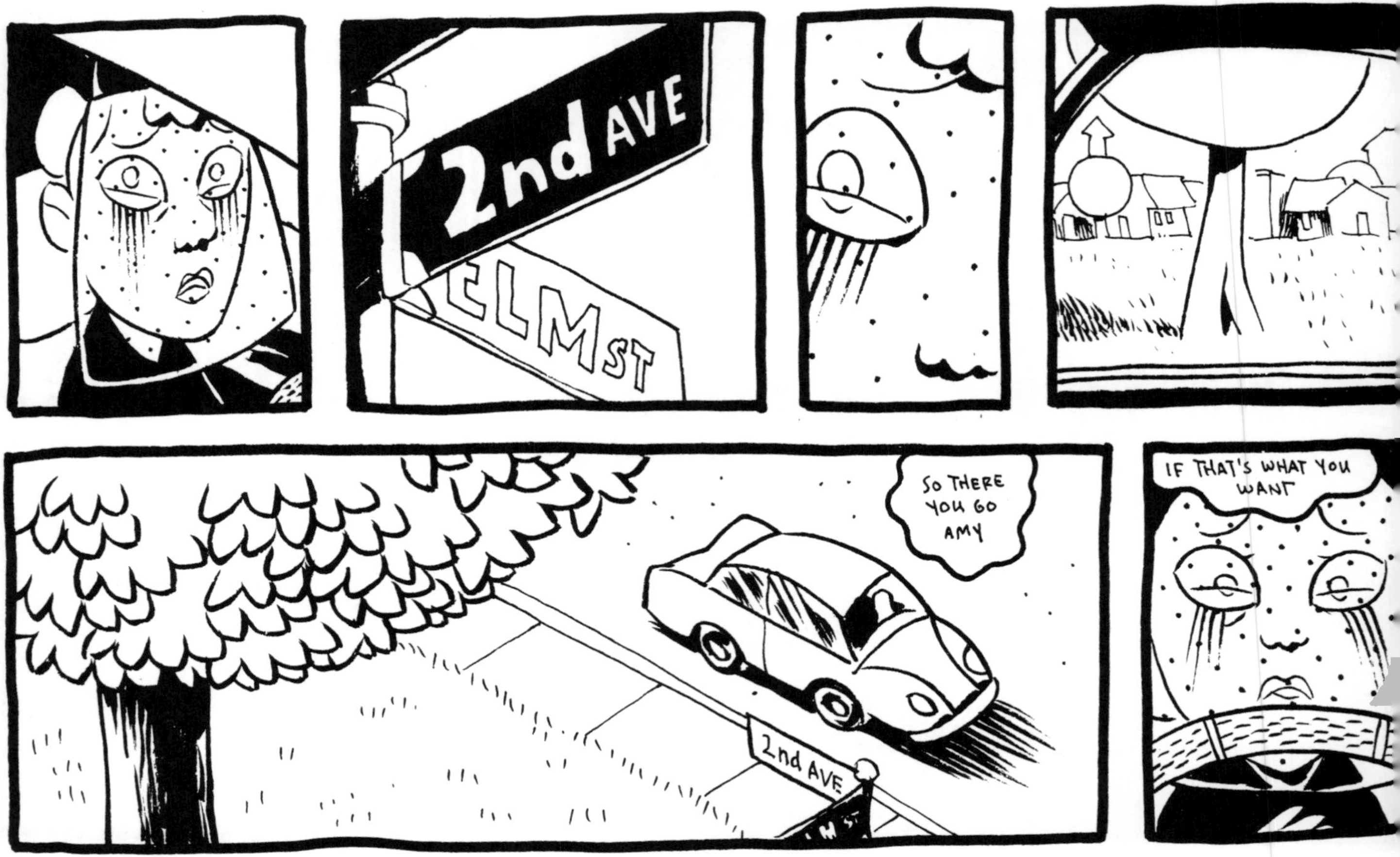
2nd AVE
ELM ST
SO THERE YOU GO AMY
2nd AVE
IF THAT'S WHAT YOU WANT

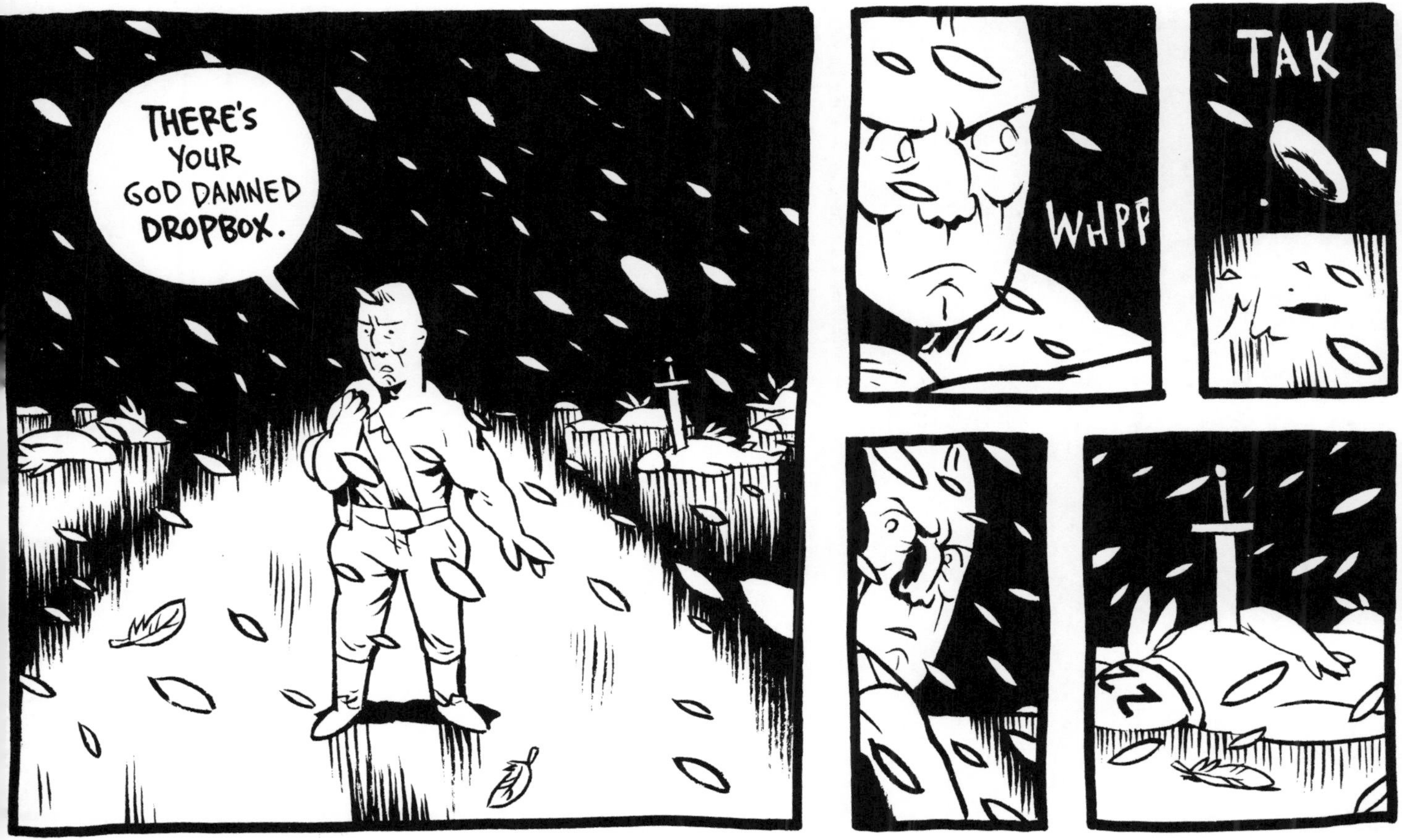
THERE'S YOUR GOD DAMNED DROPBOX.
WHPP
TAK

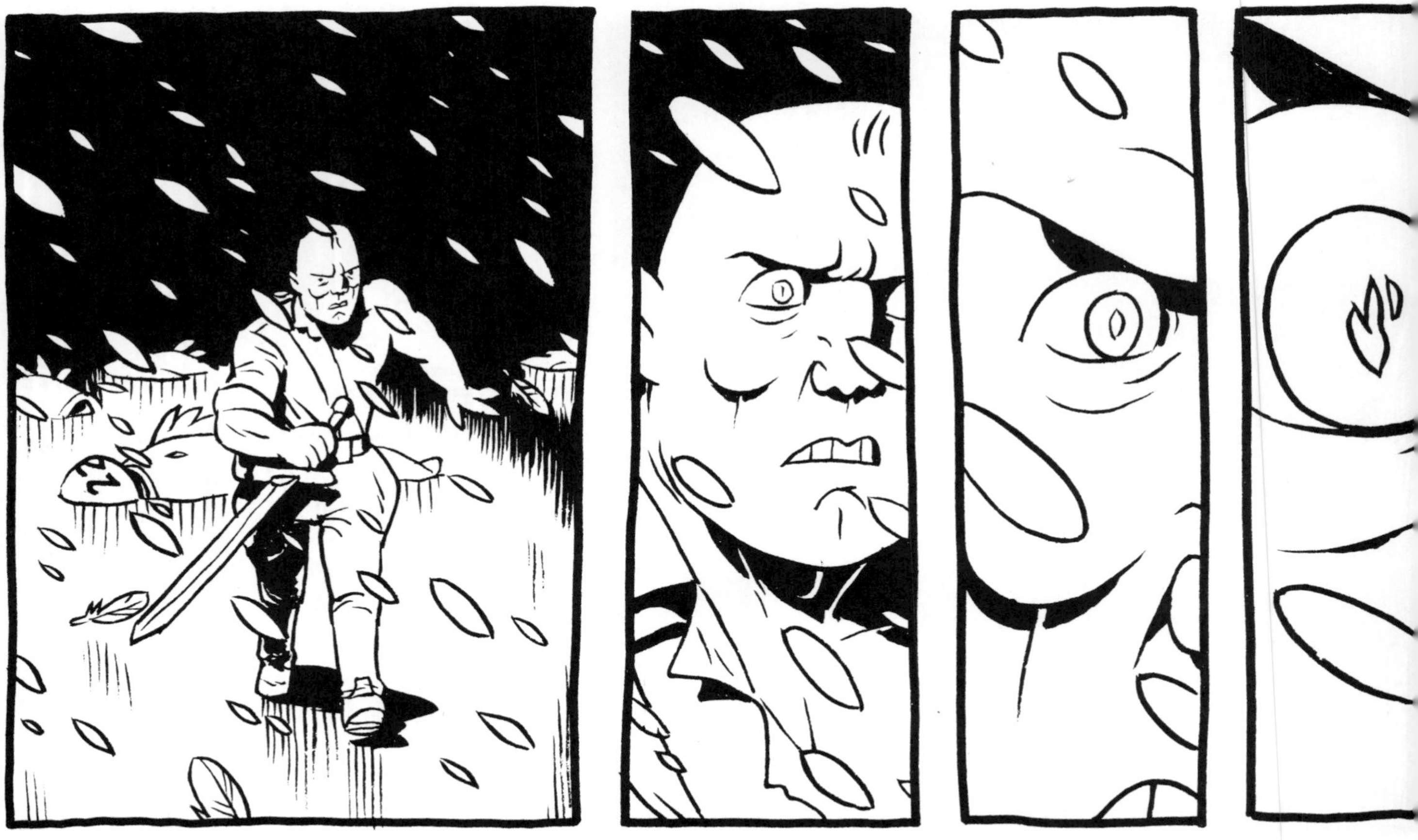

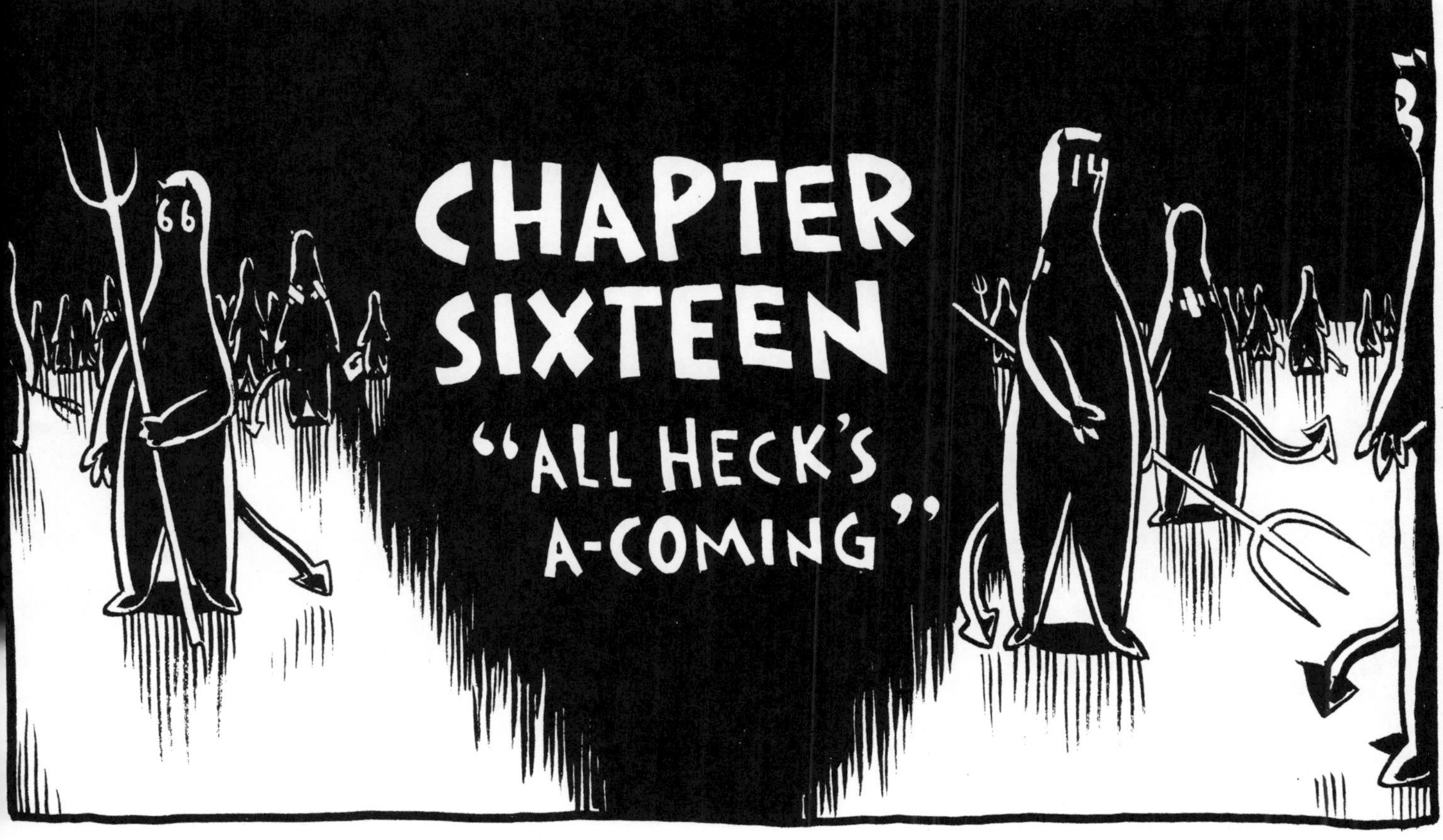
CHAPTER
SIXTEEN
"ALL HECK'S
A-COMING"
66
14

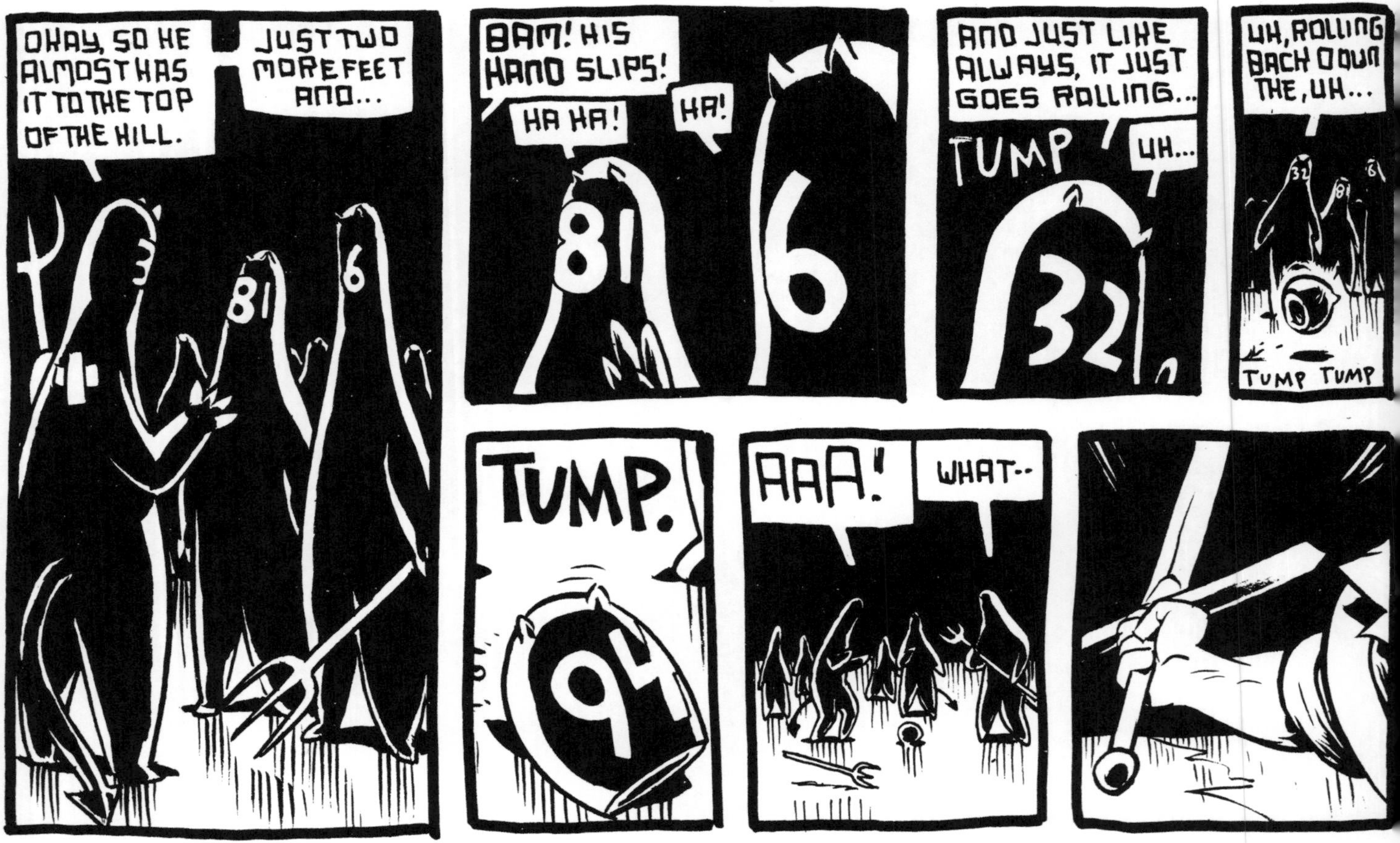
OKAY, SO HE ALMOST HAS IT TO THE TOP OF THE HILL.
JUST TWO MORE FEET AND...
BAM! HIS HAND SLIPS!
HA HA!
HA!
AND JUST LIKE ALWAYS, IT JUST GOES ROLLING...
TUMP
UH...
UH, ROLLING BACK DOWN THE, UH...
TUMP TUMP
TUMP.
AAA!
WHAT--

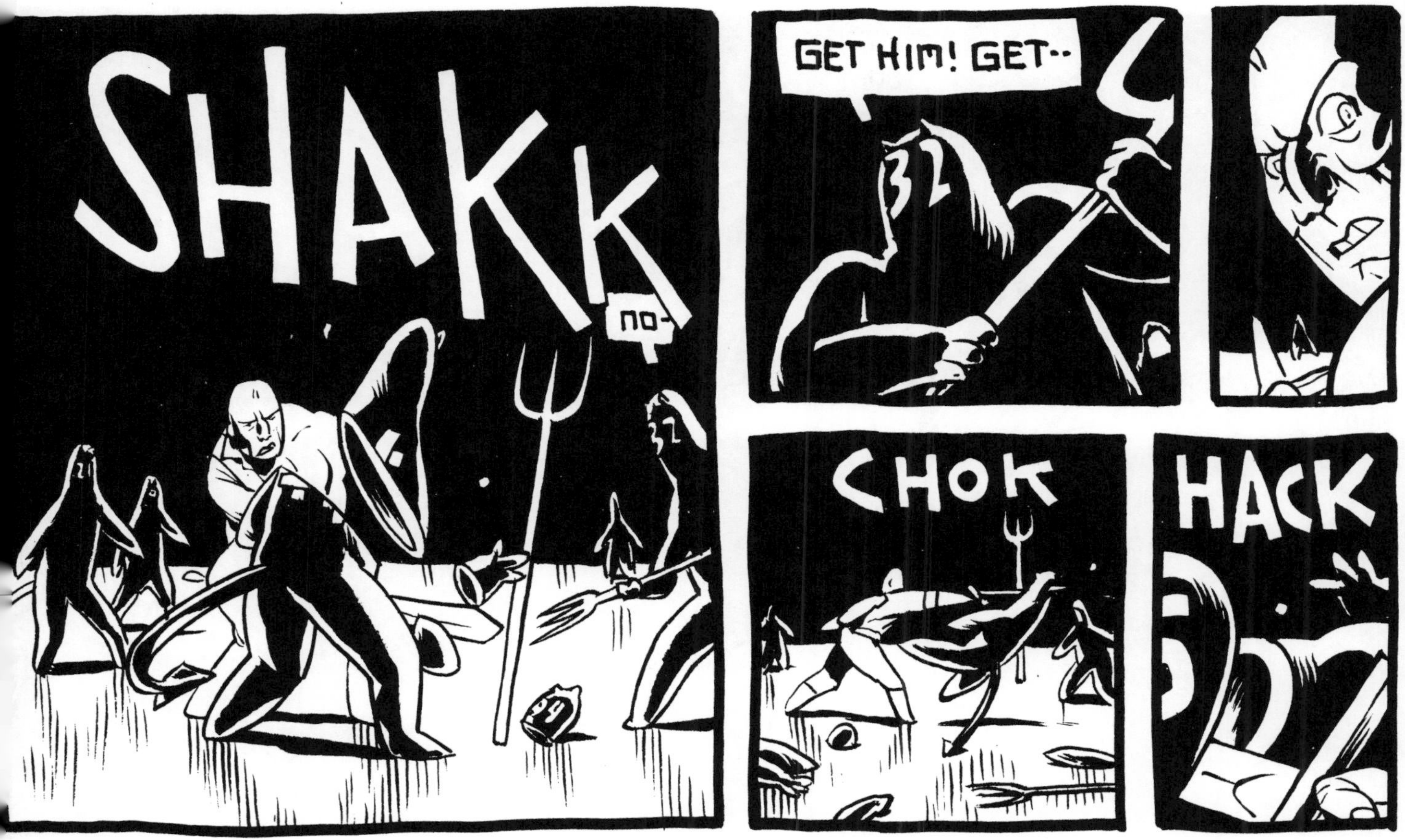
SHAKK
NO-
GET HIM! GET--
CHOK
HACK

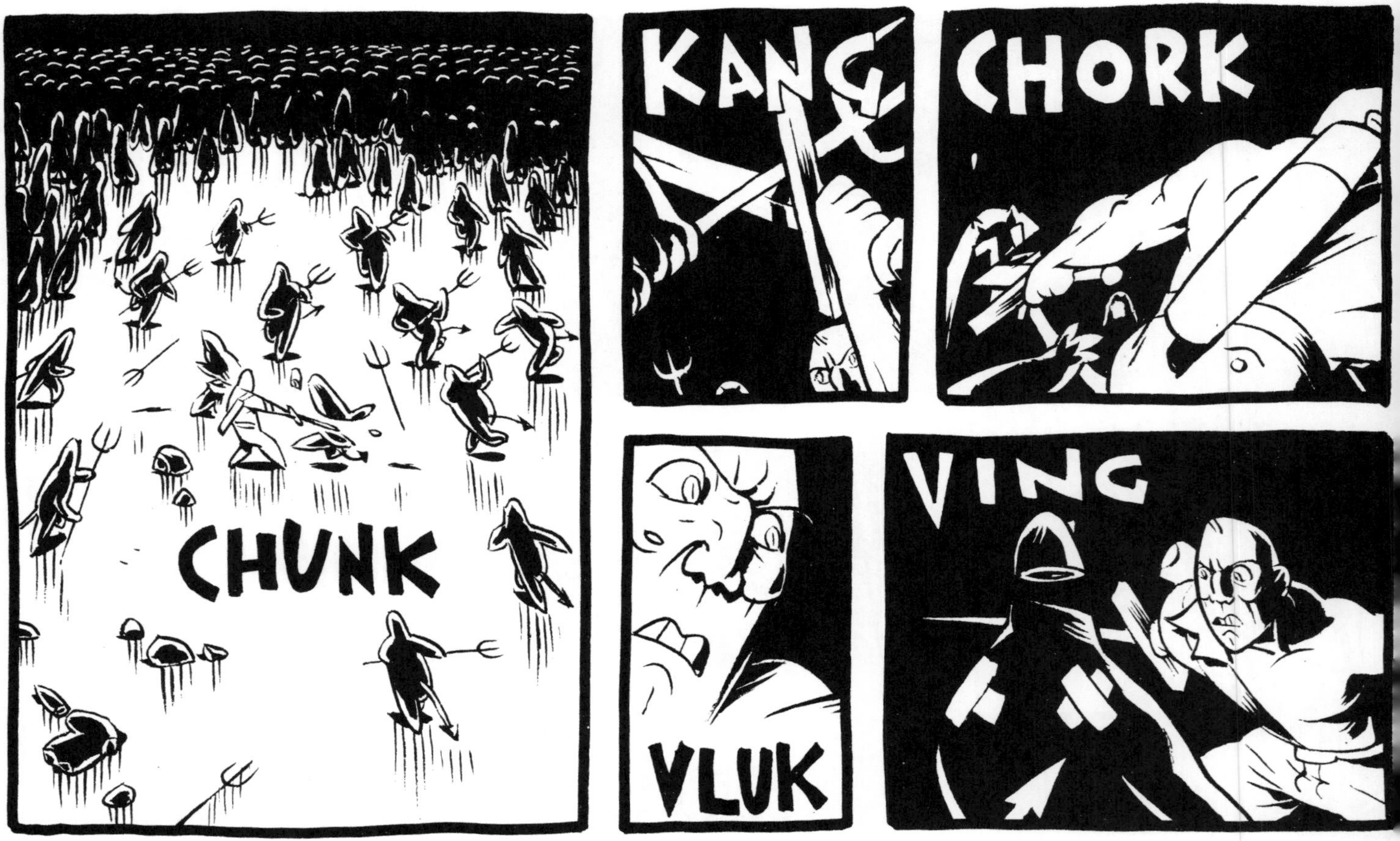
CHUNK
KANG
CHORK
VLUK
VING

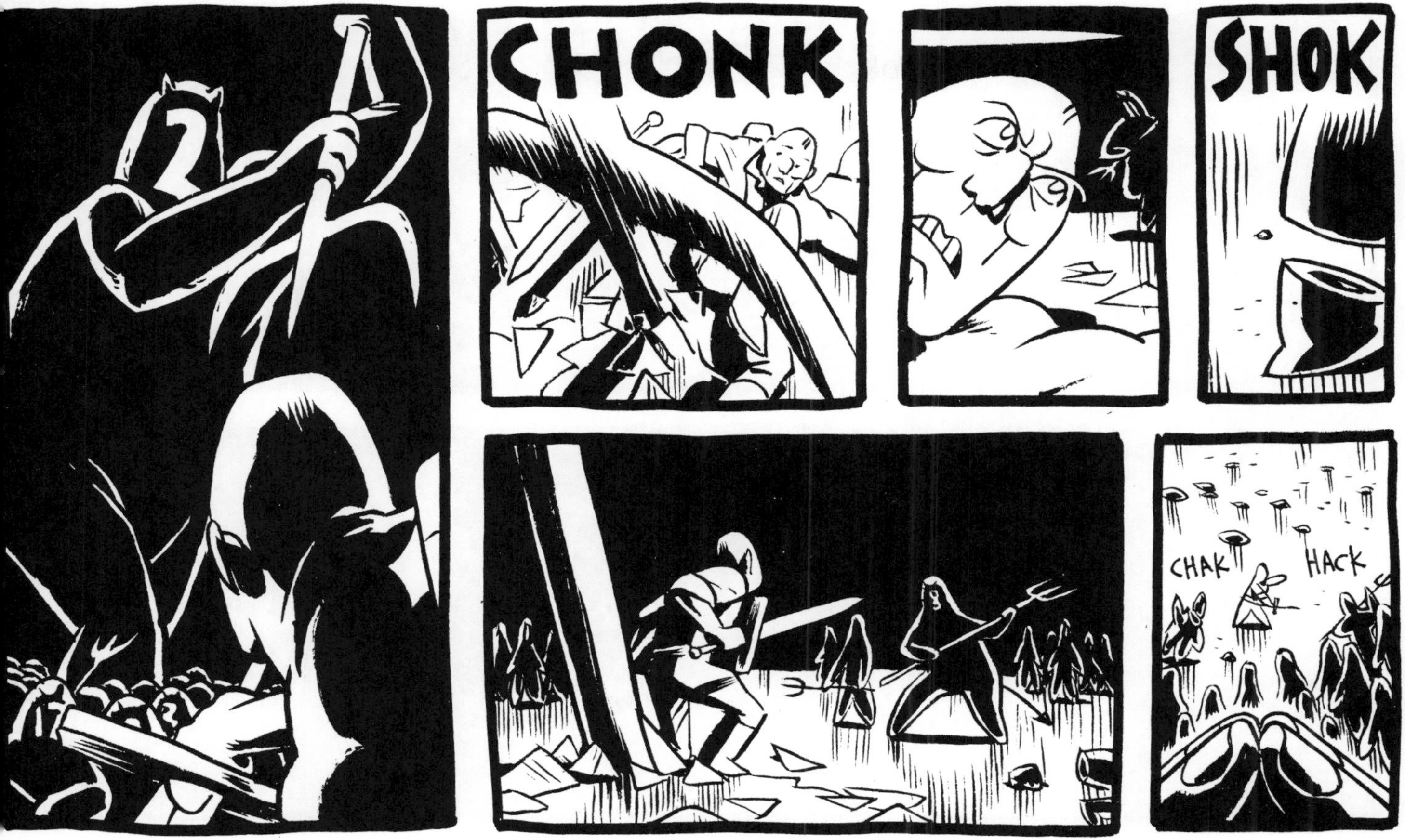
CHONK
SHOK
CHAK
HACK

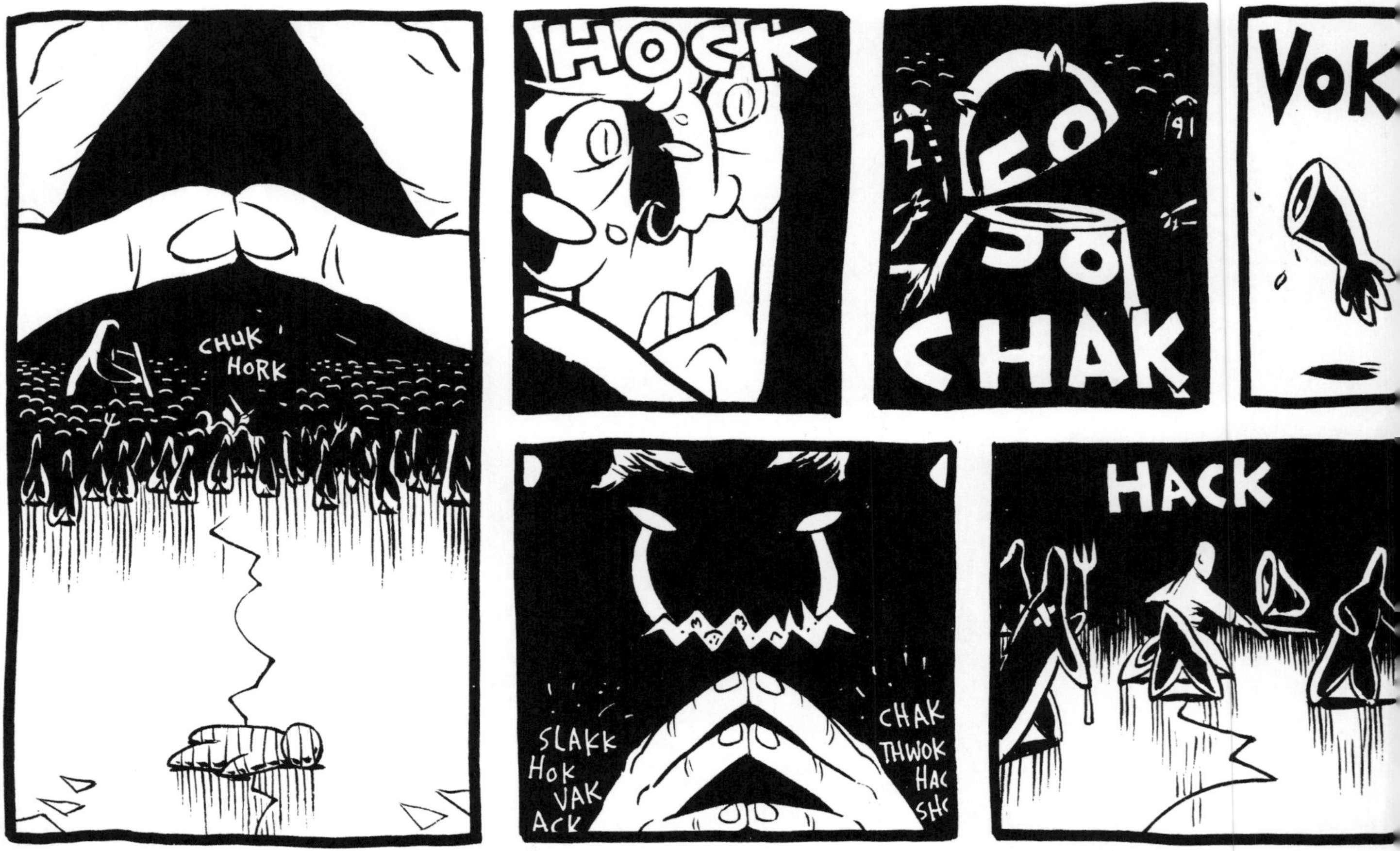
CHUK
HORK
HOCK
CHAK
VOK
SLAKK
HOK
VAK
ACK
CHAK
THWOK
HAC
HACK

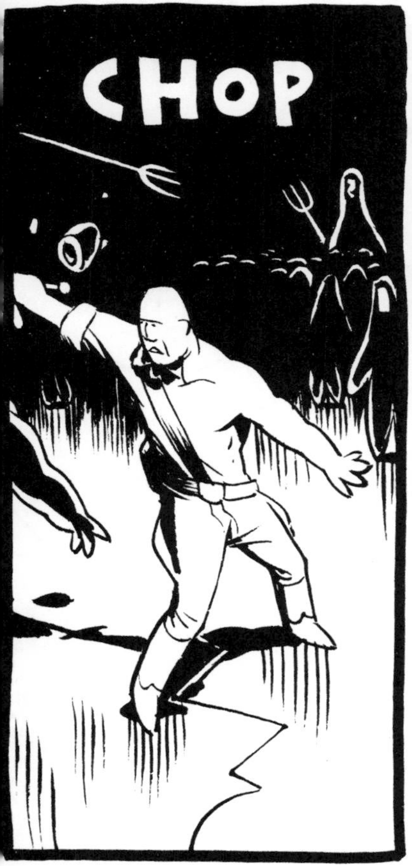
CHOP
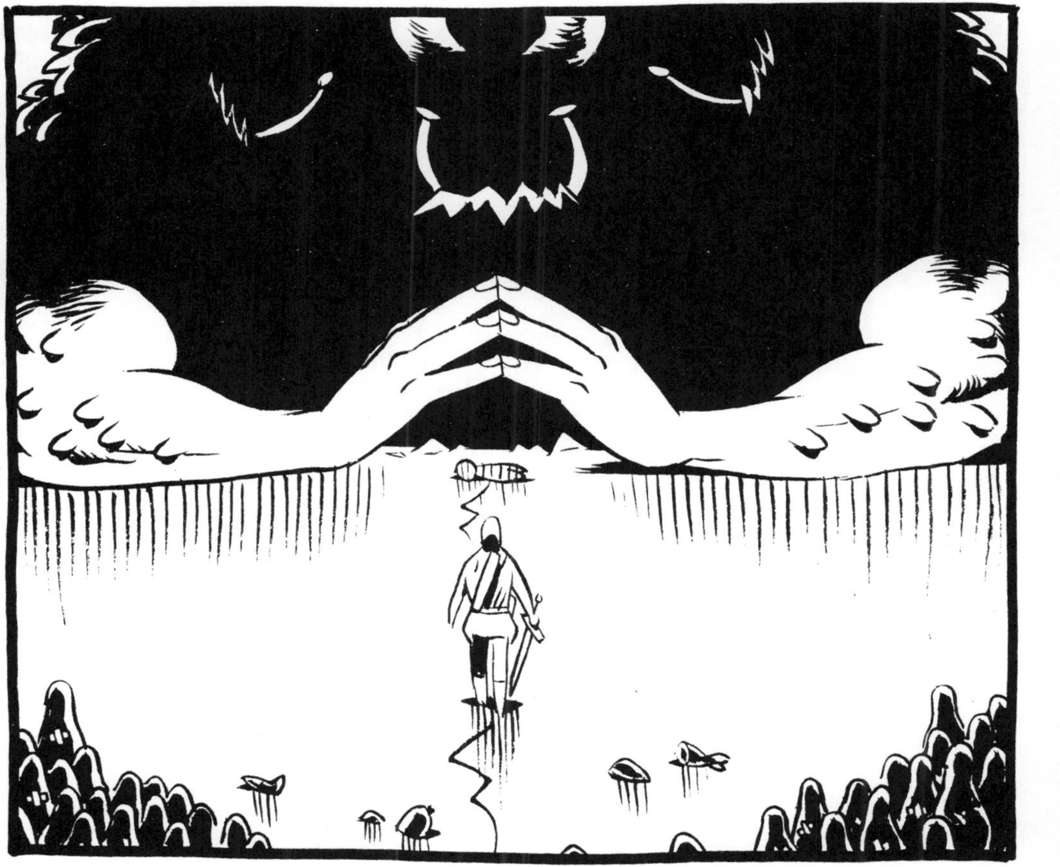

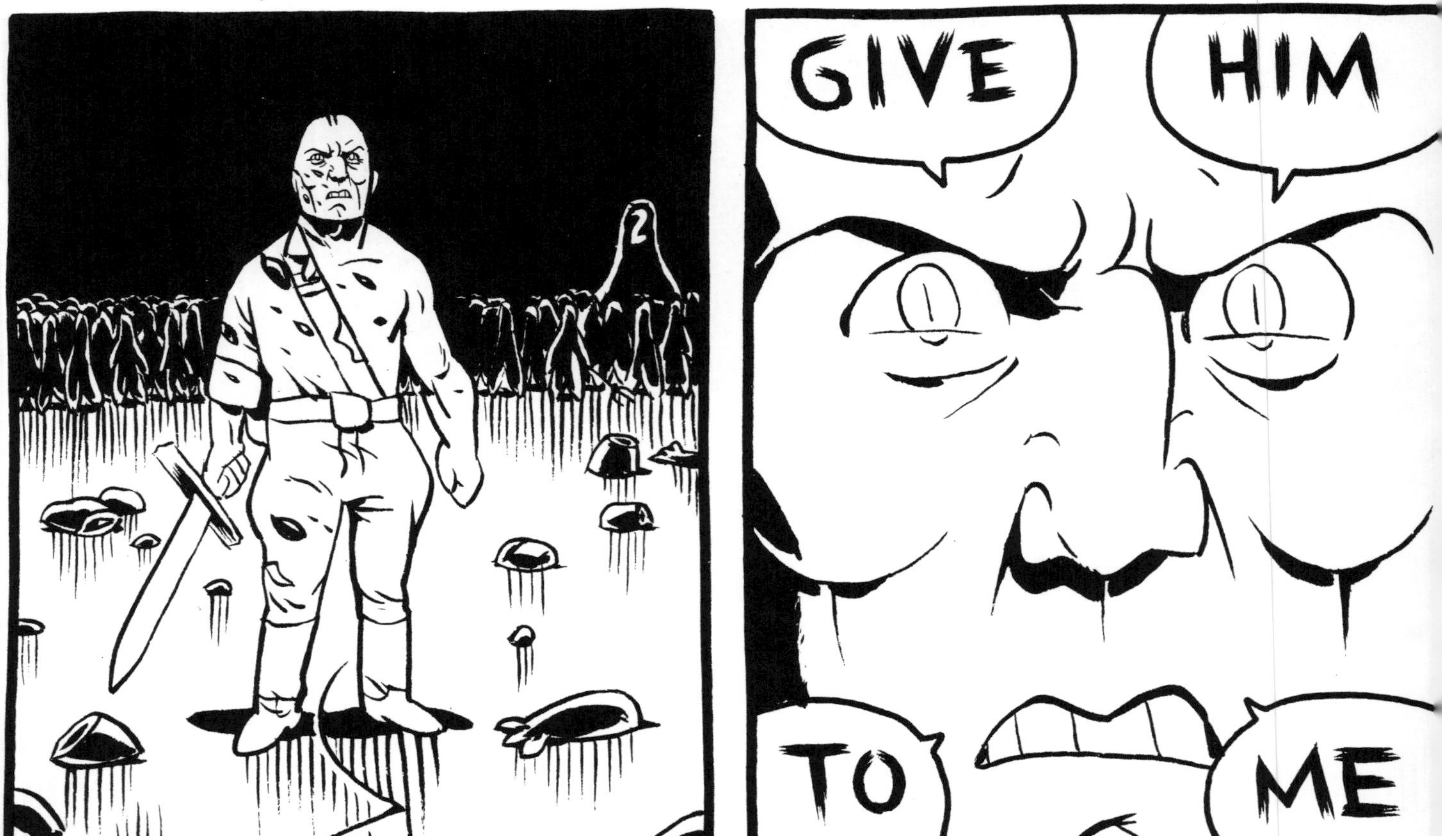
2
GIVE
HIM
TO
ME

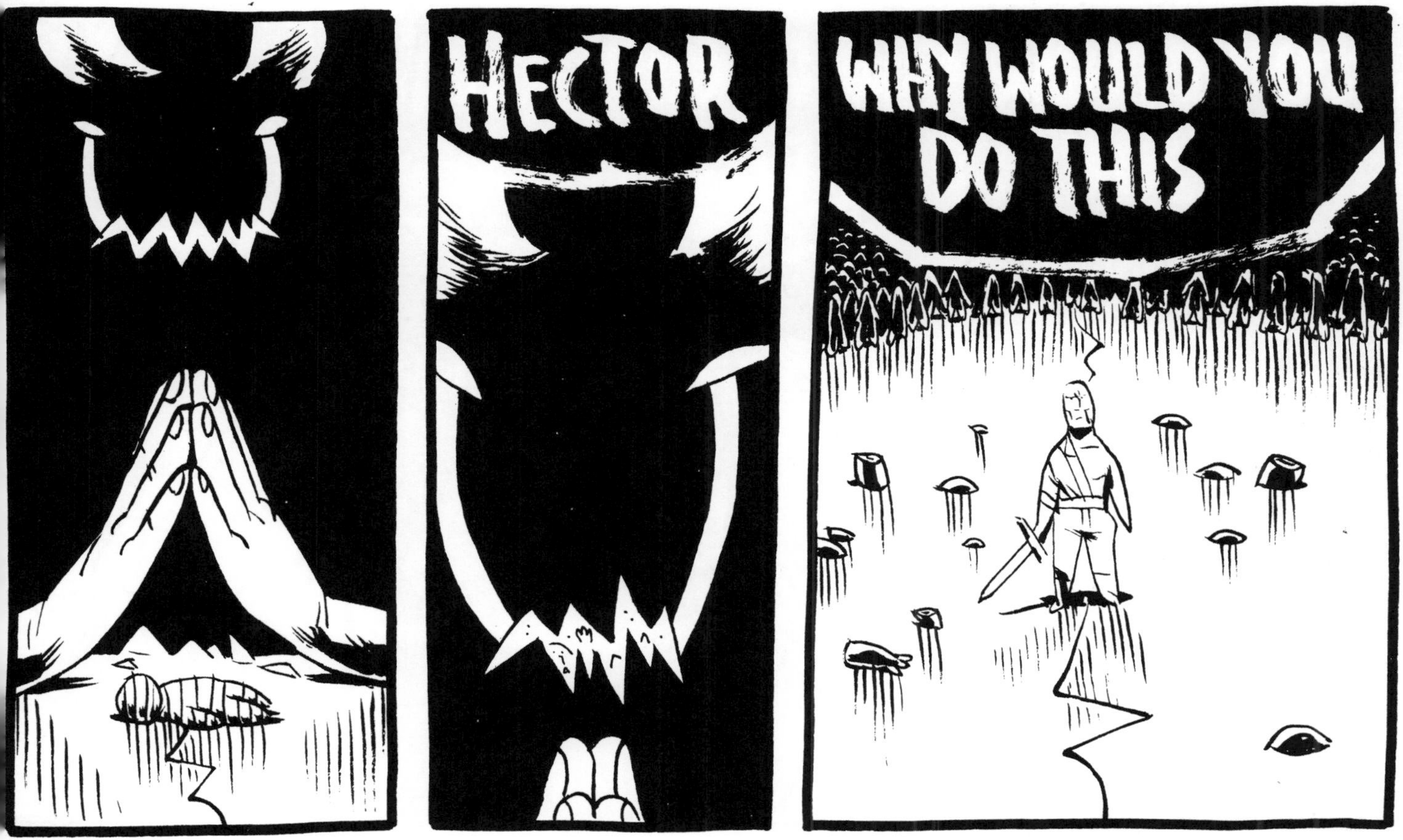
HECTOR
WHY WOULD YOU DO THIS

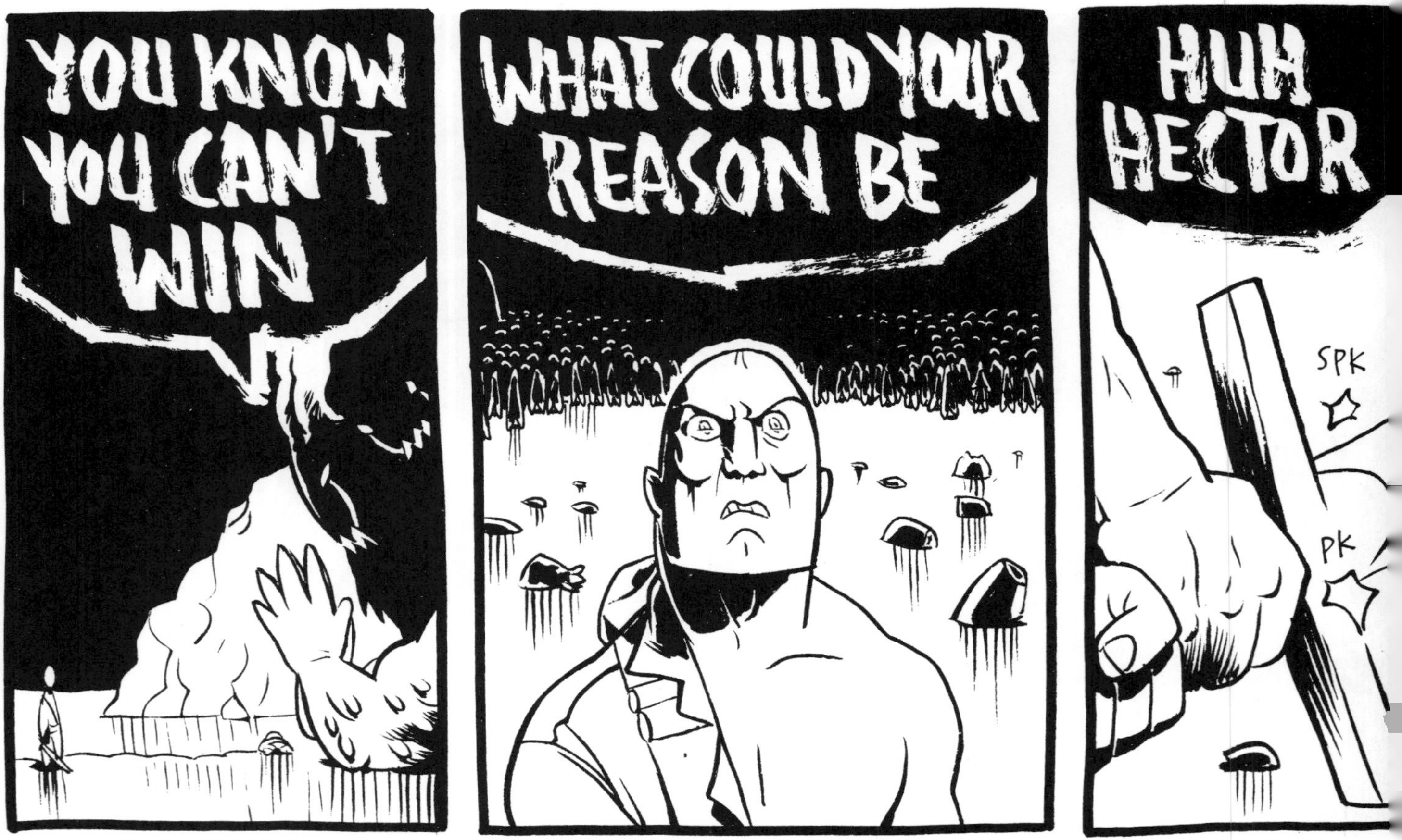
YOU KNOW
YOU CAN'T
WIN
WHAT COULD YOUR
REASON BE
HUH
HECTOR
SPK
PK

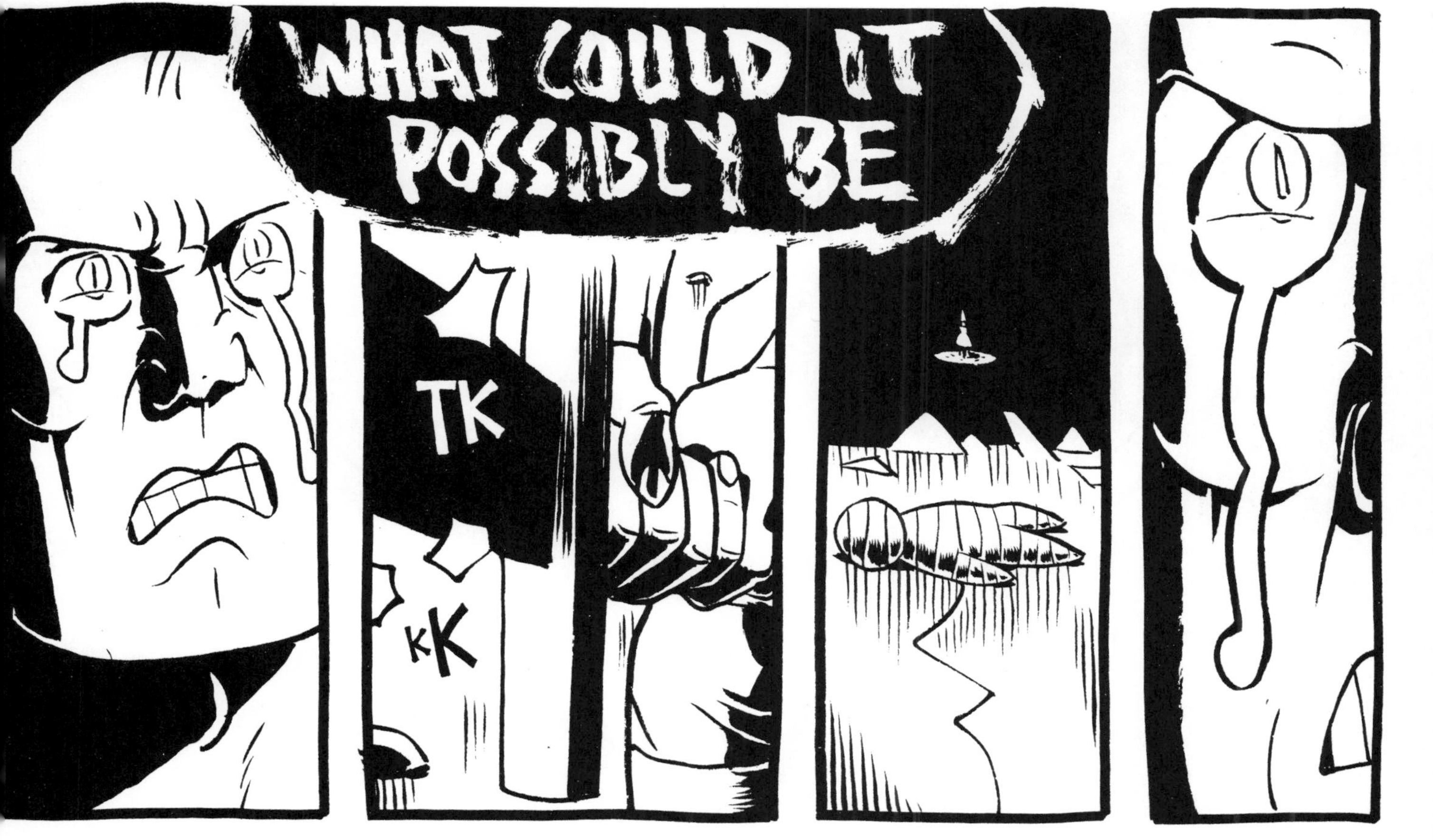
WHAT COULD IT POSSIBLY BE
TK
KK

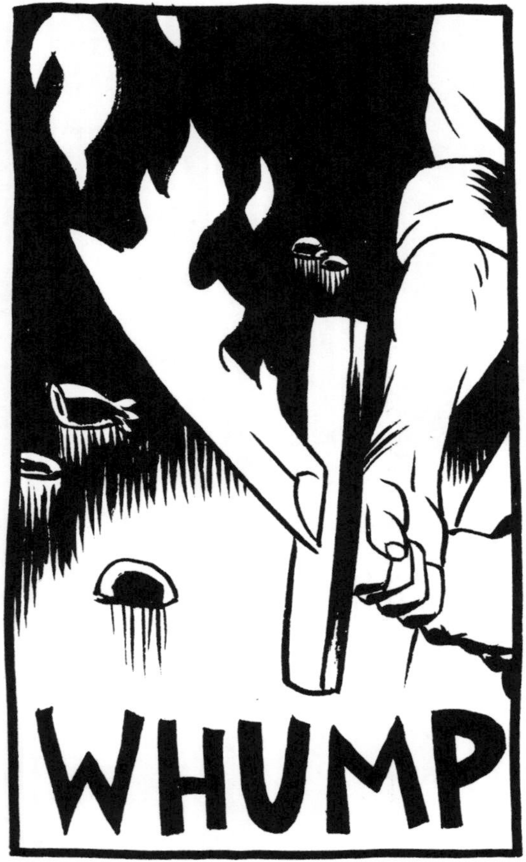
WHUMP

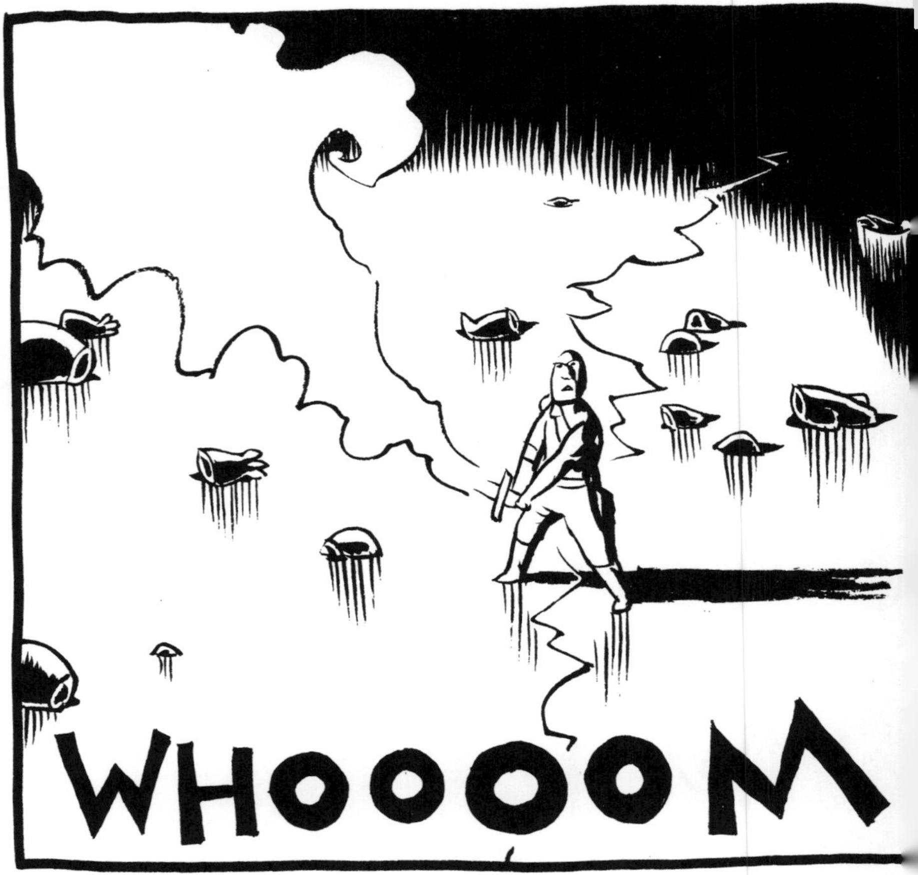
WHOOOOM

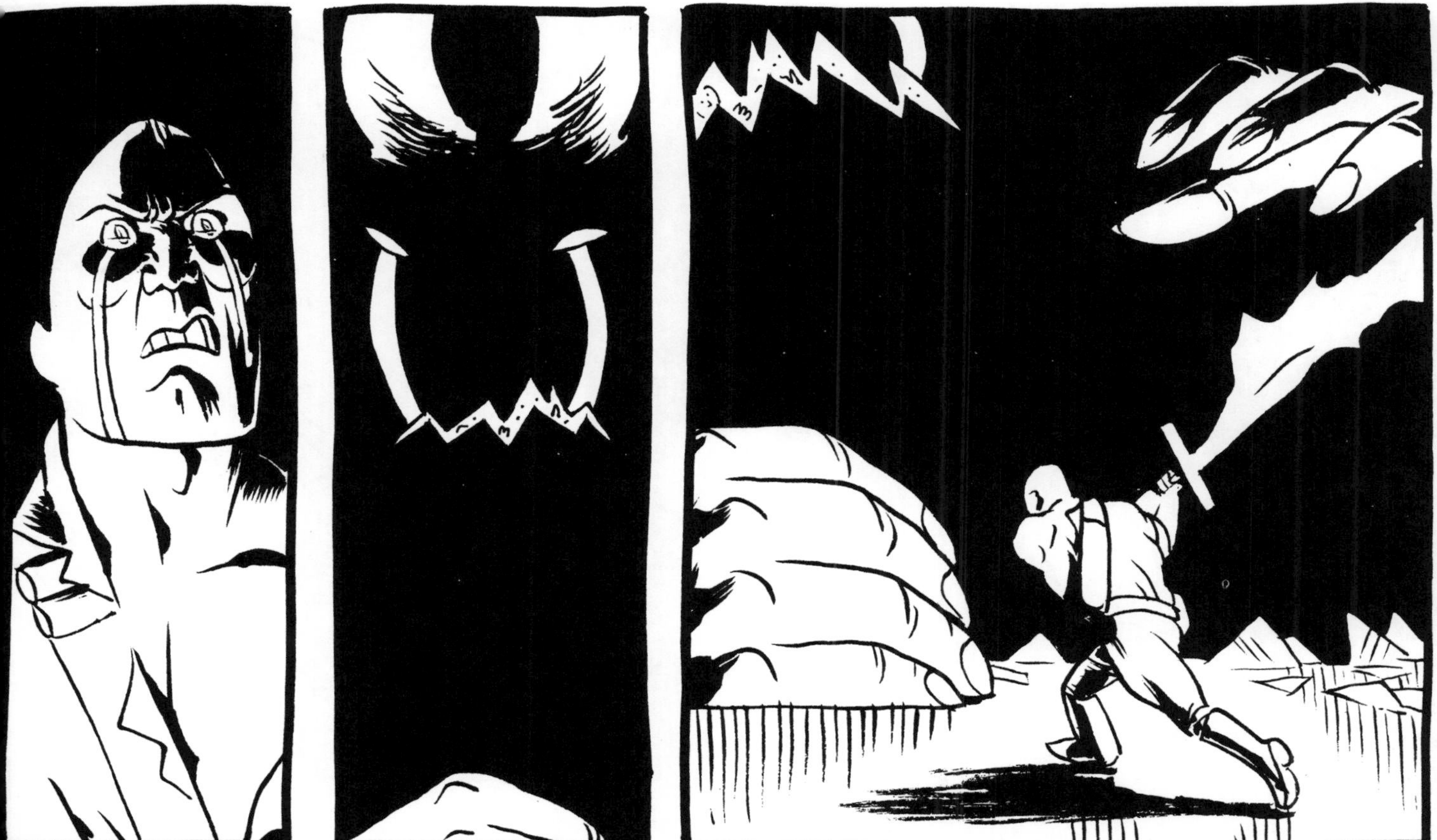

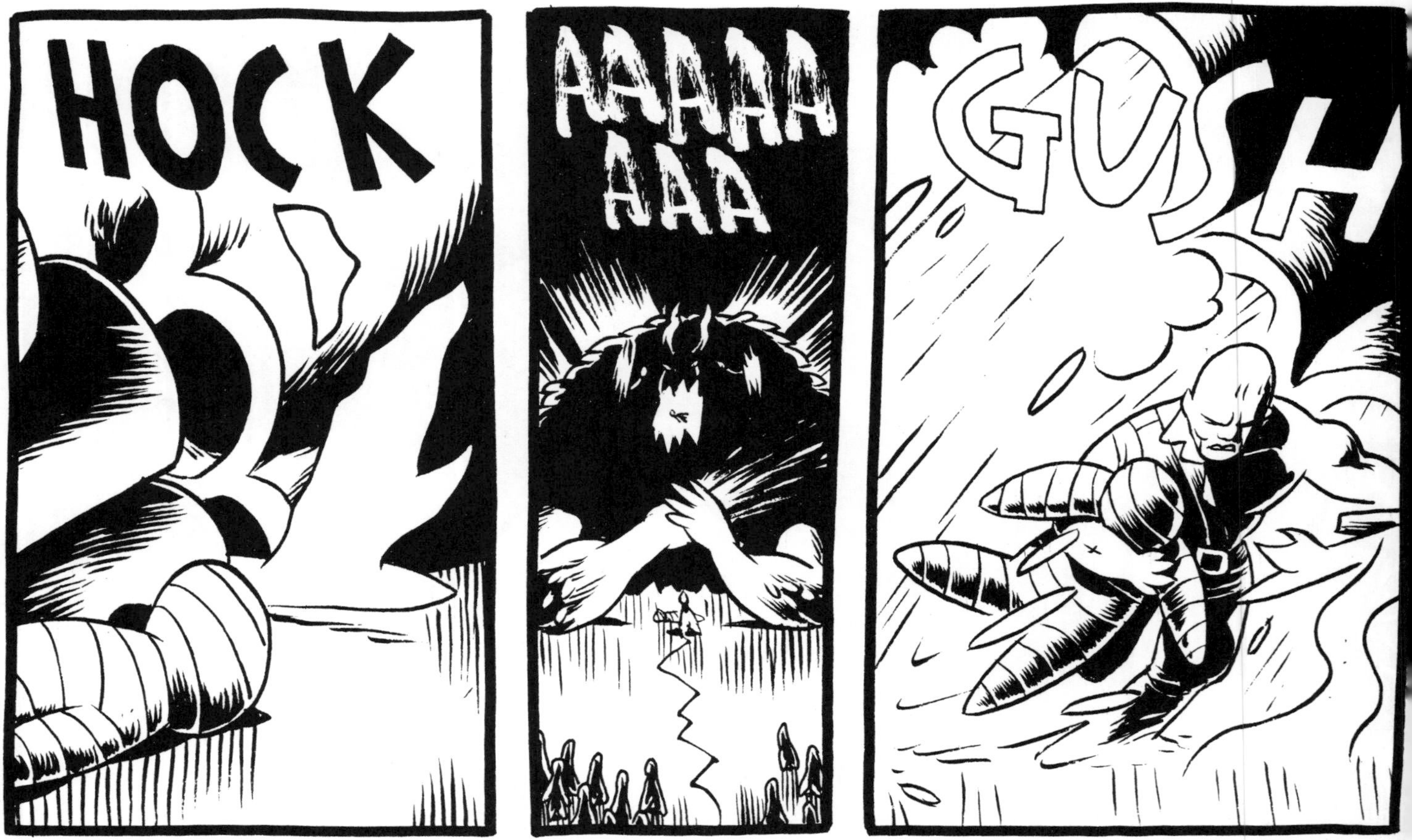
HOCK
AAAAA
AAA
GUSH

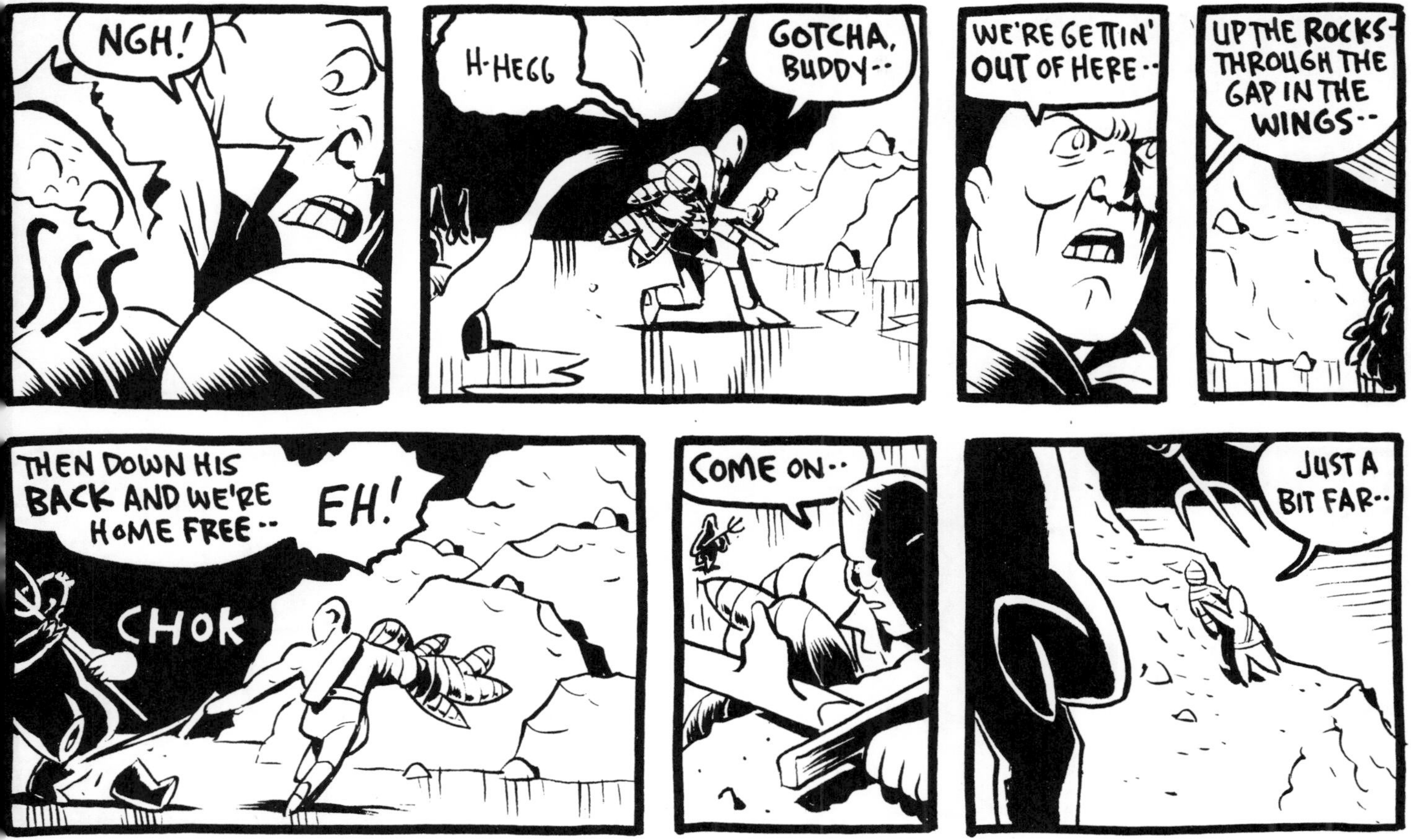
NGH!
H-HEGG
GOTCHA, BUDDY--
WE'RE GETTIN' OUT OF HERE--
UP THE ROCKS-THROUGH THE GAP IN THE WINGS--
THEN DOWN HIS BACK AND WE'RE HOME FREE--
EH!
CHOK
COME ON--
JUST A BIT FAR--

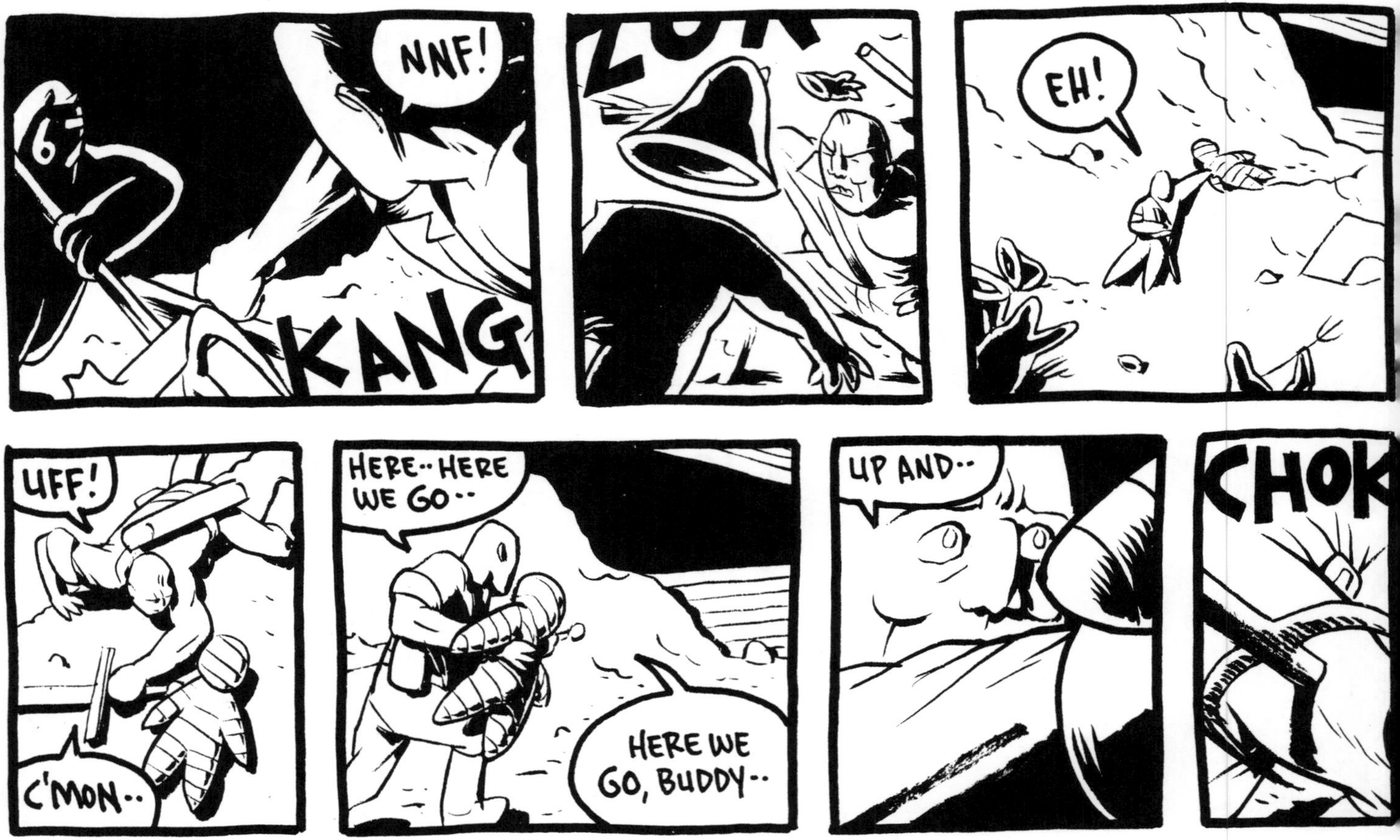
NNF!
KANG
EH!
UFF!
C'MON..
HERE.. HERE WE GO..
HERE WE GO, BUDDY..
UP AND..
CHOK

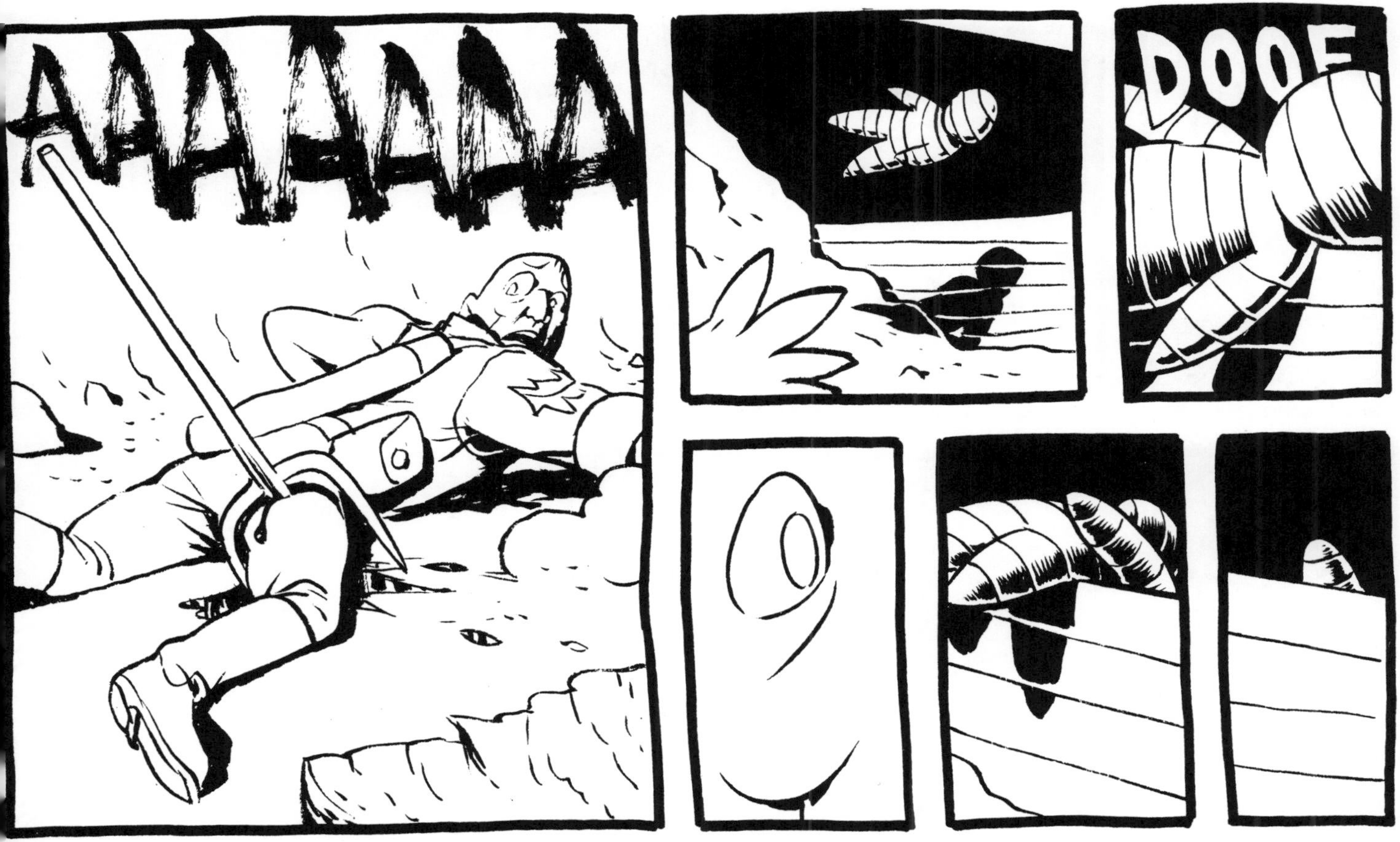
AAAAAAA
DOOF

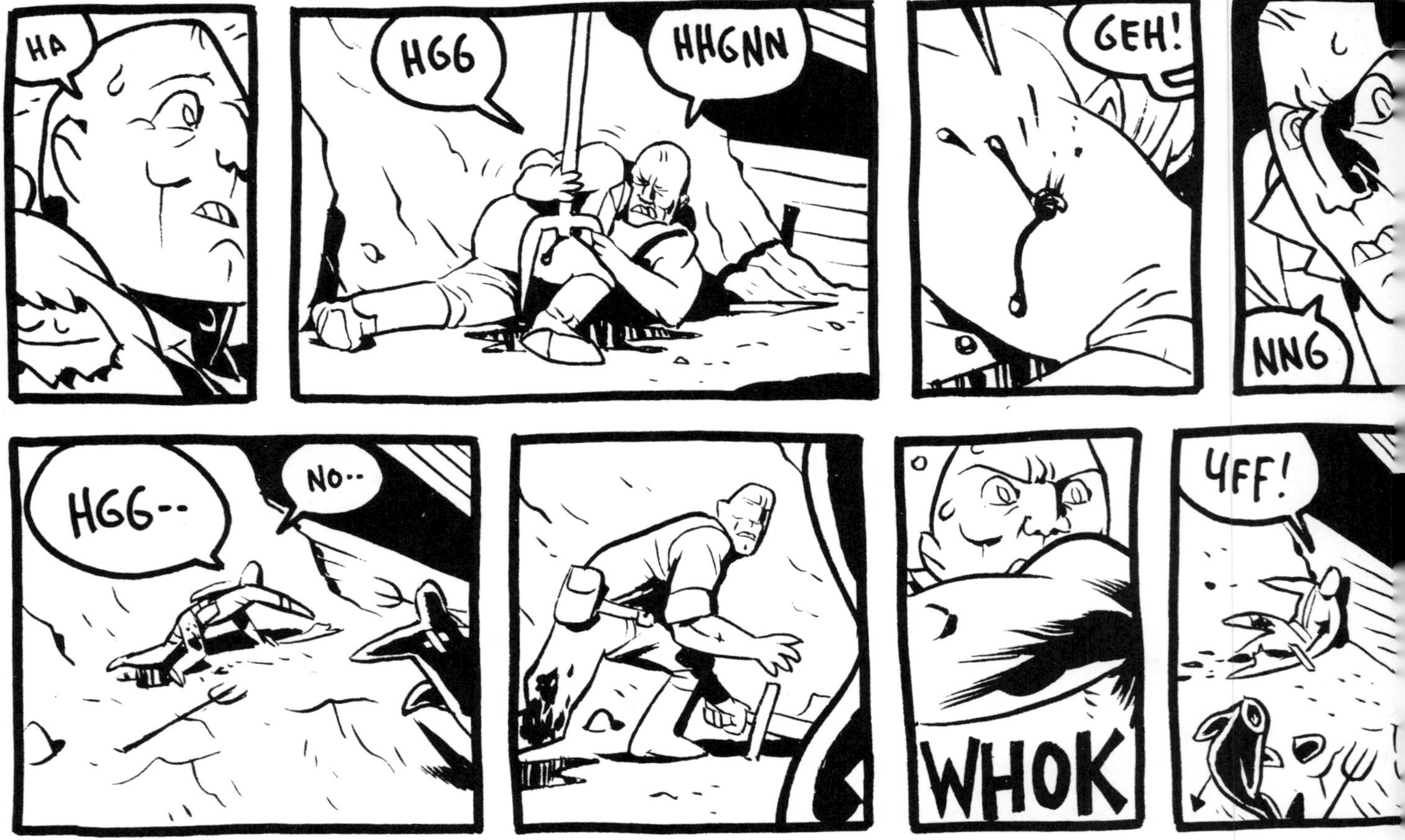
HA
HGG
HHGNN
GEH!
NNG
HGG--
NO..
WHOK
UFF!

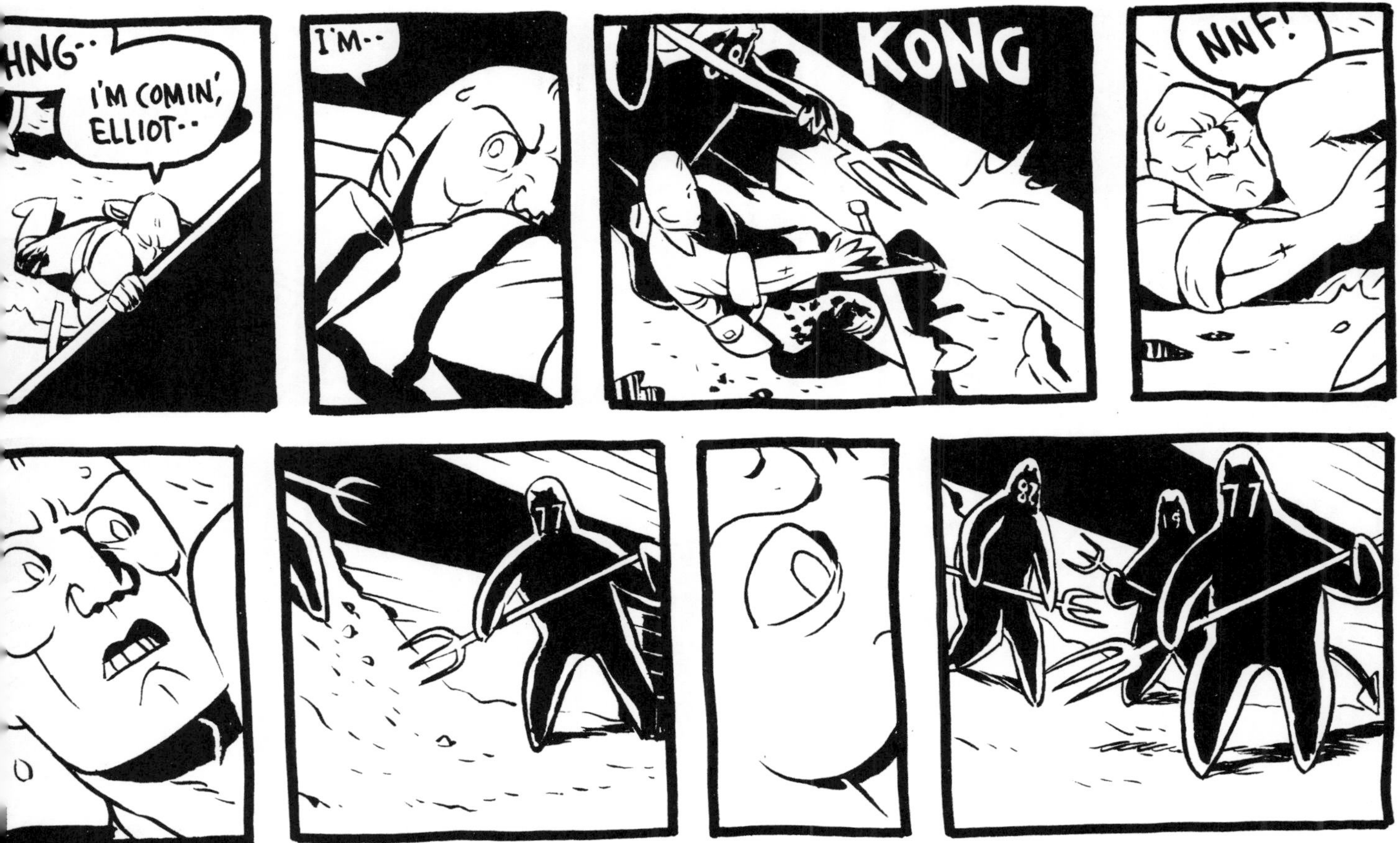
HNG··
I'M COMIN',
ELLIOT··
I'M··
KONG
NNF!
77
82
19
77

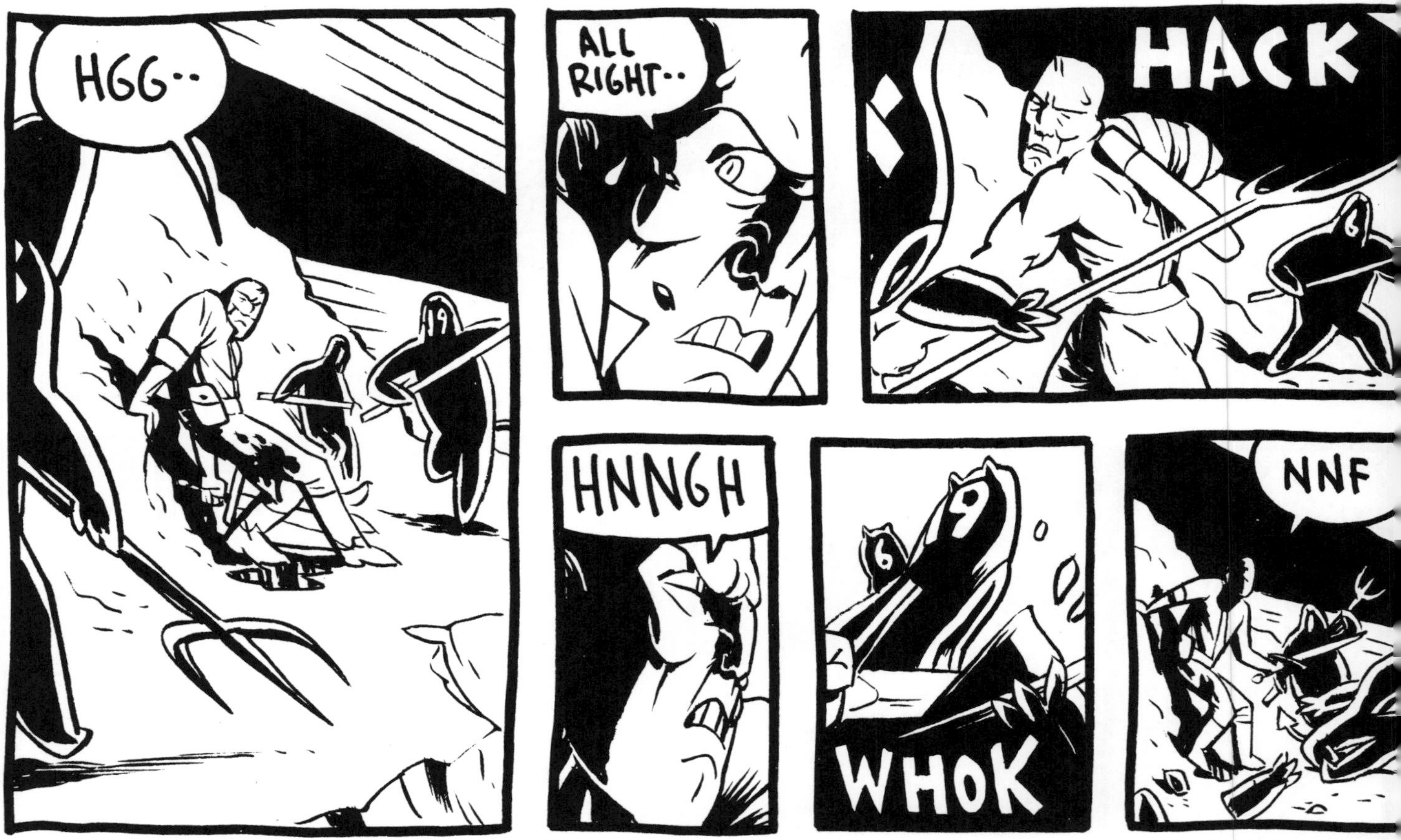
HGG..
ALL RIGHT..
HACK
HNNGH
WHOK
NNF

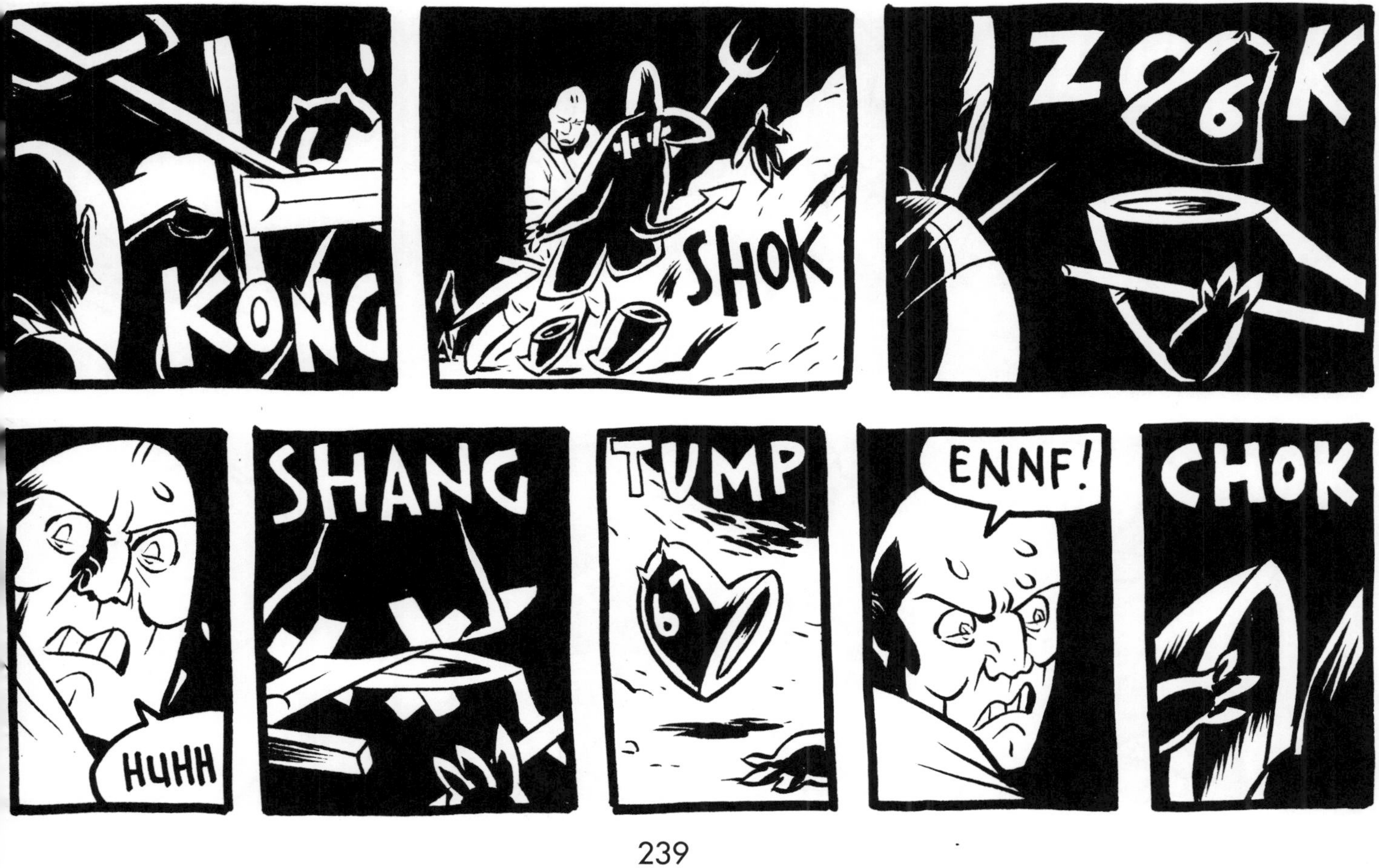
KONG
SHOK
HUHH
SHANG
TUMP
ENNF!
CHOK

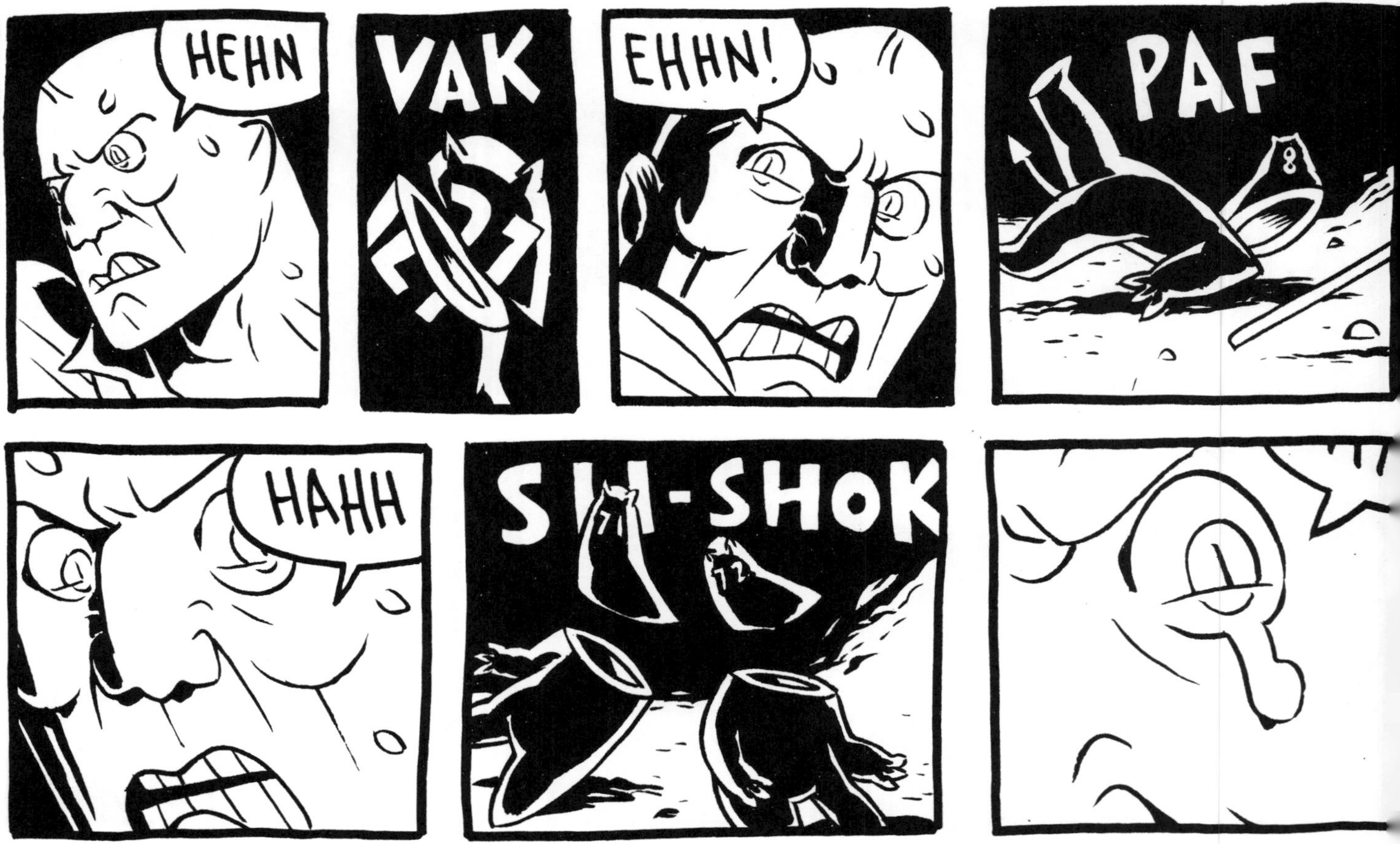
HEHN
VAK
EHHN!
PAF
HAHH
SH-SHOK

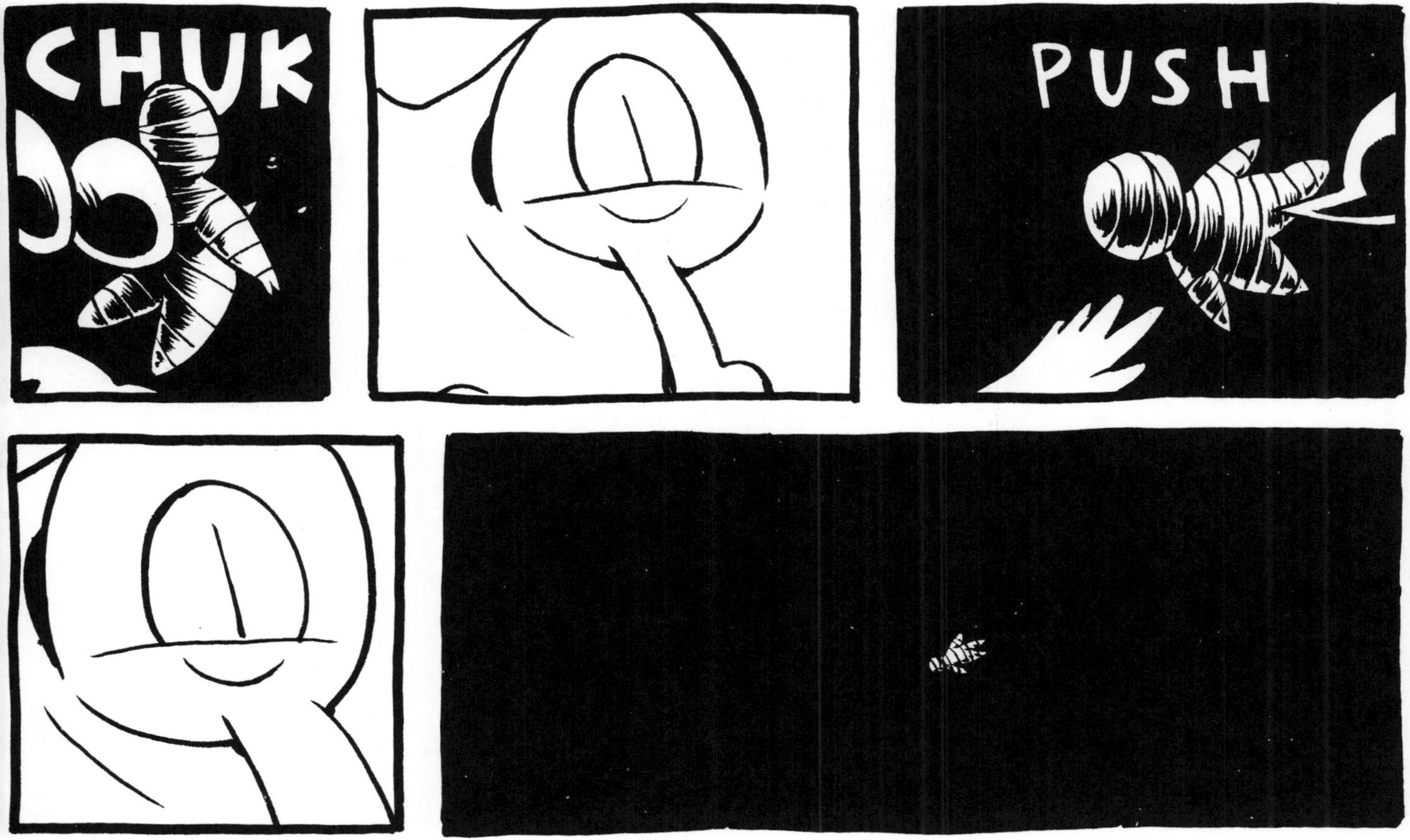
CHUK
PUSH

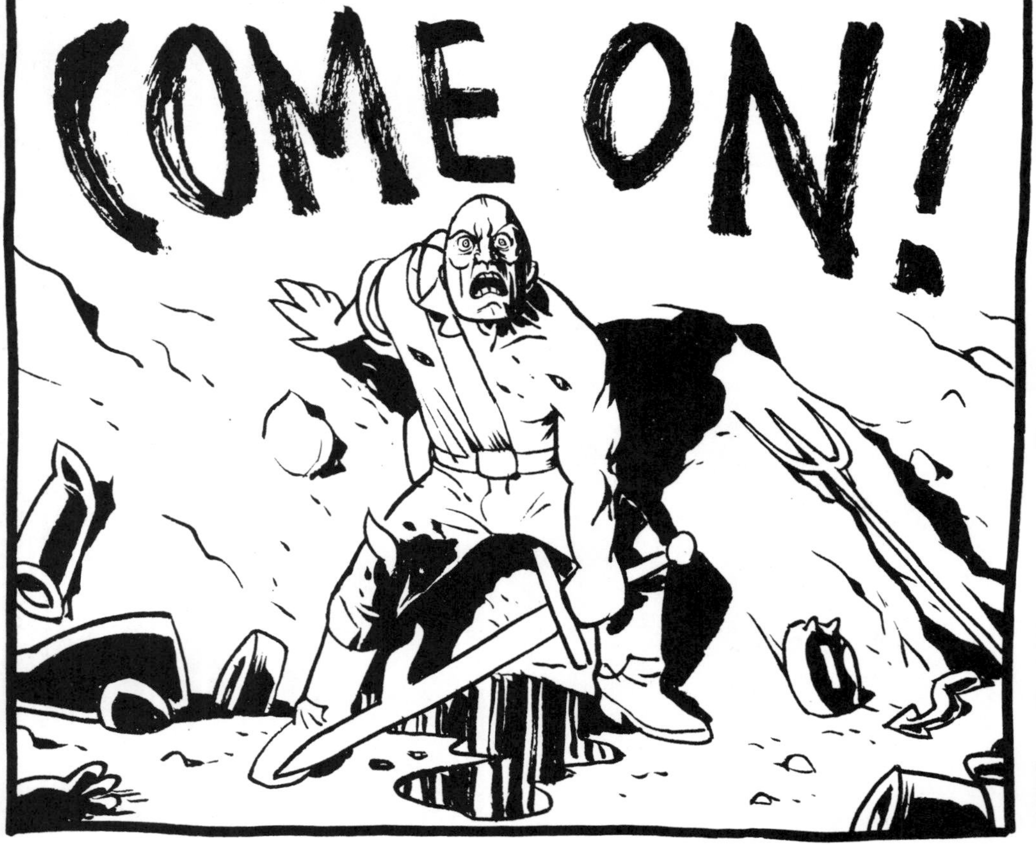
COME ON!

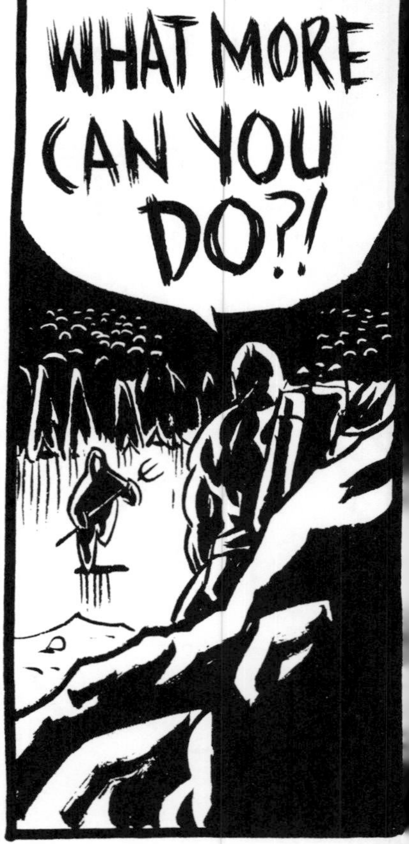
WHAT MORE CAN YOU DO?!

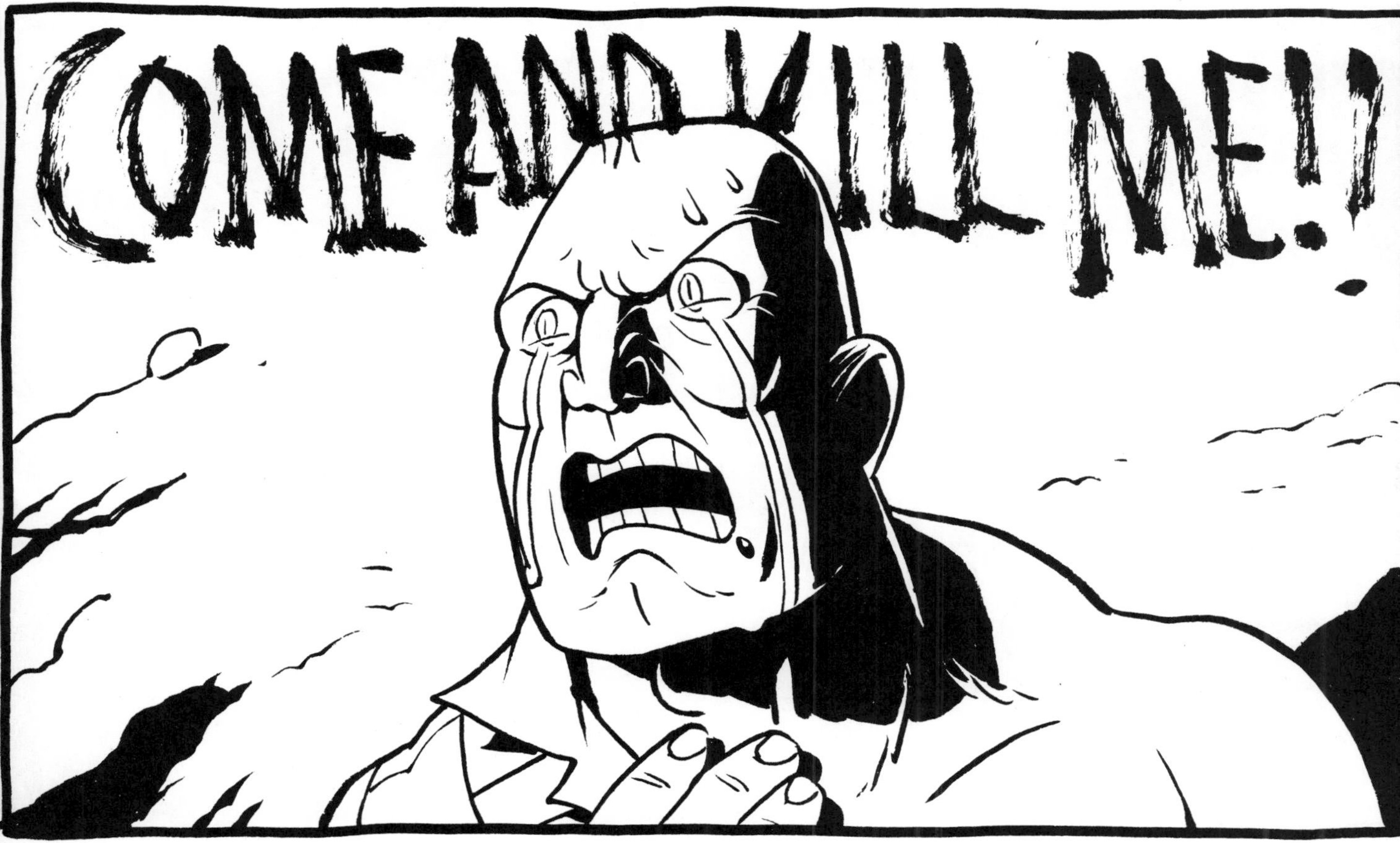
COME AND KILL ME!!

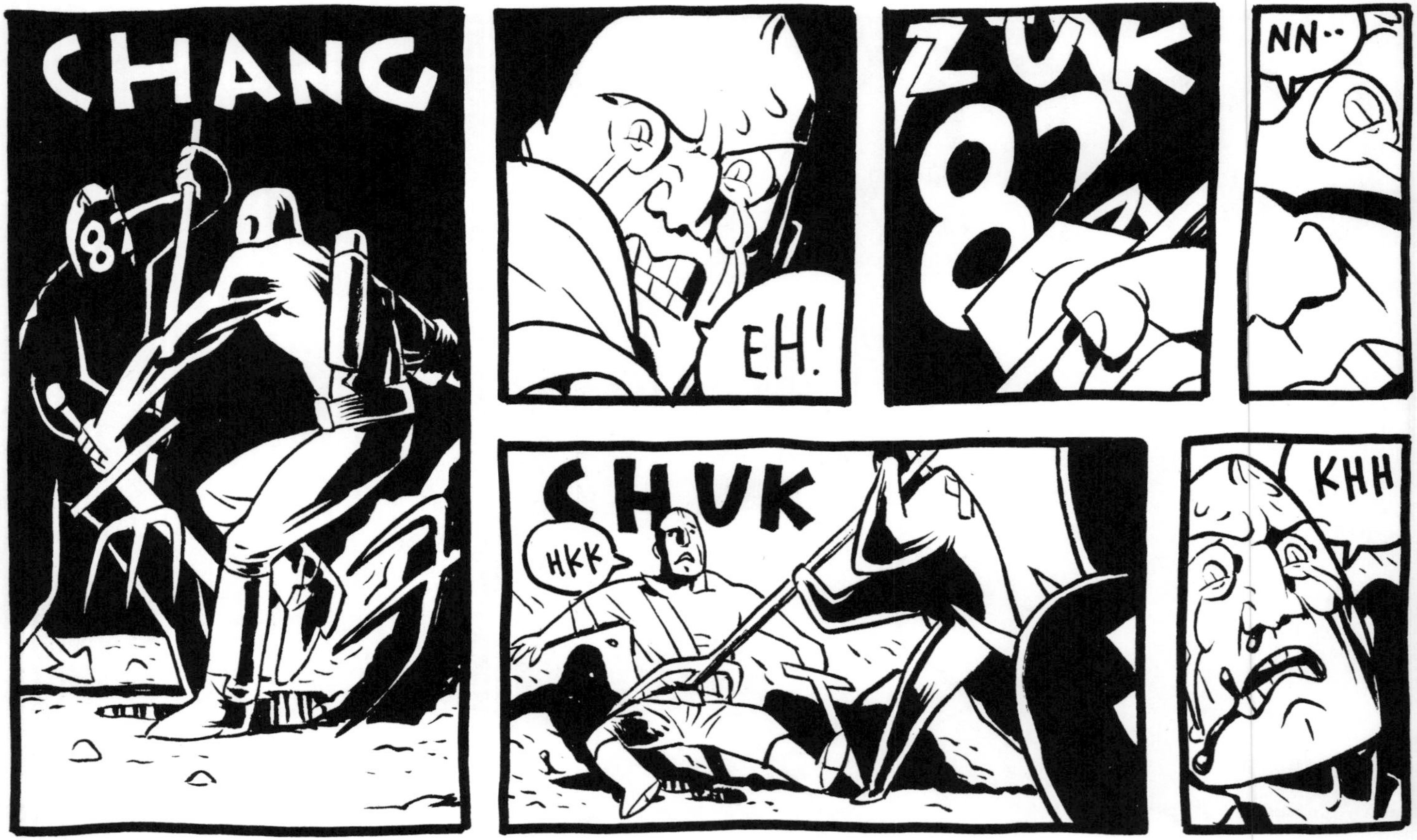
CHANG
EH!
ZUK
NN..
CHUK
HKK
KHH

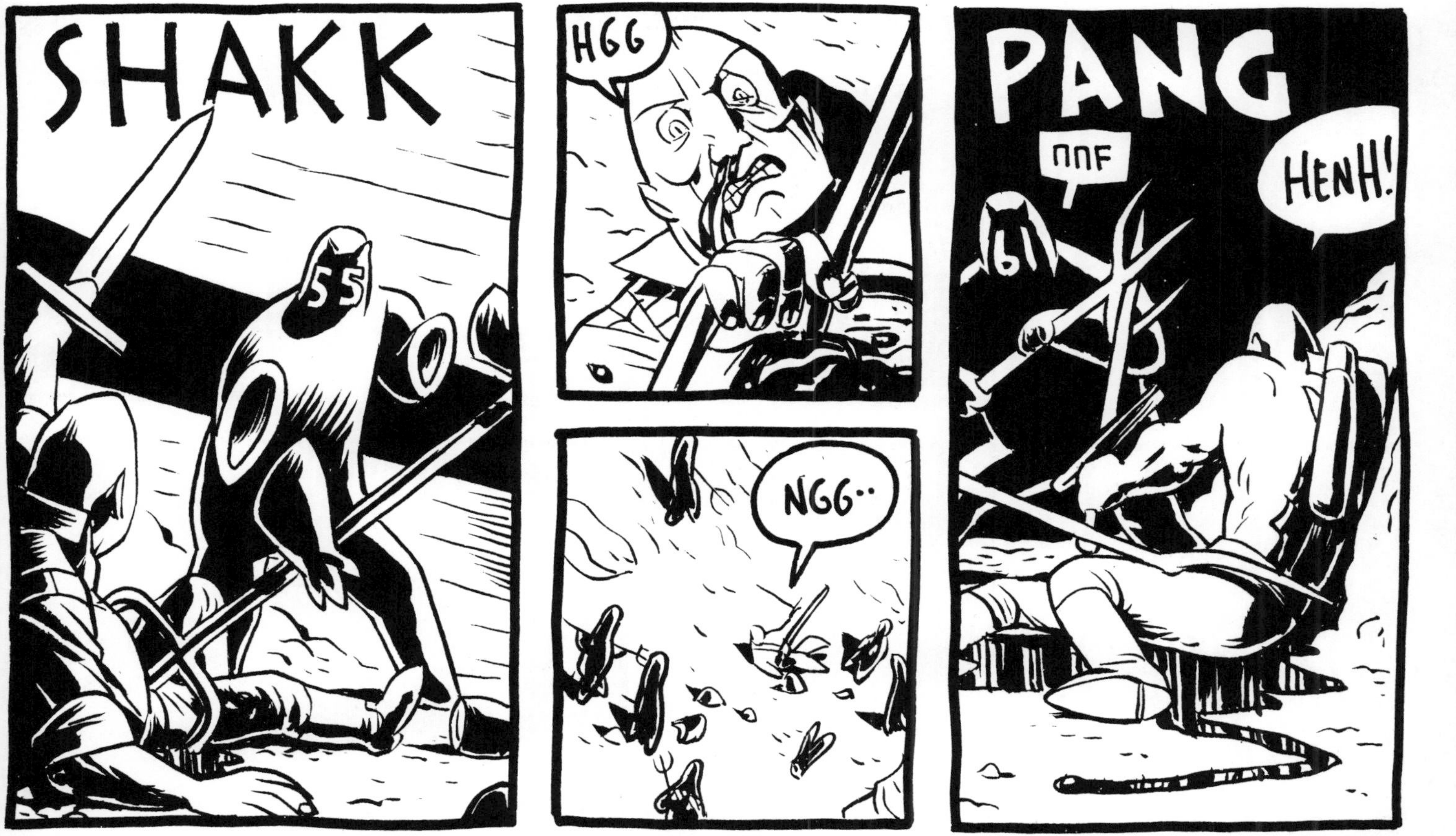
SHAKK
HGG
NGG..
PANG
nnF
HENH!

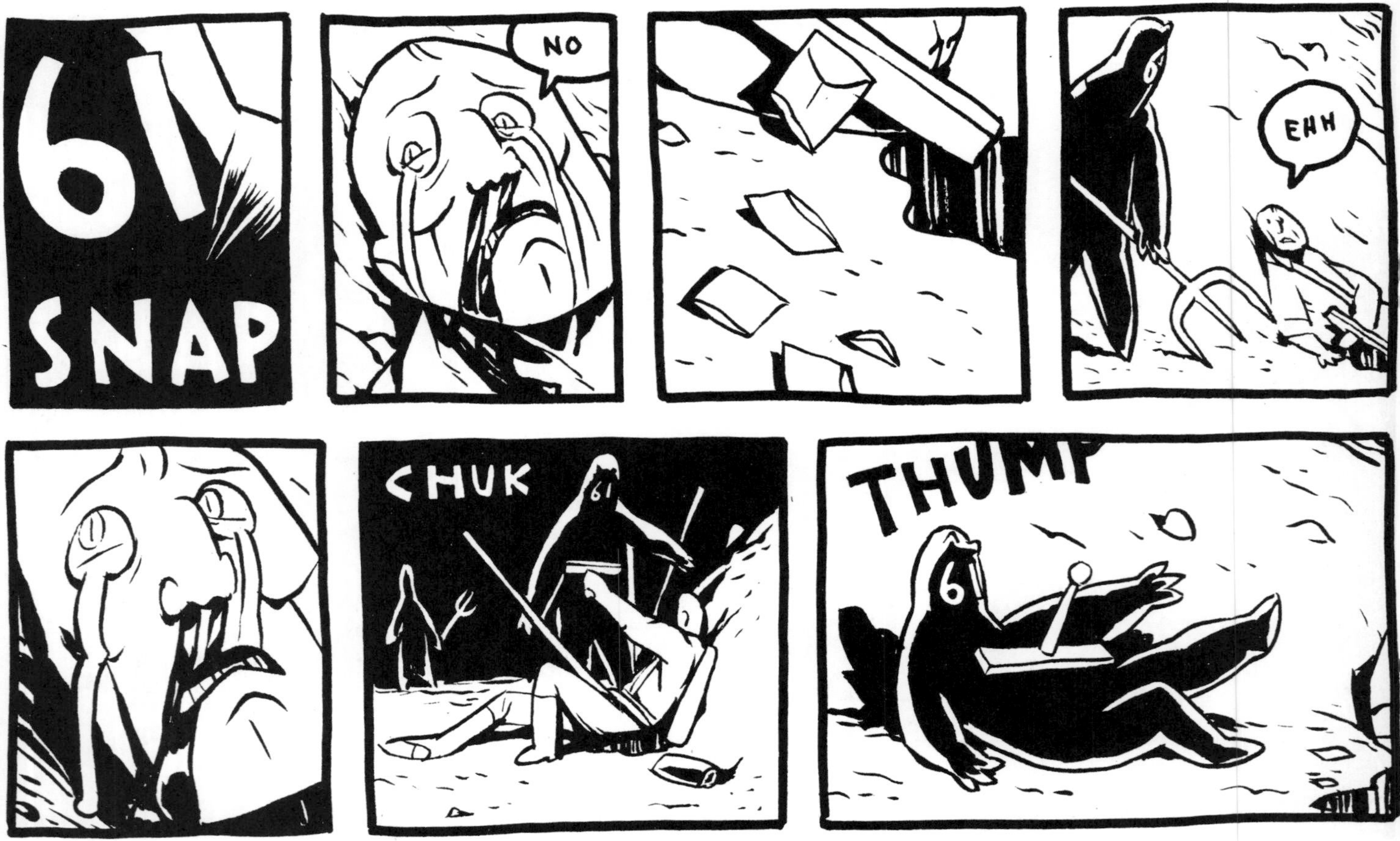
61
SNAP
NO
EHH
CHUK
61
61
THUMP
6

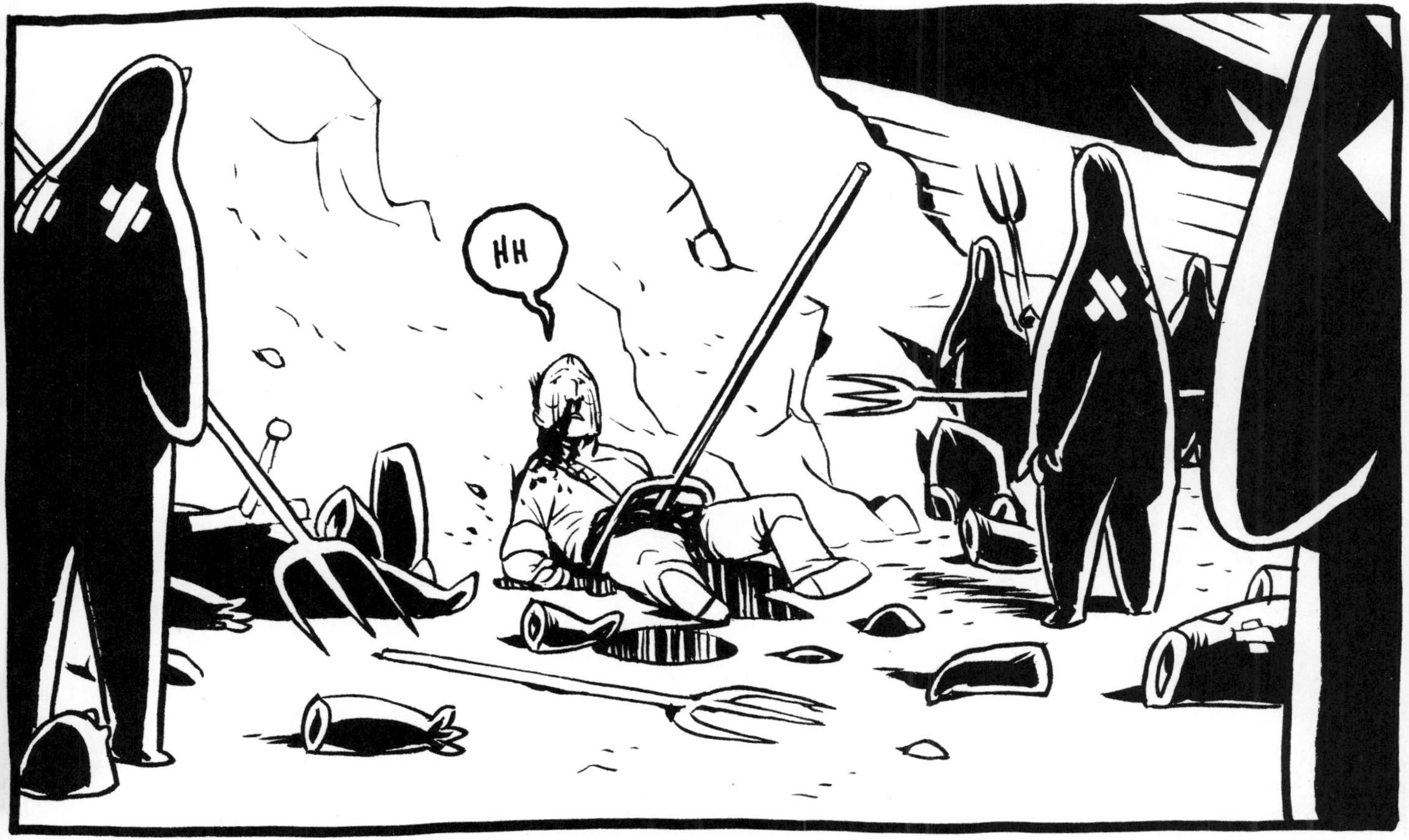
HH

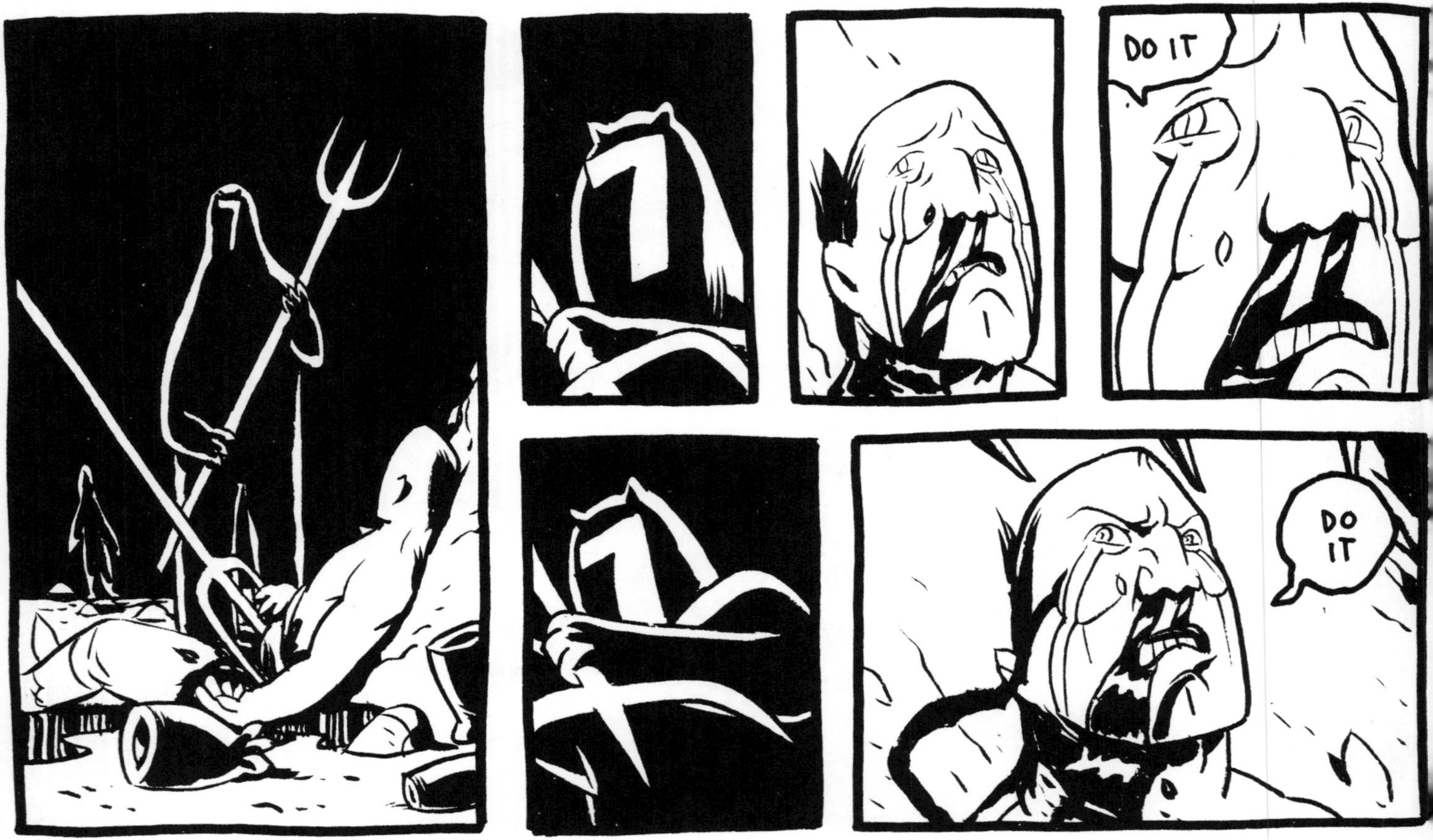
DO IT
DO IT

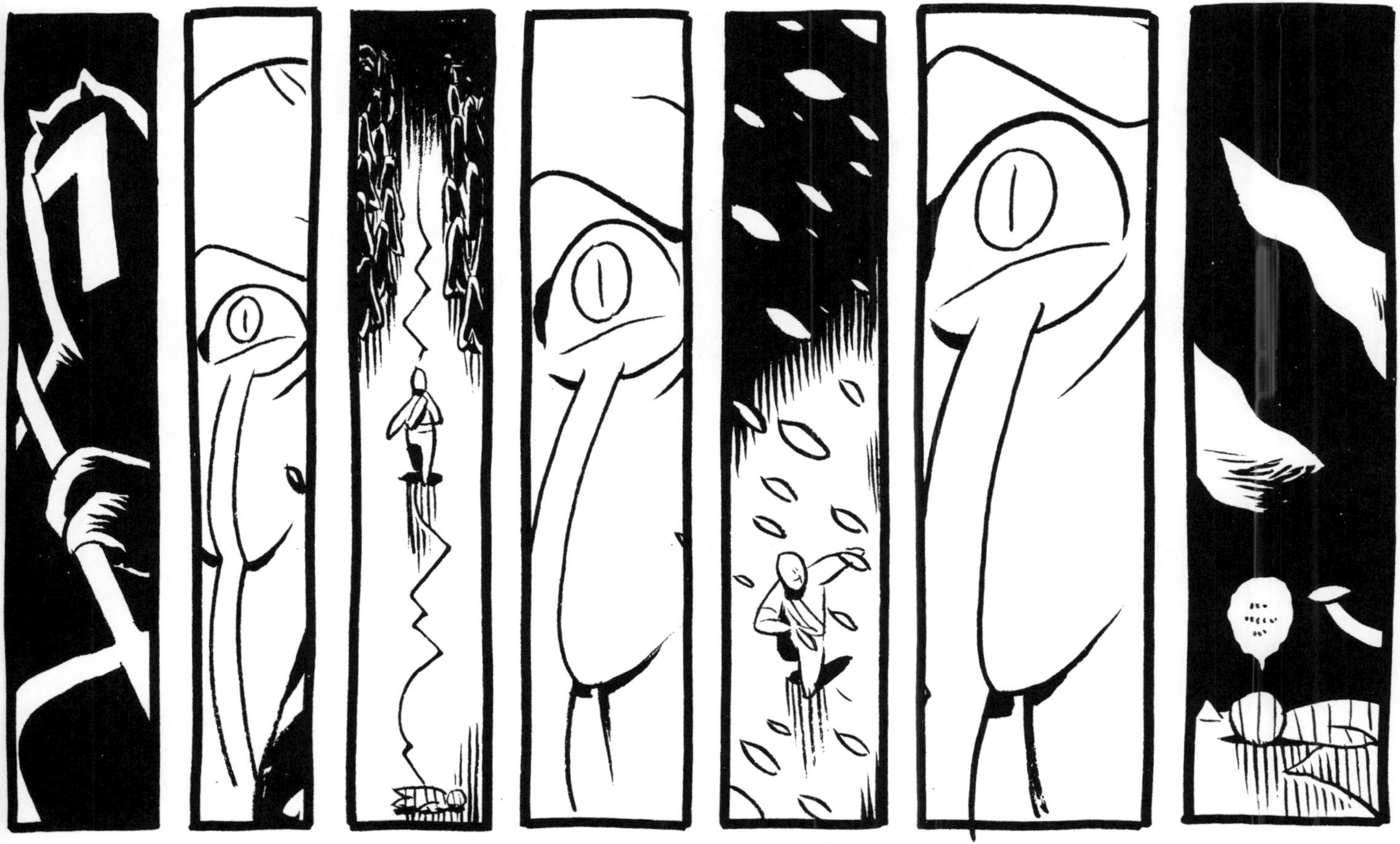

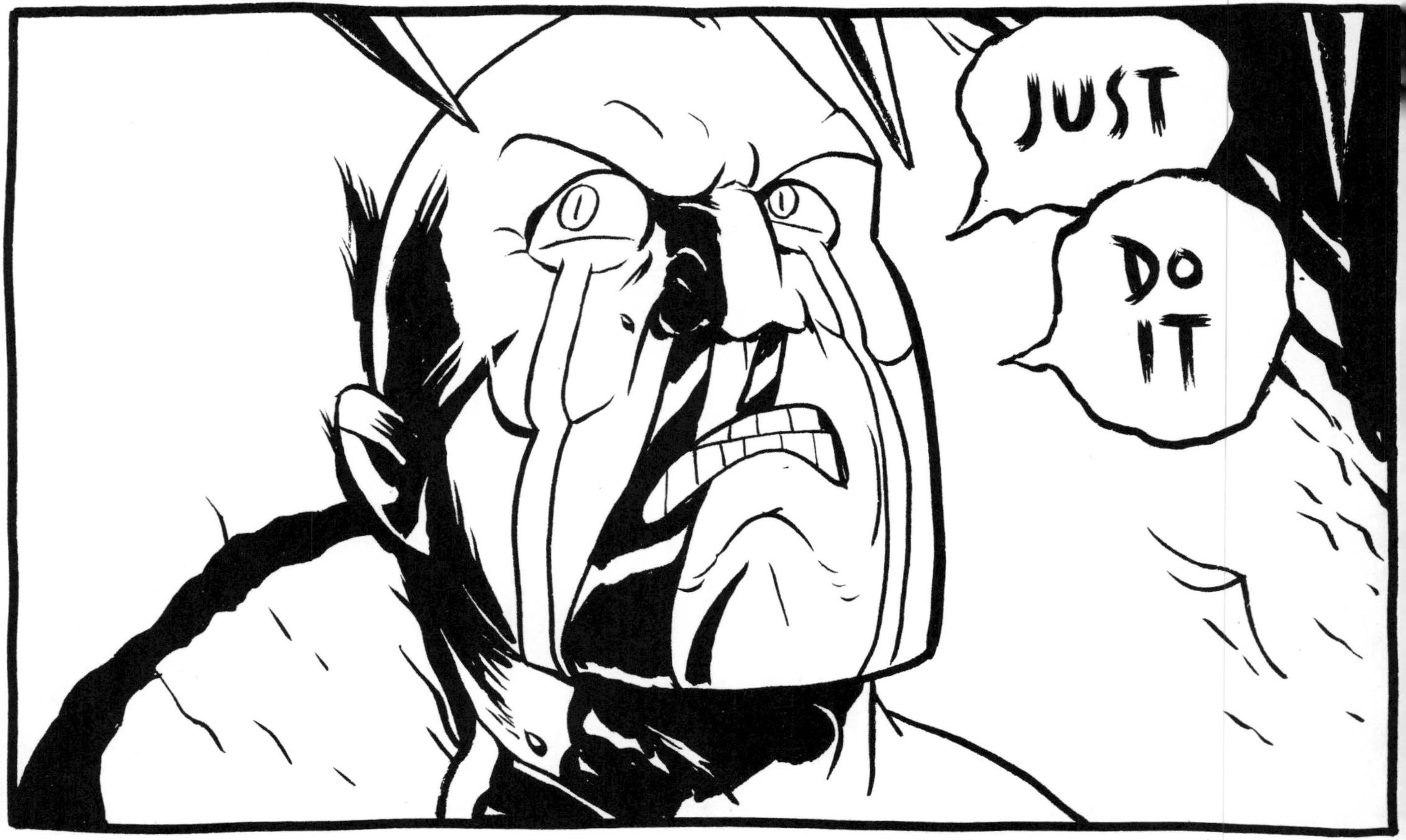
JUST
DO IT

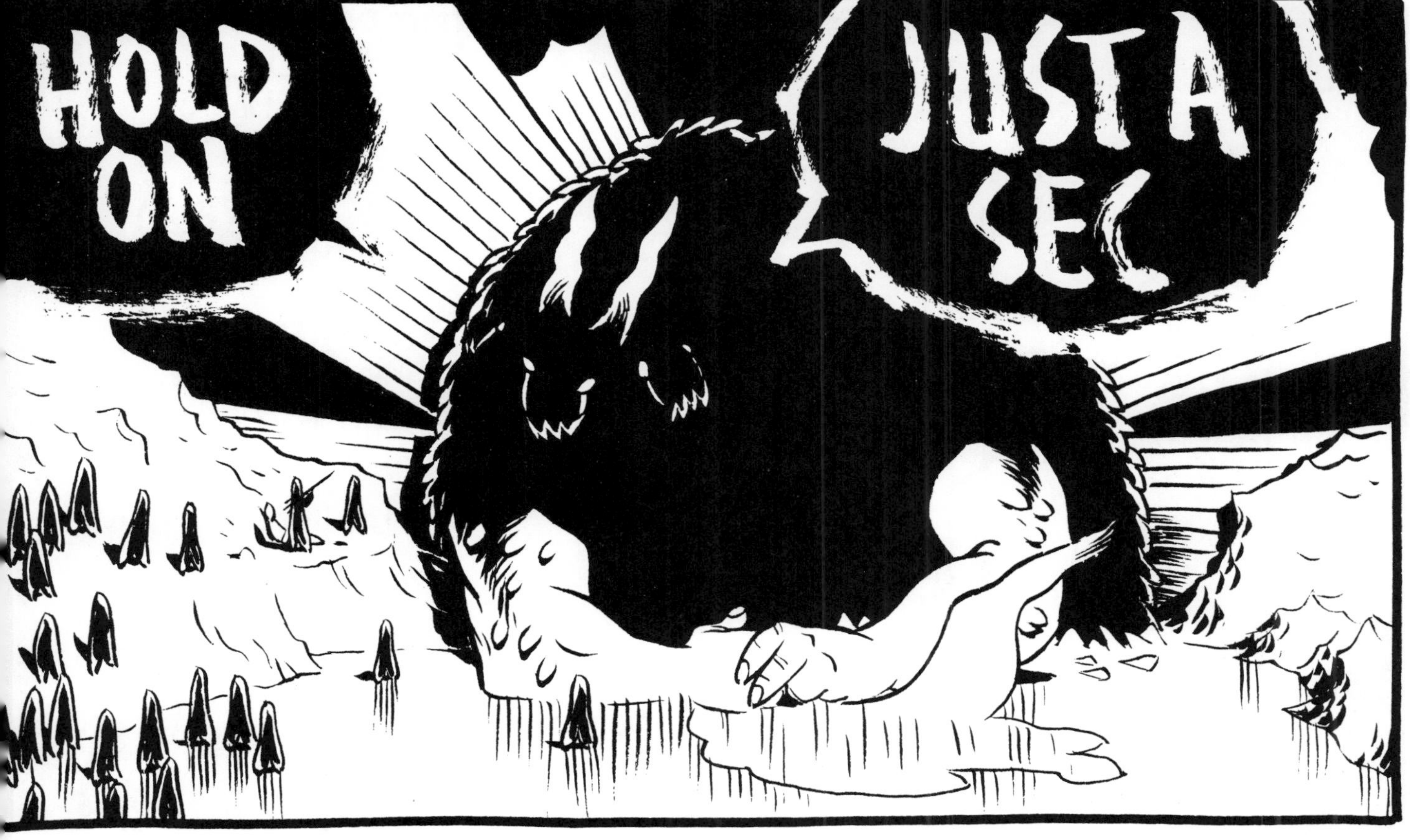
HOLD ON
JUST A SEC

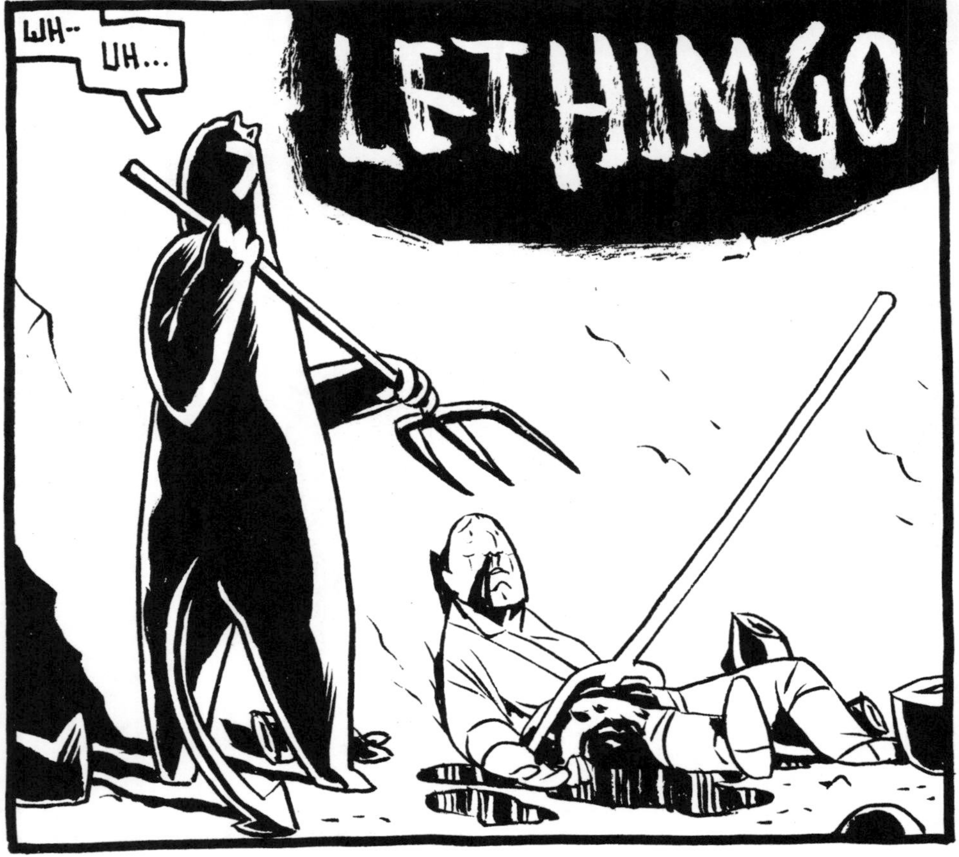
WH--
UH...
LETHIMGO

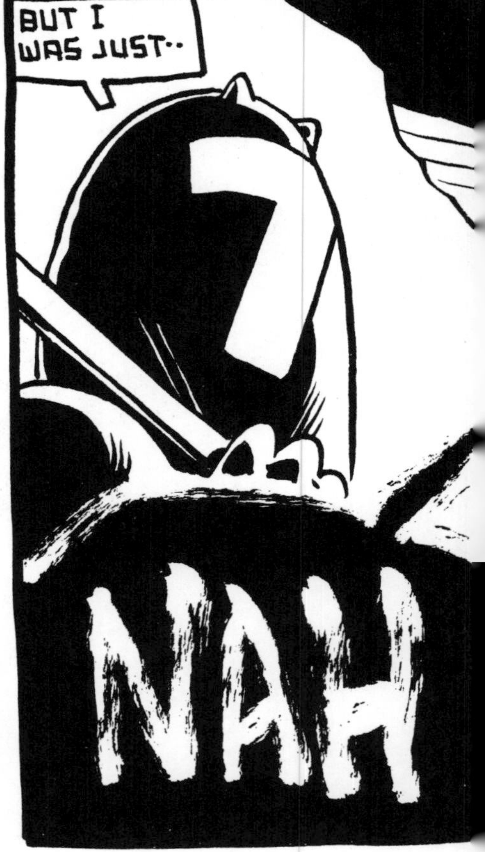
BUT I WAS JUST--
NAH

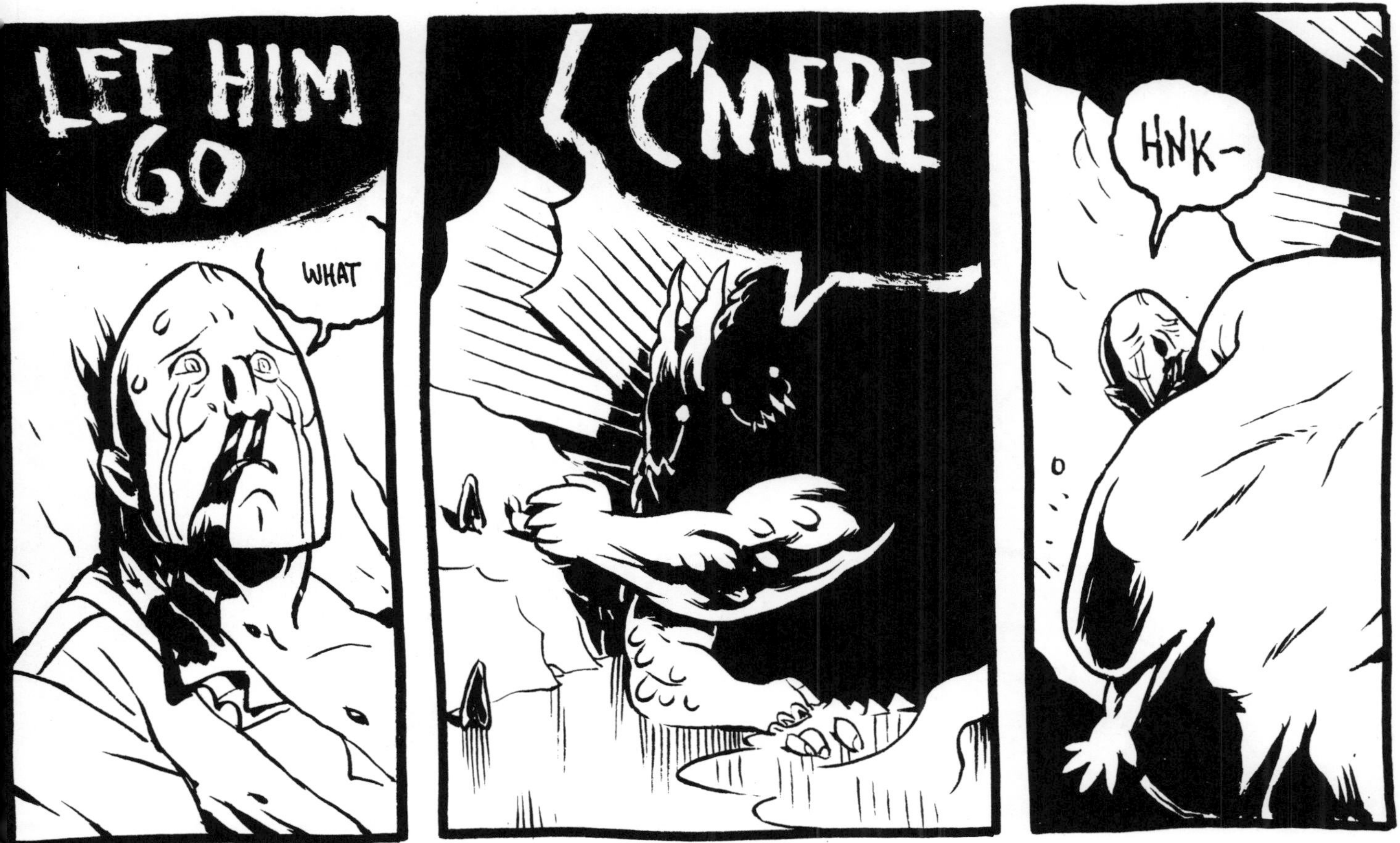
LET HIM GO
WHAT
C'MERE
HNK-

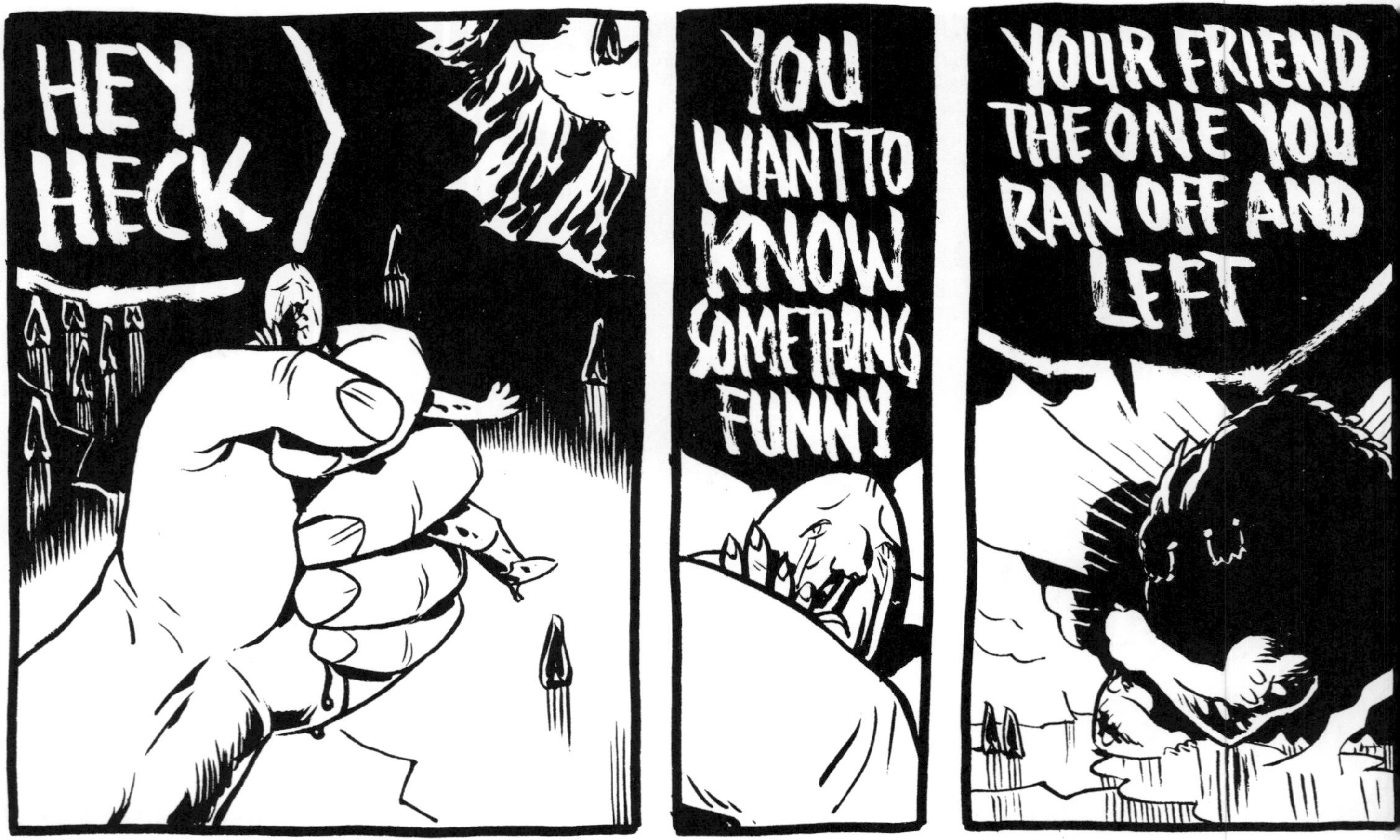
HEY HECK
YOU WANT TO KNOW SOMETHING FUNNY
YOUR FRIEND THE ONE YOU RAN OFF AND LEFT

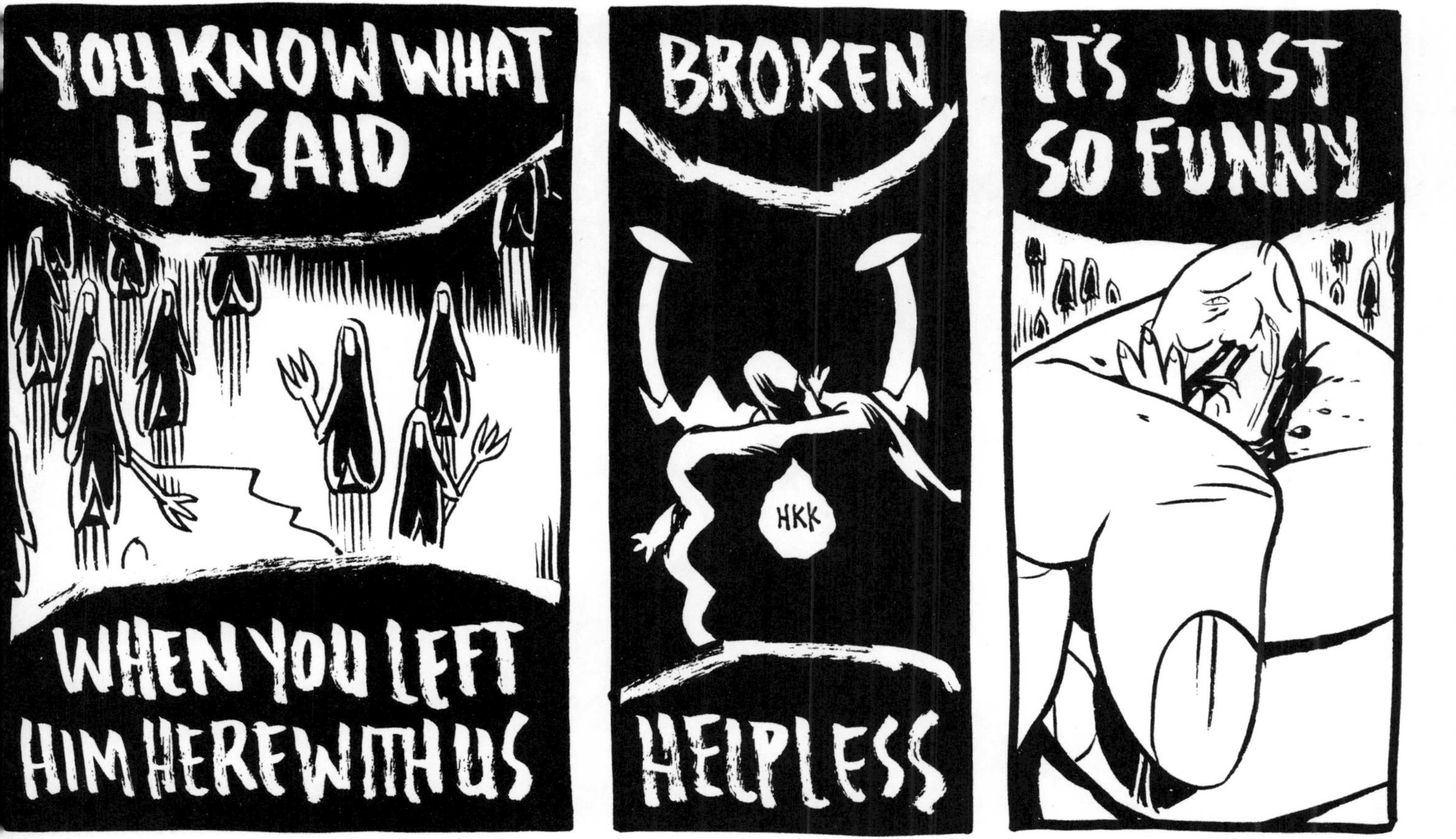
YOU KNOW WHAT HE SAID
WHEN YOU LEFT HIM HERE WITH US
BROKEN
HKK
HELPLESS
IT'S JUST SO FUNNY

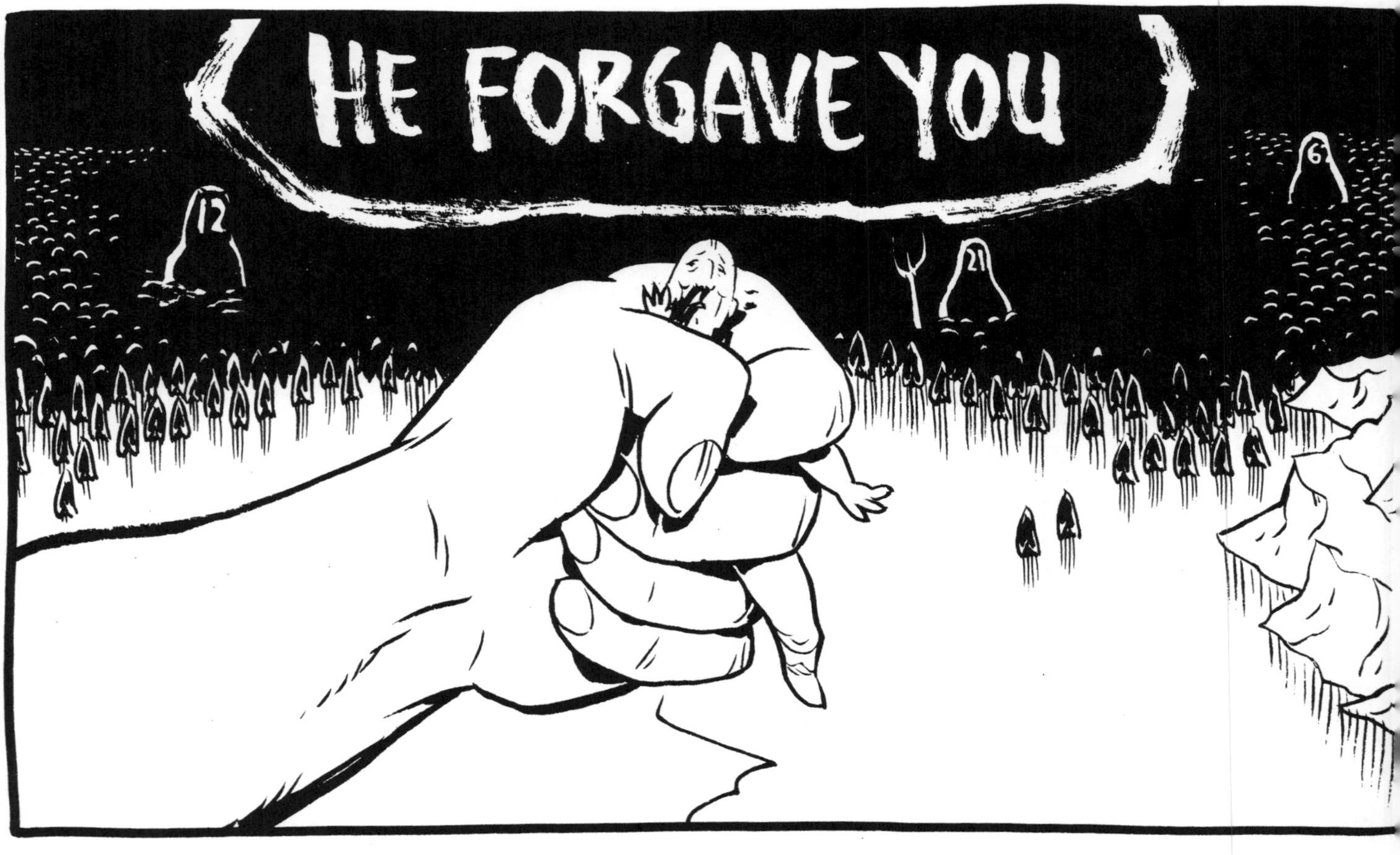
HE FORGAVE YOU
12
21
6

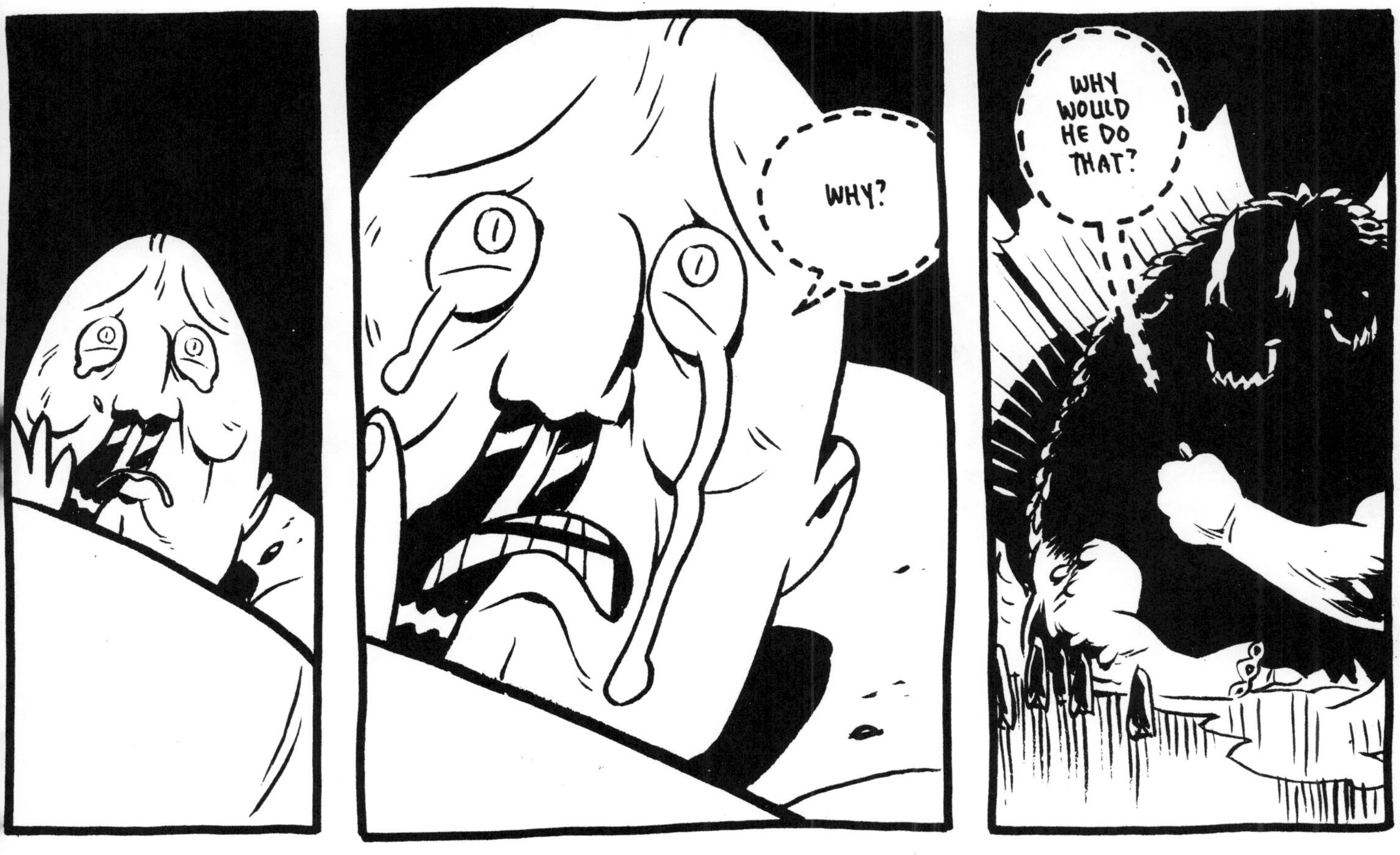
WHY?
WHY WOULD HE DO THAT?

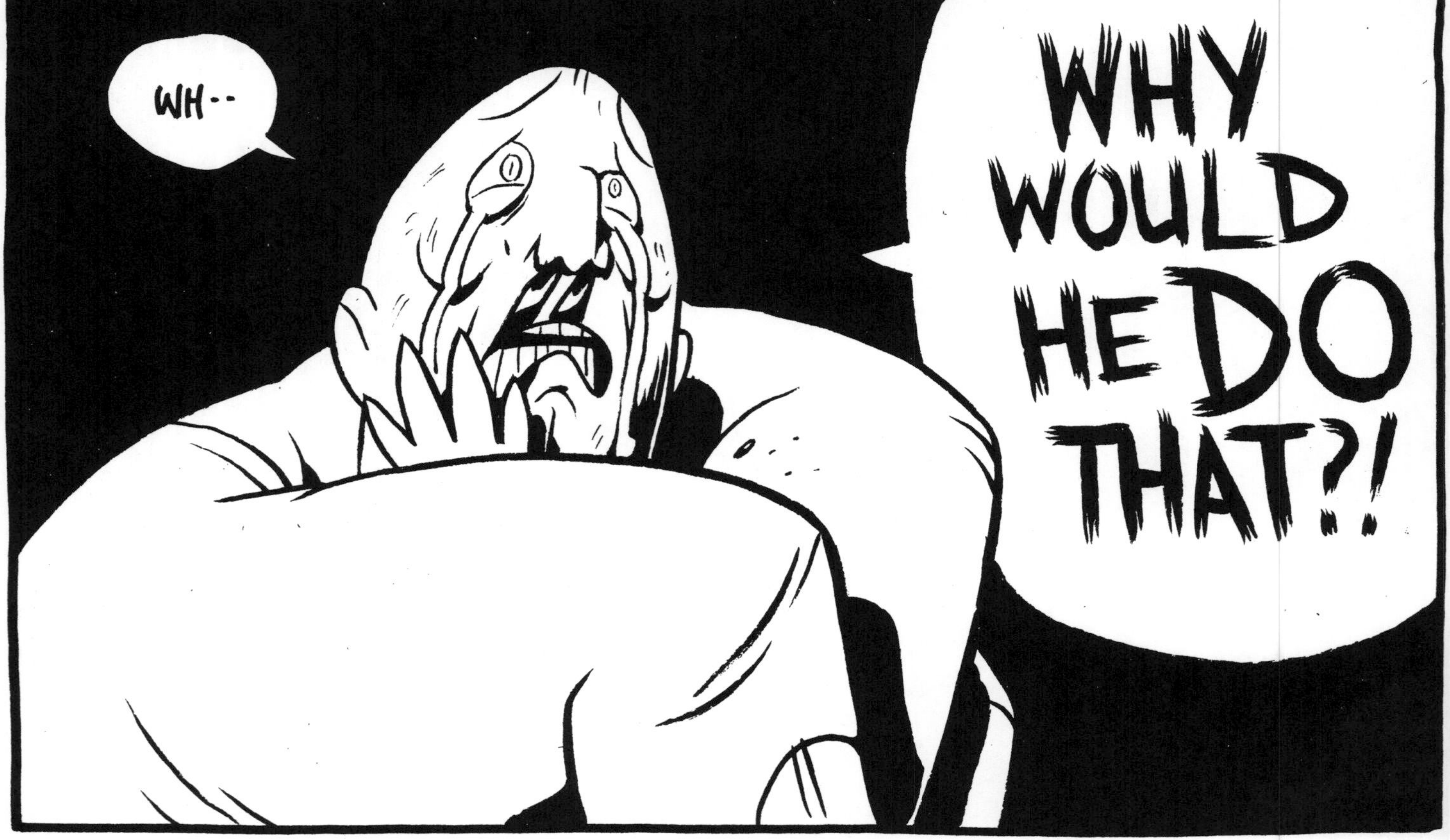
WH--
WHY WOULD HE DO THAT?!

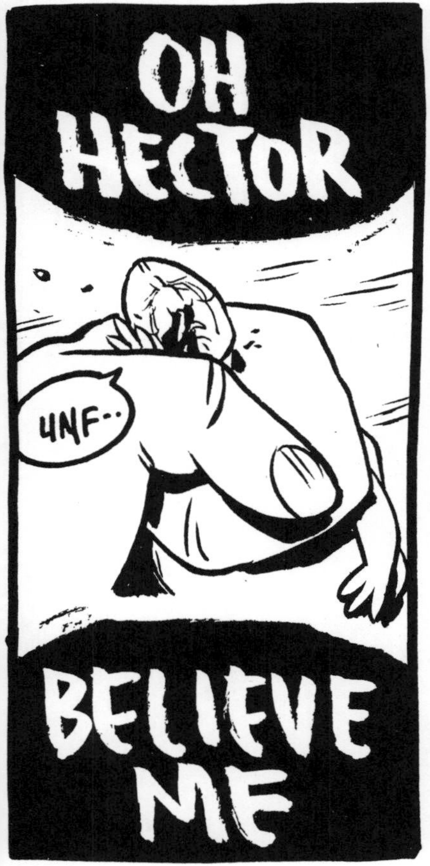
OH HECTOR
UNF..
BELIEVE ME

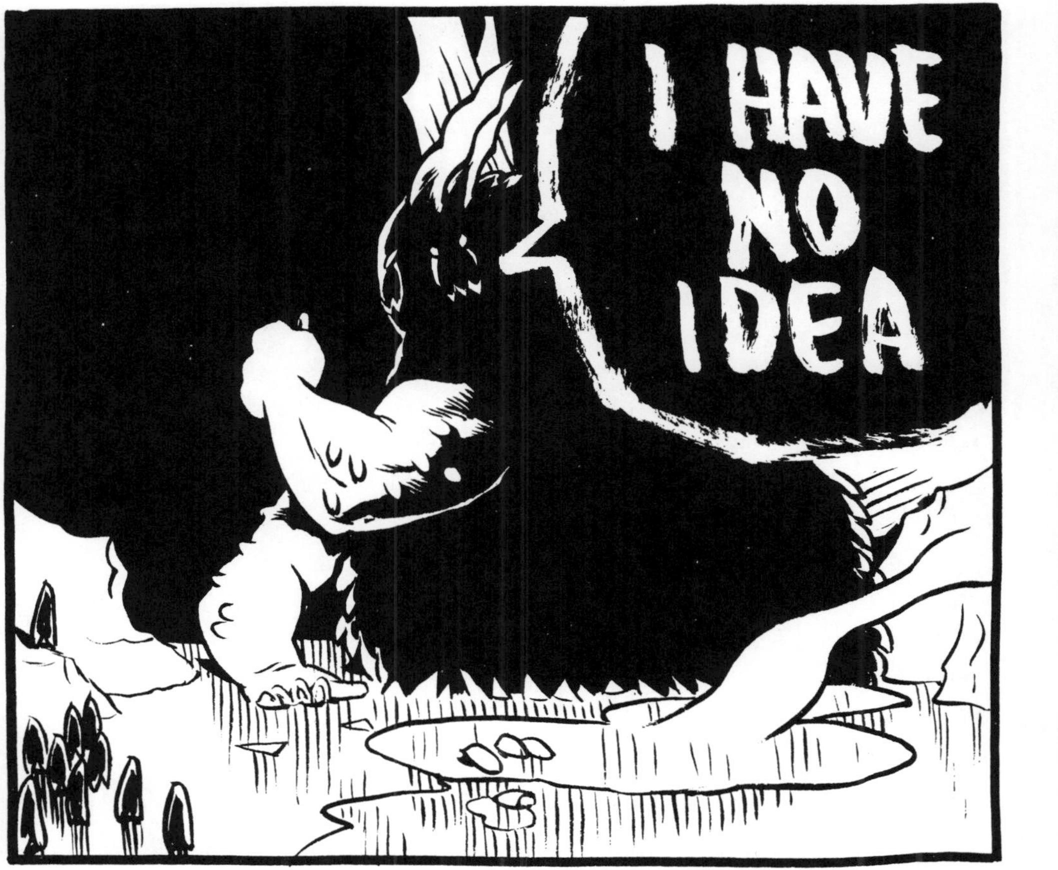
I HAVE NO IDEA

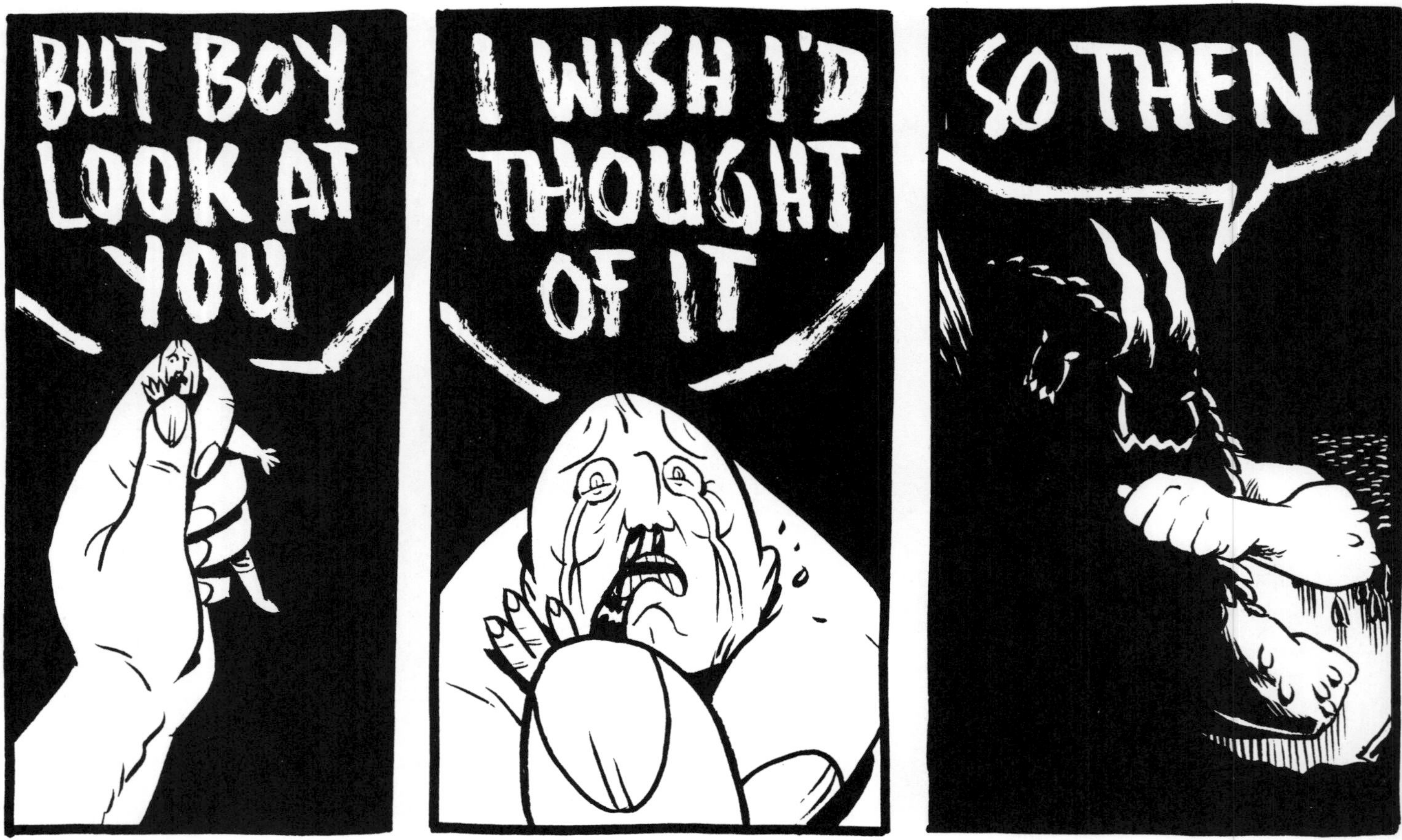
BUT BOY LOOK AT YOU
I WISH I'D THOUGHT OF IT
SO THEN

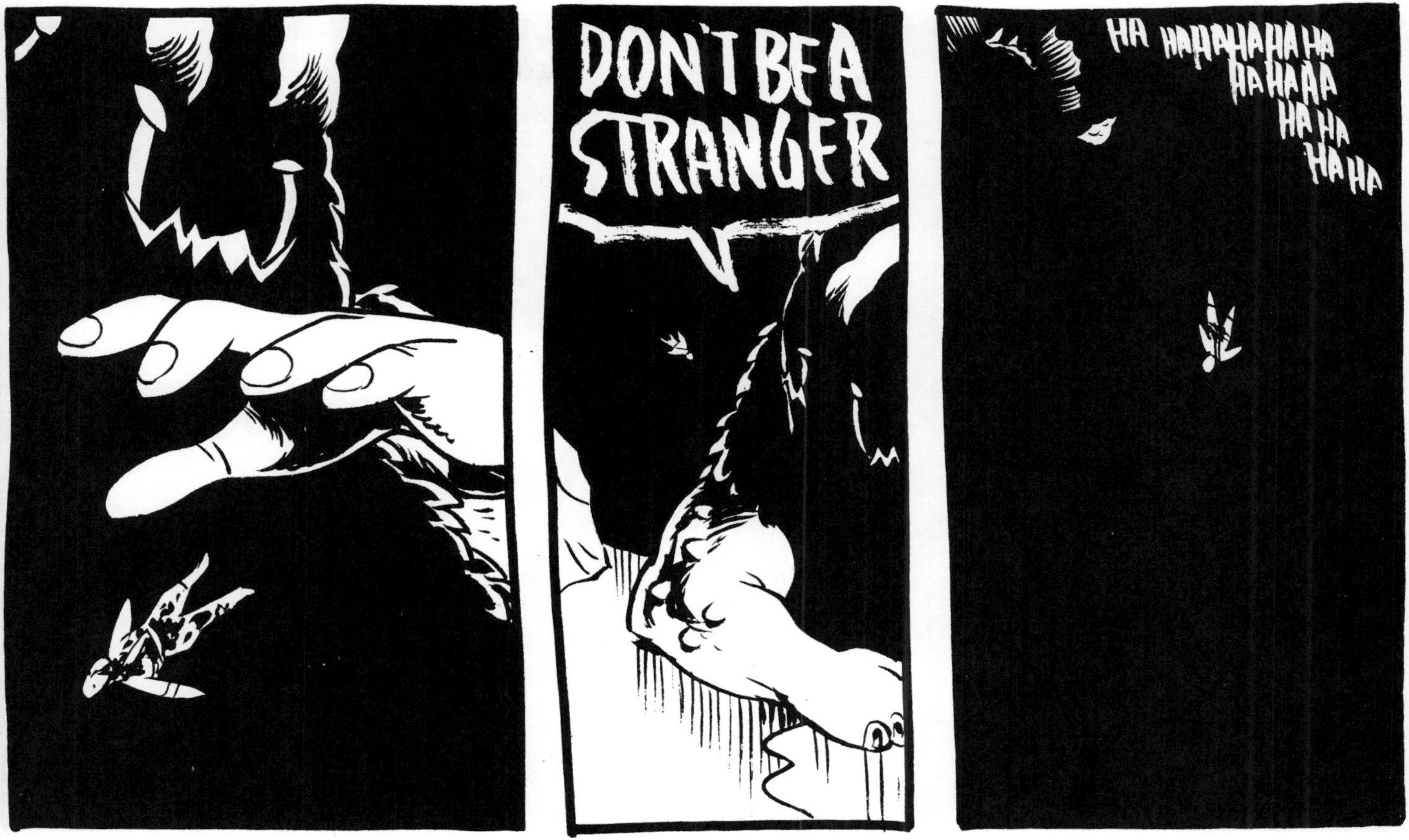
DON'T BE A STRANGER
HA HAHAHAHAHA HA
HA HAAA
HA HA
HA HA

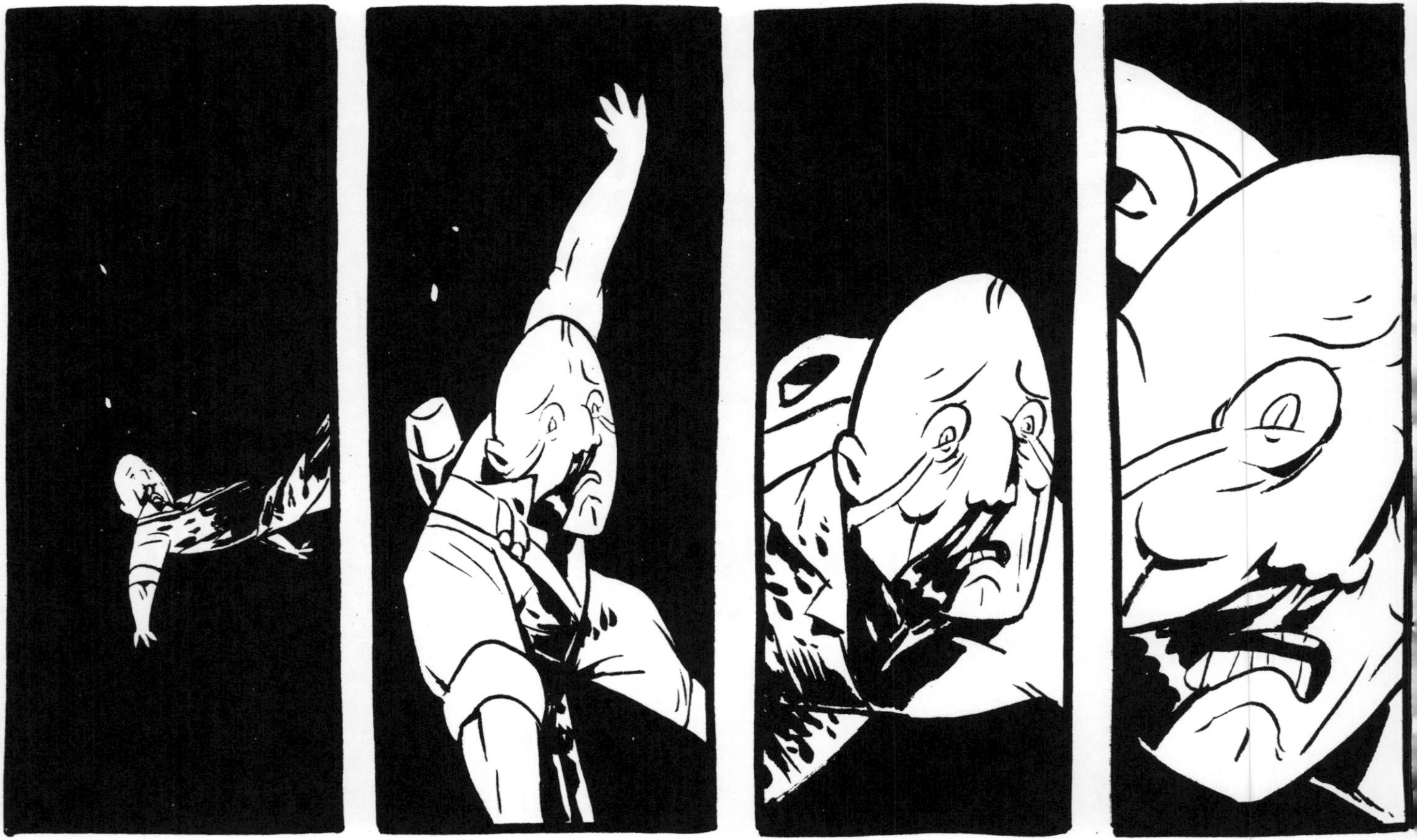

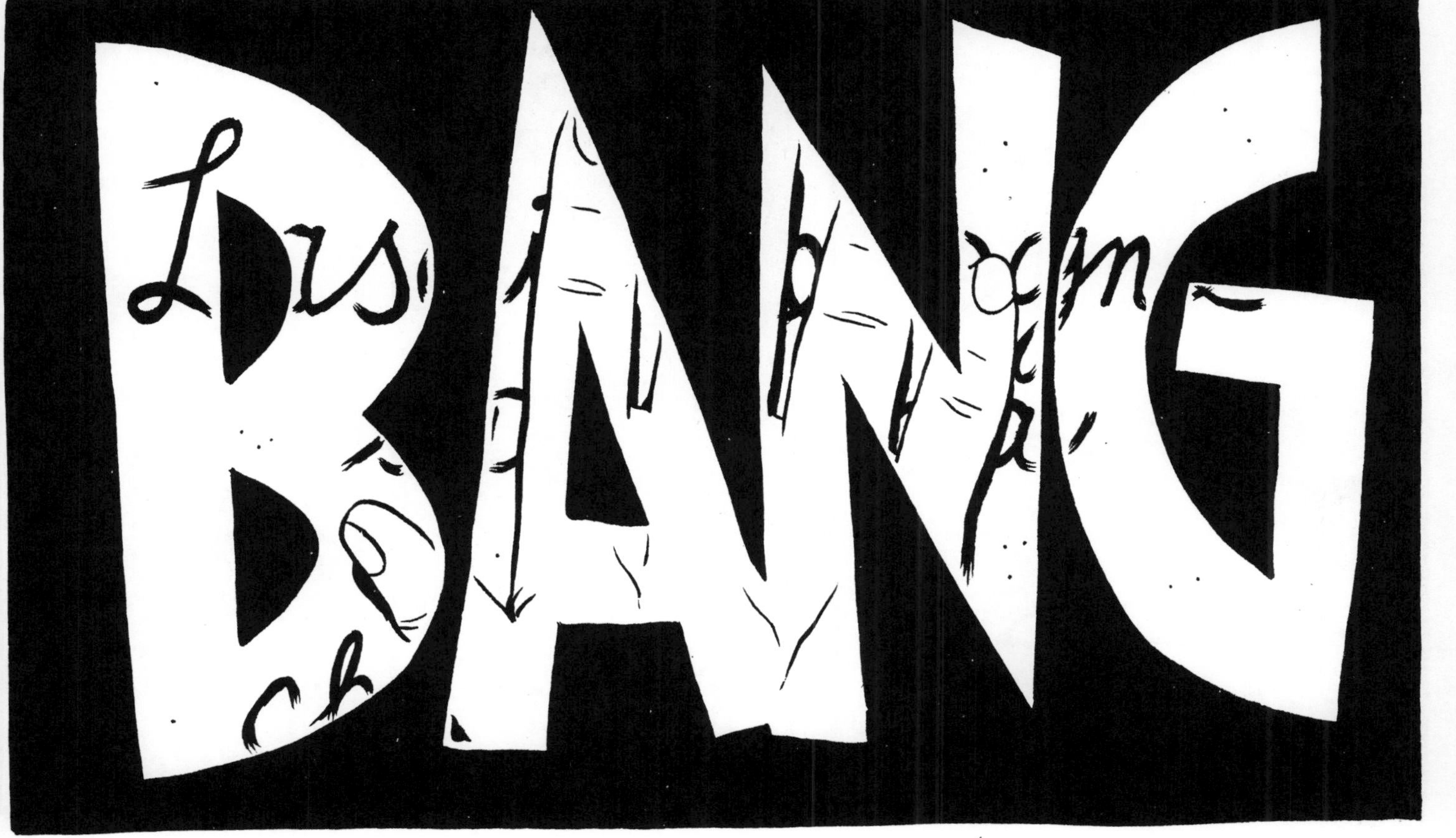
BANG

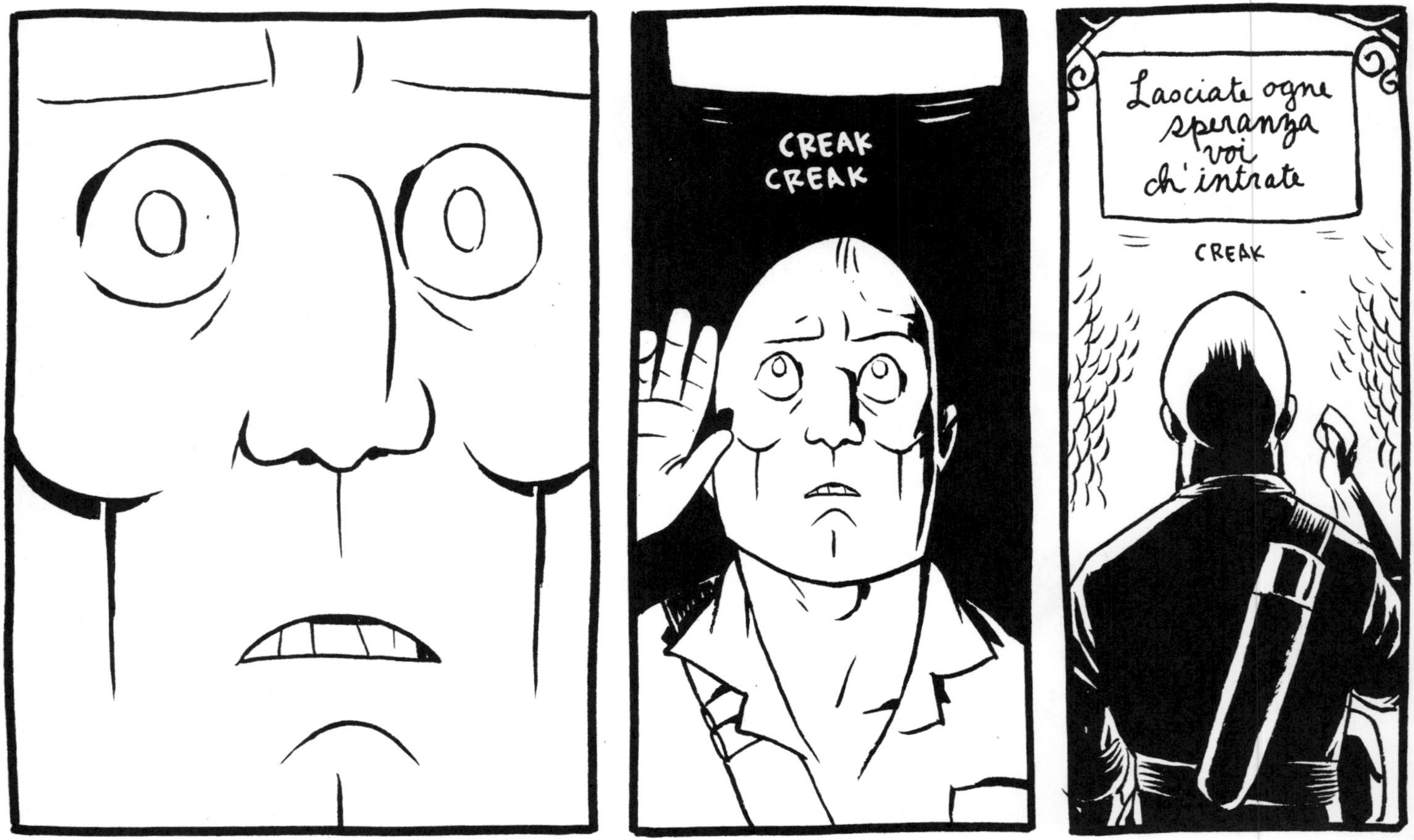
CREAK
CREAK
Lasciate ogne speranza voi ch'intrate
CREAK

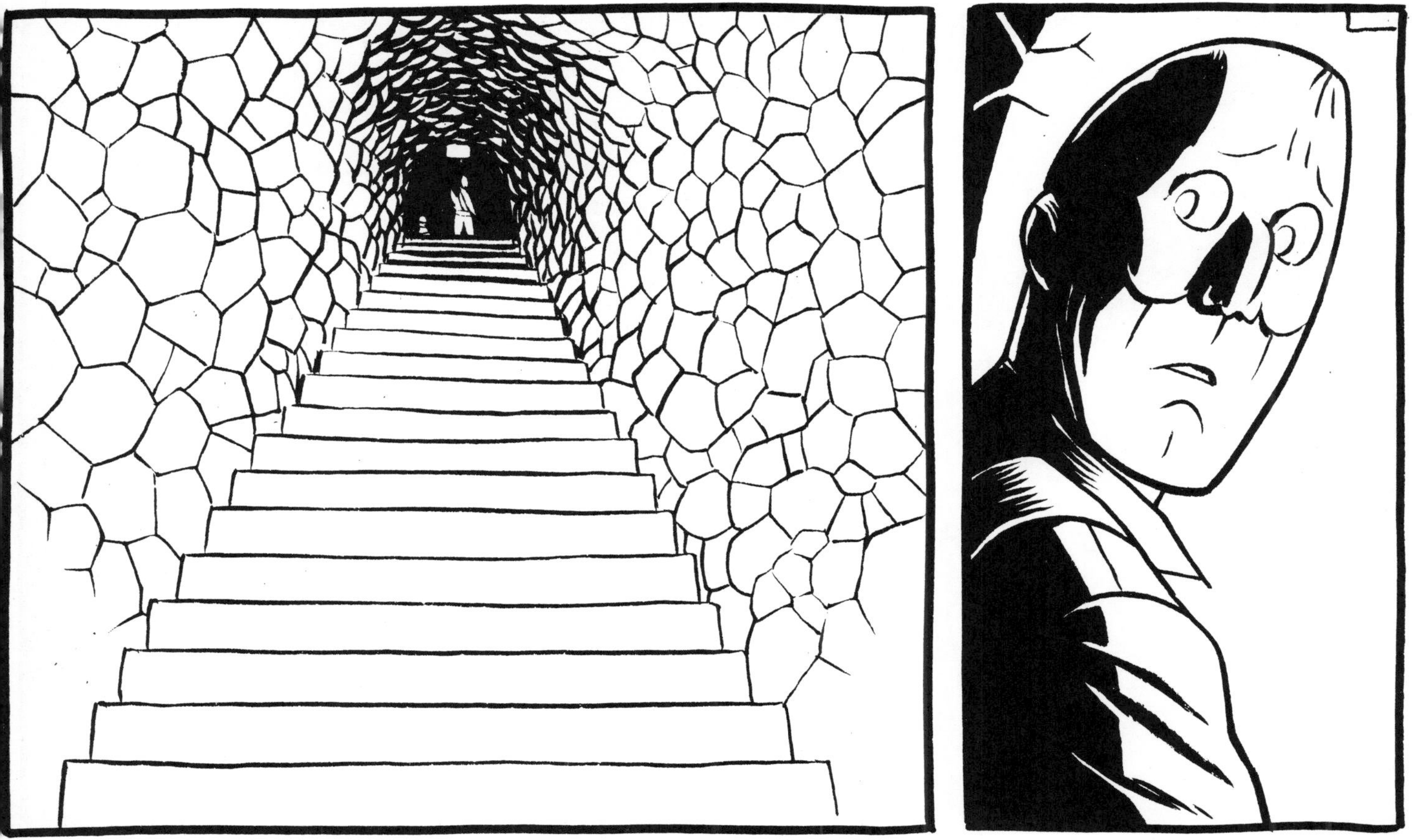

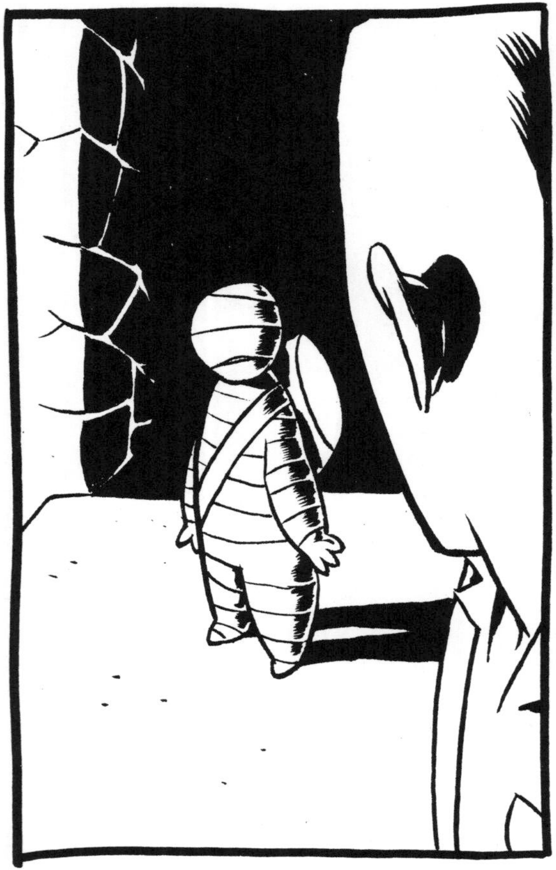

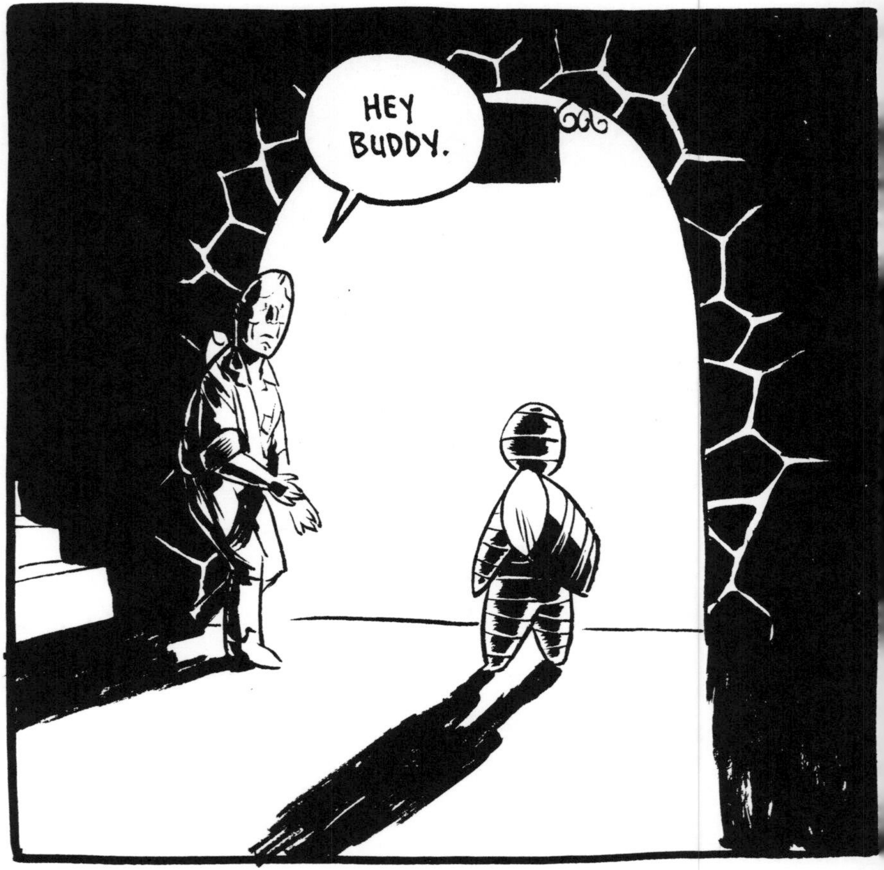
HEY BUDDY.

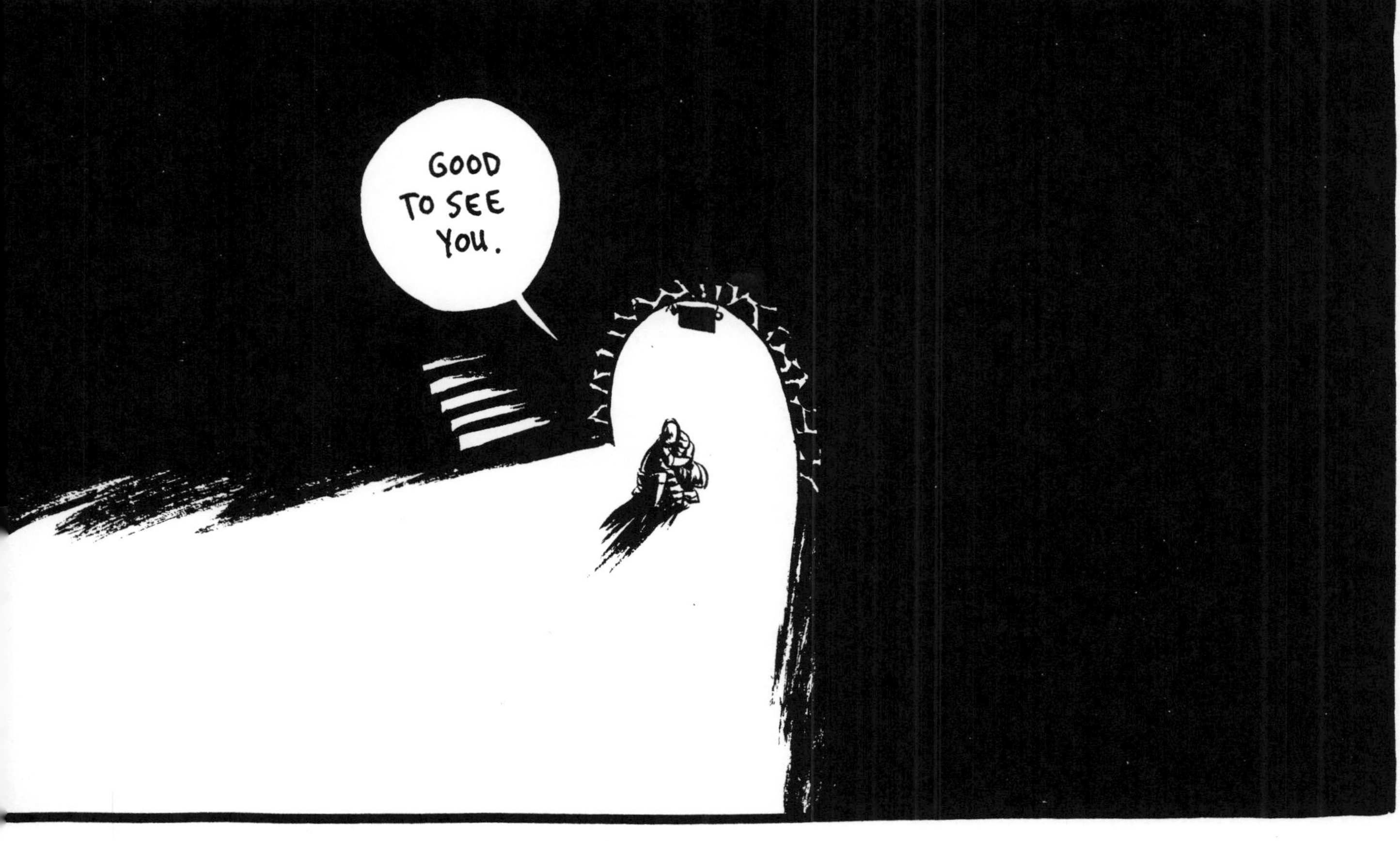
GOOD TO SEE YOU.

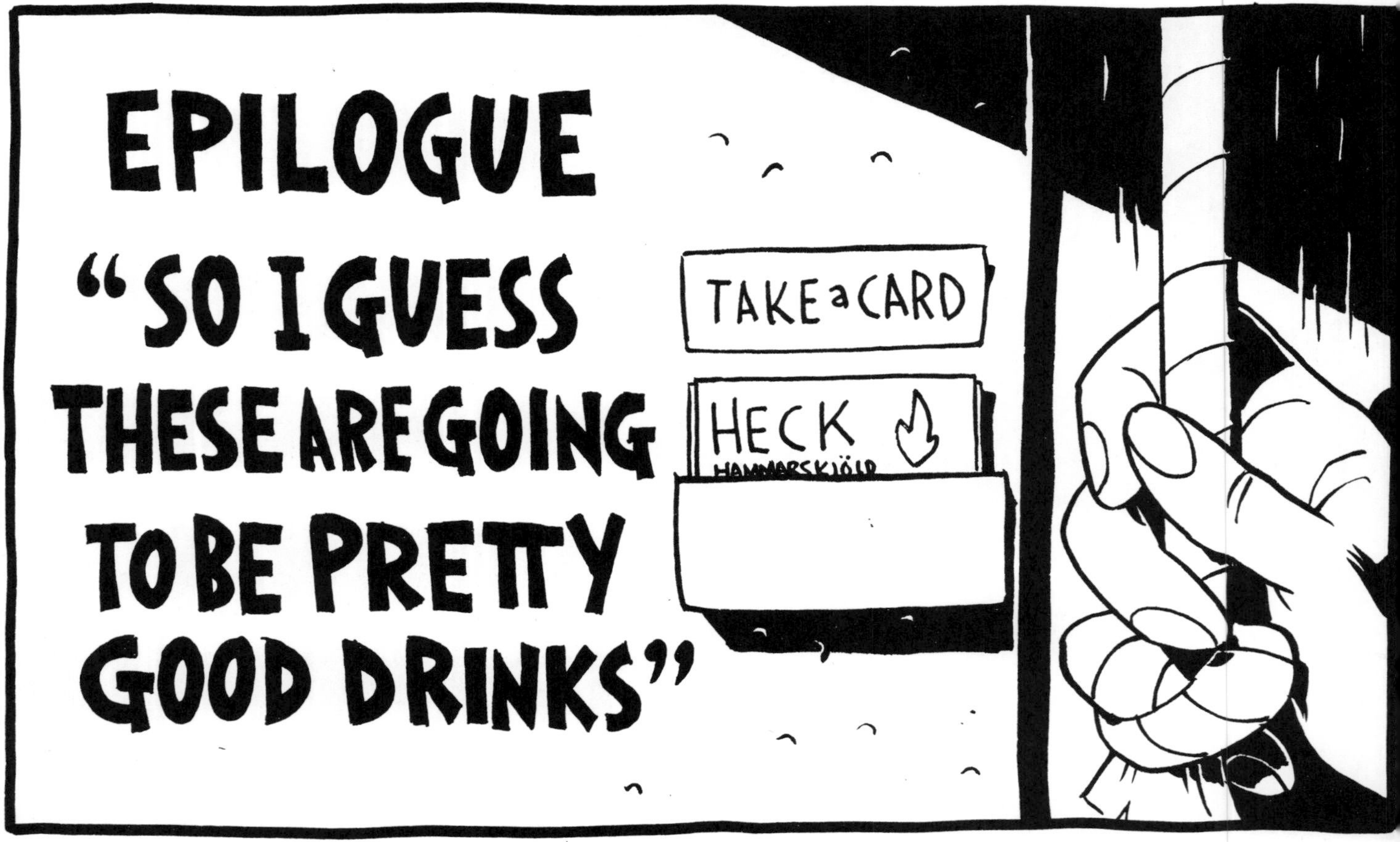
EPILOGUE
"SO I GUESS THESE ARE GOING TO BE PRETTY GOOD DRINKS"
TAKE a CARD
HECK
HAMMARSKJÖLD

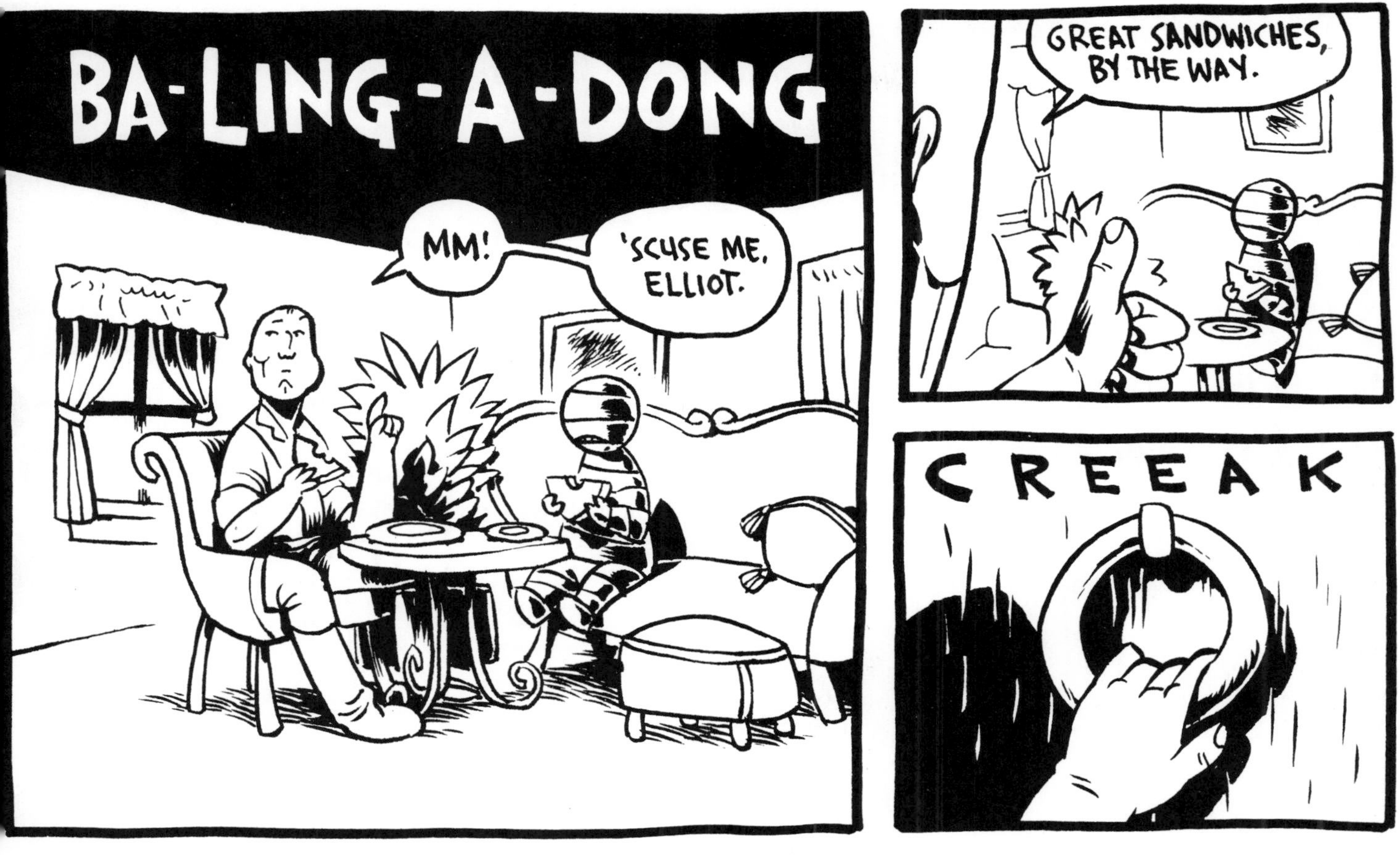
BA-LING-A-DONG
MM!
'SCUSE ME, ELLIOT.
GREAT SANDWICHES, BY THE WAY.
CREEAK

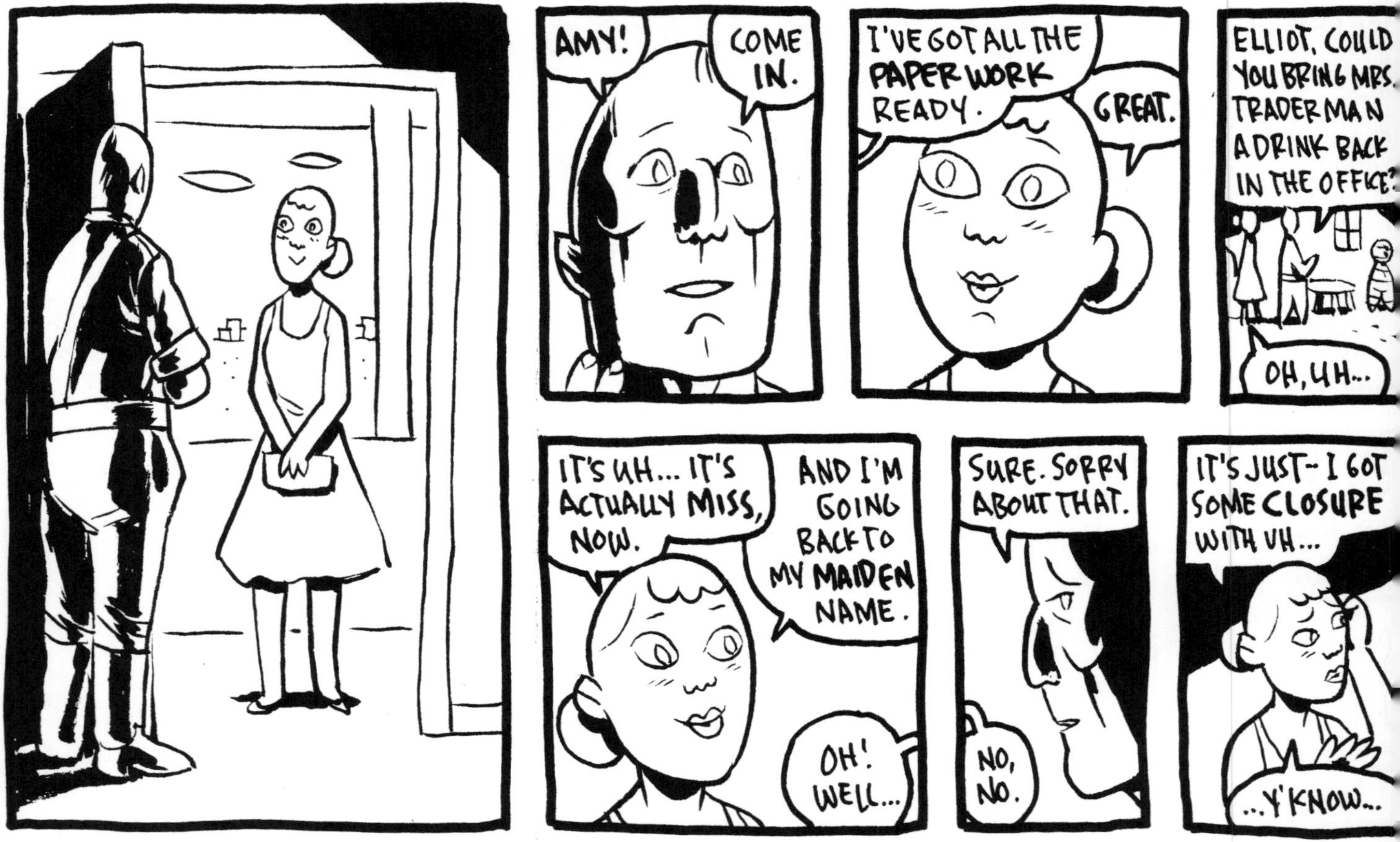
AMY!
COME IN.
I'VE GOT ALL THE PAPER WORK READY.
GREAT.
ELLIOT, COULD YOU BRING MRS. TRADERMAN A DRINK BACK IN THE OFFICE?
OH, UH...
IT'S UH... IT'S ACTUALLY MISS, NOW.
AND I'M GOING BACK TO MY MAIDEN NAME.
OH! WELL...
SURE. SORRY ABOUT THAT.
NO, NO.
IT'S JUST-- I GOT SOME CLOSURE WITH UH...
...Y'KNOW...

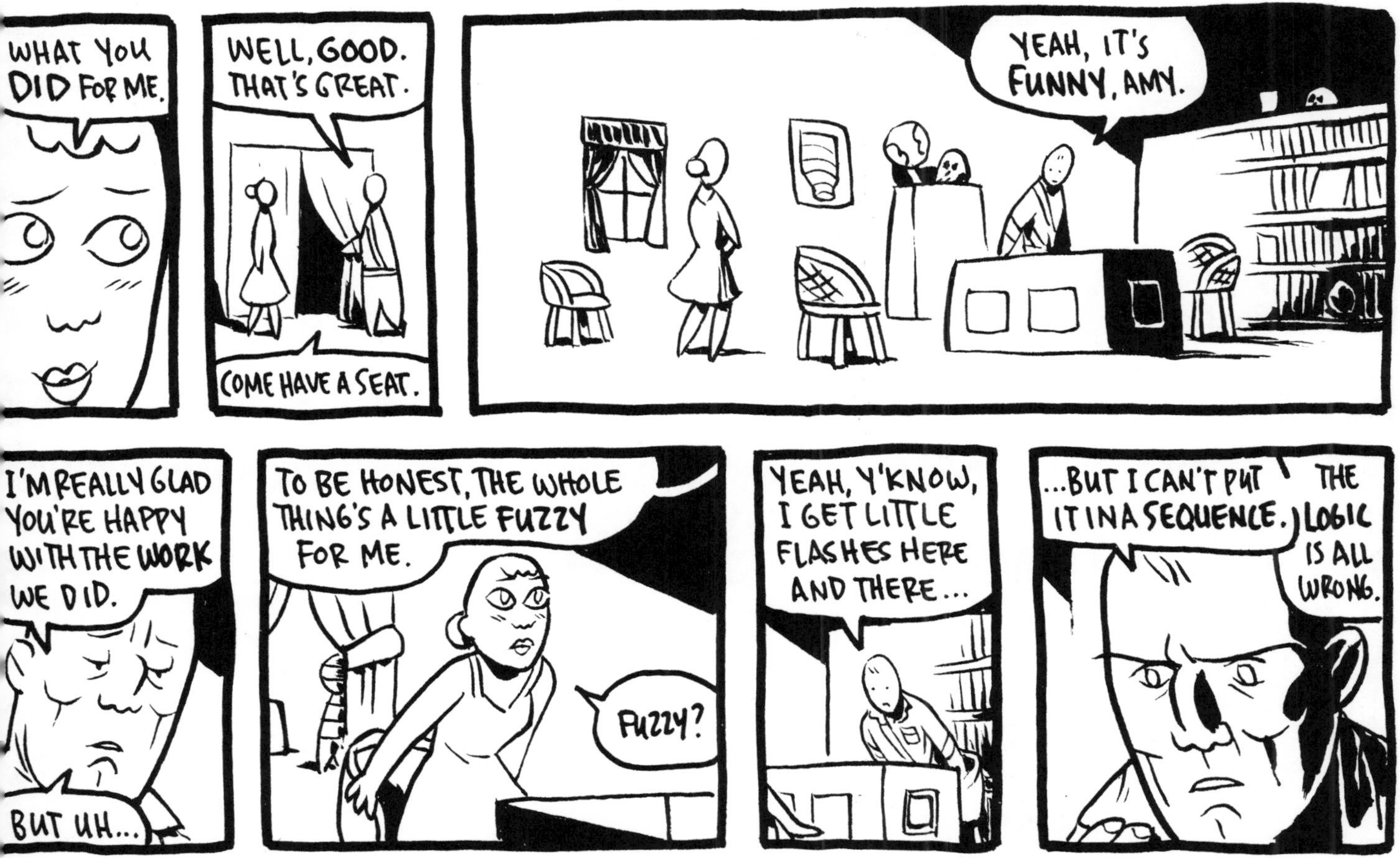
WHAT YOU DID FOR ME.
WELL, GOOD. THAT'S GREAT.
COME HAVE A SEAT.
YEAH, IT'S FUNNY, AMY.
I'M REALLY GLAD YOU'RE HAPPY WITH THE WORK WE DID.
BUT UH...
TO BE HONEST, THE WHOLE THING'S A LITTLE FUZZY FOR ME.
FUZZY?
YEAH, Y'KNOW, I GET LITTLE FLASHES HERE AND THERE...
...BUT I CAN'T PUT IT IN A SEQUENCE.
THE LOGIC IS ALL WRONG.

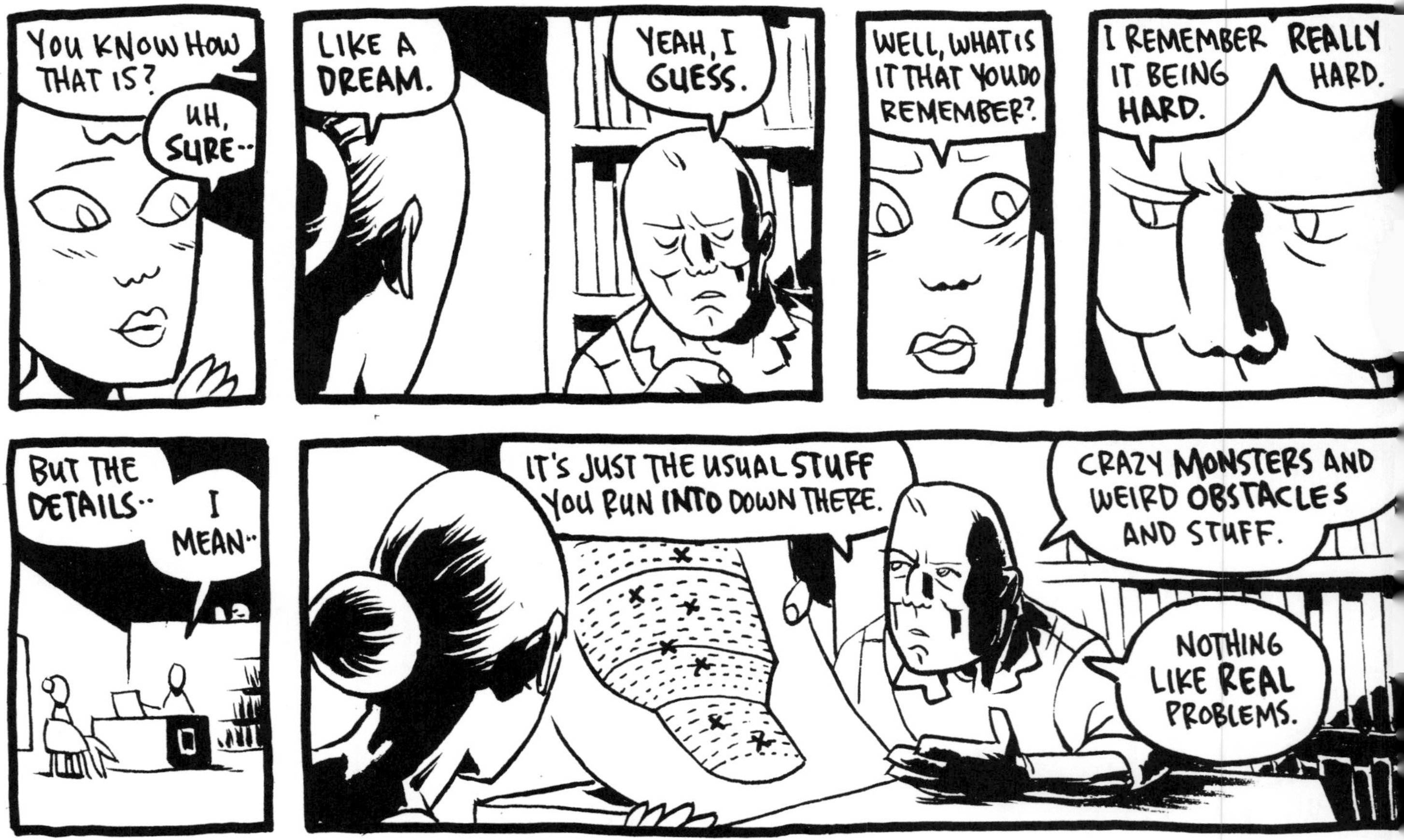
YOU KNOW HOW THAT IS?
UH, SURE..
LIKE A DREAM.
YEAH, I GUESS.
WELL, WHAT IS IT THAT YOU DO REMEMBER?
I REMEMBER IT BEING HARD.
REALLY HARD.
BUT THE DETAILS..
I MEAN..
IT'S JUST THE USUAL STUFF YOU RUN INTO DOWN THERE.
CRAZY MONSTERS AND WEIRD OBSTACLES AND STUFF.
NOTHING LIKE REAL PROBLEMS.

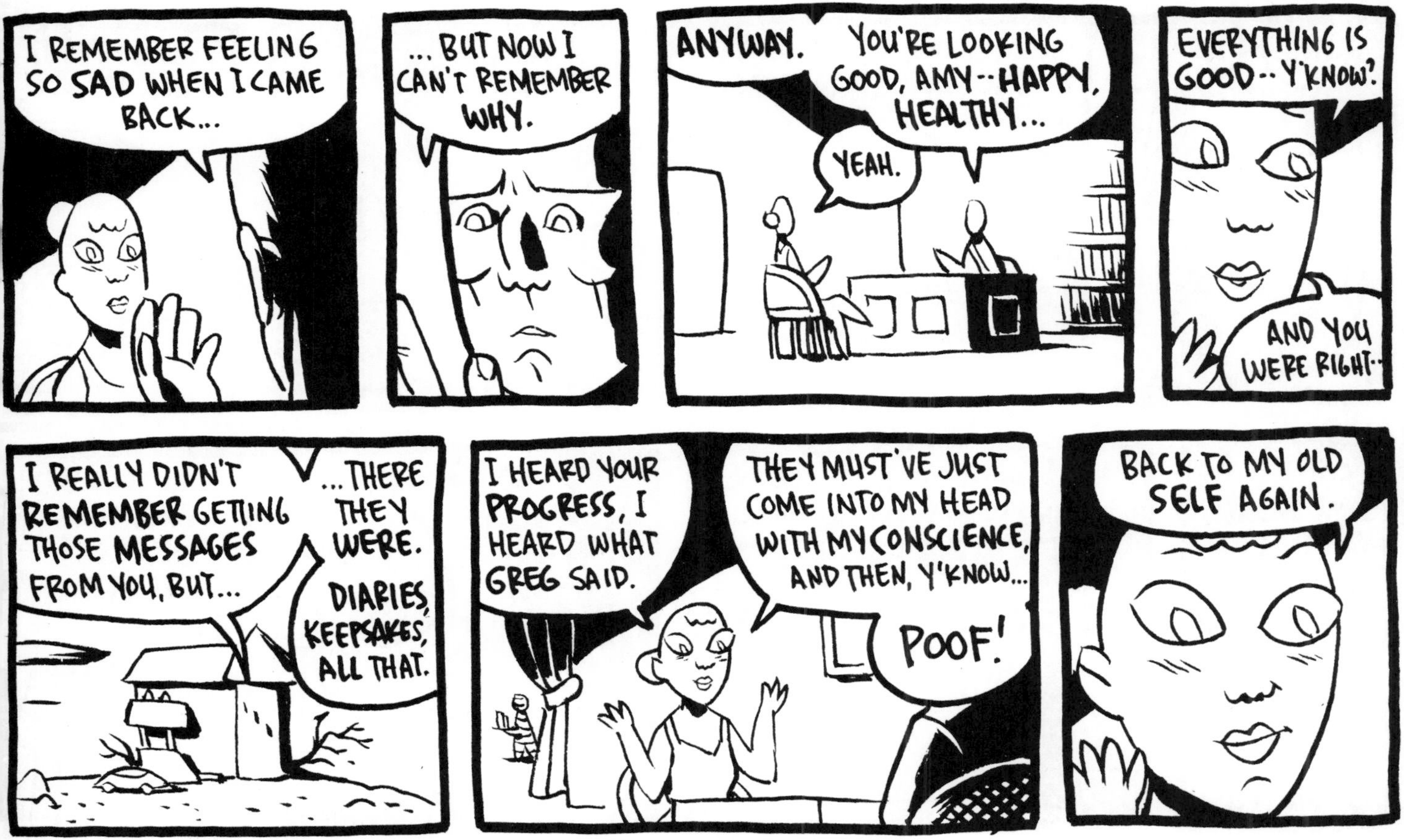
I REMEMBER FEELING SO SAD WHEN I CAME BACK...
... BUT NOW I CAN'T REMEMBER WHY.
ANYWAY.
YOU'RE LOOKING GOOD, AMY--HAPPY, HEALTHY...
YEAH.
EVERYTHING IS GOOD--Y'KNOW?
AND YOU WERE RIGHT--
I REALLY DIDN'T REMEMBER GETTING THOSE MESSAGES FROM YOU, BUT...
...THERE THEY WERE.
DIARIES, KEEPSAKES, ALL THAT.
I HEARD YOUR PROGRESS, I HEARD WHAT GREG SAID.
THEY MUST'VE JUST COME INTO MY HEAD WITH MY CONSCIENCE, AND THEN, Y'KNOW...
POOF!
BACK TO MY OLD SELF AGAIN.

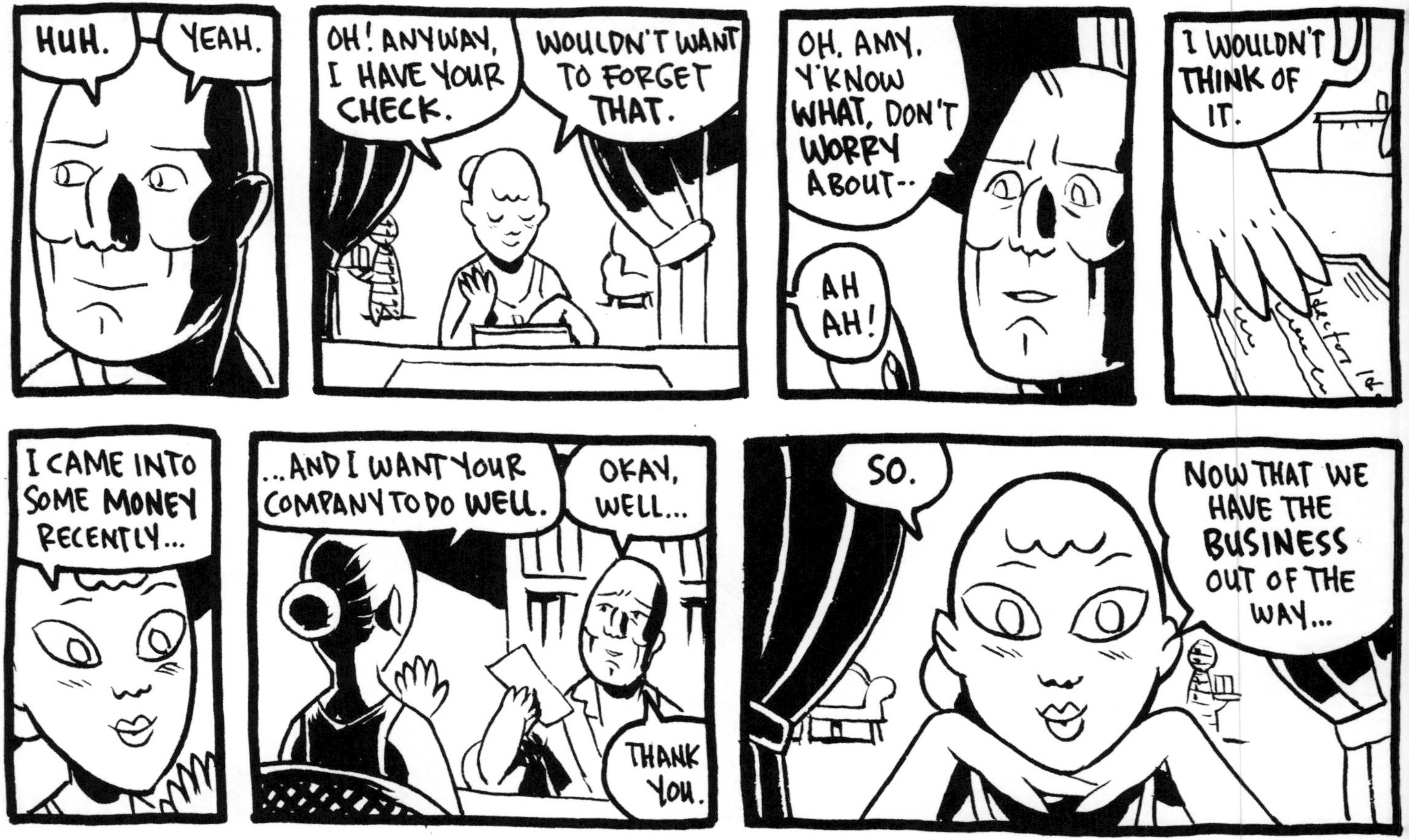
HUH.
YEAH.
OH! ANYWAY, I HAVE YOUR CHECK.
WOULDN'T WANT TO FORGET THAT.
OH. AMY. Y'KNOW WHAT, DON'T WORRY ABOUT--
AH AH!
I WOULDN'T THINK OF IT.
I CAME INTO SOME MONEY RECENTLY...
...AND I WANT YOUR COMPANY TO DO WELL.
OKAY, WELL...
THANK YOU.
SO.
NOW THAT WE HAVE THE BUSINESS OUT OF THE WAY...

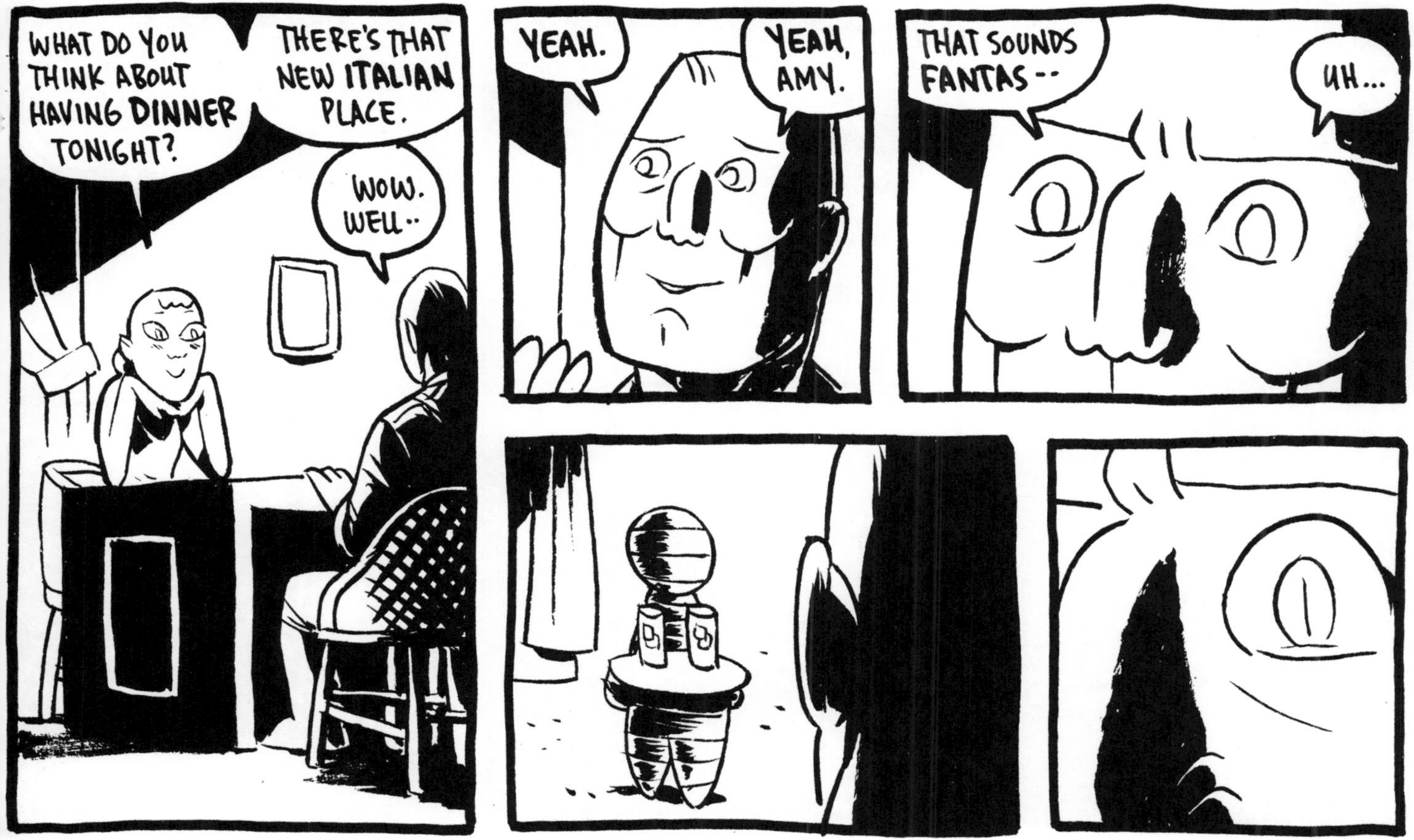
WHAT DO YOU THINK ABOUT HAVING DINNER TONIGHT?
THERE'S THAT NEW ITALIAN PLACE.
WOW. WELL..
YEAH.
YEAH, AMY.
THAT SOUNDS FANTAS--
UH...

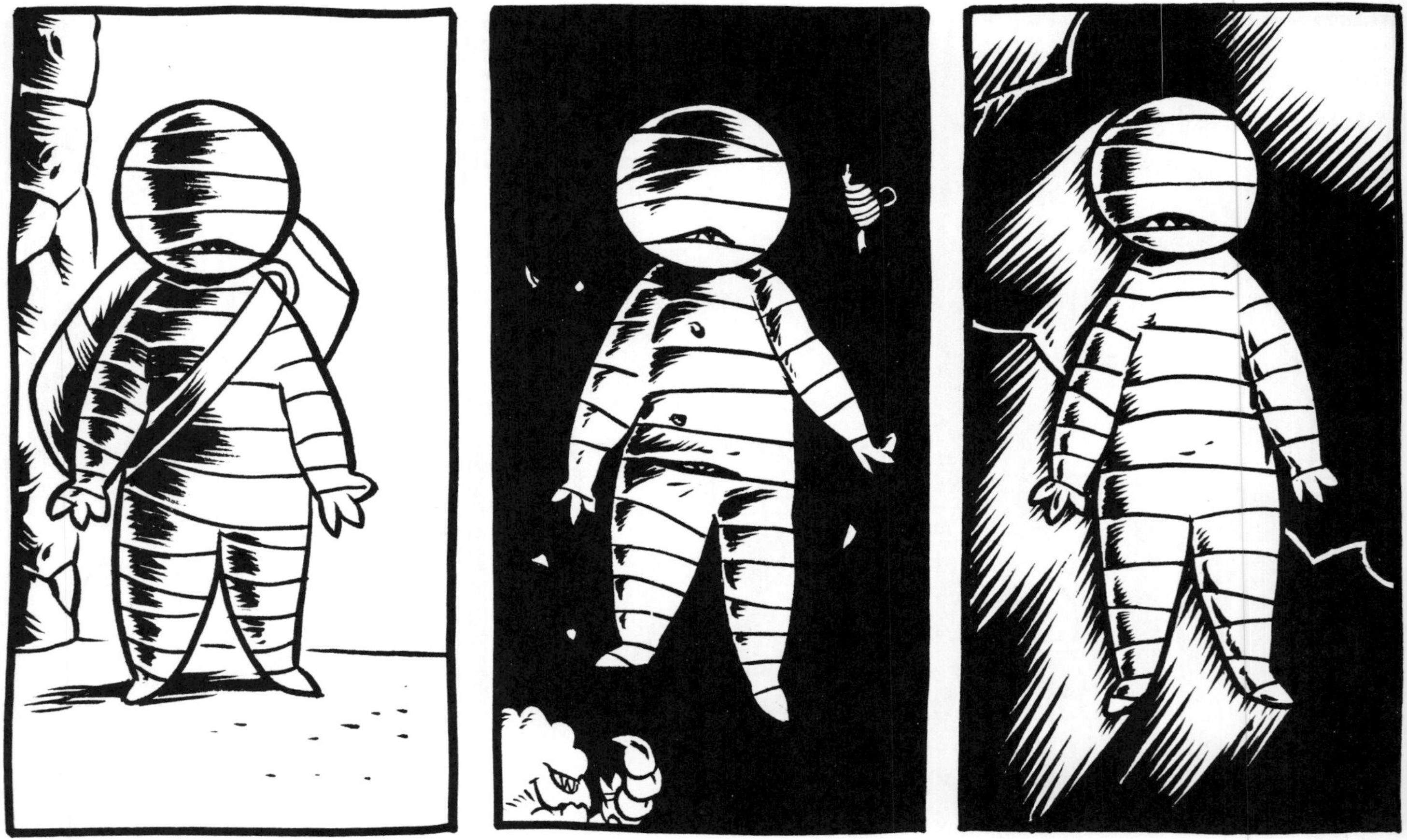

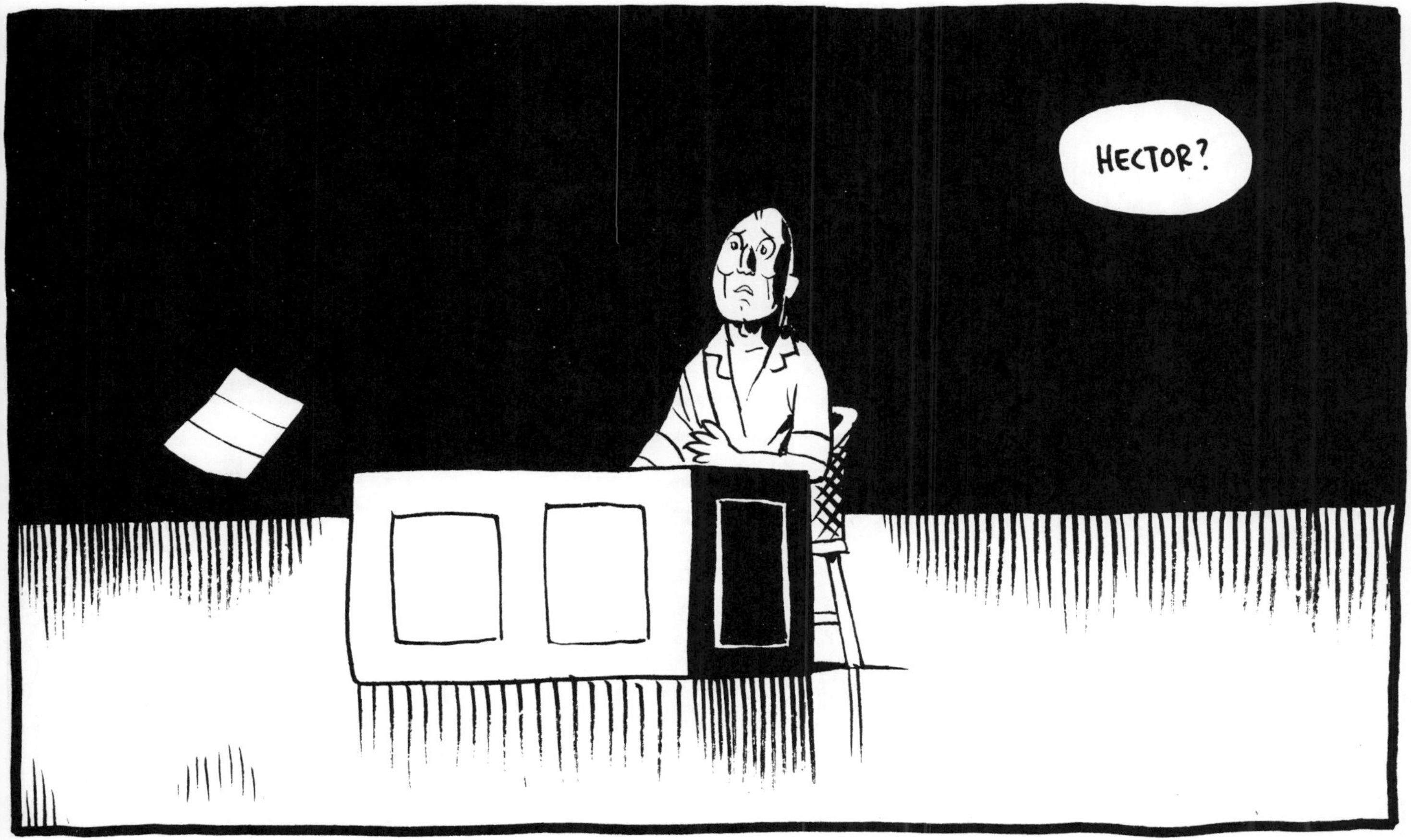
HECTOR?

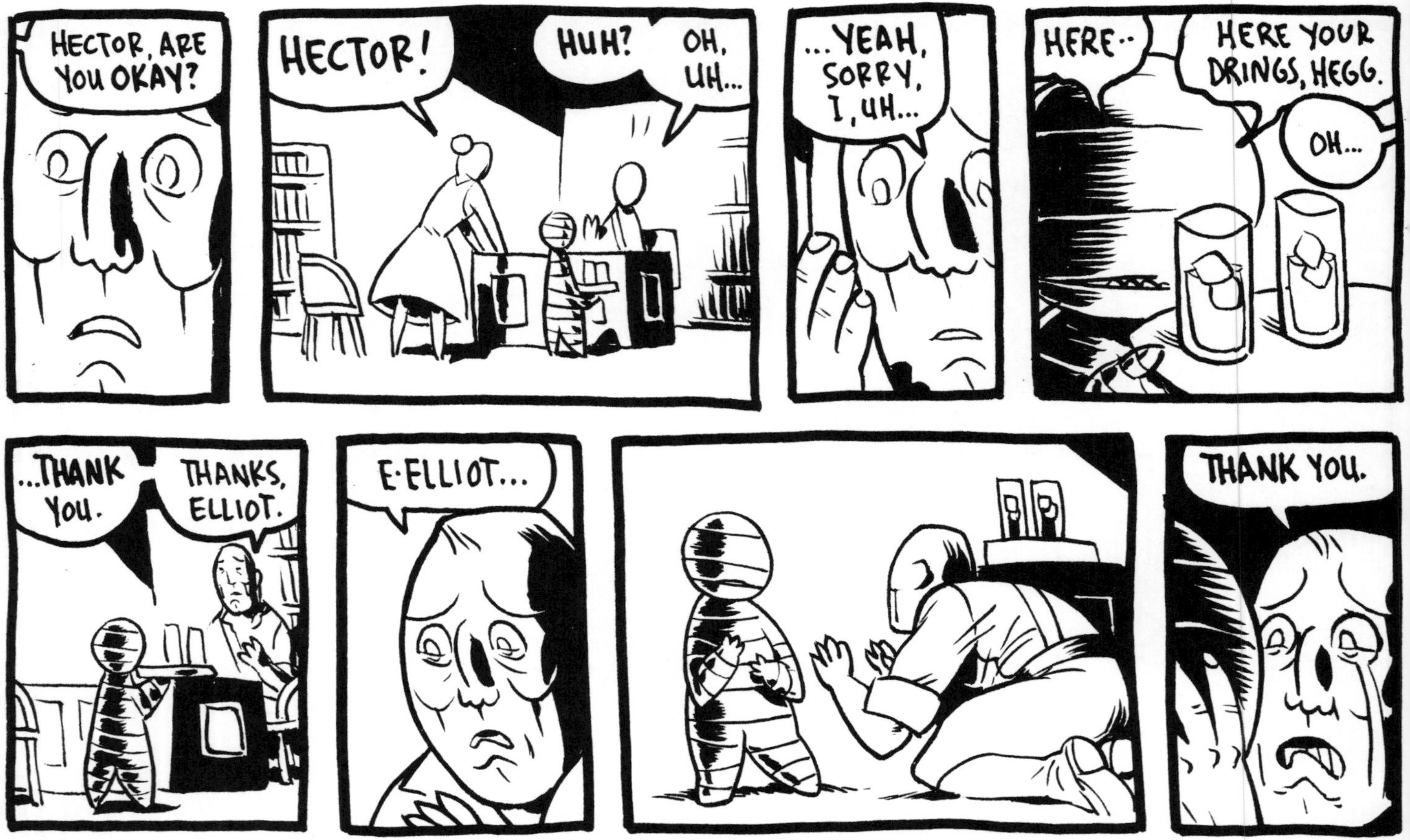
HECTOR, ARE YOU OKAY?
HECTOR!
HUH?
OH, UH...
...YEAH, SORRY, I, UH...
HERE..
HERE YOUR DRINGS, HEGG.
OH...
...THANK YOU.
THANKS, ELLIOT.
E-ELLIOT...
THANK YOU.

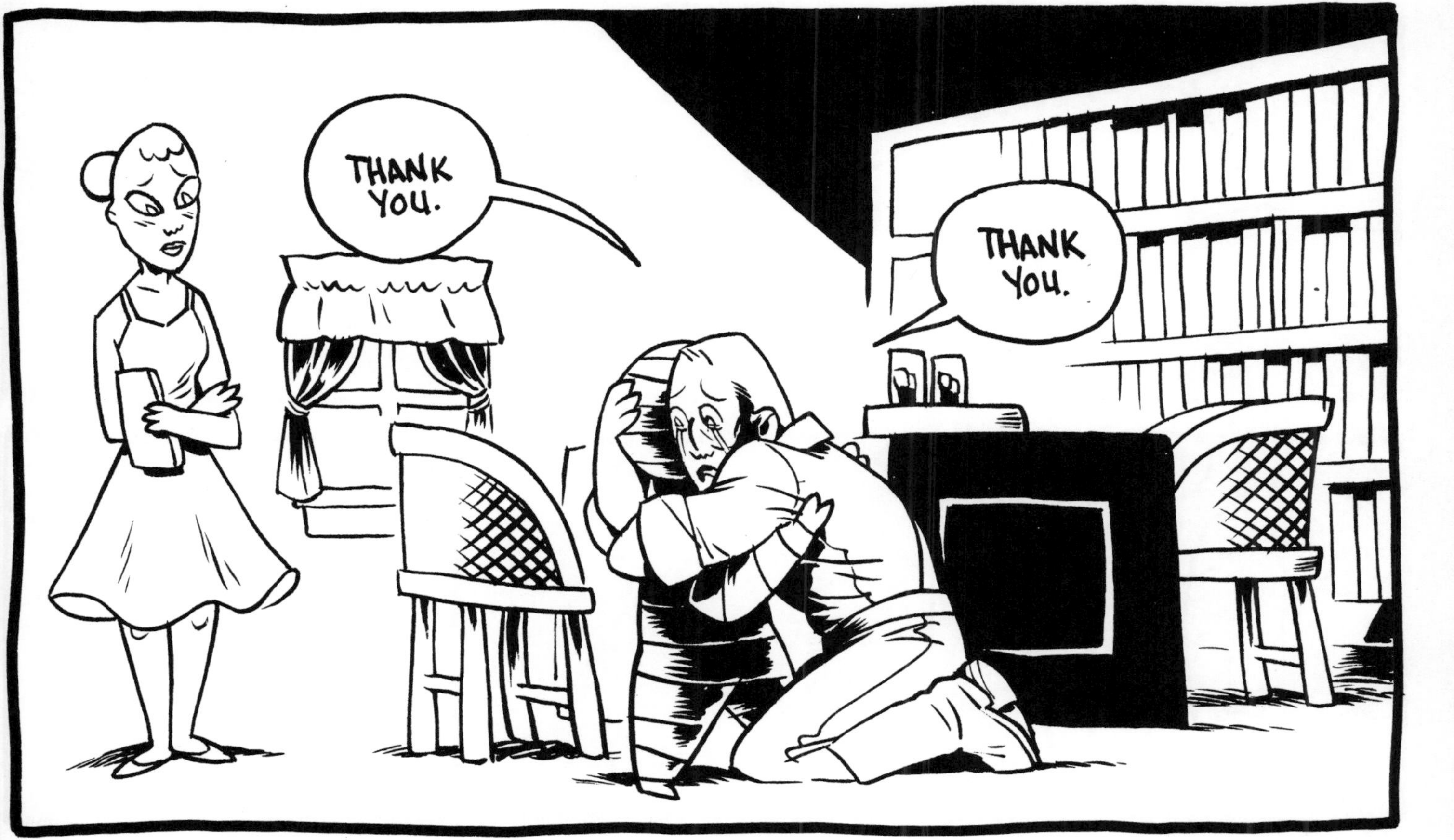
THANK YOU.
THANK YOU.

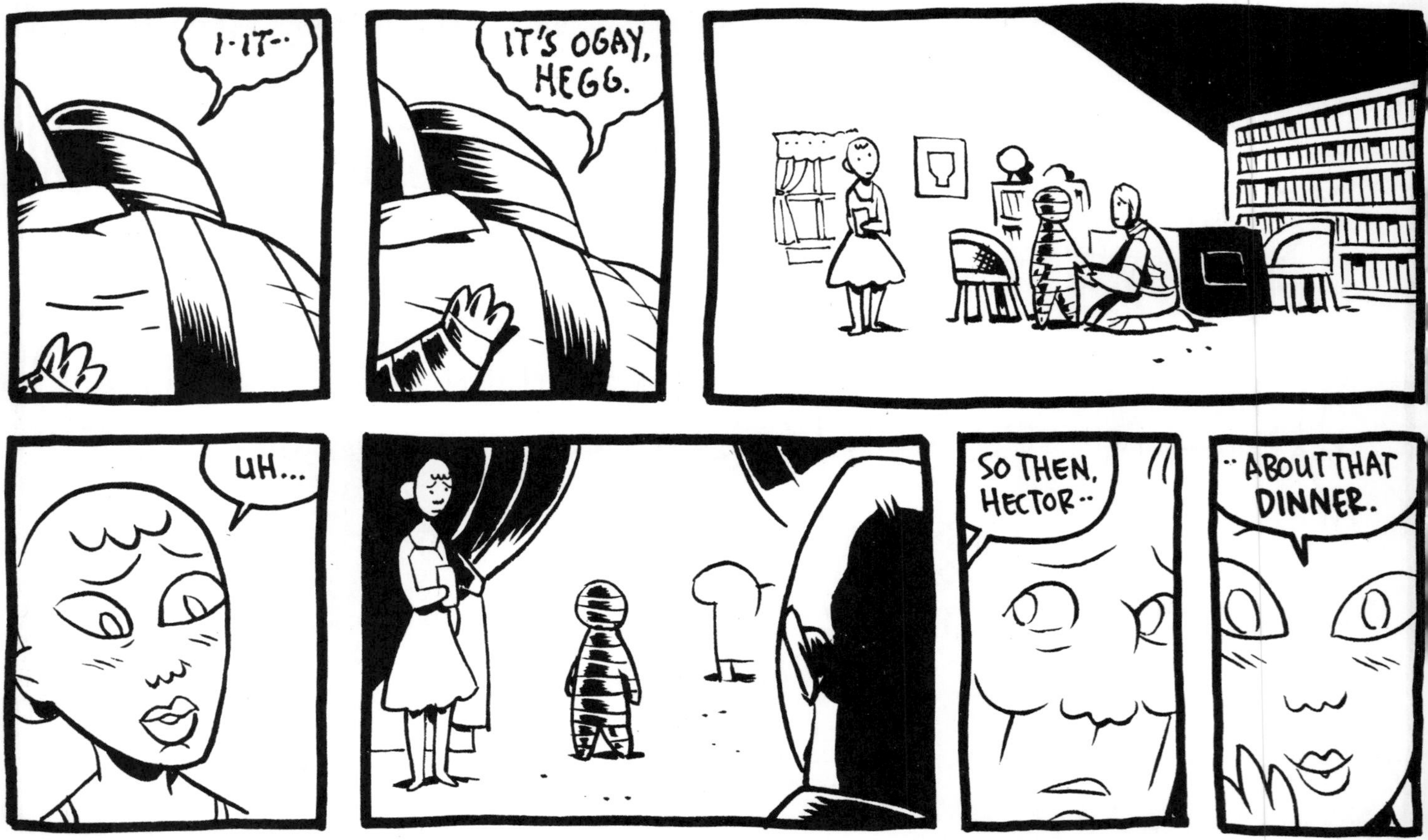
I-IT--
IT'S OGAY, HEGG.
UH...
SO THEN, HECTOR--
--ABOUT THAT DINNER.

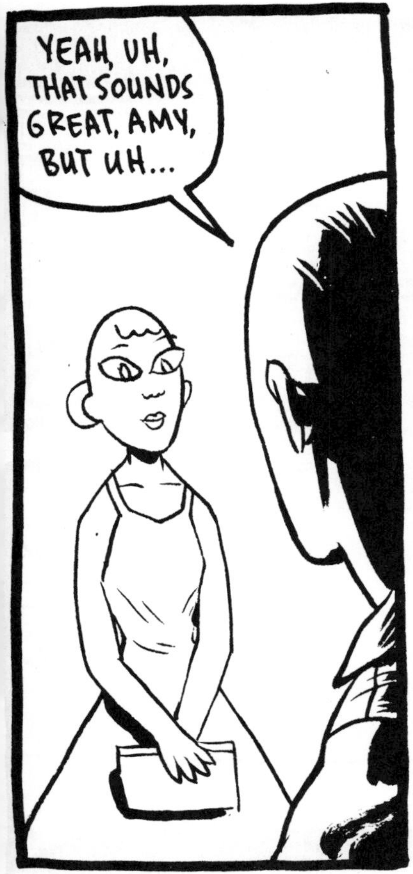
YEAH, UH, THAT SOUNDS GREAT, AMY, BUT UH...

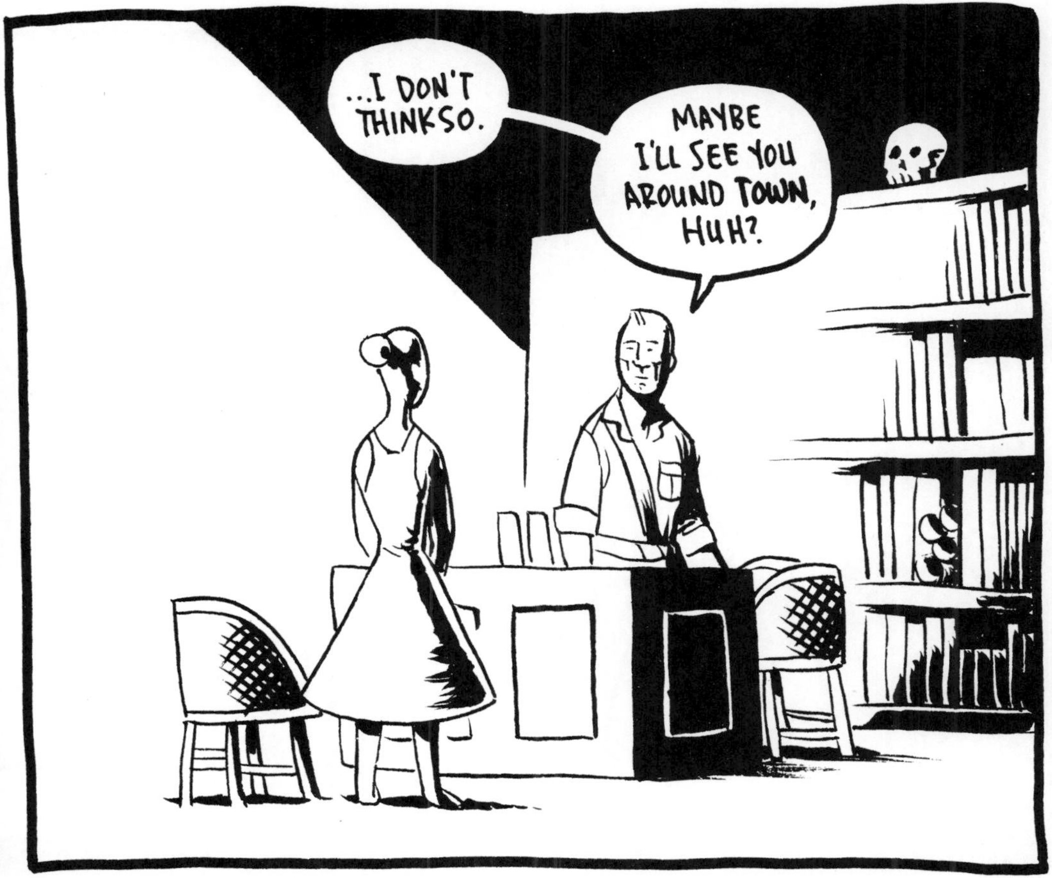
...I DON'T THINK SO.
MAYBE I'LL SEE YOU AROUND TOWN, HUH?

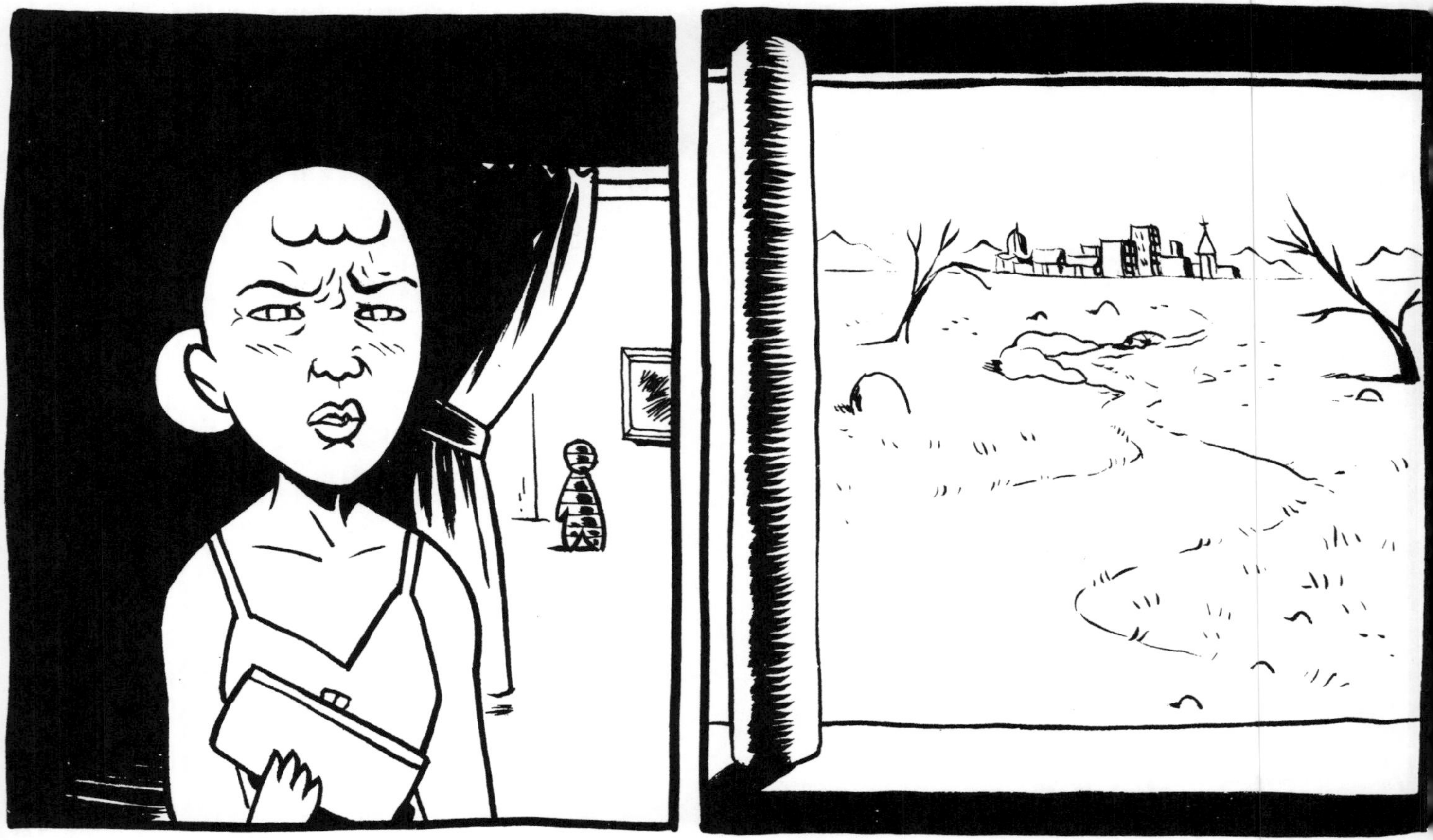

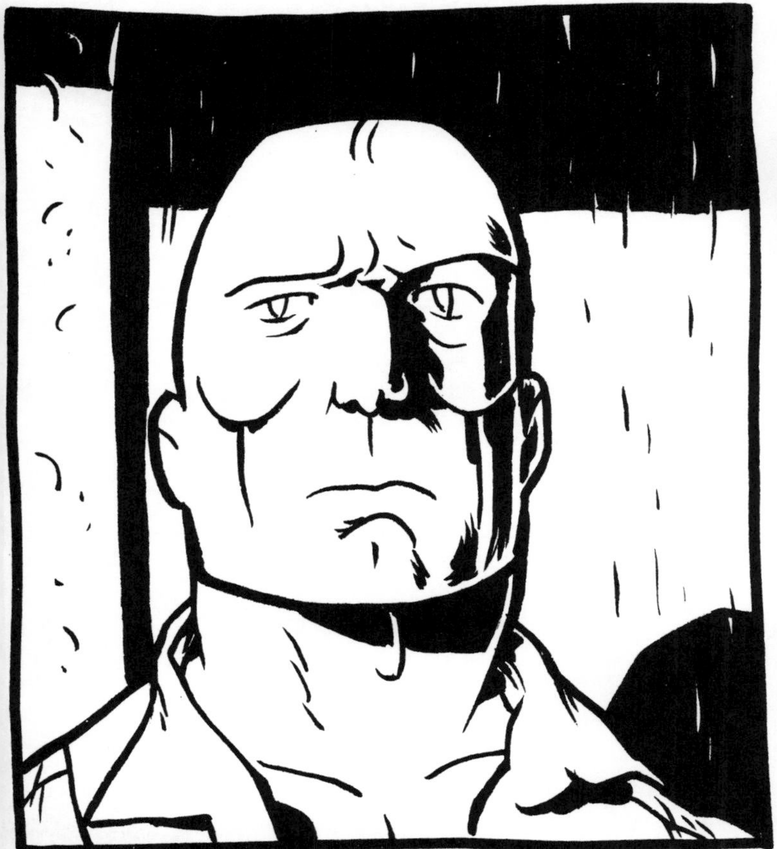

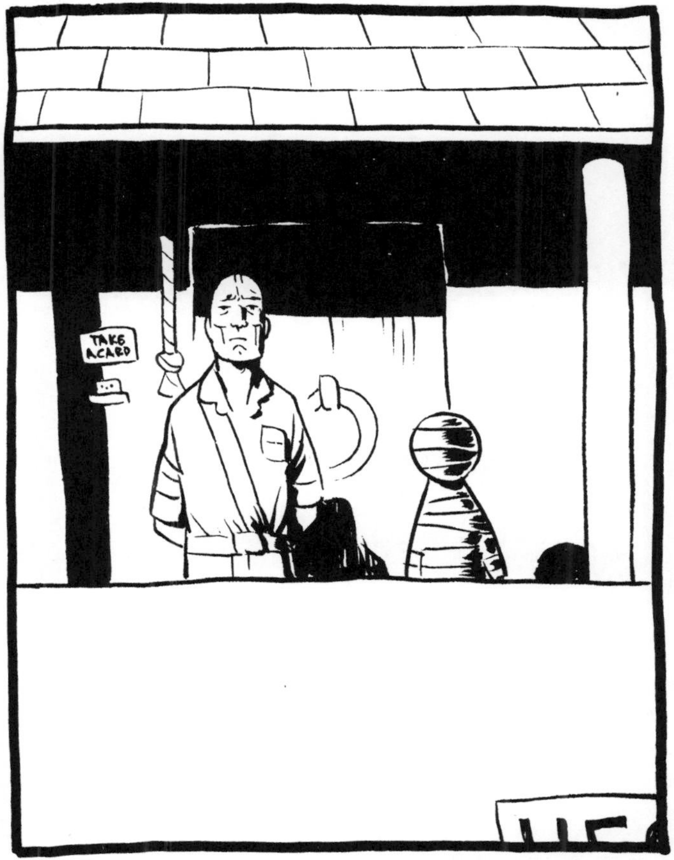
TAKE A CARD

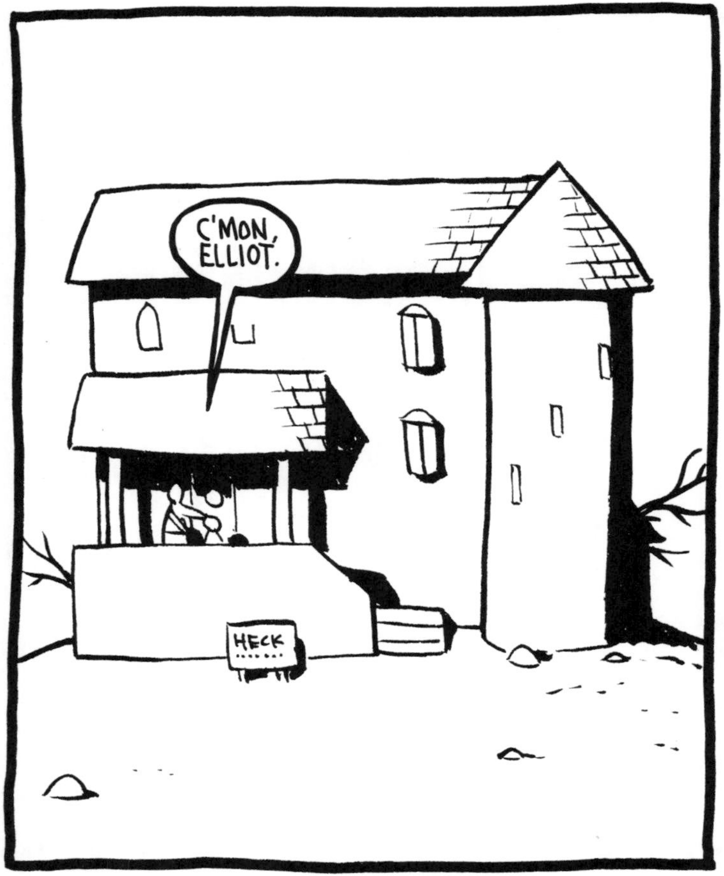
C'MON, ELLIOT.
HECK

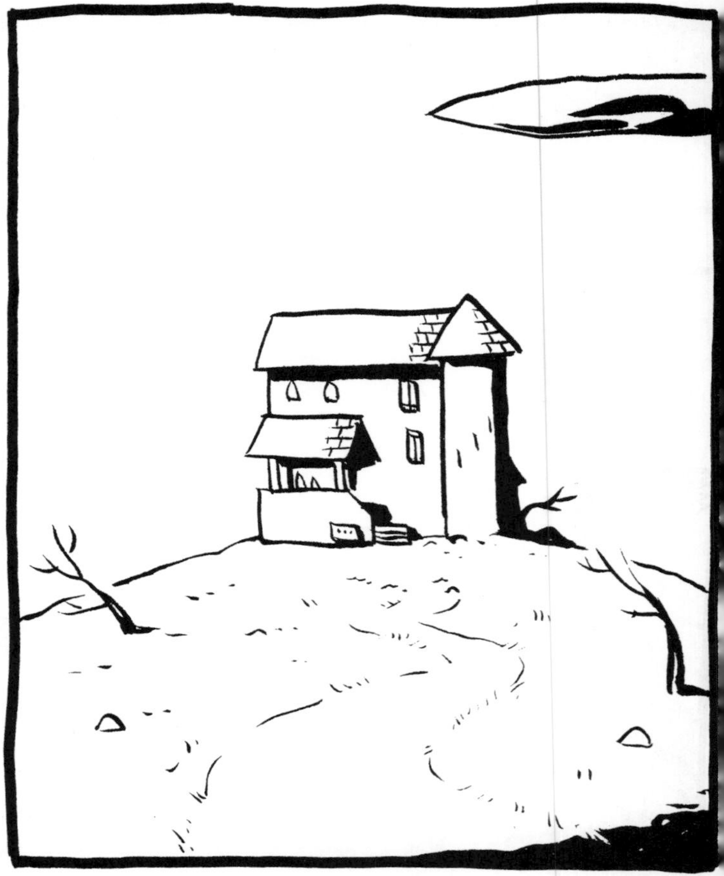

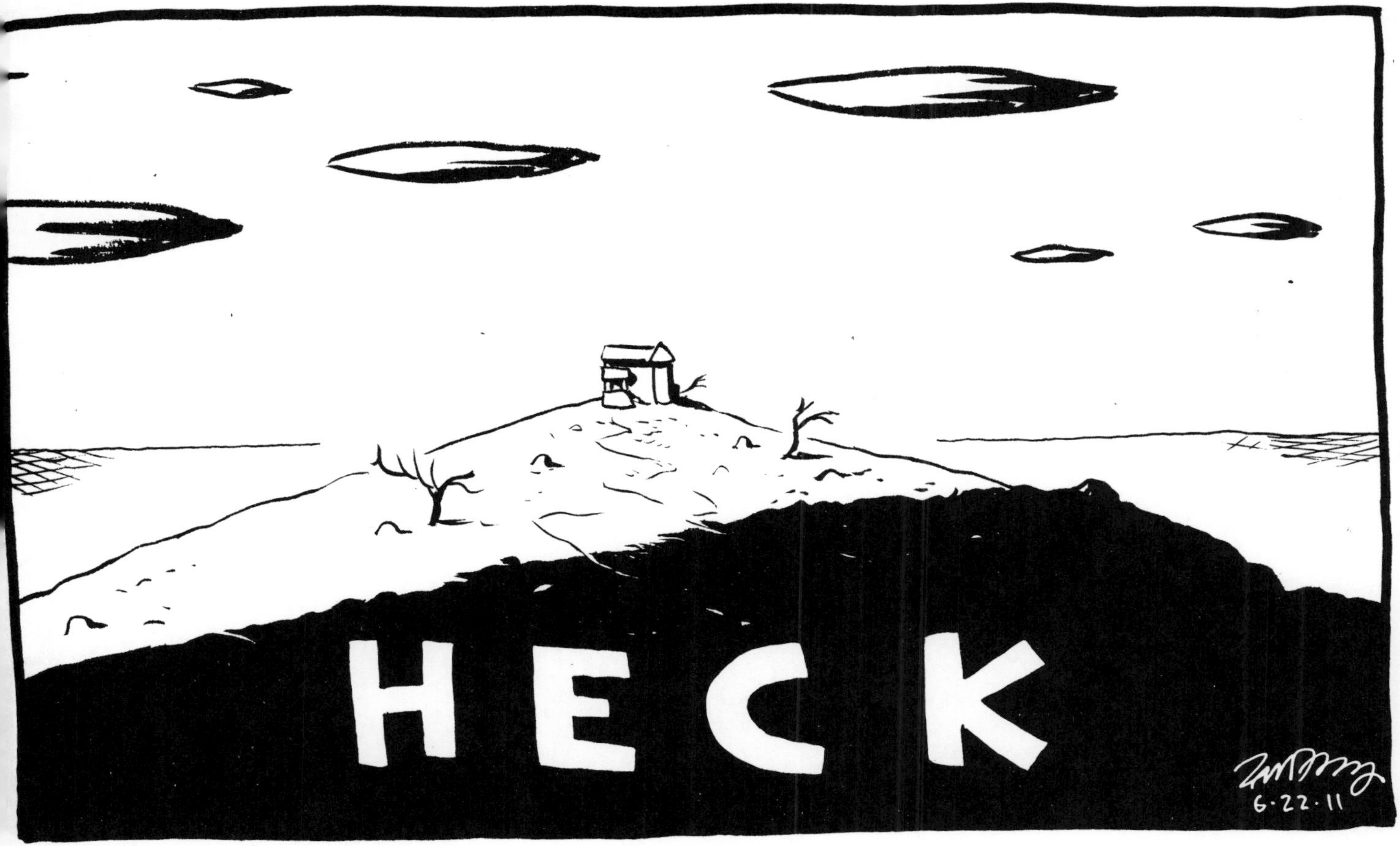
HECK
6-22-11

ZANDER CANNON IS AN AMERICAN
CARTOONIST WHO HAS BEEN WRITING
AND DRAWING COMIC BOOKS SINCE 1993.
HE LIVES IN MINNEAPOLIS WITH HIS
STRONG WIFE JULIE AND THEIR
ABOVE-AVERAGE SON JIN.

- * -

THANKS TO:
KEVIN CANNON
CHRIS ROSS, LEIGH WALTON,
CHRIS STAROS, & BRETT WARNOCK
at TOP SHELF
LAURIE and BETSY CANNON
JULIE and JIN

AFTERWORD

Heck is a project that was born out of a local Minneapolis–St. Paul project called the 144-Hour Graphic Novel Project. Each 12-page chapter would be produced in a single 12-hour session, for a year, which would culminate in a decent-sized graphic novel without significantly impacting one's free time. Naturally this project collapsed for all involved, myself included, when the reality of burning a whole Saturday once a month started to impede on our spouses, children, and more interesting weekend plans.

By that time, however, this project had grown to the point where I could not abandon it. The concept was plucked out of a shuffle of old mid-quality ideas as a modest pulp adventure, but as I wrote and drew it (simultaneously, in most cases, and very quickly), the characters by necessity came to life and started to possess dimensions that I hadn't planned on. The various forces that were shaping my mid-thirties horned their way in and made the relationship between a man with a shotgun and his tiny mummy sidekick the representation of a lot of my own thoughts about fatherhood, responsibility, guilt, and heartbreak.

I know. It's ridiculous.

MINNEAPOLIS
2013